CURRICULUM

FOUNDATIONS, PRINCIPLES AND ISSUES

SECOND EDITION

ALLAN C. ORNSTEIN
Loyola University of Chicago

FRANCIS P. HUNKINS
University of Washington, Seattle

ALLYN AND BACON
Boston   London   Sydney   Toronto   Tokyo   Singapore

To Joel, Stacey, and Jason
and to Leah and Francis, Jr.
from Allan and Francis

Series Editor: Virginia Lanigan
Series Editorial Assistant: Nicole DePalma
Production Administrator: Marjorie Payne
Editorial-Production Supervisor: Raeia Maes
Cover Administrator: Linda Dickinson
Composition Buyer: Linda Cox
Manufacturing Buyer: Megan Cochran

Library of Congress Cataloging-in-Publication Data

Ornstein, Allan C.
    Curriculum—foundations, principles, and issues / Allan C.
Ornstein, Francis P. Hunkins. —2nd ed.
      p. cm.
    Includes bibliographical references and indexes.
    ISBN 0-205-14145-5
     1. Curriculum planning—United States. 2. Curriculum evaluation—
United States.   I. Hunkins, Francis P.   II. Title.
LB2806.15.O76 1993
375′.001′0973—dc20   92-20517
                                               CIP

Printed in the United States of America

10 9 8 7 6 5 4   98 97 96 95 94

BRIEF CONTENTS

CONTENTS

PART III
ISSUES OF CURRICULUM

CURRICULUM TIPS

PREFACE

Curriculum: Foundations, Principles, and Issues, Second Edition, is a book for researchers, theoreticians, and practitioners of curriculum. It is a basic text for those studying curriculum development, design, and/or planning, as well as a reference for teachers, supervisors, and administrators who participate in curriculum making.

The book is a comprehensive and documented overview of the foundations, principles, and issues of curriculum: *Foundations* are the areas of study outside of curriculum that impact on the field; *principles* refer to the technical aspects, including techniques and methods, for developing, designing, implementing, and evaluating curriculum; *issues* are the theories and trends that influence the field.

The book consists of a one-chapter introduction to the field plus three major parts: foundations, principles, and issues. Part I has five chapters: one each on the philosophical, historical, psychological, social, and theoretical *Foundations of Curriculum.* Part II, *Principles of Curriculum,* comprises five chapters: aims, goals, and objectives; design; development; implementation; and evaluation. Part III, *Issues of Curriculum,* includes two chapters that discuss present issues and trends and future directions.

This book differs from other curriculum texts in several ways. Most texts tend to focus on either theory or practice; we try to blend both aspects of curriculum. Most curriculum writers emphasize either the foundations, principles, or issues of curriculum; the majority focus on principles and many others focus on foundations. We have attempted to balance all three areas of curriculum. Most texts take a particular philosophical or theoretical position; we, however, have tried to present various philosophies and theories. We provide readers with alternatives and choices for formulating their own views and values on curriculum foundations, principles, and issues.

We have also attempted to maintain a foot in the past while keeping our eyes and ears open to the future by combining traditional concepts of philosophy, history, and sociology with emerging and futuristic perspectives of the field. We have analyzed several competing theories, models, and paradigms, and we have recommended several practical guidelines. In short, we have supplied a mix of material to help researchers, theoreticians, and practitioners develop their own interpretations of past, present, and future curriculum domains.

In addition to updating the first edition of the book, we have provided three new instructional and learning tools. In keeping with our intent to blend theory with practice, we have introduced curriculum tips for each chapter. These tips are designed to give practical meaning to the research and insights into the curriculum process. To facilitate learning, each chapter now has a series of focusing questions at the beginning to help orient the reader and set the stage for the main ideas in the chapter. Next, overview tables are incorporated in each chapter to make learning more meaningful and to provide summaries of the major concepts and principles conveyed in the chapters.

We extend a note of thanks to our respective mentors of curriculum: Virgil Clift, Hilda Grobman, and O. L. Davis, Jr. Finally, our sincere appreciation goes to the reviewers who provided valuable insights and comments at the manuscript stage: William F. Benjamin, University of South Florida; Breda Bova, University of New Mexico; Jack Cross, University of North Texas; Sister Mary D'Amico, University of Dayton; Robert Isaf, State University of New York at Cortland; Gerald Skoog, Texas Tech University; and John A. Zahorik, University of Wisconsin, Milwaukee.

A.C.O.
F.P.H.

CHAPTER 1

THE FIELD OF CURRICULUM

Focusing Questions

1. *What approach to curriculum do most educators adopt? Why?*
2. *What approach to curriculum do you prefer? Why?*
3. *How do you define curriculum?*
4. *Why do most theorists define curriculum in terms of generic principles or processes, not specific subject matter?*
5. *What fundamental questions guide the field of curriculum?*
6. *How do the foundations of education influence curriculum? Which foundation areas are more important? Why?*
7. *What are the differences between curriculum development and design?*
8. *How can theory and practice be integrated into the planning of curriculum?*
9. *How do you define the role of the principal (teacher) in curriculum planning?*

Curriculum as a field of study is elusive and fragmentary, and what it is supposed to entail is open to a good deal of debate and even misunderstanding. Curriculum is both a subject to be taught at colleges and universities and a field in which practitioners work. Students who enroll in curriculum courses, as a minor or major field of study in education, usually study these courses at the graduate level. People who teach or train others, who engage in program development, instruction, supervision, and/or evaluation in schools and colleges, businesses, hospitals and health agencies, as well as governmental agencies are practicing curriculum.

What we mean by curriculum, what it involves, and who is involved are best understood by analyzing curriculum in a broad context. We thus look at curriculum in this text in terms of *approach* (or what others call an orientation, perspective, or position), and *definition*. We consider, also, the relationship and differences between the foundations and domains of curriculum, the theory and practice of curriculum, and roles of curriculum workers.

In much of our discussion, we point to various curriculum texts published since 1985. This should not only help introduce the field, but it should also help put this text in context with other curriculum texts.

CURRICULUM APPROACHES

An individual's approach to curriculum reflects that person's view of the world, including what the person perceives as reality, the values he or she deems important, and the amount of knowledge he or she possesses. A curriculum approach reflects a *holistic* position or a *metaorientation,* encompassing the foundations of curriculum (the person's philosophy, view of history, view of psychology and learning theory, and view of social issues), domains of curriculum (common and important knowledge within the field), and the theoretical and practical principles of curriculum. An approach expresses a viewpoint about the development and design of curriculum, the role of the learner, teacher, and curriculum specialist in planning curriculum, the goals and objectives of

1

the curriculum, and the important issues that need to be examined.

A curriculum approach reflects our views of schools and society; to some extent it may even become an all-encompassing outlook if we feel strongly about these views. By understanding one's curriculum approach, and the prevailing curriculum approach of the school or school district in which one works, it is possible to conclude whether one's professional view conflicts with the formal organizational view.

Although schools, over time, tend to become committed to a particular curriculum approach, many educators are not strongly committed to one approach. Many of them do not have a single or pure approach; rather, in some situations they emphasize one approach, and in other cases they advocate several approaches. In still other cases, they fail to recognize that they even reflect a particular attitudinal or behavioral curriculum approach, or that they are in fact influenced by many approaches. They need to recognize that curriculum textbook writers sometimes adhere to more than one curriculum approach. Moreover, curriculum specialists, even curriculum students, need to examine their approaches.

Curriculum approaches can be viewed from a technical and nontechnical, or scientific and nonscientific, perspective. (Note that the terms *nontechnical* and *nonscientific* do not suggest a negative or disparaging approach; rather, these two terms denote a contrast.) Technical-scientific approaches coincide with traditional theories and models of education, and reflect established and formal methods of schooling. Nontechnical and nonscientific approaches have evolved as part of avant-garde and experimental philosophies and politics of education; they tend to challenge established and formalized practices of education.

The remainder of this section outlines five curriculum approaches. The first three may be classified as technical or scientific, the latter two as nontechnical and/or nonscientific.

Behavioral Approach

Rooted in the University of Chicago school (from Bobbitt and Charters to Tyler and Taba), this is the oldest and still the major approach to curriculum.[1] As a means-ends approach it is logical and

prescriptive. It relies on technical and scientific principles, and includes paradigms, models, and step-by-step strategies for formulating curriculum. Usually based on a plan, and sometimes called a blueprint or document, goals and objectives are specified, content and activities are sequenced to coincide with the objectives, and learning outcomes are evaluated in relation to the goals and objectives.

This curriculum approach, which has been applied to all subjects for more than two-thirds of this century, constitutes a frame of reference against which other approaches to curriculum are compared. Other names that have been used to identify this approach—including logical-positivist, conceptual-empiricist, experientalist, rational-scientific, and technocratic[2]—suggest that the approach is also technical and scientific and that it deals with principles for theoreticians and practitioners.

The behavioral approach started with the idea of efficiency, influenced by business and industry, and the scientific management theories of Frederick Taylor, who analyzed factory efficiency in terms of time and motion studies and concluded that each worker should be paid on the basis of his or her individual output, as measured by the number of units produced in a specified period of time. Efficient operation of the schools (and other social systems), sometimes called **machine theory** by its critics, became a major goal in the 1920s.

Often ensuring efficiency in schools meant eliminating small classes, increasing student-teacher ratios, hiring few administrators, cutting costs in teacher salaries, maintaining or reducing operational costs, and so on, and then preparing charts and graphs to show the resultant lower costs. Raymond Callahan later branded this idea the "cult of efficiency."[3] The goals or effects were to make schools in general and curriculum making more scientific, at least more precise, and to reduce teaching and learning to precise behaviors with corresponding activities that could be measured.

Franklin Bobbitt described the problems as he set out to organize a course of studies for the elementary grades. "We need principles of curriculum making. We did not know that we should first determine objectives from a study of social needs. . . . We had not learned that [plans] are means, not ends."[4]

Bobbitt developed his objectives and activities approach in the early 1920s in *How to Make a Curriculum*. In the book, he outlined more than 800 objectives and related activities to coincide with predetermined student needs. These activities ranged from the "ability to care for [one's] teeth . . . eyes . . . nose, and throat; . . . to keep home appliances in good working condition; . . . to spelling and grammar."[5] Bobbitt's methods were quite sophisticated for the day, but taken out of context, his list of hundreds of objectives and activities, along with the machine or factory analogy that he advocated, was easy to criticize.

It was left to Ralph Tyler, who took a number of courses with Bobbitt at the University of Chicago, to recognize the need for behavioral objectives that were not so tiny or lockstep; instead, basic techniques of curriculum, instruction, and evaluation were combined in a simple plan. His idea was to use the philosophy of the school (or school district) "in making decisions about objectives." Thus he provided greater latitude and value judgments for those responsible for planning the curriculum. Tyler's approach combined behaviorism (objectives were an important consideration), and thus noted the influence of Thorndike, with progressivism (the emphasis on the needs of the learner), and the influence of Dewey, with the "scientific movement of curriculum [making] during the past thirty years" prior to his classic text.[6]

Current texts written from this behavioral approach, such as those of James Beane, Peter Oliva, J. Galen Saylor, and Jon Wiles and Joseph Bondi, tend to stress other approaches as well.[7] Few pure behaviorists today are writing curriculum textbooks, because new, competing philosophies and learning theories are evolving and expanding. Nonetheless, authors who cluster around the behavioral approach rely on prescriptive blueprints for curriculum making, consider the curriculum to be a plan with sequential and structured activities, and maintain that there are specific roles that curriculum persons can play. The technical issues of development and design receive much attention. Most people who plan and develop curriculum utilize the behavioral-rational approach, regardless of how they may classify themselves or how others may classify them.

Managerial Approach

This approach considers the school as a social system, reminiscent of organizational theory, whereby groups of people such as students, teachers, curriculum specialists, and administrators interact according to certain norms and behaviors. Educators who rely on this approach plan the curriculum in terms of programs, schedules, space, resources and equipment, and personnel. This approach advocates, among other things, the need for selecting, organizing, communicating with, and supervising people involved in curriculum decisions. Consideration is given to committee and group processes, human relations, leadership styles and methods, and decision making.[8]

An offshoot of the behavioral approach, the managerial approach, also relies on a plan, rational principles, and logical steps, but not necessarily behavioral approaches. The managerial aspect tends to focus on the supervisory and administrative aspects of curriculum, especially the organizational and implementation process. See Curriculum Tips 1-1.

Advocates of this approach are interested in change and innovation, and in how curriculum specialists, supervisors, and administrators can facilitate these processes. The curriculum specialist and supervisor (sometimes the same person) is considered to be a practitioner, not a theoretician—a change agent, resource person, and facilitator. He or she reports to an administrator and follows the mission and goals of the school. If the school does not appreciate change, then the change role of the job is minimized. If the school is innovative or reform minded, then changes are expected and the school culture tends to create and sustain a culture for change.[9] However, if the school emphasizes the "three R's," then the curriculum specialist introduces plans accordingly. Most of the cues related to change or stability are communicated to subordinates (teachers) from managers through formal and informal (body language, conversations, and the like) communication networks.

The managerial approach is rooted in the organizational and administrative school models of the early 1900s—a period that combined a host of innovative plans involving curriculum and instruction that centered around individualization, departmentalization, nongrading, classroom grouping, and homeroom and work-study activities. It was an era when various school district plans were introduced by their respective superintendents in an attempt to modify the horizontal and vertical organization of the schools. The names of the plans were usually based either on the school district's name or organizational concept, such as the Batavia (New York) Plan, Denver (Colorado) Plan, Elizabeth (New Jersey) Plan, Pueblo (Colorado) Plan, Platoon (Gary, Indiana) Plan, Portland (Oregon) Plan, Santa Barbara (California) Plan, Study Hall (New York City) Plan, and Winnetka (Illinois) Plan. Superintendents and associate superintendents were very much involved in curriculum leadership,

often developing a plan in one school district and being hired by another to implement the plan in the new district. Hence, there was a good deal of hopscotching around of administrators who combined managerial and curriculum leadership skills.[10]

The managerial approach became the dominant curriculum approach in the 1950s and 1960s. During this period, the notion of the principal as a curriculum leader and instructional leader was popularized and fused with the idea of general manager. It was in this era when Midwest school administrators and professors (with administrative backgrounds) dominated the field of curriculum in terms of setting policies and priorities, establishing the direction of change and innovation, and planning and organizing curriculum and instruction.

The pace setters for this era were such school superintendents (or associate superintendents) as Robert Anderson (Park Forest, Illinois), Leslee

Bishop (Livonia, Michigan), William Cornog (New Trier Township High School, Winnetka. Illinois), Robert Gilchrist (University City, Missouri), Arthur Lewis (Minneapolis, Minnesota), Sidney Marland (Winnetka, Illinois), Lloyd Michael (Evanston, Illinois), Gordon McAndrew (Gary, Indiana). Stuart Rankin (Detroit), J. Lloyd Trump (Waukegan, Illinois), and Glenys Unruh (University City, Missouri). Of course, there were other superintendents (or associate superintendents) from outside the Midwest who were also influential, such as Chester Babcock (Seattle, Washington), Muriel Crosby (Wilmington, Delaware), Gerald Firth (Roselyn, New York), John McNeil (San Diego, California), and Harold Shafer (Wyckoff, New Jersey).

These administrators were very active politically. They used the supervisory and curriculum associations and their respective journals and yearbooks as platforms to publicize their ideas. Many, like Anderson, Bishop, Firth, Gilchrist, Lewis, and McNeil, became curriculum professors at major universities; others became active as board directors and executive committee members of professional organizations that had major impact on curriculum, supervision, and administration. Still others, like Bishop, Firth, Gilchrist, Lewis, McNeil, Trump, and Unruh, published curriculum books that expressed this managerial view.[11]

These school administrators were less concerned about content than about organization and implementation. And they were less concerned about subject matter, methods, and materials than about improving curriculum in light of policies, plans, and people on a system-wide basis. They envisioned curriculum changes and innovation as they administered the resources and restructured the schools.

Today, many of our "new" ideas of school reform and restructuring are rooted in the ideas of change and innovation that characterized the 1950s and 1960s: then local control was a sacred cow, while today the state is playing a major role in reform. Many current plans related to school-based management and empowerment are based on the older career ladder and differential staffing models of this previous era. Much of the new legislative and administrative support for improving curriculum and instruction is based on

the changing role of the superintendent and principal, as curriculum and instructional leaders, that blossomed during the 1950s and 1960s and is now shaping the profession again.

Current texts that tend to stress a managerial view of curriculum, with emphasis on the school district's central administration or school's principal and supervisors, are books written by David Armstrong, Ronald Doll, Allan Glatthorn, Edward Pajak, and Glenys and Adolph Unruh.[12] In all these texts, the authors examine the relationships among administrators, supervisors, and teachers; techniques of networking, planning, goal setting, and communicating; the practical world and tasks of the curriculum leader; and the politics of decision making and policy making.

The Systems Approach

It was not far to leap from organizing people and policies, a managerial view, to organizing curriculum into a system. The systems aspect tends to view various units and subunits of the organization in relation to the whole, and organizational diagrams, flow charts, and committee structures are often diagrammed as the curriculum plan is introduced and monitored. Sometimes referred to as **curriculum engineering,** the approach includes the processes necessary to plan the curriculum by such *engineers* as superintendents, directors, coordinators, and principals: *the stages* (development, design, implementation, and evaluation) and *structures* (subjects, courses, unit plans, and lesson plans).

The systems approach to curriculum was influenced by systems theory, systems analysis. and systems engineering. These concepts, originally developed by social scientists in the 1950s and 1960s, are used or at least discussed widely by school managers as part of administrative and organizational theory. The largest users of the systems approach are the military, business, and industry, since it is critical that all learners master whatever tasks they perform (our nation's defense or a company's profits largely depend on people performing their jobs), and they can afford the start-up costs necessary to introduce the system.[13] (A new curriculum is expensive in terms of personnel, resources, and materials.)

In the systems approach to curriculum, the parts of the total school district or school are closely examined in terms of their interrelatedness and influence on each other. Components like departments, personnel, equipment, and schedules are planned to create changes in people's behavior and expectations. Information is usually communicated to administrators who consider alternatives and choices.

One particular application of the systems approach was developed by Rand Corporation and has rapidly spread from government to business agencies. It is called Planning, Programming, Budgeting System (PPBS), and it brings together the components of planning, programming, and budgeting with the system's structure, functions, and capabilities. In our case, the system is curriculum.

Another well-known systems approach is the Program Evaluation and Review Technique (PERT), which was introduced by the Defense Department and subsequently spread to business and industry in the 1960s. Like PPBS, it has been introduced into education. Progress and interruptions of various facets of the program, in this case the curriculum, are computed, analyzed, and made available to administrators. Progress reports are continuously updated, reflecting changes in schedule, possible difficulties, and achievement rates. In both systems approaches, the curriculum is closely monitored by administrators; revisions and corrective action are introduced on a continuous basis.

George Beauchamp described the first systems theory of curriculum. He divided theories of education into five major theories of equal importance: (1) administration, (2) counseling, (3) curriculum, (4) instruction, and (5) evaluation.[14] Many professors of education (outside of curriculum) do not accept this notion of equal theories, for they view their own field as their major system or area of study—and curriculum as a component or subsystem of the major system. For example, school administrators often delegate supervisors to take care of curriculum matters, especially if the administrators view their leadership role chiefly in terms of management. On the other hand, curriculum specialists usually view curriculum as the major system, and related fields such as teaching, instruction, and supervision are seen as subsystems that help implement the curriculum.[15]

However, what Beauchamp was trying to convey is that the five theories of education are applied realms of knowledge that draw their ideas from the foundations of education: psychology, sociology, history, philosophy, and so on. Rather than dispute what are the major systems or subsystems, it is more important to design procedures that are applicable to the real world and use whatever theory that can be helpful to the practitioner.

Curriculum specialists who value the systems approach take a macro or broad view of curriculum and are concerned with curriculum issues and questions that relate to the entire school or school system—not just in terms of particular subjects or grades. They are concerned with how the curriculum is related across different programs and content areas, to what extent the curriculum reflects the hierarchy or organizational arrangements of the school (or school system), the needs and training of the participants, and various methods for monitoring and evaluating results. Long-term planning is fused with short-range or incidental planning.

Although no one curriculum text emphasizes curriculum systems, the systems approach is discussed widely in texts that emphasize development or design, such as those authored by James Beane, Francis Hunkins, Peter Oliva, and David Pratt.[16]

Academic Approach

Sometimes referred to as the traditional, encyclopedic, synoptic, intellectual, or knowledge-oriented approach, the academic approach attempts to analyze and synthesize major positions, trends, and concepts of curriculum. The approach tends to be historical or philosophical, and, to a lesser extent, social in nature. The discussion of curriculum making is usually scholarly and theoretical (not practical), and concerned with many broad aspects of schooling, including the study of education. This expansion of curriculum boundaries relative to the subject of schooling, and the treatment of curriculum as intellectual thought, are reflected in a good deal of background information and broad overview of events and people.

This approach is rooted in the philosophical and intellectual works of John Dewey, Henry Morrison, and Boyd Bode.[17] It became popular between the 1930s and 1950s, and is illustrated by the lengthy and intellectual curriculum works of Hollis Caswell and Doak Campbell, L. Thomas Hopkins, John and Mary Norton, B. Othanel Smith, and Florence Stratemeyer.[18] The influx of new topics related to curriculum during this period expanded the boundaries of the field to include a good number of trends and issues, and the integration of various instructional, teaching, learning, guidance, evaluation, supervision, and administrative procedures. The field became all-encompassing because the books published accumulated a great deal of curriculum knowledge and subject matter.

After the 1950s, major interest in curriculum centered around the structure of disciplines and qualitative methods. Thus the academic approach lost some of its glamor among curricularists. The texts that still reflect this approach (such as those by John Miller and Wayne Seller, William Schubert, and Daniel and Laurel Tanner) frequently overwhelm beginning curriculum students who usually lack sufficient background information and philosophical and/or historical insights on the subject.[19] These texts tend to be more appreciated by advanced students of the field and by professors of curriculum. Critics argue that these authors are compilers of information and sometimes the focus is unclear or cumbersome.

Other academics try to cover a host of foundations topics (usually historical, philosophical, social, and political), thus presenting a broad or general overview of curriculum.[20] While some of these authors do an admirable job in presenting such an overview, the content of these texts is sometimes presented in highly abbreviated form, offering little opportunity for analysis of important concepts and technical methods (development and design); indeed, there is a tendency to skim essential material because too much is being attempted.

Humanistic Approach

Some curriculum leaders reflect on the field and contend that the above approaches are too technocratic and rigid. They contend that in attempting be scientific and rational, curricularists miss the personal and social aspects of curriculum and instruction; ignore the artistic, physical, and cultural aspects of subject matter; rarely consider the need for self-reflectiveness and self-actualization among learners; and, finally, overlook the sociopsychological dynamics of classrooms and schools.

This view is rooted in progressive philosophy and the child-centered movement of the early 1900s (first spearheaded at the University of Chicago when John Dewey, Charles Judd, and Francis Parker developed progressive methods of teaching, based on the student's natural development and curiosity).[21] In the 1920s and 1930s, the progressive movement moved east and was dominated by Teachers College, Columbia University, and by such professors as Frederick Bosner, Hollis Caswell, L. Thomas Hopkins, William Kilpatrick, Harold Rugg, and John Dewey (who had changed professional affiliations and was now at Columbia).[22] This approach gained further impetus in the 1940s and 1950s with the growth of child psychology (which deals with the needs and interests of children) and humanistic psychology (which deals with valuing, ego identity, psychological health, freedom to learn, and personal fulfillment).

From this approach, numerous curriculum activities have emerged, mainly at the elementary school level, including lessons based on life experiences, group games, group projects, artistic endeavors, dramatizations, field trips, social enterprises, learning and interest centers, and homework and tutoring stations (or corners). These activities include creative problem solving and active student participation; they emphasize socialization and life adjustment for students, as well as stronger family and school-community ties. They are representative of Parker, Dewey, Kilpatrick, and Washburne's (Parker and Washburne were superintendents) ideal school and the kinds of curriculum activities they put into practice—and that are still practiced in the Parker School in Chicago, Dewey's lab school at the University of Chicago, Washburne's school district in Winnetka, Illinois, and Kilpatrick's Lincoln School of Teachers College, as well as in many other private and university lab schools and upper-middle-class school districts across the country. (Actually, the Lincoln School was founded by Abraham Flexner, but many of Kilpatrick's ideas were developed at the school.)

The humanistic curriculum seems more conducive for middle- and upper-middle-class students, as well as higher achievers. Evidence suggests that these students exhibit high independence in learning and are better off in low-structured situations in which they can exercise their own initiative. Low-class and low-achieving students often lack the inner controls necessary for self-discipline and the cognitive skills necessary for independent learning. These students usually need high conforming rules and highly structured activities in class.[23]

Various developmental theories (Erikson, Havighurst, and Maslow) and child-centered methods (Frobel, Pestalozzi, and Neill) for curriculum are derived from the humanistic approach. The formal or planned curriculum is not the only curriculum to consider; the informal and hidden curricula are also worthwhile. Also, this approach considers the whole child, not only the cognitive dimension. Humanistic theories of learning are given equal billing, and sometimes greater emphasis, than behavioral and cognitive theories. Music, art, literature, health education, and the humanities are just as important as science and math (and other academic subjects).

Curriculum specialists who believe in this approach tend to put faith in cooperative learning, independent learning, small-group learning, and social activities, as opposed to competitive, teacher-dominated, large-group learning and only cognitive instruction. Each child, according to this approach, has considerable input in the curriculum and shares responsibility with parents, teachers, and curriculum specialists in planning classroom instruction. Curriculum leaders and supervisors tend to permit teachers more input in curriculum decisions, and the ideas of professional collegiality and mentor systems are more pronounced in the schools adopting this approach. Curriculum committees are *bottom up* instead of *top down,* and often students are invited into curriculum meetings to express their views on content and experiences related to curriculum development.[24]

The humanistic approach became popular again in the 1970s as relevancy, radical school reform, open education, and alternative education became part of the reform movement in education. Today, however, demands for educational excellence and academic productivity have resulted in emphasis on cognition, and not humanism, and on subjects such as science and math, and not art or music. The humanistic approach has usually represented a minority view among curriculum leaders in schools. Most educators are usually more concerned with the "nuts and bolts" of curriculum, that is the "three R's" in elementary school and the core or basic academic subjects in secondary school. And now humanism has been relegated almost to a fringe view, overshadowed by a return to back to basics, critical thinking, and tougher academic standards.

Current curriculum texts that reflect the humanistic approach are authored by Elliott Eisner, Glenn Hass, and Gene Shepherd and William Ragan.[25] These books tend to stress the personal and social development of the child, theories of learning (cognitive and affective), and the self-concept and self-esteem of learners. They envision the teacher as a facilitator and resource for their students—interacting, problem solving, and inquiring. Students are not passive, but active learners who are involved with planning classroom and school activities.

Reconceptualists

Some curriculum textbook writers consider that reconceptualists represent an approach to curriculum.[26] But reconceptionalists lack a model for developing and designing curriculum (or for dealing with technical matters); rather, they tend to focus on larger ideological and moral issues of education (not only curriculum) and economic and political institutions of society (not only schools). For this reason, and because they lack a model for planning curriculum, we feel they should be discussed more in a philosophical or political context—not as a curriculum approach.

Reconceptionalists view schools as an extension of society. They hold that the purpose of curriculum ought to be emancipatory but that instead it has become controlling and preserving of the existing order. Most of these curricularists are not textbook writers (broad based, objective, nonpolitical, nonpartisan); rather, they tend to be educational critics—advocates of a particular philosophical and political position.[27]

Rooted in the philosophy and social activism of such early reconstructionists as Counts, Rugg, and Benjamin,[28] these new curricularists wish to rethink, reconsider, and reconceptualize the curriculum. Not only do they challenge the traditional, scientific, and rational views of curriculum, but they also criticize those holding them for embodying their own subjective and imperfect sets of values. They assert that other ways of knowing are not quantifiable or objective as the dominant notion of "good research" in education. Their approach to curriculum is subjective, political, and ideological, and they do not rely on either the hard sciences or empirical methods for answers.

DEFINITION OF CURRICULUM

What is curriculum? What is its purpose? How does it affect students and teachers? The way we define curriculum by and large reflects our approach to it. But the relationship between approach and definition is neither perfect nor mutually exclusive; approaches and definitions overlap. We can specify five basic views or definitions of curriculum. The first two, the most popular, delineate two extremes: specific and prescriptive versus broad and general.

A curriculum can be defined as a *plan* for action or a written document that includes strategies for achieving desired goals or ends. This position, popularized by Ralph Tyler and Hilda Taba, exemplifies a linear view of curriculum. The steps of the planner are sequenced in advance. The plan has a beginning and end, as well as a process (or means) so that the beginning can progress to an end. Most behavioral and some managerial and systems people today agree with this definition. For example, J. Galen Saylor defines curriculum "as a plan for providing sets of learning opportunities for persons to be educated."[29] Writes David Pratt, "Curriculum is an organized set of formal education and/or training intentions."[30] Jon Wiles and Joseph Bondi view

"curriculum as a plan for learning [whereby] objectives determine what learning is important."[31]

Curriculum can, however, be defined broadly—as dealing with the *experiences* of the learner. This view considers almost anything in school, even outside of school (as long as it is planned) as part of the curriculum. It is rooted in Dewey's definition of experience and education, as well as in Caswell and Campbell's view, from the 1930s, that curriculum was "all the experiences children have under the guidance of teachers."[32]

Humanistic curricularists and elementary school curricularists subscribe to this definition, which, over the years, has been interpreted more broadly by textbook writers. State Shepherd and Ragan, "The curriculum consists of the ongoing experiences of children under the guidance of the school." It represents "a special environment . . . for helping children achieve self-realization through active participation within the school."[33] Eisner points out that the curriculum "is a program [the school] offers to its students." It consists of a "preplanned series of educational hurdles" and "an entire range of experiences a child has within the school."[34] Finally, Hass contends that "curriculum is all of the experiences that individuals have in a program of education . . . which is planned in terms of . . . theory and research or past and present professional practice."[35]

Three other definitions fall in between these two common, almost extreme definitions. Curriculum can be considered as a system for dealing with people and the processes or the organization of personnel and procedures for implementing that system. The system can be either linear or nonlinear. A linear system is a simple means-ends view of curriculum whereby a process or means is determined to achieve a desired end. A nonlinear system, however, permits the curriculum specialist to operate with flexibility and to enter at various points of the model, skip components or parts, reverse order, and work on more than one component at a time. Many managerial and systems curricularists adopt this definition.[36]

Curriculum can also be viewed as a *field of study,* comprising its own foundations and domains of knowledge, as well as its own research, theory, and principles and its own specialists to interpret this knowledge. The discussion of curriculum is usually scholarly and theoretical, not practical, and concerned with broad historical, philosophical, or social issues. Academics, such as McNeill, Schubert, and the Tanners, often subscribe to this view of curriculum.[37]

Finally, curriculum can be considered in terms of *subject matter* (mathematics, science, English, history, and so on) or content (the way we organize and assimilate information). We can also talk about subject matter or content in terms of different *grade levels*. Nonetheless, the emphasis from this viewpoint would be on facts. concepts, and generalizations of a particular subject or group of subjects, as opposed to generic concepts and principles of curriculum making that cut across the field of curriculum. There is no particular curriculum approach that adheres to this definition, and any curriculum approach could adopt this definition. Of all the current texts, only Shepherd and Ragan examine subject matter in depth and at the elementary school level. Glatthorn and Wiles and Bondi examine subject matter K-12, but the discussion is limited.[38]

Beauchamp asserts that only definitions involving a plan, system, and field of study represent key or legitimate uses of the word curriculum.[39] But the other two definitions (dealing with experiences and subjects) are also consistent with good theory and practice. Surprisingly, there are no real curriculum advocates of subjects and grades. Because most school systems across the country develop curriculum in terms of different subjects and grades, it would seem that we need to view curriculum more in line with this definition than others. The fact that practitioners use this form of curriculum on a daily basis, whereas theoreticians rarely do (usually professing that they wish to examine generic concepts and principles that are applicable to most subjects and grades) suggests that the two groups are not really talking to each other. Although many university curriculum departments offer courses in elementary and secondary school curriculum, they rarely offer curriculum courses by subjects—mathematics curriculum, science curriculum, and so on. (Curricularists commonly contend that too few students would enroll in these courses to justify them.)

The Problem of Definition

The varied definitions of curriculum create confusion and trivialize the field. Definitional debates take away time and energy from substantive problems and issues, from research and theoretical and practical approaches. Because curricularists cannot agree on just what is curriculum, it follows that they lack common terms and have trouble communicating with each other.

Consider the two most common definitions. The more precise one's definition of curriculum, and the more a person relies on a preconceived plan or document, the greater the tendency to omit, ignore, or miss relevant factors related to teaching and learning because they are not part of the written plan. As Doll points out, "Every school has a planned, formal acknowledged curriculum," but it also has "an unplanned, informal and hidden one" that must be considered.[40] The planned, formal curriculum focuses on goals, objectives, subject matter, and organization of instruction; the unplanned, informal curriculum deals with social-psychological interaction among students and teachers, especially their feelings, attitudes, and behaviors.

If we only consider the planned curriculum, or if we are too prescriptive in our approach, we ignore the unintended and dysfunctional (negative) consequences of our plans and actions (that is, suppose the student begins to dislike history or English, even though the teacher's intention was to teach DuBois). The point is, we cannot be too rigid or close-ended and try to fill in all the boxes. There are too many gray areas in education, and too many human variables that we cannot control or plan for in advance. The curriculum must consider the smells and sounds of the classroom, the intuitive judgments and hunches of the teacher, and the needs and interests of the students that evolve and cannot always be planned by the student, teacher, or curriculum specialist.

On the other hand, a broad umbrellalike definition of curriculum as school experiences results in other problems. It assumes that almost everything that goes on in school can be classified or discussed in terms of curriculum. It even suggests that curriculum is synonymous with education. It also connotes that almost every field or discipline in schools of education has implications for curriculum or is part of the curriculum field. If nearly everything in schools and in the study of education is related to curriculum, classifying what is not curriculum is meaningless. The content of curriculum becomes so diffuse that no one can have sufficient knowledge, or knowledge that is agreed to be of sufficient value, in the field. Given this macro view of curriculum, it is extremely difficult to become a specialist or expert in the field. When the content and scope of any field become all-encompassing, or so enlarged that they overlap with those of many other fields, then it becomes too difficult to delineate that field (say, curriculum) and separate it from other fields.

Background Issues for Defining the Field

Content or subject matter issues are relevant too. Is it appropriate to talk about a social studies or mathematics curriculum or about curriculum in general? Are there general principles of curriculum that apply to all subjects, or specific principles that apply to specific subjects? Should subject matter be organized around separate disciplines or based on interdisciplinary and core approaches? To what extent is subject a matter of student choice, professional choice, or parent choice? Should it be determined by the community, state, or nation? How should subjects be organized: around graded or nongraded approaches, behavioral objectives, student activities, social or community values, future jobs? What portion of subject matter should be classified as general, specialized, or elective? What is the appropriate mix of common subjects versus optional subjects? And what is the appropriate stress on facts, concepts, and principles of subject matter? As Beauchamp writes, "The posture . . . one assumes with respect to the content of a curriculum inevitably will be of great influence upon . . . theory and planning."[41] Actually, it has a major influence on everything that follows, from developing, designing, implementing, and evaluating the curriculum, from planning the policies and programs to determining the processes and products of the curriculum.

Other issues are related to people. Who are the major participants? To what extent should students, teachers, parents, and community members be involved in curriculum planning? Why are school administrators assuming greater roles in curriculum matters, and curriculum specialists assuming fewer roles? What are the roles and responsibilities of researchers and practitioners in curriculum making? And, how do we improve their communication?

Fundamental Questions

Asking the right questions is crucial for addressing basic concerns in curriculum and for determining the basic concepts, principles, and research methods of the field. If we ask the wrong questions, the discussions that follow (even the answers) are of little value. The danger in listing a host of fundamental questions, however, is that they tend to become translated as a set of principles or steps to be blindly followed. Indeed, appropriate questions can be used as a base for raising issues and problems that curriculum specialists need to address, whether they deal in theory or practice or both.

The first list of fundamental questions was formulated by a famous twelve-person committee on curriculum making, headed by Harold Rugg and organized in 1930 for the Twenty-Sixth Yearbook of the National Society for the Study of Education (NSSE). This group of curriculum specialists, perhaps the most prestigious ever convened to present a general system on the principles of curriculum making, started the second volume of the Yearbook with eighteen "fundamental questions" to serve as a basis for "viewing . . . the issues and problems of curriculum" for that era.[42] These questions are shown in column 1 of Table 1.1.

A more recent set of questions was presented more than 50 years later and is shown in column 2 of the same table. In general the sets of both questions focus on the role of school in American society, the place and function of subject matter, the methods and materials for facilitating learning, the role of the curriculum specialist, and the relationship between curriculum, instruction, supervision, and governmental levels of curriculum making.

TABLE 1-1 Fundamental Questions of Curriculum

18 QUESTIONS , 1930	15 QUESTIONS , 1987
1. What period of life does schooling primarily contemplate as its end?	1. How is curriculum defined?
2. How can the curriculum prepare for effective participation in adult life?	2. What philosophies and theories are we communicating, intentionally or not, in our curriculum?
3. Are the curriculum-makers of the schools obliged to formulate a point of view concerning the merits or deficiencies of American civilization?	3. What social and political forces influence curriculum? Which ones are most pertinent? Which constrain or impose limitations?
4. Should the school be regarded as a conscious agency for social improvement?	4. How does learning take place? What learning activities are most suitable for meeting the needs of our learners? How can these activities best be organized?
5. How shall the content of the curriculum be conceived and stated?	5. What are the domains of curriculum knowledge? What types of curriculum knowledge are essential?
6. What is the place and function of subject matter in the education process?	6. What are the essential parts of a curriculum?
7. What portion of education should be classified as "general" and what portions as "specialized" or "vocational" or purely "optional"? To what extent is general education to run parallel with vocational education, and to what extent is the latter to follow on the completion of the former?	7. Why do changes in curriculum take place? How does change affect the curriculum?
8. Is the curriculum to be made in advance?	8. What are the role's and responsibilities of the curriculum specialist?
9. To what extent is the "organization" of subject matter a matter of pupil-thinking and construction of, or planning by, the professional curriculum-maker as a result of experimentation?	9. How is the curriculum best organized?
10. From the point of view of the educator, when has "learning" taken place?	10. What are the roles and responsibilities of the teacher and student in organizing curriculum?
11. To what extent should traits be learned in their "natural" setting (that is, in a "life-situation")?	11. What are our aims and goals? How do we translate them into objectives?
12. To what degree should the curriculum provide for individual differences?	12. How do we define our educational needs? Whose needs? How do we prioritize these needs?
13. To what degree is the concept of "minimal essentials" to be used in curriculum construction?	13. What subject matter or content is most worthwhile? What are the best forms of content? How do we organize them?

(continued)

TABLE 1-1   Continued

18 QUESTIONS , 1930	15 QUESTIONS , 1987

14. What should be the form of organization of the curriculum? Shall it be one of the following or will you adopt others?

   a. A flexibly graded series of suggestive activities with reference to subject matter which may be used in connection with the activities? Or,

   b. A rigidly graded series of activities with subject matter included with each respective activity? Or,

   c. A graded sequence of subject matter with suggestion for activities to which the subject matter is related? Or,

   d. A statement of achievements expected for each grade, a list of suggested activities, and an outline of related subject matter, through the use of which the grade object may be achieved? Or,

   e. A statement of grade objectives in terms of subject matter and textual and reference materials which will provide this subject matter without any specific reference to activities?

15. What, if any, use shall be made of the spontaneous interests of children?

16. What types of material (activities, reading, discussions problems and topics, group projects, and so on) should the curriculum-maker analyze [for] activities in which [students] actually engage?

17. How far shall methods of learning be standardized?

18. Administrative questions of curriculum-making.

   a. For what time units shall the curriculum be organized?

   b. For what geographic units shall the curriculum be made [national, state, school district, local school]? What is the optimal form in which to publish the course of study?

---

14. How do we measure or verify what we are trying to achieve? Who is accountable, for what, and to whom?

15. What is the appropriate relationship between curriculum and instruction? Curriculum and supervision? Curriculum and evaluation?

Source: Harold Rugg et al., ''List of Fundamental Questions on Curriculum Making,'' in G. M. Whipple, ed., *The Foundations of Curriculum-making,* Twenty-sixth Yearbook of the National Society for the Study of Education, Part II (Bloomington, Ill.: Public School Publishing Co., 1930), p. 8; Allan C. Ornstein. ''The Theory and Practice of Curriculum.'' *Kappa Delta Pi Record* (Fall 1987), p. 16.

Most important, it can be argued that these fundamental questions help establish what Tyler called the "rationale" of curriculum, that later Saylor, Alexander, and Lewis called the "purpose," and that Schubert more recently maintained was the "paradigm,"—which governs how inquiry in the field of curriculum may be established.[43] By asking these "what" and "how" questions, curriculum specialists can delineate important theories, concepts, and methods in the field.

FOUNDATIONS OF CURRICULUM

Debates continue on what is curriculum, and on how to outline the basic foundations (or boundaries) and domains (knowledge) of the field. An optimistic view would be that almost all, if not all, the knowledge concerning curriculum is available in the literature, but at present it is "widely scattered" and is either "unknown or unread" by a majority of those who teach or practice curriculum.[44] A pessimistic view is that the field lacks purpose and direction because it has extensively "adapted and borrowed subject matter from a number of [other] disciplines," including its major "principles, knowledge and skills."[45] This is basically the same criticism that Joseph Schwab made some 20 years ago, when he complained that the field was "morbid [because] it has adopted theories from outside the field of education . . . from which to deduce . . . aims and procedures for schools and classrooms."[46]

Some argue that until these problems are resolved, curriculum as a field of study will be characterized by considerable confusion, conflict, and lack of coherence, and that it will continue to lack a well-organized professional and political constituency. A more optimistic view, however, considers this openness or lack of closure as a source of richness and challenge. It illustrates that curriculum is dynamic and subject to change, like schools and society.

Major Foundations: Philosophy, History, Psychology, and Sociology

The foundations of curriculum set the external boundaries of the knowledge of curriculum and define what constitutes valid sources of information from which come accepted theories, principles, and ideas relevant to the field of curriculum.

The commonly accepted foundations of curriculum include the following knowledge areas: philosophical, historical, psychological, and social (sometimes cultural, political, or economical foundations are included as part of or separate from the social foundations). Although curriculum writers generally agree on the foundation areas, few attempt to analyze or discuss these four areas in depth. Of all the recent texts in curriculum, Miller and Seller put the most emphasis on the foundation areas—50 percent of their text deals with historical, philosophical, social, cultural, and psychological foundations.[47] They assert that the foundation areas serve as the basis for theory in curriculum, a view that corresponds somewhat with the intellectual-academic approach to curriculum. Not since Robert Zais, another academic, has such emphasis been put on the major foundation areas of curriculum.[48] Other curricularists do not put as much emphasis on the foundation areas, but still seriously discuss the foundations in their respective textbooks.[49]

Most texts emphasize one or two foundation areas. The texts of Hunkins and Saylor and others, for example, emphasize the social foundations. They examine various social, as well as related political and economic issues.[50] Although Shepherd and Ragan examine some historical and social foundations, they also examine psychological principles and ideas (without the label foundations) extensively throughout the text. Eisner also puts strong emphasis on psychological foundations, especially the psychology of teaching and learning.[51] Schubert and the Tanners present an extensive historical overview of curriculum, but weave some social and philosophical overtones throughout their respective historical treatments of the field.[52]

Of course, merely examining the foundation areas is insufficient. Curricularists need to show the relationship of the foundation areas and curriculum. They must analyze and synthesize what is known about each of the foundations and present implications that are relevant to curriculum. In this connection, Herbert Kliebard claims that the field of curriculum is a synoptic one. The specialist in curriculum brings perspectives from other fields to bear on curriculum. This means the curriculum person examines and uses the concepts, methods, and research tools of the philosopher, historian, psychologist, sociologist, economist, and political scientist.[53]

Regardless of their approach or their philosophical, historical, social, or psychological views, it is natural for curriculum people to rely on the foundation areas as a means of studying and practicing curriculum. This text examines four foundation areas (in four chapters) with the intention of presenting important sources of information from other fields that are pertinent to curriculum. It is important that the readers analyze and interpret the knowledge of foundations presented to establish and clarify the external boundaries of curriculum.

We need to point out, also, the growing influence upon curriculum and instruction of one particular foundation area. Recent trends since the Sputnik era of the 1950s show the increasing impact of psychology. This was illustrated by the behaviorist and cognitive models of compensatory education in the 1960s, the humanistic models of learning in the 1970s, and the cognitive theories dealing with educational productivity and critical thinking in the 1980s and 1990s. It is further evidenced by the shift of subject matter to disciplinary inquiry and modes of thinking, and from emphasis on traditional materials and media to whole language and reading processes.

Finally, the growing influence of psychology is considered to be a major support of instruction, learning, and teaching—in the professional literature and research dealing with individualized learning, cooperative learning, academic learning time, direct instruction, mastery learning, and more effective schooling, as well as by the empirical emphasis on teaching methods, teacher behavior, teacher competencies, and teacher effectiveness. What has happened is that such instructional and learning theorists as David Berliner, Benjamin Bloom, Jere Brophy, Walter Doyle, Nate Gage, Thomas Good, Carolyn Evertson, and Herb Walberg, who have strong research and statistical backgrounds, seem to have filled a void left by curricularists who in the past addressed these twin areas and envisioned instruction and learning as integral to the discussion of curriculum.

This trend is especially exemplified by the educational psychologists, who deliver most of the papers at the American Educational Research Association (AERA) in Division C, "Learning and Instruction," and by their growing influence even in Division B, "Curriculum Studies."[54] Even in two popular curriculum journals, *Educational Leadership* and *Phi Delta Kappan,* articles on instruction and learning (as well as teaching) are increasingly written by educational psychologists.[55]

Indeed, some curricularists seem to have lost some of their initiative and influence in instruction and learning, what they did well (between the 1920s and 1950s) when the field of curriculum was expanding and including many aspects of instruction and learning. At that time, many curriculum leaders (Harold Alberty, Nelson Bossing, Gertrude Noar, John and Mary Norton, Hilda Taba, Ralph Tyler, B. Othanel Smith, and others) had strong psychology backgrounds and greater interest in educational measurement and assessment.

Some curricularists feel uncomfortable about the inroads of psychology; moreover, many appear to be less familiar with this foundation area compared with others. In this connection, we note the scant discussion of psychological foundations in curriculum texts. (Only two current curriculum texts, Eisner's and Shepherd and Ragan's, reflect a strong psychological approach.)[56] Prior to these texts, one would have to turn back to Taba to find a basic text in curriculum that emphasized psychology.[57]

DOMAINS OF CURRICULUM

Whereas the foundations of curriculum represent the external boundaries of the field, the domains of curriculum define the internal boundaries, or accepted knowledge, of the field that can be derived from examining published textbooks, articles, and research papers. Although curriculum specialists generally agree on the foundation areas, they often do not agree on what represents the domains or common knowledge of curriculum. The latter problem suggests that the field is neither a disciplined body nor a full profession based upon a defined body of knowledge. Many efforts have been made to structure a matrix or map of the knowledge in curriculum so as to help conceptualize or set the boundaries within the field. According to some observers, the problem is that the knowledge is diffused in several sources, many unrecognized as curriculum sources. In addition, many known sources are unread because there is so much literature to read.[58]

The lack of consensus of the domains of curriculum is illustrated by the experts themselves. For example, George Beauchamp divided curriculum knowledge into planning, implementation, and evaluation.[59] Fenwick English viewed curriculum in terms of ideological (or philosophical-scientific), technical (or design), and operational (or managerial) issues.[60] Finally, Edmund Short outlined the domains of curriculum into policy making, development, evaluation, change, decision making, activities or fields of study, and forms and language of inquiry (or theory).[61]

Linda Behar was the first to establish an empirical format for identifying *curriculum domains* (broad areas of knowledge based on the most influential curriculum textbooks over a 20-year period) and *curriculum practices* (precise activities teachers and curriculum specialists engage in while inquiring about, planning, or implementing the curriculum). As many as 49 curriculum practices were validated and then rated in importance by professors of curriculum across the nation. These practices were categorized into and used to define and support the existence of nine curriculum domains: (1) curriculum philosophy, (2) curriculum theory, (3) curriculum research, (4) curriculum history, (5) curriculum development, (6) curriculum design, (7) curriculum evaluation, (8) curriculum policy, and (9) curriculum as a field of study.[62] Although these curriculum domains vary from one theorist to another, so that a knowledge base in the field is difficult to agree upon, the reader might infer that Behar's work helps establish recommended content for a curriculum text.

Despite this lack of consensus, however, it is important to establish a framework for conceptualizing the domains of curriculum—that is, the significant and indispensable curriculum knowledge necessary to conduct research and make theoretical and practical decisions about curriculum. The problem is that few curriculum writers can agree on the domains of curriculum knowledge; in some cases, no framework exists that

connotes curriculum as a distinct enterprise with its own boundaries, internal structures, relations, and activities. We maintain that, of all the domains of curriculum knowledge, the *development* and *design* of the curriculum—what some observers refer to as the theoretical aspects and what others call the technical aspects of curriculum—are crucial for any text.

Curriculum Development

Analyzing curriculum in terms of development is the traditional and most common approach to the field. The idea is to show how curriculum evolves or is planned, implemented, and evaluated, as well as what various people, processes, and procedures are involved in constructing the curriculum. Such development is usually examined in a logical step-by-step fashion, based on behavioral and managerial approaches to curriculum and rooted in scientific principles of education. In other words, the principles are generalizable. Many curriculum texts today use the terms *development* and *plan* in their titles—and thus reflect this thinking. See Curriculum Tips 1-2.

Saylor and others, for example, outline a concise four-step planning model, which includes goals and objectives, curriculum design (or specifications), curriculum implementation (or instruction), and curriculum evaluation. The planning model is influenced by several social forces and three social sources of curriculum—society, learners, and knowledge.[63] Another easy-to-understand approach is by Unruh and Unruh, who outline five developmental steps: goals and objectives, needs assessment, content, implementation, and evaluation.[64] Francis Hunkins has designed a similar linear model, in seven corresponding steps: curriculum conceptualization and legitimization, curriculum diagnosis, content selection, experience selection, curriculum implementation, curriculum evaluation, and curriculum maintenance.[65]

There are more complicated curriculum development models, but they are geared for the more advanced student of curriculum. All these development models, however, attempt to show the relationship of curriculum to various decisions, activities, and processes. They provide us

**CURRICULUM TIPS 1-2   Steps in Curriculum
Planning**

The following questions are based on three stages of curriculum planning: development, implementation, and evaluation. The questions presented are essential in the process leading to a new or revised curriculum. They are starting points or guides to help clarify curriculum planning in any subject area or grade level.

1. When the school system is developing a new curriculum:
    a. Who determines priorities?
    b. Who develops the time line?
    c. Who assigns members to curriculum committees?
    d. Who coordinates the efforts of curriculum committees?
    e. Who devises the curriculum development process?
2. After the curriculum has been approved and it is time to put it into place:
    a. Who decides on the materials and activities?
    b. Who determines how much money will be needed?
    c. Who decides what staff development will be offered to prepare teachers to use it?
3. Finally, to determine if the curriculum is meeting expectations:
    a. Who decides how the curriculum will be evaluated?
    b. Who is responsible for carrying out the evaluation?
    c. Who is responsible for reporting the results of the evaluation to teachers, administrators, school board members, and the public?

Source: Michael Campbell, Judy Carr, and Douglas Harris, "Board Members Needn't Be Experts to Play a Vital Role in Curriculum," *American School Board Journal* (April 1989) p. 30.

with guideposts and structure to clarify our thinking. The models tend to be graphically or pictorially illustrated, and in terms of input, transformations, and output, they are sequential and rational, the curriculum is viewed as a total system, and all enterprises within the model are conceived as subsystems. The development models are also theoretical and scientific, and they are designed to increase understanding of facts, correlates, and relationships of curriculum. Finally, the models are conceived in technical terms—with the assumption that one must be knowledgeable of the field to fully appreciate and understand them.

Many curriculum textbook writers tend to formulate developmental models. However, some curricularists use the term *development* in their respective textbook titles without either formulating their own developmental models or even paying much attention to other models.[66] But the emphasis on development is not without pitfalls. By basing their developmental models around scientific and technical terms, writers tend to overlook the human aspects of teaching and learning. By formulating steps that are concrete, prescriptive, and measurable, they tend to ignore processes that are not readily observable or measurable, that are not precisely consistent, or that are not applicable to a good deal of control. What they sometimes ignore are the personal attitudes, emotions, and feelings linked to teaching and learning, and the values and beliefs involved in curriculum making.

By adopting developmental models, curricularists tend to constrain curriculum choices and to limit flexibility in the various curriculum sequences or steps—from aims and objectives to evaluation of learning tasks and outcomes. They sometimes forget that the path to curriculum development is strewn with many concessions to social and political realities, qualitative judgments that require familiarity with teaching effectiveness and allowable choices in teaching methods and learning activities, and alternatives that recognize that one kind of curriculum may be more suitable and successful with one school (or with one population of students and teachers) than another.

However, adopting one or more of these developmental models does not prevent one from being mindful of these pitfalls. Some of the models' advocates would argue that by being systematic, they are able to consider students in all of their complexity and to manage the dynamics and decisions of curriculum activity; moreover, they might argue that their models consider multiple variables and permit choices.

Curriculum Design

Curriculum design refers to the way we conceptualize the curriculum and arrange its major components (subject matter content, instructional methods and materials, learner experiences or activities) to provide direction and guidance as we develop the curriculum. Most curriculum writers do not have a single or pure design for curriculum; they tend to be influenced by many designs, as they are by many approaches, and they are likely to draw bits and pieces from different designs. Unless they are highly motivated or compelled by one curriculum approach or a set of values or tools for analyzing the world around them, they tend to use eclectic designs and to intermix ideas from several sources.

Nonetheless, the way someone designs a curriculum is partially rooted in his or her approach to and definition of curriculum. For example, those who view curriculum in behaviorist terms with a prescribed plan and set of learning outcomes and those who consider curriculum to be a system of managing people and organizing procedures will produce different curriculum designs. Those who have strong psychological views of teaching and learning will also present different designs for curriculum from those who have strong social or political views of schools. Whereas curriculum development tends to be technical and scientific, curriculum design is more varied, because it is based on curricularists' values and beliefs about education, priorities of schooling, and views of how students learn. Just asking questions such as what are schools for, what shall we teach, how shall we teach, and what learning theories should we stress evokes considerable controversy. The positions educa-

tors adopt to these questions, however, reflect their preferred designs in curriculum.

A number of current curriculum texts focus on a particular curriculum design choice of designs. For example, Saylor and coauthors distinguish five curriculum designs: (1) subject matter/disciplines, which involve subject matter and knowledge; (2) competencies/technology, which are sequential, analytical, and behaviorist; (3) human traits/processes, which focus on human behavior and group behavior; (4) social functions/activities, which pertain to social living and societal needs; and (5) individual needs and interests, which comprise student-oriented or child-centered activities.[67]

Wiles and Bondi present six different designs: (1) conservative-liberal arts designs, which emphasize knowledge and intellectual pursuits; (2) educational technology designs, which focus on goals and ends, objectivity, and efficiency; (3) humanistic designs, which propose student-centered curricula; (4) vocational designs, which are concerned with vocational and economic aspects of schooling; (5) social-reconstruction designs, which are aimed at social improvement of society; and (6) deschooling designs, which emphasize the de-emphasis of formal schooling.[68]

In general, a curriculum design should provide a basic frame of reference for planning—or more precisely, for developing—curriculum. A curriculum design is influenced to some extent by the writer's curriculum approach, but more precisely by his or her views of teaching, learning, and instruction.

The people who go into teaching, and eventually become curriculum specialists in schools, are often traditional and content oriented. This is good. Because schools usually adopt conservative and cognitive designs to curriculum, highly liberal and humanistic designs are likely to encounter difficulty in most formal school settings. Schools in our society, and almost everywhere else, are given the traditional task of socializing students in accordance with the norms of society (a conservative function) and pursuing intellectual tasks (a cognitive function).

Other Domains of Curriculum

Those who study curriculum and who contribute to the professional literature must constantly deal with other domains of curriculum. Opinions about what curriculum knowledge is essential vary from one scholar to another and from one textbook writer to another. There appears to be more disagreement than agreement in the status and scope of remaining domains of curriculum. As Rosales-Dordelly and Short assert, "The status of the body of curriculum knowledge has been described by scholars in the field as amorphous, diffuse, incoherent, and fragmentary. . . . Few advances have been made in conceptualizing the field."[69] In introducing his text, McNeil puts it another way: "I have left much to the reader and instructor. Everything that ought to be known about curriculum has not been put into the book."[70]

Perhaps one reason for the confusion is that much of curriculum involves values, choices, and options, as well as personal reflection and various views (or perspectives) in different contexts. Presumably, we do not deliberately plan the curriculum or carry it out because it is required; we teach content and organize experiences in certain ways because of our personal and professional beliefs and because we understand the impact on our students. Hence our values, choices, and reflective processes lead to competing versions of the good curriculum and the appropriate domains of curriculum.

The minimum consensus for which we can strive is that a curriculum text include a discussion of development and design. Some might argue that it is important to include, also, discussions of curriculum foundations, curriculum change and innovation, curriculum research and inquiry, and other critiquing ways in which the field is understood. Behar's work comes closest for helping to establish recommended content for a curriculum text, since the domains she outlined were based on assessing the most influential texts in the field over a 20-year span.[71] Whatever other curriculum knowledge we can agree upon in the future as essential would facilitate theoretical and practical decisions in curriculum.

THEORY AND PRACTICE

A field of study basically involves theoretical and practical knowledge. By theory we mean the most advanced and valid knowledge available that can be generalized and applied to many situ-

ations. Theory often establishes the framework of the field and helps persons (researchers and practitioners) within the field analyze and synthesize data, organize concepts and principles, suggest new ideas and relations, and even speculate about the future. According to Beauchamp, theory may be defined as the knowledge and statements that "give functional meaning to a series of events [and] take the form of definitions, operational constructs, assumptions, postulates, hypothesis, generalizations, laws or theorems." In the case of curriculum theory, the subject matter involves "decisions about . . . the use of a curriculum, the development of curriculum, curriculum design and curriculum evaluation."[72] This definition suggests a scientific and technical approach that emphasizes the domain of knowledge that corresponds with curriculum development and also with most textbooks today.

Good theory in curriculum, or in education for that matter, describes and explains the various relationships that exist in the field. It also implies that there are elements of predictability, or that there are rigorous laws that yield high probability and control. Good theory should also prescribe actions to be taken; however, we do not always use theory productively in our practice or in education in general.

The more variable, complex, or unpredictable one views the teaching-learning process, the more one is compelled toward a belief that it is impossible to determine or agree upon generalizations or to obtain high predictability of outcomes. Curriculum, like other aspects of education, involves the use of judgments, hunches, and insights that are not always conducive to laws, principles, or even generalizations. A curriculum often does not emerge as a tightly regulated, predictable, or concise set of enterprises, or as a result of a single or theoretical mix of principles or processes; rather, it evolves as one act and one choice that lead to others, as interests emerge, and, finally, as educators reflect and quietly self-analyze their thinking.

Nonetheless, all curriculum texts should try to incorporate theory throughout the discussion to be systematic in their approach and to establish worthwhile practices. In fact, according to Taba, "any enterprise as complex as curriculum requires some kind of theoretical or conceptual framework of thinking to guide it."[73] There are many theories and theoretical constructs to examine, depending on the author's knowledge and interpretation of curriculum. Ideally, the data should be what we might call *hard* data—scientifically verifiable, quantifiable, and/or based on research principles that can be generalized in similar situations. *Model, paradigm,* or *system* referents can be developed, too, to show various relationships that exist. Most theoretical discussions in curriculum, in fact, rely on one or more of these three referents.

Most curriculum textbook authors would argue that their approaches are grounded in good theory, and that they examine the various theoretical structures and relationships that exist in curriculum. Some authors, such as Glatthorn, Unruh and Unruh, and Walker, include (like we do) separate chapters on theory.[74] Others, like McNeil, combine theory and research in one chapter.[75]

Recent reconceptualist curricularists, however, rely on nonverifiable and nonquantifiable data, what we might call *soft* data. Instead of presenting logical, rational, or objective models, paradigms, or systems to show various curriculum relationships, they emphasize personal biographies, literary criticism, philosophical inquiry, psychoanalysis, and esthetic and artistic knowledge, as well as ideological (or social and political) analysis—which can sometimes be construed as provocative and subjective. Their tools of inquiry are value laden, not objective; their emphasis is on qualitative matters, not quantitative data. By most social science standards, their perspective would not be considered scientific in terms of basic or traditional standards. They tend to focus on contemporary issues and to carefully select proofs and arguments that support preconceived beliefs.

Reconceptualists would argue that traditional social science methods have dominated, under the guise of certainty, logic, and objectivity, but that their methods introduce new knowledge, new ways of knowing, and new tools of research.[76] They argue that traditional curriculum thinkers and theorizers are ideological, and that their methods and models are also based on preconceived assumptions and values.[77]

From Theory to Practice

The test of good theory is whether it can guide practice. In reverse, good practice is based on theory. By practice, we mean the procedures, methods, and skills that apply to the working world, where a person is on the job or actively involved in his or her profession. These procedures and methods are teachable and can be applied in different situations. When applied they should result in the practitioner being considered successful or effective.

Regardless of the theories discussed in any book, those who work with, shape, or formulate curriculum in one way or another have to deal with practice. Such people include administrators, supervisors, and teachers; curriculum developers and curriculum evaluators; textbook authors and test makers; and individuals assigned to curriculum committees, accrediting agencies, school boards, and local, regional, state, and federal educational agencies. The idea is to present theories that are workable for these practitioners, that make sense, and that can explain and be applied to the real world of classrooms and schools. See Curriculum Tips 1-3.

According to Elizabeth Vallance, "much ado [is] made about the split between theory and practice in the dialogues and concerns about professional curriculum workers." The crux of the matter is to provide "practical answers to very practical questions having to do with design, development, implementation, and evaluation of curricula." The distinctions between theory and practice are secondary to Vallance, because both aspects of curriculum focus on the "same curriculum problems."[78]

The problem is, however, that most curricularists, including those who write textbooks, have difficulty in fusing theory with practice. This is true even though many books in curriculum today emphasize "theory" and "practice"[79] or "principles" and "processes"[80] to reflect some form of theory and practice in their titles. Perhaps the reason curricularists have difficulty making the connection between theory and practice is that their methods of inquiry lend themselves more to theoretical discussions and less to practical matters. Also, good theory is recognized

CURRICULUM TIPS 1-3   Translating Theory into Practice

Blending theory with practice is an old ideal. To make serious progress toward this goal in curriculum, we need to recognize certain basic steps.

1. *Read the literature.* Any attempt to relate theory and practice must be based on knowledge of the professional literature.
2. *Identify the major terms.* The need is for curriculum theorists and practitioners to identify and agree on the major constructs, concepts, and questions for discussion.
3. *Check the soundness of existing theories.* Existing theories need to be analyzed in terms of validity, evidence, accuracy, underlying assumptions, logic of argument, coherence, generalizability, values, and biases.
4. *Avoid fads.* Fads must not be introduced to practitioners under the guise of a new theory, or even as reform or innovation. When a new program or method is introduced to the profession, we must resist jumping on the bandwagon, much less calling it "theory"; we should wait for evaluations or complaints to surface.
5. *Align theory with practice.* Theory must be considered in context with the real world of schools; it must be plausible, applicable, and realistic in terms of practice.
6. *Test theory.* If the theory is credible and makes common sense, it must be empirically tested and the results measured. It should be introduced first on a small scale, comparing experimental and control schools.
7. *Interpret theory.* The results must be tested and interpreted in realistic conditions over realistic time periods. The theory must be evaluated in schools for a minimum of 1 year, and ideally over a 3-year period, to test for "fading out."
8. *Modify theory, reduce its complexity.* A theory is a generalizable construct supported by language or quantitative data. Nonetheless, theory must be modified from paper to practice, from the abstract to the concrete world, from complex concepts to lay terms. When we move theory to practice, we include many people (and resources) to make it work. Theory must fit with people (not mold people to theory) to move it from an idea to action.

by professors of the field (and the research community in general) as a worthwhile endeavor; however, good practice is often misconstrued by theoreticians as a "cookbook" or as "do's and dont's" that are second rate or unimportant.

Decker Walker is more critical, noting the benefits of a theory in any field as being to provide a framework to conceptualize and clarify important problems and techniques. But "curriculum theories . . . that are correct and complete to serve as . . . a basis for practical decisions do not exist." Educators, including curricularists, tend to embrace "theory as an ideology," even though much of what they say is suspect and closes us to "other aspects of reality and other values."[81]

Most curriculum texts are more theoretical than practical, but so are education textbooks in general. Despite their claims, curricularists seem unable to make the leap from theory to practice, from the textbook and college course to the classroom and school (or other organizations). Good theory in curriculum (and in other fields of education) often gets lost as practitioners (say, teachers) try to apply what they learned in college to the job setting in a search for practical solutions to common, everyday problems.

The problem of translating theory into practice is further aggravated by practitioners who feel that practical considerations are more worthwhile than theory; most teachers and principals view theory as unpractical and "how to do" approaches as helpful. In short, many theoreticians ignore the practitioners, and many practitioners ignore the theoreticians. Moreover, many theoretical discussions of curriculum are divorced from practical application in the classroom, and many practical discussions of curriculum rarely consider theoretical relationships.[82]

Practice involves selecting strategies and rules that apply to various situations, like good theory, but all situations are not the same. This becomes especially evident when practitioners try to apply the theory they learn in their textbooks. Adopting the right method for the appropriate situation is not an easy task and involves a good deal of common sense and experience, which no one can learn from theoretical discussions. No matter how scientific we think our theories are, a certain amount of art is involved in the practice of curriculum—intuitive judgments and hunches that cannot be easily predicted or generalized from one situation to another, and this confounds theory.

Just what, then, does curriculum practice involve? The response is open to debate. But we might say that curriculum practice includes understanding the constraints and specifics operating within the school (or organization in which one is working) and comprehending the goals and priorities of the school and the needs of the students and staff. It also involves planning and working with procedures and processes that can be implemented in classrooms (or any formal group setting) and schools (or any formal organization). A successful practitioner in curriculum is capable of developing, implementing, and evaluating the curriculum; that is, he or she can select and organize (1) goals and objectives; (2) subject matter; (3) methods, materials, and media; (4) learning experiences and activities that are suitable for learners and then (5) assess these processes.

In the final analysis, it is up to the curriculum specialist to recognize that the theoretician and practitioner have different agendas and perceptions of what is important. The practitioner does not function as the mere user of the theoretician's or researcher's product, and the theoretician is often interested in knowledge that has little value to practitioners. One role for the curriculum specialist, what some educators call the "reflective practitioner," is to generate dialogue between the theoretician and practitioner and establish modes of collaboration that can benefit both groups.[83]

Curriculum Certification

The fact that curriculum lacks certification in most states (specified or professional requirements) adds to the problem of defining and conceptualizing the field and agreeing on curriculum courses at the college and university level. This lack of certification should be considered seriously, because we need competent people who can make wise curriculum decisions.

The closest thing to certification is an endorsement or license as a supervisor or principal. Curriculum making is a complicated procedure that cannot be left to just anyone or any group. We need people qualified to serve as generalists and specialists in curriculum, both as resource agents and decision makers. And we need people who can maintain a curriculum balance in terms of goals, subject matter, and learning activities, given the numerous special-interest groups who wish to impose their brand of education on schools. Not only do minimum requirements for curriculum personnel vary among school systems within the same state, not to mention among states, but the programs in curriculum vary considerably among colleges and universities as well. Because there are no state or professional regulations, each school of education usually decides its own requirements and the courses it will use to meet these requirements. The result is a proliferation of elective courses in curriculum programs and a lack of specialized and general, agreed-upon courses. Even when curriculum course titles are similar, wide differences in content and level of instruction are common.

The irony is that there is great confusion about content and experiences in a field that should be very clear about its curriculum. Although there are many good curriculum programs at the university level, there is little guarantee that curricularists who graduate from a program know how to develop, implement, and evaluate a curriculum—or that they can translate theory into practice. Some curriculum students may not have taken courses in development, implementation, or evaluation (especially students in administration), whereas others may have taken several. And no test or screening device helps school systems or school board officials make choices about curriculum personnel, and their expertise in curriculum. This also adds to the problem of defining who curriculum specialists or generalists, and what their respective job titles, roles, and responsibilities, are. Is a supervisor a curriculum generalist or specialist? What about a principal who is supposed to be a curriculum and instructional leader? Is a resource teacher, consultant, or director a curriculum person? And what about the classroom teacher?

Professionals are certified in such other fields as teaching, counseling, school psychology, supervision, administration, and so on. Job descriptions and related course requirements are defined. Students can major in curriculum but they are at risk, because curriculum jobs are not well defined and there are few certification requirements or licenses that protect their jobs. Curriculum positions are definitely available in schools, universities, and local, regional, state, and federal education agencies, but without certification someone other than a curriculum person can obtain the same job.

Actually, many curriculum specialists who work in schools are certified in other fields, which means that their loyalties are not often in curriculum or that their educational preparation and professional reading habits may be closely aligned to other fields. Similarly, professors of curriculum, unlike professors of elementary education, reading, counseling, educational administration, and so on, are usually schooled in many disciplines, not only curriculum per se. Thus, the field is open to several interpretations by the experts themselves—what curriculum should encompass, what knowledge is of tangible substance, and what content and experiences are essential.

The lack of certification weakens the role of curricularists in the schools and the influence of curricularists at the university level. It also encourages local and state policy makers and legislators to develop and design the school curriculum—to impose standards and approve programs in terms of goals, content, and subject matter. This is especially true in large states like California, Florida, Illinois, New York, and Texas, where standards and programs are often changed and influenced by pressure groups. Because the field lacks professional certification, the responsibilities of curriculum leaders are vague and diffuse, and a strong and organized constituency is lacking at the school and university levels.

Hence, it behooves the professional organizations that perceive themselves as curriculum based (for example, the Association for Supervision and Curriculum Development, Division B of AERA) and leading professors of curriculum, as well as practitioners, to put pressure first on a national level, then state level, to formulate a certification policy in curriculum. This is a call for reform.

THE ROLES OF THE CURRICULUM WORKER

Much has been written about the roles and responsibilities of the curriculum worker. Confusion exists for several reasons. First, the term is used interchangeably with curriculum supervisor, curriculum leader, curriculum coordinator, and curriculum specialist. A *curriculum worker* is a general term and includes various educators, from a teacher to a superintendent. Any person involved in some form of curriculum development, implementation, or evaluation is a curriculum worker. A *curriculum supervisor* is usually a chairperson, assistant principal, or principal; he or she usually works at the school level. A *curriculum leader* can be a supervisor or administrator—not only a chairperson or principal but also a director or associate superintendent of curriculum. A *curriculum coordinator* usually heads a program at the school district, regional, or state level; it may be a special government-funded program or a traditional subject area program involving math or English. A *curriculum specialist* is a technical consultant from the district level, regional or state department of education, or university. The person provides advice or in-service assistance, sometimes in the classroom but usually at meetings, conferences, or staff sessions. Most of the terms, as well as the related responsibilities and functions of these people, depend on the philosophy and organization of the school district (or state education agency) and the personal preferences and views of the administration.

Another problem is the confusion on whether curriculum planning or development takes place at the local, state, or national level. In the past, emphasis on curriculum development was at the school or school district level; since the mid 1980s, the school reform movement has shifted some of the curriculum responsibilities to the state level, and there is serious talk of moving to the national level. (Bear in mind that most other nations have a national ministry of education with major curriculum responsibilities.)

Curriculum roles, in the past, have been defined at the local level, and decisions were made to develop curriculum leaders at the chair and principal's level. The majority of school districts depend on school people (teachers and supervisors) to develop curriculum and usually without pay, unless they meet in the summer; parents are also included in many curriculum committees at the school level. Staff limitations make unlikely the provision of curriculum specialists from the central office, and if such a person exists it is one person (possibly two) whose time is limited because of other responsibilities. Only large school districts can afford to have a curriculum department, with a full staff of specialists. In such school districts, most curriculum development takes place at the central level and teachers often complain that their professional input is minimal—relegated to implementing predetermined and prepackaged materials from the district office.

Responsibilities of the Curriculum Worker

What are the responsibilities of a curriculum worker? Assigned responsibilities within the school structure are important, but unclear, because different people (teachers, supervisors, principals, district personnel, and others) are usually expected to serve in the role of curriculum worker. Each position holder has different professional responsibilities, needs, and expectations. Adjustments must be made by each holder of a position. For example, teachers are usually expected among other things to

provide instruction, but principals are expected to manage a school and provide assistance to teachers.

The curriculum worker has many different titles; nonetheless, the teacher is a member of the curriculum team and works with supervisors and administrators as part of the team. Early identification of teachers to serve in the capacity of a curriculum worker is essential for the growth of the teacher and vitality of the school (and school district). Where there is need or attention for clarifying the responsibilities of curriculum workers, consider the following:

1. Develop technical methods and tools to carry out curriculum planning in the school (or school district or state agency).

2. Blend theory building with practice; obtain curriculum knowledge and apply it in the real world of classrooms and schools.

3. Agree on what is involved in curriculum development and design, including the relationships that exist among the elements of curriculum.

4. Agree on the relationship between curriculum, instruction, and supervision, including the explicit language of each area and how each aids the work of the other.

5. Act as a change agent who considers schools in context with society; balance the demands and views of the local community with state and national goals and interests.

6. Create a mission or goal statement to provide direction and focused behavior within the organization.

7. Be open to new curriculum trends and thoughts; examine various proposals and suggest modifications, while not falling victim to fads and frills or to a particular pressure group.

8. Confer with various parental, community, and professional groups; have skills in human relations and in working with groups and individuals.

9. Encourage colleagues and other professionals to solve professional problems, innovate, and become familiar with and use new programs and ideas.

10. Develop a program for continuous curriculum development, implementation, and evaluation.

11. Balance and integrate subject areas and grade levels into the total curriculum; pay close attention to scope and sequence by subject and grade level.

12. Understand current research in teaching and learning, as well as new programs that are relevant to target students for teaching and learning.

Other texts identify other responsibilities and duties of curriculum leaders. Table 1-2 shows the functions of curriculum leaders as purported by Doll in column 1 and Glatthorn in column 2. Those by Doll tend to be process oriented and diffuse; those by Glatthorn are task oriented and outcome based. Both lists are geared for the traditional curriculum leader, which excludes the teacher and emphasizes the school (school district) supervisor or administrator. Depending on one's philosophy and view of curriculum leadership, the reader may prefer one column over the other or borrow from both.

The authors' list of twelve responsibilities for the curriculum worker tends to be more theoretical and conceptual than the lists by Doll and Glatthorn, who tend to be more practical and action oriented. The authors' view implies curriculum workers, who may be teachers, supervisors, principals, and directors employed at the school, school district, or state level. Doll and Glatthorn examine the activities of curriculum leaders and connote a narrower view, which suggests a chair or principal operating at the school level. Finally, the authors' concept of the curriculum worker views the person in terms of broad responsibilities and the whole organization. Doll and Glatthorn zero in on explicit responsibilities or activities that are considered important for the curriculum leader—such as the school principal—and thus consider a limited part of the organization.

The Teacher and the Curriculum

Although Doll views the curriculum expert primarily as a chair or principal, he is concerned with the teacher's role in planning and implementing the curriculum at three levels: classroom, school, and district. In his opinion, the teacher should be involved "in every phase" of curriculum making, including the planning of "specific goals, . . . materials, content, and methods." Teachers should have a curriculum "coordinating body" to unify their work and develop "relationships with supervisors [and] other teachers" involved in curriculum.[84]

Oliva adopts a broader view of the teacher's role. For him, teachers are seen as the "primary group in curriculum development." They constitute the "majority or the totality of the membership of curriculum committees and councils." Their role is to develop, implement, and evaluate curriculum. In his words, teachers work in committees and "initiate proposals, . . . review proposals, gather data, conduct research, make contact with parents and other lay people, write and create curriculum materials, . . . obtain feedback from learners, and evaluate programs."[85]

The views of Doll and Oliva suggest a *bottom-up* approach to curriculum, whereby the teacher has a major role to perform, a view popularized by Taba in her classic text on curriculum development,[86] but actually first introduced and elaborated by Harold Rugg, who argued that teachers needed to be released from all classroom duties "to prepare courses of study, and assemble materials, and develop outlines of the entire curriculum," and later by Caswell and Campbell, who envisioned teachers participating in curriculum committees at the school, district, and state levels during the summers and sometimes as a special assignment during the school year.[87]

Beane adopts a more moderate position for the teacher. Although teachers may emerge as curriculum leaders, the "major responsibility of administrative and supervisory personnel should be to provide leadership and assistance in curriculum development and implementation." Other aspects of curriculum work, such as "budget development, grant writing, and interaction with school boards," should be carried out by supervisors and administrators "in such a way as to facilitate curriculum planning." Nonetheless, the school district has the ultimate responsibility to employ support personnel who have skill in curriculum planning, and such per-

TABLE 1-2 Responsibilities and Activities of the Curriculum Leader

DOLL	GLATTHORN
1. Planning for improvement of the curriculum and of the curriculum development program	1. Determining the locus of planning decisions: differentiating between district and school planning responsibilities
2. Helping evaluate continuously both the appropriateness of the curriculum and the quality of the curriculum development program	2. Determining the organizational structures needed to facilitate planning and setting up those structures
3. Directing the formation of point of view, policies, and philosophy of education	3. Identifying leadership functions and allocating those functions properly
4. Directing the development of curriculum materials	4. Aligning the district's educational goals with appropriate curricular fields
5. Using ready-made research data and promoting local research	5. Developing a curriculum data base
6. Coordinating the activities of other special instructional personnel, supervisors or librarians, for example	6. Developing a planning calendar based on leader's assessments of organizational priorities
7. Working with guidance personnel to integrate curriculum and guidance functions	7. Conducting needs assessment in high-priority areas by using standardized tests, curriculum-referenced tests, and other measures and data sources; using assessment results to determine the need for curriculum development or improvement
8. Providing for lay participation in curriculum improvement	8. Organizing task forces to carry out development or improvement projects and monitoring their work
9. Arranging time, facilities, and materials for curriculum improvement	9. Evaluating development or improvement projects
10. Serving school personnel as technical consultant and advisor regarding curriculum problems	10. Making necessary organizational changes and provisions for effective implementation
11. Organizing and directing special in-service education projects	11. Securing resources needed for new or revised curricula
12. Interpreting the curriculum to the public and, in certain situations, to the board of education	12. Providing staff development needed for effective implementation
13. Encouraging articulation among levels of the school system	

Source: Adapted from Ronald C. Doll, *Curriculum Improvement: Decision Making and Process,* 8th ed. (Boston: Allyn and Bacon, 1992), pp. 494–496; Allan A. Glatthorn, *Curriculum Leadership* (Glenview, Ill.: Scott, Foresman, 1987), p. 144.

sonnel may include "teachers, school officials, and citizens."[88]

On the other side of the continuum, Glatthorn makes little provision for teacher input. He discusses the role of the "coordinators" at the district level and the principal, assistant principal, and chair at the school level. Only in elementary schools is he willing to recognize the role of a "teacher specialist" as a member of a subject or grade-level team and mainly confined to "reading and mathematics."[89]

Walker's view is even narrower. He confines the curriculum role of teachers mainly to classroom responsibilities; he or she is involved in "selecting, scheduling, presenting, and adapting and adjusting activities. . . . These actions define the purpose, content and structure of the classroom—the classroom curriculum."[90] Hence, the role of teachers is confined to implementing the goals and related subject or curriculum areas that are planned at a higher level. They are permitted little input in interpreting or managing the curriculum, a *top-down* method of organizing schools. Even worse, it can be argued that such an interpretation leads to a teacher-proof curriculum and disempowered teachers.

Based on traditional theories of social organization and open systems and the latest we know about effective schools, our interpretation of the teachers' role in curriculum making is central. They are seen as part of a professional team, working with supervisors, administrators (and other colleagues) at all levels—at the school, district, and state level. In small and medium-sized school districts, teachers also work with parents where lay input is common in curriculum committees.

In our view, the teacher sees the curriculum as a whole and, at several points, serves as a resource and agent: developing it in committees, implementing it in classrooms, and evaluating it as part of a technical team. To guarantee continuity, integration, and unification of the curriculum, within and among subjects and grade levels, teachers must be actively involved in the curriculum. It is the experienced teacher who has a broad and deep understanding of teaching and

learning, the needs and interests of students, and the content, methods, and materials that are realistic; therefore, it is the teacher (not the supervisor or administrator) who has the best chance of taking curriculum making out of the realm of theory or judgment and translating it into practice and utility. To be sure, the supervisor or administrator acts as a facilitator, lends support, coordinates, and communicates so that the mission can be achieved. But it is the teacher who should play a major role in planning, implementing, and evaluating the curriculum.

CONCLUSION

We have discussed curriculum in a variety of ways. We have tried to define it, to show the relationship between foundations and domains of curriculum, to illustrate how theory and practice interrelate with curriculum, and to describe the roles and responsibilities of the curriculum worker. In effect, we have told the reader that he or she can focus on approaches and definitions, foundations and domains, theory and practice, or curriculum and instruction. We feel that no one can fully integrate the entire field of curriculum. Eventually, each individual should choose an approach and definition, a school of philosophy and psychology, developmental and design models, theory and practice relationships, and curriculum responsibilities he or she wishes to promote. In this chapter, we outlined some options; we continue to do so in the remaining text.

In presenting this broad overview of curriculum, we have also tried to show how current texts in curriculum examine these theoretical dimensions or issues, and how, in terms of philosophy and direction, they fit into the field of curriculum. This information is summarized in Table 1-3. However, we caution the reader that it is not easy to categorize authors and textbooks into pure types. Not only may they overlap in some cases, but some text writers may represent more than one category, at least on different issues. Finally, we have attempted to set the stage for the discussions that follow on the foundations, domains, and issues of curriculum.

TABLE 1-3 Overview of Curriculum Texts Since 1985

AUTHOR	CURRICULUM APPROACH	CURRICULUM DEFINITION	CURRICULUM FOUNDATIONS	CURRICULUM DOMAINS	TEACHER'S ROLE IN CURRICULUM
Armstrong (1989) *Developing and Documenting the Curriculum*	Behavioral, managerial	Plan, grades	Philosophical	Development, design	Top down
Beane et al. (1986) *Curriculum Planning and Development*	Behavioral, managerial	Plan	Social	Change	Middle
Doll (1992) *Curriculum Improvement: Decision Making and Process*	Managerial, systems	Plan, system	Social, psychological	Change	Bottom up
Eisner (1993) *The Educational Imagination*	Humanistic	Plan, experiences	Psychological	Teaching-learning	Middle
Ellis et al. (1988) *The School Curriculum*	Behavioral	Plan, experiences	Social, psychological	Teaching-learning	Top down
Glatthorn (1987) *Curriculum Leadership*	Behavioral, managerial	Plan, system	Historical, social, political	Change	Top down
Hass (1993) *Curriculum Planning: A New Approach*	Humanistic	Plan, experiences	Philosophical, social, psychological	Teaching-learning	Bottom up
McNeil (1990) *Curriculum: A Comprehensive Introduction*	Systems, academic	System, field	Historical, social, political	Change, issues	Middle

Reference				
Miller and Seller (1985) *Curriculum: Perspectives and Practice*	Academic	Field	Historical, philosophical, social, psychological	Development	Top down
Oliva (1988) *Developing the Curriculum*	Behavioral	Plan, experiences	Social	Development, design	Bottom up
Pajak (1989) *The Central Office Supervisor and Curriculum and Instruction*	Managerial	Plan	Social, political	Development, change	Top down
Schubert (1986) *Curriculum: Perspective, Paradigm and Possibility*	Academic	Field	Historical, social	Development, Issues	Bottom up
Shepherd & Ragan (1992) *Modern Elementary Curriculum*	Academic, humanistic	Field, experiences, subjects	Psychological	Teaching-learning	Middle
Walker (1990) *Fundamentals of Curriculum*	Academic	Field	Historical, social, political	Change, issues	Top down
Wiles and Bondi (1989) *Curriculum Development: A Guide to Practice*	Systems	Plan, grades	Philosophical, social	Development, design	Top down

ENDNOTES

1. Franklin Bobbitt, *The Curriculum* (Boston: Houghton Mifflin, 1918); W.W. Charters, *Curriculum Construction* (New York: Macmillan, 1923); Ralph W. Tyler, *Basic Principles of Curriculum and Instruction* (Chicago: University of Chicago Press, 1949); and Hilda Taba, *Curriculum Development: Theory and Practice* (New York: Harcourt Brace Jovanovich, 1962).

2. William Pinar, "Notes on the Curriculum Field," *Educational Researcher* (September 1978), pp. 5–12; William H. Schubert, *Curriculum Books: The First Eighty Years* (Lanham, Md.: University Press of America, 1980); and James T. Sears and J. Dan Marshall, eds., *Teaching and Thinking about Curriculum* (New York: Teachers College Press, Columbia University, 1990).

3. Raymond Callahan, *Education and the Cult of Efficiency* (Chicago: University of Chicago Press, 1962).

4. Bobbitt, *The Curriculum,* p. 283.

5. Franklin Bobbitt, *How to Make a Curriculum* (Boston: Houghton Mifflin, 1924), pp. 14, 28.

6. Tyler, *Basic Principles of Curriculum and Instruction,* p. 4.

7. James A. Beane, Conrad E. Toepfer, and Samuel J. Alessi, *Curriculum Planning and Development* (Boston: Allyn and Bacon, 1986); Peter F. Oliva, *Developing the Curriculum,* 3rd ed. (Glenview, Ill.: Scott, Foresman, 1988); and J. Gaylen Saylor, William M. Alexander, and Arthur J. Lewis, *Curriculum Planning for Better Teaching and Learning,* 4th ed. (New York: Holt, Rinehart and Winston, 1981); and Jon Wiles and Joseph C. Bondi, *Curriculum Development: A Guide to Practice,* 3rd ed. (Columbus, Ohio, Merrill, 1989). Many of these authors can also be classified as representative of the managerial and systems approaches.

8. Allan C. Ornstein, "The Field of Curriculum: What Approach?" *High School Journal* (April–May 1987), pp. 208–216.

9. See Matthew B. Miles and Karen Seashore Louis, "Mustering the Will and Skill for Change," *Educational Leadership* (May 1990), pp. 57–61; Allan C. Ornstein and Daniel U. Levine, "School Effectiveness and Reform: Guidelines for Action," *Clearing House* (November–December 1990), pp. 115–118.

10. Allan C. Ornstein, "Analyzing Curriculum," *NASSP Bulletin* (in press, 1993).

11. Leslee J. Bishop, *Staff Development and Instructional Improvement* (Boston: Allyn and Bacon, 1976); Gerald R. Firth and Richard Kimpston, *The Curriculum Continuum in Perspective* (Itasca, Ill.: Peacock, 1973); Robert S. Gilchrist, *Using Current Curriculum Developments* (Alexandria, Va.: Association for Supervision and Curriculum Development, 1963); Arthur J. Lewis and Alice Miel, *Supervision for Improved Instruction* (Belmont, Calif.: Wadsworth, 1972); John McNeil and William H. Lucio, *Supervision: A Synthesis of Thought and Action.* 2nd ed. (New York: McGraw-Hill, 1969); J. Lloyd Trump and Dorsey Baynham, *Focus on Change* (Chicago: Rand McNally. 1961); and Glenys G. Unruh and William A. Alexander, *Innovations in Secondary Education,* 2nd ed. (New York: Holt, Rinehart and Winston, 1971).

12. David C. Armstrong, *Developing and Documenting the Curriculum* (Boston: Allyn and Bacon, 1989); Ronald C. Doll, *Curriculum Improvement: Decision Making and Process,* 8th ed. (Boston: Allyn and Bacon, 1992); Allan A. Glatthorn, *Curriculum Leadership* (Glenview, Ill.: Scott, Foresman, 1987); Edward Pajak, *The Central Office Supervisor of Curriculum and Instruction* (Boston: Allyn and Bacon, 1989); and Glenys G. Unruh and Adolph Unruh, *Curriculum Development: Problems, Processes, and Progress* (Berkeley, Calif.: McCutchan, 1984).

13. Walter Dick, "Instructional Design and the Curriculum Development Process," *Educational Leadership* (December–January 1987), pp. 54–56; Walter Dick and Robert A. Reiser, *Planning Effective Instruction* (Englewood Cliffs, N.J.: Prentice Hall, 1989); and Bruce Joyce, Marsha Weil, and Beverly Showers, *Models of Teaching,* 4th ed. (Boston: Allyn and Bacon, 1992).

14. George A. Beauchamp, *Curriculum Theory,* 4th ed. (Itasca, Ill.: Peacock, 1981).

15. Allan C. Ornstein, "Curriculum, Instruction, and Supervision—Their Relationship and the Role of the Principal," *NASSP Bulletin* (April 1986), pp. 74–81.

16. Beane, Toepfer, and Alessi, *Curriculum Planning and Development.* Francis P. Hunkins, *Curriculum Development: Program Improvement* (Columbus, Ohio: Merrill, 1980); Oliva, *Developing the Curriculum;* and David Pratt, *Curriculum Design and Development* (New York: Macmillan, 1980).

17. John Dewey, *Democracy and Education* (New York: Macmillan. 1916); Henry C. Morrison, *The Practice of Teaching in the Secondary School* (Chicago: University of Chicago Press, 1926); and Boyd H. Bode, *Modern Educational Theories* (New York: Macmillan, 1927).

18. Hollis L. Caswell and Doak S. Campbell, *Curriculum Development* (New York: American Books, 1935); L. Thomas Hopkins, *Integration: Its Meaning and Application* (New York: Appleton-Century, 1937); John K. Norton and Mary A. Norton, *Foundations of Curriculum Building* (Boston: Ginn, 1936); B. Othanel Smith, William O. Stanley, and J. Harlan

Shores, *Fundamentals of Curriculum Development* (New York: World Books, 1950); and Florence B. Stratemeyer et al., *Developing a Curriculum for Modern Living* (New York: Teachers College Press, Columbia University, 1952).

19. John P. Miller and Wayne Seller, *Curriculum Perspectives and Practice* (New York: Longman, 1985); William H. Schubert, *Curriculum: Perspective, Paradigm, and Possibility* (New York: Macmillan, 1986); and Daniel Tanner and Laurel N. Tanner, *Curriculum Development: Theory into Practice,* 2nd ed. (New York: Macmillan, 1980).

20. Arthur K. Ellis, James A. Mackey, and Allen D. Glenn, *The School Curriculum* (Boston: Allyn and Bacon, 1988); John D. McNeil, *Curriculum: A Comprehensive Introduction,* 4th ed. (Glenview, Ill.: Scott, Foresman, 1990); and Decker Walker, *Fundamentals of Curriculum* (San Diego: Harcourt Brace Jovanovich, 1990).

21. John Dewey, *The Child and the Curriculum* (Chicago: University of Chicago Press, 1902); Charles Judd, *The Evolution of a Democratic School System* (Boston: Houghton Mifflin, 1918); and Francis W. Parker, *Talks on Pedagogics* (New York: Kellogg, 1894).

22. Frederick G. Bosner, *The Elementary School Curriculum* (New York: Macmillan, 1920); Hollis L. Caswell, *Program Making in Small Elementary Schools* (Nashville, Tenn.: George Peabody College for Teachers, 1932); L. Thomas Hopkins and James E. Mendenhall, *Achievement at the Lincoln School* (New York: Teachers College Press, Columbia University, 1934); William H. Kilpatrick, *Foundations of Method* (New York: Macmillan, 1925); and Harold Rugg and Ann Shumaker, *The Child-centered School* (New York: World Books, 1928).

23. Beau Fly Jones, "Thinking and Learning: New Curricula for the 21st Century," *Educational Psychologist* (Spring 1991), pp. 129–144; Robert E. Slavin and Nancy A. Madden, "What Works for Students at Risk," Educational Leadership (February 1989), pp. 4–13; and Richard E. Snow, "Individual Differences and the Design of Educational Programs," *American Psychologist* (October 1986), pp. 1029–1039.

24. Allan C. Ornstein and Daniel U. Levine, "Urban School Effectiveness and Improvement," *Illinois School Research and Development* (Spring 1991), pp. 111–117; Ornstein and Levine, "School Effectiveness and Reform: Guidelines for Action."

25. Elliot W. Eisner, *The Educational Imagination,* 3rd ed. (New York: Macmillan, 1993); Glen Hass, ed., *Curriculum Planning: A New Approach,* 6th ed. (Boston: Allyn and Bacon, 1993); and Gene D. Shepherd and William B. Ragan, *Modern Elementary Curriculum,* 7th ed. (New York: Holt, Rinehart and Winston, 1992).

26. McNeil, *Curriculum: A Comprehensive Introduction;* Miller and Seller, *Curriculum: Perspectives and Practice.* (The latter uses the term *social change orientation* to classify the reconceptualists.)

27. Recent reconstructionist publications that are close to textbook writings are Henry A. Giroux, *Teachers as Intellectuals: Toward a Critical Pedagogy of Learning* (Westport, Conn.: Bergin & Garvey, 1988); Henry A. Giroux and David E. Purpel, *The Hidden Curriculum and Moral Education* (Berkeley, Calif.: McCutchan, 1983); and James A. Gress and David E. Purpel, *Curriculum: An Introduction to the Field,* 2nd ed. (Berkeley, Calif.: McCutchan, 1988).

28. George S. Counts, *Dare the School Build a New Social Order?* (New York: John Day, 1932); Harold O. Rugg, ed., *Democracy and the Curriculum* (New York: Appleton-Century, 1939); Rugg et al., *American Life and the School Curriculum* (Boston: Ginn, 1936); and Harold Benjamin, *The Saber-tooth Curriculum* (New York: McGraw-Hill, 1939).

29. Saylor, Alexander, and Lewis, *Curriculum Planning for Better Teaching and Learning,* p. 10.

30. Pratt, *Curriculum: Design and Development,* p. 4.

31. Wiles and Bondi, *Curriculum Development: A Guide to Practice,* p. 131.

32. John Dewey, *Experience and Education* (New York: Macmillan, 1938); Caswell and Campbell, *Curriculum Development,* p. 69.

33. Shepherd and Ragan, *Modern Elementary Curriculum,* pp. 3–4.

34. Eisner, *The Educational Imagination,* p. 41.

35. Hass, *Curriculum Planning: A New Approach,* p. 54.

36. Doll, *Curriculum Improvement: Decision Making and Process*; Pajak, *The Central Office Supervisor and Curriculum and Instruction*; and Unruh and Unruh, *Curriculum Development: Problems, Process, and Progress.*

37. McNeil, *Curriculum: A Comprehensive Introduction;* Schubert, *Curriculum: Perspective, Paradigm, and Possibility;* and Tanner and Tanner, *Curriculum Development: Theory into Practice.*

38. Glatthorn, *Curriculum Leadership;* Shepherd and Ragan, *Modern Elementary Curriculum*; and Wiles and Bondi, *Curriculum Development: A Guide to Practice.*

39. Beauchamp, *Curriculum Theory.*

40. Doll, *Curriculum Improvement: Decision Making and Process,* p. 5.

41. Beauchamp, *Curriculum Theory,* p. 81.

42. Harold Rugg, "Introduction," in G. M. Whipple, ed., *The Foundations of Curriculum Making,* Twenty-Sixth Yearbook of the National Society for the Study

of Education, Part II (Bloomington, Ill.: Public School Publishing Co., 1930), p. 8.

43. Saylor, Alexander, and Lewis, *Curriculum Planning for Better Teaching and Learning;* Schubert, *Curriculum: Perspective, Paradigm, and Possibility;* and Tyler, *Basic Principles of Curriculum and Instruction,* Also see Charles P. McFadden, "Author-Publisher-Educator Relationships and Curriculum Reform," *Journal of Curriculum Studies* (January–February 1992), pp. 71–88.

44. Carmen L. Rosales-Dordelly and Edmund C. Short, *Curriculum Professors' Specialized Knowledge* (New York: Lanham, 1985), p. 23.

45. Oliva, *Developing the Curriculum,* p. 15.

46. Joseph J. Schwab, "The Practical: A Language of Curriculum," *School Review* (November 1969), p. 1.

47. Miller and Seller, *Curriculum: Perspectives and Practice.*

48. Robert S. Zais, *Curriculum: Principles and Foundations* (New York: Harper & Row, 1976).

49. Doll, *Curriculum Improvement: Decision Making and Process*; Hass, *Curriculum Planning: A New Approach*; McNeil, *Curriculum: A Comprehensive Introduction*; and Walker, *Fundamentals of Curriculum.*

50. Hunkins, *Curriculum Development: Program Improvement*; Saylor et al., *Curriculum Planning for Better Teaching and Learning.*

51. Shepherd and Ragan, *Modern Elementary Curriculum*; Eisner, *The Educational Imagination.*

52. Schubert, *Curriculum: Perspective, Paradigm, and Possibility*; Tanner and Tanner, *Curriculum Development: Theory into Practice.* Also see John Rogan and Jean Luekowski, "Curriculum Texts," *Journal of Curriculum Studies* (January–February 1990), pp. 17–40.

53. Herbert Kliebard, "Curriculum Theory as Metaphor," *Theory into Practice* (Winter 1982), pp. 11–17; Kliebard, "Problems of Definition of Curriculum," *Journal of Curriculum and Supervision* (Fall 1989), pp. 1–5.

54. About 75 to 80 percent of all Division C papers between 1985 and 1990 at AERA annual meetings were delivered by educational psychologists, especially research, measurement, and evaluation professors. The percentage was about 25 to 30 in Division B for the same period.

55. In letters written to one of the authors of this text, Ronald Brandt (editor of *Educational Leadership)* concurs with this viewpoint about both journals. Bob Cole (former editor of *Phi Delta Kappan*) is less enthusiastic about this viewpoint; his argument is basically that people like Bloom and Gage can be considered curricularists.

56. Eisner, *The Educational Imagination*; Shepherd and Ragan, *Modern Elementary Curriculum.*

57. Taba, *Curriculum Development: Theory and Practice.*

58. William M. Reynolds, "Comprehensiveness and Multidimensionality in Synoptic Curriculum Texts," *Journal of Curriculum and Supervision* (Winter 1990), pp. 189–193.

59. Beauchamp, *Curriculum Theory.*

60. Fenwick W. English, "Contemporary Curriculum Circumstances," in F. W. English, ed., *Fundamental Curriculum Decisions* (Alexandria, Va.: Association for Supervision and Curriculum Development, 1983), pp. 1–17.

61. Edmund C. Short, "Curriculum Decision Making in Teacher Education," *Journal of Teacher Education* (July–August 1987), pp. 2–12; Short, "Organizing What We Know about Curriculum," unpublished paper, 1984.

62. Linda Behar, "A Study of Domains and Subsystems in the Most Influential Textbooks in the Field of Curriculum 1970–1990," unpublished doctoral dissertation. Loyola University of Chicago, 1992.

63. Saylor et al., *Curriculum Planning for Better Teaching and Learning.*

64. Unruh and Unruh, *Curriculum Development: Problems, Processes, and Progress.*

65. Francis P. Hunkins, "Fostering Doubt and Suspicion: Goal of Curriculum," *Journal of Curriculum and Supervision* (Fall 1989), pp. 81–90; Hunkins, *Curriculum Development Program Improvement.*

66. Beane, Toepfer, and Alessi, *Curriculum Planning and Development*; and Tanner and Tanner, *Curriculum Development: Theory into Practice.*

67. Saylor et al., *Curriculum Planning for Better Teaching and Learning.*

68. Wiles and Bondi, *Curriculum Development: A Guide to Practice.*

69. Rosales-Dordelly and Short, *Curriculum Professors' Specialized Knowledge,* p. 22.

70. McNeil, *Curriculum: A Comprehensive Introduction,* pp. iii–iv.

71. Behar, "A Study of Domains and Subsystems in the Most Influential Textbooks in the Field of Curriculum 1970–1990."

72. Beauchamp, *Curriculum Theory,* p. 58.

73. Taba, *Curriculum Development: Theory and Practice,* p. 413.

74. Glatthorn, *Curriculum Leadership*; Unruh and Unruh, *Curriculum Development: Problems, Process, and Progress*; and Walker, *Fundamentals of Curriculum.*

75. McNeil, *Curriculum: A Comprehensive Introduction.*

76. Elaine Atkins, "Power and Criticism: Poststructural Investigations in Education," *Journal of Curriculum Studies* (January–February 1990), pp. 77–81; Robert J. Graham, "Currere and Reconceptualism: The Progress of Pilgrimage 1975–1990," *Journal of Curriculum Studies* (January–February 1992), pp. 27–42.

77. Michael W. Apple, "Curricula and Teaching: Are They Headed Toward Excellence?" *NASSP Bulletin* (September 1988), pp. 14–25; William Pinar, "Reply to My Critics," *Curriculum Inquiry* (Summer 1980), pp. 199-206.

78. Elizabeth Vallance, "Curriculum as a Field of Practice," in English, ed., *Fundamental Curriculum Decisions*, p. 155.

79. Miller and Seller, *Curriculum: Perspectives and Practice*; Tanner and Tanner, *Curriculum Development: Theory into Practice*, and Wiles and Bondi, *Curriculum Development: A Guide to Practice*.

80. Doll, *Curriculum Improvement: Decision Making and Process*; Unruh and Unruh, *Curriculum Development: Problems, Processes, and Progress*.

81. Walker, *Fundamentals of Curriculum*, p. 200.

82. Allan C. Ornstein and Francis P. Hunkins, "Theorizing about Curriculum Theory," *High School Journal* (December-January 1989), pp. 77–82.

83. Karen F. Osterman, "Reflective Practice: A New Agenda for Education," *Education and Urban Society* (February 1990), pp. 133–154; Donald A. Schon, *Educating the Reflective Practitioner* (San Francisco: Jossey-Bass, 1987); and Schon, "Critiques, Commentaries, Illustrations," *Journal of Curriculum and Supervision* (Fall 1989), pp. 6–9.

84. Doll, *Curriculum Improvement: Decision Making and Process*, p. 334.

85. Oliva, *Developing the Curriculum*, p. 120.

86. Taba, *Curriculum Development: Theory and Practice*.

87. Caswell and Campbell, *Curriculum Development*; Harold Rugg, "The Foundations of Curriculum Making," in G. Whipple, ed., *The Foundations of Curriculum Making*, Twenty-sixth Yearbook of the National Society for the Study of Education, Part II (Bloomington, Ill.: Public School Publishers, 1930), pp. 439–440.

88. Beane, Toepfer, and Alessi, *Curriculum Planning and Development*, pp. 355, 358.

89. Glatthorn, *Curriculum Leadership*, pp. 148–149.

90. Walker, *Fundamentals of Curriculum*, p. 227.

CHAPTER 2

PHILOSOPHICAL FOUNDATIONS OF CURRICULUM

Focusing Questions

1. *How does philosophy influence curriculum workers?*
2. *In what way is philosophy the main curriculum source? Or only one of many curriculum sources?*
3. *What are the differences (in terms of knowledge and values) between idealism, realism, pragmatism, and existentialism?*
4. *What are the differences (in terms of content and methods) between perennialism, essentialism, progressivism, and reconstructionism?*
5. *What common ideas do Adler, Bloom, and Hirsch embrace?*
6. *Can schools promote the ideas of equality and excellence at the same time? Why? Why not?*
7. *In what ways are reconstructionists both realistic and idealistic? Mainstream and radical?*

Philosophy is an important foundation of curriculum because the philosophy advocated or reflected by a particular school and its officials influences its goals or aims and content, as well as the organization of its curriculum. Studying philosophy helps us deal with our own personal system of beliefs and values: the way we perceive the world around us, and how we define what is important to us. It helps us understand who we are, why we are, and, to some extent, where we are going.

Philosophy deals with the larger aspects of life, the problems and prospects of living, and the way we organize our thoughts and facts. It is an effort to see life and its problems in full perspective. It requires looking beyond the immediate to causes and relationships and to future developments. It involves questioning one's own point of view as well as the views of others; it involves searching for defined and defensible values, clarifying one's beliefs and attitudes, and formulating a framework for making decisions and acting on these decisions.

Philosophical issues have always and still do impact on schools and society. Contemporary society and the schools in it are changing fundamentally and rapidly, much more so than in the past. The special urgency that dictates continuous appraisal and reappraisal calls for a philosophy of education. As William Van Til puts it, "Our source of direction is found in our guiding philosophy. . . . Without philosophy, [we make] mindless vaults into the saddle like Stephen Leacock's character who 'flung himself from the room, flung himself upon his horse, and rode madly off in all directions.' "[1] In short, our philosophy of education influences, and to a large extent determines, our educational decisions, choices, and alternatives.

PHILOSOPHY AND CURRICULUM

Philosophy provides educators, especially curriculum workers, with a framework or base for organizing schools and classrooms.

It helps them answer what schools are for, what subjects are of value, how students learn, and what methods and materials to use. It provides them with a framework for broad issues and tasks, such as determining the goals of education, the content and its organization, the process of teaching and learning, and in general what experiences and activities they wish to stress in schools and classrooms. It also provides them with a basis for dealing with precise tasks and for making such decisions as what workbooks, textbooks, or other cognitive and noncognitive activities to utilize and how to utilize them, what homework to assign and how much of it, how to test students and how to use the test results, and what courses or subject matter to emphasize.

The importance of philosophy in determining curriculum decisions is expressed well by L. Thomas Hopkins:

> *Philosophy has entered into every important decision that has ever been made about curriculum and teaching in the past and will continue to be the basis of every important decision in the future.*
>
> *When a state office of education suggests a pupil-teacher time schedule, this is based upon philosophy, either hidden or consciously formulated. When a course of study is prepared in advance in a school system by a selected group of teachers, this represents philosophy because a course of action was selected from many choices involving different values. When high school teachers assign to pupils more homework for an evening than any one of them could possibly do satisfactorily in six hours, they are acting on philosophy although they are certainly not aware of its effects. When a teacher in an elementary school tells a child to put away his geography and study his arithmetic she is acting on philosophy for she has made a choice of values . . . When teachers shift subject matter from one grade to another, they act on philosophy. When measurement experts interpret their test results to a group of teachers, they act upon philosophy, for the facts have meaning only within some basic assumptions. There is rarely a moment in a school day when a teacher is not confronted with occasions where philosophy is a vital part of action. An inventory of situations where philosophy was not used in curriculum and teaching would lead to a pile of chaff thrown out of educative experiences.*[2]

Hopkins's statement reminds us how important philosophy is to all aspects of curriculum

decisions, whether it operates overtly or covertly, whether we know that it is operating or not. Indeed, almost all elements of curriculum are based on philosophy. As John Goodlad points out, philosophy is the beginning point in curriculum decision making and is the basis for all subsequent decisions regarding curriculum.[3] Philosophy becomes the criterion for determining the aims, means, and ends of curriculum. The aims are statements of value, based on philosophical beliefs; the means represent processes and methods, which reflect philosophical choices; and the ends connote the facts, concepts, and principles of the knowledge or behavior learned, or what we feel is important to learning, which is also philosophical in nature.

B. Othanel Smith, William Stanley, and J. Harlan Shores also put great emphasis on the role of philosophy in developing curriculum; it is essential, they posit, when (1) formulating and justifying educational purposes; (2) selecting and organizing knowledge; (3) formulating basic procedures and activities; and (4) dealing with verbal traps (what we see versus what is real).[4] Curriculum theorists, they point out, often fail to recognize both how important philosophy is and how it influences other aspects of curriculum.

Philosophy and the Curriculum Worker

The philosophy of the curriculum worker reflects his or her life experiences, common sense, social and economic background, education, and general beliefs about himself or herself and people. An individual's philosophy evolves and continues to evolve as long as he or she continues to grow and develop, and as long as he or she learns from experience. One's philosophy is a description, explanation, and evaluation of the world as seen from one's own perspective, or through what some social scientists call "social lenses."

Curriculum workers can turn to many sources, but no matter how many sources they may draw upon or how many authorities they may read or listen to, the decision is theirs to accept or reject the explanations and truths presented. Their decision is shaped by past and contemporary events and experiences that have affected them and the social groups with which they identify; it is based on values (attitudes and beliefs) that they have developed, and their knowledge and interpretation of causes, events, and their consequences. Philosophy becomes principles for guiding action.

No one can be totally objective in a cultural or social setting, but curriculum workers can broaden their base of knowledge and experiences, try to understand other people's sense of values, and analyze problems from various perspectives. They can also try to modify their own critical analyses and points of view by learning from their experiences and others. Curriculum workers who are unwilling to modify their points of view or compromise philosophical positions, when school officials or the majority of their colleagues lean toward another philosophy, are at risk of causing conflict and disrupting the school. Ronald Doll puts it this way: "Conflict among curriculum planners occurs when persons . . . hold positions along a continuum of [different] beliefs and . . . persuasions." The conflict may become so intense that "curriculum study grinds to a halt." Most of the time, the differences can be reconciled "temporarily in deference to the demands of a temporary, immediate task. However, teachers and administrators who are clearly divided in philosophy can seldom work together in close proximity for long periods of time."[5]

The more mature and understanding one is, and the less personally threatened and ego-involved one is, the more capable one is of reexamining or modifying his or her philosophy, or at least of being willing to appreciate other points of view. It is important for curriculum workers to consider their attitudes and beliefs as tentative—as subject to reexamination whenever facts or trends challenge them.

Equally dangerous for curriculum workers is the opposite: indecision or lack of any philosophy, which can be reflected in attempts to avoid commitment to sets of values. A measure of positive conviction is essential to prudent action, even though total objectivity is not humanly possible. Having a personal philosophy that is tentative or subject to modification does not lead to lack of conviction or disorganized behavior. Curriculum workers can arrive at their conclusions on the best evidence available, and they can change when better evidence surfaces.

Philosophy as a Curriculum Source

The function of philosophy can be conceived as either (1) the base or starting point in curriculum development or (2) an interdependent function with other functions in curriculum development. John Dewey represents the first school of thought. He contended that "philosophy may . . . be defined as the general theory of education," and that "the business of philosophy is to provide" the framework for the "aims and methods" of schools. For Dewey, philosophy provides a generalized meaning to our lives and a way of thinking; it is "an explicit formulation of the . . . mental and moral habitudes in respect to the difficulties of contemporary social life."[6] Philosophy is not only a starting point for schools, it is also crucial for all curriculum activities. For Dewey, "education is the laboratory in which philosophic distinctions become concrete and are tested."[7]

In Ralph Tyler's framework of curriculum, philosophy is commonly one of five criteria for selecting educational purposes. The relationships between philosophy and the other criteria—studies of learners, studies of contemporary life, suggestions from subject specialists, and the psychology of learning—are shown in Figure 2-1. Although philosophy is not the starting point in Tyler's curriculum, but rather interacts on an equal basis with the other criteria, Tyler, highly influenced by Dewey, seems to place more importance on philosophy than other criteria for developing educational purposes. He writes, "The educational and social philosophy to which the school is committed can serve as the first screen for developing the social program." He concludes that "philosophy attempts to define the nature of the good life and a good society," and that the educational philosophies in a democratic society are likely "to emphasize strongly democratic values in schools."[8]

For John Goodlad, there can be no serious discussion about philosophy until we embrace the question of what education is. When we agree on what education is, we can ask what schools are for. Then we can pursue philosophy, aims,

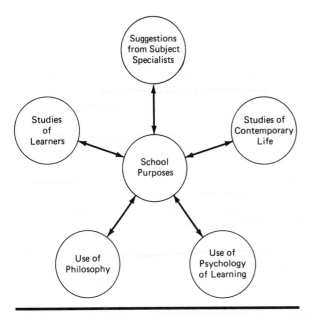

FIGURE 2-1 Tyler's View of Philosophy in Relation to School Purposes

and goals of curriculum. According to Goodlad, the school's first responsibility is to the social order, what he calls the "nation-state," but in our society the sense of individual growth and potential is paramount, too.[9] This duality—society versus the individual—has been a major philosophical issue in western society for centuries, and was very important in Dewey's works. As the latter claimed, we not only wish "to make [good] citizens and workers," but also we ultimately want "to make human beings who will live life to the fullest."

This duality—allegiance to the nation and fulfillment of the individual—is a noble aim that should guide all curriculum specialists—from the means to the ends. When many individuals grow and prosper, then that society flourishes since it is comprised of many individuals. The original question set forth by Goodlad can be answered now. Education is growth and the meaning that the growth has for the individual and society; it is a never ending process (so long as life exists), and the richer the meaning the better the quality of the educational process.

MAJOR PHILOSOPHIES

In any consideration of the influence of philosophical thought on curriculum, several classifi-

cation schemes are possible; no superiority is thus claimed for the categories used in the following discussion. The cluster of ideas as organized here are those that often evolve during curriculum development.

Labeling a philosophical idea, method, or proponent may give rise to argument. Differences within philosophical groups are sometimes greater than differences between groups. Also, anyone who embraces an extreme point of view may very likely be critical of other views.

Four major philosophies have influenced education in the United States: idealism, realism, pragmatism, and existentialism. Here, we present short overviews to define and identify each philosophy. The first two philosophies are traditional, and the latter two are contemporary.

Idealism

Plato is often identified as giving classic formulation to idealist philosophy, one of the oldest that exists. The German philosopher Hegel created a comprehensive view of the historical world based on idealism. In the United States, transcendentalist philosophers Ralph Waldo

Emerson and Henry Thoreau outlined an idealist conception of reality. In education, Fredrich Froebel, the founder of kindergarten, was a proponent of idealist pedagogy. William Harris, who popularized the kindergarten movement when he was superintendent of schools in St. Louis, Missouri, and who became U.S. Commissioner of Education at the turn of the twentieth century, used idealism as a source for this administrative philosophy. The leading contemporary proponent of idealism is J. Donald Butler.[10]

Idealism emphasizes moral and spiritual reality as the chief explanation of the world. Truth and values are seen as absolute, timeless, and universal. The world of mind and ideas is permanent, regular, and orderly; it represents a perfect order. Eternal ideas are unalterable and timeless. To know is to rethink the latent ideas that are already present in the mind. The teacher's task is to bring this latent knowledge to consciousness. As a primarily intellectual process, learning involves recalling and working with ideas; education is properly concerned with conceptual matters.[11]

The idealist educator prefers the order and pattern of a subject matter curriculum that relates ideas and concepts to each other. The most important subjects and highest form of knowledge recognize relationships and integrate concepts to each other. In this vein, the curriculum is hierarchical, and it constitutes the cultural heritage of humankind; it is based on learned disciplines, illustrated by the liberal arts curriculum.

At the top of this hierarchy are the most general or abstract subjects: philosophy and theology; they cut across time, place, and circumstances, and they apply to a wide range of situations and experiences. Mathematics is important because it cultivates the power to deal with abstract thinking. History and literature also rank high because they are sources of moral and cultural models. Lower in the curricular ladder are the natural and physical sciences, which deal with particular cause and effect relationships. Language is also an important subject, because it is necessary for communication and facilitates conception of thought.

Realism

Aristotle is often linked to the development of realism, another traditional school of thought. Thomas Aquinas's philosophy, which combined realism with Christian doctrine, developed an offshoot of realism, called Thomism, on which much of Catholic education and religious studies today are rooted. Pestalozzian instructional principles, which began with concrete objects and ended with abstract concepts, were based on realism. Such modern educators as Harry Broudy and John Wild are leading realists.[12]

The realist views the world in terms of objects and matter. People can come to know the world through their senses and their reason. Everything is derived from nature and is subject to its laws. Human behavior is rational when it conforms to the laws of nature and when it is governed by physical and social laws.

Like the idealist, the realist stresses a curriculum consisting of organized, separate subject matter, content, and knowledge that classifies objects. For example, the experiences of humankind comprise history. Animals can be studied as zoology. Like the idealist, the realist locates the most general and abstract subjects at the top of the curricular hierarchy and gives particular and transitory subjects a lower order of priority. Logic and lessons that exercise the mind and that cultivate rational thought are stressed. Concepts and systems that can be organized into subjects— such as ethical, political, and economic thought—are also included in the curriculum. The three R's (reading, writing, and arithmetic) are also necessary in a person's basic education.[13]

Whereas the idealist considers the classics to be the ideal subject matter, because the curriculum can be fixed and will not vary with time, the realist views subject matter experts as the source of authority. For the idealist, knowledge comes from studying the external ideas and universal truths found in the arts, but for the realist reality and truth emanate from both science and art.

Pragmatism

In contrast to the traditional philosophies, pragmatism, also referred to as experimentalism, is based on change, process, and relativity. Whereas idealism and realism emphasize subject matter, disciplines, and content or ideas, pragmatism construes knowledge as a process in which reality is constantly changing. Learning occurs as the person engages in problem solving; problem solving is, moreover, transferable to a wide variety of subjects and situations. Knowing is considered a transaction between learner and environment. Basic to this interaction is the notion of change. Both the learner and environment are constantly changing, as are the transactions or experiences. To disregard social change and to consider only what is changeless, as the idealists do, or only our heritage, as the realists do, is unrealistic and unwise. Concepts of unchanging or universal truths, such as the traditional philosophies advocate, are based on faith. The only guides that people have in their interaction with the social world or environment are established generalizations or tentative assertions that are subject to further research and verification.

To a pragmatist, nothing can be viewed intelligently except in relation to a pattern. The whole affects the parts, and the parts and the whole are all relative. The ideal teaching method is concerned not so much with teaching the learner what to think as with teaching him or her to critically think. Teaching is more exploratory than explanatory. The method is more important than the subject matter. What is needed is a method for dealing with change and scientific investigation in an intelligent manner.

Scientific developments at the turn of the twentieth century accelerated the pragmatic philosophy. Society's accepting scientific explanations for phenomena and its recognizing the forces of change challenged the long-standing traditional views of idealism and realism. In 1859, Charles Darwin's *Origin of the Species* shook the foundations of the classic view of human's notion of the universe. Charles Pierce, a mathematician, and William James, a psychologist, developed the principles of pragmatism, which (1) rejected the dogmas of preconceived truths and eternal values, and (2) promoted the method of testing and verifying ideas. The truth was no longer absolute or universal, but rather it had to be proven in relation to facts, experience, and/or behaviors.[14]

The great educational pragmatist was John Dewey, who viewed education as a process for improving (not accepting) the human condition. The school was seen as a specialized environment that coincided with the social environment. No demarcation exists between school and society. The curriculum ideally, is based on the child's experiences and interests, and prepares him or her for life's affairs and for the future.[15] The subject matter is interdisciplinary, rather than located within a single or group of disciplines. The stress is on problem solving, not mastering organized subject matter, and using the scientific method, not a bunch of facts or a point of view.

The pragmatists consider teaching and learning to be a process of reconstructing experience according to the scientific method. Learning takes place in an active way as learners, either individually or in groups, solve problems. These problems, as well as the subject matter, will vary in response to the changing world. For the learner, it is most important to acquire the method or process of solving problems in an intelligent manner.

Existentialism

Whereas pragmatism is mainly an American philosophy that evolved just prior to the turn of the twentieth century, existentialism is mainly a European philosophy that originated years before the turn of the century but became popular after World War II. In American education, such people as Maxine Greene, George Kneller, and Van Cleve Morris are well-known existentialists who stress individualism and personal self-fulfillment.[16]

According to existentialist philosophy, people are thrust into a number of choice-making situations. Some choices are minor and others are significant, but the choice is the individual's, and the decisions lead to personal self-definition. A person creates his or her own definition and in doing so makes his or her own essence. We are what we choose to be. The essence we create is a product of our choices; this varies, of course, among individuals.

Existentialists prefer to free learners to choose what to study and also to determine what is true and by what criteria to determine these truths. The curriculum would avoid systematic knowledge or structured disciplines, and the students would be free to select from many available learning situations. The learners would choose the knowledge they wish to possess. On both of these curricular points, some educators would criticize the philosophy as too unsystematic or laissez-faire to be included at the elementary school level.

Existentialists believe that the most important kind of knowledge is about the human condition and the choices that each person has to make, and that education is a process of developing consciousness about the freedom to choose and the meaning of and responsibility for one's choices.[17] Hence, the notion of group norms, authority, and established order—social, political, philosophical, religious, and so on—is rejected. The existentialists recognize few standards, customs or traditions, or eternal truths; in this respect, existentialism is at odds with the ideas of idealism and realism.

Some critics (mainly traditionalists or conservatives) claim that existentialism as a philosophy for the schools has limited application because education in our society, and in most other modern societies, involves institutionalized learning and socialization, which require group instruction, restrictions on individuals' behavior, and bureaucratic organization. Schooling is a process that limits students' freedom and that is based on adult authority and on the norms and beliefs of the mass or common culture. The individual existentialist, exerting his or her will and choice, will encounter difficulty in school—and in other large, formal organizations.

An existentialist curriculum would consist of experiences and subjects that lend themselves to philosophical dialogue and acts of choice making. Because the choice is personal and subjective, subjects that are emotional, esthetic, and philosophical are appropriate. Literature, drama, film making, art, and so on, are important, because they portray the human condition and choice-making conditions. The curriculum would stress self-expressive activities, experimentation, and methods and media that illustrate emotions, feelings, and insights. The classroom would be rich in materials that lend themselves to self-ex-

pression, and the school would be a place in which the teacher and students could pursue dialogue and discussion about their lives and choices.[18] See Table 2-1.

EDUCATIONAL PHILOSOPHIES

Although aspects of educational philosophy can be derived from the roots of idealism, realism, pragmatism, and existentialism, a common approach is to provide a pattern of educational philosophies. Four agreed-upon philosophies of education have emerged: perennialism, essentialism, progressivism, and reconstructionism. Each of these four philosophies of education has roots in one or more of the four major philosophical traditions. For example, perennialism draws heavily on the principles of realism, essentialism is rooted in idealism and realism, and progressivism and reconstructionism stem from pragmatism. Some reconstructionism has linkages to existentialist knowing and teaching. See Curriculum Tips 2-1.

Perennialism

Perennialism, the oldest and most conservative educational philosophy, is rooted in realism. Much of colonial and postcolonial American education, up to the late nineteenth century, was dominated by perennialist thinking. At the elementary school level, the curriculum stressed the three Rs, as well as moral and religious training; at the secondary level, it emphasized such subjects as Latin, Greek, grammar, rhetoric, logic, and geometry.

As a philosophy of education, perennialism relies on the past, especially the past asserted by agreed-upon, universal knowledge and cherished values of society. It is a plea for the permanency of knowledge that has stood the test of time and for values that have moral, spiritual, and/or physical constancies of existence. It is a view of the unchanging nature of the universe, human nature, truth, knowledge, virtue, beauty, and so on. As Robert Hutchins, a long-time advocate of perennialism, noted: "The function of man as man is the same in every society. . . . The aim of the educational system is the same in every age and in every society where such a system can exist; it

Table 2-1 Overview of Major Philosophies

PHILOSOPHY	REALITY	KNOWLEDGE	VALUES	TEACHER'S ROLE	EMPHASIS ON LEARNING	EMPHASIS ON CURRICULUM
Idealism	Spiritual, moral, or mental; unchanging	Rethinking latent ideas	Absolute and eternal	To bring latent knowledge and ideas to consciousness; to be a moral and spiritual leader	Recalling knowledge and ideas; abstract thinking as the highest form	Knowledge based; subject based; classics or liberal arts; hierarchy of subjects: philosophy, theology, and mathematics are most important
Realism	Based on natural laws; objective and composed of matter	Consisting of sensation and abstraction	Absolute and eternal; based on nature's laws	To cultivate rational thought; to be a moral and spiritual leader; to be a source of authority	Exercising the mind; logical and abstract thinking are highest form	Knowledge based; subject based; arts and sciences; hierarchy of subjects: humanistic and scientific subjects
Pragmatism	Interaction of individual with environment; always changing	Based on experience; use of scientific method	Situational and relative; subject to change and verification	To cultivate critical thinking and scientific processes	Methods for dealing with changing environment and scientific explanations	No permanent knowledge or subjects; appropriate experiences that transmit culture and prepare individual for change; problem-solving topics
Existentialism	Subjective	Knowledge for personal choice	Freely chosen; based on individuals's perception	To cultivate personal choice and individual self-definition	Knowledge and principles of the human condition; acts of choice making	Choices in subject matter, electives; emotional, esthetic, and philosophical subjects

is to improve a man as man."[19] With this interpretation, education becomes constant, absolute, and universal.

For perennialists, the answers to all educational questions derive from the answer to one question: What is human nature? The perennialists contend that human nature is constant. Humans have the ability to reason and to understand the universal truths of nature. The goal of education is to develop the rational person and to uncover universal truths by carefully training the intellect. Character training is also important as a means of developing one's moral and spiritual being.

The curriculum of the perennialist is subject centered; it draws heavily on defined disciplines or logically organized bodies of content—what proponents call "liberal" education—with emphasis on language, literature, and mathematics, on the arts and sciences. The teacher is viewed as an authority in the field whose knowledge and expertise are unquestionable. The teacher, accordingly, must be a master of the subject or discipline and must be able to guide discussion. Teaching is, in fact, the art of stimulating discussion and the inherent rational powers of the students. Teaching is primarily based on the Socratic method: oral exposition, lecture, and explication.

Students' interests are irrelevant for curriculum development because students are immature and lack the judgment to determine what are the best knowledge and values to learn. Whether the students dislike the subject matter is secondary.[20] There is only one common curriculum for all students, with little room for elective subjects, vocational, or technical subject matter.

Permanent Studies.   The notion of permanent or essential studies addresses knowledge and truths today. According to perennialists, it is permanent studies that comprise our intellectual heritage. This content is based on what is commonly called the liberal arts, or, according to Robert Hutchins the "Great Books" of the Western world that cover the foundations of Western thought and its scientific and cultural knowledge. The approach is to read and discuss the great works of great thinkers, which, in turn, should discipline the mind and cultivate the intellect. Among the great books are the works of Plato, Aristotle, St. Augustine, St. Thomas Aquinas, Erasmus, and Shakespeare.

The idea is to read these writers in their original language, which is why students must learn Latin and Greek. In addition to the classics, and the study of language, Hutchins urges the study of the three Rs, as well as grammar, rhetoric, logic, advanced mathematics, and philosophy.[21] This is basically the curriculum of the past; it treats human nature as rational and knowledge as absolute and unchanging. For Hutchins, this type of education "develops intellectual power . . . it is not a specialized education or a pre-professional education; it is not a utilitarian education. It is an education calculated to develop the mind."[22] It is a universal, broad education that prepares the individual to think, to prepare for many possible jobs, and to deal with life and the real world. By studying the great ideas of the past, one can better cope with the future.

Paideia Proposal.   A recent revival of perennialism appeared with the publication *Paideia Proposal* by Mortimer Adler. Adler developed three types of curriculum and instruction to improve the intellect: acquisition of *organized knowledge* to be taught by didactic instruction, development of *basic learning skills* by coaching and understanding of *ideas,* and *values* to be taught by the Socratic method.[23] Further outlined in Table 2-2, the three areas of concentration are the same as outlined by John Dewey in *Democracy and Education* and later by Ralph Tyler in *Basic Principles of Curriculum and Instruction.* (It should be noted all three professors taught the great bulk of their careers at the University of Chicago and were influenced by similar ideas.)

A broad liberal education is considered the best and only type of education for *all* students; in short, the same curriculum and quality of teaching and learning should be provided to all students. An academic or broad curriculum is considered to have the most practical value, as compared to vocational or specialized training for future employment. Anyone trained for a particular job will have to be retrained when he or she starts the job. Among the subjects identified as indispensable for all students are language, literature, fine arts, mathematics, natural sciences, history, and geography. Although it emphasized fundamental subjects, the Paideia group did not consider subject matter as an end in itself but rather as the context for developing intellectual skills. Among the sought-after intellectual skills were the three Rs, speaking, listening, observing, measuring, estimating, and problem solving. Together, the fundamental subjects and intellectual skills lead to a still higher level of learning, reflection, and awareness. For Adler, like Hutchins, the purpose of education is to cultivate significant knowledge and thinking skills; the "best books"—great books, as they were called by Hutchins—are recommended by the Paideia program.

The education advocated by perennialist appeals to a small group of educators who tend to stress intellectual meritocracy. Such educators emphasize testing students, enforcing tougher academic standards and programs, and identifying gifted and talented students. Their education fosters a common curriculum, usually liberal arts, and offers little or no opportunity for students to choose electives related to their interests or goals. For the perennialists, genuine equality of education is maintained by providing quality of education for all—of high intellectual fiber. To track some students into a vocational curriculum is to deny the latter genuine equality of educational opportunity. True equity can be satisfied only by access to quality education: a *common,* perennial curriculum.

Returning to the Liberal Arts.   More recently, Allan Bloom, in *The Closing of the American Mind,* has voiced concern about education being relative to particular times and places, instead of being consistent with universal standards and

TABLE 2-2 The Paideia Course of Study

CURRICULUM/INSTRUCTIONAL CONCENTRATION	METHOD	CONTENT
Acquisition of knowledge	Didactic instruction, teaching by telling	Language[a]
		Literature
	Lectures, explanations	Math
	Standard questions	Science
	Laboratory demonstrations	History, geography
	Use of textbooks	Fine arts
Learning (intellectual) skills	Coaching	Reading, writing[b],
	Exercises, problems	speaking, listening
	Supervised practice	Observing, measuring,
	Use of computers and other	estimating
	instructional tools	Critical judgment
Ideas and values	Socratic questioning	Discussion of major books,
	Active participation	not texts
	Philosophical essays and	Interdisciplinary subject matter
	debates	(literature, history, science,
	Creative products[c]	philosophy, etc.)
		Involvement in linguistic and
		artistic activities

Source: Adapted from Mortimer J. Adler, *The Paideia Proposal: An Educational Manifesto* (New York: Macmillan, 1982), pp. 23–32. [a]Traditional academic subject matter. [b]Linguistic, math, and science skills. [c]Highly creative and individualized projects.

But equality in the curve of no tracking (handwritten margin note)

subjects.[24] Like other perennialists, Bloom asserts that cultural relativism—with its emphasis on trivial pursuits, quick fixes, relevancy and self-esteem—has eroded the quality of American education. Our media and educational institutions are marked by an easy-going, flippant, indifference to critical thought. Deprived of a serious liberal arts and science education, avoiding an engagement with the great works and great ideas of the past, our youth lack educational depth.

On a national level, Bloom contends we are heading for educational nihilism—a disrespect for tough academics and critical thought. Our schools, and especially universities, are not places where serious thought occurs. Our educational institutions fail in their fundamental task of educating people and providing a place for serious learning and scholarship. We have welcomed the false doctrine of equality and have rejected universal standards of excellence. We refuse to take a position on what is right and wrong, based on standards of truth (of course, we can argue whose truth); rather, we welcome no-fault choices.

Indeed, if we want to ask ourselves how and where we went wrong, why we are in social and economic decline, Bloom offers a conservative analysis and sense of fundamental reform. To remedy American education and to neutralize the problems caused by cultural relativism, Bloom, as did Hutchins some 25 years ago, seeks to reestablish the idea of an educated person along the great books and great thinkers line and to reestablish the virtues of a liberal education.

Essentialism

Another traditional and conservative philosophy is essentialism. This philosophy is rooted in both idealism and realism and surfaced in the 1930s as a reaction to progressivism and developed into a major position during the Cold War and the Sputnik era of the 1950s and early 1960s. The ideas of essentialism were formulated by William Bagley of Teachers College, Columbia University, and were later developed by Arthur Bestor of the University of Illinois and Admiral Hyman Rickover.[25]

According to essentialists, the school curriculum should be geared to the fundamentals or essentials: the three Rs at the elementary school level and five academic or essential subjects—that is, English, mathematics, science, history, and foreign language—at the secondary school level. Although subject centered like perennialism, essentialism is not rooted in the past but is more concerned with the contemporary scene. Both perennialism and essentialism reject such subjects as art, music, physical education, homemaking, and vocational education as fads and frills, and thus appeal to those who favor limiting educational expenses (because these subjects are more expensive in terms of facilities, materials, and student-teacher ratios than academic subjects). Perennialists, however, totally reject these subjects as wasteful and senseless, whereas essentialists grudgingly award half-credit for these so-called minor subjects, although they do limit the number and hours that students can take them. This latter requirement tends to parallel the present secondary school curriculum.

Perennialists tend to regard the student's mind as a sponge for absorbing knowledge; essentialists, too, are concerned with facts and knowledge, but they are also interested in conceptual thought and principles and theories of subject matter. Both groups feel that all students, regardless of abilities and interests, are to be offered the same common curriculum—intellectual in content—but with the quantity and rate adjusted to the capacity of the individual learner.[26] Just how far each student should go is related to his or her specific abilities. This, in fact, was the majority view before the turn of the twentieth

century, when the perennialist era introduced many viable employment opportunities—farming, manual, and, later, industrial—that did not require formal educations.

Many essentialists, like the perennialists, embrace the past mental discipline approach that the educational process should emphasize the mastery of essential skills and facts that form the basis of the subject matter. Wrote Admiral Rickover, "For all children, the educational process must be one of collecting factual knowledge to the limit of their absorptive capacity."[27] A curriculum that takes into account student interests or social issues is wasteful, as are teaching methods that rely on psychological theories. As Bestor declared, "Concern with the personal problems of adolescents has grown so excessive as to push into the background what should be the schools' central concern, the intellectual development of its students."[28] The school is viewed as being sidetracked, from its original mission when it deemphasizes cognitive needs, and attends to the social and psychological problems of students. (Most current task force reports on academic excellence, incidentally, agree with this assessment.) Tough discipline and training, and a good deal of homework and serious studies, permeate the curriculum. As Rickover asserted: "The student must be made to work hard" at his or her studies, and "nothing can really make it fun."[29]

The role of the essentialist teacher follows the perennialist philosophy. The teacher is considered a master of a particular subject and a model worthy of emulation. A teacher is to be respected as an authority because of the knowledge and high standards he or she holds. The teacher is very much in control of the classroom, and decides on the classroom curriculum with minimal student input (because the students do not really know what they want).

Essentialism today is reflected in the public demand to raise academic standards and to improve the students' work and minds. It is evidenced in such reports as *A Nation at Risk* (and other reports on excellence discussed in Chapter 5) and in the current proposals outlined in Ernest Boyer's *High School* and Theodore Sizer's *Hornace's Compromise* (also about high school). Although current essentialist philosophy is more moderate than it was during the Sputnik era—it provides, for example, for less able students—it still emphasizes academics (not play) and cognitive thinking (not the whole child). It is reflected in the two current movements below that emerged in response to the general relaxation of academic standards during the late 1960s and 1970s.

Back-to-Basics Curriculum.   Automatic promotion of marginal students, the dizzy array of elective courses, and textbooks designed more to entertain than to educate are frequently cited as sources of the decline in students' basic skills. Today's concerns parallel, to some extent, those voiced immediately after the Sputnik era. The call is less for academic excellence and rigor, however, than for a return to basics. Annual Gallup polls have asked the public to suggest ways to improve education; since 1976 "devoting more attention to teaching the basics" and improving curriculum standards" have ranked no lower than fifth in the list of responses; in the 1980s these suggestions surfaced as the number one, two, or three concern each year.[30]

By 1988, all the states had implemented statewide testing programs for various grade levels; the tests were, in fact, mandated in twenty-seven states. As an offshoot of this movement, as many as thirty-six states required beginning teachers to evidence minimum competencies in basic skills (spelling, grammar, mathematics), academic knowledge (English, social studies, science, mathematics, arts, etc.) and/or pedagogical practices for the purpose of certification.[31]

Although the back-to-basics movement means different things to different people, it usually connotes an essentialist curriculum with heavy emphasis on reading, writing, and mathematics. "Solid" subjects—English, history, science, and mathematics—are taught in all grades. English means traditional grammar, not linguistics or nonstandard English; it means Shakespeare and not *Lolita*. History means U.S. and European history, and perhaps Asian and African history, but not African-American history or ethnic studies. Science means biology, chemistry, and physics, not ecology. Math means old math, not new math. Furthermore, these subjects are required for everyone. Elective courses, minicourses, even the integrated social science

and general science courses, are considered too "soft."

Proponents of the movement are concerned that too many illiterate students are passed from grade to grade and eventually graduate, that high school and college diplomas are meaningless as measures of academic performance, that minimum standards must be established, and that the basic skills and subjects are essential for employment and self-survival in modern society. Some of these advocates are college educators who would do away with open admissions, credit for life experiences or for remedial courses, and grade inflation. They would simply insist on reasonable high school and college standards, and they would use tests (a dirty word for some educators) to monitor educational standards over time and to pressure students, teachers, and parents to perform their responsibilities.[32]

Although the movement is spreading, and state legislators and the public seem convinced of the need for minimum standards, some unanswered questions remain: What standards should be considered minimum? What do we do with students who fail to meet these standards? Are we punishing the victims for the schools' inability to educate them? How will the courts and then the school districts deal with the fact that proportionately more minority than white students fail the competency tests in nearly every case? Is the issue minimum competency or equal educational opportunity? And, when all is said and done, are we not, educationally speaking, reinventing the academic wheel?

Worried reformers also point out that parental involvement in education has been victimized by a change in family structure: rising divorce rates, percentages of children in single-family homes, numbers of married mothers of young children working outside the home, and a corresponding number of latchkey children which has tripled in the last 20 years.[33] The result is that parents have less time and energy to devote to their children's basic education or to supervise them. Regardless of the reform movement we wish to push, the fact is we cannot get increased student output (even in the "basics") because parental input has declined. Hence, it can be argued that the family revolution is the greatest single cause for the decline in student achievement.

Emphasizing Content, De-emphasizing Process.
E. D. Hirsch's *Cultural Literacy,* a national
bestseller, focuses on the background *knowledge*
necessary for cultural (Hirsch calls it "functional") literacy and effective communication for
our nation's populace. Complementing his narrative is a compilation of some 5,000 "essential"
items from history, geography, literature, science, and technology.[34] Table 2-3 lists a sample
of 50 names, phrases, and concepts (dates are not
listed) from the text to test your own literacy.

Although the items are supposedly a mix of
historical and current names, people, places, and
terms—national and international in scope—
most of the items reflect a conservative interpretation of literacy: More than 80 percent of the
total items refer to events, people, or places from
previous centuries, and about 25 percent deal

with the classics. The list, originally based on
testing lawyers' knowledge, has questionable
validity, but people who like "Trivial Pursuit"
and other knowledge games seem to enjoy discussing the list, which is one reason for the
book's popularity. One might also ask if the
items appear with any frequency in *Atlantic, Com-
monweal, Harper's, New Republic,* or *Saturday
Review,* American magazines that highly literate
people usually read.

Instead of placing emphasis on process or
teaching students how to think, Hirsch stresses
the importance of specific information in all
levels of schooling. Knowing the facts, for him
and a growing number of other essentialists
(William Bennett, Chester Finn, Diane Ravitch,
and others), increases the students' capacity to
comprehend what they read, see, and hear. The

Table 2-3 Fifty Names, Phrases, and Concepts Essential for Literate Americans

Absolute monarchy	Centigrade
Acculturation	Chamberlain
Acid rain	Chekhov, Anton
Aeneas	Chernobyl
Aesop's fables	Cholesterol
Alien and Sedition Acts	Chutzpah
Apollo program	Cid (title)
Auxiliary verb	Clemens, Samuel
Babylon	Cobb, Ty
Bacillus	Cohan, George M.
Bangkok	Cologne
Bard of Avon	Colon
Bay of Biscay	Common Market
Becket, Saint Thomas à	Communist Manifesto
Berlin, Irving	Congressional Record
Big Ben	Congress of Vienna
Black, Hugo	Cyclops
Brussels	Czar
Brutus	Damascus
Calvin, John	Dante
Candide (title)	Darrow, Clarence
Canterbury Tales	D-Day
Cape Hatteras	Degas, Edgar
Capital expenditure	Detente
Catch-22 (title)	Dien Bien Phu

Source: E. D. Hirsch, *Cultural Literacy: What Every American Needs to Know,* rev. ed. (Boston: Houghton Mifflin. 1987), Appendix.

need for background knowledge or a core of essential knowledge is judged important for future communication and specialization. In recent years these people argue we have overlooked content and have stressed process—or thinking skills—without regard to subject matter. The outcome has been a decline in national literacy.

For Hirsch and other essentialists, the notion that learning to think, even learning to read, involves a process of acquiring a certain set of skills—without regard to content—is wrong. The idea breaks down very quickly as soon as students advance beyond simple subject matter and/or begin to read for information. Processes or skills are only part of the picture. An educated person has command of knowledge. For traditional educators, the goal of education is not to prepare youth for the future, but rather to enculturate the young. The need is to transmit the shared knowledge and values of adult society to youth. Without the transmission of a shared cultural core to the young, traditionalists argue that our society will become fragmented and our ability to accumulate and communicate information to various segments of the populace will become limited.

Excellence in Education.   A spin-off to the back-to-basics movement was the demand in the 1980s for educational excellence and tougher academics. This trend was also in tune with the past Cold War–Sputnik era, when essentialists exerted a considerable influence on the school curriculum; today, it coincides with a broader theme of not only military defense but also technology and economic competition. The dimensions of the problem of academic quality were amply documented in several policy reports on academic excellence—the best known being *A Nation at Risk,* released in the mid-1980s, and the *National Goals for Education,* published in 1990—all calling for reform to improve the quality of education in the United States and emphasizing international "competition" and "survival"—themes reminiscent of the post-Sputnik era as well.[35]

Overall, the trend is for higher achievement (not just minimum competency) for all children (not just college-bound students) in the academic

areas, which means that we need to stress cognitive achievement (not the whole child) and rigorous grading, testing, and discipline (not relaxed standards). The emphasis is on higher standards for passing courses and meeting graduation requirements.

For some this approach means more than emphasizing the basic ability to think, reason, and problem solve: It means promoting such serious subjects such as calculus, physics, and advanced foreign languages at the high school level; it means upgrading our definition of basic skills to include advanced skills and knowledge, including computer skills as the fourth R—which are required for tomorrow's technological world. Stress is on increasing and improving the quality of instruction, upgrading our teachers and schools, and making the most of our human capital so we can compete on an economic basis. Unquestionably, the emphasis is on productivity. Moreover, the health and vitality of our country's economy and political position are linked to strengthening our educational institutions.

Others allow wider latitude in defining excellence and permit various models or criteria of excellence. Some still criticize the overemphasis on mathematical and scientific excellence in the schools, and the consequent underemphasis or ignoring of other conceptions of excellence—linguistic, humanistic, musical, spatial, bodily kinesthetic, moral, interpersonal, intrapersonal, and information processing areas.[36] Some are also concerned that equity and equality will be shoved under the rug, with too much stress on cognitive excellence—a return to a post-Sputnik-type emphasis on academically talented students but not high school dropouts.[37] Some fear that this emphasis on excellence will lead to disappointment; they say it is wrong to assume that increased testing and more course requirements will automatically raise the level of student performance. Students, teachers, and parents must also be motivated, and technical and financial support at the school and school district level must be evidenced. See Curriculum Tips 2-2.

In any event, the general theme of this movement is excellence, not adequacy, and many forms of it. The focus is on productivity, increased testing, more homework, better selection of textbooks, and more competent personnel. Both educators and the public agree that students must not only master basic or prerequisite skills, but they must also excel, think creatively, solve problems, and develop their fullest human potential. Finally, the public even seems willing to spend increased monies for real school reform and for upgraded curricula.

Progressivism

Progressivism developed from pragmatic philosophy and as a protest against perennialist think-ing in education. The progressive movement in education was also part of the largest social and political movement of reform that characterized much of American society at the turn of the twentieth century. It grew out of the political thought of such progressives as Robert LaFollette, Theodore Roosevelt, and Woodrow Wilson, as well as from the muckraker movement of the 1920s. Progressivism is considered a contemporary reform movement in educational, social, and political affairs.

The educational roots of progressivism can be traced to the reform writings of Horace Mann and Henry Barnard of the nineteenth century, and later to the work of John Dewey in the early twentieth century.[38] In his most comprehensive work, *Democracy and Education,* Dewey claimed that democracy and education went hand in hand; democratic society and democratic education are participatory and emergent, not preparatory and absolute. Dewey viewed the school as a miniature democratic society in which students could learn and practice the skills and tools necessary for democratic living.[39]

According to progressivist thought, the skills and tools of learning include problem-solving methods and scientific inquiry; in addition, learning experiences should include cooperative behaviors and self-discipline, both of which are important for democratic living. Through these skills and experiences the school can transmit the culture of society while it prepares the students for a changing world. Because reality is constantly changing, Dewey saw little need to focus upon a fixed body of knowledge, as did the perennialists and essentialists. Progressivism, instead, placed heavy emphasis on *how* to think, not *what* to think. Traditional education, with its "method of imposition from the side of the teacher and reception, [and] absorption from the side of the pupil," wrote Dewey, "may be compared to inscribing records upon a passive phonographic disc to result in giving back what has been inscribed when the proper button is pressed in recitation or examination."[40]

For Dewey and other progressivist thinkers, the curriculum was interdisciplinary in nature, and books and subject matter were part of the learning process rather than sources of ultimate knowledge. The role of the teacher was unique when operating under progressive thinking. The teacher served as a guide for students in their problem-solving and scientific projects. Dewey and William Kilpatrick both referred to this role as the "leader of group activities." The teacher and students planned activities together (although Dewey later affirmed that the final authority rested with the teacher), but the teacher was to help students locate, analyze, interpret, and evaluate data—to formulate their own conclusions.[41]

The progressive movement became splintered by several different wings, including the child-centered, activity-centered, creative, and neo-Freudian groups. Dewey criticized these groups for misinterpreting and misusing his ideas. Just as he condemned the old philosophies that pursued knowledge for its own sake, he attacked those who thought knowledge had little or no value. Not only did he attack "traditional ideas as erecting silence as a virtue," he also criticized those who sought to liberate the child from adult authority and social controls. He declared "progressive extremists" and "laissez-faire" philosophies to be destructive to the ideas of progressivism, and he warned that "any movement that thinks and acts in terms of an ism becomes so involved in reaction against other isms that it is unwittingly controlled by them."[42]

Dewey was not alone in his criticism of progressive educators. As criticisms mounted, Boyd Bode, another leading proponent of progressivism, warned his associates of the impending crisis in a book entitled *Progressive Education at the Crossroads.*[43] He cautioned that "progressive education stands at the parting of the ways." The movement "nurtured the pathetic hope that it could find out how to educate by relying on such notions as interests, needs, growth and freedom." In its social and psychological approach to learning, in its "one-sided devotion to the child, it betrayed the child," and deprived him or her of appropriate subject matter. If progressivism continued its present course without changing its focus, "it would be circumvented and left behind."[44] Bode's words proved prophetic. More and more progressivists responded to the growing criticism and self-justifying theories and educational ideas that involved trivialities and errors.

Although the progressive movement in education encompassed many different theories and practices, it was united in its opposition to certain traditional school practices: (1) the authoritarian teacher; (2) excessive reliance on textbook methods; (3) memorization of factual data and techniques by drill; (4) static aims and materials that reject the notion of a changing world; (5) use of fear or corporal punishment as a form of discipline; and (6) attempts to isolate education from individual experiences and social reality. However, the movement's inability to outline a uniform theory of the purpose of schooling, or even to establish a set of principles, contributed to its downfall.[45]

Progressive education was both a movement within the broad framework of American education and a theory that urged the liberation of the child from the traditional emphasis on rote learning, lesson recitations, and textbook authority. In opposition to the conventional subject matter of the traditional curriculum, progressives experimented with alternative modes of curricular organization—utilizing activities, experiences, problem solving, and the project method. Progressive education focused on the child as the learner rather than on the subject, emphasized activities and experiences rather than verbal and literary skills, and encouraged cooperative group-learning activities rather than competitive individualized lesson learning. The use of democratic school procedures was considered a prelude to community and social reform. Progressivism also cultivated a cultural relativism that critically appraised and often rejected traditional value commitments.

Although the major thrust of progressive education waned in the 1940s and 1950s, with the advent of essentialism, the philosophy did leave its imprint on education and the schools of today. Contemporary progressivism is expressed in several movements, including those for a relevant curriculum, humanistic education, and radical school reform.

Relevant Curriculum. As the 1960s unfolded, students took a more active role in their education, as a spin off to the student movement, and perceived the subject-centered curriculum as irrelevant to the social times and demanded a more progressive and student-centered curriculum. It was now argued that learners must be motivated and interested in the learning task, and the classroom should build on real-life experiences.

The call for relevance came, in fact, from both students and educators. Advocates of this approach saw as needs (1) the individualization of instruction through such teaching methods as independent study and special projects; (2) revised and new courses on such topics of student concern as sex education, drug addiction, race relations, urban problems, and so on; (3)

educational alternatives, as well as electives, minicourses, and open classrooms; (4) the extension of the curriculum beyond the school's walls through such innovations as work-study programs, credit for life experiences, off-campus courses, and external degree programs; and (5) the relaxation of academic standards and admission standards to schools and colleges.[46]

Humanistic Curriculum. The humanistic curriculum also began as a reaction to what was viewed as an overemphasis on subject matter and cognitive learning in the 1960s and 1970s. In his best-selling book, *Crisis in the Classroom,* Charles Silberman advocated humanizing American schools.[47] He charged that schools are repressive, and that they teach students docility and conformity. He believed that schools must be reformed, even at the price of de-emphasizing cognitive learning and student discipline. He suggested that elementary schools adopt the methods of the British infant schools. At the secondary level, he suggested independent study, peer tutoring, and community and work experiences.

The humanistic model of education stems from the human potential movement in psychology. Within education it is rooted in the work of Arthur Jersild who linked good teaching with knowledge of self and students, and in the work of Arthur Combs and Donald Snygg, who explored the impact of self-concept and motivation on achievement.[48] Combs and Snygg considered self-concept the most important determinant of behavior.

A humanistic curriculum emphasizes affective rather than cognitive outcomes. Such a curriculum draws heavily on the works of Abraham Maslow and Carl Rogers.[49] Its goal is to produce "self-actualizing people," in Maslow's words, or "total human beings," in Rogers's. The works of both psychologists are laced with such terms as maintaining, striving, enhancing, and experiencing—as well as independence, self-determination, integration, and self-actualization.

Advocates of humanistic education contend that the present school curriculum has failed miserably by humanistic standards, that teachers and schools are determined to stress cognitive behaviors and to control students *not* for their own good but for the good of adults.[50] Humanists emphasize more than affective processes; they seek higher domains of consciousness. But they see the schools as unconcerned about higher planes of understanding, enhancement of the mind, or self-knowledge. Students must therefore turn to such out-of-school activities as drugs, yoga, transcendental meditation, group encounters, T-groups, psychotherapy, and sexual therapy.

But such activities lead many observers to put down the humanistic movement. Mario Fantini, an advocate of humanistic education, warns that too many Americans view the humanistic approach negatively. They are suspicious of what appears to be bizarre procedures and touch-feel sexual experiences. "In certain professional circles, the movement is . . . referred to as the 'touchfeeling crowd' connoting an almost illegitimate status among the established disciplines."[51]

Humanists would attempt to form more meaningful relationships between students and teachers; they would foster student independence and self-direction, and they would promote greater acceptance of self and others. The teacher's role would be to help learners cope with their psychological needs and problems, to facilitate self-understanding among students, and to help them develop fully.

A drawback to humanist theory is its lack of attention to cognitive learning and intellectual development. When asked to judge the effectiveness of their curriculum, humanists generally rely on testimonials and subjective assessments by students and teachers. They may also present such materials as students paintings and poems or talk about "marked improvement" in student behavior and attitudes. They present very little empirical evidence, however, to support their stance. See Curriculum Tips 2-3.

Radical School Reform. During the late 1960s and 1970s, intense attacks were leveled on teachers and schools by radical critics of education, sometimes called "radical romanticists" or "neoprogressives." The criticisms were widely published in the mass media, especially in magazines that politically liberal and college-educated adults read (*Atlantic, Harper's, New Republic, The New York Times Magazine,* and

Saturday Review). These radicals also published many popular books on their views; in fact, they were superverbalizers who enchanted their readers.[52]

Among the most prominent wave of radicals are Edgar Friedenberg, John Holt, Paul Goodman, A. S. Neill, and Ivan Illich. They expressed considerable disdain toward established methods of schooling, compulsory schooling, adult authority, and school rules. They referred to students as prisoners, to teachers as prison guards (who disliked their students), and to schools as prisons (which keep youths locked up, restricted from free expression and democratic procedures). In general, school is considered to be a highly discriminatory place that sorts and tracks students for various jobs that extend class differences in society.

In particular, Friedenberg argued that teachers "dislike and distrust" the students they teach, and that they "fear being involved with young people in any situation that is not under their complete control." Teachers have a "repressed hostility toward their students" and "resentment," a kind of ill temper, suppressed anger, and jealousy because of students' youthful energy and freedom.[53]

John Holt's book, *How Children Fail,* is his most influential text.[54] There is nothing positive in it about teachers or the school processes; it deals instead with how teachers and schools turn off students. Holt describes the conventions of the classroom: teachers' enforcing rigid rules and children's focusing on right answers, learning to be stupid, and learning not to learn. He goes into great detail about how children adopt strategies of fear and failure to please their teachers. The successful students become cunning strategists in a game of beating the system—figuring out how to outsmart the teacher, how to get the answer out of the teacher, or how to fake the answer.

Paul Goodman's thesis is that our society is sick and full of spurious and false values that have produced sick schools. He contends that schools have little to do with education; they provide jobs for millions of people and a market for textbook companies, building contractors, and graduates of schools of education. In the early grades, the schools provide "a baby-sitting service" for the parents and keep kids off the

CURRICULUM TIPS 2-3 Affective Methods to Enhance Learning

Progressive philosophy and humanistic education increase the student's self-understanding and self-awareness, allow students to personalize and individualize learning, and match (at least consider) their personal needs and interests with academic experiences. The classroom is characterized by activity, not passivity; cooperation, not competition; and many learning opportunities other than textbooks and teacher-dominated situations. To help the teacher and curriculum worker provide a leadership role in progressive and humanistic approaches, we provide the following guidelines.

1. Demonstrate real interest and concern for each student.
2. Challenge students to become personally and actively involved in their own learning; encourage them to grow toward self-direction and self-control over learning.
3. Help students define personal goals; recognize their efforts in pursuit of a chosen goal.
4. Structure learning activities so that each student can accomplish his or her own personal goals and experience success.
5. Relate content to students' personal goals, needs, and interests.
6. Match task requirements to students' age, development, and abilities.
7. Offer constructive and corrective feedback, but put the emphasis on being constructive.
8. Test students if necessary, but delay grading their performance (say until the fourth or fifth grade).
9. Use local resources to obtain information and solve problems; actively involve students in learning that involves different materials, people, and places.
10. Provide alternative ways for learning; minimize memory, rote. and drill activities.
11. Help students achieve their own competence and mastery; let them know that their learning is the result of their own efforts, for which they are responsible.
12. Recognize students' improvement and achievement.
13. Encourage students to share materials and resources and to work in groups.
14. Encourage students to contribute their ideas and feelings, to accept and support each other—not to criticize or ridicule one another—and to be considerate to others who need help or are slow to learn.

street. In the middle and senior years, "they are the arm of the police, providing cops and concentration camps paid for in the budget under the heading of 'Board of Education.'" From kindergarten to college, schools teach youth to adjust to a sick society and provide "a universal trap [in which] democracy begins to look like regimentation."[55] Goodman's solution is to do away with compulsory education, to which he refers as "miseducation" and to "drastically cut back formal schooling because the present extended tutelage is against nature and arrests growth."[56]

A. S. Neill, the fourth member of the earlier generation of romantic progressivists, recounts the way he operated his school, Summerhill, in Suffolk, England. He wrote about the innate goodness of the child, and about the replacement of authority for freedom against which Dewey warned:

> . . .we set out to make a school in which we should allow children to be themselves. In order to do this, we had to renounce all discipline, all direction, all suggestion, all moral training. . . . All it required was what we had—a complete belief in the child as a good, not an evil being. For almost forty years, this belief in the goodness of the child has never wavered; it rather has become a final faith.[57]

Neill claimed that the "child is innately wise and realistic. If left to himself without adult suggestions of any kind," he will develop on his own. Those "who are to become scholars will be scholars," and those "who are only fit to sweep the streets will sweep streets."[58] Neill is not concerned with formal teaching or instruction; he does not believe in examinations or in homework. Those who want to study will study, and those who prefer not to study will not—regardless of how teachers teach or what they say. If a child wants to go to class, great; if not, so what? Neill's criteria for success have nothing to do with school or economic outcomes; rather they relate to the ability to "work joyfully" and "live positively." Following these guidelines, most of the students who attend Summerhill allegedly turn out to be successful in life.

Ivan Illich, another radical critic, goes beyond his contemporaries in his plans for remaking schools. He argues for a new society that requires the prior deschooling of society.[59] In this sense Illich may also be a reconstructionist philosopher. Although the other radical critics are very angry and see little possibility of school reform, given the present educational process, Illich, who completely rejects school as a viable agency, is the center of controversy. His criticism of current schools is that they are coercive, discriminatory, and destructive toward their clients. If schools were eliminated, education could be open to all and could become a genuine instrument of human liberation: Learners would no longer have an obligatory curriculum imposed upon them; they would be liberated from institutional and capitalistic indoctrination. There would no longer be discrimination and a class society based on possession of a certificate.

In lieu of school, Illich recommends small learning networks characterized by the following: *Educational objects,* that is, shops, libraries, museums, art galleries, and so on that are open to learners; *peer matching,* that is, identifying and bringing together students who wish to engage in a particular learning activity; *skill exchanges,* that is, exchanges between those who are competent in a particular skill, and who wish to teach it, and those who wish to learn it; and *educators-at-large,* that is, counselors who serve as advisors to students and parents and intellectual initiators and administrators who operate the networks.

Even though Illich is considered a neo-Marxist educator, he has stimulated large numbers of disciples to further the idea of deschooling, and a good deal of radical reform

literature related to the political and economic concept of educational "revisionism."[60]

Reconstructionism

The reconstructionist philosophy itself is based on early socialistic and utopian ideas of the nineteenth century; nonetheless, it was the Economic Depression that gave it rebirth and new life. The progressive educational movement was at its height in popularity then, but a small yet significant group of progressive educators still became disillusioned with American society and impatient for reform. This group argued that progressivism put too much emphasis on child-centered education that mainly served the individual child and the middle class, with its play theories and private schools. What was needed was more emphasis on society-centered education that took into consideration the needs of society (not the individual) and all classes (not only the middle class).

At the 1932 annual meeting of the Progressive Education Association, George Counts urged progressive educators to consider the social and economic problems of the era and to use the schools to help reform society. In his speech, "Dare the School Build a New Social Order?" (which was later published as a book), Counts suggested that the schools become the agent of social change and institution for social reform. In a rhetorical and highly charged statement, Counts stunned his progressive colleagues with the following statement:

> . . . If Progressive Education is to be genuinely progressive, it must . . . face squarely and courageously every social issue, come to grips with life in all its stark reality, establish an organic relation with the community, develop a realistic and comprehensive theory of welfare, fashion a compelling and challenging vision of human destiny, and become less frightened than it is today at the bogeys of imposition and indoctrination.[61]

The social issues of the 1930s, according to Counts, involved racial and class discrimination, poverty, and unemployment—and progressive education had ignored these issues. The social issues today are similar, although the list is larger: racial, ethnic, and sexual inequality; poverty, unemployment, and welfare; computers and technology; political oppression and war; the threat of nuclear disaster; environmental pollution; disease; hunger; AIDS; and depletion of the earth's resources.

Theodore Brameld, who is often considered the originator of the term reconstructionism in 1950 (actually Dewey coined the term),[62] has asserted that reconstructionism is a crisis philosophy, appropriate for a society in crisis, which is the essence of our society and international society today.[63] According to Brameld, students and teachers must not only take positions; they must also become change agents to improve society. Neutrality in the classrooms or schools, that in which we often engage under the guise of objective and scientific inquiry, is not appropriate for the democratic process. Writes Brameld, "Teachers and students have a right to take sides, to stand up for the best reasoned and informed partialities they can reach as a result of free, meticulous examination and communication of all relevant evidence." In particular, teachers must measure up to their social responsibilities. Brameld goes on: "The immediate task before the [teaching] profession is to draw upon this strength and thus to strengthen control of the schools by and for the goal-seeking interests of the overwhelming majority of mankind."[64]

As for the curriculum, it had to be transformed to coincide with a new social-economic-political education; it had, in other words, to incorporate realistic reform strategies. For reconstructionists, analysis, interpretation, and evaluation of problems are insufficient; commitment and action by students and teachers are needed. Society is always changing, and the curriculum has to change; students and teachers must be change agents. A curriculum based on social issues and social services is ideal.

The reconstructionists, including such recent proponents as Mario Fantini, Harold Shane, and Alvin Toffler, seek a curriculum that emphasizes cultural pluralism, equality, and futurism.[65] Students are taught to appreciate life in a world of many nations. A reconstructionist program of education (1) critically examines the cultural heritage of a society as well as the entire civilization, (2) is not afraid to examine controversial issues, (3) is deliberately committed to bring about so-

cial and constructive change, (4) cultivates a future planning attitude that considers the realities of the world, and (5) enlists students and teachers in a definite program to enhance cultural renewal and interculturalism. In such a program, teachers are considered the prime agents of social change, cultural renewal, and internationalism. Teachers are organized not to strengthen their own professional security, but rather to encourage widespread experimentation in the schools and to challenge the outdated structures of society. They are considered to be the vanguard for a new social order—somewhat utopian in nature.

Internationalists. A reconstructionist educator tends to be very sensitive to global issues and analyzes them as part of the larger social order. Although, historically, the United States has taken a relatively isolationist position, interdependence among nations no longer allows Americans to remain ignorant of developments in distant countries. Educators now feel the need to place a greater emphasis on understanding other nations and cultures than they have in the past.

Such terms as "global village," "global interdependence," "shrinking world," and "greenhouse effect" reflect our new concerns that the oceans no longer protect us and we are forced to reflect on the international tendencies of the times. Increasingly, one group of curriculum experts is seeking an *international component* in national curricula. This does not suggest a common curriculum, but rather that the goals, content, and experiences of each nation's school curricula enhance its mutual understanding about international society and global cooperation. Sometimes called a world curriculum or universal core, each nation would continue to promote its own culture, values, and political/economic systems, but students would learn a common core of knowledge and skills essential for global peace and cooperation.[66]

One advocate of this international curriculum is Kenneth Boulding; he maintains that students need to acquire an awareness of global events and tools for understanding "worldwide systems." These systems, are social, and political, economic, physical, biological, communicative, and evaluative.[67] This new curriculum would focus on understanding the earth's ecosystem and world problems. Some might argue the idea is unrealistic, too encompassing, or not possible to implement as schools are presently organized. Indeed, there are some 15,000 school districts, each with their own curricula, multiple textbooks, and ideal teaching methods. Perhaps all these global concepts cannot be fully implemented, but the idea of a new core or worldwide curriculum for all students is certainly intriguing and worth considering.

When discussion about an international curriculum surfaces, another group of educators answers the question, "What knowledge is most needed?" in one word: history. (Others say geography.) Although not reconstructionists, but essentialists, people like William Bennett, Chester Finn, and Diane Ravitch argue that our students are internationally ignorant and need greater historical understanding—a core history curriculum with greater emphasis on content.[68] Similarly, the Bradley Commission on History points out that at least 50 percent of U.S. high school students never studied Western civilization or world history; 15 percent never even took American history. The commission concludes that American students are ignorant of great ideas and events that have shaped the world. They lack a sense of history, which negatively affects their overall education, that is, their personal growth, preparation for work, and intelligent citizenship.[69]

These spokespeople point to the National Assessment of Education Progress (NAEP), the nationwide assessment among students aged 9, 13, and 17 (as well as young adults aged 21 to 25). As many as 33 percent of the high school juniors (age 17) could not recognize the principal enemies of the United States during World War II, 40 percent could not tell in which 50-year period the U.S. Constitution was written or when World War I was fought, and 75 percent did not know that the United Nations was founded after World War II or that when it is winter in the United States it is summer in Argentina and Australia.[70]

Still another group of international educators point out that, in the national interest, the implications of internationally ignorant Americans are far reaching and frightening. An increasing percentage of our gross national product, jobs at home, and standard of living are influenced by global activities. Oil prices in Iraq or Saudi Arabia influence jobs in Houston and Tulsa and prices at the gas pump nationally. Automobile and steel output in Korea and Japan influences the local economy in Detroit and Pittsburgh and national economy in general.

While the political and economic advantages of learning foreign languages are evident, which languages are more important results in controversy. For example, some of us feel Spanish is crucial for U.S. students, given our growing Hispanic immigrant and ethnic population trends. Others who are seemingly outdated, still feel that the truly educated person must speak French, or that a social scientist or scholar must read German. During the Cold War period, and fostered by the Conant era of reform, Russian was considered essential; today, it seems almost irrelevant. Some feel that Japanese, today, is crucial to learn if we are to remain economically competitive. Then there are others (including the authors of this text) who feel that the economy (and related demographic trends) is market driven, and the future is in learning Mandarin (Chinese) and Hindi (Indian)—to learn the culture and customs of over 1 billion and 850,000 people, respectively—or nearly 40 percent of the world's population.*

The ten most commonly spoken languages in the world in rank order are (1) Mandarin, (2) English, (3) Hindi, (4) Spanish, (5) Russian, (6) Arabic, (7) Bengali, (8) Portuguese, (9) Malay-Indonesian, and (10) Japanese.[71] (Interestingly French and German don't make the top ten list.) Of all students enrolled in foreign language courses in U.S. secondary schools, 58 percent were studying Spanish, 28 percent French, and 8 percent German.[72] Less than 0.2 percent took Russian and sadly so few were enrolled in Mandarin or Japanese that these two languages were grouped into "other languages." And to our international embarrassment, we need only ask one question: What percentage of Chinese and Japanese students study English?

---

*Most educated Chinese and Indians already know English, and it can be argued that English is the worldwide language for conducting international government and business activities. A question can be made raised: why study these languages? Answer: We cannot afford to ignore so many people, at least not in our "shrinking" world.

American language enrollment trends seem to connote the "saber-tooth" curriculum and Western provincialism. We might as well be in the Paleolithic period, according to hard-driving reconstructionists who wish to bring American schools into the twenty-first century and combine both global politics and economics with academic and especially modern language considerations. While other nations attain direct access to our mass media and information sources and while foreign diplomats and business people speak fluent English, U.S. people doing business abroad must rely on second-hand translations—and hope that the interpretation is accurate. See Curriculum Tips 2-4.

Reconceptualists. The reconceptualists have criticized the majority of curricularists as exemplifying a lock-step, means-ends approach, based on technocratic and bureaucratic school models that are not sensitive to the inner feelings and experiences of people. The majority of curricularists, in turn, have claimed that the reconceptualists are unable to quantify or verify the components of their curriculum and are unclear about their philosophical and methodological tools. Most people in the field, representing a conservative outlook, believe that the empirical-analytical and scientific approaches contribute the most to the field of curriculum. Nonetheless, the reconceptualists's approach is enriching and introduces aesthetic, existentialist, and social science procedures previously not deemed appropriate.

Reconceptualists have expanded the field to include other dimensions of curriculum, including intuitive, personal, mystical, linguistic, political, and social systems of theorizing. They stress broad problems and issues, and they attempt to reflect, refine, rethink, reinterpret, and reconceptualize the field of curriculum. It is doubtful, however, that reconceptualists really reinterpret or reconceptualize anything. They are basically socially sensitive and politically concerned intellectuals who reflect and refine important issues that have philosophical, psychological, social, political, and economic implications. Unfortunately for the field of curriculum, they have been labeled reconceptualists.[73]

Reconceptualists accept many aspects of progressive philosophy, including learner-centered, relevant, humanistic, and radical school-reform models. However, they reiterate and detail a bit more of the dynamic, holistic, transcendental, linguistic, and artistic meaning of teaching learning. They are more concerned with personal self-knowledge, inner self, personal reflection, psychologies of consciousness, and spiritual and moral introspection. They contend there is more to knowledge and knowing than empirical or even logical, verifiable data. Expanded ideas of inner consciousness, "third force," or humanistic psychology, and existentialist ideas serve as the foundations for their views.

Content and experiences that emphasize language and communication skills, personal biographies, art, poetry, dance, drama, literature, psychology, ethics, religion, and other aesthetic, humanistic, and spiritual subject matter comprise a good part of the reconstructionist curriculum—subjects not part of the normal curriculum or certainly not the major foci. Maxine Greene advocates this curriculum, which she calls "personal expression," "intellectual consciousness," and "reflective self-consciousness." Paulo Freire refers to this as a curriculum of "human phenomenon," "problematic situations," and "background awareness" that has the potential "to transform the world."[75] According to William Pinar, this subject matter deals with "personal becoming," "autonomy," the "soul" and "heart," "affiliative needs," "mature personality," "trust" and "love," "self-direction," "sensitivity," and "enjoyment"[76]—that is, psychological, philosophical, spiritual, and existentialist attitudes and behaviors.

Reconceputualists are also concerned with social, political, and economic ideas and ideology, and in this context reflect reconstructionist philosophy. Many of their ideas, rooted in the school of Dewey, Counts, and Rugg, deal with inequities and/or conflict concerned with socioeconomic relationships, sexual and racial roles and attitudes, the relationship between labor and capital, and the consequences of political power. Reconceptualists are also concerned with current technocratic and bureaucratic systems that dominate the individual and that reduce the person to a powerless and manipulated cog. They envision

It is time for Americans to get to know more about their global neighbors (and competitors). A recent study of Japanese education summarized the lessons Americans might learn. The emphasis is on academic excellence and productivity—and there is good reason to try to incorporate these ideas in our schooling process.

1. *Parental engagement with the education of their children is high,* from infancy through high school, and makes a difference in how well children learn.

2. *Schools are clear about their purposes* and both children and parents are too. They know their mission, and while not exclusively "cognitive," it is the object of sustained purpose.

3. *Motivation and hard work count.* Throughout school there is the conviction that progress can be made by everyone who tries hard enough, and there is a sense that significant rewards accompany school success.

4. *Expectations and standards matter too.* Students learn more when more is expected of them, and these expectations are communicated first by the family and then by the school.

5. *All students are provided with the same basic education.* There are limited choices and minimal specialization at the high-school level. The curriculum is planned by teachers and administrators, not students.

6. *The school transmits the shared and inherited culture to the next generation.* Emphasis is on common historical knowledge, shared values, and cultural understanding.

7. *Sound character, ethical behavior, and traditional values are reinforced and nurtured through the "regular" and "implicit" curriculum.* Japanese schools designate certain hours for moral education—for establishing standards of behavior and integrity.

8. *The school and classroom setting reflect an orderly environment,* including formal discipline and self-discipline and good study habits. It is possible to converse in normal tones with no interruptions in the corridor, yet students are not fearful or inhibited.

9. *Maximum and effective use of academic time is devoted to learning.* The school day and school year are considerably longer than in American schools. By the end of the twelfth grade, Japanese students have accumulated more than one extra year of schooling than have our students.

10. *Education money is focused on quality teaching and instructional materials.* Fad and frills, lavish facilities, special programs or electives, and special consultants and bureaucratic layers are all minimized. Teachers are well paid and the instructional materials are relevant and up to date.

11. *Teachers are dedicated but society offers teachers reasonable remuneration and respected status.* Dedicated teachers make for good schools, but in order to retain good teachers, society must be willing to pay them decent salaries.

12. *Students are held accountable.* Notwithstanding reports of pressure on Japanese youngsters, attendance, graduation, and knowledge acquisition are higher than in American Schools.

Source: Adapted from William J. Bennett, "Looking at Japanese Education—Implications for American Education," *NASSP Bulletin* (May 1987), pp. 102–108.

schools as an oppressive instrument of society that controls and coerces, even oppresses, students through various customs and mores and teaching-learning practices.

Some reconceptualists have been labeled neo-Marxists. Michael Apple, for one, has tried to highlight the relationship between what he perceives to be political, economic, and cultural domination of the individual in relation to schools and society. Such domination "is vested in the constitutive principles, codes, and especially the common sense consciousness and practices underlying our lives, as well as by overt division and manipulation."[77] In other words, the everyday structures and institutions of our society, including schools, convey meaning and conditions that shape our lives and that take control over us; the dominant social, political, and economic system pervades in all critical aspects of the curriculum.

Elsewhere, Apple points out that just as there is "unequal distribution of economic capital in society, so, too is there a similar system of distribution surrounding cultural capital." In technological societies, schools become "distributors of this cultural capital."[78] They play a major role in distributing various forms of knowledge, which in turn leads to power and control over others.

Both Illich and Freire contend that the larger system is oppressive and in need of major overhaul. Illich, who is also considered to be a radical critic, outlines a curriculum that is less institutionalized, formal, and discriminatory for purposes of "emancipation." He relies on a "grass-roots" curriculum that seeks to engage students, teachers, and community members.[79] Freire develops a "pedagogy for the oppressed" for students and the poor, and describes how people can move through different stages to ultimately be able to take action and overcome oppression. To effect major change, at what Freire calls the "critical transforming stage," people must become active participants in changing their own status through social action that aims at changing the larger social order. Freire calls for a dialogue or match between students and adults who are sensitive to change. The curriculum is to focus on community, national, and world problems—and is to be based on a core or interdisciplinary approach.[80]

In general, the curriculum advocated by in this wing of reconceptualists emphasizes the social sciences—history, political science, economics, sociology, and some psychology and philosophy—and not the hard sciences. The thrust is to develop individual self-realization

and freedom through cognitive and intellectual activities and then to liberate people from the restrictions, limitations, and controls of society. The idea is to move from knowledge to activity, from reflections to action. The curriculum attempts to create new conditions and environments that improve the human condition and the institutions of society. It is, according to James Macdonald, "a form of 'utopianism,' a form of political and social philosophizing."[81] All the oppressed—youth, poor, minorities, women, and so on—are considered agents for change. The model, in essence, is an updated version of old reconstructionism, which viewed students and teachers as agents of change. In the new version, reconceptualism, the teacher is often construed as an agent of oppression, representative of the larger and coercive society.

Equality of Educational Opportunity. No country has taken the idea of equality more seriously than ours. Politically, the idea is rooted in our Constitution, written more than 150 years prior to the emergence of reconstructionism as a philosophy. The origins of American public schools are also dominated by the concept of equal opportunity and the notion of universal, free education. The rise of the "common school" was spearheaded by Horace Mann who asserted, "Education beyond all other devices of human origin is the greatest equalizer of the condition of men—the balance-wheel of the social machinery."[82]

Equality of opportunity in this context would not lead to equality of outcomes; this concept did not attempt a classless society. As David Tyack wrote, "For the most part, working men did not seek to pull down the rich; rather they sought equality of opportunity for their children, an equal chance at the main chance."[83] Equality of opportunity in the nineteenth and early twentieth centuries meant an equal start for all children, but the assumption was that some would go farther than others. Differences in backgrounds and abilities, as well as motivation and luck, would create differences in outcomes among individuals, but the school would assure that children born into any class would have the opportunity to achieve status as persons born into other classes. Implicit in this view was that the "schools represented the means of achieving the goal . . . of equal chances of success" relative to all children in all stratum.[84]

In retrospect, the schools did not fully achieve this goal, according to some observers, because school achievement and economic outcomes are highly related to social class and family background.[85] Had the schools not existed, however, social mobility would have been further reduced. The failure of the common school to provide social mobility raises the question of the role of school in achieving equality—and the question of just what the school can and cannot do to affect cognitive and economic outcomes.

The modern view of educational equality, which emerged in the 1950s through the 1970s, goes much further than the old view. In light of this, James Coleman has outlined five views of inequality of educational opportunity, the latter four of which parallel reconstructionist philosophy: (1) inequality defined by the same curriculum for all children, with the intent that school facilities be equal; (2) inequality defined in terms of the racial composition of the schools; (3) inequality defined in terms of such intangible characteristic as teacher morale and teacher expectations of students; (4) inequality based on school consequences or outcomes for students with equal backgrounds and abilities; and (5) inequality based on school consequences for students with unequal backgrounds and abilities.[86]

The first two definitions deal with race and social class; the next definition deals with concepts that are hard to define; the fourth definition deals with school expenditures and school finances. The fifth definition is an extreme interpretation: Equality is reached only when the outcomes of schooling are similar for all students—those in minority as well as dominant student groups.

When inequality is defined, in terms of equal outcomes (both cognitive and economic), we start comparing racial, ethnic, and religious groups. In a heterogeneous society like ours, this results in some hot issues, including how much to invest in human capital, how to determine the cost-effectiveness of social and educational programs, who should be taxed and how much, to what extent are we to handicap our brightest and most talented minds (the swift racers) to enable those who are slow to finish at the same time, and

whether affirmative action policies lead to reverse discrimination.[87] Indeed, we cannot treat these issues lightly, because they affect most of us in one way or another and lead to questions over which wars have been fought.

All these issues involve balancing acts and what effect these balancing acts have on individuals, groups, and society. Many reconstructionists, not to mention perennialists and essentialists, who have their own ideas about excellence in education, have problems with these issues. Many of us are unable to agree on what is equitable and just, and how much we can stretch the embodiment of reform ideas or the fiber of society. Too much egalitarianism can lead to mediocrity, indifference, and economic decline within society. On the other hand, excellence carried too far can create wide social and economic gaps, hostilities among groups, and a stratified society. The idea is to search for the golden mean.

In his classic text on excellence and equality, John Gardner points out that in a democracy the differences among groups cannot be dwelled on and we go out of the way to ignore them. He describes the dilemma.

> *Extreme equalitarianism—or what I would prefer to say equalitaranism wrongly conceived—which ignores differences in native capacity and achievement, has not served democracy well. Carried far enough, it means . . . the end of that striving for excellence which has produced mankind's greatest achievements.*
>
> *. . . no democracy can give itself over to extreme emphasis on individual performance and still remain a democracy—or to extreme equalitarianism and retain its vitality. A society such as ours has no choice but to seek the development of human potentialities at all levels. It takes more than educated elite to run a complex, technological society. Every modern industrialized society is learning that hard lesson.*[88]

The issues that Gardner raised directly affected the social fabric of the country and have echoed loudly in the past twenty-five years. They have given rise to educational equality and equal opportunity legislation that has permeated many aspects of school and society. The reconstructionists, among other educators, have raised many of the same issues, including school desegregation, compensatory education, multicultural education, handicapped education, more effective schooling, and affirmative action (who goes to college, who gets what jobs, and who manages society). These issues have no easy answers, and they will continue to plague us in the 1990s. See Table 2-4.

CONCLUSION

Philosophy gives meaning to our decisions and actions. In the absence of a philosophy, the educator is vulnerable to externally imposed prescriptions, to fads and frills, to authoritarian schemes, and to other "isms." Dewey was so convinced of the importance of philosophy that he viewed it as the all-encompassing aspect of the educational process—as necessary for "forming fundamental dispositions, intellectual and emotional, toward nature and fellow man." [89] *If one accepts this conclusion, it becomes evident that many aspects of curriculum, if not most of the educational process in school, are developed around philosophy. Even if we believe that Dewey's point is an overstatement, we should still recognize the pervasiveness of philosophy in determining our views of reality, what values and knowledge are worthwhile, and decisions in education in general and curriculum making in particular.*

Major philosophical viewpoints that have emerged within the curriculum field may be viewed along a continuum—traditional and conservative versus contemporary and liberal—idealism, realism, pragmatism, and existentialism. These general or world philosophies have influenced educational philosophies, sometimes called educational theories or views, along the same continuum: perennialism and essentialism as traditional and conservative, and progressivism and reconstructionism as contemporary and liberal. (See Table 2-5.) Very few schools adopt a single philosophy; in practice, most schools combine various philosophies. Moreover, our position is that no single philosophy, old or new, should serve as the exclusive guide for making decisions about schools or about the curriculum. All philosophical groups (outlined in this chapter) want the same thing of education, that is,

they wish to improve the educational process, to enhance the achievement of the learner, to produce better and more productive citizens, and to improve society. Because of their different views of reality, values, and knowledge, however, they find it difficult to agree on how to achieve these ends.

What we need to do, as curricularists, is to search for the middle road, a highly elusive and abstract concept, where there is no extreme emphasis on subject matter or student; cognitive development or sociopsychological development; excellence or equality. What we need is a prudent school philosophy, one that is politically and economically feasible and that serves the needs of students and society. Implicit in this view of education is that too much emphasis on any one philosophy, sometimes at the expense of another, may do harm and cause conflict. How much we emphasize one philosophy, under the guise of reform or for whatever reason, is critical because no one society can give itself over to extreme "isms" or political views and still remain a democracy. The kind of society into which we evolve is in part reflected in our educational system, which is influenced by the philosophy that we eventually define and develop.

In the final analysis, curriculum workers must understand that they are continuously faced with curriculum decisions and that philosophy is important in determining these decisions. Indeed, few school people scrutinize their curriculum with regard to the school's philosophy or mission statements. Often teachers and administrators plan and implement long reams of behavioral objectives with minimal regard to the overall philosophy of the school." [90] *Curriculum workers need to provide assistance in developing and designing school practices that coincide with the philosophy of the school and community. Teaching, learning, and curriulum are all interwoven in our school practices and should reflect a school philosophy. It is important, then, for school people, especially curricularists, to make decisions and take action in relation to the philosophy of their school and community.*

TABLE 2-4 Overview of Educational Philosophies

EDUCATIONAL PHILOSOPHY	PHILOSOPHICAL BASE	AIM OF EDUCATION	KNOWLEDGE	ROLE OF EDUCATION	CURRICULUM FOCUS	RELATED CURRICULUM TRENDS
Perennialism	Realism	To educate the rational person; to cultivate the intellect	Focus on past and permanent studies; mastery of facts and timeless knowledge	Teacher helps students think rationally; based on Socratic method, oral exposition; explicit teaching of traditional values	Classical subjects; literary analysis; constant curriculum	Great books; Paideia proposal; returning to the liberal arts
Essentialism	Idealism, realism	To promote the intellectual growth of the individual; to educate the competent person	Essential skills and academic subjects; mastery of concepts and principles of subject matter	Teacher is authority in his or her subject field; explicit teaching of traditional values	Essential skills (three Rs) and essential subjects (English, science, history, math, and foreign language)	Back to basics; cultural literacy; excellence in education
Progressivism	Pragmatism	To promote democratic, social living	Knowledge leads to growth and development; a living-learning process; focus on active and relevant learning	Teacher is guide for problem solving and scientific inquiry	Based on student's interests; involves the application of human problems and affairs; interdisciplinary subject matter; activities and projects	Relevant curriculum; humanistic education; radical school reform
Reconstructionism	Pragmatism	To improve and reconstruct society; education for change and social reform	Skills and subjects needed to identify and ameliorate problems of society; learning is active and concerned with contemporary and future society	Teacher serves as an agent of change and reform; acts as a project director and research leader; helps students become aware of problems confronting humankind	Emphasis on social sciences and social research methods; examination of social, economic, and political problems; focus on present and future trends as well as on national and international issues	International education; reconceptualism; equality of educational opportunity

TABLE 2-5 Traditional and Contemporary Education Philosophies

TRADITIONAL PHILOSOPHY (Perennialism, Essentialism)	CONTEMPORARY PHILOSOPHY (Progressivism, Reconstructionism)

Society and Education

1. Formal education begins with the school; schools are considered the major institution of the child's education.
2. School transmits the common culture; individual's major responsibility is to society, performing societal roles; conformity and cooperation are important.
3. Education is for the aims of society; it involves authority and moral restraint.
4. Certain subjects and knowledge prepare students for democracy and freedom.
5. Education formulated mainly in cognitive terms; focus on academic subjects.
6. Values and beliefs tend to be objective and, if not absolute, then based on agreed standards or truths.

1. Formal education begins with the family; the parents are considered the most important influence in the child's education.
2. School improves society; individual's fulfillment and development can benefit society; independence and creativity are important.
3. Education involves varied opportunities to develop one's potential and engage in personal choices.
4. Democratic experiences in school help prepare students for democracy and freedom.
5. Education concerned with social, moral, and cognitive terms; focus on the whole child.
6. Values and beliefs are subjective, based on the individual's view of the world.

Knowledge and Learning

7. Emphasis on knowledge and information.
8. Emphasis on subjects (content).
9. Subject matter selected and organized by teacher.
10. Subject matter organized in terms of simple to complex, centered on the past.
11. Unit/lesson plans organized according to topics or concepts.
12. Subject matter is compartmentalized according to distinct fields, disciplines, or study areas.

7. Emphasis on resolving problems and functioning in one's social environment.
8. Emphasis on students (learners).
9. Subject matter planned by teacher and students.
10. Subject matter organized in terms of understanding relationships, centered on present or future.
11. Unit/lesson plans organized according to problems or student interests.
12. Subject matter is integrated; includes more than one related subject.

Instruction

13. Textbooks and workbooks dominate; teaching and learning largely contained to classroom.
14. Whole-group learning, fixed schedules, and uniform time periods.
15. Homogeneous grouping; tracking of students into special programs.

13. Varied instructional materials; teaching and learning include community resources.
14. Whole, small, and individualized groups, flexible schedules, and adjustable time periods.
15. Heterogeneous grouping; some tracking of students but widely differentiated programs.

(continued)

TABLE 2-5 Continued

TRADITIONAL PHILOSOPHY (Perennialism, Essentialism)	CONTEMPORARY PHILOSOPHY (Progressivism, Reconstructionism)
16. Passive involvement of students in assimilating what teacher or textbook says.	16. Active involvement of students in seeking information that can be used or applied.
17. Emphasis on uniformity of classroom experiences and instructional situations.	17. Emphasis on variability of classroom experiences and instructional situations.

Purpose and Programs

18. Emphasis on liberal arts and science.	18. Mix of liberal arts, practical, and vocational subjects.
19. Emphasis is on specialization or scholarship.	19. Emphasis is general and for the layperson.
20. Curriculum is prescribed; little room for electives.	20. Curriculum based on student needs or interests; room for electives.
21. Excellence and high standards; special consideration for high achievers.	21. Equality and flexible standards; special consideration for low achievers.

Source: Adapted from Allan C. Ornstein, "Philosophy as a Basis for Curriculum Decisions," *High School Journal* (December–January 1991), pp. 106–107.

ENDNOTES

1. William Van Til, "In a Climate of Change," in R. R. Leeper, ed., *Role of Supervisor and Curriculum Director in a Climate of Change* (Washington, D.C.: Association for Supervision and Curriculum Development, 1965), p. 18.
2. L. Thomas Hopkins, *Interaction: The Democratic Process* (Boston: D. C. Heath, 1941), pp. 198–200.
3. John I. Goodlad et al., *Curriculum Inquiry* (New York: McGraw-Hill, 1979).
4. B. Othanel Smith, William O. Stanley, and J. Harlan Shores, *Fundamentals of Curriculum Development,* rev. ed. (New York: World Book, 1957). See also B. Othanel Smith, "Curriculum Content," in F. W. English, ed., *Fundamental Curriculum Decisions* (Alexandria, Va.: Association for Supervision and Curriculum Development, 1983), pp. 30–39.
5. Ronald C. Doll, *Curriculum Improvement: Decision Making and Process,* 8th ed. (Boston: Allyn and Bacon, 1992), p. 27.
6. John Dewey, *Democracy and Education* (New York: Macmillan, 1916), pp. 186, 383–384.
7. Ibid., p. 384.
8. Ralph W. Tyler, *Basic Principles of Curriculum and Instruction* (Chicago: University of Chicago Press, 1949), pp. 33–34.
9. John I. Goodlad, *What Schools Are For* (Bloomington, Ind.: Phi Delta Kappan Educational Foundation, 1979). See also Goodlad, *A Place Called School* (New York: McGraw-Hill, 1984).
10. J. Donald Butler, *Idealism in Education* (New York: Harper & Row, 1966).
11. Morris L. Bigge, *Educational Philosophies for Teachers* (Columbus, Ohio: Merrill, 1982); Howard Ozman and Sam Craver, *Philosophical Foundations of Education,* 3rd ed. (Columbus, Ohio: Merrill, 1986).
12. Harry S. Broudy, *Building a Philosophy of Education* (Englewood Cliffs, N.J.: Prentice Hall, 1961); John Wild, *Introduction to a Realist Philosophy* (New York: Harper & Row, 1948).
13. Broudy, *Building a Philosophy of Education;* William O. Martin, *Realism in Education* (New York: Harper & Row, 1969).
14. Ernest E. Bayles, *Pragmatism in Education* (New York: Harper & Row, 1966); John L. Childs, *Pragmatism and Education* (New York: Holt, Rinehart and Winston, 1956).
15. John Dewey, *Experience and Education* (New York: Macmillan, 1938).
16. Maxine Greene, *Existential Encounters for Teachers* (New York: Random House, 1967); George F. Kneller, *Existentialism in Education* (New York: Wiley, 1958); and Van Cleve Morris, *Existentialism and Education* (New York: Harper & Row, 1966).
17. Harold Soderquist, *The Person and Education* (Columbus, Ohio: Merrill, 1966); Donald Vandenberg, *Human Rights in Education* (New York: Philosophical Library, 1983). See also Israel Scheffler, *Of Human*

Potential: An Essay in the Philosophy of Education (Boston: Routledge & Kegan Paul, 1986).

18. Maxine Greene, *Landscapes of Learning* (New York: Teachers College Press, Columbia University, 1978); Donald Vandenberg, "Human Dignity, Three Human Rights, and Pedagogy," *Educational Theory* (Winter 1986), pp. 33–44.

19. Robert M. Hutchins, *The Conflict in Education* (New York: Harper & Row, 1953), p. 68.

20. Bigge, *Educational Philosophies for Teachers*; Daniel Tanner and Laurel N. Tanner, *Curriculum Development: Theory into Practice* (New York: Macmillan, 1980).

21. Robert M. Hutchins, *The Higher Learning in America* (New Haven, Conn: Yale University Press, 1936).

22. Robert M. Hutchins, *A Conversation on Education* (Santa Barbara, Calif.: The Fund for the Republic, 1963), p. 1.

23. Mortimer J. Adler, *The Paideia Proposal: An Educational Manifesto* (New York: Macmillan, 1982); Adler, *Paideia Problems and Possibilities* (New York: Macmillan, 1983); and Adler, *The Paideia Program: An Educational Syllabus* (New York: Macmillan, 1984).

24. Allan Bloom, *The Closing of the American Mind* (New York: Simon & Schuster, 1987).

25. See William Bagley, "Just What Is the Crux and the Conflict between the Progressives and the Essentialists?" *Educational Administration and Supervision* (September 1940), pp. 508–511; Arthur Bestor, *Educational Wastelands* (Urbana, Ill.: University of Illinois Press, 1953); and Hyman Rickover, *Education and Freedom* (New York: E. P. Dutton, 1959).

26. See Daniel Tanner, "Curriculum History," in H. E. Mitzel, ed., *Encyclopedia of Educational Research*, 5th ed. (New York: Macmillan, 1982), pp. 412–420.

27. Hyman G. Rickover, "European vs. American Secondary Schools," *Phi Delta Kappan* (November 1958), p. 61.

28. Arthur Bestor, *The Restoration of Learning* (New York: Knopf, 1955), p. 120.

29. Rickover, "European vs. American Secondary Schools," p. 61.

30. Stanley M. Elam, "The Gallup Education Surveys," *Phi Delta Kappan* (September 1983), p. 26. See also Gallup polls published in the September or October issues of *Phi Delta Kappan*, 1984 to 1990.

31. *The Condition of Education 1989* (Washington, D.C., U.S. Government Printing Office, 1989), Table 1.30–1, p. 127; Allan C. Ornstein, "National Reform and Instructional Accountability," *High School Journal* (October–November 1990), pp. 51–56.

32. Gregory R. Anig, "Educational Standards, Testing, and Equity," *Phi Delta Kappan* (May 1985), pp.

623–625; David Hill, "What Has the 1980s Reform Movement Accomplished?" *Education Digest* (February 1990), pp. 3–6; and Daniel U. Levine and Allan C. Ornstein, "Research on Classroom and School Effectiveness," *Urban Review* (July 1989), pp. 81–95.

33. Kenneth H. Bacon, "Many Educators View Involved Parents as Key to Children's Success in School," *Wall Street Journal*, July 31, 1990, pp. 1B, 4B. Lynette Long and Thomas L. Long, "Latchkey Adolescents: How Administrators Can Respond to Their Needs," *NASSP Bulletin* (February 1989), pp. 102–108.

34. E. D. Hirsh, *Cultural Literacy: What Every American Needs to Know*, rev. ed. (Boston: Houghton Mifflin, 1987).

35. Larry Cuban, "Four Stories About National Goals for American Education," *Phi Delta Kappan* (December 1990), pp. 264–271; Bill Honig, "Target Areas for Reaching National Goals," *Education Digest* (October 1990), pp. 18–22; and Allan C. Ornstein, "The National Reform of Education," *NASSP Bulletin* (May 1992).

36. Howard Gardner, "National Education Goals and the Academic Community," *Education Digest* (February 1990), pp. 41–43; Elliot W. Eisner, "What Really Counts in School," *Educational Leadership* (February 1991), pp. 10–17.

37. Harold Howe II, "American 2000: A Bumpy Ride on Four Trains," *Phi Delta Kappan* (November 1991), pp. 192–203; David S. Seeley, "Carrying School Reform into the 1990s," *Future Choices* (Fall 1989), pp. 53–57; and Grant Wiggins, "Standards, Not Standardization, " *Educational Leadership* (February 1991). pp. 18–25.

38. R. Freeman Butts, *Public Education in the United States* (New York: Holt, Rinehart and Winston, 1978); Lawrence A. Cremin, *The Transformation of the School* (New York: Knopf, 1961).

39. John Dewey, *Democracy and Education* (New York: Macmillan, 1916).

40. John Dewey, "Need for a Philosophy of Education," *New Era in Home and School* (November 1934), p. 212.

41. John Dewey, *How We Think*, rev. ed. (Lexington, Mass.: D.C. Heath, 1933); William Kilpatrick, *Foundations of Method* (New York: Macmillan, 1925).

42. John Dewey, *The Child and the Curriculum* (Chicago: University of Chicago Press, 1902), pp. 30–31; Dewey, *Experience and Education* (New York: Macmillan, 1938), p. vii.

43. Boyd H. Bode, *Progressive Education at the Crossroads* (New York: Newson, 1938).

44. Ibid., p. 44.

45. Cremin, *The Transformation of the School*; Joel Spring, *The American School: 1642–1990* (New York: Longman, 1990).

46. Herbert Kohl, *The Open Classroom* (New York: Random House, 1969); Jonathan Kozol, *Free Schools* (Boston: Houghton Mifflin, 1972). See C. M. Bowers and David J. Flinders, *Responsive Teaching* (New York: Teachers College Press, Columbia University, 1990).

47. Charles A. Silberman, *Crisis in the Classroom* (New York: Random House, 1971).

48. Arthur T. Jersild, *In Search of Self* (New York: Teachers College Press, 1952); Jersild, *When Teachers Face Themselves* (New York: Teachers College Press, 1955); and Arthur Combs and Donald Snygg, *Individual Behavior,* 2nd ed. (New York: Harper & Row, 1959). See also Arthur Combs, ed., *Perceiving, Behavioring, Becoming* (Washington, D.C.: Association for Supervision and Curriculum Development, 1962); Combs, *A Personal Approach to Teaching* (Boston: Allyn and Bacon, 1982).

49. Abraham H. Maslow, *Toward a Psychology of Being* (New York: Van Nostrand Reinhold, 1962); Maslow, *Motivation and Personality,* 2nd ed. (New York: Harper & Row, 1970); Carl R. Rogers, *Client-Centered Therapy* (Boston: Houghton Mifflin, 1951); Rogers, *On Becoming a Person* (Boston: Houghton Mifflin, 1961); and, Rogers, *Freedom to Learn for the 1980s,* 2nd ed. (Columbus, Ohio: Merrill, 1983).

50. Michael W. Apple, "The Politics of Official Knowledge in the United States," *Journal of Curriculum Studies* (July–August 1990), pp. 377–383; Eisner, "What Really Counts in Schools"; and Herbert Kohl, "Toward Educational Change and Economic Justice," *Phi Delta Kappan* (May 1991), pp. 678–681.

51. Mario D. Fantini, "Humanizing the Humanistic Movement," *Phi Delta Kappan* (February 1974), p. 400.

52. For a discussion of these radical critics, see Philip W. Jackson, "Deschooling? No," *Today's Education* (November 1972), pp. 18–21; Allan C. Ornstein, "Critics and Criticism of Education," *Educational Forum* (November 1977), pp. 21–30. See also Diane Ravitch, *The Troubled Crusade: American Education 1945–1980* (New York: Basic Books, 1983).

53. Edgar Z. Friedenberg, *The Vanishing Adolescent* (Boston: Beacon Press, 1959), pp. 26, 91, 110. See also Edgar Z. Friedenberg, *Coming of Age in America* (New York: Random House, 1967).

54. John Holt, *How Children Fail* (New York: Pitman, 1964).

55. Paul Goodman, *Compulsory Mis-education* (New York: Horizon Press, 1964), pp. 20–22.

56. Paul Goodman, *New Reformation* (New York: Random House, 1970), p. 86.

57. A. S. Neill, *Summerhill: A Radical Approach to Child Rearing* (New York: Hart, 1960), p. 4.

58. Ibid., pp. 4, 14.

59. Ivan Illich, *Deschooling Society* (New York: Harper & Row, 1971).

60. See Samuel Bowles and Herbert Gintis, *Schooling in Capitalist America* (New York: Basic Books, 1976); Alan J. DeYoung, *Economics and American Education* (New York: Longman, 1990); and Henry A. Giroux, *Theory and Resistance in Education* (Westport, Conn.: Bergin & Garvey, 1989).

61. George S. Counts, *Dare the School Build a New Social Order?* (New York: Day, 1932), pp. 7–8. See also Robert R. Sherman, "Dare the School Build a New Social Order—Again?" *Educational Theory* (Winter 1986), pp. 87–92.

62. See John Dewey, *Reconstruction in Philosophy* (New York: Holt, 1920).

63. Theodore Brameld, *Ends and Means in Education* (New York: Harper & Row, 1950); Brameld, *Patterns of Educational Philosophy* (New York: World, 1950).

64. Theodore Brameld, "Reconstructionism as Radical Philosophy of Education," *Educational Forum* (November 1977), p. 70.

65. Mario D. Fantini, *Regaining Excellence in Education* (Columbus, Ohio: Merrill, 1986); Harold Shane, *Educating for a New Millennium* (Bloomington, Ind.: Phi Delta Kappa, 1981); and Alvin Toffler, *Previews and Premises* (New York: Morrow, 1983).

66. Ruud J. Garter, "International Collaboration in Curriculum Development," *Educational Leadership* (December–January 1987), pp. 4–7; David Hill, "Rediscovering Geography: It's Five Fundamental Themes," *NASSP Bulletin* (December 1989), pp. 1–7; and Jon Nixon, "Reclaiming Coherence: Cross-Curriculum Provision and the National Curriculum," *Journal of Curriculum Studies* (March–April 1991), pp. 187–192.

67. Kenneth B. Boulding, *The World as a Total System* (Beverly Hills, Calif.: Sage, 1985).

68. Chester Finn, "The Biggest Reform of All," *Phi Delta Kappan* (April 1990), pp. 584–592.

69. *The Bradley Commission on History in Schools* (New York: Macmillan, 1990). Also see Howard D. Mehlinger, "The National Commission on Social Studies in the Schools," *Journal of Curriculum Studies* (September–October 1991), pp. 449–458.

70. *The Condition of Education,* 1989, Vol. 1 (Washington, D.C.: U.S. Government Printing Office, 1989), Table 1.6, p. 84; *The Bradley Commission on History in Schools.*

71. *The World Almanac and Book of Facts* (New York: Pharos Books, 1989), pp. 224–225. The almanac lists Russian as 5 and Arabic as 6. We feel that more

people speak Arabic than Russian (based on world population figures).

72. Myrian Met, "Which Foreign Languages Should Students Learn?" *Educational Leadership* (September 1989), pp. 54–58.

73. Michael W. Apple, in a telephone conversation with one of the authors, August 8, 1985; Herbert M. Kliebard, in a personal conversation with one of the authors, April 17, 1991.

74. Maxine Greene, "Interpretation and Re-Vision: Toward Another Story," in J. T. Sears and J. D. Marshall, eds., *Teaching and Thinking About Curriculum* (New York: Teachers College Press, Columbia University, 1990), pp. 75–78; Greene, *Landscapes of Learning*, p. 163.

75. Paulo Freire, *Pedagogy of the Oppressed* (New York: Herder & Herder, 1970), pp. 75, 100, 108; *The Politics of Education: Culture, Power and Liberation* (Westport, Conn.: Bergin & Garvey, 1985).

76. William Pinar, "Sanity, Madness, and the School," in W. Pinar, ed., *Curriculum Theorizing: The Reconceptualists* (Berkeley, Calif.: McCutchan, 1974), pp. 364–366; 369–373, 381.

77. Michael W. Apple, *Ideology and Curriculum* (Boston: Routledge & Kegan Paul, 1979), p. 4. See also Apple, *Teachers and Texts* (Boston: Routledge & Kegan Paul, 1986).

78. Michael Apple and Nancy R. King, "What Do Schools Teach?" in R. H. Weller, ed., *Humanistic Education* (Berkeley, Calif.: McCutchan, 1977), p. 30.

79. Illich, *Deschooling Society.*

80. Paulo Freire and Donaldo Macedo, *Literacy: Reading the Word and the World* (Westport, Conn.: Bergin & Garvey, 1989); Freire, *Pedagogy of the Oppressed.*

81. Macdonald, "Curriculum and Human Interests," p. 293.

82. Horace Mann, *The Republic and the School,* rev. ed. (New York: Teachers College Press, Columbia University, 1957), p. 39.

83. David B. Tyack, *Turning Points in American Educational History* (Waltham, Mass.: Blaisdell, 1967), p. 114.

84. Henry M. Levin, "Equal Educational Opportunity and the Distribution of Educational Expenditures," in A. Kopan and H. J. Walberg, eds., *Rethinking Educational Equality* (Berkeley, Calif.: McCutchan, 1974), p. 30.

85. See James S. Coleman et al., *Equality of Educational Opportunity* (Washington, D.C.: U.S. Government Printing Office, 1966); Christopher Jencks et al., *Inequality: A Reassessment of the Effect of Family and Schools in America* (New York: Basic Books, 1972). Also see Kathleen Bennett and Margarett D. LeCompte, *How Schools Work: A Sociological Analysis of Education* (New York, Longman, 1990).

86. James S. Coleman, "The Concept of Equality of Educational Opportunity," *Harvard Educational Review* (Winter 1968), pp. 7–22.

87. Nathan Glazer, "The Affirmative Action Stalemate," *Public Interest* (Winter 1988), pp. 99–114; Also see Herman Belz, *Equality Transformed* (New Brunswick, N.J.: Transaction, 1992).

88. John W. Gardner, *Excellence: Can We Be Equal and Excellent Too?* (New York: Harper & Row, 1961), pp. 17–18, 83, 90.

89. Dewey, *Democracy and Education,* p. 383.

CHAPTER 3

HISTORICAL FOUNDATIONS OF CURRICULUM

Focusing Questions

1. *How were European educational ideas modified by American schools?*
2. *How did American democratic ideas contribute to the rise of public schooling in the United States?*
3. *In what ways did American nationalism during the first half of the nineteenth century influence the curriculum?*
4. *How did nineteenth-century European pioneers of pedagogy influence the American school curriculum?*
5. *What unique problems were evidenced in the nineteenth century as the elementary (secondary) school curriculum developed?*
6. *How did the Committee of Fifteen and Committee of Ten influence curriculum for the twentieth century?*
7. *How did scientism in education influence curriculum making?*
8. *What basic principles of curriculum making have persisted for the last 50 or more years? Why?*

Because many scholars in the field of curriculum often lack historical perspective, they rely on the history of American education to analyze the heritage of our curriculum. By analyzing the first 200 years (or more) of curriculum, up to the turn of the twentieth century, we can view curriculum primarily in terms of evolving subject matter or content and the dominant philosophy of perennialism. Not until the rise of progressivism, followed by the early period of behaviorism and scientism in education (the use of empirical methods, analysis of human behavior, and generalizations), did attention in the curriculum field expand to include principles of curriculum development. This shift occurred in the early years of the twentieth century.

We begin our discussion with the colonial period and proceed through the eighteenth, nineteenth, and twentieth centuries. Most of our discussion focuses on the last 100 years. In the interest of brevity, we examine only the broad sweep of curriculum and how the curriculum evolved.

THE COLONIAL PERIOD: 1642–1776

The historical foundations of curriculum are largely rooted in the educational experiences of colonial Massachusetts. Massachusetts was settled mainly by Puritans who adhered to strict principles of theology. Unlike contemporary schools, the first schools in New England were closely related to the Puritan church. The major purpose of school, according to educational historians, was to teach children to read the Scriptures and notices of civil affairs.[1]

Reading, therefore, was the most important subject, followed by writing and spelling, for purposes of understanding the catechism and common law. Since colonial days, then, reading and related language skills have been basic to American education and basic to the elementary school curriculum.

Three Colonial Regions

Colonial schools established in Massachusetts were derived from two sources: legislation of

1642, which required parents and guardians of children to make certain that their charges could read and understand the principles of religion and the laws of the Commonwealth; and the "Old Deluder Satan" Act of 1647, which required every town of fifty or more families to appoint a reading and writing teacher. Towns of 100 or more families were to employ a teacher of Latin so that students could be prepared for entry to Harvard College.[2] The other New England colonies, except Rhode Island, followed the Massachusetts example.

These early laws reveal how important education was to the Puritan settlers. Some historians have regarded these laws as the roots of American school law and the public school movement. It is obvious that the Puritans did not want an illiterate class to grow in colonial America. They feared that such a class might comprise a group of dependent poor, an underclass, which would be reminiscent of that in England and other parts of Europe, and which they wanted to avoid. They also wanted to ensure that their children would grow up being committed to the religious doctrines.

In the middle colonies, unlike New England, no common language or religion existed. Writes George Beauchamp, "Competition among political and religious groups retarded willingness to expend the public funds for educational purposes."[3] No single system of schools could be established. What evolved instead were parochial and independent schools, related to different ethnic and religious groups, and the idea of community or local control of schools (as opposed to New England's concept of central or district-wide schools). The current notion of cultural pluralism thus took shape and form some 200 years ago. Just as the schools and the curriculum were uniform and centralized in the New England colonies, they were divergent and localized in the middle Atlantic colonies.

Until the end of the eighteenth century educational decisions in the Southern colonies were generally left to the family. Legislative action was taken, however, in behalf of poor children, orphans and illegitimate children—to ensure that their guardians provided private educational or vocational skills. Nevertheless, the plantation system of landholding, slavery, and

gentry created a small privileged class of white children (children of plantation owners) who had the benefit of private tutors. For most poor whites who tilled the soil, formal education was nonexistent. Unable to read and write, many of them grew up to be subsistence farmers like their parents before them. Black slaves' children were forbidden to learn to read or write and were relegated as the underclass of the plantation system. In short, the economic and political system of the early South "tended to retard the development of a large-scale system of schools. This education [handicap] was felt long after the Civil War period."[4]

Despite the regional variations between the schools of New England, the middle Atlantic colonies, and the South, all three areas were influenced by English political ideas. And, despite differences in language, religion, and economic systems, religious commitment had a high priority throughout all schools and society; the family, too, played a major role in the socialization and education of all children. What was later to become the three Rs evolved from these schools as well.

"The curriculum of the colonial schools consisted of reading, writing, and [some] arithmetic along with the rudiments of religious faith and lessons designed to develop manners and morals."[5] It was a traditional curriculum, stressing basic-skill acquisition, timeless and absolute values, social and religious conformity, faith in authority, knowledge for the sake of knowledge, rote learning, and memorization. It was based on the notion of child depravity (children were born in sin, play was idleness, and child's talk gibberish), and thus the teacher needed to apply constant discipline. This approach to the curriculum dominated American education until the rise of progressivism.

Colonial Schools

The schools were important institutions for colonial society, as they are for today's. One difference is that a smaller percentage of the school-aged children attended elementary school on a regular basis compared to today, and a much smaller percentage of youth attended secondary school, much less graduated.

The Town School.   In the New England colonies, the town school was a locally controlled and
popular elementary school. Often it was a crude,
one-room structure, dominated by the teacher's
pulpit at the front of the room and attended by
both boys and girls of the community. Students
sat on benches and studied their assignments
until called on to recite by the schoolmaster. The
children ranged in age from 5 or 6 to 13 and 14.
Attendance was not always regular; it depended
on weather conditions and on individual families'
needs for their children to work on their farms.[6]

Parochial and Private Schools.   In the middle
colonies, parochial schools and private schools
predominated; the elementary schools were established by missionary societies and various religious and ethnic groups to educate their own
children. Like the New England town schools,
these schools focused on reading and writing and
religious sermons. In the South, upper-class children attended private schools oriented to reading,
writing, arithmetic, and studying the primer and
Bible; less fortunate children attended charity
schools (if they were lucky) to be trained in the
three Rs, to recite religious hymns (which was
less demanding than reading the Bible), and to
learn vocational skills.

Latin Grammar Schools.   At the secondary
level, the sons of the upper class attended Latin
grammar schools, first established in Boston in
1635, to be prepared for entry into college. These
schools catered to those who planned to enter the
professions (medicine, law, teaching, and the
ministry) or to spend their lives as business owners or merchants.[7]

   A boy would enter a Latin grammar school
at the age of 8 or 9 and remain for eight years. His
curriculum consisted of studying the classics.
"There were some courses in Greek, rhetoric . . .
and logic, but Latin was apparently three-quar-
ters of the curriculum in most of the grammar
schools, or more. . . ."[8] Little or no attention was
given to the other arts and sciences. "The religious atmosphere was quite as evident . . . as it
was in the elementary school" with the "master
praying regularly with his pupils" and quizzing
them "thoroughly on the sermons. . . ."[9] The reg-
imen of study was exhausting and unexciting,
and the school's role that of handmaiden of the
church. As Samuel Morrison reminds us, the
Latin grammar school was one of colonial
America's closest links to European schools, and
its curriculum resembled the classical humanist
curriculum of the Renaissance (when schools
were primarily intended for children of the upper
classes and their role was to support the religious
and social institution of that era).[10]

The Academy.   The academy, established in
1751, was the second American institution to
provide education at the secondary level. Based
on the ideas of Benjamin Franklin, and intended
to offer a practical curriculum for those not going
to college, it had a diversified curriculum of English grammar, classics, composition, rhetoric,
and public speaking.[11] Latin was no longer considered a crucial subject. Students could choose a
foreign language based on their vocational
needs—for example, a prospective clergyman
could study Latin or Greek, and a future busi-
nessman could learn French, German, or Spanish.
Mathematics was to be taught for its practical
application to a job rather than as an abstract
intellectual exercise. History was the chief ethical study, not religion. The academy also introduced many practical and manual skills into the
formal curriculum; these formed the basis of vocational curriculum in the twentieth century: car-
pentry, engraving, printing, painting, cabinet
making, farming, bookkeeping, and so on.

College.   Most students went to Harvard or
Yale after they graduated from Latin grammar
schools. College was based on the Puritan conception that those called to the ministry needed to
be soundly educated in the classics and scriptures. The students had to demonstrate their competency in Latin and Greek and the classics.

   Latin grammar schools prepared students for
Harvard or Yale college—much like high school
academic programs prepare students for college
today. The current relationship between the
course offerings of secondary school and college
admission requirements was, in fact, set in motion more than 200 years ago. Writes Ellwood
Cubberley, "The student would be admitted into
college 'upon Examination' whereby he could
show competency 'to Read, Construe, Parce

Tully, Vergil and the Greek Testament; and to write Latin in Prose and to understand the Rules of Prosodia and Common Arithmetic' as well as to bring 'testimony of his blameless and inoffensive life.' "[12]

The Harvard/Yale curriculum consisted of courses in Latin, grammar, logic, rhetoric, arithmetic, astronomy, ethics, metaphysics, and natural sciences. The curriculum for the ministry or other professions also included Greek, Hebrew, and ancient history.

Old Textbooks, Old Readers

Because the hornbook, primer, Psalter, Testament, and Bible were considered textbooks, they were widely read (depending on the reading ability of the students). By and large, most elementary textbooks, until the time of the American Revolution, were of English origin or were direct imitations of English texts.[13] Children learned the alphabet, Lord's Prayer, some syllables, words, and sentences by memorizing the *hornbook*—a paddle-shaped board to which was attached a single sheet of parchment covered by a transparent sheath made by flattening cattle horns.

When the *New England Primer* was published in the last decade of the seventeenth century, it replaced the English primer. It was not only the first American basal reader, it was also the most widely used textbook in the colonies for over 100 years; more than 3 million copies were sold. The *New England Primer* was permeated with religious and moral doctrines. The somber caste of the Puritan religion and morals was evident as students memorized sermons and learned their ABCs through rote and drill:

> A—In Adam's Fall
> We sinned all
> B—Thy Life to mend
> This book attend
> C—The Cat doth play
> And after slay . . .
> Z—Zacheus he
> Did climb the tree
> His Lord to see.[14]

In 1740 Thomas Dilworth published a *New Guide to the English Tongue,* which contained a mixture of grammar, spelling, and religious material. It was followed a few years later by the *School Master's Assistant,* a widely used mathematics text.

The narrowness of the elementary curriculum and the limited use of textbooks were illustrated by Noah Webster, an ardent cultural nationalist, years later in a letter to Henry Barnard, then Commissioner of Education of Connecticut:

> *before the Revolution . . . the books used were chiefly or wholly Dilworth's Spelling Books, the Psalter, Testament, and Bible. No geography was studied before the publication of Dr. Morse's small books on that subject, about the year 1786 or 1787. No history was read, as far as my knowledge extends, for there was no abridged history of the United States. Except the books above mentioned, no book for reading was used before the publication of the Third Part of my Institute, in 1785. . . . The Introduction of my Spelling Book, first published in 1783, produced a great change in the department of spelling. . . . No English grammar was generally taught in common schools when I was young, except that in Dilworth, and that to no good purpose.*[15]

THE NATIONAL PERIOD: 1776–1850

A new mission for education, which began to emerge during the Revolutionary period, continued through the early national period. Many leaders began to link free public schooling with the ideas of popular government and political freedom. Wrote President Madison, "A popular government without popular information, or the means of acquiring it, is but a prologue to a farce or a tragedy or perhaps both." Jefferson expressed a similar belief when he asserted: "If a nation expects to be ignorant and free in a state of civilization, it expects what never was and never will be."

The emphasis on life, liberty, and equality was highlighted in the great documents of the era: the Declaration of Independence, the Bill of Rights, and the Northwest Ordinances. In 1785 these ordinances divided the Northwest Territory into townships and reserved the sixteenth section of "every township for the maintenance of public schools." In 1787, they reaffirmed that "schools and the means of education shall forever be encouraged" by the states. The federal government thus recognized its commitment to education and exhibited its willingness to advance its cause, while assuring the autonomy of state and local schools, guaranteed by the U.S. Constitution. As a result of these Ordinances, thirty-nine states received over 154 million acres of land for schools from the federal government.[16]

By the turn of the nineteenth century, secular forces had developed sufficiently to challenge and ultimately cause the decline of religious influence over elementary and secondary schools. Among these secular forces were the development of democracy, the development of a strong federal government, the idea of religious freedom, and new discoveries in natural sciences.

Even though some leaders of the country mistrusted the mass of the people and continued to favor the classical curriculum, the popular movement in government mobilized against the money class and the old curriculum based on English traditions. Accompanying this growing political liberalism was an emerging cultural nationalism—a demand for an American language, an American culture, and an American educational system free of English ideas from the past. As a new nation, America sought its own political system and culture—and this thinking spilled over into the schools.

Rush: Science, Progress, and Free Education

Dr. Benjamin Rush (1745–1813) represented this new era. In 1791, he wrote that the emphasis on the classics led to the prejudice the masses felt for institutions of learning. As long as Latin and Greek dominated the curriculum, universal education beyond the rudiments was wishful thinking. In a new country, in which the chief task was to explore and develop natural resources, as well as to promote democracy, education should be functional to these concerns. "Under these circumstances, to spend four or five years in learning two dead languages, is to turn our backs upon a gold mine, in order to amuse ourselves catching butterflies." If the time spent on Latin and Greek were devoted to science, continued this champion pragmatist, "the human condition would be

much improved."[17] For Rush, science was the chief instrument of social progress.

Rush went on to outline a plan of education for Pennsylvania and the new Republic: free elementary schools in every township consisting of 100 families or more, a free academy at the county level, and free colleges and universities at the state level for the future leaders of society. The public would pay for the expenses, but, in the end, Rush argued, the educational system would reduce our taxes because a productive and well-managed workforce and entrepreneur force would result. (It was the same argument among other points that Horace Mann was to make 30 years later when he spearheaded the common school movement.) Rush's curriculum emphasized reading, writing, and arithmetic at the elementary school level; English, German, the arts, and especially the sciences at the secondary and college level; and good manners and moral principles from the beginning to the end of the educational sequence.

Jefferson: Education for Citizenship

Faith in the agrarian society and distrust toward the proletariat of the cities were basic in Thomas Jefferson's (1743–1826) idea of democracy. A man of wide-ranging interests that embraced politics, agriculture, science, and education, Jefferson assumed the state had the responsibility to cultivate an educated and liberated citizenry to ensure a democratic society. In "A Bill for the More General Diffusion of Knowledge," introduced in the Virginia legislature in 1779, Jefferson advocated a plan that provided educational opportunities for both common people and landed gentry "at the expense of all."[18] To Jefferson, formal education was largely a state or civic concern, rather than a matter reserved to religious or upper-class groups. Schools should be financed through public taxes.

Jefferson's plan subdivided the counties of Virginia into wards, each of which would have a free elementary school to teach reading, writing, arithmetic, and history. His proposal also provided for the establishment of twenty grammar schools at the secondary level, for which gifted students who could not afford to pay tuition would be provided scholarships. There, the students would study Latin, Greek, English, geography, and higher mathematics. Upon completing grammar school, half the scholarship students would be assigned positions as elementary or ward school teachers. The ten scholarship students of highest achievement would attend William and Mary College. Jefferson's plan promoted the idea of school as a selective agency to identify bright students for continuing education, as well as the traditional idea of equality of opportunity for economically less fortunate students.

Neither Jefferson's proposal for Virginia nor Rush's proposal for Pennsylvania was enacted. Nonetheless, the bills indicate the type of educational theorizing characteristic of the young nation. Coupled with Franklin's academy, and its practical curriculum based on business and commercial principles of education rather than classical and religious principles, these bills demonstrated the purpose of education to be to promote good citizenship, social progress, and utilitarianism. The classical curriculum and religious influence were, in effect, beginning to decline. Rush and Jefferson (and to a lesser extent Franklin) were all concerned with equality of educational opportunity—that is, they proposed universal education for the masses of children and youth, and methods for identifying students of superior ability, who were to receive free secondary and college educations at public expense.

Webster: Schoolmaster and Cultural Nationalism

The United States differed from most new countries struggling for identity in that it lacked a shared cultural identity and national literature. In its struggle against the "older" cultures and "older" ideas, the new nation went to great lengths to differentiate itself from England.[19] Noah Webster (1758–1843) called passionately upon his fellow Americans to "unshackle [their] minds and act like independent beings. You have been children long enough, subject to the control and subservient to the interests of a haughty parent. . . . You have an empire to raise . . . and a

national character to establish and extend by your wisdom and judgment."[20]

In 1789, when the Constitution went into effect as the law of the land, Webster argued that the United States should have its own system of "language as well as government." The language of Great Britain, he reasoned, "should no longer be our standard; for the taste of her writers is already completed, and her language on the decline."[21] By the act of revolution, the American people had declared their political independence from England, and now they needed to declare their cultural independence as well.

Realizing that a sense of national identity was conveyed through a distinctive national language and literature, Webster set out to reshape the English language used in the United States. He believed that a uniquely American language would (1) eliminate the remains of European usage, (2) create a uniform American speech that would be free of localism and provincialism, and (3) promote self-conscious American cultural nationalism.[22] The creation of an American language would become the linguistic mortar or national union; it would, however, have to be phonetically simple to render it more suitable to the common people.

Webster directly related the learning of language to organized education. As they learned the American language, children also would learn to think and act as Americans. The American language that Webster proposed would have to be taught deliberately and systematically to the young in the nation's schools. Because the curriculum of these Americanized schools would be shaped by the books that the students read, Webster spent much of his life writing spelling and reading books. His *Grammatical Institute of the English Language* was published in 1783. The first part of the *Institute* was later printed as *The American Spelling Book,* which was widely used throughout the United States in the first half of the nineteenth century.[23] Webster's *Spelling Book* went through many editions; it is estimated that 15 million copies had been sold by 1837. Webster's great work was *The American Dictionary,* which was completed in 1825 after twenty-five years of laborious research.[24] Often termed the "schoolmaster of the Republic,"

Noah Webster was an educational statesman of the early national period whose work helped to create a sense of American language, identity, and nationality.

McGuffey: The Reader and American Virtues

William Holmes McGuffey (1800–1873) who taught most of his life in Ohio colleges, also entered the debate on American cultural nationalism. The author of America's most popular textbooks of the period, called the *Readers,* McGuffey acknowledged with respect and gratitude America's "obligations to Europe and the descendants of the English stock" in science, art, law, literature, and manners. America had made its own contributions to humankind, however; they "were not literary or cultural, but moral and political." The seeds of popular liberty "first germinated from our English ancestors, but it shot up to its fullest heights in our land."[25] America had furnished to Europe proof that "popular institutions, founded on equality and the principle of representation, are capable of maintaining governments," that it was practical to elevate the masses, what Europe called the laboring and lower class, "to the great right and great duty of self-government."[26] Thus, McGuffey balanced the cultural indebtedness of the country with its political and social promise, the full realization of liberalism and traditions of the American common folk.

It is estimated that over 120 million copies of McGuffey's five *Readers* were sold between 1836 and 1920.[27] What McGuffey did was to combine the virtues of the Protestant faith with those of rural America—patriotism, heroism, hard work, diligence, and virtuous living. The tone was moral, religious, capitalistic, and pro-American; the selections of American literature included orations by George Washington, Patrick Henry, Benjamin Franklin, and Daniel Webster. Through his *Readers,* McGuffey taught several generations of Americans. He also provided the first graded *Readers* for our schools and paved the way for a graded system, which had its beginnings in 1840. So popular were his *Readers,* and so vivid and timeless his patriotism and faith in American institutions—home, work, church, and

nationhood—that many of his *Readers* (also his *Pictorial Primer*) have been reintroduced today in some rural, conservative, and/or fundamentalist schools. See Curriculum Tips 3.1.

NINETEENTH-CENTURY EUROPEAN EDUCATORS

Even though much criticism was leveled against European thought, American education was greatly influenced by it. At the college level, German educators influenced the fields of natural science, psychology, and sociology; many of our research-oriented universities were based on the German model. At the public school level, K-12, German (and Swiss) thought introduced romantic and progressive ideas—and a curriculum and instructional method that were psychologically oriented and considered the needs and interests of the students. The English also affected American education by providing models of schooling that ranged from efficient to romantic.

However strongly American patriots may have desired a distinctive cultural life, they could not, as men and women of common sense and learning, turn their backs on the wealth and wisdom of European ideas. Moreover, the rising current of educational thought in the Old World was not all steeped in old-fashioned and classical ideas, because progressive and scientific principles were beginning to evolve.

The theme of reform characterized much of the educational discussions of the time. The limitations of the "traditional curriculum and typical school of this era were recognized by educational leaders in Europe and America, and many of the features that were now firmly established in [curriculum] theory and practice can be traced to the ideas of the men and women who were ahead of their time."[28] The traditional curriculum, which emphasized Latin, Greek, and the classics, was de-emphasized. New pedagogical practices were developed that ran contrary to the methods of rote learning, memorization, and corporal punishment.

Pestalozzi: General and Special Methods

During the early American period of education, educational reformers were influenced by Johann

Heinrich Pestalozzi (1746–1827), a Swiss educator. According to one educational historian,
"Pestalozzi, probably more than any other educational reformer, laid the basis for the modern
elementary school and helped to reform elemen-
tary-school practice."[29] Pestalozzi maintained
that the educational process should be based on
the natural development of the child and his or
her sensory influences—similar thinking to that
of current progressives and environmentalists.
Pestalozzi's basic pedagogical innovation was
his insistence that children learn through the
senses rather than with words. He labeled rote
learning as mindless, and he emphasized instead
linking the curriculum to children's experiences
in their homes and family lives.

    Education, according to Pestalozzi, was to
develop by considering the "general" method and
"special" method. The general method called for
educators, who were loving persons, to provide
emotional security, trust, and affection for the
children. The special method considered the auditory and visual senses of the children in the
teaching process. To this end, Pestalozzi devised
the "object" lesson, in which children studied
common objects that they saw and experienced in
their daily environments—plants, rocks, artifacts,
and so on. The object lesson enhanced three types
of learning—form, number, and sound. Children
would first determine the form of the object, then
draw it, then name it. From the lessons in form,
number, and sound came more formal instruction
in the three Rs.

    Pestalozzi's ideas had great impact on early
nineteenth-century American education. William
McClure and Joseph Neef, and later Horace
Mann and Henry Barnard, when the latter was
U.S. Commissioner of Education, all worked to
introduce his ideas into American schools.[30] His
basic concepts of education became part of progressive schooling and later appeared in the move
for curriculum relevancy and humanistic curriculum. When educators discovered the "disadvantaged" in the 1960s and later promoted the ideas of
Project Head Start and compensatory education,
Pestalozzi's theories had special imprint.

Froebel: The Kindergarten Movement

Friedrich Froebel (1782–1852), a German educator, is known for his development of the kindergarten, what he called the "child's garden." Froebel formulated his educational principles around 3- and 4-year-old children; he believed that their schooling should be organized around play and individual and group interests and activities. This suggested a less formal and lockstep curriculum—one based on love, trust, and freedom, as well as the child's self-development.

Froebel's kindergarten was a prepared environment in which learning was based on the children's self-activities and self-development and on the children's trust and affection along the lines of Pestalozzi. Songs, stories, colorful materials, and games—what classical curriculum advocates would criticize as wasteful—were part of the formal curriculum. The children could manipulate objects (spheres, cubes, and circles), shape and construct materials (clay, sand, cardboard), and engage in playful activities (build castles and mountains, run and exercise).[31] Together these activities were to comprise the learning environment and provide a secure and pleasant place where children could grow naturally.

The kindergarten concept was brought to America by German immigrants, and the first American kindergarten was established in Watertown, Wisconsin, in 1855 by Margaret Schurz. William Harris, Superintendent of Schools in St. Louis, Missouri, and later U.S. Commissioner of Education, was instrumental in implementing the idea on a broader scale. The kindergarten is now an established part of American education, and many of Froebel's ideas of childhood experiences and methods of play are incorporated into current theories of early childhood education and progressive schooling.

Herbart: Moral and Intellectual Development

A famous German philosopher, Johann Freidrich Herbart (1776–1841), maintained that the chief aim of education was moral education, and that the traditional curriculum was too rigid and limited for this purpose. The need was to expand curriculum offerings and educate the good person who had diversified interests and a balanced perspective on life. Herbart specified two major bodies of subject matter: knowledge interests and ethical interests. Knowledge interests involved empirical data, factual data, and theoretical ideas; ethical interests involved personal convictions, benevolence, and regard for the social welfare of others, justice, and equity. Herbart wanted history, English, mathematics, and science integrated into all stages and grade levels of the curriculum. He also introduced the idea of *correlation* of all subjects to integrate the curriculum, an idea that influenced curriculum specialists who favored a core curriculum in the 1940s and 1950s.

Herbart was influential in integrating the techniques of instruction with learning, whereby the teacher would address the needs and interests of the students. It was a psychological process and involved the following:

1. *Preparation:* The teacher considers previous learning experiences and stimulates readiness of the learner.
2. *Presentation:* The new lesson is introduced.
3. *Association:* The new lesson is related to ideas or materials previously studied.
4. *Systemization:* Rules, principles, or generalizations of the new ideas are mastered by the learner.
5. *Application:* The new lesson is given meaning by testing and applying the new ideas to pertinent problems or activities.[32]

Speaking of Herbart's contribution to the instruction of teaching, John Dewey said: "Few attempts have been made to formulate a method, resting on general principles, of conducting a recitation. One of these is of great importance, and has probably had more influence upon the learning of lessons than all others put together; namely, the analysis by Herbart of a recitation into five successive steps."[33]

Herbart's formal steps of instruction were not only adopted by classroom teachers, they were applied to teacher training as well. In theory, teachers were asked to prepare their lessons by thinking of five steps and asking: What do my students know? What questions should I ask? What events should I relate? What conclusions should be reached? How can students apply what they have learned? To a large extent, these instructional principles influenced the teaching-learning principles Dewey expressed in *How We Think*; they still serve as guidelines for teachers who use the developmental lesson approach.

Pragmatism

Spencer: Utilitarian and Scientific Education

Herbert Spencer (1820–1903) was an English social scientist who based his ideas of education on Charles Darwin's theories of biological evolution and survival of the fittest. Spencer maintained that social development takes place according to the evolutionary process by which simple societies had evolved to more complex social systems, characterized by an increased variety of specialized professions and occupations.[34] Because of the laws of nature, only intelligent and productive populations would adapt to environmental changes. Less intelligent, weak, or lazy people would slowly disappear. The doctrine had immense implications for education based on excellence, the notion of social-economic progress, and the idea of intellectual development based on heredity.

Spencer also criticized religious doctrines and classical subject matter in education as nonscientific and unrelated to contemporary society. Rather, he advocated a curriculum fit for industrialized society—one that was scientific and practical (utilitarian). He believed that traditional schools were impractical and ornamental, a luxury for the upper class that failed to meet the needs of the people living in modern society.

For Spencer, the major purpose of education was to "prepare for complete living." Curriculum needed to be arranged according to this purpose. Spencer constructed a curriculum by prioritizing human activities so as to advance human survival and progress. His curriculum included the following activities, in order of importance: activities that (1) sustain life, (2) enhance life, (3) aid in rearing children, (4) maintain one's social and political relations, and (5) enhance leisure, tasks, and feelings.[35]

In his famous essay, "What Knowledge Is Most Worth?," Spencer argued that science was the most practical subject for the survival of the individual and society, yet it occupied minimal space in the curriculum because impractical and ornamental traditions prevailed. Spencer also maintained that students should be taught how to think (or problem solve) and not what to think.[36]

Although many of Spencer's ideas about religion, evolution, and social progress created a furor—and they still do among religious and political observers today—the ideas fitted well with those of thinkers in the second half of the nineteenth century, which was characterized by industrial growth, colonial expansion, and manifest destiny among European countries and the United States. Spencer's notion of discovery learning also influenced twentieth-century curricularists, both Deweyite progressive educators and later academic disciplinary educators. His demand for a curriculum steeped in science and linked with political survival and economic competition had special meaning during the Cold War-Sputnik era and still does—in light of present-day competition with Japan, Korea, and Germany.

THE RISE OF UNIVERSAL EDUCATION: 1820–1920

During the early nineteenth century America expanded westward. Life on the new frontier deepened America's faith in the common or average person, who built the new nation. Equality and rugged individualism were important concepts, expressed in the Declaration of Independence and reaffirmed by Westerners, who believed that all people were important and that in order to survive each had a job to do—despite different backgrounds. The common person, whether educated or not, was elected to various political offices; faith abounded in the capacity of humans to improve their lives. This kind of faith in the common people and in American civilization underscored to the frontier people the necessity of school.[37]

In the cities of the East, especially among the immigrant populations, there was also faith in the common person, in social mobility, and in the American dream of life, liberty, and equality. The upper class may not have had the same faith;

nonetheless, the traditional argument (since Franklin, Rush, and Jefferson)—that mass education was necessary for intelligent participation in political democracy and that it must extend beyond the common school to high schools and colleges—helped convert the American populace to supporting free schooling.

Monitorial Schools

The monitorial school was a European invention, based on Joseph Lancaster's model of education. It spread quickly to the large American urban centers, where the immigrant population was increasing, and to the frontier, where there was need for a system of schools. Its attraction, in the 1820s and the following decades, was its economy and efficiency: Bright student monitors served as instructors. The teacher taught the lesson to the monitors (high-achieving students) and they in turn presented the materials to their classmates—what some observers today might call "cooperative learning." The instruction was highly structured, and it was based on rote learning and drilling the three Rs.

Proponents of such teaching stressed that besides its economy, it kept potentially idle students busy while the teacher was occupied with other students. The class was divided into smaller groups, with a monitor in charge of each group. The students were kept actively involved in practice and drill activities and moved along at their own pace. Teachers were freed from some of their instructional chores and permitted to adopt new instructional roles—but mostly as inspectors and supervisors. The monitorial system was thus also considered "efficient" education.[38]

The monitorial system deemphasized classical education for the three Rs and religious theory for moral doctrines and citizenship, demonstrated the need for and possibility of systematic instruction, acquainted many people with formal education, and made educational opportunities more widely available. Most important, it promoted mass education and tax-supported elementary schools.[39] At the peak of its popularity, in the 1840s, it was organized in some high schools and suggested for the colleges.

But the monitorial system was considered too mechanical, and it was criticized for using students who knew little to teach those who knew even less. By the middle of the nineteenth century, its popularity waned. One hundred years later, however, the virtues of mechanical education resurfaced with the notion of programmed instruction. Instruction through self-pacing and drill could now be measured.

Common Schools

The common school was established in 1826 in Massachusetts, when the state passed a law requiring every town to choose a school board to be responsible for all the schools in the local area. Eleven years later, the Massachusetts legislature created the first state board of education, and Massachusetts organized the public common schools under a single authority. Connecticut quickly followed the example of its neighbor.[40] These common schools were devoted to elementary education with emphasis on the three Rs. The movement was spearheaded by Horace Mann and rooted in the ideas of progressive thought.

As a member of the Massachusetts legislature and later as the first Massachusetts Commissioner of Education, Horace Mann skillfully rallied public support for the common school by appealing to various segments of the population. To enlist the business community, Mann sought to demonstrate that "education has a market value" with a yield similar to "common bullion." The "aim of industry . . . and wealth of the country" would be augmented "in proportion to the diffusion of knowledge."[41] Workers would be more diligent and more productive. Mann also established a stewardship theory, aimed at the upper class, that the public good would be enhanced by public education. Schools for all children would create a stable society in which people would obey the laws and add to the nation's political and economic well-being. To the workers and farmers, Mann asserted that the common school would be a great equalizer, a means of social mobility for their children. To the Protestant community, he argued that the common school would assimilate ethnic and religious groups, promote a common culture, and help immigrant children learn English and the customs and laws of the land.[42] He was convinced that the common school was crucial for the American system of equality and opportunity, for a sense of community to be shared by all Americans, and for the promotion of a national identity.

Although the pattern for establishing common schools varied among the states, and the quality of education varied as well, the foundation of the American public school was being forged through this system. The schools were common in the sense that they housed youngsters of all socioeconomic and religious backgrounds, from age 6 to 14 or 15, and were jointly owned, cared for, and used by the local community. Because a variety of subjects was taught to children of all ages, teachers had to plan as many as ten to twenty different lessons a day.[43] Teachers also had to try to keep their schoolrooms warm in the winter—a responsibility shared by the older boys, who cut and fetched wood—and cool in the summer. Schoolhouses were often in need of considerable repair, and teachers were paid miserably low salaries.

In New England, the state legislatures encouraged the establishment of school districts and elected school boards and state laws to govern the schools. But it was on the frontier where the common school flourished, where there was faith in the common person and a common destiny. The common one-room schoolhouse "eventually led to one of America's most lasting, sentimentalized pictures—the 'Little Red Schoolhouse'. . . in almost every community." It had problems and critics, but it symbolized the pioneers' spirit and desire to provide free education for their children. "It was a manifestation of the belief held by most of the frontier leaders that a school was necessary to raise the level of American civilization."[44]

This small school, meager in outlook and thwarted by inadequate funding and insufficient teachers, nevertheless fit with the conditions of the American frontier—of expansion and equality. It was a "blab school," according to Abe Lincoln, but it was the kind of school in which the common person's children—even those born in log cabins—could begin their "readin," "writin," and "cipherin,"[45] and could advance to limitless achievements. It was a school local citizens could use as a polling place, a center for Grange activities, a site for

dances, and a location for community activities; it was a school controlled and supported by the local community.

The traditions built around the common school—the idea of neighborhood schools, local control of schools, and government support of schools—took a firm hold on the hearts and minds of Americans. America's confidence in the common school helped fashion the public schools later in the nineteenth century; it also influenced our present system of universal education.

The Elementary School Curriculum Evolves.
There was no agreement on an appropriate or common curriculum for the elementary school. The trend, throughout the nineteenth century, was to add courses to the essential or basic subjects of reading, spelling, grammar, and arithmetic. Religious doctrine changed to "manners" and "moral" instruction by 1825; the subject matter of textbooks was heavily moralistic (one reason for the popularity of McGuffey), and teachers provided extensive training in character building. By 1875 lessons in morality were replaced by courses in "conduct," which remained part of the twentieth-century curriculum. The traditional emphasis on curriculum was slowly altered, as more and more subjects were added—including geography and history by 1850; science, art (or drawing), and physical education by 1875; and nature study (or biology and zoology), music, and home and manual training by 1900. Table 3-1 shows this evolution of the elementary school curriculum.

Secondary Schools

The common school created the basis for a tax-supported and locally controlled elementary school education. The American high school was established on this base. By 1900 the majority of children aged 6 to 13 were enrolled in public elementary school, but only 11.5 percent of those aged 14 to 17 were enrolled in public secondary schools (and only 6.5 percent of the 17-year olds graduated). As shown in Table 3-2, not until 1930 did the secondary school enrollment figure exceed 50 percent. By 1970, the percentage of elementary aged children attending school was 98

TABLE 3-1 Evolution of the Elementary School Curriculum, 1800–1900

1800	1825	1850	1875	1900
Reading	*Reading*	*Reading*	*Reading*	*Reading*
	Declamation	*Declamation*	Literary selections	*Literature*
Spelling	*Spelling*	*Spelling*	*Spelling*	Spelling
Writing	Writing	*Writing*	Penmanship	Writing
Catechism	Good behavior	Conduct	Conduct	Conduct
Bible	Manners and morals	Manners		
Arithmetic	*Arithmetic*	*Mental arithmetic*	*Primary arithmetic*	*Arithmetic*
		Ciphering	Advanced arithmetic	
	Bookkeeping	Bookkeeping		
	Grammar	*Grammar*	*Grammar*	Grammar
		Elementary language	Oral language	*Oral language*
	Geography	Geography	Home geography	Home geography
			Text geography	*Text geography*
		U.S. history	U.S. history	History studies
			Constitution	
		Object lessons	Object lessons	Nature study
			Elementary science	Elementary science
			Drawing	Drawing
				Music
			Physical exercises	Physical training
				Play
	Sewing			Sewing
				Cooking
				Manual training

Source: From E. P. Cubberley, *The History of Education* (Boston: Houghton Mifflin, 1920), p. 756.
Note: Italics indicate the most important subjects.

Pragmatist view

percent, and the percentage of secondary aged children was 94 percent (and 75 percent were graduating). The great enrollment revolution for elementary schools took place between 1850 and 1900; for high schools it evolved between 1900 and 1970. Since the 1980s to the present, enrollment percentages have leveled off—and are beginning to gradually decline.

The Academy

In the early nineteenth century, the academy began to replace the Latin grammar school; by the middle of the century, it was dominant. It offered a wide range of curricula, and it was designed to provide a practical program (for terminal students) as well as a college preparatory course of study. By 1855 more than 6,000 academies had an enrollment totalling 263,000 students[46] (more than two-thirds of the total secondary school enrollment of that period).

"One of the main purposes" of the academy, according to Ellwood Cubberley, "was the establishment of . . . subjects having value aside from mere preparation for college, particularly subjects of modern nature, useful in preparing youth for the changed conditions of society. The study of real things rather than words about things, and useful things rather than subjects merely preparatory to college became prominent features of the new course of study."[47]

By 1828 as many as fifty different subjects were offered by the academies of the state of New York. The top fifteen, in rank order, were: (1) Latin, (2) Greek, (3) English grammar, (4) geography, (5) arithmetic, (6) algebra, (7) composition and declamation, (8) natural philosophy, (9) rhetoric, (10) philosophy, (11) U.S. history, (12) French, (13) chemistry, (14) logic, and (15) astronomy. By 1837, the state Board of Regents reported seventy-two different subjects.[48]

TABLE 3-2 Percentage of Students Enrolled in Secondary School
and College, 1900–1980

	14-TO 17-YEAR-OLDS ENROLLED IN SECONDARY SCHOOL	17-YEAR-OLDS GRADUATING HIGH SCHOOL	18-TO 21-YEAR-OLDS ENROLLED IN COLLEGE
1900	11.5	6.5	3.9
1910	15.4	8.8	5.0
1920	32.3	16.8	7.9
1930	51.4	29.0	11.9
1940	73.3	50.8	14.5
1950	76.8	59.0	26.9
1960	86.1	65.1	31.3
1970	93.4	76.5	45.2
1980	93.7	74.4	46.3
1990[a]	92.8	72.6	47.1

Source: From *Digest of Educational Statistics, 1982, 1985–1986, 1989* (Washington, D.C.: U.S. Government Printing Office, 1982, 1986, 1989), Table 35, p. 44; Table 9, p. 11. Tables 6, 49, pp. 13,62; *Projections of Education Statistics 1992–1993* (Washington, D.C.: U.S. Government Printing Office, 1988), Table 15, p. 19.
[a]Projections based on governmental sources.

Although no typical academy existed, with so many different course offerings, the academy inadvertently served the major function of preparing students for college. The traditional curriculum, or the classical side of the academy, continued in the new setting. Writes Elmer Brown, "The college preparatory course was the backbone of the whole system of instruction" in the better academies. Although practical courses were offered, "it was the admission requirements of the colleges, more than anything else, that determined their standards of scholarship."[49] And, writes Paul Monroe, "The core of academy education yet remained the old classical curriculum . . . just as the core of the student body in the more flourishing academies remained the group preparing for college."[50]

The era of the academies extended to the 1870s, when academies were replaced by public high schools. The academies, nevertheless, served as finishing schools for young ladies—with courses in classical and modern language, science, mathematics, art, music, and homemaking. Also, they offered the "normal" program for prospective common school teachers by combining courses in the classics with principles of ped-

agogy. A few private military and elite academic academies still exist today.

The High School

Although a few high schools existed in the early half of the nineteenth century (the first one was founded in 1821 in Boston), the high school did not become a major American institution until after 1874, when the Michigan court ruled, in the Kalamazoo decision, that the people could establish and support high schools with tax funds if they consented. There was some initial resistance—the fear that the taxes for the high schools would only benefit a small portion of the youth population—but after the court decision, the high school spread rapidly and compulsory attendance laws were established on a state-by-state basis. The idea of high school attendance for all youth, based on the notion of equality of educational opportunity, was a major educational reform.

Students were permitted to attend private schools, but the states had the right to establish minimum standards for all. By 1890, the 2,525 public high schools in the United States enrolled more than 200,000 students, compared to 1,600 private secondary schools, which had fewer than 95,000 students. By 1900 the number of high schools had soared to 6,000, while the number of academies had declined to 1,200.[51] The public high school system, contiguous with common schools, had evolved. Although as late as 1900 the high schools were still attended by only a small percentage of the total youth population, the inclusion of terminal and college preparatory students as well as rich and poor students under one roof was evidence that the American people had rejected the European dual system of secondary education. Fifty years later, when the American high school had fully evolved, James Conant was to present his argument for the comprehensive high school on the basis that it integrated all types of learners and helped eliminate class distinctions. The comprehensive high school provided curriculum options for all students.

The high schools stressed the college preparatory program, but they also served to complete the formal education of terminal students. They offered, in addition, a more diversified curriculum than the academies. At the turn of the century, high schools began to offer vocational and industrial courses as well as commercial and clerical training courses. Despite all their problems and criticisms, the public high schools evolved into democratic and comprehensive institutions for social and political reform. They produced a skilled workforce in an expanding industrial economy, and they assimilated and Americanized millions of immigrant children in our cities. They emphasized that our society, unlike most others, could afford to educate the masses of 14 to 18 year olds. When the high school became a dominant institution, a student could attend a publicly supported and supervised institution from age 5 to 18. The high school, moreover, was a bridge to college and the university.

The Secondary School Curriculum Evolves.
The curriculum of the Latin grammar school was virtually the same at the beginning and end of the colonial period. Table 3-3 lists the most popular courses. As indicated, Latin, Greek, arithmetic, and the classics were stressed. The academy introduced greater variation—courses for practical studies, for example—in the curriculum. By 1800, the academy offered about twenty-five different subjects (the table lists the seventeen most popular courses). Between 1850 and 1875, the peak period of the academy, estimates are that some 150 courses were offered.[52] The fifteen most popular ones in rank order were as follows: (1) algebra; (2) higher arithmetic; (3) English grammar; (4) Latin: (5) geometry; (6) U.S. history; (7) physiology; (8) natural philosophy; (9) physical geography; (10) German; (11) general history; (12) rhetoric; (13) bookkeeping; (14) French; and (15) zoology.[53]

There was no real philosophy or aim to these courses, except that most were college preparatory in nature, even though the original aim of the academy was to offer a practical program. It was believed then that a broad program with several course offerings was the hallmark of a better academy. The curriculum just expanded.[54]

After 1875, the high school rapidly grew and the academy rapidly declined. The secondary courses listed in Table 3-3 between 1875 and 1900 were high school courses. The curriculum continued to expand. The great variety in course offerings would allegedly allow the students to find where their interests and capabilities might be.[55] See Curriculum Tips 3-2.

THE TRANSITIONAL PERIOD: 1893–1918

From the colonial period until the turn of the twentieth century, the traditional curriculum, which emphasized classical studies for college-bound students, dominated at the elementary and secondary levels. The rationale for this emphasis was that the classics were difficult, and were thus the best source for intellectualizing and for developing mental abilities (a view later supported by the mental discipline approach to learning). The more difficult the subject and the more the students had to exercise their minds, the greater the subject's value. Such ideas of knowledge and subject matter, as well as mental rigor, were rooted in the philosophy of perennialism.

Along with the classics, more and more subjects were added to the curriculum. As a result the need was growing to bring some unity or a pattern for curriculum organization out of the

TABLE 3-3 Evolution of Secondary School Curriculum, 1800–1900

1800–1825	1825–1850	1850–1875	1875–1900

Latin Grammar School

1800–1825	1825–1850	1850–1875	1875–1900
Latin	Latin		
Greek	Greek		
Arithmetic	Arithmetic		
Classical literature	Classical literature		
	Ancient history		

Academy and High School

1800–1825	1825–1850	1850–1875	1875–1900
Latin	Latin	Latin	Latin
Greek	Greek	Greek	Greek†
Classical literature	Classical literature	English literature	English literature
Writing*	Writing*	Composition*	Composition*
Arithmetic*	Arithmetic*	Arithmetic*	Arithmetic*
		Higher arithmetic	
Geometry	Geometry	Geometry	Geometry
Trigonometry	Trigonometry	Trigonometry	Trigonometry
	Algebra	Algebra	Algebra
Bookkeeping*	Bookkeeping*	Bookkeeping*	Bookkeeping*†
English grammar	English grammar	English grammar	English
Rhetoric	Rhetoric	Rhetoric	Rhetoric*
Oratory	Oratory†		
	Debating	Debating†	
Surveying*	Surveying*		
Astronomy*	Astronomy*	Astronomy	Astronomy*
Navigation*	Navigation*†		
Geography	Geography	Physical geography	Physical geography†
	Natural philosophy	Natural philosophy†	
		Meteorology	Meteorology†
		Chemistry	Chemistry
		Physiology	Physiology†
			Health education
		Botany	Botany†
		Zoology	Zoology†
			Biology
			Physics
Foreign language* (French, Spanish, German)	Foreign language* (French, Spanish, German)	Foreign language (French, Spanish, German)	Foreign language (French, Spanish, German, Italian)
Philosophy	Philosophy	Mental philosophy	
		Moral philosophy†	
	History	General history†	World history
	Greek history	Greek history†	Ancient history

(continued)

TABLE 3-3 Continued

1800–1825	1825–1850	1850–1875	1875–1900
	U.S. history	U.S. history	U.S. history
			Civil government
			Political economy
			Manual training*
			Home economics*
			Agriculture*
			Music
			Art
			Physical education

Source: Adapted from Calvin Davis, *Our Evolving High School Curriculum* (New York: World Book, 1927), p. 38; Committee of Ten, *Report of the Committee on Secondary Studies* (Washington, D.C.: National Education Association, 1893), p. 4; Newton Edwards and Herman G. Richey, *The School in the American Social Order,* 2nd ed. (Boston: Houghton Mifflin, 1963), p. 250; and Gerald R. Firth and Richard D. Kimpston, *The Curricular Continuum in Perspective* (Itasca, Ill.: Peacock, 1973), pp. 102–104.
*Considered as part of practical studies.
†All but disappeared; limited enrollments.

chaotic and confused situation, especially at the secondary level, where subject matter was expanding the most. According to two educators, "subjects taught varied from school to school. There was no uniformity as to time allotments, and grade placements of topics or subjects pursued" differed from school to school.[56]

A companion problem existed. Most children, even as late as the turn of the century, completed their formal education at the elementary school level, and those students who did go to secondary schools usually ended their formal education upon graduation. As late as 1890, only 14.5 percent of the students enrolled in high school were preparing for college, and less than 3 percent went on to college.[57] Hence, the needs of more than 85 percent of these students were still being overlooked for only the top 15 percent; the discrepancy was more lopsided if the college track was considered. Reformers began to question the need for two curriculum tracks at the elementary level—one for high school-bound and the other for nonhigh school-bound children—the dominance of college over the high school, and the emphasis on mental discipline and the classics.

Reaffirming the Traditional Curriculum: Three Committees

With these unsettled questions as background, the National Education Association (NEA) organized three major committees between 1893 and 1895: the Committee of Fifteen on Elementary Education, the Committee of Ten on Secondary School Studies, and the Committee on College Entrance Requirements. These committees were to determine the specifics of the curricula for these schools. Their reports "standardized" the curriculum for much of this century. In the words of Ellwood Cubberley, "The committees were dominated by subject-matter specialists, possessed of a profound faith in mental discipline." No concern for student "abilities, social needs, interest, or capabilities . . . found a place in their . . . deliberations."[58]

The Committee of Fifteen. The Committee of Fifteen was heavily influenced by Charles Eliot, president of Harvard University, who had initiated vigorous discussion on the need for school reform in the years preceding, and by William Harris, then the U.S. Commissioner of Education, a staunch perennialist, who believed in strict teacher authority and discipline. Both Eliot and Harris wanted the traditional curriculum to remain intact. Eliot's plan, which was adapted by the Committee, was to reduce the elementary grades from ten to eight. The Committee stressed the three Rs, as well as English grammar, literature, geography, and history. Hygiene, culture, vocal music, and drawing were given 60 minutes, or one lesson, per week. Manual training, sewing, and/or cooking, as well as algebra and Latin, were introduced in the seventh and eighth grades.

In general, the Committee resisted the idea of newer subjects and the principles of pedagogy or teaching that had characterized the reform movement of the European pioneers since the early 1800s. The Committee also rejected the idea of kindergarten and the idea that the children's needs or interests should be considered when planning the curriculum.[59] Any idea of interdisciplinary subjects or curriculum synthesis was rejected. Isolation of each branch of knowledge, or what John Dewey, in *Democracy and Education,* and Ralph Tyler, in *Basic Principles of Curriculum and Instruction,* later referred to as "compartmentalization" of subject matter, was considered the norm; it still is today in most schools.

The Committee of Ten.   The Committee of Ten was the most influential of the three committees. Its recommendations best illustrate the tough-minded, mental discipline approach supported by Eliot, who was the chair. The Committee identified nine academic subjects as central to the high school curriculum. As shown in Table 3-4, they were: (1) Latin; (2) Greek; (3) English; (4) other modern languages; (5) mathematics (algebra, geometry, trigonometry, and higher or advanced algebra); (6) physical sciences (physics, astronomy, and chemistry); (7) natural history or biological sciences (biology, botany, zoology, and physiology); (8) social sciences (history, civil government, and political economy); and (9) geography, geology, and meteorology.

The Committee recommended four different programs or tracks: (1) classical; (2) Latin scientific; (3) modern languages; and (4) English. The first two required four years of Latin; the first program emphasized English (mostly classical) literature and math, and the second program, math and science. The modern language program required four years of French or German (Spanish was considered not only too easy, but also not as important a culture or language as French or German). The English program permitted four years of either Latin, German, or French. Both of

TABLE 3-4 Secondary School Programs and Subjects Proposed by Committee of Ten, 1893

FIRST YEAR		SECOND YEAR		THIRD YEAR		FOURTH YEAR	
Latin	5 p.*	Latin	4 p.	Latin	4 p.	Latin	4 p.
English Literature 2 p. }	4 p.	Greek	5 p.	Greek	4 p.	Greek	4 p.
English Composition 2 p. }		English Literature 2 p. }	4 p.	English Literature, 2 p. }	4 p.	English Literature 2 p. }	4 p.
German [or French]	5 p.	English Composition 2 p. }		English Composition, 1 p. }		English Composition 1 p. }	
Algebra	4 p.	German continued	4 p.	Rhetoric, 1 p. }		Grammar, 1 p. }	
History of Italy, Spain, and France	3 p.	French, begun		German	4 p.	German	4 p.
Applied Geography (European political-continental and oceanic flora and fauna)	4 p.	Algebra,* 2 p. }	5 p.	French	4 p.	French	4 p.
		Geometry 2 p. }	4 p.	Algebra,* 2 p. }	4 p.	Trigonometry }	2 p.
		Botany or Zoology	4 p.	Geometry, 2 p. }		Higher Algebra }	
		English History to 1688	3 p.	Physics	4 p.	Chemistry	4 p.
				History, English and U.S.	3 p.	History (intensive) and Civil Government	3 p.
				Astronomy, 3 p. 1st 1/2 yr. }	3 p.	Geology or Physiography, 4 p. 1st 1/2 yr. }	4 p.
				Meterology, 3 p. 2nd 1/2 yr. }		Anatomy, Physiology, and Hygiene, 4 p. 2nd 1/2 yr. }	
	25 p.		33 p.		34 p.		33 p.

Source: From Committee of Ten, *Report of the Committee of Ten on Secondary School Studies* (Washington, D. C.: National Educational Association, 1893), p. 4.

*p. = periods.

these programs also included literature, composition, and history.

The Committee of Ten took a position and claimed that the latter two programs, which did not require Latin or emphasize literature, science, or mathematics, were "in practice distinctly inferior to the other two."[60] In taking this position, the Committee indirectly tracked college-bound students into the first two or superior programs and noncollege-bound students into the latter two or inferior programs. To some extent, this bias reflected the Committee's composition—eight of the ten members represented college and private preparatory school interests.

The Committee ignored art, music, physical education, and vocational education, maintaining that these subjects contributed little to mental discipline. In analyzing the effects of the Committee's action, two curricularists wrote: "The choice of these subjects and the omission of others from consideration was enough to set the course for secondary education" for many years and to indirectly set the tone at the elementary level, too. As "might be expected," the Committee suggested that "the nine subjects be taught sooner" and that all subjects except Latin and Greek be taught at the elementary school level.[61]

Even though very few students at that time went to college, this college preparatory program established a curriculum hierarchy, from elementary school to college, that promoted academics and ignored the majority of students, who were noncollege bound. Today, even though we offer vocational, industrial, and/or technical programs, the academic program is still considered superior to and of more status than the other programs.

The Committee on College Entrance Requirements. When this Committee met in 1895, it reaffirmed college dominance over the high school, in terms of admission requirements and classical subjects for mental training at the high school and college levels. Consisting mainly of college and university presidents, including Eliot, the Committee recommended to strengthen the college preparatory aspect of the high school curriculum, believing that it best served all students. It also made recommendations regarding the number of credits required in different subjects for college admission; it served as a model for the Carnegie Unit, a means for evaluating credits for college admission, imposed on the high schools in 1909 and still in existence today in most high schools.

Pressure for a Modern Curriculum

Gradually, demands were made for various changes to be made in the schools to meet the needs of a changing society. The pace of immigration and industrial development led a growing number of educators to question the classical curriculum and the constant emphasis on mental discipline and incessant drill. This shift in curriculum was influenced by the scientific movement in psychology and education in the late nineteenth and early twentieth centuries, particularly the pragmatic theories of Charles Pierce and William James; the social theories of Darwin, Herbart, and Spencer; and the impact of Pestalozzi, Froebel, Montessori, and others on pedagogy. The movement rejected the mental discipline approach and classic curriculum (both of which stressed that certain traditional and "cultural" subjects were best for disciplining the mind), as well as faculty psychology (that is, enhancing the "faculties" or mind of the child through stimulation of the senses). Instead, the new scientism put emphasis on vocational, technical, and scientific subjects—fitting into the concurrent age of industrialism, colonialism, and materialism.

Increased pressure against the traditional curriculum was evident at the turn of the century—with the educational ideas of John Dewey and Francis Parker, the Gestalt psychology and child psychology movements (which focused on the whole child), the learning theories of behaviorism and transfer learning (which involved connections between stimuli and responses), and the progressive movement in schools and society.

The argument eventually appeared that the classics had no greater disciplinary or mental value than other subjects, and that mental discipline (which emphasized rote, drill, and memorization) was not conducive to the inductive method of science or compatible with contemporary educational theory. Wrote Edward Thorndike, the most influential learning psychologist of the era:

The expectation of any large difference in general improvement of the mind from one study rather than another seems doomed to disappointment. The chief reason why good thinkers seem superficially to have been made such by having taken certain school studies is that good thinkers have taken such studies. . . . Now that good thinkers study Physics and Trigonometry, these seem to make good thinkers. If abler pupils should all study Physical Education and Dramatic Art, these subjects would seem to make good thinkers.[62]

Even Latin came under attack, by none other than old-time perennialists. In 1917, for example, Charles Eliot, a former advocate of Latin, was saying Latin should no longer be compulsory for high school or college students.[63] Abraham Flexner, a former teacher of the classics who had become a celebrity with his exposé of the American medical schools, claimed that Latin had "no purpose" in the curriculum and that the classics were out of step with scientific developments.[64] Flexner, who had become a strong advocate of utilitarianism, argued that tradition was an inadequate criterion for justifying subject matter. In short, society was changing and people could alter the conditions around them; the stress on psychology and science and the concern for social and educational reform made evident the need for a new curriculum.

Flexner: A Modern Curriculum.   In a famous paper, "A Modern School," published in 1916, Abraham Flexner (1866–1959) rejected the traditional curriculum of the secondary school and proposed a "modern" curriculum for contemporary society. Flexner's curriculum consisted of four basic areas: (1) science (the major emphasis of the curriculum); (2) industry (occupations and trades of the industrial world); (3) civics (history, economics, and government); and (4) esthetics (literature, languages, art, and music).[65] Modern languages would replace Latin and Greek. Flexner concluded that, unless a utilitarian argument could be made for a subject, it had little value in the curriculum, regardless of traditional value.

Flexner's concepts of utility and modern subject matter tend to resemble Spencer's views on science and subject matter. The difference is that Flexner's timing was on the mark, and Spen-

cer was ahead of his time. Flexner was tuned to the changing social and political times during which many educators were willing to listen to his proposals. In 1917, for example, Flexner's "Modern School" was established at the Lincoln School of Teachers College, Columbia University. The school combined the four core areas of study, with emphasis on scientific inquiry; it represented Dewey's type of progressivism and science of education, and it also reflected the fact that Dewey was now teaching at Columbia University.

Dewey: Pragmatic and Scientific Principles of Education.   The same year Flexner published his modern school report, John Dewey (1859–1952) published *Democracy and Education,* in which can be found all elements of his philosophy as well as their implications for the educational process.[66] In the book, Dewey showed the relationship between education and democracy and set forth the notion that democracy itself was a social process that could be enhanced through the school. Dewey considered schools as neutral institutions that could serve the ends of either freedom or repression and authority. Dewey envisioned school in America as an instrument of democracy.

Thus, the aims of education went hand in hand with the particular type of society involved; conversely, the society that evolved influenced the aims of education.

Dewey argued that subjects could not be placed in a value hierarchy and that attempts to do so were misguided. Any study or body of knowledge was capable of expanding the child's experience, and "experiencing"—that is, being stimulated to develop and internalize intellectual capabilities—was the process of educating the child. Traditional subjects such as Latin or Greek were no more valuable than music or art.

One subject that may be more important to Dewey is science. Science, for Dewey, was another name for knowledge, and it represented "the perfected outcome of learning—its consummation. . . . What is known, certain, settled" and what "we think with rather than that which we think about" is science or rationalized knowledge. Dewey considered scientific inquiry to be the best form of knowledge for a society, because it consisted of the "special . . . methods which the race has slowly worked out in order to conduct reflection under conditions whereby its procedures and results are tested."[67] He thus elevated the place of science in education.

What is relevant to educating an individual to function well as a free person in a free society remained constant for Dewey. His emphasis on the "method of inquiry," which is really synonymous with "intelligent behavior," is as valued today as it was seventy-five years ago.

Judd: Systematic Studies and Social Sciences.

Charles Judd (1873–1946) was the colleague of John Dewey; in fact, he was the head of the Department of Education at the University of Chicago when Dewey directed the lab school. Along with Dewey and others, he constructed a science of education based on the methods of finding facts and then applying them as a basis for reasoning out solutions to problems and for making decisions. Whereas Charles Pierce and William James referred to this method as pragmatism, Judd referred to it as "scientism in education."

Judd was an evolutionist and felt the laws of nature could be used to educate the young. He used statistical research (which was then in its infancy stage) to determine the worth of curriculum content, that is, which subjects would best promote thinking and dealing with the problems of contemporary life. By preparing students to deal with problems, not acquire endless knowledge, he argued students would be prepared to deal with the changing world and the problems they would encounter as adults.

The justification for the method of determining subject matter was outlined in Judd's book *The Scientific Study of Education,* which was concerned with what he called "systematic studies . . . of the curriculum."[68] His emphasis was on reading, writing, and spelling based on words shown statistically to be used by successful adults, as well as on math problems applied to practical problems of everyday life. Utilitarian and pragmatic in philosophy, he urged that elementary students be exposed to "career education" to help them formulate ideas about the world of work and thus prepare them for the evolving social order. At the secondary level, Judd sought practical subjects that had a voca-

tional or technical orientation, not a "cultural" or elitist one. For slower students, he advocated English, business math, mechanics or stenography, and office management—what later was to become part of the commercial and vocational tracks in high school. For average and talented students, he urged a curriculum consisting of science, mathematics, modern language, and the social sciences—what later was to be labeled the academic track.

Although, today, we might criticize Judd's evolutionary ideas as prejudicial, his ideas fit into the scientific and social science era of the day, that is, the "survival of the fittest." The same ideas resurfaced during the Sputnik and Cold War era, especially with regard to James Conant's ideas of tracking students and separating them into vocational and academic programs; it appears in slightly different form as we enter the 1990s and engage in economic combat with Germany, Japan, and Korea.

On a less philosophical basis, one which is more focused on curriculum, Judd was to influence the next generation of theorists, who sought to systematize curriculum making by applying scientific methods to curriculum development. These new theorists, sometimes called *technicians,* starting with Bobbitt and Charters in the 1920s and ending with Tyler in the 1950s, evoked his educational utility and social science/research methods.

Commission on the Reorganization of Secondary Education.

In 1918 the NEA Commission on the Reorganization of Secondary Education published the famous *Cardinal Principles of Secondary Education,*[69] a highly progressive document. Influenced by Flexner's "A Modern School" and Dewey's *Democracy and Education,* the Commission stressed the whole child (not just the cognitive area of study), education for all youth (not just college-bound youth), diversified areas of study (not classical or traditional studies), common culture, ideas, and ideals for a democratic society (not religious, elitist, or mental, discipline learning).

The Commission noted the following:

1. *Seven major aims or "Cardinal Principles" should comprise education: health, command of*

the fundamentals, worthy home membership, vocation, citizenship, leisure, and ethical character.

2. *High school should be a comprehensive institution based on the various social and economic groups that populate the nation.*

3. *The high school curriculum should offer various programs to meet various student needs—agricultural, business and commercial, vocational, and college preparatory.*

4. *The current ideas of psychology of education, principles of pedagogy, measurement, and evaluation should be applied to the curriculum and instruction of the high school.*

5. *American education comprises a set of defined institutions that should function in conjunction with, rather than in isolation from, each other.*

Indeed, the high school was assuming its modern curricular patterns—combining academic programs with several nonacademic programs. The choice of subject matter was being fine-tuned to emphasize five basic or essential subjects such as English, math, science, social science, and modern language. Classical languages and classical literature took a back seat to modern languages and English literature. Aims and subjects were related, not separated or compartmentalized. The idea of mental discipline was replaced by utilitarian modes of thought and scientific inquiry. There was a growing recognition that curriculum, too, should not be compartmentalized but interdisciplinary, and that it should not be static, but change as society changed. The needs and interests of the students were now considered. Most important, there was recognition of the responsibility of schools (including the high school) to serve all children and youth, not just college-bound youth. The era of progressive education was about to begin impacting the schools—and traditional education (which had dominated American education for so long) was vanishing.

CURRICULUM AS A FIELD IS BORN: 1918–1949

The early twentieth century was a period of educational ferment. Scientific methods of research, the influence of psychology, the child study movement, the idea of efficiency in industry, and the muckracker-progressive movement in society all influenced education. Many of the resulting ideas were applied to curriculum: From them evolved the process and how-to-do aspects of curriculum. Curriculum was now viewed as a science, with principles and methodology, not just as content or subject matter. The ideas of planning and describing a curriculum, as opposed to describing curriculum in terms of subjects and the amount of time needed to study each subject, appeared in the literature.

Bobbitt and Charters: Behaviorism and Scientific Principles

Franklin Bobbitt (1876–1956) and Werrett Charters (1875–1952) were influenced by the idea of efficiency, promoted by business and industry, and the scientific management theories of Frederick Taylor, who analyzed factory efficiency in terms of time and motion studies and concluded that each worker should be paid on the basis of his or her individual output (as measured by the number of units produced in a specified period of time).[70] Efficient operation of the schools, sometimes called "machine" theory by sociologists and economists, became a major goal in the 1920s. Often ensuring efficiency meant eliminating small classes, increasing the student-teacher ratio, cutting costs in teacher salaries, and so on, and then preparing charts and graphs to show the resultant lower costs. Raymond Callahan later branded this idea the "cult of efficiency."[71] The effects were to make curriculum making more scientific and to reduce teaching and learning to precise behaviors with corresponding activities and learning experiences that could be measured. These ideas were cultivated by Taylor's faithful followers, Bobbitt and Charters.

Bobbitt's book, *The Curriculum,* published in 1918, is considered by some observers as the first book devoted solely to curriculum as a science and to curriculum in all its phases. Bobbitt outlined the principles of curriculum planning by focusing on an activities approach, which he defined as "a series of things which children and youth must do and experience by way of developing abilities to do things well and make up the affairs of adult life."[72] To Bobbitt the purpose of curriculum was to outline what knowledge was important for each subject, and then to develop various activities to train the learner and enhance his or her performance.

Bobbitt understood the importance of analyzing the process of curriculum making, especially the need for specifications, tasks, and detail to what one wanted to accomplish and then measure—all part of machine theory and the cult of efficiency, as well as the behaviorist movement of the era. Adherence to the traditional curriculum, which emphasized subject matter, did not provide educators with methods for developing curricula. Bobbitt described the problems as he set out to organize a course of studies for the elementary grades:

> We need principles of curriculum making. We did not know that we should first determine objectives from a study of social needs. We supposed education consisted only of teaching the familiar subjects. We had not come to see that it is essentially a process of unfolding the potential abilities of [students]. . . . We had not learned that studies are means, not ends."[73]

Bobbitt further developed his objectives and activities approach in the early 1920s in *How to Make a Curriculum.* Here he outlined more than 800 objectives and related activities to coincide with student needs. These activities ranged from the "ability to care for [one's] teeth. . . . eyes, . . . nose, and throat, . . . ability to keep the heart and blood vessels in normal working condition, . . . to keep home appliances in good working condition . . . to spelling and grammar."[74]

Bobbitt's methods were quite sophisticated for the period. Moreover, his guidelines for selecting objectives can be applied today: (1) *eliminate* objectives that are impractical or cannot be accomplished through normal living; (2) *emphasize* objectives that are important for success and adult living; (3) *avoid* objectives opposed by the community; (4) *involve* the community in selecting objectives; (5) *differentiate* between objectives that are for all students and those that are for only a portion of the student population; and (6) *sequence* the objectives in such a way as to establish how far students should go each year in attaining them—that is, establish criteria for achievement.

Taken out of context, however, Bobbitt's list of hundreds of objectives and activities, along

with the machine or factory analogy that he advocated, were easy to criticize.[75] Nevertheless, Bobbitt's insistence that curriculum making was a specialty based on scientific methods and procedures was important for elevating curriculum to a field of study, or what he called a "new specialization." His offer was that educators try his method with the intention of improving it or suggesting a better one. He was one of the first to propose the idea of a curriculum specialist, with special training.

Charters advocated the same behaviorist, precise approach, which he termed a "scientific" approach. He viewed the curriculum as a series of objectives that students must attain by way of a series of learning experiences. In his book on *Curriculum Construction,* Charters, who was influenced by the machine theory of business, envisioned curriculum as the analysis of definite operations—a process he termed *job analysis*—such as those involved in running a machine.[76]

Charters's statement about the weakness of curriculum is still relevant today: that even though curriculum writers often begin "with the statement of aim, none has been able to derive a curriculum logically from his statement of aim." In almost every case, a "mental leap [is made] from the aim to the subject matter, without providing adequate principles such as would bridge the gap . . . and lead us from aim to selection of materials."[77] Charters attempted to bridge the gap by proposing a curriculum derived from specific objectives and precise activities. He considered objectives to be observable and measurable, an outlook that is similar to today's notion that behavioral objectives can be sound and definable. He felt the state of knowledge at that time did not permit scientific measurement that would specifically identify the outcomes of the objectives, but he set out to develop a method for selecting objectives, based on social consensus, and for applying subject matter and student activities to analysis and verification. Although Charters did not use the term *evaluation* during this period, he was laying the groundwork for curriculum evaluation, which surfaced twenty years later.

As prime initiators of the behavioral and scientific movements in curriculum, Bobbitt and Charters had a profound impact on curriculum. They (1) developed principles for curriculum making, involving aims, objectives, needs, and learning experiences (which they called activities); (2) highlighted the use of behavioral objectives, which has a legacy in various contemporary educational ideas, such as the use of instructional objectives and curriculum evaluation; (3) introduced the ideas that objectives are derived from the study of needs (later called needs assessment) and that objectives and activities are subject to analysis and verification (later called evaluation); and (4) emphasized that curriculum making cuts across subject matter, and that a curriculum specialist need not necessarily be a specialist in any *subject,* rather a professional in *method* or *process.*

Finally, Bobbitt and Charters taught at the University of Chicago when Tyler was a graduate student in the department of education (in fact, Tyler was Charters's graduate assistant). Tyler was highly influenced by their behaviorist ideas, particularly that (1) objectives derive from student needs and society, (2) learning experiences relate to objectives, (3) activities organized by the teacher should be integrated into the subject matter, and (4) instructional outcomes should be evaluated. Tyler's stress on evaluation as a component of curriculum is rooted in the research background of Charters, who helped his graduate student get appointed to his first teaching and evaluation position in 1929 as Head of Testing and Evaluation for the Ohio State Bureau of Educational Research (Charters had assumed the directorship of the bureau the previous year). Tyler's principles of curriculum and instruction, especially his four major components (objectives, learning experiences, methods of organization, and evaluation), are rooted in Bobbitt's and especially Charters's ideas.

Kilpatrick: The Progressive Influence

The increasing rise of progressive education and universal education, that is, education for the masses, led to an attack against the rigidity and rote memorization of the classical curriculum, the emphasis on tough subject matter, and the high school curriculum standardized on the basis of preparation for college. The progressive movement consisted of many wings. and among the most influential were the child-centered and

activity-centered curricularists. Subject matter emphasis was replaced by emphasis on the student or learner; the needs and interests of the child dominated the new thinking, and cognitive processes were replaced by social processes. The curriculum was organized around classroom and school social activities, group enterprises, and group projects. See Curriculum Tips 3-3.

Creative self-expression and freedom were the major goals of the child-centered movement, and this was a reaction against the rigid and domineering influence of the traditional curriculum. While the method relied on Dewey's progressivism, it was Dewey who made several criticisms in the 1920s and 1930s about this new education, which he felt to be a distortion of his original ideas and to lack purpose and method as well as teacher direction. According to Dewey, the method of surrounding students with materials but not suggesting a purpose or a plan, but rather allowing students to respond according to their interests, "is really stupid [and] attempts the impossible which is always stupid."[78]

William Kilpatrick, a colleague of Dewey when he moved to Teachers College, Columbia University, attempted to merge the current behaviorist psychology of the day, particularly Thorndike's (connectionism) and Watson's (conditioning) theories with Dewey's and Judd's progressive philosophy, which became known as the "Project Method,"[79] or what was later called *purposeful activity.* Kilpatrick combined four steps in methodology, which were actually more behaviorist than progressive: purposing, planning, executing, and judging, with his projects (ranging from classroom projects to school and community projects).

Two of his doctoral students applied many of his ideas in the Missouri schools. One was Junius Merian, who called Kilpatrick's projects "subjects of study" and organized them into four areas: observation, play, stories, and hard work.[80] The second student, Ellsworth Collings, developed a curriculum around the real-life experiences of children. He had both teachers and students present several guided experiences or activities that were related and developmental in nature; one activity led to another. "The curriculum was continuously made 'on the spot' by the joint action of pupils and teachers." The idea was that such a joint endeavor "would mean most for

CURRICULUM TIPS 3-3   Enriching the Curriculum

The following suggestions combine Kilpatrick's activities curriculum and Rugg's child-centered curriculum. In general, the suggestions integrate elementary's schooling with the philosophy of progressivism, which evolved during the first half of the twentieth century. The specific suggestions are still viable today for those schools and teachers who stress a student-centered curriculum.

1. Study the cumulative record of each child.
2. Compare the achievement score with ability indices.
3. Examine a pupil's creative production for words, symbols, and topics that are used frequently.
4. Listen to pupils talk about themselves.
5. Provide opportunity for a choice of activities.
6. Visit each pupil's home, if possible.
7. Help each pupil learn as much as possible about his or her values, attitudes, purposes, skills, interests, and abilities.
8. Be willing to allow pupils to say what they think.
9. Encourage students to reflect on their beliefs and values.
10. Analyze with pupils their interpretations of their in-class and out-of-class experiences.
11. Organize class activities around individual or group study of problems important to the individuals involved.
12. Help each pupil to state his or her purposes, both immediate and long term. Share with pupils the information available about their present status.
13. Clarify with pupils the limitations (in time, materials, and resources) of the situation.
14. Ask each pupil to formulate a plan of work.
15. Encourage each pupil to collect and share materials.
16. Make possible the collection of information in out-of-class situations.
17. Use record-keeping as a way of helping the individual student to organize his or her learning.

Source: Kimball Wiles, *Teaching for Better Schools* (Englewood Cliffs, N.J.: Prentice Hall, 1952), p. 286.

the children."[81] His projects were similar to Merian's four study areas, but included more field trips and community activities.

Although advocates such as Boyd Bode and John Childs treated these ideas as "innovative" and "new,"[82] there was almost nothing new with the idea of purposeful activity. The idea was rooted in the curriculum ideas of Bobbitt and Charters, as expressed by their stress on objectives and related activities, and the philosophy of Dewey, particularly his doctrine of growth, which was derived from "purposeful activity," and "modes of action" to meet the needs and interests of students.

Kilpatrick's project method was mainly implemented at the elementary schools, like the activity movement, because both were child centered. His method was fully developed in his text, *Foundations of Method,* and became part of the activity movement. Nonetheless, he argued that the difference was that his doctrine had "social purpose," whereas the activity-centered curriculum had only "child purpose." When forced to decide who should plan the curriculum, the child or teacher, Kilpatrick opted for the child, arguing that "if you want to educate the boy to think and plan for himself, then let him make his own plan."[83] In this respect, he differed from Dewey, who put more emphasis on the role of the teacher.

For Kilpatrick, the child had to learn to "search . . . compare . . . think why . . . and in the end . . . make his own decision."[84] The teacher could serve as a guide, but not as the source of information or dispenser of knowledge. When Kilpatrick's project method was eventually introduced in the high school curriculum, it became fused with social studies and the core curriculum. All these curriculum experiences meshed subject matter, social issues, and social problems important to students involved.[85]

Kilpatrick was also part of the wing of the radical progressive movement, later called reconstructionism, which was concerned with social issues and saw traditional education (expressed in perennialist terms) as reactionary. Bode, Caswell, Counts, and Rugg were part of this new social movement. Although these radicals criticized the Committee of Ten and felt its members had legitimatized traditional systems of education, Kilpatrick (like members of the Committee) was concerned about "a curriculum containing a bewildering variety of more or less unrelated subjects." New subjects were being added "as occasion arose," lacking in philosophy or related goals.[86] But whereas the traditional curricularists of the Committee of Ten urged a curriculum based on perennialist philosophy, clearly compartmentalized and tough academics, with emphasis on Latin, language, and science, Kilpatrick argued for progressive philosophy, integrated subject matter, and a general education with emphasis on values and social issues. Whereas the Committee of Ten saw school as a place where students go to primarily acquire knowledge, Kilpatrick and his progressive colleagues saw school as a "way of life" and "ideal community" where students practiced "cooperation, self-government . . . and application of intelligence . . . to problems as they may arise."[87]

The traditional practice of education focused on certain subjects, usually the three Rs at the elementary level and basic academic subjects at the secondary level. These were considered as logically organized bodies of subject matter. The basic method for teaching these subjects was through rote practices. Kilpatrick and his followers challenged both of these positions regarding method and the assumption about logically organized subject matter. As Collings asserted, the activities movement made the individual child the focus of thinking in a social context. The child's growth along social lines, not the mastery of content, was the purpose of education.[88] School was preparation for life; it had social purpose.

In the end, the emphasis in education was the student—interested, active, and interacting with peers in school and adults in the community. Students had needs, interests, and problems growing out of their experiences with each other, their family, and community. Hence, the curriculum had to be derived not from organized bodies of subject matter, but from real-life experiences and expressed in terms of purposeful activities.

The Twenty-Sixth Yearbook

In 1930, the National Society for the Study of Education (NSSE), an honor society with headquarters at the University of Chicago, published its twenty-sixth yearbook in two parts, *Curriculum-Making: Past and Present* and *The Foundations of Curriculum Making*.[89]

The committee that developed the two volumes consisted of twelve members, including Harold Rugg (the chairperson) and William Bagley, Franklin Bobbitt, Werrett Charters, George Counts, Charles Judd, and William Kilpatrick, among others. Leaders of curriculum development during that period were mainly scientific-oriented (including Bobbitt and Charters) and progressive (including Counts, Judd, and Kilpatrick), and many were affiliated with the University of Chicago, which emphasized this science of education.

The Yearbook comprised two parts. The first part began as a harsh criticism of traditional education and its emphasis on subject matter, rote learning, drill, and mental discipline. It then became a synthesis of progressive practices and programs—the best and most innovative since the turn of the century—in public and private schools across the country. Part II has become a landmark text. It described the state of the art in curriculum making up to that period of time, and it included a consensual statement by the group on the nature of curriculum making. It is still relevant today.

The committee recognized the need for curriculum reform and the need for "those who are constructing our school curriculum" to determine "an overview . . . [and] orientation . . . to curriculum making."[90] With this idea in mind, the Yearbook outlined characteristics of the ideal curriculum—a curriculum that:

1. *Focuses on the affairs of human life.*
2. *Deals with the facts and problems of the local, national, and international community.*
3. *Enables students to think critically about various forms of government.*
4. *Informs and develops an attitude of open mindedness.*
5. *Considers student interests and needs as well as opportunities for debate, discussion, and exchange of ideas.*
6. *Deals with the issues of modern life and the cultural and historical aspects of society.*
7. *Considers problem-solving activities and practice in choosing alternatives.*
8. *Consists of carefully graded organization of problems and exercises.*
9. *Deals with humanitarian themes, and purposeful and constructive attitudes and insights.*[91]

This description of the ideal curriculum is basically one that might be developed today. The problems and issues identified by the committee are chiefly those that another curriculum committee could recognize as important for the 1990s.

In the same vein, Harold Rugg maintained that the people should formulate the aims and purposes of education through committees or legislative groups; the appropriate materials and methods of instruction "through which to achieve those aims and purposes [were] . . . technical . . . demanding special professional preparation." The role of trained curriculum specialists was to plan the curriculum in advance and to include four tasks (which were later to become the basis of Tyler's four principles): (1) "a statement of objectives, (2) a sequence of experiences [to achieve] the objectives, (3) subject matter found to be . . . the best means of engaging in the experiences, and (4) statements of immediate outcomes of achievements to be derived from the experiences." Rugg concluded that curriculum was adapting scientific methods and that there was need "for specialization and for professional . . . training."[92] Experienced teachers and specialists in curriculum making should work together to organize the content and materials within the various fields of subject matter—what many schools do today.

The Yearbook represented a tremendous advance in clarifying problems curriculum workers were encountering and in proposing procedures for the future in curriculum making. It had major

influence in many school districts (both large and small, as well as city, suburban, and rural), as illustrated by the plan that was later called "The Eight-Year Study," and by the ideas that Ralph Tyler and Hilda Taba expressed in their classic texts 20 and 30 years later.

Rugg and Caswell: The Development Period

During the late 1920s, the 1930s, and the early 1940s, a number of important books were published on curriculum principles and processes and on techniques for helping the teacher in curriculum making. Harold Rugg (1886–1960) the chairperson of the NSSE Yearbook, shared the faith of Bobbitt and Charters in a "science of curriculum." By training Rugg was an engineer, but, like Dewey, he had a broad view of curriculum that focused on the whole child and the way the child would grapple with the changing society. In this respect, Rugg was a progressive thinker as well as a forerunner of reconstructionism.

In 1928, Rugg and Shumaker coauthored their controversial text, *The Child-centered School.* In an era which stressed student input in planning the curriculum, the authors stressed the need for curriculum specialists to construct the curriculum.[83] They also stressed the role of the teacher in implementing the curriculum at the classroom and instructional level. Hence, the teacher needed to preplan; the idea of student input was rejected by Rugg, as was the idea of a curriculum based on the needs and interests of students. Such a curriculum would lack direction and logic. But the idea of a preplanned, fixed curriculum was antithetical to the progressive doctrine that was becoming more influential during this period. More in line with progressivism, however, Rugg advocated cooperation among educational professionals from different areas, including teachers, administrators, test experts, and curriculum specialists from various fields.

Rugg's attention in the 1930s and the 1940s shifted almost entirely to the integration of history, geography, civics, and economics—commonly called social studies. Some of his ideas about labor history and collectivism and his criticisms of American life, compounded by his activities with the teachers' union, resulted in a great deal of criticism from Establishment groups. Like Counts and Dewey, Rugg, too, had the distinction of having an FBI file.[94]

During the mid-1920s and 1930s, most school districts and state education departments were developing curriculum guides. However, the selection of methods and activities was left to the teachers. Hollis Caswell (1901–1989) was concerned that this practice was limited; he wanted to shift emphasis from formulating a course of study to improving instruction. He envisioned curriculum making as a means of helping teachers coordinate their instructional activities with subject matter and students' needs and interests. He considered courses of study as guides or sources that teachers could use to plan their daily work, but not as plans they should follow in detail. He sought to combine three major curriculum components: content, teacher's instruction, and student's learning.

Caswell attempted to assist teachers by providing a step-by-step procedure for curriculum making. He and his colleagues outlined seven points, in question form, that still have relevancy today:

1. *What is a curriculum?*
2. *Why is there need for curriculum revision?*
3. *What is the function of subject matter?*
4. *How do we determine educational objectives?*
5. *How do we organize curriculum?*
6. *How do we select subject matter?*
7. *How do we measure the outcomes of instruction?*[95]

Influenced by Bobbitt's definition of curriculum as "that series of things which children and youth must do and experience," Caswell and Campbell, in their classic text *Curriculum Development,* maintained that the curriculum must consider "all elements in the experience of the learner."[96] They thought curriculum should synthesize the fields of philosophy, psychology, and sociology—what other curricularists would later refer to as the foundations of curriculum. To a large extent, Caswell envisioned curriculum as a field with few limitations on content; rather, he thought curriculum represented a procedure or process that incorporated scientific steps of development, organization, instruction, and evaluation.

Caswell and Campbell believed that the curriculum must address three basic elements: children's interests, social functions, and organized knowledge. The curriculum was to provide the proper scope and sequence of subject matter at every grade level. The *scope* was to represent broad themes based on social functions (similar to educational aims), such as conservation of natural resources, worthy home membership, democratic living, and so on. The *sequence* was based on experiences according to the children's interests. *Subject matter* was suggested to match the social functions and the learner's interests; the knowledge that was taught was to be measured as outcomes of instruction.

Caswell and Campbell's book "became heavily prominent during the next two decades, almost becoming synonymous with curriculum study at large."[97] Their three elements of curriculum, as well as scope and sequence, heavily influenced Taba's book *Curriculum Development: Theory and Practice.* Their three foundations and elements of curriculum also influenced the classic textbook written by B. Othanel Smith and his colleagues, *Fundamentals of Curriculum Development.* Both textbooks served as bridges between Caswell and Campbell and many present curriculum textbooks (which stress foundations and principles of curriculum).

Eight Year Study. Although traditional subject matter and methods dominated the school curriculum, the progressive movement was still influential in certain parts of the country, particularly in Denver, St. Louis, and Winnetka. While most high schools implemented the mainstream curriculum, there were sharp criticism and outspoken differences among elementary school progressive educators. Most high school teachers and principals were reluctant to implement progressive changes because the curriculum was (as it is today) test driven and dominated by college admission requirements.[98]

The Progressive Education Association launched the "Eight Year Study," from 1932 to 1940, to show that a new curriculum designed to meet the needs and interests of students was just as effective as one designed around traditional tests and admission requirements to college. As many as 30 progressive or experimental high schools and 1,475 graduates were matched with corresponding schools and students from traditional college preparatory tracks. It was found that the experimental or progressive group did just as well as or better than the control or traditional group on cognitive, social, and psychological bases.

Despite the evidence suggesting that the progressive curriculum was as good or better for college preparation, the traditional academic program prevailed. Nevertheless, the study demonstrated the essential principles of curriculum making as purported by the Twenth-sixth Yearbook of the National Society for the Study of Education (NSSE). The study established a curriculum commission largely around the ideas of Rugg (and the Yearbook), and it led to several books; among the best known are those by Wilford Aiken and Harry Giles.[99] One major participant in the project was Giles's colleague Ralph Tyler. Many of Tyler's ideas, later to be published in *Basic Principles of Curriculum and Instruction,* stemmed from the principles and ideas generated by the Study (as well as the NSSE Yearbook).

Although the idea of stating objectives in behavioral terms had been introduced 20 years prior to the Study, it was this group of curriculum specialists that first introduced it on a national level; and, because of the visibility of the Study, it has remained a standard approach since. The Study group insisted on classifying or grouping objectives into homogeneous types or related categories. Tyler and Taba were both later to use this idea as a basis for classifying objectives into the (1) acquisition of knowledge, (2) intellectual skills, (3) attitudes and feelings, and (4) academic skills or study habits.[100] See Curriculum Tips 3-4.

Members of the Eight Year Study understood that education was designed to change people (an idea rooted in Dewey and Thorndike) and that objectives would classify the desired behavioral changes. It was further understood that the nature of objectives required an evaluation to determine whether the objectives had been achieved or to what extent. The Study confirmed the need for comprehensive evaluation, as part of curriculum making, including data on (1) *student achievement,* such as initial levels of mastery,

standardized tests, social and psychological skills, and creativity; (2) *social factors,* social class, peer group, community patterns, and motivational abilities; (3) *teaching-learning processes,* such as classroom management, homework assignments, and student-teacher interaction; and (4) *instructional methods,* such as discussions, demonstrations, problem solving, and discovery.

Taba worked on the evaluation team of the Study, along with Tyler, and later developed the idea of comprehensive evaluation in her work as chair of the ASCD's Commission on Evaluation in the 1940s and 1950s and in her classic text, *Curriculum Development: Theory and Practice,* in 1962. Tyler also played a key role in the evaluation of the Study, and some of his ideas were the basis of the evaluation component of the Study; they were further elaborated in his classic text, *Basic Principles of Curriculum and Instruction,* in 1949.

It later became apparent that the ideas of curriculum making developed by the Study did not filter down to the schools because teachers were not deeply involved in the curriculum. Most curriculum committees failed to include teachers, and restricted them to examining classroom textbooks and materials or modifying curriculum guides developed by central district offices. The exclusion of teachers from clarifying school goals and program objectives, organizing subject matter and learning activities, and participating in the evaluation process confirmed the traditional top-down practice of curriculum making of the period.

Tyler: Basic Principles

An account of curriculum as a field is not complete without discussion of Ralph Tyler, (1902-). Although Tyler published more than 700 articles and sixteen books (eleven of which are coauthored) on the subjects of curriculum, instruction, and evaluation, he is best known for his small book, *Basic Principles of Curriculum and Instruction.*[101] Originally written as a course syllabus for his students at the University of Chicago, the book was published in 1949; it has already gone through over thirty-five print-

Those in charge of formulating objectives should pay close attention in translating school goals into objectives. The process is twofold: (1) formulating objectives into subject areas and/or grade levels, often called program objectives, and (2) categorizing objectives into related categories or clusters. The example below, derived from the South Bend school district, involves elementary social studies and was developed during the era of the Eight Year Study. It includes three of four categories later advocated by Tyler and Taba as a method for grouping objectives. Most interesting, the objectives are still relevant today.

1. Children need to understand (knowledge):
   a. That all peoples of the world are in some way dependent on each other and must get along with each other.
   b. That our world is constantly changing.
   c. That events, discoveries, and inventions may improve some ways of living but create problems in others.
   d. That people have established communities and governments to meet their needs.
   e. That groups develop traditions, values, and ways of doing things, and new generations learn these from their elders.
   f. That the physical geography of a place affects way people live.
2. Children need to learn how (skills):
   a. To seek information from many sources and to judge its validity.
   b. To organize facts and form generalizations based on facts.
   c. To carry on a discussion based on facts and to make generalizations or conclusions.
   d. To plan, to carry out plans. and to evaluate the work and the planning.
   e. To accept responsibility as part of living.
   f. To develop a set of values for judging right and wrong actions.
3. Children need to become (attitudes):
   a. Willing to undertake and carry through a job to completion.
   b. Anxious to help others and to work with others for desirable group goals.
   c. Appreciative of others like and unlike themselves.

Source: For Our Time: A Handbook for Elementary Social Studies Teachers (South Bend, Ind.: School City of South Bend, 1949). pp. 229–230.

ings. It is, in fact, considered by some as a "mini-Bible" of curriculum.

In 128 pages, Tyler covers the basic questions that he believes should be answered by anyone involved in planning or writing a curriculum for any subject or grade level:

1. *What educational purposes should the school seek to attain?*
2. *What educational experiences can be provided that are likely to attain these purposes?*
3. *How can these educational experiences be effectively organized?*
4. *How can we determine whether these purposes are being attained?*[102]

Tyler was highly influenced by the progressive social theories of Judd and Dewey, as well as the learning theories of Thorndike and Piaget. He drew from the behaviorists, too, including Bobbitt and Charters. His philosophy and principles of curriculum were influenced by older contemporaries, such as George Counts (while Tyler was at the University of Chicago) and Boyd Bode (while he was at Ohio State University).

Not much in Tyler's model is new; we might consider it an elaboration of Rugg's four major tasks in curriculum and a condensed version of the NSSE's Twenty-Sixth Yearbook. One critic claims that "it clearly paraphrased, restated, and elaborated the position taken by the NSSE committee."[103] Others infer that the four questions and related discussions closely resemble the companion curriculum report, *Exploring the Curriculum,* submitted with "The Eight Year Study."[104] The model was not fully developed at that time, however; Tyler fully developed it later.

To some extent, also, Tyler's model can be considered an elaboration of an earlier work he did with Douglas Waples, when Tyler was at Ohio State University. In their publication, Tyler and Waples outlined the major elements in curriculum and instruction: (1) defining objectives, organizing content, and adopting materials; (2) selecting learning experiences and diagnosing learners; (3) managing students; and (4) outlining techniques of instruction and evaluation.[105]

Tyler, also, was highly influenced by Hilda Taba, his colleague for over 20 years at Ohio State and the University of Chicago. Tyler had a close professional relationship with Taba, and together they served on numerous research projects involving curriculum and evaluation. Because Taba's classic book on *Curriculum Development* was published several years after Tyler's book, most people think that Tyler influenced Taba. Actually, they influenced each other, but Tyler was the first to lay out four linear steps, which Taba further developed into seven linear steps.

The Tyler model depicts a rational, logical, and systematic approach to curriculum making. Although it embraces no philosophical or political bias in the sense that any subject can be organized around the model, its ideas are rooted in progressivism (it emphasizes the needs of the learner), scientific procedures (its principles are applicable in varying situations), and behaviorism (its objectives are the most important consideration, in Tyler's own words).

As the NSSE Yearbook put little emphasis on the teachers' role in curriculum making, Tyler said very little about the students' or the principals' roles. Although Tyler claims the book deals with principles and processes, the work is a "cookbook" approach to curriculum making. Nevertheless, the book is highly influential, because of its rational, no-nonsense, and sequential approach. In just over 100 pages, Tyler laid out a basic procedure to follow with easy-to-understand examples—different from the complex and cumbersome writings of other texts. Tyler gives students a manageable description, a series of concise steps, through which to plan curriculum.

Although critics have judged Tyler's model to be inadequate, naive, overly lockstep, and technocratic, and have censured it for its oversimplifying view of curriculum making as the collection of small bits of behavior,[106] it still works for many. Because it is simple to grasp, it serves as a starting point for curriculum students (which was its original intention). Remember that Tyler did not attempt anything more than to provide a basic guideline for students; his contemporaries inflated the significance of the book. When a treatise in social science becomes popular, as this one did, it becomes fair game for analysis and criticism by others in the field—as this one did as well.

Perhaps the most important reason Tyler is so influential is that he worked closely with a number of influential colleagues, besides Taba, such as Paul Diederich, Harold Dunkel, Maurice Hartung, Virgil Herrick, and Joseph Schwab, who accepted many of his ideas and who also influenced curriculum. In addition, many of Tyler's students at Ohio State University, such as Edgar Dale, Louis Heil, Louis Raths, and Harold Shane, and at the University of Chicago, such as Elliot Eisner, Ned Flanders, Thomas Hastings, David Krathwohl, Malcolm Provus, and Louise Tyler were influenced by Tyler and also became prominent in the field. Most important, a number of Tyler's other students, including Ben Bloom, Lee Cronbach, John Goodlad, Ken Rehage, Ole Sand, and Herbert Thelen, were also his colleagues for many years.[107] With the exception of Eisner, these colleagues continuously praised Tyler's work in the professional literature. Like Tyler, these men and women were (or are) known for their scientific assumptions, systematic procedures, and traditional views on education. See Table 3-5.

CURRENT FOCUS

The Tyler model, despite its criticism, summed up the best principles of curriculum making during the first half of the twentieth century. The model has been utilized and adapted by many

TABLE 3-5 Overview of Curriculum Theorists 1918–1949

THEORIST	PURPOSE	PRINCIPLES	CONTENT	MAJOR BOOK
Franklin Bobbitt (1876–1956)	Curriculum as a science; Emphasis on student needs; Prepare students for adult life; Clarify objectives; Cost-effective education	Grouping and sequencing objectives with corresponding activities; Clarifying instructional specifications and tasks	Basic three Rs in elementary schools; Academic subjects in high school; Subject matter and related activities planned by teacher	*The Curriculum,* 1918; *How to Make a Curriculum,* 1924
Werrett Charters (1875–1952)	Curriculum as a science; Emphasis on student needs (and needs assessment); Bridging theory and practice in curriculum	Curriculum process, described as job analysis; Listing of objectives and corresponding activities; Verification of objectives through evaluation	Subject matter related to objectives; Subject matter and corresponding activities planned by teacher	*Curriculum Construction,* 1923
William Kilpatrick (1871–1965)	School as a social and community experience; Curriculum identified as purposeful activities; Child-centered curriculum; Child development and growth	Project method, a blend of behaviorism and progressivism; Teacher and student planning, emphasis on the student; Emphasis on pedagogy or instructional activities: creative projects, social relationships, and small-group instruction	Educating a generalist, not a specialist; Integrated subject matter; Problem solving	*Foundations of Method,* 1926

Harold Rugg (1886–1960)	Education in context with society Child-centered curriculum Whole child Curriculum specialist as an engineer	Statement of objectives, related learning experiences, and outcomes Teacher plans curriculum in advance	Emphasis on social studies	*The Child Centered Curriculum* (with Ann Shumaker), 1928
Hollis Caswell (1901–1989)	Foundations of education (history, philosophy, etc.) influence curriculum development Relationship of three major components: curriculum, instruction, and learning Student needs and interests Curriculum organized around social functions (themes), organized knowledge, and learners' interests	Curriculum as a set of experiences Curriculum guides as a source of teacher planning Teachers coordinate instructional activities to implement curriculum	Subject matter organized in relation to student needs and interests Subject matter developed around social functions and learners' interests	*Curriculum Development* (with Doak Campbell), 1935
Ralph W. Tyler (1902–)	Curriculum as a science and extension of school's philosophy Clarify purposes (objectives) by studies of learners and contemporary life, suggestions from subject specialists, and use of philosophy and psychology Student needs and interests Relationship between curriculum and instruction	Curriculum as a rational process Using objectives to select and organize learning experiences Using evaluation to determine outcomes (whether objectives have been achieved) Vertical and horizontal relationship of curriculum	Subject matter organized in terms of knowledge, skills, and values Emphasis on problem solving Educating a generalist, not a specialist	*Basic Principles of Curriculum and Instruction*, 1949

curricularists, including some of Tyler's students, like Taba and Goodlad.[108] Although Tyler and his predecessors did a great deal toward outlining a science of curriculum, the major concepts and principles of the field remain ill-defined and open to dispute. According to Bruce Joyce, there are "no agreed upon concepts or modes which are known and used. . . . The curriculum field has no overarching 'metasystem,' known to most of its practitioners, which enables comparisons of and choices between all alternative approaches which are taken." In general, curriculum people still "do their own thing."[109]

On the other hand, Elliot Eisner points out that the "kind of science that has dominated educational research, . . . including [curriculum] development . . . uses knowledge provided by the social scientist as the primary bases for . . . management and control.[110] This has led to prescriptive models of curriculum and instruction, uniform methods of teaching and testing, and outcomes of learning that can be standardized and measured. This tendency toward scientific principles of curriculum making, and educational research in general, has resulted in nonexpressive and nonemotional forms of education, according to Eisner, and what he labels as "value-neutral," "technical," "cool," and "dispassionate objective."[111] The inference is that the Bobbitt-Tyler era, and its science of curriculum, has taken the joy, humor, and fun out of teaching and learning.

Although this analysis may be construed as an overstatement, especially by those who believe in behavioral, managerial, or systems approaches to curriculum, several curricularists today—like Mike Apple, Maxine Greene, Herb Kliebard, James Macdonald, Gail McCutcheon, and William Pinar—have lost faith in the ability of scientific principles and technical models to solve curriculum problems. Like Eisner, they have turned to various personal, esthetic, and linguistic concepts to formulate—or better yet, to reformulate—curriculum.

To some extent, the problem with curriculum is that its concepts and principles are abstract, not precise, and a good deal of subjectivity and inference is sometimes introduced in our curriculum discussions. Decker Walker feels that defining curriculum in abstract terms is a double-edged process: It "makes it harder to explain [its

concepts and principles] to a person unacquainted with curriculum, but gives the serious student of the subject a more flexible and powerful concept." If we are to engage in curriculum dialogue and try to "improve it," we will have "to attend to wide ranges of interrelated processes."[112] However, the more processes or relationships we introduce, the more complex our discussion and the more we fall victim to our imprecision. But, then, we can argue that so much of education is already vague and fuzzy— and why should curriculum or more precisely the history of curriculum be any different?

Even though we cannot agree on the concepts and principles of curriculum, much less on a science of curriculum making, the field of curriculum is expanding, and certain trends are taking shape. During the 1980s, the notion of global competition has resurfaced, along with the cry for tougher standards and educational productivity. The academic curriculum is also being expanded and upgraded, and the idea of academic excellence is once more being debated in educational circles. The notion of a fourth R—computer literacy for students—is also being seriously considered (the authors would introduce a fifth R as well—Spanish because of our country's ethnic population trends), along with a renewed emphasis on science, mathematics, and foreign languages.

The field of curriculum is also maturing. It is moving beyond schools and including programs in business, industry, military, government, and health fields. It is also incorporating many disciplines, such as philosophy, psychology, sociology, and politics. Finally, the field is developing an international character, and curriculum specialists are adapting the tools of research methodology, computers, instructional technology, and systems analysis. In short, curriculum as a field of study is becoming more interdisciplinary, scientific, and qualitative.

CONCLUSION

From the colonial period to around World War I, curriculum was a matter of evolving subject matter. Some reform ideas concerned pedagogical principles, mainly as a result of European influence and the emerging progressive reform move-

ment of the mid and late nineteenth century. But these ideas were limited to theoretical discussions and a few isolated and innovative schools. The perennialist curriculum, which emphasized the classics and timeless and absolute values based around religious and then moral doctrines, remained dominant for the first 150 years of our nation's history.

The idea of principles and processes of curriculum began to take shape after the turn of the twentieth century, along with emphasis on scientific principles and progressive philosophy. Curriculum as a field of study, with its own methods and theories and ways of solving problems, has made real advances ever since the 1920s. Most of the advances have actually taken place since Tyler wrote his basic text on curriculum. Many of these advances are discussed elsewhere in this text.

ENDNOTES

1. John S. Brubacher, *A History of the Problems of Education* (New York: McGraw-Hill, 1947); R. Freeman Butts and Lawrence A. Cremin, *A History of Education in American Culture* (New York: Holt, Rinehart and Winston, 1953).

2. Warren H. Button and Eugene Provenzo, *History of Education and Culture in America*, 2nd ed. (Englewood Cliffs, N.J.: Prentice Hall, 1989); Butts and Cremin, *A History of Education in American Culture*.

3. George A. Beauchamp, *The Curriculum of the Elementary School* (Boston: Allyn and Bacon, 1964), p. 34.

4. Allan C. Ornstein and Daniel U. Levine, *An Introduction to the Foundations of Education*, 5th ed. (Boston: Houghton Mifflin, 1993), p. 161. See also S. Alexander Rippa, *Education in a Free Society*, 7th ed. (New York: Longman, 1992).

5. Beauchamp, *The Curriculum of the Elementary School*, p. 36.

6. Paul Monroe, *Founding of the American Public School System* (New York: Macmillan, 1940); Samuel E. Morrison, *The Intellectual Life of Colonial New England* (New York: New York University Press, 1956).

7. Robert Middlekauff, *Ancients and Axioms: Secondary Education in the Eighteenth-Century New England* (New Haven, Conn.: Yale University Press, 1963).

8. Elmer E. Brown, *The Making of Our Middle School* (New York: Longman, 1926), p. 133.

9. Newton Edwards and Herman G. Richey, *The School in the American Social Order*, 2nd ed. (Boston: Houghton Mifflin, 1963), p. 102.

10. Morrison, *The Intellectual Life of Colonial New England*. Joel Spring, *The American School: 1642–1990* (New York: Longman, 1990).

11. John H. Best, *Benjamin Franklin on Education* (New York: Teachers College Press, Columbia University, 1962).

12. Ellwood P. Cubberley, *Public Education in the United States*, rev. ed. (Boston: Houghton Mifflin, 1947), p. 30.

13. R. Freeman Butts, *The American Tradition in Religion and Education* (Boston: Beacon Press, 1950); Gerald R. Firth and Richard D. Kimpston, *The Curricular Continuum in Perspective* (Itasca, Ill.: Peacock, 1973).

14. Paul L. Ford, *The New England Primer: A History of Its Origins and Development*, rev. ed. (New York: Dodd, Mead, 1897), pp. 329–330.

15. Henry Barnard, *Educational Developments in the United States* (Hartford, Conn.: Connecticut Department of Education, 1867), p. 367.

16. Cubberley, *Public Education in the United States;* Merle Curti, *The Social Ideas of American Educators* (New York: Littlefield, Adams, 1959).

17. Benjamin Rush, *A Plan for the Establishment of Public Schools* (Philadelphia: Thomas Dobson, 1786), pp. 29–30.

18. Thomas Jefferson, "A Bill for the More General Diffusion of Knowledge," in P. L. Ford, ed., *The Writings of Thomas Jefferson* (New York: Putnam, 1893), p. 221.

19. Merle Curti, *The Growth of American Thought*, rev. ed. (New York: Harper & Row, 1951).

20. Hans Kohn, *American Nationalism: An Interpretive Essay* (New York: Macmillan, 1957), p. 47.

21. Noah Webster, *Dissertations on the English Language* (Boston: Isaiah Thomas, 1789), p. 27.

22. Harvey R. Warfel, *Noah Webster: Schoolmaster to America* (New York: Macmillan, 1936).

23. Henry Steele Commager, ed., *Noah Webster's American Spelling Book* (New York: Teachers College Press, Columbia University, 1962).

24. Robert K. Leavitt, *Noah's Ark, New England Yankees and the Endless Quest* (Springfield, Mass.: Merriam, 1947); Richard M. Rollins, "Words as Social Control: Noah Webster and the Creation of the Amer-

ican Dictionary," *American Quarterly* (Fall 1976), pp. 415–430.

25. William H. McGuffey, *New Fifth Eclectic Reader* (Cincinnati: Winthrop Smith, 1857), p. 271.

26. William H. McGuffey, *Newly Revised Eclectic Fourth Reader* (Cincinnati: Winthrop Smith, 1853), p. 313.

27. John H. Westerhoff, *McGuffey and His Readers: Piety, Morality, and Education in Nineteenth Century America* (Nashville, Tenn.: Abingdon, 1978).

28. William B. Ragan and Gene D. Shepherd, *Modern Elementary Curriculum,* 7th ed. (New York: Holt, Rinehart and Winston, 1992), p. 23.

29. Edgar W. Knight, *Education in the United States,* 3rd ed. (Boston: Ginn, 1951), p. 512.

30. See Henry Barnard, *Pestalozzi and Pestalozzianism* (New York: Brownell, 1862).

31. Friedrich Froebel, *The Education of Man,* trans. W. Hailman (New York: Appleton, 1889).

32. Johann F. Herbart, *Textbook of Psychology* (New York: Appleton, 1894).

33. John Dewey, *How We Think* (Boston: D. C. Heath, 1910), p. 202.

34. Andreas Kazamias, *Herbert Spencer on Education* (New York: Teachers College Press, Columbia University, 1966).

35. Herbert Spencer, *Education: Intellectual, Moral and Physical* (New York: Appleton, 1860).

36. Michael W. Apple, "The Politics of Official Knowledge in the United States," *Journal of Curriculum Studies* (July–August 1990), pp. 377–383.

37. See Everett Dick, *Vanguards of the Frontier* (New York: Appleton-Century, 1940); William W. Folwell, *The Autobiography and Letters of a Pioneer Culture* (Minneapolis: University of Minnesota Press, 1923).

38. Joel Spring, *The Storting Machine Revisited* (New York: Longman, 1989).

39. Button and Provenzo, *History of Education and Culture in America;* Monroe, *Founding of the American Public School System.*

40. Frederick M. Binder, *The Age of the Common School: 1830–1865* (New York: Wiley, 1974).

41. V. T. Thayer and Martin Levit, *The Role of the School in American Society,* 2nd ed. (New York: Dodd, Mead, 1966), p. 6.

42. Lawrence A. Cremin, *The Republic and the School: Horace Mann on the Education of Free Man* (New York: Teachers College Press, Columbia University Press, 1957); Jonathan Messerlie, *Horace Mann: A Biography* (New York: Knopf, 1972).

43. Andrew Gulliford, *America's Country Schools* (Washington, D.C.: National Trust for Historic Preservation, 1985).

44. James H. Hughes, *Education in America,* 3rd ed. (New York: Harper & Row, 1970), p. 233.

45. Carl Sandburg, *Abraham Lincoln: The Prairie Years* (New York: Harcourt, Brace, 1926), p. 19.

46. Theodore R. Sizer, *The Age of Academies* (New York: Teachers College Press, Columbia University, 1964).

47. E. P. Cubberley, *The History of Education* (Boston: Houghton Mifflin, 1920), p. 697.

48. Edwards and Richey, *The School in the American Social Order;* Firth and Kimpston, *The Curricular Continuum in Perspective.*

49. Brown, *The Making of Our Middle Schools,* p. 230.

50. Monroe, *Founding of the American Public School System,* p. 404.

51. Edward A. Krug, *The Shaping of the American High School: 1880–1920* (New York: Harper & Row, 1964); Daniel Tanner, *Secondary Education: Perspectives and Prospects* (New York: Macmillan, 1972).

52. Cubberley, *Public Education in the United States;* Edwards and Richey, *The School in the American Social Order;* and Monroe, *Founding of the American Public School System.*

53. Davis, *Our Evolving High School Curriculum;* David H. Kamens and Yun-Kyung Cha, "The Legitimation of New Subjects in Mass Schooling," *Journal of Curriculum Studies* (January–February 1992), pp. 43–60.

54. Krug, *The Shaping of the American High School.*

55. John H. Bishop, "The Productivity Consequences of What Is Learned in High School," *Journal of Curriculum Studies* (March–April 1990), pp. 101–126; Kamens and Cha, "The Legatimation of New Subjects in Mass Schooling."

56. Thayer and Levit, *The Role of the School in American Society,* p. 382.

57. *Report of the Year 1889–90* (Washington, D.C.: U.S. Bureau of Education, 1893), pp. 1388–1389. See also Table 3–2.

58. Cubberley, *Public Education in the United States,* p. 543.

59. Paul Gagnon, *Historical Literacy: The Case of History in American Education;* Robert S. Zais, *Curriculum: Principles and Foundations* (New York: Harper & Row, 1976).

60. *Report of the Committee of Ten on Secondary School Studies,* book ed. (New York: American Book, 1894), p. 48.

61. Daniel Tanner and Laurel Tanner, *Curriculum Development: Theory into Practice,* 2nd ed. (New York: Macmillan, 1980), p. 233. See also Richard Pratte, *The Civic Imperative* (New York: Teachers College Press, Columbia University Press, 1988).

62. Edward L. Thorndike, "Mental Discipline in High School Studies," *Journal of Educational Psychology* (February 1924), p. 98.

63. Charles W. Eliot, "The Case against Compulsory Latin," *Atlantic* (March 1917), pp. 356–359.
64. Abraham Flexner, "Parents and School," *Atlantic* (July 1916), p. 30.
65. Abraham Flexner, "A Modern School," *Occasional Papers,* No. 3 (New York: General Education Board, 1916); Flexner, *A Modern College and a Modern School* (New York: Doubleday, 1923).
66. John Dewey, *Democracy and Education* (New York: Macmillan, 1916).
67. Ibid., p. 190.
68. Charles H. Judd, *Introduction to the Scientific Study of Education* (Boston: Ginn, 1918).
69. Commission on the Reorganization of Secondary Education, *Cardinal Principles of Secondary Education,* Bulletin No. 35 (Washington, D.C.: U.S. Government Printing Office, 1918).
70. Frederick W. Taylor, *The Principles of Scientific Management* (New York: Harper & Row, 1911).
71. Raymond E. Callahan, *Education and the Cult of Efficiency* (Chicago: University of Chicago Press, 1962).
72. Franklin Bobbitt, *The Curriculum* (Boston: Houghton Mifflin, 1918), p. 42.
73. Ibid., p. 283.
74. Franklin Bobbitt, *How to Make a Curriculum* (Boston: Houghton Mifflin, 1924), pp. 14, 28.
75. Elliot W. Eisner, *The Educational Imagination,* 3rd ed. (New York: Macmillan, 1993); Herbert Kliebard, *The Struggle for the American Curriculum: 1893–1951* (Boston: Routledge, 1986).
76. W. W. Charters, *Curriculum Construction* (New York: Macmillan, 1923).
77. Ibid., pp. 6–7. See also W. W. Charters, "Idea Men and Engineers in Education," *Educational Forum* (Spring 1986), pp. 263–272. Originally published in *Educational Forum* (May 1948), pp. 399–406.
78. John Dewey, "Individuality and Experience," in J. Dewey, ed., *Art and Education* (Marion, Pa.: Barnes Foundation, 1929), p. 180.
79. William H. Kilpatrick, "The Project Method," *Teachers College Record* (September 1918), pp. 319–335.
80. Junius L. Merian, *Child Life and the School Curriculum* (New York: World Book, 1920).
81. Ellsworth Collings, *An Experiment with a Project Curriculum* (New York: Macmillan, 1923).
82. Boyd Bode, *Modern Educational Theories* (New York: Macmillan, 1927); John L. Childs, *Education and the Philosophy of Experimentalism* (New York: Appleton, 1931).
83. William H. Kilpatrick, *Foundations of Education* (New York: Macmillan, 1926), p. 212.
84. Ibid., p. 213.
85. John McNeil, *Curriculum: A Comprehensive Introduction* (Glenview, Ill.: Scott, Foresman, 1990); Tanner and Tanner, *Curriculum Development.*
86. William H. Kilpatrick, ed., *The Educational Frontier* (New York: Century, 1933), pp. 4–5.
87. Ibid., p. 19
88. Ellsworth Collings, *Project Teaching in Elementary Schools* (New York: Century, 1928).
89. Guy M. Whipple, ed., *Curriculum-Making: Past and Present,* Twenty-Sixth Yearbook of the National Society for the Study of Education, Part I (Bloomington, Ill.: Public School Publishing Co., 1930; Whipple, ed., *The Foundations of Curriculum-Making,* Twenty-Sixth Yearbook of the National Society for the Study of Education, Part II (Bloomington, Ill.: Public School Publishing Co., 1930).
90. Harold Rugg, "Forward," in Whipple, ed., *Curriculum-Making: Past and Present,* p. 1.
91. Harold Rugg, "The School Curriculum and the Drama of American Life," in Whipple, ed., *Curriculum-Making: Past and Present,* pp. 3–16.
92. Harold Rugg, "Three Decades of Mental Discipline: Curriculum-Making via National Committees," in Whipple, ed., *Curriculum-Making: Past and Present,* pp. 52–53.
93. Harold Rugg and Ann Shumaker, *The Child-Centered School* (New York: World Book, 1928), p. 118.
94. David Pratt, *Curriculum: Design and Development* (New York: Harcourt, Brace, 1980). Also see Henry J. Perkinson, *The Imperfect Panacea: American Faith in Education, 1865–1990,* 3rd ed. (New York: McGraw-Hill, 1991).
95. Sidney B. Hall, D. W. Peters, and Hollis L. Caswell, *Study Course for Virginia State Curriculum* (Richmond: Virginia State Board of Education, 1932), p. 363.
96. Hollis L. Caswell and Doak S. Campbell, *Curriculum Development* (New York: American Book, 1935), p. 69.
97. William H. Schubert, *Curriculum Books: The First Eighty Years* (Lanham, Md.: University Press, 1980), p. 77. See also Schubert, *Curriculum: Perspective, Paradigm, and Possibility* (New York: Macmillan, 1986).
98. Ralph W. Tyler, "Curriculum Development in the Twenties and Thirties," in R. M. McClure, ed., *The Curriculum: Retrospect and Prospect,* Seventieth Yearbook of the National Society for the Study of Education, Part I (Chicago: University of Chicago Press, 1971), pp. 26–44; Tyler, "The Five Most Significant Curriculum Events in the Twentieth Century," *Educational Leadership* (December–January 1987), pp. 36–38. Also see Louis Rubin, "Educational Evaluation: Classic Works of Ralph W. Tyler," *Journal of Curriculum Studies* (March–April 1991). pp. 193–198.

99. Wilford Aiken, *The Story of the Eight Year Study* (New York: Harper & Row, 1942); H. H. Giles, S. P. McCutchen, and A. N. Zechiel, *Exploring the Curriculum* (New York: Harper & Row, 1942).

100. Hilda Taba, "Evaluation in High Schools and Junior Colleges," in W. S. Gray, ed., *Reading in Relation to Experience and Language* (Chicago: University of Chicago Press, 1944), pp. 199–204; Taba, *Curriculum Development: Theory and Practice* (New York: Harcourt, Brace, 1962); Ralph W. Tyler, *Basic Principles of Curriculum and Instruction* (Chicago: University of Chicago Press, 1949); and E. R. Smith and Ralph W. Tyler, eds., *Appraising and Recording Student Progress* (New York: Harper & Row, 1942).

101. Ralph W. Tyler, *Basic Principles of Curriculum and Instruction* (Chicago: University of Chicago Press, 1949).

102. Ibid., p. 1.

103. Pratt, *Curriculum: Design and Development*, p. 34.

104. Tanner and Tanner, *Curriculum Development: Theory into Practice.*

105. Douglas Waples and Ralph W. Tyler, *Research Methods and Teachers' Problems: A Manual for Systematic Studies of Classroom Procedure* (New York: Macmillan, 1930).

106. Henry Giroux, *Teachers as Intellectuals* (Westport, Conn.: Bergin & Garvey, 1988); Herbert M. Kliebard, "Reappraisal: the Tyler Rationale," in A. A. Bellack and H. M. Kliebard, eds., *Curriculum and Evaluation* (Berkeley, Calif.: McCutchen, 1977), pp. 34–69; and James T. Sears and J. Dan Marshall, eds., *Teaching and Thinking About Curriculum* (New York: Teachers College Press, Columbia University, 1990).

107. Marie K. Stone, *Principles of Curriculum, Instruction, and Evaluation: Past Influence and Present Effects.* Ph.D. dissertation, Loyola University of Chicago, January 1985. Also from conversations by one of the authors with John Beck, April 12, 1991.

108. Taba, *Curriculum Development: Theory and Practice*; John I. Goodlad et al., *Curriculum Inquiry: The Study of Curriculum Practice* (New York: McGraw-Hill, 1979).

109. Bruce R. Joyce, "The Curriculum Worker of the Future," in R. M. McClure, ed., *The Curriculum: Retrospect and Prospect,* Seventieth Yearbook of the National Society for the Study of Education, Part I (Chicago: University of Chicago Press, 1971), pp. 312–313.

110. Eisner, *The Educational Imagination,* pp. 17–18.

111. Ibid., p. 20. Also see Elliot W. Eisner and Alan Peshkin, eds., *Qualitative Inquiry in Education* (New York: Teachers College Press, Columbia University, 1990).

112. Decker Walker, *Fundamentals of Curriculum* (San Diego, Calif.: Harcourt, Brace, 1990), pp. 6–7.

CHAPTER 4

PSYCHOLOGICAL FOUNDATIONS
OF CURRICULUM

Focusing Questions

1. *What are the main differences between the three major theories of learning?*
2. *How can these learning theories be applied to curriculum planning?*
3. *How can traditional S-R behavior be differentiated from operant behavior?*
4. *What are the various steps involved in problem solving?*
5. *How would you define creativity?*
6. *What constitutes humanistic learning in schools?*
7. *How do we organize the classroom so as to promote valuing?*
8. *To what extent does cooperative learning promote academic achievement? Hinder academic achievement?*

How do people learn? Psychology is concerned with this question. Curriculum specialists, however, ask, How does psychology contribute to curriculum? Psychology provides a basis for understanding the teaching and learning process. As long as teaching and learning are important considerations for curriculum specialists, then psychology will be important as well. Other questions that interest psychologists and curriculum specialists are: Why do learners respond as they do to the efforts of the teachers? How should the curriculum be organized to enhance learning?

Teaching and learning are interrelated, and psychology cements the relationship; it provides the theories and principles that influence teacher-student behavior within the context of the curriculum. For John Dewey, psychology was the basis for understanding how the individual learner interacts with objects and persons in the environment. The process goes on for life, and the quality of interaction determines the amount and type of learning. Ralph Tyler considered psychology to be a "screen" for helping determine what our objectives are and how our learning takes place.[1] More recently, Jerome Bruner linked psychology with modes of thinking that underlie the methods employed in various bodies of knowledge comprising specific disciplines. The goal of utilizing these methods is to formulate concepts, principles, and generalizations that form the structure of the disciplines.[2] In short, psychology is the unifying element of the learning process; it forms the basis for the methods, materials, and activities of learning, and it subsequently serves as the impetus for many curriculum decisions.

Historically, the major theories of learning have been classified into three groups: (1) behaviorist or association theories, the oldest one of which deals with various aspects of stimulus-response and reinforcers; (2) cognitive-information processing theories, which view the learner in relationship to the total environment and consider the way the learner applies information; and (3) phenomenological and humanistic theories, which consider the whole child, including his or her social, psychological and cognitive development. When behaviorist theories are discussed separately, learning tends to focus on conditioning, modifying, or shaping behavior through reinforcement and rewards. When cognitive information processing theories are stressed,

107

the learning process focuses on the student's developmental stages and multiple forms of intelligence, as well as problem solving, critical thinking, and creativity. The phenomenological aspects of learning deal with needs, attitudes, and feelings of the learner and entail more alternatives in learning.

BEHAVIORISM

The behaviorists, who represent traditional psychology, are rooted in philosophical speculation about the nature of learning—the ideas of Aristotle, Descartes, Locke, and Rousseau. They emphasize conditioning behavior and altering the environment to elicit selected responses from the learner. This theory has dominated twentieth-century psychology, especially during the first half of the century; it has recently returned as a major school to explain the learning process.

Connectionism

One of the first Americans to conduct experimental testing of the stimulus-response (or classical conditioning) idea was Edward Thorndike. At Harvard, Thorndike began his work with animals, a course of experimentation other behaviorists adopted as well.[3] Thorndike defined learning as habit formation—as connecting more and more habits into a complex structure. He defined teaching, then, as arranging the classroom so as to enhance desirable connections as bonds.

Thorndike developed three major laws of learning: (1) the *Law of Readiness*—when a "conduction" unit is ready to conduct, to do so is satisfying and not to do so is annoying; (2) the *Law of Exercise*—a connection is strengthened in proportion to the number of times it occurs, and in proportion to average intensity and duration; and (3) the *Law of Effect*—responses accompanied by satisfaction are important for strengthening the connection; conversely, responses accompanied by discomfort weaken the connection.[4]

The Law of Readiness suggests that, when the nervous system is ready to conduct, it leads to a satisfying state of affairs; this has been misinterpreted by some educators as referring to educational readiness, such as readiness to read. The Law of Exercise provides justification for drill, repetition, and review and is best illustrated today by behavioral modification and basic-skill instructional approaches. Although rewards and punishments were used in schools for centuries prior to Thorndike's formulation of the Law of Effect, his theory did make more explicit and furnished justification for what was already being done. B. F. Skinner's operant model of behavior, programmed instruction, and many current ideas based on providing satisfying experiences to the learner, as well as reinforcement in the form of feedback, are rooted in this law.

Thorndike maintained that (1) behavior was influenced more likely by conditions of learning; (2) attitudes and abilities of learners could change (and improve) over time through proper stimuli; (3) instructional experiences could be designed and controlled; and (4) it was important to select appropriate stimuli or learning experiences that were integrated and consistent—and that reinforced each other. For Thorndike, no one subject was more likely than another to improve the mind; rather, learning was a matter of relating new learning to previous learning. Thus, the "psychology" of mental discipline was attacked, and this attack meant that there was no hierarchy of subject matter.

Although connectionism no longer enjoys the wide appeal it once had in the schools, practices related to it continue under different behaviorist labels. And even though Thorndike's model of learning has minimal direct influence today, many of his assumptions related to learning are evident nonetheless.

Thorndike's Influence: Tyler, Taba, and Bruner

Coinciding with Thorndike's (1874–1949) theories, both Tyler and Taba maintained that learning had application and thus could be transferred to other situations.[5] This meant that rote learning and memorization of knowledge were unnecessary. The student could organize and classify information into existing mental schemata or patterns and use it in different situations. Much of Thorndike's theories of learning impacted on the behaviorist and logical approach outlined by

Tyler and Taba. However, both Tyler and Taba disagreed with Thorndike's view of connections between specific stimuli and specific responses. Rather, they outlined a more generalized view of learning, one that more closely corresponds with a cognitive approach. Whereas Bobbitt and Charters opted for the more precise behavioral approach to learning, along Thorndike's lines, which viewed objectives in context with highly specific habits to be acquired, Tyler and Taba were inclined to take Dewey's and Judd's approach: That learning was based on *generalizations* and the teaching of important *principles* (terms used by the latter four educators) to explain concrete phenomena.[6]

Note that both Tyler and Taba gave credit to Thorndike in their classic texts. Tyler's recognition of Thorndike was minimal; nevertheless, he spent considerable space discussing connectionism and organizing learning principles along Thorndike's transfer theories. Taba devoted an entire chapter to "the transfer of learning," as well as the influence that Thorndike and others had on this learning theory. Like Thorndike, Taba argued that practice alone does not necessarily strengthen memory or the transfer of learning, which served to free the curriculum from the rigid roteness and drill of the past. "Since no program, no matter how thorough, can teach everything, the task of all education is to cause a maximum amount of transfer."[7] The idea was to develop content or methods that led to generalizations and that had wide transfer value; this led to Taba's advocating problem-solving and inquiry-discovery techniques.

The notions of "learning how to learn" and "inquiry discovery," although popularized by Bruner, are rooted in Thorndike. Thorndike, and later Bruner, assumed that learning that involves meaningful organization of experiences can be transferred more readily than learning acquired by rote.[8] The more abstract the principles and generalizations, the greater the possibility of transfer. (This also corresponds with Dewey's idea of reflective thinking and the steps that he outlined for problem solving.)

For Bruner, learning the structure of a discipline provided the basis for the specific transfer of learning. The abilities to learn and to recall and use some information later are directly related to the learner's having a structural pattern by which information can be transferred to new situations. Transfer of learning is much more frequent when learning is of a basic, general nature. One difference between Thorndike and Bruner should be noted, however. Whereas Thorndike found that no one subject was more important than another subject for meaningful learning, Bruner gave great emphasis to science and mathematics as the major disciplines for teaching structure. In this context, Thorndike was more progressive than Bruner—he gave equal weight and equal importance to various subjects—and he broke from traditional thinking about the hierarchy of subject matter.

Classical Conditioning

The classical conditioning theory of learning emphasizes that learning consists of eliciting a response by means of previously neutral or inadequate stimuli; some neutral stimulus associated with an unconditioned stimulus at the time of response gradually acquires the ability to elicit the response. The classical conditioning experiment by Ivan Pavlov is widely known. In this experiment, a dog learned to salivate at the sound of a bell. The bell, a biologically neutral or inadequate stimulus, was being presented simultaneously with food, a biologically nonneutral or adequate stimulus. So closely were the two stimuli associated by the dog that the bell came to be substituted for the food, and the dog reacted to the bell as he originally had to the food.[9]

The implications for human learning were important. Some neutral stimulus (bell) associated with an unconditioned stimulus (food) at the time of the response gradually acquired the association to elicit the response (salivation). The theory has led to a wealth of laboratory investigations about learning and has become a focal point in social and political discussions—for example, Aldous Huxley's futuristic novel *Brave New World* and the movies *The Deer Hunter, Jacob's Ladder,* and *Silence of the Lambs.*

On the American scene, James Watson used Pavlov's research as a foundation for building a new science of psychology based on behaviorism. The new science emphasized that learning was based on the science of behavior, what was observable or measurable, and not on cognitive processes. The laws of behavior were derived from animal and then human studies and were expected to have all the objectivity of the laws of science.[10]

For Watson and others, the key to learning was to condition the child in the early years of life, based on the method Pavlov had demonstrated for animals. Thus, Watson once boasted:

> *Give me a dozen healthy infants, well-informed, and my own specified world to bring them up and I'll guarantee to take anyone at random and train him to be any type of specialist I might select—a doctor, lawyer, artist . . . and yes, even into beggarman and thief, regardless of his talents, . . . abilities, vocations, and race.*[11]

Operant Conditioning

Perhaps more than any other recent behaviorist, B. Frederick Skinner attempted to apply his theories to the classroom situation. Basing a major part of his theories on experiments with mice and pigeons, Skinner distinguishes two kinds of responses: *elicited*, a response identified with a definite stimulus, and *emitted*, a response that is apparently unrelated to an identifiable stimulus. When a response is elicited, the behavior is termed *respondent*. When it is emitted, the behavior is *operant*—that is, no observable or measurable stimuli explain the appearance of the response.[12] In operant conditioning, the role of stimuli is less definite; often, the emitted behavior cannot be connected to a specific stimulus.

Reinforcers can be classified, also, as primary, secondary, or generalized. A *primary* reinforcer applies to any stimulus that helps satisfy a basic drive, such as for food, water, or sex. (This reinforcer is also paramount in classical conditioning.) A *secondary* reinforcer is important for people, such as getting approval from friends or teachers, receiving money, or winning school awards. Although secondary reinforcers do not satisfy primary drives, they can be converted into primary reinforcers. Because of the choice and range of secondary reinforcers, Skinner refers to them as *generalized* reinforcers. Classroom teachers have a variety of secondary reinforcers

at their disposal, ranging from words of praise or smiles to words of admonishment or punishment.

Operant behavior will discontinue when it is not followed by reinforcement. Skinner classifies reinforcers as positive or negative. A *positive* reinforcer is simply the presentation of a reinforcing stimulus. A student receives positive reinforcement when a test paper is returned with a grade of A or a note that says "Keep up the good work." A *negative* reinforcement is the removal or withdrawal of a stimulus. When the teacher shouts to the class, "Keep quiet," and the students quiet down, the students' silence reinforces the teacher's shouting. Punishment, on the other hand, calls for the presentation of unpleasant or harmful stimuli or the withdrawal of a (positive) reinforcer, but it is not always a negative reinforcer.[13] Although Skinner believes in both positive and negative reinforcement, he rejects punishment because he feels it inhibits learning. He maintains that a considerable amount of teaching and learning is based on punitive procedures and faulty reinforcement—a practice that has led to disappointing results.[14]

Acquiring New Operants

Skinner's approach of selective reinforcement, whereby only desired responses are reinforced, has wide appeal to educators because he has demonstrated its application to the instructional and learning process. An essential principle in the reinforcement interpretation of learning is the variability of human behavior, which makes change possible. Individuals can acquire *new operants*—that is, behavior can be shaped or modified and complex concepts can be taught to students. The individual's capability for the desired response is what makes the shaping of behavior or the learning possible. Behavior and learning can be shaped through a series of successive approximations or a sequence of responses that increasingly approximate the desired one. Thus, through a combination of reinforcing and sequencing desired responses, new behavior is shaped; this is what some people today refer to as *behavioral modification.*

Although behavioral modification approaches vary according to the student and the behavior being sought, they are widely used in conjunction with individualized-instructional techniques, programmed learning, and classroom management techniques. Student activities are specified, structured, paced, reinforced, rewarded, and frequently assessed in terms of learning outcomes or behaviors desired. With this approach, curriculum may be defined by Popham and Baker's definition: "all planned outcomes for which the school is responsible" and "the desired consequences of instruction."[15]

Observational Learning and Modeling.   Albert Bandura has contributed extensively to what we know today about how students learn through observation and modeling. In a classic study, he showed how aggressive behavior can be learned from viewing human adults acting agressively in real situations as well as in films and cartoons. The same children also learned nonaggressive behavior by observing humans of subdued temperaments.[16]

The repeated demonstration that people can learn and have their behavior shaped by observing another person or even film (obviously, the influence of TV is immense) has tremendous implications for modifying tastes and attitudes, how we learn and perform, or whether we want to develop soldiers or artists. For behaviorists, the idea suggests that cognitive factors are unnecessary in explaining learning; through modeling, students can learn how to perform at sophisticated levels of performance. While recognizing the value of reinforcement and reward, the learner needs mainly to attend and acquire the necessary responses through observation and then to model the behavior later. See Curriculum Tips 4-1. Coaches in various sports and instructors in military settings make use of this type of instruction; teachers who use coaching techniques should find the modeling concept and specific tips useful.

Hierarchical Learning.   Robert Gagné has presented a hierarchical arrangement of eight types of learning sets or behaviors that has become a classic model. The first five may be defined as behavioral operations, the next two as both behavioral and cognitive, and the last (and highest form of thinking) as cognitive in nature. The behaviors are based on prerequisite conditions, resulting in a cumulative process of learning. The eight types of learning and examples of each follow:

1. *Signal learning* (classical conditioning, a response to a given signal). Example: Fear response to a rat.
2. *Stimulus response* (operant conditioning [S-R], a response to a given stimulus). Example: Student's response to the command, "Please sit."
3. *Motor chains* (linking together two or more S-R connections to form a more complex skill). Example: Dotting the i and crossing the t to write a word with an i and t.
4. *Verbal associations* (linking together two or more words or ideas). Example: Translating a foreign word.
5. *Multiple discriminations* (responding in different ways to different items of a particular set). Example: Discriminating between grass and trees.
6. *Concepts* (reacting to stimuli in an abstract way). Examples: animals, grammar, and so on.
7. *Rules* (chaining two or more stimulus situations or concepts). Examples: Animals have offspring. An adjective modifies a noun.
8. *Problem solving* (combining known rules or principles into new elements to solve a problem). Example: Finding the area of a triangle given the dimensions of two sides.[17]

Gagné also describes five learning outcomes that can be observed and measured and for him encompass all the domains of learning: (1) *intellectual skills,* "knowing how" to categorize and use verbal and mathematical symbols, forming concepts through rules, and problem solving; (2) *information,* which can be described as "knowing what," knowledge about facts, names, and dates; (3) *cognitive strategies,* skills needed to process and organize information, what today is called "learning strategies" or "learning skills"; (4) *motor skills,* the ability to coordinate movements, including simple muscle movements and complex movements, which comes with practice and coaching; and (5) *attitudes,* feelings and emotions learned through positive and negative experiences.[18]

CURRICULUM TIPS 4-1 Behaviorism in Classroom Learning Situations

A wide range of behaviors can be used when applying behavioral theories in the classroom. These suggestions have meaning for behaviorist teaching and learning situations.

1. Consider that behavior is the result of particular conditions; alter conditions to achieve desired behaviors.
2. Use reinforcement and rewards to strengthen the behavior you wish to encourage.
3. Consider extinction or forgetting by reducing the frequency of undesirable behaviors.
4. Reduce undesirable behaviors as follows:
   a. Withhold reinforcement or ignore the behavior.
   b. Call attention to rewards that will follow the desired behavior.
   c. Take away a privilege or resort to punishment.
5. When students are learning factual material, provide frequent feedback; for abstract or complex material, provide delayed feedback.
6. Provide practice, drill, and review exercises; monitor learners' progress.
7. Consider workbooks, programmed materials, and computer programs that rely on sequenced approaches.
8. When students struggle with uninteresting material, use special reinforcers and rewards to motivate them.
   a. Select a variety of reinforcers students enjoy (candy bars, bubble gum, baseball cards).
   b. Establish a contract for work to be performed to earn a particular reward or grade.
   c. Provide frequent, immediate rewards.
9. Make use of observational learning.
   a. Select the most appropriate model.
   b. Model the behavior clearly and accurately.
   c. Insist that learners attend to what is being modeled.
   d. Provide praise when the desired behavior is exhibited.
   e. Have the learner practice the observed behavior.
   f. Provide corrective feedback during practice.
   g. Repeat demonstrations when necessary.
   h. Reinforce desired behaviors.
   i. Model behavior in similar settings in which learners will use the new skills.
10. Assess changes in learning and behavior.
   a. Diagnose learning problems.
   b. Establish levels of competency or mastery.
   c. Provide feedback.
   d. Integrate old tasks or skills with new ones.
   e. Reteach, when necessary.
   f. Take other actions.

The five outcomes overlap with the three domains (cognitive, psychomotor, and affective) of the taxonomy of educational objectives (see Chapter 7). The first three capabilities mainly fall within the cognitive domain, motor skills correspond with the psychomotor domain, and attitudes correspond with the affective domain. The mental operations and conditions involved in each of the five outcomes are different. Writes Gagné, "Learning intellectual skills requires a different design of instructional events from those required for learning verbal information or from those required for learning motor skills, and so on."[19]

As part of the instructional process, Gagné introduced the idea of *task analysis,* which is a common procedure used in business, industry, and the military. A task is broken down into the small and sequenced steps necessary to achieve an intended outcome. By breaking down a learning task into skills required, a teacher can pinpoint problem areas, make appropriate corrections, and make sure students have the necessary skills and subskills to complete the task. Following are some examples of task analysis:

1. To solve subtraction problems:
   a. To arrange sets of numbers to be subtracted
   b. To add numbers
   c. To identify plus and minus signs
   d. To recognize the meaning of numbers
   e. To write numbers
2. To evaluate statements made by government officials concerning the economy:
   a. To know economic principles and relationships
   b. To comprehend national and international events
   c. To distinguish between evidence and opinion
   d. To identify limitations of evidence
   e. To draw conclusions from evidence

Behaviorism and Curriculum. Behaviorism exerts a major impact on education. Educators who are behaviorists and who are in charge of curricula use many principles of behaviorism to guide the creation of new programs. Although what influences learning differs for different students, curriculum specialists can adopt procedures to increase the likelihood that each student will find learning relevant and enjoyable. When new topics or activities are introduced, connections should be built on positive experiences each student has had. Things about which each student is likely to have negative feelings should be identified and modified, if possible, to produce positive results.

The behaviorists believe that the curriculum should be organized so students experience success in mastering the subject matter. Of course, all curriculum persons, regardless of their psychological camps, have this view. The difference is that the behaviorists are highly prescriptive and diagnostic in their approach, and they rely on

step-by-step, structured methods for learning. For students who have difficulty learning, curriculum and instruction can be broken down into small units with appropriate sequencing of tasks and reinforcement of desired behavior.

Behaviorist theories, it should be noted, have been criticized as describing learning too simply and mechanically—and as perhaps reflecting overreliance on classical animal experimentation. Human learning involves complex thinking processes beyond respondent conditioning (or recall and habit) and operant conditioning (or emitted and reinforced behavior). According to Robert Travers, a further concern is that there is little justification to define learning in terms of a "collection of small bits of behavior each of which has to be learned separately." Although behavior consists of organized sequences, it is not a collection of tiny bits of behavior. The stress of prescribed, lockstep procedures and tasks—and a "belief that a behavioral science should be definable in terms of observable events—[are] hardly justifiable today."[20]

The latter criticism may be an overstatement, because many behaviorists today recognize cognitive processes much more than classical or S-R theorists, and they are flexible enough to hold that learning can occur without the individual's having to act on the environment or exhibit overt behavior. To the extent that traditional behavioral theory can be faulted for having to rely on identifying all behavior, many behaviorists today are willing to consider that cognitive processes partially explain aspects of learning.

But behaviorism is alive and well; it is linked to many current educational practices impacting on classrooms and schools. Writes Robert Glaser:

> *Much of the application of psychological theory currently going on in schools represents the earlier behavioristic approach. The concepts of behavioral objectives, and behavior modification, for example, now pervade all levels of education, including special education, elementary school instruction in basic literary skills, and personalized systems of instruction . . .*[21]

In general, combining behaviorism with learning includes careful analyzing and sequencing of the learners' needs and behaviors. Principles of testing, monitoring, drilling, and feed-back are characteristic. The learning conditions needed for successful outcomes are carefully planned through small instructional steps and se-quences of responses that increasingly approxi-mate the desired behavior or learning. These basic principles tend to coincide with today's basic skill training programs in reading and lan-guage development (such as DISTAR, SQ3R, and Continuous Progress), as well as methods of individualized instruction, direct instruction, mastery learning, instructional training (design), and competency-based education. These steps and sequences are shown in Table 4-1. Although these procedures are predetermined and planned in advance, some observers might claim they have a cognitive flavor, too.

With the above behavioral approaches to learning, as shown in the table, the emphasis is on (1) remediation, skill acquisition, and basic or advanced learning (from learning to read to flying an airplane); (2) well-defined, short-term, and long-term objectives; (3) matching instructional materials and media to the learners' abilities; (4) shaping behavior through prescribed tasks, step-by-step activities, close supervision of activities, and modeling; (5) rep-etition, practice and drill, probing and other methods for eliciting correct responses; (6) re-inforcement, review, homework, and other re-tention-ensuring methods; and (7) diagnosing, assessing, and reassessing the learners' needs, objectives, and tasks.

Many of the traditional and contemporary ideas of behaviorism are popular not only in classrooms and schools but also in business and industry, government, and allied health profes-sions. With these behaviorist models, it is com-mon to reject value-laden, qualitative influences and to accept fixed quantitative components. Stripped of their scientific and technocratic con-cepts, however, the models are sometimes viewed to be narrow and mechanistic.[22] On the other hand, they are the types of designs and models that people who deal with intended out-comes in prescribed tasks, numbers, and in pre-cise boxes and bottom lines are inclined to favor. Many behaviorists today are aware of these rigid doctrines and thus integrate cogni-tive developmental theory with their approaches

to human learning. The teaching-learning prac-tices shown in Table 4-1 combine behaviorism with cognitivism.

COGNITIVE DEVELOPMENT

Today most psychologists classify human growth and development as *cognitive, social, psycholog-ical,* and *physical*—but they note that learning in school is mainly cognitive in nature. Growth and development refer to changes in the structure and function of human characteristics. The changes occur in a steady progression; they are not uni-form, but result from the interaction of inherited potential (heredity) and environment. Whether a person is a rapid or slow learner, has a pleasing or disturbing personality, is tall or short largely depend on the interaction of hereditary tenden-cies and environmental influences.

There is no agreed-upon way to determine exactly to what extent the characteristics (cogni-tive, social, psychological, and physical) of an individual are the result of inherited limitations or potential or the harmful or favoring circum-stances in the person's environment. In fact, there is considerable controversy about the extent or role of heredity versus environment in determin-ing cognitive outcomes (that is, IQ scores and achievement scores) in school. Unfortunately, the evidence remains open to debate and to a variety of interpretations because of factors that cannot be adequately controlled and separated from one another. Most curriculum specialists avoid involvement in this controversy, even though the issue affects education and learning theories in general.

Cognitive Stages of Development

Most cognitive theory is developmental; that is, it supposes that growth and development occur in progressive stages. Jean Piaget presents the most comprehensive view of this theory.[23] The Swiss psychologist's work came to the attention of American educators during the 1950s and 1960s—coinciding with the rising influence of cognitive developmental psychology, the envi-ronmentalist theories, and the compensatory edu-cation movement. (Remember, behaviorism was the first and foremost theory of behavior and

TABLE 4-1 Instructional Components by Current Authorities: A Behaviorist Approach to Teaching and Learning

DIRECT INSTRUCTION: ROSENSHINE MODEL	MASTERY LEARNING: BLOCK AND ANDERSON MODEL
1. *State learning objectives.* Begin lesson with a short statement of objectives.	1. *Clarify.* Explain to students what they are expected to learn.
2. *Review.* Introduce short review of previous or prerequisite learning.	2. *Inform.* Teach the lesson, relying on whole-group instruction.
3. *Present new materials.* Present new materials in small, sequenced steps.	3. *Pretest.* Give a *formative* quiz on a no-fault basis; students can check their own papers.
4. *Explain.* Give clear and detailed instructions and explanations.	4. *Group.* Based on results, divide the class into mastery and nonmastery groups (80 percent is considered mastery).
5. *Practice.* Provide active practice for all students.	5. *Enrich and correct.* Give enrichment instruction to mastery group; give corrective (practice/drill) to nonmastery group.
6. *Guide.* Guide students during initial practice; provide seatwork activities.	6. *Monitor.* Monitor student progress; vary amount of teacher time and support for each group based on group size and performance.
7. *Check for understanding.* Ask several questions; assess student comprehension.	7. *Post test.* Give a *summative* quiz to nonmastery group.
8. *Provide feedback.* Provide systematic feedback and corrections.	8. *Assess performance.* At least 75 percent of students should achieve mastery by the summative test.
9. *Assess performance.* Obtain student success rate of 80 percent or more during practice session.	9. *Reteach.* If not, repeat procedures starting with corrective instruction (small study groups, individual tutoring, alternative instructional materials, extra homework, reading materials, practice and drill).
10. *Review and test.* Provide for spaced review and testing.	

GUIDED INSTRUCTION: HUNTER MODEL	SYSTEMATIC INSTRUCTION:[a] GOOD AND BROPHY MODEL
1. *Review.* Focus on previous lesson; ask students to summarize main points.	1. *Review.* Review concepts and skills related to homework; provide review exercises.
2. *Anticipatory set.* Focus students' attention on new lesson; stimulate interest in new materials.	2. *Development.* Promote student understanding; provide examples, explanations, demonstrations.
3. *Objective.* State explicitly what is to be learned; state rationale or how it will be useful.	3. *Assess comprehension.* Ask questions; provide controlled practice.
4. *Input.* Identify needed knowledge and skills for learning new lesson; present material in sequenced steps.	4. *Seatwork.* Provide uninterrupted-seatwork; get everyone involved; sustain momentum.
5. *Modeling.* Provide several examples or demonstrations throughout the lesson.	5. *Accountability.* Check the students' work.

(continued)

TABLE 4-1 Continued

GUIDED INSTRUCTION: HUNTER MODEL	SYSTEMATIC INSTRUCTION: [a] GOOD AND BROPHY MODEL
6. *Check for understanding.* Monitor students' work before they become involved in lesson activities; check to see they understand directions or tasks.	6. *Homework.* Assign homework regularly; provide review problems.
7. *Guided practice.* Periodically ask students questions or problems and check their answers. Again monitor for understanding.	7. *Special reviews.* Provide weekly reviews to check and enhance learning; provide monthly reviews to further maintain and enhance learning.
8. *Independent practice.* Assign independent work or practice when it is reasonably sure that students can work on their own with minimal frustration and understanding.	

[a] Originally developed for math instruction.

learning during the first half of this century.) Piaget is now probably the most quoted and influential person in the area of cognitive growth and child development.

Like many other investigators today, Piaget describes cognitive development in terms of stages from birth to maturity. The overall stages can be summarized as follows:[24]

1. *Sensorimotor stage* (birth to age 2). The child progresses from reflex operations and undifferentiated surroundings to complex sensorimotor actions in relation to environmental patterns. The child comes to realize that objects have permanence; they can be found again. The child begins to establish simple relations between similar objects.

2. *Preoperational stage* (ages 2 to 7). In this stage objects and events begin to take on symbolic meaning. For example, a chair is for sitting; clothing is what we wear. The child shows an increased ability to learn more complex concepts from experience as long as familiar examples are provided from which to extract criteria that define the concept. (For example, oranges, apples, and bananas are fruit; the child must have the chance to touch and eat them.)

3. *Concrete operations stage* (ages 7 to 11). The child begins to organize data into logical relationships and gains facility in manipulating data in problem-solving situations. This learning situation occurs, however, only if concrete ob-

jects are available or if actual past experiences can be drawn upon. This child is able to make judgments in terms of reversibility and reciprocal relations (for example, that the left and right are relative to spatial relations) and conservation (that is, a long, narrow glass may hold the same amount of water as a short, wide one).

4. *Formal operations stage* (age 11 onward). This stage is characterized by the development of formal and abstract operations. The adolescent is able to analyze ideas and comprehend spatial and temporal relationships. The young person can think logically about abstract data, evaluate data according to acceptable criteria, formulate hypotheses, and deduce possible consequences from them. He or she can construct theories and reach conclusions without having had direct experience in the subject. At this stage there are few or no limitations on what the adolescent can learn; learning depends on his or her intellectual potential and environmental experiences.

Piaget's cognitive stages presuppose a *maturation* process in the sense that development is a continuation and is based on previous growth. The mental operations are sequential and successive. The stages are hierarchical, and they form an order of increasingly sophisticated and integrated mental operations. Although the succession of stages is constant, stages of attainment vary within certain limits that are a function of

Piaget's, Dewey's & Bruner's
Tyler's & "Three Part Concepts"

heredity and environment. Although hereditary or environmental factors may speed up or slow down cognitive development, they do not change the stages or the sequence.

Environmental experience is the key to Piaget's cognitive theories, as it was also the crux of Dewey's learning principles. The educator's role involves "the shaping of actual experience by environing conditions" and knowing "what surroundings are conducive to having experiences that lead to growth."[25] Three basic cognitive processes form the basis of the environmental and experiential theories of both Piaget and Dewey.

For Piaget, *assimilation* is the incorporation of new experiences into existing experiences; it represents a coordination of the child's experiences into his or her environment. But assimilation, alone, does not have the capacity to handle new situations and new problems in context with present cognitive structures. The child must organize and develop new cognitive structures in context with existing structures— that is, how he or she thinks. This is *accommodation,* whereby the child's existing cognitive structures are modified and adapted in response to his or her environment. *Equilibration* is the process of achieving balance between those things that were previously understood and those yet to be understood; it refers to the dual process of assimilation and accommodation of one's environment.[26]

This coincides with Dewey's conceptions of situation and interaction [which] are inseparable from each other" and which form the basis of continuity.[27] For Dewey, a *situation* represents the experiences of the environment affecting the child, similar to assimilation. *Interaction* is concerned with current or latitudinal transactions taking place between the child and his or her environment, including his or her capacities to establish meaning, similar to accommodation. *Continuity* refers to longitudinal learning or to situations and interactions that follow, similar to equilibration.

It is difficult to determine who influenced whom, because both Piaget and Dewey formulated most of their learning theories during the same period, in the 1920s and 1930s. Most authorities recognize Dewey's influence on Tyler, Taba, and Bruner, but Piaget had considerable influence on them, too.

Piaget's Influence: Tyler, Taba, and Bruner

Piaget's (1896–1980) three cognitive processes (and Dewey's educational experiences) also serve as a basis for Tyler's three methods of organizing learning experiences: (1) *continuity* suggests that the curriculum should possess vertical reiteration; that is, the skills and concepts should be "recurring" and there should be "continuing opportunity for these skills to be practiced"; (2) *sequence* suggests that the curriculum should include progressive development of understanding and that "each successive experience builds upon the preceding one [and] go more broadly and deeply into matters involved"; (3) *integration* "refers to the horizontal relationships of curriculum experiences" and means that the organization of experiences should be "unified . . . in relation to other elements" of the curriculum being taught and that subjects "should not be isolated . . . or taught as a single course" from the rest of the subjects.[28]

Taba not only spends considerable time reviewing Piaget's four stages of cognitive development and the implications they have for intelligence and mental development; she also concludes that learning experiences must be "designed to match assessment of age levels at which certain processes of thought can occur." The idea is to transform complex concepts and subject matter into mental operations appropriate to the learner and to develop a curriculum that provides for "increasing deeper and more formal levels" of thinking. "Building such a curriculum would naturally also involve a better understanding of the hierarchies [Piaget's stages] of concept formation and mental operations [and] a better understanding of the sequences in the development of thought."[29]

Similarly, Taba notes Piaget's cognitive processes—assimilation, accommodation, and equilibration—in her discussion of generalizations and abstract thinking. She is concerned with organizing curricula and teaching new experiences so they are compatible with existing experiences (assimilation), moving from concrete experiences to concepts and principles (accommodation), and classifying and understanding new relationships (equilibration). The basis of what Taba calls "curriculum strategies for productive learning" are rooted in Piaget's synthesis of experiences into more complex forms and levels.

For Bruner, learning how things are related means learning the structure of knowledge. Such learning is based on Piaget's ideas of assimilation and accommodation.[30] The student who comes to grasp how bits of information within a subject area are related is able to continually and independently relate additional information to a field of study. Learning some "thing" should not be an end of learning, but, as Piaget and Dewey suggest, should be related to other aspects of subject matter and should be general enough to apply in other problems or situations. The structure of knowledge provides the basis for this kind of specific transfer of learning.

Piaget's equilibration forms the basis of Bruner's notion of a "spiral curriculum": previous learning is the basis of subsequent learning, that learning should be continuous, and that subject matter is related to and built on a foundation (from grade to grade). Bruner is also influenced by Dewey, who uses the term *continuity* in learning to explain that what a person has already learned "becomes an instrument of understanding and dealing effectively with the situations that follow."[31] Bruner also uses the term continuity, in the same way as Piaget and Dewey, to describe the spiral curriculum: how subject matter and mental operations can be "continually deepened by using them in a progressively more complex form."[32]

Bruner considers that the act of learning consists of three related processes, similar to Piaget's cognitive processes:

1. *Acquisition* is the grasping of new information; it mainly corresponds to assimilation. Such information may be "new" to one's store of data; it may also replace previously acquired information, or it may merely refine or further qualify previous information.

2. *Transformation* is the individual's capacity to process new information so as to transcend or go beyond it. Means for processing such information are extrapolation, interpolation, or transla-

tion into another form. This process mainly overlaps with accommodation.

3. *Evaluation* is the determination of whether or not information has been processed in a way that renders it appropriate for dealing with a particular task or problem. It closely corresponds with equilibration.

What is educationally critical is that the teacher (in conjunction with learning psychologists and curriculum specialists) should determine the appropriate emphasis to be given to each of Piaget's stages of cognitive development and processes of thinking. Piaget's cognitive processes overlap with Tyler's methods, Taba's strategies, and Bruner's processes. The ability to match appropriate learning experiences with Piaget's four stages of development and three processes of thinking is especially important for elementary school teachers. It is during the elementary school period, to be sure, when children move from the second stage to the third and fourth stages.

Levels of Thinking

Educators concerned with learning are also concerned with thinking. Thinking can be classified in various ways. One way is to describe the mental structure of intelligence and still another way is to describe various types of intelligences.

Structure of Intellect. The complexity of thinking can be described in numerous ways. One model by J. P. Guilford classifies mental abilities three dimensionally.[33] It comprises:

1. *Operations:* mental operations dealing with the processing of certain content.
   a. Evaluation (making assessments or decisions)
   b. Convergent thinking (generating relationships and analogies)
   c. Divergent thinking (creative thinking and production)
   d. Memory (remembering of knowledge)
   e. Cognition (knowledge)
2. *Products:* mental operations related to the application of operations to content.
   a. Units (comprehending figural, symbolic, and semantic data)

b. Classes (classifying units)

c. Relations (perceiving connections between items)

d. Systems (a coherent body of knowledge)

e. Transformations (changes in preexisting data)

f. Implications (association of previously unrelated items)

3. *Contents:* mental operations confined to information and comprehension.

    a. Figural (material perceived by the senses)

    b. Symbolic (letters and digits organized in a general system—that is, an alphabet or number system)

    c. Semantic (a form of ideas or verbal meanings)

    d. Behavioral content (social intelligence or understanding of oneself and others)

These three dimensions, represented graphically in Figure 4-1 by a 5 × 6 × 4 geometric model of five operations, six products, and four contents, yield 120 cells or distinct mental abilities. By 1985, more than 100 abilities had been recognized and separated by factor analysis. Guilford concluded that the vacant cells indicate uncovered mental abilities. It is possible, however, that our cognitive tests do not measure the other mental operations or that such abilities do not exist. The Guilford model is highly abstract and theoretical and involves administering and grading many extra tests. Rather than a single index of IQ (or of aptitude), we are required to report several scores. Thus, the theoretical issues surrounding intelligence and cognitive operations take on added complexity. Although some critics might argue that the model is dated because it lacks information-processing concepts, the theory and operations behind the model are still very relevant. The model of 120 specific abilities requires curriculum specialists, test specialists, and learning theorists to consider multiple thinking processes, as well as a three-dimensional model for learning with several categories under each dimension.

Multiple Intelligences. Howard Gardner also argues for a theory of multiple intelligences and,

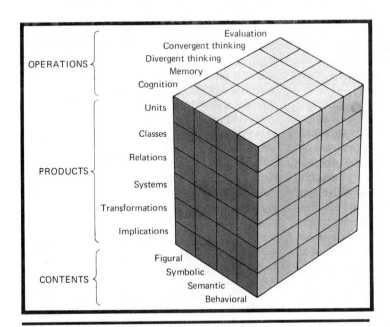

FIGURE 4-1 The Structure of Intellect

Source: From J.P. Guilford, *The Nature of Human Intelligence* (New York: McGraw-Hill, 1967), p. i.

like Guilford, he contends that there are different mental operations associated with intelligence. But Gardner feels the search for empirically grounded structures or components of intellience may be misleading, since it avoids many roles and skills valued by human cultures. However, Guilford maintains that the criteria for intelligence and the related mental operations and a priori schemes can be quantified. Gardner maintains that there are many different types of intelligence and that too often (at least in a technological society) we emphasize only verbal or linguistic factors. He outlines six types of intelligence: (1) linguistic, (2) musical, (3) logical-mathematical, (4) spatial, (5) bodily kinesthetic, and (6) personal/social.[34]

The implications seem clear. Too often, curriculum workers, especially teachers, do not recognize achievement and skills associated with noncognitive domains—and at the expense of low achievers who usually have difficulties in cognitive areas. We write off too many students who are below average in reading or writing, overlooking the fact that many of them can develop in other areas of expertise. Indeed, there are many different forms of excellence, and a viable society needs to reward both its scholars and bricklayers.

In connection with Gardner's ideas, we might conclude that there is a place in school not only for the 3 R's, or core academic subjects, but also for music, art, speech, and even people skills (winning friends, influencing people, negotiating, and the like). These bodies of knowledge and processes can be considered part of multiple intelligence. They have a place in our "other-directed" society and help people interpret and deal with social situations that can foster economic achievement and success in adulthood.

Subscribing to Gardner's ideas means not only being a cognitivist but also a "positive cognitivist," if we can coin a new term. It means there are many opportunities and chances in life. Someone who can dance, sing, act, or hit a baseball or golf ball can rise to the ranks of the masters. If encouraged and given a chance, many of our school dropouts would not be wasted. Therefore, those in charge of planning and implementing the curriculum must expand their vision beyond intellectual and academic pursuits, without creating "soft" subjects or a "watered down curriculum." We must nurture all types of intelligence and all types of excellence that contribute to the worth of the individual and society. We must be guided by reason and balance and consider the versatility of children and youth. We need to be aware of their multiple strengths and abilities and the multiple ways of thinking and learning—and that there are multiple ways of reaching Rome or finding the end of the rainbow.

Problem Solving/Creative Thinking

Since the Sputnik era, many curriculum theorists have renewed their examination of various aspects of problem solving and creative thinking. The common belief is that these methods of thinking constitute a highly sophisticated form of processing information. Some curricularists, especially those who talk about the structure of disciplines, feel they are complementary: students must be given supportive conditions in which they can develop different forms of creativity, but at the same time they must be held responsible for confirming or disproving the value or correctness of their assumptions. Problem-solving procedures are their means of doing so, for they do not lead to creative discovery, but rather they establish the validity of the discoveries. In this context, problem solving and creative thinking are considered methods of inquiry conducive of scholars and scientists.[35]

An opposing view is that problem solving (in the past referred to as reflective thinking and today called critical thinking) is based on inductive thinking, analytical procedures, and *convergent* processes. Creative thinking, which includes intuitiveness and discovery, is based on deductive thinking, originality, and *divergent* processes. Problem solving, in this second view, is conducive to rational and scientific thinking and is the *method* of arriving at a solution to a task or to a correct answer, whereas creativity is conducive to artistic and literary thinking and is a *quality* of thought. There is no right solution or answer when creativity is the goal.

Actually, problem solving and creativity may or may not go hand in hand. Some people perform well on problems without being creative, and others can be highly creative but do poorly in problem-solving tasks. But the fact that we can distinguish between both thinking processes does not necessarily suggest that they are mutually independent of each other; research does suggest that a creative individual is just as likely or unlikely to be a good problem solver, and, in reverse, that a good problem solver may or may not be creative.[36]

Perhaps the most important thing to note is that these complex cognitive tasks should be taught as generic skills and principles—relevant for all subject matter. The idea is to develop metacognitive strategies that students can transfer to many curriculum areas and content materials, as opposed to repeating the mistakes of an earlier period whereby experts claimed that each discipline had its own structure and thinking manner. The need is to develop reflective-thinking, critical-thinking, intuitive-thinking, and discovery-thinking strategies that fit a wide variety of course and content situations, not for mathematicians or historians to claim their own metacognitive strategies.

Reflective Thinking.   Problem solving played a major role in Dewey's overall concept of education. Dewey not only believed that problem-solving activities in school developed intelligence and social growth, but also that the skills developed in problem solving could be transferred to resolving everyday problems of society. Dewey's concept of problem solving is rooted in his idea of the scientific method and has become a classic model:

1. Becoming aware of a difficulty (or a felt difficulty).
2. Identifying the problem.
3. Assembling and classifying data and formulating hypotheses.
4. Accepting or rejecting the tentative hypotheses.
5. Formulating conclusions and evaluating them.[37]

Dewey's problem-solving method encourages systemic interpretation of everyday experiences through the reasoning process. This method coincides with his strong belief in a science of education (see Chapter 2). Because Dewey considers

that the chief function of the school is to improve the reasoning process, he recommends adapting this problem-solving method to other subjects at all levels. Problems selected for study should be derived from student interests, for a student who is not motivated will not really perceive a problem.

Others, however, criticize the problem-solving method as producing the misconception that scientists have a be-all and end-all formula for finding answers to practical problems. James Conant, for example, defines the problem-solving approach as a series of six steps that can be used both by experimental scientists in the laboratory and by laypersons confronted with everyday situations that need to be solved:

1. Recognizing a problem and formulating objectives.
2. Collecting relevant information.
3. Formulating an hypothesis.
4. Deducing from the hypothesis.
5. Using tests by actual trial.
6. Depending on the outcome, accepting, modifying, or discarding the hypothesis.[38]

Conant believes that problem solving is not enhanced by science. The scientific method is not readily applied to everyday problems, he claims; rather, science has simply borrowed the method of testing hypotheses from the practical person. Whereas Dewey's model, developed for all disciplines, involved social problem solving, Conant's model was used by the advocates of science and math (not social thinking) during the Sputnik era. The predominant notion then was that each discipline had its own method of problem solving.

Both models and their derivatives are considered by some researchers to be incomplete. First, the analysis occurs after the person has solved the problem. Second, the models ignore intuition, insight, and ideas that are nonlogical and perhaps even personal—in short, procedures that cannot be easily observed or tested but that are sometimes used successfully in problem solving. Present theories of cognitive processes suggest that logical and observable steps are not always used in problem solving, nor are the steps always related. Finally, different problem-solving techniques are used for different subjects or disciplines and different grade levels. Presumably, they have common features, but they also involve specific variance.

Critical Thinking.   Critical thinking and thinking skills are the terms used today to connote problem solving and related behaviors. This old idea under a new label is endorsed by the outpouring of articles in the professional literature, by a host of conferences and reports on the subject, and by the majority of states taking steps to bolster critical thinking for all students.

Although several teaching procedures, teacher-training programs, and taxonomies of critical thinking have surfaced in recent years, the latest opinion is that critical thinking is a form of intelligence that can be taught (it is not a fixed entity). The leading proponents of this school are Robert Ennis, Matthew Lipman, and Robert Sternberg.

Ennis identifies 13 attributes of critical thinkers. They tend to (1) be open minded, (2) take a position (or change a position) when the evidence calls for it, (3) take into account the entire situation, (4) seek information, (5) seek precision in information, (6) deal in an orderly manner with parts of a complex whole, (7) look for options, (8) search for reasons, (9) seek a clear statement of the issue. (10) keep the original problem in mind, (11) use credible sources, (12) remain relevant to the point, and (13) exhibit sensitivity to the feelings and knowledge level of others.[39]

Lipman distinguishes between *ordinary thinking* and *critical thinking*. Ordinary thinking is simple and lacks standards; critical thinking is more complex and is based on standards of objectivity, utility, or consistency. He wants teachers to help students change (1) from guessing to estimating, (2) from preferring to evaluating, (3) from grouping to classifying, (4) from believing to assuming, (5) from inferring to inferring logically, (6) from associating concepts to grasping principles, (7) from noting relationships to noting relationships among relationships, (8) from supposing to hypothesizing, (9) from offering opinions without reasons to offering opinions with reasons, and (10) from making judgments without criteria to making judgments with criteria.[40]

In a series of texts, called *Philosophy for Children,* Lipman outlines a strategy for teaching critical thinking. Children spend a considerable portion of their time thinking about thinking, and about ways in which effective thinking is distinguished from ineffective thinking. After reading the stories in the text, children engage in classroom discussions and exercises that encourage them to adapt the thinking process depicted in the stories.[41] The assumption behind Lipman's program is that children are by nature interested in such philosophical issues as truth, fairness, and personal identity. Children can and should learn to think for themselves, to explore alternatives to their own viewpoints, to consider evidence, and to make distinctions and draw conclusions. (See Curriculum Tips 4-2.)

Sternberg seeks to foster many of the same intellectual skills, listed in Table 4-2, albeit in a very different way. He points out three mental processes that enhance critical thinking: (1) *meta components*—high-order mental processes used to plan what we are going to do, monitor what we are doing, and evaluate what we are doing; (2) *performance components*—the actual steps or strategies we take; and (3) *knowledge-acquisition components*—processes used to relate old material to new material and to apply and use new material.[42] Sternberg does not outline a "how" approach like Lipman; rather, he outlines general guidelines for developing and/or selecting a program. See Table 4-2.

Note that some educators, including most phenomenologists and humanistic theorists, contend that teaching a person to think is like teaching someone to swing a golf club or tennis racket; it involves a holistic approach, not a piecemeal effort, as implied by Ennis, Lipman, and Sternberg. "Trying to break thinking skills into discrete units may be helpful for diagnostic proposals," according to two critics, "but it does not seem to be the right way to move in the teaching of such skills." Critical thinking is too complex of a mental operation to divide into small processes; the approach depends on "a student's total intellectual functioning, not on a set of narrowly defined skills."[43]

Perhaps the major criticism has been raised by the method's own proponent. Sternberg cautions that the kinds of critical thinking skills we

CURRICULUM TIPS 4-2   Teaching Critical Thinking

Teachers must understand the cognitive processes that constitute critical thinking, be familiar with the tasks, skills, and situations to which these processes can be applied, and employ varied classroom activities that develop these processes. Robert Ennis provides a framework for such instruction. He divides critical thinking into four components, each consisting of several specific skills that can be taught to students.

1. Defining and clarifying:
   a. Identifying conclusions
   b. Identifying stated reasons
   c. Identifying unstated reasons
   d. Seeing similarities and differences
   e. Identifying and handling irrelevance
   f. Summarizing
2. Asking appropriate questions to clarify or challenge:
   a. Why?
   b. What is the main point?
   c. What does this mean?
   d. What is an example?
   e. What is not an example?
   f. How does this apply to the case?
   g. What difference does it make?
   h. What are the facts?
   i. Is this what is being said?
   j. What more is to be said?
3. Judging the credibility of a source:
   a. Expertise
   b. Lack of conflict of interest
   c. Agreement among sources
   d. Reputation
   e. Use of established procedures
   f. Known risk to reputation
   g. Ability to give reasons
   h. Careful habits
4. Solving problems and drawing conclusions:
   a. Deducing and judging validity
   b. Inducing and judging conclusions
   c. Predicting probable consequences

Source: Robert H. Ennis, "A Logical Basis for Measuring Critical Thinking," *Educational Leadership* (October 1985), p. 46.

stress in school and the way we teach them "inadequately prepares students for the kinds of problems they will face in everyday life."[44] We believe that because our critical skill programs stress "right" answers and "objectively scorable" test items, they are removed from real-world relevance. Most problems in real life have social, economic, and psychological implications. They involve interpersonal relations and judgments about people, personal stress and crisis, and dilemmas involving choice, responsibility, and survival. How we deal with illness, aging, or death

TABLE 4-2 Principal Thinking Skills Underlying Intelligent Behavior

Recognizing and defining the nature of a problem
Deciding on the processes needed to solve the problem
Sequencing the processes into an optimal strategy
Deciding on how to represent problem information
Allocating mental and physical resources to the problem
Monitoring and evaluating one's solution processing
Responding adequately to external feedback
Encoding stimulus elements effectively
Inferring relations between stimulus elements
Mapping relations between relations
Applying old relations to new situations
Comparing stimulus elements
Responding effectively to novel kinds of tasks and situations
Effectively automatizing information processing
Adapting effectively to the environment in which one resides
Selecting environments as needed to achieve a better fit of one's abilities and
    interests to the environment
Shaping environments so as to increase one's effective utilization of one's abilities
    and interests

Source: From Robert J. Sternberg, "How Can We Teach Intelligence?" *Educational Leadership* (September 1984), p. 40. Reprinted with permission of the Association for Supervision and Curriculum Development. Copyright © 1984 by the Association for Supervision and Curriculum Development. All rights reserved.

(someone else's or even our own eventual demise), or with simple things like starting new jobs or meeting new people, has little to do with the way we think in class or on critical thinking tests. But they are important matters. By stressing cognitive skills in classrooms and schools, we ignore the realities and milieu of life. Except for college, being an A student or good problem solver in school guarantees us very little in real life.

Creative Thinking. Standardized tests do not always accurately measure creativity; in fact, we have difficulty agreeing on what creativity is and who is creative. There are many types of creativity—artistic, musical, scientific, manual, and so on—yet we tend to talk about creativity as an all-encompassing term. Creative students are often puzzling to teachers. They are difficult to characterize; their novel answers frequently seem threatening to teachers, and their behavior often deviates from what is considered "normal." Sometimes, teachers discourage creativity and

punish creative students. Curriculum specialists also tend to ignore them in their curriculum plans (subject matter or course descriptions, subject guides, and subject materials and activities), because they represent only a small proportion (about 2 to 5 percent, depending on the definition) of the student population. Also, curriculum specialists have little money earmarked to support special programs and personnel for these students. Frequently, educators lump creative children in with highly intelligent or gifted children, even though high intelligence and high creativity are not necessarily related; and there are many types of creative children.

In a classic, cross-cultural study, E. P. Torrance used sixty-two statements to investigate elementary and secondary teachers' ratings of the "ideal" creative personality. From 95 to 375 teachers in each of the following countries were sampled: United States, Germany, India, Greece, and the Philippines.[45]

For example, the United States and Germany (technologically developed countries) both encourage independent thinking, industriousness, and curiosity; these traits do not appear important in the less developed countries. Greece and the Philippines reward remembering, which connotes convergent thinking, but many American researchers consider this type of thinking anti-creative. Teachers in all the countries, especially the less developed ones, stress that being well-liked, considerate of others, and obedient are important ideals.

There is little agreement on a definition of creativity except that all believe it represents a quality of mind: It comprises both a cognitive and humanistic component in learning; although no one agrees upon an exact mix, it is probably more cognitive than humanistic. According to Carl Rogers, the essence of creativity is its novelty, and, hence, we have no standard by which to judge it. In fact, the more original the product, the more likely it is to be judged by contemporaries as foolish or evil.[46] The individual creates primarily because creating is self-satisfying and because the behavior or product is self-actualizing. (This is the humanistic side of creativity, even though the process and intellect involved in creating are cognitive in nature.) Eric Fromm defines the creative attitude as (1) the willingness to be puzzled—to orient oneself to something new without frustration; (2) the ability to concentrate; (3) the ability to experience oneself as a true originator of one's acts; and (4) the willingness to accept conflict and tension caused by the climate of opinion or lack of tolerance for creative ideas.[47]

Robert Sternberg identified six attributes associated with creativity from a list of 131 mentioned by American laypeople and professors in the arts, science, and business: (1) lack of conventionality, (2) integration of ideas or things, (3) esthetic taste and imagination, (4) decision-making skills and flexibility, (5) perspicacity (in questioning social norms), and (6) drive for accomplishment and recognition.[48] He also makes important distinctions among creativity, intelligence, and wisdom. Creativity overlaps more with intelligence ($r = 0.55$) than it does with wisdom ($r = 0.27$), but there is more emphasis on imagination and unconventional methods with creativity, as opposed to intelligence, which deals with logical

and analytical absolutes. Wisdom and intelligence are most closely related ($r = 0.68$), but differ in emphasis on mature judgment and use of experience with different situations.

All three types of people, creative, intelligent, and wise, can solve problems, but they do so in different ways. Creative people tend to be divergent thinkers, and teachers must understand that creative students go beyond ordinary limitations of classrooms and schools and think and act in unconventional and even imaginary ways. This sometimes upsets teachers, and it is not uncommon to mislabel these learners as "disabled" or "difficult." (Indeed, our schools sometimes commit an injustice to those who are nonconforming.) Intelligent people rely on logic, have a good vocabulary, and store of information. Such students tend to be convergent thinkers, score high on conventional tests, and probably perform well on Hirsch's cultural literary test (see Chapter 2). Few students exhibit wisdom, since this comes with age and experience. Nonetheless, there are sufficiently mature students who show good judgment, make expedient use of information, and profit from the advice of others and their own experiences. They "read between the lines" and have a good understanding of peers and adults (including their teachers). They usually exhibit cognitive intelligence, what we would label as traditional intelligence, and also social intelligence, what we might label as "people" skills.

For teachers, the definition of creativity comes down to how new ideas have their origin. We are dealing with both logical and observable processes and unconscious and unrecognizable processes. The latter processes give teachers trouble in the classroom and sometimes lead to misunderstanding between teachers and creative students. For some students the methods of Edison and Einstein seem appropriate—theoretical, deductive, and developmental. For others, creativity may correspond more closely to the insights and originality of Kafka, Picasso, Bob Dylan, or Michael Jackson. Because few curriculum specialists think like the Edison or Kafka groups, there is a void, a real lack of attention to these students in our curriculum literature. See Table 4-3.

Table 4-3 Appropriate Curriculum and Instruction for Gifted Students

CHARACTERISTICS	LEARNING NEEDS	CURRICULUM IMPLICATIONS	INSTRUCTIONAL IMPLICATIONS
Ability to handle abstractions	Presentation of symbol systems at higher levels of abstraction	• Reduce basic skills curriculum • Introduction of new symbol systems at earlier stages of development (computers, foreign language, statistics, and so on)	• Develop advanced materials and products related to content • Integration of content by key ideas, issues, and themes • Include high-level and divergent questioning strategies
Power of concentration	Longer time frame that allows focused, in-depth work in an area of interest and challenge	• Diversified scheduling of curriculum work • Chunks of time for special project work and small-group efforts	• Advanced reading materials • Faster-paced instruction • Problem solving and special projects
Ability to make connections and establish relationships among disparate data	Exposure to multiple perspectives and domains of inquiry	• Interdisciplinary curriculum opportunities such as special concept units, humanities, and the interrelated arts • Use of multiple text materials and resources	• Reorganize content according to concepts and high-level skills • Integrate ideas across related content • More frequent discussions
Ability to memorize well and learn rapidly	Rapid movement through basic skills and concepts in traditional areas; economical organization of new areas of learning	• Restructured learning frames (that is, speed up and reduce reinforcement activities) • New curriculum organized according to its underlying structure	• Special programs organized around global and technological issues • Accelerate instruction
Multiple interests; wide information base	Opportunity to choose area(s) of interest and to study a chosen area in greater depth	• Learning center areas in the school for extended time use • Self-directed learning packets • Individual learning contracts	• Small-group and independent study • Extension, enrichment, and in-depth study • Connect multiple areas of curriculum • Cluster by abilities and interests

Source: Adapted from Joyce Van Tassel-Baska, "Appropriate Curriculum for Gifted Learners," *Educational Leadership* (March 1989), Tables 1–2, pp. 13–14.

Intuitive Thinking.   Intuitive thinking is not new. But this thinking process was either overlooked because teaching practices have relied instead on facts and rote, or ignored, because it was difficult to define and measure. Bruner popularized the idea in his book about the *Process of Education.* The good thinker not only has knowledge, but also an intuitive grasp of the subject. Intuitive thinking is part of a process of discovery that is similar to the scholar-specialist's engaging in hunches, playing with ideas, and understanding relationships so that he or she can make discoveries or add to the storehouse of new knowledge.

The following explanation by Bruner is a good description of how some people work with intuitive thinking:

> Intuitive thinking characteristically does not advance in careful, well-defined steps. Indeed, it tends to involve maneuvers based seemingly on implicit perception of the total problem. The thinker arrives at an answer, which may be right or wrong, with little, if any, awareness of the process by which he reached it. He rarely can provide an adequate account of how he obtained his answer, and he may be unaware of just what aspects of the problem situation he was responding to. Usually intuitive thinking rests on familiarity with the domain of knowledge involved and with its structure, which makes it possible for the thinker to leap about skipping steps and employing shortcuts in a manner that requires later rechecking of conclusions by more analytical means.[49]

This has very little to do with a convergent or step-by-step approach. It speaks of the revelation of discovery—the "sheer knowing the stuff—but coupled with the ability to put knowledge to use and to find new ways in which to fit things together. According to this interpretation, problem solving and free discovery come together; knowledge is dynamic, built around the process of discovery, without precise steps or rules to follow.

Discovery Learning.   Since the Sputnik era, the inquiry-discovery method has been examined in conjunction with the discipline-centered curriculum—as a unifying element related to the knowledge and methodology of a domain of study.

Taba, Bruner, Phenix, and Inlow were products of this era[50] (the latter's influence on curriculum planning and instructional methods is underrated and almost ignored by present curricularists). Taba was influenced by Bruner, Phenix was to a lesser extent influenced by both of them, and Inlow was influenced by all three. (Their respective books, including the content and citations, illustrate these relationships.) All four educators were more concerned about *how* we think than with *what* we think or what knowledge we possess.

Although Bruner went to great lengths to fuse the inquiry-discovery methods in the sciences and mathematics, Phenix, Taba, and Inlow claimed that the discovery method was separate from inquiry and that both methods of thinking cut across all subjects (not just science and math). Phenix, for example, proposed that discovery was a form of inquiry that dealt with new knowledge, hypothesis, and hunches. Most of his efforts were spent defining inquiry, which he claimed was the method of deriving, organizing, analyzing, and evaluating knowledge (like problem solving). Inquiry was considered to bind together all the separate aspects of knowledge into a coherent discipline; it was viewed as more important than discovery.

Taba and Inlow contrasted discovery learning with verbal and concrete learning. Most of traditional learning was described as a process of *transmitting* verbal and concrete information to the learner; it was authority centered, subject centered, highly organized, also flexible and open. Discovery, on the other hand, involved extensive exploration of the concrete at the elementary level. For older students, according to Inlow, it involved "problem identification, data organization and application, postulation, . . . evaluation and generalization."[51] For Taba, it meant "abstracting, deducing, comparing, contrasting, inferring, and contemplating."[52] All these discovery processes are rational and logical, and thus infer a problem-solving or convergent component. Inlow and Taba, however, were quick to point out that discovery also included divergent thinking and intuitiveness; Taba also added creativity and limitless learning to help define discovery.

Bruner, who is well known for elaborating the idea of discovery, defined it as the learning that takes place when students are not presented with subject matter in its final form, when subject matter is not organized by the teacher but by the students themselves. Discovery is the formation of coding systems, whereby students discover relationships that exist among the data presented.

The most obvious characteristic of discovery as a teaching technique is perhaps that after the initial stages it requires less teacher input or guidance than do other strategies. Discovery is, in fact, less teacher centered than other approaches to learning, and students assume more responsibility for their own learning. Recall the influence of Thorndike's theory of transfer on Bruner. To be part of discovery, learning must be transferable. Increased transferability is evidenced by what Bruner calls "intellectual potency," an elusive term that infers a high degree of intelligence. Bruner also contends that discovery learning leads to greater skill acquisition in problem solving (in Bruner's terms, a learner acquires the heuristics of discovery) and motivation (a shift from extrinsic to intrinsic reward). Successful discovery experiences make the learner more capable of discovering new experiences and more willing to learn for the sake of learning.

Cognition and Curriculum

Most curriculum specialists, and learning theorists and teachers, tend to be cognitive oriented, because (1) the cognitive approach constitutes a logical method for organizing and interpreting learning, (2) the approach is rooted in the tradition of subject matter, and (3) educators have been trained in cognitive approaches and better understand them. Even many contemporary behaviorists, as previously mentioned, incorporate cognitive processes in their theories of learning. Because learning in school involves cognitive processes, and because schools emphasize the cognitive domain of learning, it follows that most educators feel that learning is synonymous with cognitive developmental theory.

The teacher who has a structured style of teaching would prefer the problem-solving method, based on reflective thinking and/or the scientific method. Most curricularists tend to be cognitive oriented in their approach to learning,

but we feel that this learning model is incomplete and that something gets lost in its translation to the classroom. For example, we feel that many schools are not pleasant places for learners and that the "quality of life" in classrooms can be improved.

We are reminded of John Goodlad's description of schools. After visiting more than 1000 elementary and secondary schools, Goodlad concluded that most students are not engaged in problem-solving tasks, but passive-rote tasks, and that they are rarely asked to "initiate anything . . . or create their own products."[53] In short, real and meaningful learning rarely takes place in schools. Although Goodlad is a cognitive curricularist, he finds that the teaching-learning process boils down to teachers predominantly talking and students mostly responding to the teachers. The workbook and textbook are the main sources of instruction; rarely are students permitted to talk to each other, and rarely do they become involved in problem-solving or creative activities. According to Goodlad, much of the so-called learning theories and educational reforms have been blunted at the classroom door.

We are also influenced by John Holt, a humanistic and radical critic of schools.[54] Holt points out that the schooling process encourages *producers* (students who seek to please adults and find right answers, but who, if they fail to obtain the right answers, plunge into despair) and discourages *thinkers* (students who are not concerned with pleasing adults, who can grapple with ideas, cope with uncertainty, and solve problems under consideration).

In a system run primarily on right answers, those who are thinkers find school an unpleasant place. Many students cannot bear to be wrong. They must be right; they wait for the magic words "right" or "wrong." According to Holt, those who produce the right answers are relieved. Those who are wrong no longer want to think about the problem; they give up. When teachers ask questions and they do not know the right answers, they stall, make up excuses, and, in some cases, become "paralyzed" with fear. Thinkers, on the other hand, are curious, challenged by problems rather than frustrated, and independent and inclined to risk—so that they do not need teacher approval. The trouble is, many teachers and schools do not know what to do with thinkers.

Curriculum specialists must understand that school should be a place where students are not afraid of asking questions, not afraid of being wrong, not afraid of not pleasing their teachers, and not afraid of taking cognitive risks and playing with ideas. With all our cognitive theory, we would expect students to want to learn and know how to learn, but we observe, both in the literature and in the real world of schools, that after a few years of school most students have to be cajoled to learn and have learned how not to learn. So-called "successful" students become cunning strategists in a game of beating the system and figuring out the teacher. To be sure, schools should be more humane places where students can fulfill their human potential. With this in mind, we turn to humanistic learning.

PHENOMENOLOGY/HUMANISTIC PSYCHOLOGY

Traditional psychologists do not recognize phenomenology or humanistic psychology as a school of psychology, much less a wing or form of psychology. Their contention is that most psychologists are humanistic, because they are concerned with people and with bettering society. Moreover, they claim that the label *humanism* should not be used as a mask for generalizations based on little knowledge and "soft" research.[55] Nonetheless, a number of observers have viewed phenomenology, sometimes called humanistic psychology, as a "third force" learning theory— after behaviorism and cognitive development.[56] Phenomenology is sometimes considered a cognitive theory because it emphasizes the total organism or person. The distinct difference between the cognitive and affective aspects of learning, however, have led us to separate these domains.

The most obvious contrast with the mechanistic and deterministic view of behaviorism is the phenomenological version of learning, illustrated by the individual's awareness that he or she is an "I" who has feelings and attitudes, who experiences stimuli, and who acts on the environment. We carry some sense of control and freedom to produce certain conditions in our environment. When we speak of this awareness, we are speaking of the self. The study of immediate experiences as one's reality is called *phenomenology* and is influenced by, and perhaps even based on, an existentialist philosophy. Most phenomenological ideas are derived from and for clinical settings; nevertheless, educators are becoming aware that they have implications for the classroom as well.

Phenomenologists point out that the way we look at ourselves is basic for understanding our behavior. What we do, even to what extent we learn, is determined by our concepts of ourselves.[57] If someone thinks he or she is Napoleon, he or she will act like Napoleon, or at least convey his or her concept of Napoleon. If someone thinks he or she is dull or stupid, his or her cognitive performance will be influenced by that self-concept.

Gestalt Theory

Phenomenologist ideas are rooted in early field theories and field-ground ideas, which view the total organism in relationship to the environment, or what is called the "field," and the learner's perception of this environment and the personal meaning in a given situation. Learning must be explained in terms of the *wholeness* of the problem. Human beings do not respond to isolated stimuli, but to an organization or pattern of stimuli.

Field theories are derived from Gestalt psychology of the 1930s and 1940s. The German word *Gestalt* connotes shape, form, and configuration. In this context, various stimuli are perceived in relation to others within a field. What one perceives will determine the meaning he or she gives to the field; likewise, one's solutions to other problems will depend on his or her recognition of relationships between individual stimuli and the whole.[58] This is considered the *field-ground* relationship, and how the individual perceives this relationship determines behavior. Perception alone is not a crucial factor in learning; rather, the crucial factor is structuring and restructuring the field relationships to form evolving patterns.

On this basis, learning is complex and abstract. When confronted with a learning situation, the learner analyzes the problem, discriminates between essential and nonessential data, and perceives relationships. The environment is continuously changing, and thus the learner is continuously reorganizing his or her perceptions. In terms of teaching, learning is conceived as a selective process by the student. Curriculum specialists must understand that learners will perceive something in relation to the whole; what they perceive and how they perceive it is related to their previous experiences.

Maslow: Self-actualizing Persons

Abraham Maslow, a well-known phenomenologist, has set forth a classic theory of human needs. Based on a hierarchy, and in order of importance, the needs are:

1. *Survival needs.* Those necessary to maintain life: needs for food, water, oxygen, and rest.
2. *Safety needs.* Those necessary for routine and the avoidance of danger.
3. *Love and belonging needs.* Those related to affectionate relations with people in general and to a place in the group.
4. *Esteem needs.* Those related to receiving recognition as a worthwhile person.
5. *Knowing and understanding needs.* Those more evident in persons of high intelligence than those of limited intelligence, a wanting to learn and organize intellectual relationships.
6. *Self-actualization needs.* Those related to becoming the best person one can be, to develop one's fullest potential.[59]

These needs have obvious implications for teaching and learning. A child whose basic needs—say, love or esteem—are not filled will not be interested in acquiring knowledge of the world. The child's goal to satisfy the need for love or esteem takes precedence over learning and directing his or her behavior. To some extent, Maslow's ideas that have classroom implications are based on Pestalozzi and Froebel, who believed in the importance of human emotions and a methodology based on love and trust.

Maslow coined the term *humanistic psychology,* which stresses three major principles: (1) centering attention on the experiencing person, and thus focusing on experience as the primary phenomenon in learning; (2) emphasizing such human qualities as choice, creativity, values, and self-realization, as opposed to thinking about people in mechanistic (or behaviorist) terms and learning in cognitive terms; and (3) showing ultimate concern for the dignity and worth of people and an interest in the psychological development and human potential of learners as individuals.[60]

The teacher's and curriculum maker's role in this scheme is to view the student as a whole person. The student is to be positive, purposeful, active, and involved in life experiences (not S-R or only cognitive experiences). Learning is to be a lifelong educational process. Learning is experimental, its essence being freedom and its outcome full human potential and reform of society.

The goal of education, for Maslow, is to produce a healthy and happy learner who can accomplish, grow, and actualize his or her human self. Self-actualization and its attendant sense of fulfillment are what the learner should strive for and what teachers should stress in the classroom situation. Self-actualizing people are psychologically healthy and mature. Maslow characterized them as (1) having an efficient perception of reality; (2) being at ease and comfortable with themselves and with others; (3) not overwhelmed with guilt, shame, or anxiety; (4) relatively spontaneous and natural; and (5) problem centered rather than ego centered.[61] Rather than dealing with the scientific approach of isolating variables for research examination, as the behaviorists and cognition people do, Maslow preferred to deal with the "whole person," which accordingly he referred to as a holistic approach. This holistic approach guides Maslow's followers, both curriculum workers and teachers.

Rogers: Nondirective and Therapeutic Learning

Carl Rogers, perhaps the most noted phenomenologist, has established counseling procedures and methods for facilitating learning. His ideas are based on those of early field theorists and field-ground theories; reality is based on what the individual learner perceives: "Man lives by a perceptual 'map' which is not reality itself."[62]

This concept of reality should make the teacher aware that the level and kind of response

Value Confussion

to a particular experience will differ among children. Children's perceptions, which are highly individualistic, influence their learning and behavior in class, for example, whether they will see meaning or confusion in what is being taught.

Rogers views therapy as a method of learning to be utilized by the curriculum worker and teacher. He believes that positive human relationships enable people to grow; therefore, interpersonal relations among learners are just as important as cognitive scores.[63] The teacher's role in nondirective teaching is that of a facilitator, very much like the existentialist teacher, who has close professional relationships with students and guides their human growth and development. In this role, the teacher helps students explore new ideas about their lives, their school work, their relations with others, and their interaction with society. The counseling method assumes that students are willing to be responsible for their own behavior and learning, that they can make intelligent choices, and that they can share ideas with the teacher and communicate honestly as people who are confronted with decisions about themselves and about life in general.

The curriculum is concerned with process, not products; personal needs, not subject matter; psychological meaning, not cognitive scores; and changing environmental situations (in terms of space and time), not predetermined environments. Indeed, there must be freedom to learn, not restrictions or preplanned activities. The psychological and social conditions of the environment limit or enhance a person's field or life space. A psychological field or life space is a necessary consideration in the curriculum, and everything that is taking place in relation to a specific learner at a given time gives meaning to the field and eventually to learning.

Value Clarification

Value clarification, sometimes called value building, is part of the teacher-learning process. Value clarificationists have a high regard for creativity, freedom, and self-realization. They prefer that learners explore their own preferences and make their own choices.

The values a person holds depend on many factors, including environment, education, and

personality. People often suffer from value confusion, whose symptoms are apathy, uncertainty, inconsistency, overconforming, or overdissenting.[64] Value clarification is designed to help persons overcome value confusion and become more positive, purposeful, and productive, as well as to have better interpersonal relations.

In a popular text, Louis Raths and his colleagues outlined the process of valuing: "(1) choosing freely . . . ; (2) choosing from alternatives . . . ; (3) choosing thoughtfully . . . ; (4) prizing and cherishing . . . ; (5) affirming . . . ; (6) acting upon choices . . . ; [and] (7) repeating . . . as a pattern of life."[65] They developed various dialogue strategies, writing strategies, discussion strategies, and activity strategies for teaching valuing on a how-to-do basis. Table 4-4 illustrates some dialogue strategies for the seven valuing processes. These are actually instructional strategies to be recommended by the curriculum specialist and used by the teacher.

It is possible to identify other ways of teaching valuing. The first is *inculcation,* teaching accepted values with the support of common law. Next is *moral development,* highlighting moral and ethical principles of application. Third is *analysis of issues* and situations involving values. Fourth is *clarification,* the method Raths emphasizes. Finally is *action learning,* trying and testing values in real-life situations.[66] In addition, the approaches used by Abraham Maslow and Carl Rogers may be described as *evocation,* calling forth from the learner personal values and the ability to make choices and become self-actualizing.

Although the stress is on attitudes and feelings, and on human processes, there is a cognitive component in value clarification, just as in the *Taxonomy of Educational Objectives* there are corresponding cognitive components within the affective domain of learning.[67] One must think and engage in various cognitive forms of analysis, synthesis, evaluation, and even problem solving to engage in value clarification. The strategies for value clarification also involve what Raths calls "choosing" and "prizing," or what we see as a stress on attitudes, feelings, aspirations, self-concept, interests—and these are not easy to quantify or measure.

Cooperative Learning. Grouping students to work together instead of competing is becoming a more and more accepted practice by teachers. In the traditional classroom structure, students compete for teacher recognition and grades. The same students tend to be "winners" and "losers" over the years. High-achieving students continually receive rewards and are motivated to learn, and low-achieving students continually experience failure (or near-failure) and frustration.

Reducing competition and increasing cooperation among students may diminish hostility, prejudice, and patterns of failure among many students. It is certainly a much more humanistic approach to teaching and learning than a competitive approach, which puts emphasis on individual achievement, often at the expense of or ignoring average and low-achieving students. This does not mean that competition has no place in the classroom or school. Even the advocates of cooperation, such as David and Roger Johnson and Robert Slavin, feel that competition under the right conditions and with evenly matched individuals or groups can be a source of motivation, excitement, fun, and improved performance, for example, in simple drill activities, speed tasks, low-anxiety games and psychomotor activities, and athletics.[68]

According to a review of the research, cooperation among participants helps build (1) positive

TABLE 4-4 Clarifying Questions Suggested by the Seven Valuing Processes

---

1. Choosing freely
    a. Where do you suppose you first got the idea?
    b. How long have you felt that way?
    c. What would people say if you weren't to do what you say you must do? . . .
2. Choosing from alternatives
    a. What else did you consider before you picked this? . . .
    b. Are there reasons behind your choice?
    c. What choices did you reject before you settled on your present idea or action? . . .
3. Choosing thoughtfully
    a. What would be the consequences of each alternative available? . . .
    b. What assumptions are involved in your choice? . . .
    c. Now if you do this, what will happen to that? . . .
4. Prizing and cherishing
    a. Are you glad you feel that way? [Why?] . . .
    b. What purpose does it serve? . . .
    c. In what way would life be different without it?
5. Affirming
    a. Would you tell the class the way you feel some time?
    b. Would you be willing to sign a petition supporting that idea? . . .
    c. Should a person who believes the way you do speak out? . . .
6. Acting upon choices
    a. Have you examined the consequences of your act? . . .
    b. Where will this lead you? How far are you willing to go?
    c. How has it already affected your life?
7. Repeating
    a. What are your plans for doing more of it?
    b. Should you get other people interested and involved? . . .
    c. How long do you think you will continue?

Source: From Louis E. Raths, Merrill Harmin, and Sidney B. Simon. *Values and Teaching,* 2nd ed. (Columbus, Ohio: Merrill, 1978), pp. 64–65.

and coherent personal identity, (2) self-actualization and mental health, (3) knowledge and trust of others, (4) communication, (5) acceptance and support of others, (6) wholesome relationships, and (7) reduction of conflicts. However, the data also suggest that cooperation and group learning are considerably more effective in fostering these social and interpersonal skills than competitive or individualistic efforts.[69]

In cooperative learning, students divide the work among themselves, help one another (especially the slow members), praise and criticize one another's efforts and contributions, and receive a group performance score. Of all the cooperative learning arrangements, the two developed by Slavin are most popular: student team achievement divisions (STAD) and team-assisted instruction (TAI). Both arrangements have been found to increase student achievement, given the proper implementation.

In STAD, *teams* of four or five members are balanced by ability, gender, and ethnicity. Students are ranked by previous test scores or grades and divided into thirds or quarters. Each team consists of one student from each of the thirds or quarters of the class ranking, with extra middle-ranked students becoming the fourth or fifth members. *Class quizzes* are given frequently to see if students have learned the material while in the group. The student scores are averaged into a team score so that group members are more likely to help each other. *Recognition* is given teams for high average scores or improvement scores. Individuals are also recognized for good performance to maintain motivation, but a balance between individual reward and team accomplishment must be found. *Teams are changed* every five or six weeks to give students an opportunity to work with other students and to give members of low-scoring teams a new chance.[70]

The steps involved in *team-assisted instruction* (TAI) are similar to those in STAD, but there is more emphasis on diagnosing through *pre- and post-testing* and on mastery of skills through practice. Instead of first studying the material together and then checking understanding through practice *quizzes* in teams, students first work on their own skill sheets and then have their team members check their answers and provide assistance. Not until a student gets 80 percent or

more correct on the practice quiz is he or she certified by the team to take the final test. Teams are given *achievement and improvement scores* and recognized as in STAD, but in addition they are labeled "super teams" (high performing), "great teams" (moderate performing), or "good teams" (minimum passing grade). Each day the teacher works for about 5 to 15 minutes (based on a 45-minute lesson) with two or three groups who are at about the same point in the curriculum. The other teams work on their own during this time.[71]

The emphasis of TAI is on teaching basic skills more through a type of mastery learning than through direct instruction. The approach is designed for the elementary and junior high school, not the senior high school, and has been successfully implemented in teaching reading and mathematics. One of the most important factors related to cooperative learning and achievement, however, is that group goals be balanced with individual accountability and recognition; group goals alone have minimal achievement effects. (If you are a skeptic, then try the Russian socialist system.)

A cooperative learning approach designed for junior high and senior high school students is called the *jigsaw classroom*. It is an old idea with a new name. Students work together in a small group on a specific academic task, assignment, or project.[72] They depend on each other for resources, information, and study assignments. It is an excellent method not only for reducing classroom competition and increasing cooperation, but also for reducing classroom or student prejudices, if any exist, and improving human relations.

While the teacher instructs the rest of the class, one group works in a study area on a special task. Students share materials, help another, and evaluate each other's ideas and assignments. Each group meets once a week for half of or a whole period. Groups can also meet outside of class, say in the library, before school, or at someone's home after school. The group is required to finish its task in a specified period of time, and, depending on the task, they may report their results to the whole class or turn in the finished product to the teacher. Students are evaluated on an individual and group basis. New groups are formed when new assignments are given by the teacher. Groups are formed according to interests, but are mixed according to ability, gender, and ethnicity, thus promoting concepts of democracy and integration. (See Curriculum Tips 4-3.)

Phenomenology and Curriculum

Phenomenologists view the individual in relation to the field in which he or she operates. But what determines behavior and learning is mainly psychological. The personal experiences of the individual are accessible to others only through inferences; thus, such data are questionable in terms of scientific evidence. But to the phenomenologist, the raw data of personal experiences are vital to understand learning. Perhaps the data cannot be measured accurately and perhaps they are vague, but they are "out there." The definitions and the processes are also subjective and evaluative, rather than precise and substantive. Besides the concept of humanistic psychology, the scope and subject matter are used synonymously with many other concepts, including existentialist psychology, neoprogressivism, creativity, love, higher consciousness, valuing, transcendentalism, psychological health, ego identity, psychoanalysis[73]—almost anything that suggests maximum "self-fulfillment," "self-actualization," and "self-realization."

Although this umbrella aspect of phenomenology makes it difficult to provide a clear, agreed-upon definition of the term, the same broadness makes the concept acceptable to educational reformers of various psychological orientations. The fact that phenomenology means different things to different people is one reason for its easy acceptance, but it is also a basis for criticism. Nonetheless, phenomenologists attempt to rescue learning theory from the narrow and rigid behaviorists and from overstress on cognitive processes.

Motivation and Achievement. Phenomenologists seek to understand what goes on inside us—our wants, desires, and feelings, and ways of perceiving and understanding. While cognitive functions are recognized, teachers and schools must first make a commitment to deal with the social and psychological factors of learning. A student who is frustrated, distraught, or emotionally upset will learn very little; rather, he or she will resist, withdraw, or act out his or her problems. Student needs must be satisfied. Similarly, their self-esteem and self-concept must be recognized as essential factors related to learning. Without good feelings about oneself, and without a sense of curiosity or motivation, there is little chance for continual cognitive (or even psychomotor) learning. A learner must feel confident about performing the skill or task required, be eager to learn, and feel that what she or he is being asked to perform is psychologically satisfying. This applies to learning the ABCs, how to hit a baseball or dance the two-step, or how to socially interact with others.

Today, many schools are employing organized approaches to try to ensure that learners feel good about themselves and about learning. William Glasser, for example, envisions schools without failure. Students understand and are involved in rules of behavior, teachers are supportive, and classrooms are characterized by openness and positive student interaction. Schools must be a friendly place, not coercive, to maximize the learning potential of students, especially those students who have experienced failure[74] (or who are unsure about themselves).

We have to reform schools not by changing the length of the school day or year or the amount of homework or by beefing up the curriculum, but by first making school more satisfying to students and more consistent with their interests, so that they gain a sense of power, fulfillment, and importance in the classroom. When we learn to deal with the psychological requirements of learners, when we become sensitive to what makes them want to learn, we can then focus on what they need to learn. *Affective needs are more important than cognitive needs.* Similarly, solutions to the problems of discipline and achievement are related to and based primarily on making students feel someone listens to them, thinks about them, cares for them, and feels that they are important.

Elementary and middle school teachers seem more concerned about these issues than high school teachers, who often feel that they are not expected to deal with social or psychological problems of students on a regular basis. More-

CURRICULUM TIPS 4-3   Guidelines for Cooperative Learning

Some specific strategies for cooperative approaches developed by David and Roger Johnson are presented here.

1. *Arrange the classroom to promote cooperative goals.* Seating arrangements should be clustered. Provide sufficient space and study areas for students to share; position media equipment so that students have easy access as a group.
2. *Present the objectives as group objectives.* The group, not the individual, is the focus. Gear the reward structure to achieving group objectives.
3. *Communicate intentions and expectations.* Students need to know what the teacher expects them to accomplish.
4. *Encourage a division of labor where appropriate.* Students should understand their roles and responsibilities. This will take time and practice.
5. *Encourage students to share ideas, materials, and resources.* Students should look to each other, not to the teacher. The teacher may act as a catalyst but should not be the major source of ideas.
6. *Supply a variety of materials.* Since the sharing of materials is essential to the group, sufficient quantities and variety are needed. If materials are insufficient, the group may bog down and perhaps become disruptive.
7. *Encourage students to communicate their ideas clearly.* Verbal messages should be clear and concise. Verbal and nonverbal messages should agree with each other.
8. *Encourage supportive behavior and point out rejecting or hostile behavior.* Behaviors such as silence, ridicule, personal criticism, one-upmanship, and superficial acceptance of an idea should be discouraged since they hinder cooperation and productive group behavior.
9. *Monitor the group.* Check the progress of both individuals and the group as a whole. Explain and discuss problems, assist, and give praise as appropriate.
10. *Evaluate and reward the individual and group.* In evaluation, focus on the group and its progress. Evaluate the individual in the context of the group's effort and achievement. Provide prompt feedback. Give appropriate rewards for completion of work for the individual and group.

over, the latter teachers tend to be more concerned with subject matter and related questions about what content and how much content is most worthwhile? The humanistic approach to learning involves a certain amount of warmth, genuineness, maturity, and concern for people, in our case children and youth. The focus is not on academic achievement, rather on the whole child—on his or her social, psychological, physical, and cognitive needs. For this reason, progressive educators are more likely to adopt many of the phenomenologists' theories, without even knowing that they are, since many of these ideas coincide with classic progressive thinkers from Pestalozzi and Froebel to Parker and Washburne.[75]

In the final analysis, learning in school occurs in groups with a formalized curriculum (although some might argue that there is also an informal or hidden curriculum). The child is but one learner among as many as thirty students, all needing some attention and following a text that usually promotes passivity, not activity. Everything in and around us competes for our attention or motivation. When we pay attention to something, it usually means we are not paying attention to something else. All of us, including our students, must make choices on how we dispense our attention and time. When attention wanders, or when students cannot focus on their tasks, this means that the tasks are too complex or signals are being sent which connote some kind of sociopsychological problem, often which needs our intervention.

The question that arises, then, is how can curriculum workers, especially teachers, motivate students to pay attention to long division problems or Shakespearean sonnets when youngsters are being bombarded by a host of needs, interests, and feelings that often compete for their attention and time? How can we better incorporate their needs, interests, and feelings into the teaching-learning process, or do we just ignore them and conclude that our students are unmotivated?

Limits of learners

For many learners, the journey into advanced learning is limited—given the increased amount of time they may need for it. A point of diminishing returns, in terms of effort and energy, is reached for many learners as they struggle with more complex knowledge. Indeed, we all reach a point when it becomes too difficult to go further. For some of us, it involves quadratic equations, Russian grammar, or hitting a golf ball with accuracy. For others, the point of diminishing returns is quickly reached with simple division problems, English nouns, or a simple swim across the short part of the pool. In these cases, gold stars or grading does little to sustain learning. The game is often quickly over for such children; their minds and bodies pay attention to other things that they can perform. Indeed, curriculum workers must be realistic about their students' abilities without stereotyping individuals or groups of learners.

As educators, we need to support and nurture various learning opportunities for our students, we need to recognize several different domains of learning, not only cognitive domains, and we need to provide rewards, at least recognition, for various forms and levels of achievement, including effort, improvement, imagination, intuition, individuality, vitality, enthusiasm and maturity—all those shades of gray that have little to do with standard achievement scores but are still important for enhancing personal wholeness and modern society and in the end make the real difference in life.

The Concept of Freedom. The idea of personal freedom is another important issue in phenomenology or humanistic psychology. We may not always use the freedom we have, or we may misuse it, but it is there. One of the early humanistic psychologists put it this way: "I think people have a great deal more freedom than they ever use, simply because they operate out of habits, prejudices, and stereotypes. . . . [T]hey have a lot more self-determinism than is reflected in the traditional . . . view of humans as reactive beings. . . . [W]e have more freedom than most of today's psychology admits."[76]

The idea of freedom is the essence of Roger's thesis for learning. The more children and youth are aware of their freedom, the more opportunity they have to discover themselves and develop fully as people.[77] Freedom permits the learners to probe, explore, and deepen their understanding of what they are studying. It permits them latitude to accomplish goals and find the fit between goals and achievements and past learning and new learning—and the direction these new meanings have for additional learning. Freedom broadens the learners' knowledge of alternative ways of perceiving themselves and the environment.

Freedom was the watchword of the radical school, free school, and alternative school movements of the 1960s and 1970s, and it was part of the educational choice and private school movements of the 1980s and 1990s. These movements increase various possibilities for learning and schooling and for enhancing diverse school environments that match the diversity of the needs, feelings, attitudes, and abilities of learners. The free school, alternative school, and radical school movements basically overlap; they were fueled by child-centered education and humanistic psychology. Even though they protested against established teaching and school practices and knew they were against traditional education, they were never able to develop a constructive, detailed plan for reform.

Unquestionably, curricularists must enhance students' opportunities and alternatives for learning without lessening the teachers' authority. They need to find the "golden mean": student freedom without license and teacher authority without control—a very elusive ideal. The idea is to design a curriculum that helps learners realize their fullest potential in a behavioral, cognitive, and humanistic sphere of learning.

My idea — Humanistic approach w/ advisor/teachers — professionals who came in to teach indiv. subjects at sec. level.

PSYCHOLOGICAL FOUNDATIONS OF CURRICULUM   137

In Search of a Curriculum.   Because each individual has specific needs and interests related to his or her self-fulfillment and self-realization, there is no generally prescribed humanistic curriculum. Rather, the learners draw on those experiences, subject matter, and intellectual skills necessary to attain full potential. The humanities and arts, especially philosophy, psychology, and esthetics, would be appropriate content because they further introspection, reflection, and creativity. A curriculum of affect, one that stresses attitudes and feelings, would also be acceptable. Math and science would be considered unnecessary. Appropriate labels might be "relevant curriculum," "humanistic curriculum," "value-laden curriculum," or "existentialist curriculum."

Should the student reject the teacher's interpretation of subject matter, it is the student's right to do so. It is more important that the student-teacher relationship be based on trust and honesty so that the student knows when the teacher's ideas of a subject are wise and deserve respect. Student choice would be crucial—the power to decide what to do and how to do it, a sense of control over one's ideas and work. School routine and rules would be minimal; learners would be left alone to do what they want to do, as long as it does not harm anyone or present a potential danger. Frequent evaluation, criticism, and competition would not be considered conducive to learning. The essence of many recent instructional trends, such as academic time, direct instruction, and mastery learning (which stress prescribed behaviors and tasks, well-defined procedures and outcomes, constant drill and testing), would be rejected as narrow, rigid, and high pressured.

Most reconceptualists would accept the phenomenologist-humanistic interpretation of learning because both these curricularists and learning theorists value the uniqueness of human personality. Both groups prefer classrooms characterized by freedom, an existential educational experience, and subjects in the humanities and arts, not the hard sciences. Reconceptualists tend to approve this learning theory because it rejects the rational means-ends approach, the same processes that the traditional or hard curricularists follow.[78] Instead of presenting empirical data to justify the means, phenomenologists and reconceptualists rely on psychological and philosophical positions for validating ends proposed.

A drawback to the phenomenologist-humanistic theories is their lack of attention to cognitive learning. When asked to judge the effectiveness of their curriculum, both phenomenologists and humanists (like reconceptualists) rely on testimonials and subjective assessments by students and teachers. They may also present such materials as students' paintings, poems, interviews, reports, biographies, and projects or talk about improvement in student behavior and attitudes.[79] They present very little empirical evidence or student achievement scores, however, to support their stance. Moreover, phenomenologists are not in agreement about how to teach self-actualization, self-determination, human striving, and so on, or about how to determine what subject matter is worthwhile, how to mesh the paintings, poems, and personal biographies with learning outcomes, and how to test or confirm many of their ideas.

There is great need to examine and construct a relevant, humanistic curriculum and to enhance the self-actualizing, self-determining learning processes. However, until the just described issues are resolved we shall continue to flounder in the phenomenologist area of learning. Those who trust the behavioral or cognitive-developmental process in teaching and learning, or the traditional or scientific spirit in curriculum making, will continue to distrust the "third force" in psychology and the "soft" approach to curriculum. Humanistic learning may enhance the mental health of the learners, personal feelings between students and teachers, and human awareness among students, teachers, and curriculum specialists. Sadly, however, their processes rely mainly on personal experiences and subjective interpretations that leave them open to criticism by traditional educators, including the majority of psychologists and curriculum specialists (who are either behaviorist or cognitive oriented).

CONCLUSION

Psychology has had significant impact on curriculum, especially in recent years. This chapter has focused on learning, one of the major compo-

nents of curriculum. Other aspects of psychology and curriculum are discussed in other parts of the book. As indicated in our discussion, as well as in Tables 4-5 and 4-6, which serve as overviews of the chapter, learning can be examined in terms of three major theories: behaviorism, cognitive development, and phenomenology.

Behaviorism is the oldest theory of learning, and its continued popularity is illustrated by such teaching-learning trends as micro teaching, instructional training models, individualized learning, direct instruction, mastery learning, and so on. We explored the difference between classical and operant conditioning; traditional behavior is related to elicited responses (a well-defined stimulus-response association) and operant behavior is related to emitted responses (no well-defined stimulus-response association).

Cognitive-developmental learning theory represents the second school of thought, which has developed rapidly in the last twenty or thirty years. This corresponds with the increasing influence of Piaget among American psychologists and the growing acceptance of environment (as opposed to heredity) as an explanation of cognitive growth and development. Cognitive learning theory is conducive for explaining various levels of thinking among humans, including concept thinking, problem solving, and creativity. Most learning theorists today are cognition oriented.

Phenomenology or humanistic psychology can be considered the third and most recent learning theory. Its emphasis is on attitudes and feelings, self-actualization, freedom to learn, and value clarification; it overlaps with existentialist philosophy.

Most textbook writers, including the authors of this text, are cognition oriented (by virtue of textbook organization and discussion of subject matter). However, we propose that the behaviorist component is needed for planning and developing curriculum. We also feel that the humanistic component of teaching and learning must also be incorporated into the curriculum—then into practice where it counts. We feel that each theory of learning is incomplete by itself, but all three theories have something to contribute to explain various aspects of behavior and learning in classrooms and schools. Readers should come to their own conclusions about what aspects of each theory they can use for their own teaching and curriculum development. Table 4-6 should help in this activity.

TABLE 4-5 Overview of Learning Theories and Principles

PSYCHOLOGIST	MAJOR THEORY OR PRINCIPLE	DEFINITION OR EXPLANATION
	Behaviorist	
Thorndike	Law of effect	When a connection between a situation and response is made, and it is accompanied by a satisfying state of affairs, that connection is strengthened; when accompanied by an annoying state of affairs, the connection is weakened.
Pavlov-Watson	Classical conditioning	Whenever a response is closely followed by the reduction of a drive, a tendency will result for the stimulus to evoke that reaction on subsequent occasions; association strength of the S-R bond depends on the conditioning of the response and stimulus.
Skinner	Operant conditioning	In contrast to classical conditioning, no specific or identifiable stimulus consistently elicits operant behavior. Based on Thorndike's law of effect, operant conditioning means that if an operant response is followed by a reinforcing stimulus, the strength of the response is increased.
Bandura	Observational learning	Behavior is best learned through observing and modeling. Emphasis is placed on vicarious, symbolic, and self-regulatory processes.
Gagné	Levels of learning	Eight types of learning are identified, from simple to complex, mostly behavioral and a few cognitive; they are based on orderly, prerequisite, and cumulative processes of learning.
	Cognitive	
Piaget	Cognitive stages of development	Four cognitive stages form a sequence of progressive mental operations; the stages are hierarchical and increasingly more complex.
	Assimilation, accommodation, and equilibration	The incorporation of new experiences, the method of modifying new experiences to derive meaning, and the process of blending new experiences into a systematic whole.
Guilford	Structure of intellect	Three major dimensions of thought—contents, operations, and products—each subdivided into several factors combine and interact to form 120 possible factors.

(continued)

TABLE 4-5 Continued

PSYCHOLOGIST	MAJOR THEORY OR PRINCIPLE	DEFINITION OR EXPLANATION
Cognitive		
Guilford	Convergent-divergent thinking	A qualitative method of thinking; the first corresponds with problem solving, reflective thinking, and the scientific method; the second corresponds with creative thinking, intuitive thinking, and the artistic method.
Gardner	Multiple intelligences	A cross-cultural, expanded concept of what is intelligence—such areas as linguistics, music, logical-mathematical, spatial, body-kinesthetic, and personal.
Dewey	Reflective thinking	Being in a situation, sensing a problem, clarifying it with information, working out suggested solutions, and testing the ideas by application.
Ennis-Lipman-Sternberg	Critical thinking	Teaching students how to think, including forming concepts, generalizations, cause-effect relationships, inferences, consistencies and contradictions, assumptions, analogies, and the like.
Bruner-Phenix	Structure of a subject	The knowledge, concepts, and principles of a subject; learning how things are related is learning the structure of a subject.
	Inquiry-discovery method	A method or quality of thinking that uses a body of organized knowledge; the first method tends to be convergent and the second tends to be divergent.
Humanistic		
Maslow	Human needs	Six human needs related to survival and psychological well-being; the needs are hierarchical and serve to direct behavior.
Rogers	Becoming a person	Becoming a person means being open to experience, developing trust, and accepting oneself.
	Freedom to learn	Becoming a full person requires freedom to learn; the learner is encouraged to be open, self-trusting, and self-accepting.
Raths	Value clarification	Analysis of personal preferences and moral issues to reveal or clarify one's values–that is, beliefs, attitudes, and opinions.
Johnson-Slavin	Cooperative learning	Cooperative and group approaches to learning are considered more effective than competitive and individualistic learning situations

TABLE 4-6 Overview of Major Learning Theories

BEHAVIORAL LEARNING

We learn by doing and observing others.

Reinforcement is essential for learning to occur.

Practice (with feedback) improves learning and retention.

Spaced recalls are essential for remembering information.

Learning through rewards is preferable than under the conditions of punishment.

Learning proceeds from simple to complex and part to whole behavior.

Learning should proceed in small, step-by-step, simple units.

Learning is hierarchical, based on sequential readiness.

Desired performance or learning outcomes should be stated in advance (and by objectives).

Learning is observable and/or measurable.

COGNITIVE-DEVELOPMENTAL LEARNING

Cognitive stages of development are related to age.

Cognitive development is sequential and based on previous growth.

The capacities of students are important; bright students are capable of learning more and at a more rapid rate than other students.

Learning can be modified as a result of the interaction of the self with the environment.

Learning involves the assimilation of new experiences with prior experiences.

Learning is best achieved through active participation in the environment; the teacher can improve the environment to stimulate learning.

There are several components and types of intelligence; there is no one single indicator or type of behavior that connotes intelligent behavior.

Students learn best when they can generalize information, that is, whole to part learning.

Students who learn how to learn will learn more in school than those who are dependent on the teacher to learn.

Transfer of learning increases when students have the opportunity to solve problems.

HUMANISTIC LEARNING

Teachers are sensitive to the students' world, not just the adult world.

Learners are viewed as individuals, with diverse needs. abilities, and aptitudes.

The learners' self-concept and self-esteem are considered as essential factors in learning.

Learning is considered holistic, not just cognitive; the act of learning involves emotions, feelings, and motor-dependent skills.

Learning is based on warm, friendly, and democratic student-teacher interactions; coercive and strict disciplinary measures are minimized.

The quality (or processes) of learning is considered as important (in some cases more important) than the quantity (or products) of learning; teachers nurture learners.

Students share ideas, work together, and tutor and help each other; homogeneous grouping, academic tracking, and competitive testing or programs are minimized.

Students and teachers plan together the experiences or activities of the curriculum.

Students are given choices (with limitations) and freedom (with responsibilities); the extent of choices and freedom is related to the maturity level and age of the students.

Learning is based on life experiences, discovery, exploring, and experimenting.

ENDNOTES

1. Ralph W. Tyler, *Basic Principles of Curriculum and Instruction* (Chicago: University of Chicago Press, 1949).

2. Jerome S. Bruner, *The Process of Education* (Cambridge, Mass.: Harvard University Press, 1959).

3. Edward L. Thorndike, *Animal Intelligence* (New York: Macmillan, 1911).

4. Edward L. Thorndike, *Psychology of Learning,* 3 vols. (New York: Teachers College Press, Columbia University, 1913); *The Fundamentals of Learning* (New York: Teachers College Press, Columbia University, 1932).

5. Tyler, *Basic Principles of Curriculum and Instruction;* Hilda Taba, *Curriculum Development: Theory and Practice* (New York: Harcourt, Brace, 1962).

6. John Dewey, *How We Think* (Boston: D. C. Heath, 1910); Dewey, *My Pedalogic Creed* (Washington, D.C.: National Education Association, 1929); and Charles H. Judd, *Education and Social Progress* (New York: Harcourt, Brace, 1934).

7. Taba, *Curriculum Development: Theory and Practice,* p. 121.

8. Bruner, *The Process of Education.*

9. Ivan P. Pavlov, *Conditioned Reflexes,* trans. G. V. Anrep (London: Oxford University Press, 1927). The experiment was conducted in 1903 and 1904.

10. John B. Watson, *Behaviorism* (New York: Norton, 1939).

11. John B. Watson, "What the Nursery Has to Say about Instincts," in C. A. Murchison, ed., *Psychologies of 1925* (Worcester, Mass.: Clark University Press: 1926), p. 10.

12. B. F. Skinner, *Science and Human Behavior* (New York: Macmillan, 1953).

13. Ibid.; B. F. Skinner, *Reflections on Behaviorism and Society* (Englewood Cliffs, N.J.: Prentice Hall, 1978).

14. B. F. Skinner, "The Science of Learning and the Art of Teaching," *Harvard Educational Review* (Spring 1954), pp. 86–97.

15. W. James Popham and Eva I. Baker, *Systematic Instruction* (Englewood Cliffs, N.J.: Prentice Hall, 1970), p. 48.

16. Albert Bandura, *Social Learning Theory* (Englewood Cliffs, N.J.: Prentice Hall, 1977).

17. Robert M. Gagné, *The Conditions of Learning,* 4th ed. (New York: Holt, Rinehart and Winston, 1987).

18. Robert M. Gagné, Leslie J. Briggs, and Walter W. Wager, *Principles of Instructional Design,* 3rd ed. (New York: Holt, Rinehart and Winston, 1988).

19. Gagné, *The Conditions of Education,* p. 245.

20. Robert M. Travers, *Essentials of Learning,* 5th ed. (New York: Macmillan, 1982), p. 505.

21. Robert Glaser, "Trends and Research Questions in Psychological Research on Learning and Schooling," *Educational Researcher* (November 1979), p. 12. See also Glaser, "Education and Thinking: The Role of Knowledge," *American Psychologists* (February 1984), pp. 93–104.

22. Bruce Joyce, Marsha Weil, and Beverly Showers, *Models of Teaching,* 4th ed. (Needham Heights, Mass.: Allyn and Bacon, 1992); Travers, *Essentials of Learning.*

23. Jean Piaget, *Judgment and Reasoning in the Child* (New York: Harcourt, Brace, 1948).

24. Jean Piaget, *The Psychology of Intelligence,* rev. ed. (London: Broadway, 1950). See also Hans Furth and Harry Wachs, *Thinking Goes to School: Piaget's Theory in Practice* (New York: Oxford University Press, 1974).

25. John Dewey, *Experience and Education* (New York: Macmillan, 1938), p. 40.

26. Jean Piaget, *The Child's Conception of Physical Causality* (New York: Harcourt, 1932). See also Piaget, *The Equilibrium of Cognitive Structures,* trans. T. Brown and K. J. Thampy (Chicago: University of Chicago Press, 1985).

27. Dewey, *Experience and Education,* p. 43.

28. Tyler, *Basic Principles of Curriculum and Instruction,* pp. 84–86.

29. Taba, *Curriculum Development: Theory and Practice,* pp. 118–119.

30. Bruner, *The Process of Education.*

31. Dewey, *Experience and Education,* p. 44.

32. Bruner, *The Process of Education,* p. 13.

33. J. P. Guilford, *The Nature of Human Intelligence* (New York: McGraw-Hill, 1967).

34. Howard Gardner, *Frames of Mind,* rev. ed. (New York: Basic Books, 1985); Gardner, *The Unschooled Mind: How Children Think and How Schools Should Teach* (New York: Basic Books, 1991).

35. Bruner, *The Process of Education;* Philip H. Phenix, *Realms of Meaning* (New York: McGraw-Hill, 1964); and Joseph J. Schwab, "The Concept of the Structure of a Discipline," *Educational Record* (July 1962), pp. 197–205.

36. See Jacob W. Getzels and Philip D. Jackson, *Creativity and Intelligence: Explorations with Gifted Students* (New York: Wiley, 1962); Robert J. Sternberg, ed., *Handbook for Human Intelligence* (New York: Cambridge University Press, 1982); and Michael A. Wallach and Nathan Kogan, *Modes of Thinking in Young Children: A Study of the Creativity-Intelligence Distinction* (New York: Holt, Rinehart, 1965).

37. Dewey, *How We Think.*

38. James B. Conant, *Science and Common Sense* (New Haven: Yale University Press, 1951).

39. Robert H. Ennis, "Logical Basis for Measuring Critical Thinking Skills," *Educational Leadership* (October 1985), pp. 44–48; Ennis, "Critical Thinking and Subject Specificity," *Educational Researcher* (April 1989), pp. 4–10.

40. Matthew Lipman, "Critical Thinking—What Can It Be?" *Educational Leadership* (September 1988), pp. 38–43.

41. Matthew Lipman et al., *Philosophy for Children,* 2nd ed. (Philadelphia: Temple University Press, 1980). Also see Lipman, *Philosophy Goes to School* (Philadelphia: Temple University Press, 1988).

42. Robert J. Sternberg, "How Can We Teach Intelligence?" *Educational Leadership* (September 1984), pp. 38–48; Sternberg, "Thinking Styles: Keys to Understanding Performance," *Phi Delta Kappan* (January 1990), pp. 366–371.

43. William A. Sadler and Arthur Whimbey, "A Holistic Approach to Improving Thinking Skills," *Phi Delta Kappan* (November 1985), p. 200. Also see John Barell, *Teaching for Thoughtfulness* (New York: Longman, 1991).

44. Robert J. Sternberg, "Teaching Critical Thinking: Possible Solutions," *Phi Delta Kappan* (December 1985), p. 277.

45. E. Paul Torrance. *Rewarding Creative Behavior* (Englewood Cliffs, N.J.: Prentice Hall, 1965).

46. Carl Rogers, "Toward a Theory of Creativity," in M. Barkan and R. L. Mooney, eds., *Conference on Creativity: A Report to the Rockefeller Foundation* (Columbus: Ohio State University Press, 1953), pp. 73–82.

47. Eric Fromm, "The Creative Attitude," in H. H. Anderson, ed., *Creativity and Its Cultivation* (New York: Harper & Row, 1959), pp. 44–54.

48. Robert J. Sternberg, "Intelligence, Wisdom, and Creativity: Three Is Better than One," *Educational Psychologist* (Summer 1986), pp. 175–190; Sternberg, "Practical Intelligence for Success in School," *Educational Leadership* (September 1990), pp. 35–39.

49. Bruner, *The Process of Education,* pp. 56–57.

50. Bruner, *The Process of Education;* Gall M. Inlow, *Maturity in High School Teaching* (Englewood Cliffs, N.J.: Prentice Hall, 1964); Philip H. Phenix, *Realms of Meaning* (New York: McGraw-Hill, 1964); and Taba, *Curriculum Development: Theory and Practice.*

51. Inlow, *Maturity in High School,* p. 78.

52. Taba, *Curriculum Development: Theory and Practice,* p. 156.

53. John I. Goodlad, "A Study of Schooling: Some Findings and Hypotheses," *Phi Delta Kappan* (March 1983), p. 468.

54. John Holt, *How Children Fail* (New York: Pitman, 1964).

55. Gordon H. Bower and Ernest R. Hilgard, *Theories of Learning,* 5th ed. (Englewood Cliffs, N.J.: Prentice Hall, 1981); Travers, *Essentials of Learning.*

56. See Henry Misiak and Virginia Sexton, *Phenomenological, Existential, and Humanistic Psychologies* (New York: Grune and Stratton, 1973); Richard Schmuck and Patricia Schmuck, *A Humanistic Psychology of Education* (Palo Alto, National Press Books, 1974); and Douglas Sloan, *Toward the Recovery of Wholeness* (New York: Teachers College Press, Columbia University, 1984).

57. Arthur W. Combs and Donald Snygg, *Individual Behavior,* 2nd ed. (New York: Harper & Row, 1959); Combs, *A Personal Approach to Teaching* (Boston: Allyn and Bacon, 1982).

58. Kurt Koffka, *Principles of Gestalt Psychology* (New York: Harcourt, 1935); Wolfgang Kohler, *Gestalt Psychology,* 2nd ed. (New York: Liveright, 1947); and Max Wertheimer, *Productive Thinking* (New York: Harper & Row, 1945).

59. Abraham H. Maslow, *Toward a Psychology of Being,* 2nd ed. (New York: Van Nostrand Reinhold, 1968); Maslow, *Motivation and Personality,* 2nd ed. (New York: Harper & Row, 1970).

60. Ibid.

61. Abraham Maslow, *The Farther Reaches of Human Nature* (New York: Viking Press, 1971); Maslow, *Motivation and Personality.*

62. Carl Rogers, *Client-Centered Therapy* (Boston: Houghton Mifflin, 1951), p. 485.

63. Carl Rogers, *A Way of Being* (Boston: Houghton Mifflin, 1981); Rogers, *Freedom to Learn for the 1980s,* 2nd ed. (Columbus, Ohio: Merrill, 1983).

64. Louise M. Berman and Jessie A. Roderick, eds., *Feeling, Valuing, and the Art of Growing* (Washington, D.C.: Association for Supervision and Curriculum Development, 1977); Maxine Greene, *The Dialectic of Freedom* (New York: Teachers College Press, Columbia University, 1988).

65. Louis E. Raths, Merrill Harmin, and Sidney B. Simon, *Values and Teaching,* 2nd ed. (Columbus, Ohio: Merrill, 1978), pp. 27–28.

66. Ronald C. Doll, *Curriculum Improvement: Decision Making and Process,* 8th ed. (Boston, Mass.: Allyn and Bacon, 1992).

67. David R. Krathwohl, Benjamin S. Bloom, and Betram Maisa, *Taxonomy of Educational Objectives, Handbook II: Affective Domain* (New York: McKay, 1964).

68. David W. Johnson and Roger T. Johnson, "Toward a Cooperative Effort," *Educational Leadership* (April 1989), pp. 80–81; Robert E. Slavin, "Grouping

for instruction in the Elementary School," *Educational Psychologist* (Spring 1987), pp. 109–128.

69. David W. Johnson and Frank P. Johnson, *Joining Together: Group Theory and Group Skills,* 4th ed. (Needham Heights, Mass.: Allyn and Bacon, 1991); David Johnson, *Reaching Out: Interpersonal Effectiveness and Self-actualization,* 4th ed. (Englewood Cliffs, N.J.: Prentice Hall, 1990).

70. Robert E. Slavin, *Student Team Learning* (Washington, D.C.: National Education Association, 1983); Slavin, *Cooperative Learning: Theory, Research, and Practice* (Englewood Cliffs, N.J.: Prentice Hall, 1990).

71. Robert E. Slavin, "Student Teams and Comparison among Equals," *Journal of Educational Psychology* (August 1978), pp. 532–538; Slavin, "Student Teams and Achievement Division," *Journal of Research and Development in Education* (Fall 1978), pp. 38–49; and Slavin, "Synthesis of Research and Development in Education," *Educational Leadership* (February 1991), pp. 71–82.

72. Elliot Aronson et al., *The Jigsaw Classroom* (Beverly Hills, Calif.: Sage, 1978); Raymond J. Wlodkowski and Judith H. Jaynes, *Eager to Learn* (San Francisco: Jossey-Bass, 1990).

73. Charlotte Buhler, "Basic Theoretical Concepts of Humanistic Psychology," *American Psychologist* (April 1971), pp. 378–386; Arthur W. Combs et al., *Perceptual Psychology: A Humanistic Approach to the Study of Persons* (New York: Harper & Row, 1976);

and Edmund V. Sullivan, *Critical Psychology and Pedagogy: Interpretation of the Personal World* (Westport, Conn.: Bergin & Garvey, 1990).

74. William R. Glasser, *Schools Without Failure* (New York: Harper & Row, 1969); Glasser, *Control Theory in the Classroom* (New York: Harper & Row, 1986).

75. Allan C. Ornstein, "Components of Curriculum Development," *Illinois School Research and Development Journal* (Spring 1990), pp. 204–212.

76. Gordon Allport, "A Conversation," *Psychology Today* (April 1971), p. 59.

77. Rogers, *Freedom to Learn.*

78. Michael Apple, *Teachers and Texts* (New York: Routledge & Kegan Paul, 1986); Henry A. Giroux, *Teachers as Intellectuals: Toward a Critical Pedagogy of Learning* (Westport, Conn.: Bergin & Garvey, 1988). Also see John McNeil, *Curriculum: A Comprehensive Introduction,* 4th ed. (Glenview, Ill.: Scott, Foresman, 1990).

79. William H. Schubert, "Reconceptualizing and the Matter of Paradigms," *Journal of Teacher Education* (January–February 1989), pp. 27–32; J. Smyth, "A Critical Pedagogy of Classroom Practice," *Journal of Curriculum Studies* (November–December 1989), pp. 483–502; and Sean A. Walmsley and Trudy P. Walp, "Integrating Literature and Composing into the Language Arts," *Elementary School Journal* (January 1990), pp. 251–274.

CHAPTER 5

SOCIAL FOUNDATIONS OF CURRICULUM

Focusing Questions

1. *What is the difference between education and schooling?*
2. *How would you define developmental tasks? Why is it important for children and youth to learn these tasks for successful growth in our society?*
3. *How would you describe the rate and direction of change?*
4. *What knowledge is most worthwhile for students? Why?*
5. *How do curricularists organize knowledge?*
6. *What knowledge should students learn to better cope with the future?*
7. *In what ways have schools and society changed the focus or priorities of education over the last 90 years?*
8. *How have the national task force reports on education influenced your school (school district)?*

Any discussion of curriculum should consider the social setting, especially the relationship between schools and society and its influence on curriculum decisions. Social astuteness is essential for curriculum planners and developers today. Curriculum decisions take place in a complex social setting, through demands that are imposed by society and that filter down to schools. Indeed, curriculum workers need to consider and use social foundations to plan and develop the curriculum.

In many curriculum texts, a consideration of social foundations often leads to discussion of schools and society, as well as discussion of individual socialization, the social implications of knowledge and change, the aims of education, and various reform strategies. This chapter, too, deals with such social issues.

SOCIETY, EDUCATION, AND SCHOOLING

Education is neutral. It can be used for constructive or destructive ends, to promote one type of political institution or ism or another. The kind of education our young receive determines the qual-ity of our society. The transmission of culture is the primary task of a society's educational system. The values, beliefs, and norms of a society are maintained and passed to the next generation not merely by teaching about them, but also by embodying them in the very operation of the educational system.

For Dewey, education is the means of perpetuating and improving society, by properly organizing the experiences of the learners. It is "a primary responsibility of educators . . . [to] be aware of the general principle of the shaping of actual experiences by environing conditions" and to understand "what surroundings are conducive to having experiences that lead to growth." For Dewey, experience must be channeled properly "for it influences the formation of attitudes of desire and purpose."[1] It is up to educators, particularly those in charge of subject matter, to judge which content and activities (or what Dewey calls "experiences") enhance individual personal and social growth and improve society and which do not (or what he calls "miseducative").

Most of us regard education as synonymous with schooling. Actually, even a society that has no formal schools still educates its young through the family or special ritual and training. "Schooling plays a major role in education in modern industrial [societies]"; it becomes more important as societies become "more complex and as the frontiers of knowledge expand. In simple, nontechnological societies, almost everyone becomes proficient over the whole range of knowledge necessary for survival." In technological societies "people acquire different proficiencies and abilities; no individual can range over the entire body of complex knowledge or expect to be proficient in all areas of learning."[2]

In traditional and nonliterate societies, education is processed through ceremonies, rituals, stories, observation and emulation of older children, parents and elders, and by strict enforcement of codes of conduct and behavior. In modern and technological societies, the educational process starts at home but "school takes on greater importance as the child becomes older." The school is a vital institution "for helping the young acquire systematic knowledge," inculcating them with the proper attitudes and values, and "bonding the gap between generations." In contemporary society, the mass media also play a major role in processing knowledge and in "redefining values and ideas."[3] But it is the function of schools to serve a modern society by educating its children and youth. The curriculum worker who helps determine the content, activities, and environment of education plays a major role in shaping and indirectly socializing students.

Society and Modal Personality

When social scientists speak of modal personality, they do not mean that all members of a particular society are exactly alike. As Ruth Benedict wrote, "No culture yet observed has been able to eradicate the differences in temperament of the persons who composed it."[4] However, members of a society do have much in common; they are nursed or fed on schedule, toilet trained a certain way, educated in similar fashion, marry one or several spouses, live by labor or perform common economic tasks, believe in one God or many deities. These shared experiences temper individual differences so that individuals behave in similar ways. According to

Benedict, the norms of society govern interpersonal relations and produce a modal personality, that is, the attitudes, feelings, and behavior patterns most members of a society share.

In a study of the American modal personality, anthropologist Margaret Mead stressed that this is the land of unlimited opportunity. Whether or not this is true, the belief that anyone can become president, which is reinforced by our notion of equality of opportunity, places a heavy burden on most Americans.[5] By implication, those who do not become president (or doctors, lawyers, engineers, or corporate executives) have shirked their "moral responsibility to succeed." Most other people in the world blame poverty, fate, or the government for failure to succeed; Americans (except some minority groups) tend to blame themselves.

Whereas European parents usually raise their children to carry on family traditions, first- and second-generation American parents want their children to leave home for better lives. Americans tend to evaluate their own self-worth according to how high they have climbed above their father's status and how they compare with their friends and neighbors. At no point do Americans feel they have truly "arrived"; the climb is endless, but within reach, and it is very much a part of our American value system—and the nature of our schools and the traditional curriculum.

Sex Roles and Sex Differences

Not only does society demand conformity to its basic values and mores, it also assigns specific roles to each of its members, and it expects them to conform to certain established behavioral patterns. A good example of this type of socialization is sex roles, that is, the way boys and girls and men and women are "supposed" to act. Sex roles vary from culture to culture, but within a given culture they are rather well defined; moreover, they are enforced through an elaborate schedule of selective reinforcement. For example, preschool boys are ridiculed for playing with dolls, and girls are supposed to be "feminine."

Both male and female children initially identify with the mother, but boys must shift their original mother identifications to establish masculine role identities. As this period begins, girls often have the same-sex parental models all day, but boys see their fathers only briefly.[6] Besides, fathers participate in some feminine roles that until very recently have been defined in American society as feminine (washing dishes, cleaning), so boys must distinguish masculine roles from the stereotypes spelled out for them by society through a system of reinforcements and rewards. As boys' identification with their mothers diminishes, it is gradually replaced by learned identification with a culturally defined masculine role. This is accomplished mainly through such negative admonishments as "Don't be a sissy," which do not even tell them what to do instead.

Girls simply learn female identification as it is presented to them, partly through imitation and partly through the mothers' reinforcing and rewarding selective behavior. Boys have the problem of making the proper sex-role identification in the partial absence of male models at home; this is even more difficult in female-headed households in which the father is completely absent (increasingly common today, among all social classes). Girls acquire a learning method that basically involves developing a personal relationship and identification with their mothers. By contrast, boys must define their goals, restructure some of their experiences, and abstract underlying principles. The result is greater learning problems for boys and greater dependency on the part of girls.

Schools are largely staffed by females, especially at the elementary level, which is a critical period in child development. Schools are dominated by female norms of politeness, cleanliness, and obedience. The curriculum, tests, and classroom activities are female-oriented as well—safe, nice, antiseptic. Schools frown on vulgar language and fighting; they suppress boys' maleness and often do not permit action-oriented, tough sports. The disadvantages that boys find at home in developing masculine identities are sometimes compounded by the schooling process.[7]

Patricia Sexton presents controversial data showing that schools are feminizing institutions that discriminate against males and subvert their identity.[8] Her data show that approximately three out of four problem students are boys, and that

because teachers tend to fail problem students, approximately two out of three students who fail are boys. Boys largely outnumber girls in school dropout rates, delinquent behaviors, mental illness, and suicides. Male students who are high achievers tend to be fat and flabby, especially at the elementary and junior high school level; those who gravitate to masculine activities, such as conflict sports and mechanics, tend to do poorly in academic areas, and they are often at odds with their teachers, who are predominantly female (but they conflict with male teachers, too, who, by virtue of their role, tend to enforce feminized school norms).

Although Sexton's conclusions may be somewhat overgeneralized and extend beyond her data, there is no question that girls receive higher grades throughout elementary school, although the gap is gradually reduced in high school. More boys are nonreaders; more boys fail; more boys are disciplinary cases; more boys drop out of school; and more men than women are prisoners or have mental breakdowns. Men die younger, too. No doubt sex roles and sex differences in school are at least in part related to role expectations that are incorporated into the self-concept very early in life.

The problem that Sexton analyzes is highlighted by the fact that, on the average, according to biochemical research, boys are more active than girls almost from the time they are born, and that this difference is related, in turn, to hormone differences.[9] Boys are at a particular disadvantage in elementary school because they tend to learn through active manipulation of their environment (which schools tend to discourage), whereas girls tend to learn through verbal communication (which schools tend to stress). Writes one researcher, after a review of several studies:

> By the time they are five or six, [all] children in ... classrooms [are] expected to behave like girls. The system requires children to remain attentive to one task and stay seated in one place for a considerable period of time.... They must ... persevere at tasks that are largely linguistic or symbolic in nature. Boys [usually] cannot sit still, they are distractible; they test the properties of objects. Such behavior interferes with the concentration they need to read and write.[10]

By way of contrast, the problems that girls experience in the schooling process generally reflect their socialization for dependency rather than aggressiveness. Until recently, most girls were not encouraged to prepare for high-status occupations in law, medicine, or business, or even for training beyond high school. Instead they were expected to prepare for roles as wives and homemakers.[11] Except for a few occupations, such as teaching, social work, or nursing (which have been classified as semiprofessions), girls traditionally were not expected to enter fields that require college preparation. Further, the few professions into which women were channeled tended to have relatively low pay and low status. Both the civil rights and feminist movements have changed old stereotypes and, given a growing information society (and decline in manufacturing and factory work in the United States), muscle power is no longer an advantage on the job. Where it still counts, say in the police or military situation, provisions are made for women to contribute to this sector of the economy, too. To be sure, textbooks no longer slot women into "feminine" roles and "feminine" jobs.

SOCIAL AND DEVELOPMENTAL THEORIES

A number of theories have been originated that focus on global aspects of human growth and development. Because they emphasize the study of behavior as a totality, starting with infancy, in a sense they combine Gestalt psychology with socialization. Developmental theories address the cumulative effects of change that occur as a consequence of learning or failing to learn appropriate tasks during the critical stages of life. Failure to learn an appropriate task at a given stage of development tends to have detrimental effects on the developmental sequence that follows.

Development proceeds through a rather fixed sequence of relatively continuous stages, and it is assumed that maturation as well as appropriate societal experiences are necessary to move the individual from stage to stage. Shifts from one stage to the next are based not only on age but also on variations in the amount and the quality of social experiences an individual accumulates over long spans of time.

Human Tasks/Needs

Robert Havighurst has identified six periods in human development: (1) infancy and early childhood, (2) middle childhood, (3) adolescence, (4) early adulthood, (5) middle age, and (6) late maturity. Developmental tasks are defined as "the tasks the individual must learn" for purposes of "healthy and satisfactory growth in our society." They are what a person must learn if he or she is to be judged and to judge him- or herself to be a reasonably happy and successful person. "A developmental task is a task that occurs at a certain stage or period in the life of that individual. Successful achievement . . . leads to happiness and to success with later tasks, while failure leads to unhappiness, disapproval by the society, and difficulty with later tasks."[12]

A youngster's schooling is concerned with the developmental tasks of the second part of the first period and the next two periods of life. The tasks are:

1. *Early childhood*
   a. *Forming concepts and learning language to describe the social and physical reality.*
   b. *Getting ready to read.*
   c. *Learning to distinguish right from wrong and beginning to develop a conscience.*
2. *Middle childhood*
   a. *Learning physical skills necessary for ordinary games.*
   b. *Building wholesome attitudes toward oneself.*
   c. *Learning to get along with age-mates.*
   d. *Learning appropriate male and female roles.*
   e. *Developing fundamental skills in reading, writing, and mathematics.*
   f. *Developing concepts for everyday living.*
   g. *Developing morality and a set of values.*
   h. *Achieving personal independence.*
   i. *Developing (democratic) attitudes toward social groups and institutions.*
3. *Adolescence*
   a. *Achieving new and more mature relations with age-mates of both sexes.*
   b. *Achieving a masculine or feminine social role.*
   c. *Accepting one's physique and using the body effectively.*
   d. *Achieving emotional independence of parents and other adults.*
   e. *Preparing for marriage and family life.*

    f. *Preparing for an economic career.*

    g. *Acquiring a set of values and an ethical system to guide behavior.*

    h. *Achieving socially responsible behavior.*[13]

Although the Havighurst model is the best known, other models have been proposed to deal with student or adolescent needs. Havighurst uses the term *human* instead of *adolescent* to connote a wider range of ages, and the term *tasks* instead of *needs* to suggest a solution, but the other models are just as comprehensive and balanced as Havighurst's. For example, Harry Giles et al. outlined four "basic needs"—personal, social, civic, and economic—each of which has three to four subdivisions.[14] Florence Stratemeyer and her colleagues categorized "ten areas of living" into three "life situations"[15]; B. Othanel Smith and his colleagues classified twenty-nine "adolescent needs" into six major social-personal classifications,[16] and Henry Harap outlined thirty "life activities" needed for successful human development.[17]

    Different as these classification schemes are, they clearly show that many common topics of concern tend to be social in nature and to include environmental, moral, civic, psychological, physical, and productive (or economic) dimensions of learning. Actually, it may well be that, in principle, this degree of broad agreement is the best we can aim for in the interest of developing a student-needs approach. All the models consider the *whole child,* as opposed to only cognitive learning; tend to stress *achievement* categories, that is, tasks or needs; recognize the concept of *readiness;* and focus on the *individual,* even though they do refer to social circumstances in which the person finds him- or herself. Whereas the Havighurst model professes to be developmental and consists of a hierarchy of human needs called tasks, with no one curriculum emphasis, the other models tend to be organized around equally important student or adolescent needs and developed in context with a core curriculum and a social-issues curriculum. This does not mean that these models cannot be used for *all* curricula. Interestingly, all the models can be used as a framework for a needs-assessment plan, discussed in greater detail in Chapter 8.

Note that the *needs-assessment* plan is basically rooted in the *student-needs* or *adolescent-needs* approach of the 1940s and 1950s. The needs-assessment plan evolved during the mid-1970s, when the federal government insisted that such a plan was required for federal funding. This requirement has filtered down to state and local guidelines and curriculum workers have adopted the idea. Whereas the student-needs approach focuses on the learner, a needs assessment may not always focus on the learner, although it often does. A needs assessment can include the needs of the professional staff, school, parents, and the community. The intent is to clarify the aims and goals of a school district; the assessment itself is conducted because school officials believe there is room for improvement.

Moral Development

Any society depends on the presence of people who share its culture, who take active roles, who are tied together by a set of codes and laws that are in part determined by tradition, and who have a sense of morality and conscience. Morality, in a practical sense, involves a strong social component, for what is considered morally right or wrong reflects the nature of a society—its customs, mores, and laws. How a person develops morally is partially, if not predominantly, based on the way he or she interacts with society—more precisely, on the social environment as well as the roles and responsibilities he or she learns and/or deems important via contact with people who are considered important. Although conscience and moral standards may start evolving in the preschool years, they do not begin to develop at a rapid rate until children are about 4. From about 4 to 6 years, conscience in most children is confined less to specific behaviors; it begins to incorporate more generalized abstract standards, and it becomes determined less by external rewards or punishments and more by internal sanctions.[18]

    Jean Piaget's theories of moral development were based on investigations that included Piaget's questioning Swiss children about moral dilemmas and events in stories. For example, Piaget might have asked, "Why shouldn't you cheat in a game?" Piaget's observations suggested that from ages 5 to 12 the child's concept of justice passes from a rigid and inflexible notion of right and wrong, learned from his or her parents, to a sense of equity in moral judgments. Eventually, the concept takes into account the specific situation or circumstances in which behavior has occurred.[19] As the child becomes older, he or she becomes more flexible and realizes that there are exceptions to the rule, that is, there are some circumstances under which lying may be justifiable.

More recently, Lawrence Kohlberg studied the development of children's moral standards and concluded that the way we think about moral issues is not simply a reflection of our society but is also based on stages of growth or age. Kohlberg outlined six developmental types of moral judgments grouped into three moral levels or stages, corresponding to Piaget's cognitive stages of development:

1. *Preconventional level.* Children at this level have not yet developed a sense of right or wrong. The level is comprised of two types of children: (1) children who do as they are told because they fear punishment, and (2) children who realize that certain actions bring rewards.

2. *Conventional level.* At this level, children are concerned about what other people think of them. As a result, their behavior becomes largely other directed. There are two types in this level: (3) children who seek their parents' approval by being "nice," and (4) children who begin thinking in terms of rules.

3. *Postconventional level.* Children's morality is based on what other people feel or on their precepts of authority. This level also includes two types: (5) children who are able to view morality in terms of contractual obligations and democratically accepted laws, and (6) children who view morality in terms of individual principles of conscience.

Kohlberg and Piaget support the cognitive developmental view of morality, that is, there is a considerable amount of reasoning in moral judgments and behavior, although they differ on specifics. Whereas Piaget stresses that there are very real differences in the way children think about morality at different ages, Kohlberg found considerable overlap at the various ages. Both

also believe that social arrangements and society play a major role; however, Piaget gives maturation more emphasis. Kohlberg says:

> As opposed to Piaget's view, the data suggest that the "natural" aspects of moral development are continuous and a reaction to the whole social world rather than a product of a certain stage, a certain concept . . . or a certain type of social relations.[20]

Existentialist educators, such as Maxine Greene and Van Cleve Morris, view morality as something beyond cognitive processes, akin to such social-psychological processes as personal sensitivity, feelings and openness to others, and esthetic awareness.[21] One is free, but one's *freedom* is essentially an inner matter involving awesome *responsibility* of *choice* operating within the medium of humankind and human *awareness*. Freedom, responsibility, choice, and awareness all involve moral judgments, and are related to social standards and personal beliefs.

Philip Phenix, a cognitive curricularist, also maintains that moral development combines social standards or norms with personal choices. Moral action presupposes an "obligation of what is to be done . . . self determination . . . and freedom." Although we can discern personal knowledge in our moral behavior, it is questionable whether we can identify a subject matter or teach it. "By far the most significant sources of such influence are the laws and customs of society. . . ." Accepted social standards "may not always be right or good, but they do embody much well-tested moral wisdom."[22]

Phenix outlines five basic moral traditions that encompass the foundations of society and that, although he does not say so, could be taught as part of the learning process to guide moral behavior: (1) human rights, which suggest conditions of life that ought to prevail, such as trial by jury, free speech and religion, and so on; (2) sex and family relations, whereby sex and family codes are carefully considered; (3) social relationships within and among class, ethnic, racial, and religious groups; (4) economic matters dealing with property rights and the distribution of goods and services; and (5) political matters dealing with distributive justice and power. Again, these concerns are mainly sociological in nature and involve social standards—various customs, mores, and laws.

In the final analysis, "moral conduct can be taught and is continuously taught, not by experts who profess the subject of ethics [or knowledge of any subject], but by participation in everyday life of society according to recognized standards of society."[23] Such learning connotes "ethical education," in Phenix's terms, not through formal schooling, but engenered by law, custom, and ritual. We can teach ethical theory in school, he maintains, and we can teach an array of standards (such as the Ten Commandments or the Golden Rule) to evaluate behavior, but an individual's final course of action is a matter of personal choice and is influenced by his or her view of what is right, good, or ideal. Phenix's position is a social and existentialist view of life—mixed with cognition.

Curriculum specialists, who must view moral development in conjunction with cognitive development, would probably feel more comfortable with Dewey's position. Dewey points out that subject matter has social and moral worth, which should be integrated "under conditions where their social significance is realized, [and] they feed moral interests and develop moral insight."[24] But the actual decisions and behaviors related to morality involve social growth and social experiences, according to Dewey, which schools can help shape. He uses such descriptors as "character," "conditions," and "environment" to describe morality and the organization of subject matter.[25] See Curriculum Tips 5-1.

CHANGE AND THE CURRICULUM

Educators, in general, and teachers and curriculum workers have a choice that has been offered to them throughout the ages. They may uncritically accept the tendencies of the times in which they find themselves and develop school programs that *mirror* current social and political forces, or they may appraise the times and develop school programs that respond to the dynamics of change. The curriculum can either reflect society or reflect upon and indirectly help shape society. Teachers may either serve as cogs in a bureaucratic school machine, keeping subject matter safe and sterile, or they may help

students think and act by offering specialized knowledge, raising controversial issues, and incorporating problem-solving activities.

The first approach views the school and educator as mirrors of society; the second approach views schools and school people as instruments of change. The former approach is based on the traditional conception of education; the latter is a progressive and reconstructionist conception of education. Sadly, the first approach tends to coincide with the *reality* of schools; the second approach borders on the *ideal*.

If we are unable to deal with change in a constructive and appropriate manner, then we become victimized by it. If we are unable to shape the world around us, then the whims of nature dictate to us and social and political forces overwhelm us. According to William Van Til, "There is a danger to individuals and to society in an education which accepts uncritically and reflects unthinkingly. . . . The danger is that some forces which mutually reinforce each other may take us down roads contrary to the American [ideal]"— the ideal of the individual who is free, morally responsible, and important. "Some tendencies of the times, if uncritically accepted and implemented by education, could lead to the powerless man in the powerful society."[26]

Society as a Source of Change

Contemporary society is changing so swiftly that we have difficulty coping with it and adjusting ourselves to the present and preparing for the future. We are forced to look to the schools for help in understanding and living with social change, but schools are conservative institutions that usually lag behind change.

The differential rates of change in different parts of society give rise to the phenomenon known as *cultural lag*. Usually, changes in the scientific, commercial, and industrial aspects of culture come first, followed by lags in the institutions of society. People seem to accept material changes more readily than institutional changes, and they seem to resist changes in fundamental ideological ideas.

The amount of cultural lag within a society varies with the amount of social change. If there is little or no social change, obviously the lag, if

CURRICULUM TIPS 5-1   Teaching Students to Reason Morally

Teachers can influence their students' moral thought and judgment in class by discussing admirable character traits and role models, permitting group discussions of value-laden issues and insisting that students be held accountable for their behavior. Then, there are practical teaching strategies for promoting moral reasoning. The strategies listed below fall into two categories: general cognitive strategies and specific cognitive strategies. In general, the 23 strategies combine critical thinking with moral issues and ideas.

I. General Cognitive Strategies

1. Avoiding oversimplification of moral issues.
2. Developing one's moral perspective.
3. Clarifying moral issues and claims.
4. Clarifying moral ideas.
5. Developing criteria for moral evaluation.
6. Evaluating moral authorities.
7. Raising and pursuing root moral questions.
8. Evaluating moral arguments.
9. Generating and assessing solutions to moral problems.
10. Identifying and clarifying moral points of view.
11. Engaging in Socratic discussion on moral issues.
12. Practicing dialogical thinking on moral issues.
13. Practicing dialectical thinking on moral issues.

II. Specific Cognitive Strategies

14. Distinguishing facts from moral principles, values, and ideals.
15. Using critical vocabulary in discussing moral issues.
16. Distinguishing moral principles or ideas.
17. Examining moral assumptions.
18. Distinguishing morally relevant from morally irrelevant facts.
19. Making plausible moral inferences.
20. Supplying evidence for a moral conclusion.
21. Recognizing moral contradictions.
22. Exploring moral implications and consequences.
23. Refining moral generalizations.

Source: Richard W. Paul, "Ethics Without Doctrination," *Educational Leadership* (May 1988), p. 12.

---

it exists, is small. In Western society, especially in the United States, consistent and fundamental change is occurring in many aspects of society. As our society has entered a period of rapid change (which has accelerated since World War II) and as each new change has set off a whole chain of other events, this lag has become acute.

Rate and Direction of Change.   There are two basic ways to conceive change—rate and direction. The rate of change has implications that are quite apart from, and sometimes more important than, the direction of change.

One way to illustrate the *rate of change* is to divide the last 100,000 years of human existence into lifetimes of approximately 75 years each (equivalent to an average lifespan in our society), or a total of 1,333 lifetimes. Only during the last sixty lifetimes has it been possible to communicate effectively from one lifetime to another through writing. Only in the last six lifetimes did humankind see a printed word. Only in the last two has anyone anywhere used a motor, and only in the last one have we used electricity.

In this connection, Alvin Toffler noted over 20 years ago that we were entering a period of *future shock:* We have too many goods and services from which to choose, and our ability to choose wisely from all these options was becoming increasingly limited because of human overload (for example, try choosing the best long-distance phone company).[27]

Another way of appreciating the rate of change is to consider that to a person born in 1940, who was 50 years old in 1990, the following occurred:

1. Telecommunications became, for practical purposes, instantaneous.
2. The speed of information processing increased a millionfold.
3. The rate of population increase went up more than a millionfold.
4. Jet aircraft, radar, space missiles, and space satellites became commonplace.
5. Major organs, such as the human heart, kidneys, and liver, were transplanted.
6. Moon and Martian landings were successfully completed.[28]

To this list, add the following:

1. Genetic engineering, test-tube babies, and sex selection became realities (and the slowing of the aging process is at our fingertips).
2. With a portable remote system (weighing less than one pound) a TV viewer can instantly (at the speed of light) tune into one or more of 100 channels and connect live to any part of the world through a satellite communication system.
3. More than 75 percent of the items on supermarket shelves today did not exist in 1940. Plastic money has since replaced paper money as the major medium of exchange.
4. Computers are common in everyday life, including in schools; robots are commonplace in commerce and industry, and they will soon be in homes as well.
5. Whereas three-fourths of Americans employed by industry in 1940 were manufacturing goods, today more than 60/75 percent are providing services; we have changed from an industrial society to a "postindustrial society" or what some

people call the third technological revolution" or "third wave."

6. The median age of the U.S. population rose from 26 in 1940 to 30 in 1980 to 34.5 in 1990 and is likely to rise to 37 by 2000. The proportion of people 65 and over increased from 7% in 1940 to 11.3% in 1980 and is expected to increase to 18% by 2000.
7. The number of working mothers increased from 18% in 1950; by 1990 two-thirds were working and the trend toward greater female participation in the labor force is expected to continue. The increase in working mothers is in part related to the general decline in the American standard of living, which started in the 1960s, and has created a new phenomenon of latchkey children. By 1990, there were some 8 million latchkey children between ages 6 and 13.

One way to illustrate the *direction of change* is to consider world population growth. Philip Hauser estimated that for 600,000 years the world population expanded by 0.02 per thousand per year. On a two-dimensional graph such as Figure 5-1, this growth appears as a straight horizontal line. During the past 500 years, however, the growth line has shifted essentially from a horizontal position to a vertical one. At the present time, population growth has expanded from 2 percent per millennium to more than 2 percent per year—a thousandfold increase per year.[29]

This shift in direction constitutes a fundamental change that simply cannot be comprehended as a mere quantitative change. (The quantitative shift represents only one dimension of change in population growth.) Other equally important directional changes in society involve advances in science, communication, transportation—all of which affect the quality of life and which have global impact. Actually, in these areas of society, as with population growth, the rate of change at a period in time reaches geometric or exponential proportions, and causes a dramatic shift or change in direction. For population growth, as well as for science, communication, and transportation, the critical time period has been the present century.

Educators, especially curriculum specialists, need to reduce educational lag and to avoid plan-

FIGURE 5-1   World Population Growth, 6000 B.C. to 2000 A.D.

ning schools for the 1990s that are suited for the 1970s—a typical 20-year lag period that often exists between schools and society. The fact of rapid change and the need to plan schools today for tomorrow bring to mind serious questions: What policies govern our society? At a global level, what should be our educational aims? How do we identify the "good" life and what role do the schools play? How do schools reduce the gap between the "haves" and "have nots"? How do the schools prepare students for the world of tomorrow, when teachers who are trusted to do the job mainly rely on a knowledge base that is quickly becoming, if it is not already, dated?

Schools as a Source of Change

If we take a broad, long view of schools, that is, a *macro* view, we can observe noticeable changes in schools over time. Historically, according to Philip Jackson, "one has only to think of the wooden benches and planked floors of the early American classroom as compared with the plastic chairs and tile flooring in today's suburban schools to note changes."[30] We can strengthen the contrast by looking back to the one-room schoolhouse: Students of many ages were crowded in

one room; the teacher stood behind the pulpit (like the church minister) preaching the daily lessons; no blackboards or chalk were used; the desks and chairs were bolted down; the sun was the major source of light; and firewood was the main source of heat. Schools, today, are dramatically different.

If we look at the school during our lifetime—that is, a *micro* view—say, when we were attending elementary school, we note that the changes have been minimal. Unruh and Alexander have summarized the milieu of change since the 1950s: "Surface changes, small and isolated innovations and lack of comprehensive approaches to changes" have prevailed in the schools. The underlying assumption, or the reason for the lack of change, has been that "the school as an institution was headed in the right direction except that it needed to exert more effort toward its previous goals and make content and instruction more palatable to students. It was taken for granted that there was nothing wrong in the schools [and] . . . it was the student" and not the schools "that needed to be changed."[31]

Although the research in education may be impressive in quantity, very few noticeable changes have resulted in schooling since our days as students. We are basically using the same instructional methods in the classroom that we were using 50 years ago, according to one observer. On the other hand, the changes and improvements in science, technology, and medicine within the last 5 years have been impressive, and they have affected almost all of our lives in some way. "Had Rip Van Winkle been a teacher and slept for fifty years, he could return to the classroom and perform relatively well; the chalk, eraser, blackboard, textbook, and pen and paper are still, today, the main tools for most teachers, as they were a half a century ago—or longer." If, however, Mr. Van Winkle's occupation "had been related to one of the other three fields, and had he dozed off for five years, he would be unable to function effectively for his knowledge and skills would be dramatically dated."[32]

We might expect educational aims and subject matter to change as society imposes new social and political demands on the schools, and as new knowledge is created. And they do! However, we should not expect the structure and organization of schools to change dramatically. This is why Rip Van Winkle could function in the schools after sleeping for so long, or why a teacher, after 10 or 20 years of retirement, could, if he or she wanted, go back into the classroom and still be effective.

We must understand that schools are highly bureaucratic and conservative (or traditional) institutions that operate with standardized norms of behavior, written rules and regulations, and well-defined tasks dispersed among administrators, teachers, and students. As parents and/or teachers who were once students, we can return to school and readily cope and function almost immediately because the behaviors and tasks, the rituals, rules, and regulations, have not changed much since we were children.

As teachers, curriculum specialists, administrators, and students interact on a daily basis in the operation of a school, a social order develops: A set of routines and rules surfaces and group norms and organizational values become pervasive and shape individual personalities and behavior. Hoy and Miskel describe this process: "The school is a system of social interaction; it is an organized whole comprised of interacting personalities bound together in an organic relation-ship." The school is "characterized by an interdependence of parts, a clearly defined population, differentiation from its environment, a complex network of social relationships, and its own unique culture."[33] The outcome is a host of institutional norms and patterns of behaviors that govern the interaction between teachers and students and between curriculum specialists and other support staff. Observers use terms like *intrinsic character, institutional realities,* or *cultural patterns,* to describe these social characteristics and interactions. When taken together, they tend to result in a persuasive method of socializing and controlling the people who attend and/or work in schools, and they tend to inhibit change.

As schools plan for change, education can no longer be reserved for the traditional age cohort, or early years of life, 5 to 16. Schooling must be expanded both downward (to cope with problems of working mothers and to better prepare at-risk students for school) and upward (to provide greater variety of educational resources at different stages of people's lives and to prepare them for second or third careers).[34] The idea of a "step-in, step-out" approach to educational systems for life-long education is gaining in popularity. Both Combs and Illich point out that education must be expanded to include "learning networks" that combine informal and formal models of schooling.[35]

Furthermore, the idea of literacy must also be expanded to include not only basic or functional literacy, but also cultural literacy, scientific literacy, computer literacy, technological literacy, television (or electronic) literacy, and research literacy.

Education for Diversity. As student populations become more diversified (by the year 2000 nearly one-third of all 5 to 13-year-olds are expected to be minorities in the United States),[36] schools will need to stop trying to organize and homogenize students into one standard or average group, as evidenced by current whole-class grouping, tracking, scheduling, and standardized testing; we need different learning goals, learning groups, school programs, time frames, acceleration lanes within grade levels, promotion practices, and flexible curriculums and schools to meet the needs and abilities of different students.

Much more attention must be focused on diversity—in terms of abilities, gender and culture, and learning styles. Although the number of at-risk students is dramatically increasing and we must not forget their schooling problems, we must never forget the gifted and talented (and that poor and minority students can be gifted, too), for they are most likely to constitute the leadership of tomorrow.

Finally, to cope with the growing number of (1) bureaucratic institutions, especially their bigness and indifference, that affect all people (including students); (2) working mothers and the resulting latchkey children and adolescents; and (3) overprogrammed and overstressed children of "fast-track" parents who want to produce superachievers (ranging from Harvard University bound children to tennis and golf pros), there is more need than ever for schools to become caring, personal, and trusting institutions—to replace the impersonal factory model that often characterizes most schools. Each student needs to be treated as special, and curriculum workers, including teachers, must become concerned not only with cognitive achievement but also the social, moral, and psychological development of children and youth, what others might call "holistic education." See Curriculum Tips 5-2.

Knowledge as a Source of Change

The accumulated body of organized knowledge about people and the world may be viewed as an extension of and interaction process with contemporary society. As society changes, so does our knowledge; in reverse, as our knowledge base increases, additional changes take place in society as well. The changes in Western society and growth in knowledge result from our striving to understand, control, and change the physical and social environment around us. (Changes take place in other societies, too, although today their growth in knowledge tends to be slower.) The schools should also be considered as a major data source for knowledge, especially for children and youth, in terms of (1) screening knowledge against aims society sets for education, (2) identifying important kinds of knowledge, and (3) determining what can and should be taught.

Explosion of Knowledge. Since the 1950s, many educators have continued to call attention to the explosion of knowledge. Every 15 years or so, our significant knowledge doubles, and this trend makes it important to continuously reappraise and revise existing curricula. "It can be affirmed unequivocally," says Bentley Glass, "that the amount of scientific knowledge available at the end of one's life will be almost one hundred times what it was when he was born." (This may be considered as an overstatement, because knowledge cannot continue to explode exponentially as it has in the past.) Moreover, 95 percent of all the scientists who ever lived are alive today.[37]

Similarly, Warren Ziegler maintains that (1) more mathematics has been created since 1900 than during the entire period of history, (2) half of what a graduate engineer studies today will be obsolete in 10 years, and (3) half of what a person learns is no longer valid by the time he or she reaches middle age.[38] We add to this list that nearly half of what we will need to know to function in scientific or technical jobs by the year 2200 is not even known today, by anyone.

The idea that knowledge is increasing exponentially or geometrically obscures the fact that the development of knowledge in many fields, especially science and technology, is more typically related to "branching": that is, the creation of several subdivisions or specialties within fields, not just simple growth. Each advance in a particular field has the potential for creating another branch. (In education, one can find some indicators of proliferation of several fields of study or branches, including curriculum and instruction, and within each field or branch several specializations of knowledge and job titles. With this increase of knowledge, there are several new curriculum journals, papers, and speeches, all adding to the proliferation of knowledge.) The almost incredible explosion of knowledge threatens to overwhelm us unless we can find ways to deal with this new and growing wealth of information; new knowledge must be constantly introduced into the curriculum while less important material is pruned away. In assessing the ongoing rush of knowledge, Alvin Toffler asserts that knowledge taught should be related to the future. "Nothing should be included in the required cur-

**Curriculum Tips 5-2   Alternative Schools for the
                        Future: Where Students
                        Come First**

The following actions might be viewed as a beginning toward modifying, or even changing, existing schools and building tomorrow's schools, which should emphasize flexibility, diversity, and acceptance. They are practices that provide transitions toward the future.

1. Replace the six or seven period day schedule with forms of flexible, smorgasbord, daily, or nonscheduled formats.
2. Eliminate A–F report cards or at least make them optional, and eliminate class rank, the separation of "smart" and "dumb" students.
3. Embrace the affective domain; students will have reduced cognitive problems if their affective needs are considered.
4. Remove group-paced instruction and requirements for group standards; instead, personalize learning and graduation goals.
5. Eliminate all labels, ability tracks, and other forms of segregation; focus on individual goals, aspirations, needs, interests, concerns, and problems.
6. Non-grade all programs. For example, all ninth graders cannot take the same science or English course; their achievement scores range over five or six grades.
7. Move into year-round education. The transition for the agriculture and industrial calendar to the information- and leisure-based calendar requires greater diversity in the school calendar.
8. Develop an interdependent, interdisciplinary curriculum by eliminating departmentalization and separate subjects; the idea of a core curriculum of basic academic subjects also segments the curriculum into separate subjects and should be avoided.
9. Consider the diverse cultural and linguistic factors associated with teaching minority students.
10. Return to the concept of the middle school, which houses grades 5 to 8 and preadolescents 10 to 14 years old. Their psychological and physical growth create a much greater range and need for special programs and personnel.
11. View the school in context with many other community institutions.
12. Use various volunteers, including other students, business people, and senior citizens, to help students learn and grow.

Source: Adapted from Don Glines, "Can Schools of Today Survive Very Far into the 21st Century?" NASSP Bulletin (February 1989), pp. 52–55.

riculum unless it can be strongly justified in terms of the future. If this means scrapping a substantial part of the formal curriculum, so be it."[39] To deal with this knowledge explosion, as it shapes the future, curriculum specialists have two major problems that require continuous attention: (1) what knowledge to select and (2) how to organize it.

What Knowledge Is of Most Worth?   This question, which was raised by Spencer more than 100 years ago, has social implications; it is certainly more relevant today, because of the complexity of and changes in society, than it was during Spencer's time. In recent years, the question has, in fact, been repeated by many different curricularists.[40] Actually, the question dates back to ancient Greece, when Plato and Aristotle questioned the value of knowledge in relation to society and governmental affairs, and to ancient Rome, when Quintilian set forth the original seven liberal arts—grammar, rhetoric, logic, arithmetic, geometry, astronomy, and music—as the ideal curriculum for educated citizens of public life: senators, lawyers, teachers, civil servants, and politicians. During the modern school period, these seven liberal arts have expanded to include many other subjects.

TABLE 5-1 Average Years of Coursework Completed by Graduating High School
Seniors, 1982 and 1987

	1982	1987
English	3.80	4.00
Mathematics	2.54	2.97
Science	2.19	2.59
Social studies (and history)	3.10	3.33
Foreign languages	1.05	1.46
Computer science	0.11	0.43

Source: *The Condition of Education, 1990,* Vol. 1 (Washington, D.C.: U.S. Government Printing
Office, 1990). Table 1.13, p. 48.

Table 5-1 shows a survey of coursework in five basic subject areas (plus computer science) for 1982 and 1987. In all subject areas, coursework among graduating high school seniors has increased, especially in mathematics and science. But the data are not so impressive when all high school students (including dropouts) are included and when comparisons are made with high school seniors in other advanced, technological countries. In any event, the percent for each subject area suggests what school officials, adult society, and students consider to be most worthwhile knowledge.

Considering that we live in a highly technocratic and scientific society, one in which knowledge has great impact on our standard of living and in a world in which the push of a button can have enormous impact on our lives, the enrollments in science and mathematics have serious implications for the future of our country. A similar concern was voiced over 30 years ago, when our standard of living was increasing more rapidly and when we were more influential as a superpower. Then, James Conant stressed that students needed to enroll in more courses in science, mathematics, and foreign language.[41] The conerns of the Sputnik era first resurfaced in the 1980s, and have continued in the 1990s, under the theme of excellence in education, and there is the same feeling of urgency. Our failure to heed Conant's warning continues and is viewed by some as one reason for our decline as the leading political and economic giant of the world, and for the general decline of our manufacturing capability and standard of living.

As a point of comparison, consider that Japanese students are required to take 23 percent of their total junior high school curricula in science and mathematics. In high school, they are required to take 1 1/4 science courses per year and 1 1/2 math courses per year (including calculus and statistics). Because 94 percent of the Japanese attend high school, this requirement produces a more scientifically literate public than ours.[42] In addition, Japanese students outperform American students in science and mathematics on the International Association for the Evaluation of Educational Achievement (IEA) study.

Because our knowledge is changing so rapidly, we must continuously ask ourselves what is the most worthwhile knowledge, and we must continuously reappraise what we mean by worthwhile. A number of paradigms have been developed along these lines. Schwab, for example, takes an eclectic approach to organizing curriculum in context with change. He is willing to accept various curriculum modes, and he points out that there are limitations to almost any approach. We need to organize a curriculum that is conducive to change, and that enables scholars and practitioners to work together and test their ideas in the context of changing problems and issues of society.[43]

Organizing Knowledge. The way we organize knowledge refers to a body of knowledge, a discipline, a field of study, or the curriculum content. These are basically synonymous terms that suggest a subject-centered approach (as opposed to a student-centered approach) to curriculum and a cognitive approach (as opposed to a behaviorist or humanistic one) to teaching and learning. This approach, according to Ruggiero and Zais, relies on logic and rational thinking to organize information, concepts, generations, and principles of school subjects, or what others call the "structure" of the subject.[44] The assumption is that the interconnection of information, concepts, and the like, constitutes bodies of information that have been validated and are the result of seeking practical, social, and educational ends; however, the result is compartmentalization of subjects.

Harry Broudy outlines four criteria for classifying knowledge: (1) agreed upon terms and concepts used for representing abstract ideas, (2) a network of related facts, generalizations, and rules or principles that are accepted as valid, (3) a method of investigation specific to itself, and (4) rules of evaluating evidence.[45] According to Phenix and Schwab, knowledge is organized into disciplines that possess their own methods of inquiry for generating new knowledge. Thus new knowledge is never ending as long as prior knowledge is organized into a true discipline or subject. For these two curricularists, disciplines prove their worth by their own ability to generate new knowledge by adhering to methods of inquiry and rules of evidence and evaluation.[46]

Knowledge classifications are not be-end, end-all categories. With time and in various social settings, they change; thus subject matter in school should also be modified on a regular basis. Indeed, old knowledge must be pruned away, while new knowledge should be assimilated and integrated into specific knowledge areas and new contexts. Ideally, new knowledge should be integrated into a moral legal context. Whose morality? The standards of that society which is governed by a constitutional process (that protects people from other people and provides people basic rights) and promotes worthwhile and just consequences.

Areas of Knowledge. The organization of knowledge into areas, bodies of information, or classifications has occupied world thinkers for centuries, from Plato and Aristotle to Whitehead and Russell. For example, Aristotle organized knowledge into three classes: (1) *theoretical,*

such as science and math; (2) *practical,* such as politics and ethics; and (3) *productive,* such as music and architecture. This classification scheme served well for his historical period; it was direct, simple, and easy to understand and lacked a hierarchical belief or position that one area or domain of knowledge was more important than the other.

Phenix organizes knowledge into six patterns or "realms of meaning": (1) *symbolics,* consisting of ordinary language, mathematics, and nondiscursive symbols (expression of feelings, values, and insights); (2) *empirics,* comprising physical science, biology, psychology, and social science; (3) *esthetics,* including music, visual arts, movement arts, and literature; (4) *synnoetics,* consisting of personal knowledge; (5) *ethics,* referring to moral knowledge and law; and (6) *synoptics,* that is history, religion, and philosophy.[47]

The ideal curriculum, according to Phenix, consists of *depth* of understanding and *mastery* in one realm, contending that "a person has to choose the one channel [or realm] into which he can pour his energies with maximum effect." He argues against an "all-around knowledgeable person . . . [for] people who scatter themselves in many directions dissipate their powers and never transcend superficiality." Thus Phenix urges that we educate the "specialist" or "scholar," and views the "generalist" as quaint and impractical. Today, Phenix would most likely resist the idea of a "common" or "core" curriculum as too general and superficial, evidenced by his "ideal curriculum," which focuses on "narrow rather than broad . . . scope." For him, "depth of knowledge and skills should be the goal," rather than what he calls "superficial acquaintance with a variety of fields."[48]

Finally, Weinstein and Fantini attempt to integrate a cognitive and humanistic view toward knowledge and learning. Referring to knowledge as "content vehicles," they contend that content should "include not only conventional subject areas (English, social studies, mathematics, science, and so on)," but also foundation disciplines such as "psychology, sociology, anthropology, philosophy," and so on, as well as "classroom situations, . . . out of school experiences, [and] the children themselves."[49] Fantini considers people more important than subject matter, but subject matter is still important for the self-actualization of people. They write, "Unless knowledge relates to feeling, it is unlikely to affect behavior appreciably."[50]

The New Core Curriculum. Considerable emphasis is being placed on a common curriculum or a core curriculum for all high school students. Some of us who are nostalgic might trace the core curriculum to the 1940s and 1950s when it suggested a block of time, two or three periods with the same teacher, who taught two or more subjects or integrated them under a different name such as "general science" or "social studies."[51] In still other cases, core suggested the blending of academic subject matter with social issues of the day (community or national), concerns or needs of youth, as well as problem-solving activities.[52] For those who wish to go farther back in a time capsule, they might recall the common curriculum proposed in 1893 by the Committee of Ten. The curriculum was geared for all secondary school students. The problem is that fewer than 10 percent of the 14 to 17 age cohort were enrolled in high school; thus, the core subjects were elitist and geared for a small number of students.

The new core, which evolved in the mid 1980s, attempts to affirm both equality and excellence by defining what is essential for all students throughout the nation. The question arises, however, whether all students should experience a common curriculum, or whether there should be a common ending point or program, given the fact that there are 50 different state departments of education and some 15,000 local school districts, each with their own brand of education and ideal curriculum.

John Goodlad's core is perhaps most controversial. In *A Place Called School,* he proposed that 80 to 90 percent of the total curriculum be reserved for the core rubrics and 10 to 20 percent be devoted to individual talents and interests—and electives.[53] Goodlad hesitates to recommend a specific core, knowing full well that it will only produce controversy and conflict. By not delineating a common curriculum, one might suggest that he is allowing room for state and local interests to prevail.

What makes Goodlad extremely controversial is his proposal to start school at age 4 and conclude at age 16, thus shortening the school system by one year (currently age 5 to 18). (Hopefully, school authorities would recognize that age 4 is a time for play and socialization; thus academic time would be minimal.) Goodlad continues: With the time saved, all vocational education would be eliminated from the curriculum, leaving room for the more common learning deemed necessary for all students. Years 16 to 20 would be devoted to vocational preparation, community or national service, or college. To be sure, the idea might be traced to Sparta and the modern Israel state, whereby youth have been recruited into national service. Goodlad does not mean to convey this nationalistic idea, but there are thinkers in our society who would push such a proposal for specific "social" or national ends.

Ernest Boyer's core curriculum is more acceptable for the establishment. He would increase required courses from one-half to three-fourths of the high school curriculum or total Carnegie units required for graduation. His curriculum would stress what he calls "traditional" courses, especially for the first two years, such as literature, history, math, and science, and give increased emphasis to foreign language, the arts, civics, non-Western cultures, technology, and the meaning of work and health. All students would complete a senior-year independent project that focuses on social issues and combines various academic core subjects; the inference is that the project would be interdisciplinary and summarize or apply what was learned in previous years.[54]

The school would offer a *single* track for *all* students for the first two years. The last two years would be a "transition period," or curriculum in which half the time would continue to be devoted to the core (and include many of the nontraditional core courses) and the other half of the time (25 percent of the total curriculum) would be devoted to *elective clusters.* These clusters would include advanced subjects for those who wished to pursue college, as well as career options for those who intended to enter the world of work upon graduation, or a combination of both. To provide the best and most comprehensive range of clusters, the schools would establish "linkages" with "learning places" (authors' words) such as local libraries, museums, galleries, theaters, colleges, science laboratories, and businesses. This coincides with the concept of "community education," whereby the school is only one of many learning institutions within the community working collaboratively with other community agencies to promote diversified and real-life learning experiences.[55]

Theodore Sizer's major work, *Horace's Compromise,* is based on his visits to 80 high schools. In his book, a teacher named Horace must choose between "covering" a multitude of low-level skills and fragmented content in the prescribed curriculum or in-depth teaching of important concepts and understandings. To develop in-depth learning, Sizer recommends that the curriculum be divided into four major areas or a common core: (1) inquiry and expression, (2) mathematics and science, (3) literature and the arts, and (4) philosophy and history.[56] He emphasizes more active learning and reduced emphasis on what he views as mindless approaches to passing achievement tests.

Sizer maintains that the four curriculum areas should meet fundamental standards of cultural literacy and civic understanding; students should be given reasonable choices in reading some instructional materials, but there should be a traditional consensus of worthwhile materials among teachers and community members; subject matter should support the students' learning of basic academic and communication skills; and subject matter chosen should be useful and interesting for students.[57] Most important, subject matter must be connected, not disconnected or isolated. The task of the curriculum worker, then, is to organize the four subject areas into a reasonable whole that includes agreed upon content, skills, and attitudes to be learned by all students.

Knowledge and Future Learning. As we begin to cope with the many changes in our society, we need to organize certain knowledge areas and knowledge assumptions to deal with and evaluate the explosion of knowledge.

In a highly theoretical book, Joseph Tykociner suggests twelve basic areas of knowledge for dealing with change:[58] (1) *arts:* architecture, choreography, dramatics, graphic arts, industrial design, landscaping, literature, music, painting, sculpture, and so on; (2) *symbolics of information:* linguistics, mathematics, logic, and information theory; (3) *hylenergetics* (sciences dealing with matter and energy): physics, chemistry, astronomy, geology, and mineralogy; (4) *biological sciences:* botany, zoology, taxonomy, morphology, cytology, genetics, and physiology; (5) *psychology:* experimental, developmental, abnormal, animal, human, and industrial; (6) *sociology:* behavioral studies, human ecology, demography, social institutions, and ethnology; (7) *exeligmology* (sciences dealing with the past): the world at large, nations, states, ethnic groups, communities, family groups in historical, cultural, literary, scientific, and philosophical context; (8) *pronoetics* (sciences related to sustaining human life): agriculture, medicine, technology, and national defense; (9) *regulative area* (harmonizing human relations): jurisprudence, political science, economics, and public administration; (10) *disseminative area* (transmission of knowledge): education, vocational guidance, library science, journalism, and mass communications; (11) *zetetics* (how knowledge can be systematized and increased): problem solving, methodology, environmental conditions and incentives, research, and development; and (12) *integrative areas* (the search for synthesis or a total picture): philosophical, aspirational, and general systems.

What Tykociner has achieved is to bind together the entire field of arts and sciences, with methods and processes for systematizing knowledge and for representing it in terms of growth, transformation, and integration. Knowledge is envisioned as a continuous process that shapes society—and links the past, present, and future. In more practical terms, Tykociner presents curriculum specialists with a total range of knowledge from which to select subject matter and organize curriculum. He provides us with various kinds of content and processes upon which the generalist or specialist can draw to develop an instructional program.

To cope with the vast array of change in society, Ornstein defines ten knowledge areas for curriculum leaders and other practitioners to consider; the knowledge areas are futuristic and form the basis of an interdisciplinary curriculum.

1. *Knowledge should comprise the basic tools.* This includes reading, writing, arithmetic, and oral communication, as well as computer literacy. The basic tools are means to an outcome, not an end in themselves. Students need to learn more than the basics, but without the basics they cannot move beyond simple knowledge or think critically in the subject fields.

2. *Knowledge should facilitate learning how to learn.* The school should help the learners acquire the skills, tools, and processes necessary to become more adept at learning and to use existing knowledge to learn new knowledge. Teachers must limit the temptation to teach a host of facts and right answers; they must encourage learners to assume responsibility for their own learning.

3. *Knowledge should be applicable to the real world.* Book knowledge that cannot be applied to everyday life is meaningless and easily forgotten. It does not help the learners participate productively in society. The schools must resist teaching theory that cannot be applied to practice. Good theory can be applied to practice.

4. *Knowledge should improve the learners' self-concepts, awareness skills, and senses of personal integrity.* Stressing cognitive learning, or facts and figures, without considering the personal, emotional, and even spiritual state of the individual, is only considering half of learning. Knowledge should be used to develop the learners' feelings and personal integrity. It should enable them to get along with themselves and others, and to be relatively content with themselves and others. Unhappy or anxiety-laden individuals cannot make the best use of their cognitive skills.

5. *Knowledge should consist of many forms and methods.* There are many roads to learning and many avenues of inquiry. What works for one learner does not always work as well as for another, because there are many different styles of learning and patterns of thinking (in part related to sex, class, culture, and intelligence). Schools need to provide various options and alternatives for acquiring knowledge and learning. Schools must also recognize they are only one of many sources of learning and intellectual authority; they compete with the home, community, peer group, and mass media, which together have greater impact on the learners, on knowledge acquisition, and on thinking than the schools.

6. *Knowledge should prepare the individual for the world of technology.* The individual, in modern society, must learn to live with computers, robots, lasers, telecommunications, and space exploration. A truly educated, productive, and well-rounded individual will be able to function in an accelerating world of science and technology (that is, individuals should be scientifically and technologically literate).

7. *Knowledge should prepare individuals for the world of bureaucracy.* Bureaucracy is a growing social phenomenon that also characterizes modern society. The school system is one of many formal institutions that is run by the complicated machinery of social organization; actually, it is the first of many bureaucratic organizations that the child will encounter in life. The individual in school, in church, in the military, in the hospital, on the job and in dealing with government must learn to cope with the enormous size of bureaucracy. He or she must be able to get along with others both on a horizontal basis (peers and colleagues) and on a vertical basis (subordinates and supervisors), in regard to rules and regulations, record keeping and "documentation, impersonal and abstract relations, experts, incompetents, seniority, and administrative hierarchy.

8. *Knowledge should permit the individual to retrieve old information.* No individual can accumulate all the knowledge necessary to fully develop his or her human potential. The individual must understand how to retrieve old knowledge and then to modify or transform it to gain new knowledge. Knowledge is a powerful tool, and in an age of information processing, those able to retrieve and then apply information intelligently will be most productive and powerful and best able to compete in contemporary society.

9. *Knowledge acquisition should be a lifelong process.* It must be recognized that schools play a diminishing role as the learners grow and develop. Schools provide only a preliminary and temporary base of knowledge that is eventually superseded by other institutions and different forms of education. Other educational tools, such as books, newspapers, television, videos, and computers, assume greater importance and more

influence than textbooks or other school materials for continuing the educations of both youngsters and adults. As adolescents develop into adults, their experiences extend beyond schools. They acquire most new learning, in fact, outside of schools.

10. *Knowledge should be taught in context with values.* Knowledge is based on facts, which are objective, neutral, and quantifiable. The knowledge that is learned becomes processed through the social and philosophical lens of the individual; it therefore becomes value laden. In a very real sense, what we learn, and what we do not learn, are based on a process of choosing, a filtering process, that is itself based on values. How we interpret knowledge, how we build and use it, partially reflect the act of valuing and the value structure we emphasize. The greatest danger in teaching knowledge is to ignore the values that shape the individual and society; this is teaching in a vacuum and without vision. Worthwhile knowledge cannot replace values, but must be incorporated into the values we cherish. The kind of society we are and the kinds of people we become reflect both the knowledge and values we learn—more precisely, how we interpret knowledge amid our values.[59]

Critical and Cautionary Choices. All these knowledge areas provide learners with the basis for coping with change—and for understanding and analyzing the events and trends that impact on society. Those who possess these skills have an enormous advantage in dealing with themselves and others and in the way they think and act in schools and society. Those who have such knowledge can deal with alternatives, possibilities, and probabilities and can thus formulate and act on convictions. Failure to achieve these knowledge skills leads to powerlessness in a powerful society.

On the other hand, we caution the reader on several fronts. Change for the sake of change is not good; change must be tempered with wisdom, compassion, and justice. Scholars throughout the ages have viewed their societies as being at the cutting edge of change and progress. We may be just as myopic as we view our society; only the future will tell. New knowledge, indeed, is not necessarily better than old knowledge: Are we to throw away most of Aristotle, Copernicus, Galileo, Kepler, Darwin, and Newton merely because they are not part of this century? If we stress only scientific and technological knowledge, we could languish physically, esthetically, and spiritually. Also, we have no guarantee that a futuristic curriculum best prevents us from repeating the mistakes of the past; as a nation we seem to lack historical perspective, and we tend to rely on our youth and future.

What knowledge to select and how to organize it require continuing attention; we must learn to prune away old and irrelevant knowledge, and sequence, balance, and integrate new and relevant knowledge into subject matter. As we modify and update the curriculum, we must not, however, throw away time-tested, enduring subjects, such as literature, history, even music or art, because of pressure groups and special-interest groups. We must learn to screen our knowledge, with subsequent emphasis on certain subjects, against the values and educational aims that, as a society, we set for schools. These are difficult tasks. Curriculum workers need to help educators make choices in a climate of change.

ESTABLISHING SOCIAL/EDUCATIONAL PRIORITIES

We look to the schools to help us cope with the elements of change. As a society, we react to change and social pressures by revising the aims or priorities of education. The schools, in turn, respond by changing their programs. The schools are also influenced by external or public groups who seek to further their interests and promote their causes and who pressure the schools to teach particular subjects. Thus, rarely will there be complete agreement, much less agreement for any length of time, on the aims or priorities of education. Pressure, popular rhetoric, and slogans of the day, as well as concerns and demands of various public groups, must be balanced for the good of the general public and the nation at large.

Education for All Students

Education prior to the turn of the twentieth century emphasized a perennialist outlook and stressed traditional subject matter, mental discipline, and schooling for academically able students. Influenced by the larger trends of society—the muckraker movement and calls for social and economic reform—the period between World War I and World War II (some educators have extended the period from the *Kalamazoo* decision, in 1874, when the Supreme Court ruled that the states had the right to levy taxes for support of public schools,[60] to the Sputnik era) may be characterized by the rise and fall of progressive education. The educational aims of this progressive era and the curriculum reflected the growing child psychology movement and endorsed meeting the diverse needs of all students, providing a common ground for teaching, enhancing American ideas and educating all citizens to function in a democratic society.

During this period, the *Cardinal Principles of Secondary Education* were formulated.[61] Only one of the seven principles or aims of secondary education was concerned with the fundamentals of cognitive learning. The aims cited in 1918 are still, in one form or another, the major aims and goals of contemporary education. The most important aspect of the document is that it emphasized that secondary schools should aim to educate all youth for "complete living," not just one segment of the student population, such as academically able students. Also, it did not emphasize subject matter or mental vigor. The Commission noted that more than two-thirds of entering high school students dropped out prior to graduation, and that an increasing number of immigrant children had to be educated, socialized, and provided with appropriate economic and civic skills.[62]

Twenty years later, the Educational Policies Commission of the NEA, which included the presidents of Harvard and Cornell Universities, the Commissioner of Education, and a number of progressive educators issued a report entitled *The Purpose of Education in American Democracy.*[63] Concerned with the problems of out-of-school youth and unemployment resulting from the Great Depression, these educators issued a comprehensive set of four goals: self-realization, human relations, economic efficiency, and civic responsibility. Each goal had several subcategories (see Chapter 7).

During the mid 1940s, the Educational Policies Commission continued to modify the aims of education. Influenced by World War II, it stressed aims related to democracy and world citizenship, as well as those related to the general needs of children and youth. According to another influential report, *Education for All American Youth,* youth must develop "Ten Imperative Needs":[64] (1) economic and vocational skills; (2) good health and physical fitness; (3) community and citizenship duties; (4) family duties; (5) consumer skills; (6) scientific skills; (7) literature, art, and music skills; (8) leisure activities; (9) ethical values; and (10) rational abilities. These needs were mostly sociopsychological and physical in nature; only two were concerned with subject matter, and a third focused on cognitive learning in general.

Recapping from the 1918 Seven Cardinal Principles to the 1944 Ten Imperative Needs, the aims are representative of an era dominated by progressivism and by an offshoot science of child psychology. During this period, emphasis was placed on the "whole child" and "life adjustment." Subject matter was de-emphasized, while social, psychological, vocational, moral, and civic responsibilities were stressed. In general, the traditional concept of curriculum as a body of subjects came under attack by progressive educators; the major emphasis focused on the "child-centered," "experience-centered," and "activity-centered" curriculum. All three approaches were used by Pestalozzi and Froebel in the nineteenth century and by Dewey in his laboratory school at the University of Chicago from 1896 to 1904.[65] All three approaches emphasized adapting curriculum to student needs and interests and ensuring that curriculum was relevant to the realities of the learner.

Focus on Academically Talented Students

After World War II, during the era of the Cold War and the Soviet Sputnik flight, the aforementioned aims and curriculum focus became targets for criticism. Americans were appalled that our country was losing the space race to the Soviet Union and that our skies were no longer impregnable.

Even though the influential Harvard Report, published at the end of World War II, looked optimistically to educating the whole person and providing a general education as means of developing the common understanding important to all citizens in a free society, powerful forces called for a return to academic essentials and old-fashioned mental discipline. Historian Arthur Bestor stated that the main subjects in elementary school should be reading, writing, and arithmetic, with some emphasis on science and history. At the high school level, the curriculum should stress math, science, history, English, and a foreign language.[66] Admiral Hyman Rickover questioned why Johnny could not read while Ivan could and did. He demanded that, in the national interest, there be a return to the basics, a beefing up of our science and mathematics courses, and "a deemphasis on life-adjustment schools and progressive educational lists."[67]

Werner von Braun, a German-educated missile expert, testified before a U.S. Senate Committee in 1958 to urge ending "family life" and "human relations" subjects and adopting the European system of education, which emphasized "technical and scientific subjects" and academic excellence.[68] As for the nonacademic or less able student, little recognition or interest seemed to exist with von Braun, or for that matter with the educational establishment.

In 1952, as Chair of the Educational Policies Commission, James Conant had endorsed a progressive policy document that urged a student-centered, whole-child approach to schooling. By 1959, Conant's vision was still "to provide a good general education for *all* the pupils," but he now emphasized "educating those with a talent for handling advanced subjects." After visiting fifty-five high schools across the country that had "a good reputation," Conant concluded that "the academically talented student, as a rule, is not being sufficiently challenged, does not work hard enough, and his program of academic subjects is not of sufficient range."[69]

In the midst of intense criticism toward schools and school people, Conant came to the defense of the educational establishment and saw little need for radically changing schools. Conant's influential book, *The American High School Today,* was a blueprint for moderate reform: for upgrading the curriculum, especially mathematics, science, and foreign language; requiring more academic subjects; tightening standards and grades; pushing students to their maximum cognitive potentials; and grouping students according to their abilities. Although Conant gave some consideration to slow and average learners, his major emphasis for reform was related to serving the needs of the highly gifted (the intellectually highest 3 percent of the student population on a national basis) and the academically talented (the top 20 percent in terms of scholastic aptitude).[70] Indeed, many of Conant's ideas could be considered a return to the mental discipline approach under the modern version of essentialist philosophy.

Many policy statements issued during this period focused on academically bright students, the three Rs at the elementary school level, and traditional academic subjects at the high school level. For example, the White House Conference on Education in 1955 stressed quality and proposed that "educational programs [must] fully exercise and develop the abilities of especially bright students."[71] Five years later the President's Commission on National Goals gave top priority to science, mathematics, and foreign languages and called for "a testing program beginning in grade one if not before . . . and ability grouping from the earliest years of school. Every effort [was to be] made in and out of school to provide enrichment for the gifted student.[72] Indeed, these were rigorous and competitive times in schools, and testing and tracking of students were considered acceptable. Scholarships based on merit and ability, not on need or athletics, were the order of the day.

Focus on Subject Matter. Hard on the heels of Sputnik and these national policy reports came federal legislation supporting training, equipment, and programs in subject fields deemed vital to defense. The major legislation, called the National Defense Act (1958), singled out science, mathematics, modern languages, and guidance (often construed as a way of steering youth into the three academic fields and into college if they had the ability). The focus on certain subjects and academically talented youth was often couched in terms of a free people's surviving in a world in

I logical statement of author

which Communism was spreading and in which the American sky was at risk.

Most important, large sums of money for beefing up the curriculum were readily available for the first time from both government and foundation sources. During the aftermath of Sputnik, William Van Til wrote, "The end result was that both national interest and available funds [in education] coincided. The scholars had a genuine opportunity to reconstruct the content of their separate subjects."[73] This was particularly true at the secondary level. To many leaders of this period, it was clear that the way to proceed to reconstruct subject matter was to call together the scientific community and university scholars, who most intimately knew the particular subject, along with some curriculum specialists, who might help with regards to methodology.

From this dialogue among scientists and scholars came a host of national curriculum projects that centered on science and math. These included the Biological Sciences Curriculum Study (BSCS), Chemical Education Material Study (CEMS), Physical Science Study Committee (PSSC), and the School Mathematics Study Group (SMSG). The new wave of curriculum reform emphasized the subject matter rather than students' needs or interests or societal problems. Most of the leaders of this movement made sweeping claims for the superiority of the new curriculum, what they often called the "new science" and the "new math."

The subject matter was reconstructed around disciplines with special methods of inquiry (that is, around major concepts and principles) and science and mathematics came to represent the highest disciplinary value as evidenced by Bruner and the Woodshole conference.[74] Proliferation of special projects in these subjects was followed by other projects in the social sciences and humanities intended to beef up the curriculum, especially the academic subjects of secondary schools, and to embrace the discipline approach for the science and math projects. But the search for structure in English, history, foreign language, and so on, proved unattainable. Even in science and mathematics, the idea of a disciplinary structure eventually declined.

Focus on Disadvantaged Students

The 1960s and early 1970s ushered in a period in which the social conscience of America burst forth, coinciding with our concern over poverty, racial discrimination, and equal educational opportunity. New aims and educational priorities surfaced to meet the climate of change. With the majority of students not going on to college and with a large percentage of students dropping out of school or graduating as functional illiterates, serious problems could be anticipated if our aims and priorities continued to be narrowly directed at our most able students. The shift to the problems of disadvantaged students gradually accelerated until this population became the number one concern in education. Exemplifying the change, James Conant, an early proponent of challenging the gifted students, gradually shifted his views.

In 1961, Conant wrote *Slums and Suburbs*. Only two years before, Conant had advocated academic rigor and upgraded academic subjects, as well as greater attention to the top 20 percent of high school students. Now he urged educators and policy makers to pay closer attention to the inner-city and disadvantaged children. He proposed that slum schools be upgraded and greater attention be paid to the less able students. Conant wrote:

> *I am concerned we are allowing social dynamite to accumulate in our large cities. . . . Leaving aside human tragedies, I submit that a continuation of this situation [youth out of school and out of work] is a menace to the social and political health of the large cities.*
>
> *The improvement of slum conditions is only in part a question of improving education. But the role of the schools is of utmost importance. . . . Added responsibility, however, requires additional funds. Indeed the whole question of financing public education in the large cities is a major national concern.*[75]

Conant's new position was a sign of the times—a shift in educational aims to focus on the disadvantaged. Historically a strong advocate of academic excellence, he was expressing a new viewpoint, one that would correct the educational discrepancies among students by placing greater emphasis on less able students, especially those in the inner city.

Given the student unrest and urban riots of the 1960s, it was easy to accept the arguments of an impacted crisis in schools and society. The government reports that were published in the 1960s strongly suggested an impending social upheaval. The needs of disadvantaged groups were stressed, both in schools and society, and these needs were reflected in such reports as the National Advisory Commission on Civil Disorders in 1967, and the HEW Urban Task Force Report in 1970. A new political bias seemed to evolve; in education it overlooked the average and above-average student, and in social and economic arenas it overlooked what was later to be called "middle America."

The outcome was a host of compensatory programs funded by the federal government, although state and local money as well as foundation money was also available. The Elementary and Secondary Education Act (ESEA), passed in 1965, immediately provided $1 billion in Title I funds (sometimes called compensatory funding) to supplement and improve the education of poor and minority group children. Ten years later, Title I money totaled $2 billion per year, or about $200 extra per disadvantaged child. By 1980, Title I expenditures were more than $3 billion per year, and other federal compensatory expenditures totaled another $2 billion or more, a total of about $500 extra per disadvantaged child. During this 15-year period, over $35 billion had been appropriated by the federal government.[76] Today, Chapter I funds have replaced most of the early ESEA money, and the amount of federal funding for the disadvantaged continues to increase: $5.3 billion in 1990, plus another $6 billion earmarked for vocational and postsecondary disadvantaged students.[77]

Expanded Priorities: New Disadvantaged Groups

The focus on the disadvantaged extended into the 1970s; in fact, the definition of the disadvantaged was enlarged to include multicultural, bilingual, and handicapped students and, to a lesser extent, women. Our multicultural and bilingual efforts were characterized by increased federal funding for Hispanic, Asian American, and Native American students; by the Bilingual Act in 1968, which expanded bilingual programs in American schools; and by the 1974 U.S. Supreme Court ruling in *Lau* v. *Nicholas,* which stated that schools must take steps to help students who "are certain to find their classroom experiences wholly incomprehensible" because they do not understand English. The courts, as well as policymakers and educators, took an active role in providing educational opportunities for limited-English speaking (LES) and non-English speaking (NES) students.[78] Despite controversies that surfaced concerning specific approaches and programs and recruitment of personnel, bilingual and multicultural education grew in importance during the 1970s. Congressional appropriations for bilingual education increased from $6.1 million in 1970 to $169 million in 1980. In 1990, appropriations were $203 million, illustrating that these funds have now leveled off [79] and in real dollars (which considers inflation) the funding has declined nearly 50 percent during the previous 10 years.

During the 1970s, much activity and concern also surfaced over special education, especially for the handicapped and for students with learning disabilities. New pressure groups, new courses, advanced degrees, new certification requirements, and new teachers and faculty at colleges and universities stimulated recognition of special education, as have new policies and programs. The Education for all Handicapped Children Act (PL 94-142) of 1975 is the cornerstone of these policies and programs, and it has been expanded by Amendment PL 99-457, passed in 1986, which extends the full rights and protection of the law to handicapped children ages 3 to 5 and was implemented in the 1990–1991 school year.[80]

Handicapped students are defined by this act as those who are mentally retarded, hard of hearing, deaf, orthopedically impaired, other health impaired, speech impaired, visually handicapped, emotionally disturbed, or learning disabled and, by reason thereof, require special education and related services. The legislation mandates a free and appropriate education for all handicapped children and youth. Handicapped students must be provided with special education and related services at public expense under public supervision and direction. Schools must not only adopt policies that serve all handicapped students, but they must conduct searches to locate such students as well.

Today, concern for the handicapped is very much alive, and the courts continue to take an active role in protecting the rights of and improving educational opportunities for the handicapped. Monies earmarked for the handicapped continue to increase in real dollars and in proportion to spending on nonhandicapped students; moreover, an increasing number of students are being identified as handicapped. Approximately 11 percent of the public school enrollments are considered handicapped, compared to 5 percent in 1975 (the year handicapped legislation went into effect).[81] This increase indicates that educators and policymakers recognize that many students who did not receive help in the past in fact need special help—not that contemporary students have more problems than students of earlier generations.

Concern for the gifted and talented students reached a low point during the 1960s and 1970s. The commitment to educating the gifted and talented was slight compared to efforts directed at the disadvantaged and at other special populations, such as bilingual, handicapped, or learning-disabled students. As two authorities stated, only "a very small percentage of the gifted and talented population [was] being serviced by existing programs, [about] 4 percent of the 1.5 to 2.5 million children."[82] A low funding priority and lack of trained personnel, coupled with few pressure groups for the gifted and talented, resulted in a scarcity of programs for these children who, in terms of numbers, represent a real minority.

National priorities in the 1970s (like those in the 1960s) for the most part did not focus on the average, ordinary students who were nonrich, nonpoor, nonminority, nongifted, and nonnewsworthy. There was (and still is) very little in the educational literature on the cultural, social, and educational diversity of students in "middle" America—in Astoria, New York, Lombard, Illinois, or Whittier, California, for example. These students were rarely defined as a special group with special characteristics and needs, so remedial or special programs for them were minimal. In the 1980s and early 1990s, some attention was

unwittingly devoted to them as a result of other trends, such as the national testing program, minimum competency testing, basic-skills programs, and the theme of national excellence in schools, but special programs and services for average children remained minimal.

Reform at the School Level

Much of what needs to be done to reform schools needs to be done at the local level; that is where the problems must be resolved, although the problems are large and multidimensional and require action at many governmental levels, as well as by businesses. Promulgating, legislating, and even packaging change are not the same as actually changing. Analysis of past efforts to improve schools has resulted in a much better understanding of the steps that must be taken to ensure that reform efforts have a significant and lasting impact. Among the lessons that can be deduced from past reform efforts at the school level are the following developed by Ornstein and Levine.

1. *Adaptive problem solving.* Reform or innovation frequently has little or no effect on students because numerous problems arise to stifle practical application. For example, experts may devise a wonderful new science curriculum for fourth graders and school districts may purchase large quantities of the new curriculum materials, but teachers may choose not to use the materials or may not know how to use them. Innovations are not likely to be implemented successfully unless the organization introducing them is *adaptive* in the sense that it can identify and solve day-by-day implementation problems.

2. *School-level focus.* Because the innovating organization must identify and solve day-to-day problems, the focus in bringing about change must be at the level of the individual school building where many of the problems occur. A school district focus helps in terms of seeking better relationships and increased funding from community and business partnerships, but it is in the schools where curriculum, instruction, teaching, and learning take place.

3. *Implementability.* Successful school reform also depends on whether changes introduced are implementable in the sense that teachers perceive that they can adopt and utilize these reforms effectively. Among the most important aspects of implementability are *compatibility* with the social context of potential users and *accessibility* to those who do not already understand or share the underlying ideas.

4. *Principal's leadership.* Implementation of a significant innovation requires change in many institutional arrangements, including scheduling of staff and student time, selection and utilization of instructional methods and materials, and mechanisms for making decisions. The building principal usually is the key person in successfully implementing change. In addition, the faculty must have a shared vision of the kinds of changes that are possible and necessary to improve their instructional program; otherwise, the staff is unlikely to seriously consider proposals that require significant modification in existing behaviors and arrangements.

5. *Teacher involvement.* Because people who are expected to alter their working patterns will not cooperate fully unless they have a voice in designing and implementing change, teachers must have an opportunity to select and evaluate innovations. Teachers must also be given the time, resources, and opportunity to collaborate and make decisions.

6. *Top-down and bottom-up approaches.* Since years of research had underlined the importance of teacher participation in decisions, researchers in the 1960s and 1970s tended to emphasize a bottom-up approach in the change process in order to encourage a sense of ownership among teachers asked to devote much time and energy to implementing improvements in curriculum and instruction. Research in the 1980s tended to underline the importance of top-down components in initiating change successfully. However, organizational specialists have delineated the stance of top-level administrators who communicate to principals and teachers an understanding that "we are going to try a new approach, you are going to implement it, and we are going to help you." They point out the need for principals to act as managers, instructional leaders, and decision makers and to mix administrative pressure and support so that teachers develop mastery of innovation and commitment to reform.

7. *Staff development.* Staff development is a core activity in the school improvement process. Staff development to support improvement should be centered on the school as the basic unit, not on the individual teacher. In the case of an elementary school, the entire staff should participate; in secondary schools, departments may be the appropriate unit for some activities. Staff development should be an interactive process in which teachers and administrators work together at every stage. Collaborative planning develops collegial responsibility for improvement.

8. *School-business cooperation.* Many schools and school districts are attempting to improve the quality of education by cooperating with other institutions, particularly business and industry. Some of the most promising programs include "partnership" or "adopt-a-school" programs in which a business or another community institution works closely with an individual school and provides assistance such as tutors or lecturers, funds, equipment or materials, and even personnel on loan (such as a computer specialist). To some extent, the old stewardship concept of business has resurfaced, reminiscent of Horace Mann's call for the private sector to become involved in the business of education for the good of business.[83] See Curriculum Tips 5-3.

Finally, reform at the school level should involve five planning processes. Based on the results of 1,500 schools in New York State, the following principles emerge among reform- and change-minded schools: (1) *curriculum change* is ongoing and involves two essential ingredients, emphasis on basic skills and advanced-level courses; (2) *research and evaluation* are prized; that is, they use instruments to assess needs, plant improvements, and evaluate results; (3) *data* are seriously considered, but the information is made clear, simple, and brief before being presented; (4) *site-based collaboration* is emphasized, that is the staff is involved in planning and making decisions to ensure their commitment to change; and (5) *instruction* is emphasized, while avoiding the tendency to be driven by test data or statewide assessments.[84] In short, these are five generic principles that school districts in all parts of the country can use as part of their mission pursuits or reform-change processes.

CURRICULUM TIPS 5-3 **Principles for Improving Schools**

A number of important principles result in school effectiveness and excellence. Based on recent efforts to improve schools and the school reform literature in general, many principles that school leaders can adapt for improving their own schools are listed here.

1. The school has a clearly stated mission or set of goals.
2. School achievement is closely monitored.
3. Provisions are made for *all* students, including tutoring for low achievers and enrichment programs for the gifted.
4. Teachers and administrators agree on what is good teaching and learning; a general philosophy and psychology of learning prevails.
5. Emphasis on cognition is balanced with concerns for students' personal, social, and moral growth; students are taught to be responsible for their behavior.
6. Teachers and administrators expect students to learn and convey these expectations to students and parents.
7. Teachers are expected to make significant contributions to school improvement.
8. Administrators provide ample support, information, and time for teacher enrichment.
9. A sense of teamwork prevails; there is interdisciplinary and interdepartmental communication.
10. Incentives, recognition, and rewards are conveyed to teachers and administrators for their efforts on behalf of the team and school mission.
11. The interests and needs of the individual staff members are matched with the expectations of the institution.
12. The staff has the opportunity to be challenged and creative; there is a sense of professional enrichment and renewal.
13. Staff development is planned by teachers and administrators to provide opportunities for continuous professional growth.
14. The school environment is safe and healthy; there is a sense of order (not control) in classrooms and hallways.
15. Parents and community members are supportive of the school and are involved in school activities.
16. The school is a learning center for the larger community; it reflects the norms and values of the community, and the community sees the school as an extension of the community.

Source: Adapted from Allan C. Ornstein, "Reforming American Schools: The Role of the States," *NASSP Bulletin* (October 1991), Table 2, p. 52.

NATIONAL TASK FORCE REPORTS ON EDUCATION

In the mid-1980s, national attention turned to the need for educational excellence and higher academic standards for all students. The educational dimensions of these needs were amply documented in several policy reports between 1983 and 1991, all calling for reforms to improve the quality of education in the United States.

To support their alarming statements about the decline of American education and the need

for academic reform, the policy reports detailed a host of gloomy trends and statistics.

1. Schools and colleges had shifted away from requiring students to take what had 20 years ago been the standard academic core curriculum for graduation: foreign language, mathematics. science, English, and history. Elective courses and remedial courses had replaced many standard academic courses.

2. Grade inflation was on the rise, and students were required to complete less homework (75

percent of high school students completed less than one hour of homework a night).

3. Average achievement scores on the Scholastic Aptitude Test (SAT) demonstrated a virtually unbroken decline from 1963 to 1988. Average verbal scores fell some 40 points (466 to 428), and mathematics scores dropped nearly 20 points (492 to 471).[85]

4. International comparisons of student achievement, completed in the 1970s, revealed that on nineteen academic tests American students were never first or second and, in comparison with other industrialized nations, were last seven times. In 1988, they scored last in math (averaging 94 points below first-ranked Korea) and second to the bottom in science (averaging 71 points below first-ranked Korea). U.S. students also scored last in geographical knowledge, more than one-third lower than their first-ranked counterparts in Sweden.[86]

5. Some 23 to 25 million American adults were functionally illiterate by the simplest tests of everyday reading and writing.

6. About 13 percent of all 17-year-old youths in the United States were considered functionally illiterate, and this illiteracy rate jumped to 40 percent among minority youth.

7. Business and military leaders complained that they were required to spend millions of dollars annually on costly remedial education and training programs in the basic skills or three Rs. Between 1975 and 1985, remedial mathematics courses in four-year colleges increased by 72 percent and by 1985 constituted one-fourth of all mathematics courses taught in these institutions. As many as 25 percent of the recruits in the Armed Forces could not read at the ninth-grade level.

8. All these sordid figures pile up and stare at us, despite the facts that our student /teacher ratios were 17 : 1 in 1988, which put us seventh lowest in the world (whereas such countries as Japan and Korea have over 30 students per teacher) and that our pupil expenditures for education were the second highest in the world (about $300 less than first-ranked Switzerland).[87]

These deficiencies have come to light at a time when the demand for highly skilled military personnel and workers in labor and industry is accelerating rapidly and amid growing concern that the United States is being overtaken by other industrialized nations in commerce, science, and technology.

The major policy reports and their sponsoring agencies are summarized in Table 5-2. Nine of the thirteen reports emphasized the need to strengthen the curriculum in the core subjects of English, math, science, foreign language, and social studies. The focus was thus on a *common curriculum.* Technology and computer courses were mentioned often, either as components of science or math or as separate subject areas (sometimes referred to as the fourth R). High-level cognitive and thinking skills were also stressed. Most of the reports concerned all students: providing various programs and personnel for disadvantaged and learning disabled students, as well as for average and above average students. The notion of *equity* was paramount, although not always loud and clear. Nevertheless, the theme of *excellence* still seemed to stress academic, college-bound, and even gifted students; emphasis was still on core academic subjects and advanced science and mathematics.

All the reports emphasized tougher standards and tougher courses, and eight out of the thirteen proposed that colleges raise their admission requirements. Most of the reports also talked about increasing homework, time for learning, and time in school, as well as instituting more rigorous grading, testing, homework, and discipline. They mentioned, too, upgrading teacher certification, increasing teacher salaries, increasing the number of and rewarding science and math teachers, and providing merit pay for outstanding teachers. Overall, they stressed excellence (not equity), academic achievement (not the whole child), and increased productivity (not relevancy or humanism).

Many of the reports expressed concern that the schools are pressed to play too many social roles, that the schools cannot meet all these expectations, and that the schools are in danger of losing sight of their key role—teaching the basic skills and the core academic subjects, new skills for computer use, and higher-level cognitive skills for the world of work, technology, and even military defense. Accordingly, many of

TABLE 5-2 Overview of Selected Recommendations of Thirteen Reports on Education, 1983–1991

REPORT AND SPONSOR	CURRICULUM OBJECTIVES	CONTENT EMPHASIS	SCHOOL ORGANIZATION	GOVERNMENT-BUSINESS ROLE
Academic Preparation for College, The College Board	Improve student competencies in reading, writing, speaking, listening, reasoning, math, and study skills Raise college entrance standards	English, math, science, computers, foreign language	Stress study and independent learning Incentives to students	Develop a national standard for academic achievement in secondary education
Action for Excellence, Education Commission of the States	Establish minimum competencies in reading, writing, speaking, listening, reasoning, and economics Strengthen programs for gifted students Raise college entrance standards	English, math, science, foreign language, history, computer literacy	Consider longer school day Emphasize order and discipline More homework More rigorous grading with periodic testing Independent learning	Foster partnerships between private sector and education Increase federal funds for education
Educating Americans for the 21st Century, National Science Foundation	Devote more time to math and science in elementary school and secondary schools Provide more advanced courses in science and math Raise college entrance standards	Math, science, technology, computers	Consider longer school day, week, and/or year Twelve-year plan for math and science	Federal input in establishing national goals for education Increase NSF role in curriculum development and teacher training

(continued)

High School, Carnegie Foundation for Achievement in Teaching	Mastery of language, including reading, writing, speaking, and listening Expand basic academic curriculum Student transition to work and further education Strengthen graduation requirements	Core of common learning, including English, history, civics, math, science, technology Computer literacy	Improve working conditions for teachers Utilize technology to enrich curriculum Flexible schedules and time allotments One track for students School-community learning activities Greater leadership role for principal	More connections between school and community, business, and universities Increase parent and community coalitions with and service to schools Utilize retired personnel from business and colleges Federal scholarships for science and math teachers
Making the Grade, Twentieth-Century Fund	Improve basic-skill programs Improve learning in English, math, and science Initiate general programs for students with learning problems and a voucher program for the disadvantaged	Basic skills English, math, and science Computer literacy	Reward teacher performance Special programs for poor, minority, handicapped, bilingual, and immigrant students	Increase federal aid for special programs for disadvantaged student populations Increase federal aid for programs to develop scientific literacy among all students and advanced math and science for academically able secondary students
A Study of High Schools, National Association of Secondary School Principals	Reduce traditional subject matter Emphasize higher-order thinking skills	Interdisciplinary curriculum Problem-solving activities and learning experiences	Eliminate age grouping Eliminate teacher specializations Incentives to students Out-of-school learning activities	Federal support for special students, including learning disabled and gifted

TABLE 5-2 Continued

REPORT AND SPONSOR	CURRICULUM OBJECTIVES	CONTENT EMPHASIS	SCHOOL ORGANIZATION	GOVERNMENT-BUSINESS ROLE
A Nation at Risk, National Commission on Excellence in Education	Improve textbooks and other instructional materials Provide more rigorous courses in vocational education, arts, and science Strengthen graduation requirements Raise college entrance requirements	Five new basics: English, math, science, social studies, and computer science	Consider seven-hour school day Tighten attendance and discipline More homework More rigorous grading and periodic testing Group students by performance rather than age	Federal cooperation with states and localities Meet needs of disadvantaged student populations as well as gifted and talented National standardized tests in context with national interest in education
The First Lesson: A Report on Elementary Education in America, The Secretary of Education	Improve basic skills for young children Improve complex learning tasks and abilities for higher-grade children Increase knowledge base essential for democratic society and national identity Improve textbook and workbook writing and selection Raise academic standards	Basic skills, especially reading through phonics Problem-solving skills in mathematics and hands-on learning and discovery in science Unified sequence stressing history, geography, and civics Computer literacy and cultural literacy	Lengthen school day More homework More rigorous testing Parental choice in children's schools Reward teacher performance	Community-wide and parental responsibility in education Teacher and school accountability Improve training programs for elementary teachers; emphasis on arts and science rather than methods courses

The Early Years, Carnegie Foundation for the Advancement of Teaching	Focus on plight of at-risk children, the nation's underclass Emphasis on basic skills Priority on childhood education	Language-development, including reading, writing, and listening skills	Flexible school schedules reflecting changing family and work patterns Longer school day and school year Reward teacher performance; attract better teachers Parental choice for after school and summer programs; end of traditional summer vacation	Increased federal aid for education of at-risk children Increased role of business and industry Greater involvement of teachers in decision-making, increased pay
Time for Results: The Governors' 1991 Report on Education, National Governors' Association	Focus on teenage pregnancy, school dropouts, adult illiteracy, and drug abuse Improve school leadership and management Better use of technology in the classroom Increase state role and responsibility in education Higher academic standards at all grade levels	Basic skills, math, science, and technology Research and development in education	Kindergarten for all children; early childhood programs for all at-risk children Parental education programs Parental choice in selecting children's school Reliable and valid assessment of student performance Year-round schooling Reorganize and regulate schools and school districts that are "academically bankrupt"	National school board to certify teachers Increased pay and accountability for teachers and principals Improved teacher training and educational leadership programs Greater involvement in education of local leaders, teachers, parents, citizens, and business people Greater state role, regulation, and spending in education Annual progress reports on what each state is doing to carry out educational reform

(continued)

TABLE 5-2 Continued

REPORT AND SPONSOR	CURRICULUM OBJECTIVES	CONTENT EMPHASIS	SCHOOL ORGANIZATION	GOVERNMENT-BUSINESS ROLE
The Disappearing Quality of the Workforce: What Can We Do to Save It? National Alliance of Business	Educate all youth in basic skills; Provide students with high-level skills required for our information and service economy; Face our education problems; Restructure education; provide financial support; Increase the quality of the nation's workforce	Basic skills; Critical thinking skills; Tutoring programs; Raise academic standards and high school graduation requirements	Reduce school dropout rates; Increase attendance rates; Improve national test scores and achievement levels; Increase adopt-a-school programs; Teacher/administrative accountability; Staff development/ mentor programs	Business leaders must take an active role in implementing education reform; Collaborative efforts between business and education groups; Reshape education at state and local levels; Involve citizen, parent, political and business groups
Investing in People: A Strategy to Address America's Workforce Crisis U.S. Department of Labor	Commitment to basic skills and literacy; Invest in human capital; Increase federal and business support in education and human resource programs; Upgrade workforce quality; Upgrade high school graduation, college entry, and labor market standards; Develop national goals and timetables to improve education and training	Basic skill programs for dropouts; Literacy programs for illiterate adults; Lifetime education and training; Combine vocational and technical education	Reduce dropout rates; Increase attendance rates; Increase parent participation; Increase business-community presence in schools; Reduce competitive learning; increase cooperative learning; More rigorous teacher training and testing of new teachers	Partnerships between business, labor, and government at all levels; Business to fund incentive programs to improve teacher/school performance; Increase government and training programs to address needs of private sector and labor; Tax credits for education and training programs for private sector

National Goals for Education, U.S. Department of Education	Focus on all students, with emphasis on at-risk students	Basic knowledge and skills	Preschool programs for all disadvantaged learners	Inspire reform at the federal, state, and local levels
	Equip students with knowledge and skills necessary for responsible citizenship and world of work	Reasoning and problem-solving skills	Parental training for child's early learning; parental choice in children's schools	Enlist assistance of parents, community, business, and civic groups; all parts of society must be involved
	Ensure readiness for school; upgrade school standards and student achievement	Math, science, English, history, and geography	Up-to-date instructional technology	Create effective apprenticeships, job training, teacher–employee exchanges, and adopt-a-school programs
	Improve adult literacy and life-long education	Drug and alcohol prevention programs	Multilayer system of vocational, technical, and community colleges	Increase flexibility, innovation, accountability, and results
	Provide a safe and drug-free school environment	Citizenship, community service, cultural literacy, and knowledge of the international community	More student loans, scholarships, and work study programs in higher education	Targets established for the year 2000
			Upgrade teacher preparation; reward teachers but hold them accountable	

Source: Revised from previous edition of book; also see Allan C. Ornstein, "The National Reform of Education," *NASSP Bulletin* (May 1992).

the reports used such terms as "emergency," "urgency," "crucial to national survival," "global competition," "act of war," "educational disarmament" and the like, reminding us of the post-Sputnik era once again. Perhaps the number one criticism of all these reports is who is to pay for all these reform measures given the decline of federal spending in education, the reported monetary deficits at the federal level, and the weakening fiscal health among most states.

PLANNING FOR EDUCATIONAL CHANGE

As long as society is dynamic and composed of a conglomeration of cultural and social groups, the debate over the aims of education will stir up controversy and change. Perhaps this is good; perhaps this is what makes a society viable and able to resist decay.

In examining the aims, priorities, or reforms of education from the turn of the century until today, we see considerable reiteration, but we also note considerable evolution linked to sweeping social change. For example, the early twentieth-century adherents of mental discipline advocated rigorous intellectual training, as did the essentialist critics and conservative thinkers of the 1950s and mid-1980s and early 1990s. At the turn of the century, public schools stressed an academic curriculum, and this priority reasserted itself during the era of the Cold War and the space race; it reappeared, too, in the 1980s and 1990s as a result of concern over economic competition with foreign countries and foreign relations with the former USSR. In the early 1900s, progressive educators sought to broaden the aims of school to serve all children and youth, especially nonacademic and vocationally oriented students; beginning in the early 1960s and continuing into the 1970s, this priority reappeared with emphasis on poor and minority students, and later bilingual and handicapped students. Although concern for disadvantaged groups remains, the pendulum has now moved to the center. Our priorities are more diffuse, and we are concerned about various other students as well, including those in average and academic groups.

Appraising and Reflecting

Educational aims should be as changeable as the changing social and political conditions and the groups of people that formulate them. Panels and commissions are often organized to formulate aims. They may operate at various government and educational levels—federal, state, regional, and local—but those at the national level have the most influence and those at the local level have the least (in terms of overall impact).

Aims are modified by the need for reform, or what is considered relevant and necessary to meet a crisis or problem. When it comes to reform, however, Americans tend to delineate a variety of proposals, often conflicting notions of where the problem is and what solutions are feasible. As Boyer notes, Americans seem addicted to school reform and become propelled by "a kind of erratic lunging from one extreme to another."[88]

Unquestionably, educational aims, and especially school reform, must be relevant or meaningful to the times. If the schools are not adaptable to changing conditions and social forces, how can they expect to produce people who are? This issue is pointedly illustrated in a satire on education entitled *The Saber-Tooth Curriculum,* which describes a society whose major tasks for survival were catching fish to eat, clubbing horses, and frightening away saber-tooth tigers.[89] The school in this society set up a curriculum to meet its needs—teaching courses in these three areas of survival. Eventually conditions changed; the streams dried up, and the horses and tigers disappeared. Social change necessitated learning new tasks for survival, but the school curriculum continued to feature courses in catching fish, clubbing horses, and frightening saber-toothed tigers.

Today we live in a highly technical, automated, and bureaucratic society; we are faced with pressing social and economic problems—aging cities, the effects of centuries of racial and sexual discrimination, an aging population, unemployment and a displaced workforce, exhaustion of our natural resources, the pollution of the physical environment, and the threat of nuclear devastation. These forces and trends are highly interrelated; they mutually reinforce each other, and they are accelerating. In an era of space technology, telecommunications, computers, and robots, schools cannot continue to teach the skills that were appropriate for the Industrial Revolution. Whether we allow the times to engulf us or whether we can cope with our new environment will depend to a large extent on what kinds of skills are taught in our schools today, in addition to the development of appropriate aims of education.

CONCLUSION

Social forces have always had a major influence on schools and in turn on curriculum decisions. Some of these forces originate from society at large and others from the local community. In either case, educators are faced with a choice: To accept and mirror the tendencies of the times or to appraise and improve the times. One view represents a perennialist notion of education, the other a reconstructionist notion; however, we would like to view the choice in terms of a traditional versus futuristic way of looking at schools. The latter approach suggests that educators can analyze and evaluate the trends taking shape in society. In doing so, they can decide on appropriate aims and curricula, and they can thus prepare students for the world of tomorrow by providing them with the knowledge and values they need to make wise decisions. Curriculum workers—indeed, all participants in curriculum decisions—play a major role in accomplishing these goals.

ENDNOTES

1. John Dewey, *Experience and Education* (New York: Macmillan, 1938), pp. 39–40.
2. Allan C. Ornstein and Daniel U. Levine, *Foundations of Education,* 5th ed. (Boston: Houghton Mifflin, 1993), p. 325.
3. Ibid.
4. Ruth Benedict, *Patterns of Culture* (Boston: Houghton Mifflin, 1934), p. 253.
5. Margaret Mead, *And Keep Your Powder Dry* (New York: William Morrow, 1941).
6. Brian K. Barber and Boyd C. Rollins, *Parent-Adolescent Relationships* (Landham, Md.: University Press of America, 1990); Burton L. White, *The First Three Years of Life* (New York: Avon Books, 1984).
7. Catherine S. Chilman, "The Development of Adolescent Sexuality," *Journal of Research and Development in Education* (Winter 1983), pp. 16–26; Nel Noddings, "The Gender Issue," *Educational Leadership* (December–January 1992), pp. 65–70.
8. Patricia C. Sexton, *The Feminized Male* (New York: Random House, 1969).
9. Ray H. Bixler, "Nature versus Nurture: The Timeless Anachronism," *Merrill-Palmer Quarterly* (April 1980) pp. 153–159.
10. Diane McGuinness, "How Schools Discriminate against Boys," *Human Nature* (February 1979), pp. 87–88.
11. Cornelius Riordan, *Girls and Boys in School* (New York: Teachers College Press, Columbia University, 1990).
12. Robert J. Havighurst, *Human Development and Education* (New York: Longman, 1953), p. 2.
13. Robert J. Havighurst, *Developmental Tasks and Education,* 3rd ed. (New York: Longman, 1972), pp. 14–35, 43–82. All rights reserved.
14. H. H. Giles, S. P. McCutchen, and A. N. Zechiel, *Exploring the Curriculum* (New York: Harper & Row, 1942).
15. Florence B. Stratemeyer, Hamden L. Forkner, Margaret G. McKim, and A. Harry Passow, *Developing a Curriculum for Modern Living,* 2nd ed. (New York: Teachers College Press, Columbia University, 1957).
16. B. Othanel Smith, William O. Stanley, and J. Harlan Shores, *Fundamentals of Curriculum Development,* rev. ed. (New York: World Book, 1957).
17. Henry Harap, *The Changing Curriculum* (New York: Appleton-Century Crofts, 1937).
18. Jerome Kagan, *The Nature of the Child* (New York: Basic Books, 1985).
19. Jean Piaget, *The Moral Judgment of the Child* (London: Routledge & Kegan Paul, 1932).
20. Lawrence Kohlberg, "Moral Development and Identification," in N. B. Henry and H. G. Richey, eds., *Child Psychology,* Sixty-second Yearbook of the National Society for the Study of Education, Part I (Chicago: University of Chicago Press, 1963), pp. 322–323.
21. Maxine Greene, *Teachers as Strangers* (Belmont, Calif.: Wadsworth, 1973); Van Cleve Morris, *Existentialism in Education* (New York: Harper & Row,

1966). Also see Landon E. Beyer and George H. Wood, "Critical Theory and Moral Action in Education," *Educational Theory* (October 1986), pp. 1–14.

22. Philip H. Phenix, *Realms of Meaning* (New York: McGraw-Hill, 1964), pp. 220–221.

23. Ibid., p. 223.

24. John Dewey, *Democracy and Education* (New York: Macmillan, 1916), p. 414.

25. Ibid., pp. 411, 415–416.

26. William Van Til, "In a Climate of Change," in R. R. Leeper, ed., *Role of Supervisor and Curriculum Director in a Climate of Change* (Washington, D.C.: Association for Supervision and Curriculum Development, 1965), p. 16. See also John O'Neil, "Preparing for the Changing Workplace," *Educational Leadership* (March 1992), pp. 6–9.

27. Alvin Toffler, *Future Shock* (New York: Random House, 1970).

28. *Curriculum Change toward the 21st Century,* an NEA Bicentennial Committee Report (Washington, D.C.: National Education Association, 1977), pp. 89–90; Thomas J. Sergiovanni and John H. Moore, *Schooling for Tomorrow* (Boston: Allyn and Bacon, 1989. Also see Daniel Bell, *The Third Technological Revolution* (New York: Basic Books, 1984); and Alvin Toffler, *The Third Wave* (New York: Morrow, 1980).

29. Philip M. Hauser, "Urbanization: An Overview," in J. K. Hadden, L. H. Masotti, and C. J. Larson, eds., *Metropolis in Crisis* (Itasca, Ill.: Peacock, 1971), pp. 51–74.

30. Philip W. Jackson, *Life in Classrooms* (New York: Holt, Rinehart and Winston, 1968), p. 6.

31. Glenys G. Unruh and William M. Alexander, *Innovations in Secondary Education,* 2nd ed. (New York: Holt, Rhinehart and Winston, 1974), p. 2.

32. Allan C. Ornstein, *Urban Education* (Columbus, Ohio: Merrill, 1972), p. 50.

33. Wayne K. Hoy and Cecil G. Miskel, *Educational Administration: Theory, Research, and Practice,* 3rd ed. (New York: Random House, 1987), p. 51.

34. Allan C. Ornstein, "Emerging Curriculum Trends: An Agenda for the Future," *NASSP Bulletin* (February 1989), pp. 37–48; Albert Shanker, "The End of the Traditional Model of Schooling," *Phi Delta Kappan* (January 1988), pp. 334–357.

35. Arthur Combs, *A Personal Approach to Teaching* (Boston: Allyn and Bacon, 1982); Ivan Illich, *Deschooling Society,* 2nd ed. (New York: World, 1983).

36. Pamela A. McCollum and Constance L. Walker, "Minorities in America 2000," *Education and Urban Society* (February 1992), pp. 178–195; Allan C. Ornstein, "Enrollment Trends in Big-City Schools," *Peabody Journal of Education* (Summer 1989), pp. 64–71.

37. Bentley Glass, *The Timely and the Timeless* (New York: Basic Books, 1980), p. 39.

38. Warren L. Ziegler, *Social and Technological Developments,* rev. ed. (Syracuse, N.Y.: Syracuse University Press, 1981).

39. Toffler, *Future Shock,* p. 132.

40. Arno Bellack, "What Knowledge Is of Most Worth?" *High School Journal* (February 1965), pp. 318–332; Donald E. Orlosky and B. Othanel Smith, *Curriculum Development: Issues and Insights* (Chicago: Rand McNally, 1978); and Decker F. Walker and Jonas F. Soltis, *Curriculum and Aims* (New York: Teachers College Press, Columbia University, 1986).

41. James B. Conant, *The American High School* (New York: McGraw-Hill, 1959).

42. Kay M. Troost, "What Accounts for Japan's Success in Science Education?" *Educational Leadership* (December–January 1984), pp. 26–29; Herbert J. Walberg, "Improving School Science in Advanced and Developing Countries," *Review of Educational Research* (Spring 1991), pp. 25–70.

43. Joseph L. Schwab, *The Practical: A Language for Curriculum* (Washington, D.C.: National Education Association, 1970).

44. Vincent R. Ruggiero, *The Art of Thinking,* 2nd ed. (New York: Harper & Row, 1988); Robert S. Zais, *Curriculum: Principles and Foundations* (New York: Harper & Row, 1976). See Jerome S. Bruner, *The Process of Education* (Cambridge, Mass.: Harvard University Press, 1960).

45. Harry S. Broudy, *Building a Philosophy of Education,* 2nd ed. (Englewood Cliffs, N.J.: Prentice Hall, 1961).

46. Phenix, *Realms of Meaning*; Joseph J. Schwab, "Problems, Topics, and Issues," in S. E. Elam, ed., *Education and the Structure of Knowledge* (Chicago: Rand McNally, 1964), pp. 4–43.

47. Phenix, *Realms of Meaning.*

48. Ibid., p. 268.

49. Gerald Weinstein and Mario D. Fantini, *Toward Humanistic Education: A Curriculum of Affect* (New York: Praeger, 1970), p. 50.

50. Mario D. Fantini, "Reducing the Behavior Gap," *NEA Journal* (January 1968), pp. 23–24.

51. J. Lloyd Trump and Dorsey Baynham, *Focus on Change* (Chicago: Rand McNally, 1961); Grace S. Wright, *Block-Time Classes and the Core Program in the Junior High School* (Washington, D.C.: U.S. Government Printing Office, 1962).

52. Harold Alberty, *Reorganizing the High School Curriculum* (New York: Macmillan, 1953); Roland C. Faunce and Nelson L. Bossing, *Developing the Core Curriculum,* 2nd ed. (Englewood Cliffs, N.J.: Prentice

Hall, 1958); and Arnold Gesell et al., *Youth: The Years from Ten to Sixteen* (New York: Harper, 1956).

53. John I. Goodlad, *A Place Called School* (New York: McGraw-Hill, 1984).

54. Ernest Boyer, *High School: A Report on Secondary Education in America* (New York: Carnegie Foundation for the Achievement of Teaching, 1983). Many high schools already have a junior- or senior-year project.

55. Mario D. Fantini et al., "Toward a Definition of Community Education," *Community Education Journal* (April 1980), pp. 11–33; Allan C. Ornstein, "Redefining Parent and Community Involvement," *Journal of Research and Development in Education* (Summer 1983), pp. 37–45.

56. Theodore Sizer, *Horace's Compromise: The Dilemma of the American High School* (Boston: Houghton Mifflin, 1984).

57. Ibid.

58. Joseph L. Tykociner, *Outline of Zetetics* (Philadelphia: Dorrance, 1966).

59. Allan C. Ornstein, "Knowledge as a Source of Change" *NASSP Bulletin* (April 1988), pp. 72–75.

60. Lawrence A. Cremin, *The Transformation of the School* (New York: Knopf, 1961).

61. Commission on the Reorganization of Secondary Education, *Cardinal Principles of Secondary Education*, Bulletin No. 35 (Washington, D.C.: U.S. Government Printing Office, 1918).

62. Allan C. Ornstein, "Aims of Education for Today and Tomorrow," *Educational Horizons* (Fall 1982), pp. 41–49.

63. Educational Policies Commission, *The Purpose of Education in American Democracy* (Washington, D.C.: National Education Association, 1938).

64. Educational Policies Commission, *Education for All American Youth* (Washington, D.C.: National Education Association, 1944).

65. Decker Walker, *Fundamentals of Curriculum* (San Diego: Harcourt, Brace, 1990). See also Allan C. Ornstein, "Curriculum Contrasts: A Historical View," *Phi Delta Kappan* (February 1982), pp. 404–408.

66. Arthur Bestor, *The Restoration of Learning* (New York: Knopf, 1956).

67. Hyman G. Rickover, *Education and Freedom* (New York: Dutton, 1959), p. 190.

68. *Science and Education for National Defense*, Hearings before the Committee of Labor and Public Welfare, U.S. Senate, Eighty-Eighth Congress (Washington, D.C.: U.S. Government Printing Office, 1958), p. 65.

69. Conant, *The American High School Today*, p. 15.

70. Ibid.

71. *Proceedings, White House Conference on Education* (Washington, D.C.: U.S. Government Printing Office, 1955), p. 12.

72. *Goals for Americans: The President's Commission on National Goals* (Englewood Cliffs, N.J.: Prentice Hall, 1960), p. 85.

73. Van Til, "In a Climate of Change," p. 21.

74. Jerome S. Bruner, *The Process of Education* (Cambridge, Mass.: Harvard University Press, 1959).

75. James B. Conant, *Slums and Suburbs* (New York: McGraw-Hill, 1961), p. 2.

76. Allan C. Ornstein and Daniel U. Levine, "Compensatory Education: Can It Be Successful? What Are the Issues?" *NASSP Bulletin* (May 1981), pp. 1–15; A. Harry Passow, "Urban Education in the 1970s," in A. H. Passow, ed., *Urban Education in the 1970s* (New York: Teachers College Press, Columbia University, 1971), pp. 1–45.

77. *Digest of Educational Statistics, 1990* (Washington, D.C.: U.S. Government Printing Office, 1990), Table 327, p. 343.

78. Carol D. Lee, "Literacy, Cultural Diversity, and Instruction," *Education and Urban Society* (February 1992), pp. 279–291; Diane Ravitch, "A Culture in Common," *Educational Leadership* (January 1992), pp. 8–11.

79. *Digest of Educational Statistics, 1990*, Table 326, p. 337.

80. Allan C. Ornstein, Daniel U. Levine, and Janet W. Lerner, "Education of Young Handicapped and At-Risk Children," *Illinois School Research and Development Journal* (Fall 1989), pp. 24–32.

81. *The Condition of Education, 1990*, Vol. 1 (Washington, D.C.: U.S. Government Printing Office, 1990), Table 1.12, p. 47; *The School-Age Handicapped* (Washington, D.C.: U.S. Government Printing Office, 1990), Table 1, p. 30.

82. A. Harry Passow and Abraham J. Tannebaum, "Education of the Gifted and Talented," *NASSP Bulletin* (March 1976), pp. 4–5; Donovan R. Walling, "Gifted Children: A Neglected Minority," *Curriculum Review* (September–October 1986), pp. 11–13.

83. Allan C. Ornstein and Daniel U. Levine, "School Effectiveness and Reform," *Clearing House* (November–December 1990), pp. 115–118.

84. Thomas F. Kelly, "Five Ways to Make Your Schools Effective," *School Administrator* (October 1989), pp. 26, 29. Also see Kenneth A. Sirotnik, "Improving Urban Schools in the Age of' Restructuring,'" *Education and Urban Society* (May 1991), pp. 256–269.

85. *Digest of Education Statistics 1989*, Table 108, p. 120.

86. *The Condition of Education 1989,* Vol. 1, Charts 1.3, 1.5, pp. 13, 17; *Digest of Education Statistics 1989,* Tables 347, 349, pp. 390–391.

87. *The Condition of Education 1989,* Chart 1.18, p. 107; *Digest of Education Statistics 1989,* Table 340, p. 385. Also see John Hood, "Education: Money Isn't Everything," *Wall Street Journal,* February 9, 1990, p. 14.

88. Ernest Boyer, "The Future Is Now," *Newsweek* (Fall–Winter 1990), p. 73. Special report.

89. Harold Benjamin, *The Saber Tooth Curriculum* (New York: McGraw-Hill, 1939).

CHAPTER 6

CURRICULUM THEORY

Focusing Questions

1. *How may we derive educational theories?*
2. *How can we interpret theory?*
3. *Which are the classic sources of curriculum theory?*
4. *What are the key functions of theory?*
5. *Why do we still lack a formal curriculum theory after so many years of dialogue?*
6. *Explain the differences among the major theoretical camps.*
7. *What is the relationship between curriculum theory and instructional theory?*
8. *Where does supervision theory fit into the curriculum picture?*
9. *What are the major trends of inquiry in curriculum, instruction, and supervision?*

A field of study basically involves both theoretical and practical knowledge. By theory, we mean the most advanced and valid knowledge available that can be generalized and applied to many situations. Theory furnishes those working with a particular realm of knowledge with a way of viewing the world and how it works. Theoretical knowledge establishes the frameworks of the field and assists persons (researchers and practitioners) within the field in analyzing and synthesizing data, organizing concepts and principles, suggesting new ideas and relations, and even speculating about the future.

Theory provides a foundation for action; it shapes individuals thinking along particular lines. For this reason, some educators have placed curriculum theory as a subset of philosophy. That is, philosophy addresses the most important questions and from the questions evolve theory. By dealing with philosophical questions that are central to our understanding that theory matures.[1]

While few curricularists would deny the importance of theory, they hold a great variety of definitions. Perhaps this is one reason that many practitioners believe theory to be of limited value. The curriculum field presents many theoretical problems, and many curriculum theorists are in an exploratory era in theory building. This exploratory era has stimulated much dialogue about curriculum theory among curriculum theorists. Elizabeth Maccia has even gone so far as to claim that talk about theory is, itself, theorizing. Even though no one would insist that the field of curriculum has any fully mature and agreed-upon theories, there is an abundance of curriculum theorizing.[2] Nevertheless, curricularists cannot agree about just what curriculum is, and curriculum theorists cannot agree about what is good curriculum theory.

THEORETICAL PERSPECTIVES

Curriculum is a complex phenomenon. Both theoreticians and practitioners would agree to the validity of this statement. For this reason, theory is both essential but slow in coming. Hilda Taba noted that "any enterprise as complex as curriculum requires some kind of theoretical or conceptual framework of thinking to guide it."[3] George

Posner argues that theoretical perspectives allow us to contemplate and "see" educational landscapes in particular ways.[4] Curricularists must advance their understanding of the theoretical aspects of the field if they are to conceptualize and develop curricula of value for students.

Over time, people have divided, subdivided, and classified their experiences into categories so as to comprehend them and to manage the masses of data associated with them. These divisions are called disciplines, areas, or realms of knowledge.

George Beauchamp has asserted that all theories are derived from three broad categories of knowledge: (1) the humanities; (2) the natural sciences; and (3) the social sciences.[5] These *divisions of knowledge* are well established as the basic realms of knowledge. For example, under the humanities are the disciplines of philosophy, music, art, and literature. Under the social sciences are the disciplines of history, sociology, psychology, and anthropology, among others. Under the natural sciences are the disciplines of chemistry, physics, botany, geology, and so on.

Beauchamp argues that from these basic knowledge divisions come areas of *applied knowledge*—architecture, medicine, engineering, education, and law, to name a few. What distinguishes applied realms of knowledge from disciplines is that applied realms draw their content and indeed their authority from theory in the disciplines. Education, for example, draws from psychology, sociology, and history and uses information from biology when referring to human growth and development. It takes much of its emphasis from philosophy. What makes education a field of knowledge is the manner in which it combines knowledge from various disciplines and formulates rules and procedures for using the knowledge.

Beauchamp has identified a series of sub-theories in education: administrative theories, counseling theories, instructional theories, evaluation theories, and curriculum theories. There are two major categories of curriculum theories—design theories and engineering theories. *Design theories* address the basic organization of the curriculum plan. For this, curricularists draw on philosophy as well as on social and psychology theory.

Engineering theories explain, describe, predict, or even guide curriculum-development activities. They involve specific plans, principles, and/or methods or procedures. Engineering theories of curriculum are also partially based on principles of measurement and statistics.

The Meaning of Theory

Despite the myriad works on the nature and function of theory, curriculum specialists have not produced a universal definition of theory. This is not too surprising because the three basic realms of knowledge—humanities, social sciences, and natural sciences—all look at reality differently and generate definitions of theory that reflect their interests.

Although differences exist among the major types of theory, some commonalities are evident as well. Most definitions of theory deal with sets of events or phenomena and the relationships among these events. Abraham Kaplan provides a useful general statement defining theory: "A theory is a way of making sense of a disturbing situation so as to allow us most effectively to bring to bear our repertoire of habits, and even more important, to modify habits or discard them altogether, replacing new ones as the situation demands. . . . "[6] Theory will appear as the device for interpreting, criticizing, and unifying established laws, modifying them to fit data unanticipated in their formation, and guiding the enterprise of discovering new and more powerful generalizations.

Richard Snow states that "a theory is essentially a symbolic construction that is designed to bring generalizable facts or laws into systematic connection." The theory itself consists of a set of units that can be "facts, concepts, or some variables, and a noting of relationships among the units identified."

Sources of Curriculum Theory

Joseph Schwab in his landmark paper on curriculum stated that we had no curriculum theory, and perhaps were not spending our time wisely in trying to develop one.[8] Notwithstanding Schwab's conclusion, there are numerous theories and theoretical orientations employed in contemplating, creating, and managing curriculum. However, many of these theories are drawn from various fields of study rather than from the curriculum field itself. A challenge for curricularists is to determine just what aspect of the field of curriculum we are processing. Our assumption is that the field of curriculum should involve curricularists in theorizing about curriculum design and curriculum development, what we refer to as the technical aspects of curriculum.

Reflecting on the nature of curriculum design draws heavily from the philosophical foundations. Often the statements we make about the nature of knowledge and the nature of reality are influenced by our philosophical views. Also, individuals concerned about creating curricula that will enhance the quality of students' lives draw from philosophical dispositions. Indeed, many theories are classified as value-oriented theories heavily influenced by philosophical underpinnings. Allan Glatthorn notes that many of the value-oriented theorists strive to raise our consciousness regarding educational issues.[9] They urge us to consider and to reflect on those value issues that form the bases of our educational programs. In many ways, these theorists draw from both the philosophical camps and from political theory.

Persons reflecting on curriculum development also have many theories outside of curriculum proper to guide their action or to employ in explaining particular phenomena. Many theories of change can be used when contemplating and engaging in curriculum development. Numerous theories of organizational development also influence curriculum development activity. Theories of group behavior also affect curriculum development. All the theories that we can consider when contemplating curriculum development tend to be based on logic and the arrangements of sequences or steps.

Most theories are still rather traditional in the sense that they draw from well-recognized areas of research and knowledge. Frances Klein points out, however, that there are some new entries into the field of curriculum theorizing. Still, even with these new entries, most curricularists do seem to agree on two points. First, curricularists agree that curriculum is of fundamental importance to our teachers and students, and to the nature of

teaching and learning. Second, curriculum development is greatly influenced by the values we bring to the process.[10]

What seems to be common among persons using alternative bases for curriculum theorizing is that they share a dissatisfaction with the traditional ways in which we either think about or create a curriculum. Many of these curriculum theorists start with essentially different beliefs and values about the curriculum. Frequently, they envision the future of the school and its curriculum in ways that greatly diverge from mainstream curricularists. Many draw their arguments from fields that until recently were never considered relevant to educational thinking, fields such as art, phenomenology, psychoanalysis, literature, critical theory, and neo-Marxism philosophy.[11]

THE CLASSIC BASES OF CURRICULUM THEORIZING

While much activity within the alternative modes of theorizing exists, there are curricularists who still divide theory either into scientific theory or humanistic theory. It is important that we not accept the posture of either-or thinking regarding scientific theory or humanistic theory. Both have value in assisting us in working within the field of curriculum.

Scientific Theory

Natural scientists in this century have made great advances in their realm of knowledge, largely because of their extensive utilization of what is called scientific theory. In many instances, scientific theory has been given the status of exemplar for theory formation and statement.

Within the natural sciences, the term *theory* sometimes refers to a set of propositions inductively derived from empirical findings. These generalizations refer to various facts, laws, or hypotheses that are related to each other in a systematic way and that form a type of whole—an entity. Scientific theory, then, is comprised of general facts, laws, or hypotheses related to each other.

Perhaps the most widely accepted definition of scientific theory is delineated by Herbert Feigl and includes a "set of assumptions from which can be derived by purely logico-mathematical procedures, a larger set of empirical laws. The theory furnishes an explanation of these empirical laws and unifies the subject matter."[12]

According to this definition, theory is a cluster of logically connected statements that generalize to and offer explanations of particular cases. In its explanations of the various cases to which it refers, theory unifies myriad data and the propositions relevant to those data.

Fred Kerlinger asserts that the basic aim of science is theory, that is, the aim of science is to identify basic statements that explain natural events. He notes that theories are general explanations that enable scientists to understand the phenomena studied.[13] Instead of attempting to explain every separate event, for example, the behavior of students in one activity, scientists formulate general statements about similar events or behavior so that they can link many events or behaviors. Instead of describing how different children each solved a particular science problem, the theorist would derive from his or her observations a general explanation of most, if not all, kinds of problem solving. The investigator would then present the general statement as a theory of problem solving.

Philosophical and Humanistic Theory

Scholars in the humanities use theory to formulate consistent and logical explanations of humans' place in the world. Such theories produce a set of assumptions or beliefs that *explain what ought to be*. These assumptions, derived inductively from the scholars' professional experiences and knowledge of the world, contrast their thinking with that of colleagues in specific disciplines. Philosophers' theories describe their outlooks—their views of reality and their place within it.

Much of the theory that relates to education, and specifically to curriculum, stems from the philosophical and/or humanistic orientation.[14] A tenet of existentialism is that to become fully human, or at least more human, people must be engaged actively in their world; without engagement, individuals become detached and isolated.

This "theory of engagement" is based on philosophical matters rather than scientific validation.

Philosophical and humanistic theory fits into the category Herbert Kliebard has identified as a concern for systematic analysis of a set of related concepts or problems.[15] Theory at this level is essentially the result of an attempt to clarify the nature of concepts and problems, and their understanding rarely depends on empirical support. Empirical considerations play only a minor role. Rather, validation of the theory relies on the logic of various positions and the articulation of values.

Philosophical and humanistic theory is largely normative (based on values). It essentially indicates what should or should not be included or done in some action. Humanistic theory emphasizes the melding of the emotional and physical with the intellectual. It addresses coherence and a way of knowing, that is, the meshing of ideas and actions together.[16] Using such theory, curricularists should have guidelines about what to do or not do in creating the curriculum, that is, about what they should include in and perhaps what they should exclude from the curriculum.

THE FUNCTIONS OF THEORY

Educators may ask, "Why do we need theory at all?" As stated earlier, the aim of science is to understand the phenomena studied. Certainly, most people would accept this statement in relation to theory. Even philosophers require theory to question what is knowledge, what is reality, and what is of value?

Theory comes from the Greek word *theoria* connoting "wakefulness of mind." It is a type of "pure viewing" of truth. Theory explains reality; it makes people aware of their world and its interactions. Many writers have ascribed four functions to theory: (1) description; (2) prediction; (3) explanation; and (4) guidance.[17] Although some writers disagree about which function is paramount, most view all as important and as closely related.

Description.   Description provides a narrative classification of knowledge in a particular theoretical field. It furnishes a structure through which individual's interpretations of complex activities can be verified. It organizes and summarizes knowledge. A theory "tells" us that there are certain variables and that they interact in particular ways or have certain relationships to other variables; it does not indicate why certain variables are important nor why they are interrelated. Theory presents an account of events. It unifies phenomena and arranges the information so that the scope and internal relationships, though not explained, are at least discernible.[18]

Prediction. The second function of theory is rather obvious. A theory can predict the occurrence of as yet unobserved events on the basis of explanatory principles embedded in it. Perhaps this is the ultimate function of theory. Of course, cautious people always regard a theory with some degree of tentativeness; for a theory, regardless of the accumulated data to support it, cannot account for all situations. If it did, it would not be a theory but a law. Nonetheless, the more diverse observations a theory can explain, the greater should be people's confidence in using it to predict the phenomena in question.

Explanation. Explanation addresses "why." It not only points out the relationships between phenomena, but suggests either explicitly or implicitly the reasons for the relationships. The best explanations relate to what people know as opposed to what they may mistakenly believe. For example, an explanation of students' learning difficulties in terms of "evil spirits" would be less believable than an explanation stressing students' motivation and interests.

Guidance. Theory also acts as a guide. It helps researchers choose data for analysis and make economical summaries of the data. The theory generated promotes further investigation. In essence, it serves a directive function. Many scientists assert that this is the true or primary responsibility of scientific theory—to serve as the guide for further study. "What is important is that laws propagate when they are united in a theory; theory serves as matchmaker, midwife, and godfather all in one."[19]

Theorists cannot divorce themselves from their values and knowledge when addressing the directive functions of theory. Values will influence, suggest, even prescribe what their behavior should be. Collecting the facts is a necessary first step in theory building—but what facts, whose rendition of the facts? Without theoretical orientations, people cannot decide what facts to gather or what issues to address. Their values influence what facts and relationships are relevant to them. Their values, in other words, guide their theorizing.

THEORY BUILDING

Essentially, the process of theory development is tied to inductive and deductive thinking. Sometimes, these are considered to be two different approaches to theory generation, but typically both are employed together to create theory.

Induction means building a theory by accumulating and summarizing a variety of inquiries. People using induction rely rather heavily on empirical data. They form propositions on the basis of research that began as tentative hypotheses they tested and validated.[20]

Deduction, in contrast to induction, is the process of inferring necessary conclusions from a combination of premises whose truth has either been accepted as given or assumed to be true. People employing deduction develop theory by constructing logical sequences.[21] They proceed from the general to the specific.

Steps in Theory Building

Theory building is for people who like to play with ideas and deal in the abstract. To engage in theory is to deal with symbols, facts, or words that can be classified into large concepts and generalizations. The ability to see and describe relationships among symbols or facts and then put these ideas into words is also part of theory building. The problem with theory is when it must be applied in the real world. To be sure, there is danger in abstracting ideas that make sense on paper and then testing or using them in specific situations. Because people are not easy to control or manipulate, our theories often faulter in real-life situations. See Curriculum Tips 6-1.

Defining Terms. One of the basic rules in theory building is to be clear about terms. According to Beauchamp, agreement on terms is an essential ingredient in the work of a theorist. The terms theorists employ and the concepts implied by those terms are the building blocks of the theory. Selecting terms is governed by two rules: (1) The wording must be clear, and (2) the terms, once defined, must be used consistently.[22]

Terms define what is to be observed. They refer to concepts, and they are the variables between which empirical relationships are to be sought. Concepts are either nominal or operational.[23] *Nominal* definitions present the attributes of a term or concept. In contrast, *operational* definitions indicate the context in which the concept is employed.

Some terms really cannot be defined either by referring to nominal attributes or by referring to other operationally defined terms. Yet they are a critical, basic part of theory. These *primitive* terms are accepted by those who use them in their theoretical work. In mathematics, for example, the terms "point" or "straight line" are primitive terms. They really cannot be nominally or operationally defined; all we can say is that a "point" is a point. In education, such terms as "felt needs" and "experience" are primitive terms.[24] Although theorists may not always be able to refrain from using primitive terms, they should try to use them as infrequently as possible.

Another category of terms used in theory is *theoretical* terms or operational constructs;

theories with any degree of sophistication contain such terms. A construct is a concept that represents relationships among things and/or events and their properties.[25] Theoretical terms cannot be defined directly by observing particular events. Rather they can be defined by their relationships to other terms that are operationally defined. Educators use a large number of such terms—motivation, cognitive dissonance, attitude, perceptual structuring, set, and social need.

Classifying. The second activity in theory building is classification. At this stage, theorists attempt to organize and integrate what they know about the areas being theorized. They begin summarizing discovered uniformities of relationships between two or more variables or concepts.[26] Their classifications or statements of classifications can have varying degrees of precision, but this does not diminish their place in theory building. Classification allows theorists to discover gaps in their knowledge that must be filled through research activities if they are to give meaning to their theorizing.

When classifying information, theorists group facts and generalizations into homogeneous groups. However, even if categories seem to be taking shape, explanations of the interrelationships among the categories or of the relationships among the facts and generalizations within any single information cluster may still be lacking.

Interpreting. To interpret the information, theorists may approach their data inductively or deductively. The inductive process tends to produce philosophical or prescriptive types of theory; the deductive approach tends to generate logical types of theory. Both processes are necessary to generate meaningful theory; both enable theorists to generate general statements.

But producing general statements is not the end of the interpretation task. Theorists must also make inferences from their general theoretical statements. In other words, they must use the statements to go beyond what they know or have recorded. They must make additional assumptions, create hypotheses, perfect generalizations from additional observations, and deduce other conclusions from observations and generalizations. They must, in effect, suggest new theories that will require additional testing to determine their soundness.[27]

Models

Sometimes, persons involved in theorizing activities engage in *model building* as a means of summarizing the phenomena investigated. Although the term model is sometimes used as a synonym for theory, it is not. Models are representations of aspects of a theory. Models aid comprehension and theory building. They are useful for economically organizing and explaining vast amounts of data. Models help theorists understand how their theories are shaping up. They also trigger questions whose answers are requisite to generating theory. Models in science act like metaphors in language. They enlighten us by suggesting arguments by analogy from known resemblances to so far unnoticed resemblances.

Of course, models do have some disadvantages. They can (1) invite overgeneralization, (2) entice people into committing logical fallacies, (3) show the relationships between variables incorrectly, (4) exhibit faulty assumptions about constructs, (5) stress invalid data, and (6) turn useful energy into nonproductive activity.[28]

Linguistic Models. Models, in terms of language, serve to organize a person's thinking by helping to describe, categorize, and conceptualize his or her knowledge and experiences. According to Herbert Kliebard, language is used to process thought, and so do theories and models of a discipline or field of study. Linguistic models represent a fundamental vehicle of human thought by which people make the complex and puzzling become more familiar and more readily understood.[29]

In discussing linguistic models, we are speaking of verbal concepts and abstractions. Most people use verbal models in everyday speech. The various systems and processes in this book to describe curriculum making are to a large extent examples of verbal models. Teachers, also, rely on verbal models in their classrooms for transmitting learning experiences to students, especially cognitive learning. The art and science of presenting information and ideas, what some of us might call "pedagogy," are based on verbal transmission.

Physical Models. Verbal models may sometimes be a bit complex to understand, but physical or working models are usually quite easy to comprehend. They are usually three-dimensional and show the actual "thing" in a reduced scale. We all are familiar with model airplanes; they look like real airplanes—some even fly—but they are not real airplanes. Chemistry students have all seen models of molecules or atoms, usually made of different colored balls. Physical models enable theorists to visualize the variables or parts under consideration and to note their interrelationships.

Mathematical Models. Sometimes, the best model for depicting the component parts or variables under consideration is a mathematical model. Such models reduce complex interactions of phenomena to the regularity of mathematical expressions. They are common in the physical sciences. Chemical equations that describe and predict the consequences of particular chemical reactions are mathematical models. Einstein's equation $E = mc^2$ is a well-known mathematical model. In decision theory, mathematical equations denote the probability that certain actions will be decided, given a particular situation.

Graphic Models. Throughout this book we have used a fourth kind of model, the graphic model. This is perhaps the most common type of model. It can be a picture, drawing, or diagram of some of the major components, and their interrelationships, of the concept being described. Graphic models help illustrate our verbal text or narrative. The old saying, "A picture is worth a thousand words" applies with good graphic models.

CURRICULUM THEORY

Theory as we have defined it is a set of statements so worded that it can be used as a means of communication among people and as a directive to those who wish to study the field of curriculum.

The challenge to curricularists is to make sense out of the complexity of the field of curriculum and to determine whether they should create their own curriculum theory or theories, borrow theories from other disciplines—such as psychology, sociology, anthropology, and philosophy—or do both. To create a single curriculum theory that would describe, and more importantly explain, curriculum is perhaps an unrealistic goal; curriculum covers too many aspects of education.

Curriculum theory has been the subject of conversation and the focus of reflection by many concerned with curriculum. Even in the early years when the field of curriculum was gaining identity and stature, curricularists were concerned with defining a theoretical basis.

Early Theory in Curriculum

The publication of Franklin Bobbitt's *The Curriculum* can probably be cited as the starting point of theorizing in curriculum. It also represented one of the early books in scientific theorizing. Bobbitt urged his fellow educators to borrow from the new technology to guide educational functioning. He believed strongly that the principles of management and the application of theory could help educators be more precise and efficient in creating and implementing their programs.[30]

Scientific theory was viewed by many to have the quality of objectivity. Theory could serve to describe and explain what is. Theory of phenomena would allow educators to predict the consequences of putting certain phenomena into action.

Many new discoveries in testing and statistics furnished those who wished to engage in theory building with tools that enabled them to manage more carefully investigations and process more precisely data gathered. Persons in curriculum theory drew guidance from the context of the times. This was especially true of Bobbitt and Charters, both of whom were expert in the field of research and evaluation. Both theorists linked the idea of activity analysis with formulating curriculum decisions. The idea was to correlate the objectives of the subject with specific activities—those tasks and skills that students had to learn to prepare for productive living. However numerous these activities were, educators had to make decisions about which activities were to be stressed in school.[31]

During the last years of the nineteenth century and the early years of this century, Dewey was engaged in creating a curriculum theory. Even though Dewey may not have considered his work to be a curriculum theory, but rather a science in education, it still holds value for curriculum theorists.[32] Dewey's theory draws on the notion that the development of the individual and the development of the human race are similar in their overall stages. His theory attempts to show the relationship between schools and society and the various aspects of experience and education as they relate to the learner.[33]

Dewey urged educators to tie knowledge in the curriculum to human experiences relevant to children; moreover, he urged that children experience knowledge through various activities. The experience-centered curriculum, which we discuss in Chapter 8, drew much of its theoretical support from this "theory" advanced by Dewey. It also gave rise to the curriculum activity movement. Dewey actually attempted to reproduce in his experimental elementary school at the University of Chicago the actual conditions of social life. Children would learn about how humans processed their environment by being involved in similar actions in school.

Educators might well ask, then, if persons such as Bobbitt or Charters approached curriculum from various theoretical stances, and Dewey attempted to test out theory in his school, why did curriculum theorizing remain undeveloped?[34] Perhaps because educators have talked a "better game" of theory than they have "played."

Theory at Mid-century

Much of the early talk about curriculum did not consider theory per se. However, in the 1940s, curriculum writings begin to discuss actual theory. The first major discussion on the topic took place at the University of Chicago in 1947. The various participants at this conference produced a paper addressing curriculum theory, but no curriculum theory emerged from the meeting. The papers, which appeared as a monograph *three years* later, did conclude with a challenge: "As a further effort in hastening the communications between groups of interested people and in the development of more adequate theory, someone might spend some time trying to describe the nature of such theory, its tasks, its subject matter, its tests, and its uses."[35]

Tyler, some might argue, took up the challenge in his book's presentation of the basic principles of curriculum and instruction. But Tyler's approach, if it can even be considered theoretical, was more attuned to curriculum development than to an overall theory of curriculum.[36] Beauchamp, however, was instrumental in adding to the field of curriculum theory. His 1950 book, *Curriculum Theory,* addressed the topic.[37] Even so, although the book has gone through four editions, it still leaves us without an agreed upon curriculum theory. Some of the major theories that have evolved are as follows:

Maccias' Theory.   During the last 25 years, the formative years of curriculum theory, a more diversified view of curriculum theory has evolved. Elizabeth and George Maccia, for example, presented four different kinds of curriculum theory. They noted that curriculum specialists speculate about forms, events, values, and practices. Consequently, they organized theory as formal theory, event theory, valuational theory, and praxiological theory.[38]

1. *Formal theory.* This theory deals with speculation about the structure of the disciplines that comprise the curriculum. Curricularists usually draw their understanding of such theory from philosophers and members of the particular disciplines in question. Such theory is nonvaluational; it deals with what is and what exists, rather than what ought to be.

2. *Event theory.* This theory, very similar to what we have been discussing as scientific theory, refers to speculation about occurrences. It attempts to predict what will occur given certain circumstances.

3. *Valuational theory.* This theory involves speculation about the appropriate means to attain the objectives most desired and to include the content judged to be the best. In contrast to event theory, valuation theory does involve values or norms. It deals with "ought-ness."

4. *Praxiological theory.* Such theory refers to speculation about appropriate means to attain what is considered valuable. It is about practices. It can support the creation of curriculum policy, the means we employ to adopt particular objectives and specific practices in schools.

The Maccias asserted that curricularists could use theory to guide their building of a definition of curriculum, as well as in the planning and development of curriculum.

Johnson's Theory.   In contrast to the Maccias, Mauritz Johnson stated that curriculum specialists should first define curriculum making and then direct their energies at theory building. He argued that most past efforts to build curriculum theory had centered on programs, with the result that attention was really on curriculum development.[39] As shown in Figure 6-1, Johnson distinguished between the curriculum plan and the process of curriculum development by defining the former as an output of the latter; he also revealed the differences among curriculum, instruction, and teacher behavior. His attention to objectives puts him in the behavioral camp. Although curricularists may not agree with Johnson's definition of curriculum— an intended series of learning outcomes—they should realize the usefulness of distinguishing between theorizing about curriculum as a plan

TABLE 6-1 Overview of Theories Affecting Curriculum Field

THEORY	AUTHOR(S)	TYPE OF THEORY	CLASSIC BASE	FUNCTION
Curriculum as systematic activity, as management	Bobbitt, Charters	Curriculum theory	Scientific	To explain, describe
Curriculum as reflecting the stages of human development	Dewey	Curriculum theory	Scientific	To explain, prescribe
Curriculum as praxis	Maccia	Curriculum theory	Scientific	To guide, prescribe
Curriculum as intended series of learning outcomes	Johnson	Curriculum theory	Scientific	To describe
Curriculum as interacting systems	Macdonald	Curriculum theory	Scientific	To describe, explain
Curriculum as metaphor	Kliebard, Freire	Curriculum theory	Humanistic	To prescribe
Curriculum as experience for social purpose	Pinar	Curriculum theory	Humanistic	To prescribe
Education as process, as structuring knowledge	Bruner	Instructional theory	Scientific	To explain, prescribe
Education as implementing the curriculum	Oliva	Instructional theory	Scientific	To explain
Teaching as interaction	Lamm	Instructional theory	Humanistic	To prescribe
Teaching as transformation	Giroux	Instructional theory	Humanistic (critical theory)	To prescribe, describe
Theory of consensual domain	Garman	Supervision theory	Scientific	To explain, prescribe
Theory of clinical supervision	Cogan	Supervision theory	Scientific	To prescribe, explain
Theory of dialogic staff development	Glatthorn, Glickman	Supervision theory	Scientific	To explain, prescribe
Theory of the human condition	Prigogine	Supervision theory	Humanistic	To explain, describe

and theorizing about the means by which such plans are generated.

Macdonald's Theory. Macdonald presented a model of the major systems in schooling: curriculum, instruction, teaching, and learning.[40] The model, not actually a theory, points out possible key components involved in the dynamics of curriculum and instruction. It presents a map indicating the key features of the educational landscape.

Though curriculum is quite large in the drawing, Macdonald's model shows it as one of four interacting systems. Macdonald defines *curriculum* as the social system that actually pro-

FIGURE 6-1   Curriculum as an Output-Input of One System.

Source: From Mauritz Johnson, "Definitions and Models in Curriculum Theory," *Educational Theory* (April 1967), p. 23.

duces a plan for *instruction,* which he in turn defines as another social system within which formal teaching and learning take place. *Teaching* is different from instruction and is defined as a personality system—the teacher—acting in a particular manner to facilitate learning. *Learning* is defined as a personality system, too; the student becomes involved in specialized task-related behaviors. All these systems come together in the center, depicted in Figure 6-2 by a shadowed spot. At this juncture, the curriculum goals become operative in the instructional encounter because of the efforts of the teacher and the behavior of the students.

While we still do not have theory, Macdonald's model does, however, clarify the interrelationships between teaching, learning, instruction, and curriculum. It points out that each can be considered a system in its own right, but that in the reality of the school, the systems interface with each other so as to produce some specialized subsystems. Still, the model leaves theorists without answers about how they would determine the nature and scope of the curriculum. The reality of the curriculum in action is certainly more complex than depicted by this model.

Educators continue to believe that theory can produce hypotheses that can be tested in the world of concrete experience. They believe still

that theory can enable them to describe reality and, more importantly, to begin to explain it. It also can serve as a policy map suggesting what they should do.

But the challenge is immense. Gail McCutcheon states that few examples of curriculum theories really integrate data resulting from analyses, interpretations, and understandings of curriculum phenomena.[41] She has argued that curriculum persons need more examples that have a clear value for them and that draw from multiple disciplines. Other curricularists have also addressed this issue, focusing on how the various psychological theories can contribute to curriculum thinking and action.[42]

Some curriculum theorists state that educators must derive curriculum theory from their analyses of curricula-in-use. Decker Walker has faulted many in the curriculum field for being so concerned with prescribing procedures for creating curricula that they have not paid sufficient attention to how curricula are created or to the nature of the programs generated.[43] He argues that curriculum theories can help curricularists view curriculum in a different light and thus generate novel interpretations of curriculum. He suggests that theories can be conceived as clustered in families, each having a different purpose and perhaps a different form. But all theories

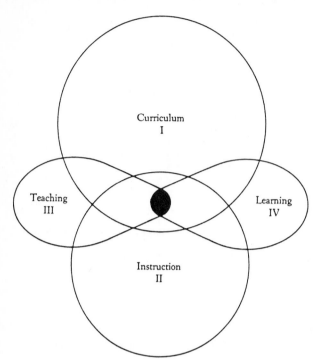

FIGURE 6-2 The Interaction of Four Systems. *Source:* From James B. Macdonald, "Educational Models for Instruction," in J. B. Macdonald and R. R. Leeper, eds., *Theories of Instruction* (Washington, D.C.: Association for Supervision and Curriculum Development, 1965), p. 95.

focus on rationalizing, conceptualizing, and explaining practice. Walker notes that some theories being advanced fit into the current society without question, whereas others are being presented within a context of a new hypothetical, as yet unformed, society. He cites Paulo Freire as one person who is relating "curriculum theory" to a better society still in need of creation. Programs are rationalized on the basis of their enabling society to attain such "utopias."

Elizabeth Vallance notes that curriculum theory is practical and based on real situations; such theorizing in curriculum occurs in every school.[44] Taking this stance, curricularists are encouraged to survey, analyze, synthesize, and test the knowledge available about curriculum problems. They should look at the data available and attempt to make practical application. Vallance notes that the data observed may be part of a new curriculum package, or the textbooks just purchased by a district, or the political climate of the school. Even though the data that theorists might view could be different data than classroom teachers might value, the process of theorizing is similar. See Curriculum Tips 6-2.

METAPHORS AND THEORETICAL CAMPS

Some curriculum theorists have argued that theoretical problems stem from faulty or nonproductive conceptions of curriculum. Dwayne Huebner has urged that educators discontinue their use of logical-rational language that stresses effectiveness, objectiveness, and behavioristic principles of learning and instead employ a language that centers on the economic and political policies that impact on education.[45] He wants educators also to use language that will direct their attention to how learners are provided with choices in subject matter—for example, how can a teacher best involve a student with the myriad cultures of the world so as to enhance the student's global awareness? Huebner has argued that educators have used a language that encourages control over the students, rather than liberation.

More recently, Henry Giroux has urged educators to employ pedagogic language that engages students in finding their own voices and experiencing other voices of diverse cultures. He also advocates a discontinuance of the logical rational language, a belief in one master narra-

CURRICULUM TIPS 6-2 Translating Theory into Practice

Blending theory with practice is an old ideal. If we are to make serious progress toward this goal in curriculum, as in other fields, we need to recognize certain basic steps.

1. *Read the literature.* Any attempt to relate theory and practice must be based on knowledge of the professional literature.
2. *Identify the major terms.* The need is for curriculum theorists and practitioners to identify and agree on the major constructs, concepts, and questions for discussion.
3. *Check the soundness of existing theories.* Existing theories need to be analyzed in terms of validity, evidence, accuracy, underlying assumptions, logic of argument, coherence, generalizability, values, and biases.
4. *Avoid fads.* New fads and hot topics must not be introduced to practitioners under the guise of a new theory—or even as reform or innovation. When a new program or method is introduced into the professional literature or at some professional conference, this is not the time to jump on the bandwagon, much less to call it theory; it is the time to pull back and wait for evaluations or complaints to surface.
5. *Align theory with practice.* Theory must be considered in context with the real world of classrooms and schools; it must be plausible, applicable, and realistic in terms of practice.
6. *Test theory.* If the theory is credible and makes common sense, then it must be empirically tested by trying it in practice and measuring the results. It should be introduced first on a small scale, comparing experimental and control schools.
7. *Interpret theory.* The results must be tested and interpreted in terms of realistic conditions over realistic time periods. The theory must be evaluated in schools for a minimum of one year and ideally over a three-year period to test for "fading out."
8. *Modify theory and reduce its complexity.* A theory is a generalizable construct supported by language or quantitative data. Nonetheless, theory must be modified from paper to practice, from the abstract to the concrete world, from complex concepts to lay terms. When we move theory to practice, we include many people (and resources) to make it work. Theory must fit with people (not mold people to theory) to move it from an idea to action.

tive, substituting instead a language that recognizes the personal, the emotional, the ethical, the uncertain.[46]

Kliebard suggests that a way in which educators can perhaps cure their myopia is to use different metaphors from those that currently influence their thinking.[47] Because a technological orientation to curriculum essentially dominates the field, the metaphor of factory and production is common. Kliebard would propose substituting a metaphor that would enable curricularists to reconceptualize their view of the school and its curriculum. He notes that some social reconstructionists employ the metaphors of culture as a form of capital.

Paulo Freire has used the metaphor of education as banking. Education in this metaphor would be an action of deposition. The students are the depositories and the teacher is the depositor.[48] Note, however, that following a metaphor too closely can be dangerous. According to a banking metaphor, for instance, the student is considered a passive receiver of the deposit; he or she is only to receive, memorize, and repeat. Moreover, this metaphor also brings into focus that educators should ensure that "cultural capital" is deposited equally into each student's account.

People do not usually think consciously about the conceptual systems by which they organize their world. In most of the things they do, they just act and think more or less automatically along pathways that have become comfortable to them. But, if they think about their language, they find themselves in conceptual (and metaphorical) camps that organize their realities. Both William Pinar and John McNeil have presented conceptual organizers that group curriculum persons into three camps.[49]

Traditionalists

Traditionalists value service to practitioners. They view curricula as plans and stress those procedures requisite for creating such plans. Traditionalists are concerned with the essential roles of the key curriculum players and the bases for the selecting, organizing, and sequencing of curriculum content.

A close relationship exists between traditionalists and school personnel. But this closeness has prevented them from creating new ways of talking about curriculum that could result in more productive educational programs.[50] While this orientation to curriculum emphasizes the role of organized subject matter, there is among these traditionalists and school practitioners some contemplation of new ways of organizing curricula. The discussion on integrated curricula, core curricula, and Science/Technology/Society (the STS curricula) exemplify this new conceptualizing and theorizing about curriculum. Such curriculum scholars as John Dewey, Franklin Bobbitt, Ralph Tyler, Hilda Taba, George Beauchamp, Ronald Doll and John Goodlad are in this camp.

Traditionalists tend to be involved in *structural theorizing* that focuses on identifying elements in the curriculum and determining their relationships. Such theorizing centers on the decisions and decision makers (sometimes called players or engineers) involved in curriculum planning. Those who focus on curriculum development and curriculum planning emphasize rationality and logic.[51]

Structural theorists contend that educational practice is not an art but rather, extensively, a science, or at least a scientific approach. They assume that the key events occurring in the educational process can be identified, described, and to some extent controlled. Frances Klein states that these traditionalists, when contemplating curricula, believe in a scientific, technological, and rational processes. They presume that curricula can be created by taking

a behavioristic reductionistic process. They also maintain that it is possible to create curricula prior to its employment within the classroom. Goals, content, and instructional experiences can be preplanned; moreover, teachers can be trained to present such curricula efficiently and effectively.[52]

Conceptual Empiricists

These persons are often researchers and/or measurement oriented and view their primary mission as engaging in research that will be theory producing. They argue that scientific knowledge of human behavior, including the curriculum, is possible. They claim that the research and the resulting theory are of practical value because they enable school practitioners to articulate the reasons for their actions. This, in turn, increases the likelihood that they will realize the traditional goals of the school.

People in this camp are Benjamin Bloom, Jerome Bruner, David Berliner, George Posner, Robert Stake, and Herb Walberg. All these people are actively exploring the application of cognitive science to curriculum and instructional research as well as to cognition and learning to guide the arrangement of curriculum content and its delivery in the classroom.

Dorothy Huenecke asserts that people who are in the conceptual empiricist camp engage in *substantive theorizing*.[53] The theory activity is designed to highlight appropriate content for the curriculum. Conceptual empiricists, engaged in substantive theorizing, analyze current situations and suggest alternatives to current patterns of content and experiences that comprise most curricula. They question what teachers are teaching, why they have arranged the school content in the ways they have, and what influence they have on learners.

Most conceptual empiricists emphasize content-based theories, in part because many are also cognition-oriented psychologists. Perhaps the best known content-based theory is the structure of disciplines which is discussed in Chapter 8. This theoretical orientation explains that knowledge can be structured according to its key concepts and that these concepts can be organized to reveal major relationships. In a curriculum so organized, students could easily grasp the conceptual basis of knowledge resulting in a more detailed understanding.

Reconceptualists

Curricularists who are in this camp maintain the view that intellectual and scientific distance from curriculum practice are required if those in charge of education are to effectively critique and theorize existing programs. Engaging in reconceptualizing theory, one attempts to actually drive a wedge between theory and practice. In theorizing, the intent is not to actually improve a particular practice at one particular juncture, but rather to gain a "wisdom" about the nature of the phenomena about which one is raising questions.

Presently, the reconceptualists are focusing on a critique of the field, which they believe is too immersed in practical and technologically oriented approaches to curriculum. They feel that true understanding will come from aesthetic, humanistic, and existential postures. Focusing on understanding oneself will lead to truly heightened consciousness.

Pinar seems to be the most visible of the reconceptualists, but James Macdonald has been credited with coining the term *reconceptualist*. Macdonald had argued that curricularists were far too concerned with logic and rationality in approaching their work, and so they often totally ignored the aesthetics of the curriculum.[54] They needed to reconceptualize—to take a new focus—to furnish new direction and to de-emphasize providing practitioners with prescriptive formulas for efficiently delivering the curricula.

A theme common to much of the work and writings of reconceptualists is liberation. Some people, who draw heavily from existentialism and phenomenology, propose that liberation comes from within the person. Both Macdonald and Pinar recommend a method of self-analysis by which learners can study their own responses to life—and, therefore, to educational situations.[55] The method for doing this involves (1) recalling and describing the past and then analyzing its psychic relation to the present, (2) describing one's imagined future and determining its relation to the present, and (3) placing this analytic understanding of one's education in its cultural and political context. We draw from this that learning is highly personal and unique for each of us. Individuals need a method for processing their experiences such that they derive meaning from them and control over their lives.

Others, such as Michael Apple, Paulo Freire, and Henry Giroux question the dynamics of power, control, and influence.[56] They raise questions about "who is in charge" of the educational system—and for what purpose? Who controls the type of knowledge that is to be experienced in the school? Who controls the amount of knowledge that will be presented to various groups of students? Who creates the criteria that will determine success? How do we liberate schools and society from the political and economic establishment?

Many of these commentators draw on critical theory. The main thrust of critical theory is to enable people to reflect and critique the dominant socioeconomic class structure and the ways in which the curriculum serves to perpetuate such structure. The theory draws from Marxism and neo-Marxist theories. Robert Young notes that the early critical theorists urged us to see schooling as part of the larger social order. For example, Marx viewed the social order as being oppressive to the workers, and as maintaining an underclass—or what he called the proletariat. It was the purpose of education to enable these workers to recognize their oppression and to use education to overcome such oppression.[57] Many of the early reconstructionists, such as George Counts and Harold Rugg, also envisioned the social order as discriminatory and oppressive toward the masses of the poor and working class. To be sure, they were considered too radical for their era, and they had FBI files. This emphasis on overcoming oppression, on liberation or emancipation, continues with current critical theorists.

To the critical theorist, liberation or emancipation means freeing oneself from the accepted ideology of current social conventions, beliefs, and modes of operation. It uses theory to get individuals to reflect on the current scene and to realize that it needs modification. People need to organize socially so that they will have the power to create new worlds and new societies. Students must be empowered by the curriculum to question the values of the current social and political scene. They are to analyze the current reality and then reflect on those beliefs and ideas that contribute to their lives.

Critical theorists contend that individuals' places in society result not from their free choices, but rather from the actions performed by the economically elite who control our competitive economy. Critical theorists argue that individuals are enslaved in our highly capitalist system. People strive to obtain meaningless certificates to the point that they are more interested in the document than in intelligence. Students, for instance, are more interested in passing tests than in gaining knowledge. The system forces us all to be passive recipients of the rewards. Critical theorists wish to use theory to enable curriculum developers to create programs that will free students of this form of existence. The main aim is to make students fully aware of themselves and of the fact that society must be altered to allow both self-freedom and collective freedom.[58]

INSTRUCTIONAL THEORY

On the basis of what happens in the classroom, we cannot separate curriculum from instruction or teaching from instruction. The actual relationship between curriculum, instruction, and teaching is not clearly defined in the professional literature or in current curriculum texts. This vagueness is reflected by the fact that about 35 percent of the curriculum departments in schools of education across the country use only the word *curriculum* in their department names, another 30 percent refer to *curriculum and instruction,* another 25 percent use the terms *educational leadership* or *curriculum leadership,* which suggest a curriculum-supervisory-administrative program, and about 10 percent use the term *curriculum and supervision* or *curriculum and teaching.*[59]

Curriculum and Instruction

Eighteenth- and nineteenth-century European educators, from Locke and Rousseau to Spencer and Herbart, were pioneers in pedagogical principles. Their concern was not curriculum as we know it, because the term itself was unknown until the twentieth century. Their concern, rather, was with content and teaching methods, which they attempted to explore as scientific principles. But what they had to say was related to curriculum, even though the field of study did not exist.

The actual relationship between curriculum and instruction was touched on slightly in the works of Bobbitt and Charters, and later in a book by Henry Harap.[60] Then, in 1930, it was examined in detail when the famous committee for the Twenty-sixth Yearbook of the NSSE formulated a composite statement about curriculum making. Of the twelve steps developed, two were linked to instruction: "the place of school subjects in instruction" and "measuring the outcomes of instruction."[61]

Both Tyler and Taba were concerned with instruction in their classic texts. This was especially true of Tyler, who considered instruction to be a plan for teaching the curriculum and "the procedures for organizing learning experiences into units, courses, and programs."[62] One of Tyler's four major questions (or chapters) examined "how learning experiences [can] be organized for effective instruction." By entitling his book *Basic Principles of Curriculum and Instruction,* he took the position that both components were equally important and part of a continuous and cyclical process, involving constant replanning and reappraisal.

Taba saw curriculum in a broader context than teaching and teaching in a broader context than instruction. Curriculum represented the substance and content of what was to be learned; teaching was identified with the general behavior and methods of the teacher for imparting the subject matter to the learner; and instruction was viewed as the specific activities introduced while teaching at various stages of the curriculum. By taking this approach, Taba identified instruction as something apart from curriculum—and something that did not have equal weight with curriculum.[63]

In the 1960s a good deal of activity occurred over theories of instruction and the relationship between curriculum and instruction. Curriculum and instruction were defined as separate entities by Jerome Bruner, who developed a theory of instruction that focused on four factors: (1) facilitating learning, (2) structuring knowledge,

(3) sequencing learning experiences, and (4) pacing rewards and punishments in the process of learning and teaching.[64] In this context, curriculum and instruction were considered as separate disciplines of education and both had equal weight.

Harry Broudy and his colleagues spoke of curriculum as a total system; instruction and teaching were subsystems, and therefore not as important. Instruction was further categorized into five content or subject areas, what they termed "study areas," and teaching was further categorized into two methods or strategies, what they termed "modes."[65] They further claimed that even though "modes of teaching are not, strictly speaking, a part of curriculum, for practical purposes it is not useful to ignore them entirely in curriculum theory."[66] This statement would not significantly differ from most current theories of curriculum; moreover, the unequal weighting of curriculum and instruction would coincide with the majority of curriculum texts today.

Among recent textbook writers is Robert Zais. He *separates* curriculum and instruction along the views of Broudy and Taba. He views curriculum as a broad concept and instruction as a specific phenomenon or subsystem (with less importance). Instruction is to be introduced at some point along a curriculum continuum. The point of introduction is flexible, to permit subjective judgment on the part of the teacher: It "is to be selected according to the teacher's personality and teacher's style, and the students' needs and interests."[67]

Most current curricularists take a middle position. Although they separate curriculum and instruction for purposes of discussion, they consider one without the other incomplete. The two components are *fused* or brought together at times, but they still retain their original characteristics or independencies, a view similar to Bruner and Tyler.

Saylor et al., for example, claim that the "two terms . . . are interlocked almost inextricably as the names . . . Romeo and Juliet. Without a curriculum or plan, there can be no effective instruction; and without instruction the curriculum has little meaning." However, both curriculum and instruction are separately defined; the latter is viewed "as the implementation of the curriculum plan."[68]

Peter Oliva considers curriculum and instruction "as two entities . . . like Siamese twins who are joined together [and] one may not function without the other." He points out that the relationship is *cyclical,* meaning that they "are separate entities with a continuing circular relationship. Curriculum makes a continuous impact on instruction and, vice versa, instruction impacts on curriculum."[69]

In the majority of cases, in which the two components are fused or depicted in a cyclical relationship (Oliva's term), curriculum is viewed as a written plan or program that serves as a guide; once the curriculum is acted upon or put into operation, the plan moves to instruction that involves implementation and methodology. Although curriculum as a plan is *inert,* instruction as an act is *alive* and evolving. The curriculum takes place in the entire school (even outside the school), and instruction takes place in the classroom (or a specific setting such as an auditorium, ballfield, etc.). In this context, curriculum deals with the *what*: what we interpret students and society to need. The basis for our decisions is largely philosophical and social in nature. Instruction deals with *how* people learn, that is, with the psychological foundations and with methods, materials, and media. However, both curriculum and instruction modify each other in a continuous and multidimensional way: curriculum decisions affect instruction, and instructional decisions affect curriculum.

Whether people wish to separate curriculum and instruction, or fuse these two components, reflects their own philosophical and psychological views on education. Curriculum students do not have strong views on this subject, and even the experts treat the matter briefly in their respective texts. Instructional experts (and learning theorists) usually have a definite position; they treat instruction as a separate field of study. Their ideas reflect the growing influence of educational psychologists in the field of curriculum.

Teaching and Instruction

Not all instructional theory emanates from psychological theory. Critical theory also relates to instruction or pedagogy. Robert Young notes that critical pedagogy has more to do with a method of teaching than with particular criticisms of the social situation. Essentially, critical theorists present teaching as interactions among individuals where reflection is valued and subjected to criticism.[70] Teachers engage in teaching to form individuals or to allow them to form themselves.

Zvi Lamm posits that the object of a theory of instruction is the teacher's behavior. This contrasts with psychological theory, which essentially focuses on the learner's behavior. Psychological or learning theory is primarily descriptive, whereas instructional theory is essentially prescriptive. It suggests how teachers *should act*. It serves to force teachers to choose among competing possible actions in the classroom. The purpose of a theory of instruction is to show what instruction *can be* and how it can be modified to address the needs of individuals or the demands of particular situations.[71] Instructional theorizing addresses those actions a teacher should take to "teach" the content or the subject matter. For those accepting the primacy of the student, instructional theorizing addresses the involvement of students in their learning. To individuals centering on political and/or social factors, instructional theory deals with those behaviors requisite for making students politically and socially aware.

Bennett and Desforges report that we are currently engaged in searching for a theory of pedagogy. We are turning away from psychology as the foundation for explaining and essentially prescribing teacher behavior. "Psychology has not delivered the goods."[72] Research in psychology has produced much literature on learning, but scant "pickings" that provide us with clear indications for teaching. One reason for the nonproductivity of the research is that much was done in laboratory settings with tight experimental controls. Such work does not transfer easily to the classroom.

For this reason, there is good reason to theorize about instruction by looking at both the classroom and social milieu within which instruction occurs. From their research, Bennett and Desforges conclude that successful instruction occurs when teachers consider their learners

as active and interpretative.[73] In the same vein, Lamm has argued that instruction is dialogic, rather than monologic. Put in different words, good teaching and good instruction are collaborative efforts between teachers and students. Teachers explain and students make sense out of the content of the curriculum.

This posture does not indicate that teachers are to lead students. Rather, teachers are to engage students in ways that help them conceptualize and interpret the content of the curriculum. Besides learning content, students begin to comprehend that knowledge results from a community of persons engaged in intellectual pursuits. From effective instruction, students gain sensitivity to and cognizance of the means people utilize to defend their views of the world and the ways in which they study their world.

Persons arguing that instruction is aimed at engaging students in interpretation might well accept the metaphor of "conversation" or "dialogue" to explain good instruction. (Indeed, this dates back to Socrates.) The ways in which people talk, the symbols they employ, the gestures they use are all influenced by the cultures or communities in which they find themselves. Conversation is a give-and-take situation. This conversation model has the teacher and student in interaction rather than the teacher talking *at* the student. But this conversation is not "blind talk"; it involves reflective statements and raising of questions. It is tied very closely to an existential posture in which students seek inner awareness in their educational talk.

Ideally, in carrying on a mental conversation, students come to realize that they actually can become different persons. Querying themselves makes them view the world differently, allows them not only to cope with their reality, but to appreciate that they can actually construct their reality in many instances. Students skilled as educational conversationalists with themselves have begun to function somewhat as young intellectuals.

Giroux talks of teachers as transformative intellectuals. In reflecting on teachers in this manner, we highlight the idea that all instructional activity involves some form of thinking. Giroux emphasizes this point, noting that it dignifies teachers to integrate thinking and practice.

Educators can indeed be, indeed are, reflective practitioners. Teachers are to be seen not merely as "implementers of the curriculum, rather they should be viewed as free men and women with a special dedication to the values of the intellect and the enhancement of the critical powers of the young."[74]

While Giroux's basic premise is nurtured by critical theory, we all can benefit from realizing that our actions in the instructional realm are to enhance the critical powers of youth. Additionally, we are to make students aware that they also are responsible for enhancing their own powers of critical thought and reflection. The nature of instruction and the roles educators play within the instructional realm are indeed influenced by philosophical orientations rather than psychological theories. See Curriculum Tips 6-3.

SUPERVISORY THEORY

We in curriculum are coming to realize that, if we wish to assure that the taught curriculum results in a learned curriculum, we will have to at least appreciate, if not fully understand, the field of supervision and how it relates to curriculum. The point is that once we have created curricula we need to "look" at, to supervise, how it is being delivered.

Supervision specialists are confronting many of the same challenges facing curricularists. Like curriculum, the term supervision has many meanings. In some instances, supervision is not defined directly, but rather in metaphoric language. Carl Glickman conceptualizes supervision as the *glue* of a successful school. It is the function that molds the myriad elements of instructional effectiveness into effective school action. This glue involves those processes employed by individuals in the school that link the individual teacher's needs with the organizations' needs so that individuals function to the benefit of both themselves and the organization. Also, this glue refers to those actions undertaken by certain individuals, called supervisors (school principals, vice principals, department heads, etc.) for adding more glue to the system when necessary.[75]

Thinking of supervision as glue makes fuzzy the picture of what supervisors do. Sometimes the title of the position does not reflect the role of the position. Expectations may differ as to supervision depending on the position one holds. Some administrators may think that the person with supervisory responsibilities is to direct and control the behavior of teachers. Others think the supervisor exists to monitor and evaluate the teacher's instruction, what some refer to as "supervision of instruction." In contrast, teachers often think that supervisors should offer encouragement and support regarding their teaching.

Supervision and Instruction

John Lovell and Kimball Wiles refer to supervision as a subsystem that interacts with a teaching subsystem designed to assure the successful learning of students. Supervision is provided by the organization for the purpose of improving teaching and instruction and learning opportunities for students.[76] Individuals with this responsibility work to assure that teachers are working optimally and that the teacher-student systems are productive and functioning.

In a sense, supervision scholars are attempting to supervise the field of supervision itself by observing the actions of those who title themselves supervisors. They are attempting to either apply theory or to organize theory to guide their actions. Thomas Sergiovanni states that the key to present-day theorizing is to reveal the workings of supervisors in action. There is a movement away from the notion of scientific theory, a departing from description and prescription, a move toward gaining information that will inform professional judgment.[77] In this sense, theorizing within the field of supervision is similar to theorizing in curriculum.

In supervision there is a person-to-person relationship, the relationship of the teacher-supervisor. Noreen Garman discusses a *theory of consensual domain* as an underpinning for explaining and understanding this relationship. This theory supports Morris Cogan's classic interpretation of "clinical supervision," which essentially follows a structure of five steps: teacher preconference, classroom observation of the teacher, analysis and interpretation of what is observed, teacher postconference, and a critique of the four steps.[78]

This person-to-person relationship is effective if the teacher and supervisor can share a belief that effective interpersonal interaction comes not from the imposition of some external model or scheme on a person but from what emerges from such joint action. Individuals do not learn and behave in particular ways as a result of following external models; rather, people learn by interacting in consensual domains in which social interaction is central. Consensual domain exists among those who share a social or professional community.

It appears that the theory of consensual domain is part of the postpositivist, postmodernist posture in which people do not function external to systems. We cannot create a model of supervision or curriculum and think that we can study it or manage it from the outside. We are part of the very models we generate. In a supervision model, we create our physical and linguistic models to represent realities. But these models only have relevance if in our discourse we tacitly agree to employ symbols in a particular way, recognizing that we have agreed to cooperate in ways that will change us. The very act of supervising a teacher assumes an agreement to collaborate in improving action within the school. Furthermore, it assumes a recognition that all parties will mutually affect one another, rather than one party being the cause and one party the effect.

Many ways exist to develop this interaction. However, it does seem that many of the procedures for "observing" teaching suggest not a theory of consensual domain, but rather an objectivistic posture that an outsider can come in and do things *to* the insider, the teacher. Granted, this is an overstatement, but consider the many principals entering classrooms with a checklist influenced by the work of Madeline Hunter. Here the principal looks for the elements of a good lesson: anticipatory set, clear objectives and purpose, presenting input or information, modeling the process of skill, furnishing guided practice, and scheduling independent practice.[79] Teachers are to conform to a narrow model that depicts teaching primarily as the setting up of situations to deliver information to students. In this model, students are to passively receive the information or skill and then to practice it until mastered.

The Hunter approach seems to suggest a classroom neatly defined. Good teaching is essentially following a recipe, and teachers' actions can be denoted on lists. However, Allan Glatthorn has suggested an approach, if not a theory of supervision, that addresses the messiness, the actual chaos, of classroom teaching. Glatthorn essentially reconceptualizes supervision to mean professional development. He talks of staff development and collegial relations. It appears that much of the current talk on supervision is drawing from an existential philosophical orientation.[80] This philosophy places the individual at the source of all reality. What exists, what is real, rests with the meaning that an individual constructs regarding his or her experiences.

Glickman might agree with Glatthorn to some degree, for he does discuss our need to match curriculum development with teacher development. If the curriculum is to be delivered or activated, then teachers must be sufficiently knowledgeable of both the content and the pedagogy embedded in it. Staff development is not something done just once prior to a curriculum being introduced. Rather, as supervisors interact with teachers who are implementors of the curriculum, there is teacher development and, we would add, supervisor development.[81]

In short, the supervisor should be mindful of how we can augment teacher control over the curriculum. A pact between supervisor and teachers should be designed so that teachers increase their effectiveness in creating, delivering, and evaluating the curriculum. The pact should also enable the supervisors to become more effective in their roles of guiding, helping, and consensus building. Drawing on existentialist philosophy, a supervisor is committed to the power of the individual to make choices. Supervisors do not exist to monitor or check off peoples' behaviors. According to Glickman, supervisors work in consensual arrangements: to nurture in teachers the powers to explore and create their own physical and mental capabilities.[82]

This existential view can be framed as a *theory of the human condition.* Ilya Prigogine and Isabelle Stengers, in writing about chaos theory, weave through their discussion the importance of humans participating in their making of meaning, in finding patterns from the analysis of chaos.[83] The issue, then, is the centrality of people. Curriculum, instruction, and supervision are very human and therefore messy activities. Rather than strive for false precision, trying to objectify reality, we should take relish in our colleagues and our own sub-

jectivity, in the chaos within which we educators work. The challenge for us is not to control and supervise the chaos, but to learn from it, to participate in it, to improve it.

DIRECTIONS FOR THE FUTURE

Theorizers focusing on curriculum, instruction, and supervision, regardless of their particular philosophical camp, do share a common concern: to make sense of human experience and human knowledge in order to promote in people (teachers and students) those competencies, skills, understandings, and values requisite for growth and prosperity. This is no small task—to account for and to affect the quality of human experiences. It is this very complexity of human experience that makes theorizers recognize the extraordinarily difficult thing that they are attempting to do—to generate theories of curriculum, instruction, and supervision so as to guide, explain, describe, and in some cases predict action.

Curriculum Inquiry

Curricularists are confronted with making sense of the world, not only to describe it but to manage it in the present and to entertain and initiate ways of modifying it in the future. The reconceptualists have suggested that curricularists take on a psychoanalytic posture in order to discover their inner worlds before describing and guiding their outer worlds. Decker Walker, who is classified by some as a conceptual curricularist, has outlined five questions:

1. What are the major features of a given curriculum?
2. What are the personal and social consequences that a given curriculum feature elicits?
3. What accounts for the stability and change in curriculum features?
4. What accounts for people's judgments of the merit or worth of various curriculum features?
5. What sorts of curriculum features should be part of a curriculum designed for a particular purpose?[84]

Walker apparently views curriculum as a practical field of study that is to create some product that, when experienced by students, will make a difference in their learning. However, Walker's concept of a "curriculum feature" is vague. Perhaps, however, a precise conception is not possible because there are so many definitions and conceptions of the curriculum.

To make sense out of the dynamics of the curriculum field, curricularists need to analyze the total educational environment in which experience occurs. This includes the school and the outside community. A "good" theory of curriculum cannot ignore the influence of the surrounding environment or the meaning generated by the theory will be incomplete. Even when approaching curriculum from a global or macroanalytic stance, however, curricularists will not be able to explain the total picture or use such theory to control the total educational drama. At best, they will be able to plan or modify portions of the curriculum and the environment affecting them.

Instructional Inquiry

Some curricularists realize the need to generate instructional theory. While we realize that we cannot have a theory that will explain the total picture, we must understand that instruction comprises a significant aspect of the curriculum-in-action. Therefore, we need to inquire into the nature of instruction and how teachers employ it, not only to deliver the curriculum, but also to share that actual message content and the manner in which it is organized with their colleagues.

We need to investigate how teachers employ instruction within various philosophical postures. We need to investigate whether we consider instruction as primarily an activity of imitation, or molding, or an activity that interacts with the developmental aspects of individuals playing both roles of student and teacher.[85] We need to probe teachers' depth of understanding of pedagogic knowledge and how such knowledge influences their perceptions of curriculum and means of delivering it.

Theories of instruction influence how educators perceive learning, even what they consider to be learning experiences. Goals of instruction, implicit in the goals of the curriculum, are affected by the philosophical and psychological postures of teachers. What is taken as student achievement, and even appropriate student behavior, is influenced by these twin theoretical notions. Presently, these are more like assumptions. But, we need continuous inquiry that will address them. We must go beyond comparing one method against another. We need to query how instruction melds into the curriculum realm and how the values, skills, and attitudes of teachers ultimately affect students' experiences and learning outcomes.

Supervisory Inquiry

As previously noted, supervision in the past has been viewed as something that a supervisor did to the person being supervised. Supervision as an area of scholarship appears as dynamic as the field of curriculum. Glickman suggests several propositions that suggest future inquiry activities. He notes that supervision can strengthen teachers' belief in a cause beyond oneself. It can make teachers aware of how they complement each other in striving for common goals. It can stimulate teachers engaging in reflection-in-action. Finally, it can challenge teachers into being more creative and more abstract in thinking about their roles.[86]

Inquiry is required to test out these propositions. Also, inquiry is necessary to determine how best to get teachers to function effectively as developing professionals. Certainly, we need to study how supervision can expand its range of functioning to the development, implementation, and maintenance of curriculum. Supervision should view the entire educational theater. Accepting this, we then need to guarantee that the key players who supervise the "school show" possess those competencies and attitudes requisite for the job. It is also likely that educators participating in teaching a curriculum, or perhaps inviting students to participate in a curriculum, will require more understanding of curriculum and supervision. How to expand this perception among educators is an interesting query. Curriculum types need to understand what supervisors do, and supervision types need to accept what curriculum is all about.

Conceptualizing the Task

There is much diversity of thought about what curriculum is, what it should be, and how it should be theorized. The same is true of instruction and supervision. Debate exists, too, about the units of analysis in theorizing about and conducting research in these three fields. With regard to curricula, is the unit of analysis the school district, the school, the classroom, or the student? With regard to instruction, is the unit of analysis the teacher or the student? In supervision, is the unit of analysis the school, the classroom, the teacher, or the student? Combining all three areas, is the unit of analysis the interacting network extant between the school and the local community? Is the unit the content, the experiences, the skills, or the values we are attempting to convey?

The task for theorizers of curriculum, instruction, and supervision is to reflect about the many dimensions of their respective fields. Curriculum types can theorize about the total curriculum field, where the field is going and why—its overall dynamics. Or they can theorize on a micro level—about the various elements or aspects of curriculum, say curriculum development, curriculum implementation, or curriculum evaluation. Instructional theories can address the overall dynamics of instruction in action. Or they may attend to the congruence of the teacher's behavior with students' actions. Also, they may investigate the influence of teacher's particular attitudes on the goals deemed important in instruction. Supervisors may study the educational program from conception to implementation, or they may just query whether teachers are following a particular prescriptive approach to teaching. Whether theorists' approach their respective fields of curriculum, instruction, or supervision globally or break them into micro elements, we must realize that a diversity of approaches exists influenced by the "mind sets" these theorists bring to their inquiries.

A Balanced Approach to Theorizing

The traditional school of theorizing has been dominant for most of this century. Especially in research, this school has relied primarily on quantitative inquiry. Empirical investigation has been the norm, and the classroom has been viewed as a laboratory in which variables are to be manipulated in a controlled atmosphere.

Although this type of research is valid and will add to the "polishing" of existing theories, much information can also be gained from qualitative inquiry in the schools. Playing "participant observers" in classrooms, theorists can note the types of materials used, the nature of classroom interactions, and the consequences for learners. Employing methods of ethnography, sociology, and history, they can ask key questions: "What do schools do?" "What are schools for?" "How do students learn?"

People in the traditional camp using well-established quantitative procedures are still influenced by their values and their views of the world. This is also true of qualitative researchers. Both quantitative and qualitative camps are approaching reality through their own perspectives—whether they are scientific or philosophical, empirical or aesthetic.

The focus of most, if not all, of this curriculum research is to discover useful generic principles. But focusing on the total field often only gives information accurate at the general level, not at the specific level—for example, a particular subject or grade level.

To get a picture of a particular subject or grade, theorists need to engage in action research, which is done in the classroom by teachers faced with particular problems. The value of action research is not judged by whether a new general principle is formulated, but rather by whether the guideline deduced from such research will lead to improved classroom practice.

CONCLUSION

In this chapter we primarily discussed the state of curriculum theory. We presented the nature of theory by outlining the various types of theory possible and the different functions that theory could serve. It is not likely that total agreement about the nature and purpose of theory will be forthcoming in the near future. Hopefully, there is some level of agreement about the steps necessary for theorizing. The first step is conceivably the greatest challenge: to come to some kind of agreement about what terms to use. Until theorists have some consensus on the meaning of major terms in curriculum, they are going to be hard pressed to produce many theories of high utility. The same applies to the fields of instruction and supervision.

Although the "slipperiness" of terms has perhaps prevented a dominant curriculum theory from arising from the field, models depicting the curriculum and its various components are certainly not lacking. We presented several in this chapter to give readers a feel for the diversity of opinion, as well as to note the common elements that draw the attention of curricularists.

Where do we go from here? What is the future of theory? Some theorists will likely continue to study curriculum, instruction, and supervision from a macro perspective and others from a micro perspective. Regardless of approach, a balance will be needed; not only a balance of approach, but also a balance among the types of professionals involved in theorizing and a balance among curricularists, instructionalists, and supervisors in schools, colleges, universities, and even in state, regional, and federal agencies.

ENDNOTES

1. William H. Schubert, *Curriculum: Perspective, Paradigm, and Possibility* (New York: Macmillan, 1986).
2. Elizabeth S. Maccia, *Curriculum Theory and Policy,* Occasional Paper 65–176 (Columbus, Ohio: Ohio State University, 1968).
3. Hilda Taba, *Curriculum Development: Theory and Practice* (New York: Harcourt Brace, 1962).
4. George J. Posner, *Analyzing the Curriculum* (New York: McGraw-Hill, 1992).
5. George A. Beauchamp, *Curriculum Theory,* 4th ed. (Itasca, Ill.: Peacock, 1981).
6. Abraham Kaplan, *The Conduct of Inquiry* (San Francisco: Chandler, 1964), p. 295.
7. Richard E. Snow, "Theory Construction for Research on Teaching," in R. M. Travers, ed., *Second Handbook of Research on Teaching* (Chicago: Rand McNally, 1973), p. 78.
8. Joseph Schwab, *The Practical: A Language for Curriculum* (Washington, D.C.: National Education Association, 1970).
9. Allan A. Glatthorn, *Curriculum Leadership* (Glenview, Ill.: Scott, Foresman, 1987).
10. M. Frances Klein, "Approaches to Curriculum Theory and Practice," in J. T. Sears and J. D. Marshall, eds., *Teaching and Thinking about Curriculum* (New York: Teachers College Press, Columbia University, 1990), pp. 3–14.
11. Ibid.
12. Herbert Feigl, "Principles and Problems of Theory Construction in Psychology," in W. Dennis, ed., *Current Trends of Psychological Theory* (Pittsburgh: University of Pittsburgh Press, 1951), pp. 182–195.
13. Fred N. Kerlinger, *Foundations of Behavioral Research,* 2nd ed. (New York: Holt, Rinehart, 1976), p. 10.

14. Ira J. Gordon, ed., *Criteria for Theories of Instruction* (Washington, D.C.: Association for Supervision and Curriculum Development, 1968).
15. Herbert M. Kliebard, "Curriculum Theory: Give Me a 'For Instance,' " *Curriculum Inquiry* (Summer 1977), pp. 257–268.
16. Richard D. Kimpston, Howard Y. Williams, and William S. Stockton, "Ways of Knowing and the Curriculum," *Educational Forum* (Winter 1992), pp. 153–172.
17. Max van Manen, "Edifying Theory: Serving the Good," *Theory into Practice* (Winter 1982), pp. 44–49.
18. May Brodbeck, "Logic and Scientific Method in Research on Teaching," in N. L. Gage, ed., *Handbook of Research on Teaching* (Chicago: Rand McNally, 1963), pp. 44–93.
19. Kaplan, *The Conduct of Inquiry,* p. 20.
20. Kenneth R. Hoover, *The Elements of Social Scientific Thinking* (New York: St. Martin's Press, 1984).
21. C. E. Noble, "Induction, Deduction, Abduction," in M. H. Marx and F. E. Goodson, eds., *Theories in Contemporary Psychology,* 2nd ed. (New York: Macmillan, 1976), pp. 300–308.
22. Beauchamp, *Curriculum Theory.*
23. Brodbeck, "Logic and Scientific Method in Research on Teaching."
24. Gordon, *Criteria for Theories of Instruction.*
25. M. H. Marx, "Theorizing," in Marx and Goodson, eds. *Theories in Contemporary Psychology,* pp. 261–285.
26. Beauchamp, *Curriculum Theory.*
27. Ibid.
28. Carter V. Good, *Introduction to Educational Research,* 2nd ed. (New York: Appleton-Century, 1963).

29. Herbert M. Kliebard, "Curriculum Theory as Metaphor," *Theory into Practice* (Winter 1982), pp. 11–17.

30. Franklin Bobbitt, *The Curriculum* (Boston: Houghton Mifflin, 1918).

31. Bobbitt, *The Curriculum;* W. W. Charters, *Curriculum Construction* (New York: Macmillan, 1923).

32. Kliebard, "Curriculum Theory: Give Me a 'For Instance.' "

33. John Dewey, *The School and Society* (Chicago: University of Chicago Press, 1900).

34. Kliebard, "Curriculum Theory: Give Me a 'For Instance.' "

35. Beauchamp, *Curriculum Theory*, p. 35.

36. Ralph W. Tyler, *Basic Principles of Curriculum and Instruction* (Chicago: University of Chicago Press, 1949).

37. Beauchamp, *Curriculum Theory.*

38. Occasional papers by Elizabeth Maccia and George Maccia (Columbus, Ohio: Bureau of Educational Research and Service, Ohio State University, 1963–1965).

39. Mauritz Johnson, "Definitions and Models in Curriculum Theory," *Educational Theory* (April 1967), pp. 17–32.

40. James B. Macdonald, "Educational Models for Instruction," in J. B. Macdonald and R. R. Leeper, eds., *Theories of Instruction* (Washington, D.C.: Association for Supervision and Curriculum Development, 1965), pp. 93–98.

41. Gail McCutcheon, "What in the World Is Curriculum Theory?" *Theory into Practice* (Winter 1982), pp. 18–23.

42. Bernice J. Wolfson, "Psychological Theory and Curricular Thinking," in A. Molnar, ed., *Current Thought on Curriculum* (Alexandria, Va.: Association for Supervision and Curriculum Development, 1985), pp. 53–72.

43. Decker F. Walker, "Curriculum Theory Is Many Things to Many People," *Theory into Practice* (Winter 1982), pp. 62–65.

44. Elizabeth Vallance, "The Practical Uses of Curriculum Theory," *Theory into Practice* (Winter 1982), pp. 4–10.

45. Dwayne Huebner, "Toward a Remaking of Curricular Language," in W. Pinar, ed., *Heightened Consciousness, Cultural Revolution, and Curriculum Theory* (Berkeley, Calif.: McCutchan, 1974), pp. 36–37.

46. Henry A. Giroux, *Postmodernism, Feminism, and Cultural Politics* (Albany, N.Y.: State University of New York Press, 1991).

47. Kliebard, "Curriculum Theory as Metaphor."

48. Paulo Freire, *The Politics of Education, Culture, Power, and Liberation* (South Hadley, Mass.: Bergin & Garvey, 1985).

49. William Pinar, "Notes on the Curriculum Field 1978," *Educational Researcher* (September 1978), pp. 5–12; John McNeil, *Curriculum: A Comprehensive Introduction,* 4th ed. (Glenview, Ill.: Scott Foresman, 1990).

50. William Pinar, "Heightened Consciousness, Cultural Revolution and Curriculum Theory: An Introduction," in W. Pinar, ed., *Heightened Consciousness, Cultural Revolution, and Curriculum Theory,* pp. 1–15.

51. Dorothy Huenecke, "What Is Curriculum Theory? What Are Its Implications for Practice?" *Educational Leadership* (January 1982), pp. 290–294.

52. Klein, "Approaches to Curriculum Theory and Practice."

53. Huenecke, "What Is Curriculum Theory? What Are Its Implications for Practice?"

54. James Macdonald, "Curriculum Theory," in J. R. Gress and D. E. Purpel, eds., *Curriculum: An Introduction to the Field* (Berkeley, Calif.: McCutchan, 1978), pp. 44–56.

55. James Macdonald, "Curriculum and Human Interests," in W. Pinar, ed., *Curriculum Theorizing: The Reconceptualists,* pp. 283–298; William Pinar and Madeline Grumet, *Toward a Poor Curriculum* (Dubuque, Ia.: Kendell-Hunt, 1976); and Pinar, *Contemporary Curriculum Discourse* (Scottsdale, Ariz.: Gorsuch Scarisbrick, 1988).

56. Apple, *Education and Power* (Boston: Rutledge and Kegan Paul, 1982); Freire, *The Politics of Education,* and Henry A. Giroux, *Theory and Resistance in Education* (New York: Bergin & Garvey, 1983).

57. Robert Young, *A Critical Theory of Education* (New York: Teachers College Press, Columbia University, 1990).

58. Klein, "Approaches to Curriculum Theory and Practice"; Schubert, *Curriculum: Perspective, Paradigm, and Possibility.*

59. There are about eighty departments in curriculum at the graduate level in universities across the country. These percentages are based on reviewing forty at random.

60. Henry Harap, *The Techniques of Curriculum Making* (New York: Macmillan, 1928).

61. "The Foundations of Curriculum Making," A Composite Statement by the Members of the Society's Committee on Curriculum Making, in G. N. Whipple, ed., *The Foundations of Curriculum Making,* Twenty-sixth Yearbook of the National Society for the Study of Education (Chicago: University of Chicago Press, 1930), p. 11.

62. Ralph Tyler, *Basic Principles of Curriculum and Instruction* (Chicago: University of Chicago Press, 1949), p. 83.

63. Taba, *Curriculum Development: Theory and Practice.*

64. Jerome S. Bruner, *Toward a Theory of Instruction* (Cambridge, Mass.: Harvard University Press, 1966).

65. Harry S. Broudy, B. Othanel Smith, and Joe R. Burnett, *Democracy and Excellence in American Secondary Education* (Chicago: Rand McNally, 1964).

66. Ibid., p. 78.

67. Robert Zais, *Curriculum: Principles and Foundations* (New York: Harper & Row, 1976), p. 12.

68. Saylor et al., *Curriculum Planning for Better Teaching and Learning* (New York: Holt, Rinehart and Winston, 1981), p. 10

69. Peter Oliva, *Developing the Curriculum,* 3rd ed. (New York: Harper Collins, 1992), p. 12.

70. Young, *A Critical Theory of Education.*

71. Zvi Lamm, *Conflicting Theories of Instruction* (Berkeley, Calif: McCutchan, 1976).

72. Neville Bennett and Charles Desforges, "Matching Classroom Tasks to Students' Attainment," *Elementary School Journal* (January 1988), p. 22.

73. Elaine Atkins, "Reframing Curriculum Theory in Terms of Interpretation and Practice," *Journal of Curriculum Studies* (Winter 1988), pp. 437–448.

74. Henry A. Giroux, *Teachers as Intellectuals* (Granby, Mass.: Bergin & Garvey, 1988), p. 125.

75. Carl D. Glickman, *Supervision of Instruction,* 2nd ed. (Boston: Allyn and Bacon, 1990).

76. John T. Lovell and Kimbal Wiles, *Supervision for Better Schools,* 5th ed. (Englewood Cliffs, N.J.: Prentice Hall, 1983).

77. Thomas J. Sergiovanni, "Emerging Scholarism of Practice," *Journal of Curriculum and Supervision* (Spring 1990), pp. 247–251.

78. Noreen Garman, "Theories Embedded in the Events of Clinical Supervision: A Humanistic Approach," *Journal of Curriculum and Supervision* (Spring 1990), pp. 201–213.

79. Madeline Hunter, "Knowing, Teaching, and Supervising," in Phil L. Hofford, ed., *Using What We Know about Teaching* (Alexandria, Va.: Association for Supervision of Curriculum Development, 1984), pp. 169–192.

80. Glatthorn, *Curriculum Leadership.*

81. Glickman, *Supervision of Instruction.*

82. Ibid.

83. Ilya Prigogine and Isabelle Stengers, *Order Out of Chaos* (New York: Bantam Books, 1984).

84. Decker Walker, "What Are the Problems Curricularists Ought to Study?" *Curriculum Theory Network* (Vol. 4, 1974), pp. 217–218.

85. Lamm, *Conflicting Theories of Instruction.*

86. Glickman, *Supervision of Instruction.*

CHAPTER 7

AIMS, GOALS, AND OBJECTIVES

Focusing Questions

1. *How can we distinguish educational aims from goals?*
2. *What are the major sources of educational aims?*
3. *What are the various types of educational objectives?*
4. *How do curriculum specialists formulate objectives?*
5. *How can the taxonomy of educational objectives be used for formulating educational objectives?*
6. *What are the differences between behavioral and nonbehavioral objectives?*
7. *How do behaviorists and humanistic educators differ in their formulation of objectives?*
8. *How do reconceptualists deal with objectives? To what extent do they accept objectives? Reject objectives?*

Education is purposeful; it is concerned with outcomes that are usually expressed at several different levels. The most general level is reflected in statements of aims; the most specific is exhibited in statements of objectives. But, whatever the level of specificity, educators use these statements to guide their development, implementation, and evaluation of educational programs. Such statements are not created in a vacuum. Their formulation is influenced to a great extent by the philosophy of the educators who are responsible for such statements.

If there were only one philosophy, only one way of viewing reality or interpreting societal needs, the tasks of curriculum specialists would indeed be easy, or so it would seem to some.[1] However, such is not the case. Because of the numerous philosophical positions, there are myriad ways to conceptualize and deliver curricula. Whether curricularists' view the outcomes of schooling as fixed terminal points or as points in a never-ending series of points, the curriculum is influenced by their philosophies.

John Dewey and others argued that the ends to which people strive are not really ends, but waypoints upon a continuous journey. Upon attaining a waypoint, the individual is then enabled to proceed to the next; thus the ends for a particular point become the means for striving to another point; for Dewey, ends lead to action, and they do not necessarily have to be preplanned. Indeed, curricularists are now realizing that the ends of education can evolve from interactions among educators and students. As much as educators are fond of stating the ends of education, it is essential to recall Dewey's comments. "Ends are, in fact, literally endless, forever coming into existence as new activities occasion new consequences." There are no "fixed self-enclosed finalities."[2]

Our purpose, however, is not to debate the various views of ends and means; it is to point out the role that philosophy and our views of the learner play in interpreting and responding to reality and in creating educational programs for students. We need to be well aware of the philosophical and psychological underpinnings of our curricular actions, perhaps even more so today than in past times, for today schools are existing in a society that is experiencing great waves of social and technological change.

It seems especially important in these times that educators consider the worth of the ends they suggest and also view them not as the final ends, but rather as leading to some other points of development or understanding. In this connection, curriculum workers would be well advised to conceptualize schooling as a philosophical enterprise. As J. Galen Saylor asserts, "Schooling is a philosophical venture, one that necessitates choosing . . . among innumerable possibilities. Those choices constitute the starting point in curriculum planning."[3]

AIMS OF EDUCATION

In times of great change, society looks to its schools to help its citizens adjust. Society often demands that the schools modify their programs so that students will be able to function more effectively in current times. Few educators would dare respond to the many demands placed on the schools without some mention of educational aims. But often they are not precise in their use of educational language. The term aims is often used interchangeably with goals, ends, functions, general objectives, and purposes.[4] However, there are differences among the terms, and it is helpful to distinguish among them. Aims are general statements that provide both shape and direction to the more specific actions designed to achieve some future product or behavior. Aims are starting points that suggest an ideal or inspirational vision of the good.[5] They reflect value judgments and value-laden statements, and they furnish educators with guides for the educational process.

Educators of every age are challenged to interpret the aims of society. Because of their global quality, only a few aims are necessary to guide education. For example, Ralph Tyler summarized the aims of American schooling as (1) developing self-realization, (2) making individuals literate, (3) encouraging social mobility, (4) providing the skills and understanding necessary for productive employment, (5) furnishing tools requisite for making effective choices regarding material and nonmaterial things and services, and (6) furnishing the tools necessary for continued learning.[6] These all-encompassing aims reflect a progressive philosophy.

Ronald Doll notes that educational aims should address the intellectual or cognitive, the social-personal or affective, and the productive.[7]

1. Aims dealing with the *intellectual dimension* focus on the acquisition and comprehension of knowledge, problem-solving, skills, and various levels and methods of thinking.

2. Aims in the *social-personal dimension* are concerned with person-to-society, person-to-person, and person-to-self interactions. These aims also subsume the emotional and psychological aspects of individuals and their adaptive aspects with regard to home, family, church, and local community.

3. Aims relating to the *productive dimension* of schooling center on those aspects of education that allow the individual to function in the home, on the job, and as a citizen and member of the larger society.

To these dimensions, we would add four others: (1) *physical,* dealing with the development and maintenance of strong and healthy bodies; (2) *aesthetic,* dealing with values and appreciation of the arts; (3) *moral,* dealing with values and behavior that reflect appropriate behavior; and (4) *spiritual,* dealing with the recognition and belief in the divine and the view of transcendence.

Sources of Aims

During every period of contemporary history, society in general and educators in particular have formulated aims. These aims are usually developed by prestigious, nationwide commissions and task forces in the context of the overriding concerns and problems of a changing society. These commissions, which have been in existence since the turn of the twentieth century, usually include descriptive studies of society to guide program creation.

Spencer's Report.   We might denote the starting point for such reports as 1859, when Herbert Spencer published his essay "What Knowledge Is of Most Worth?" From his analysis of his contemporary society, Spencer concluded that for individuals to lead successful lives they needed preparation in five realms of activities: (1) direct self-preservation, (2) indirect self-preservation (for example, securing food, shelter, and earning a living), (3) parenthood, (4) citizenship, and (5) leisure activities.[8] Since Spencer's time, hundreds of descriptive studies of all aspects of society, many conducted by blue-ribbon panels, have been utilized by educators to frame the aims of education. These aims have been formulated to sustain our way of life and to allow students to be successful in life outside the school. They have been written with the intent to preserve our social and political institutions, to maintain the current society, and to improve it.

The Cardinal Principles.   The National Education Association's Commission on the Reorganization of Secondary Education issued its report in 1918, when World War I ended. The report, called *Cardinal Principles of Secondary Education,* spoke to the role of education in our democratic society in the following manner: Education in a democracy, both within and without the school, should develop in each individual the knowledges, interest, ideas, habits, and powers whereby "he will find his place and use that place to shape both himself and society toward even nobler ends."[9]

Perhaps influenced by Spencer, the commission employed the organizational principle of important life activities to organize categories of curriculum aims. Seven major areas were presented:

1. Health
2. Command of fundamental processes
3. Worthy home membership
4. Vocational education
5. Civic education
6. Worthy use of leisure
7. Ethical character[10]

The Purpose of Education in American Democracy.   After the Great Depression, the Educational Policies Commission of the NEA issued a report entitled *The Purpose of Education in American Democracy.* The Commission noted that the definition of education needed to reflect the philosophy and practice of democracy. Education must cherish and inculcate its moral val-

ues, stress knowledge and information essential to its institutions and economy, and foster a creative and sustaining spirit.[11]

A comprehensive set of four aims, each with several corresponding goals (which the Commission called objectives) was delineated: (1) self-realization, (2) human relationships, (3) economic efficiency, and (4) civic responsibility. The aim of *self-realization* was to encourage inquiry, mental capabilities, speech, reading, writing, numbers, sight and hearing, health knowledge, health habits, public health, recreation, intellectual interests, aesthetic interests, and character formation. The aim of *human relationships* included humanity, friendship, cooperation with others, courtesy, appreciation of the home, conservation of the home, homemaking, and democracy in the home. The aims of *economic efficiency* encompassed work, occupational appreciation, personal economics, consumer judgment, efficiency in buying, and consumer protection. The aim of *civic responsibility* related to social justice, social activity, social understanding, critical judgment, tolerance, conservation of resources, social application of science, world citizenship, law of observance, economic literacy, political citizenship, and devotion to democracy.[12]

Education for All American Youth.   In 1944, the Educational Policies Commission, still concerned about the purposes of education, formulated several aims of education. Influenced by World War II, it stressed the overriding aims related to democracy and world citizenship, as well as those related to the general needs of children and youth. Its report, *Education for All American Youth,* listed ten aims, or what it called the "Ten Imperative Needs of Youth." All youth needed to develop skills and attitudes that enhance the following:

1. *Salable skills and those understandings and attitudes that make them intelligent and productive participants in economic life.*
2. *Good health and physical fitness.*
3. *Understanding of the rights and duties of citizens of a democratic society, and those necessary to serve as members of the community and citizens of the state, nation, and world.*

4. *Understanding of the significance of the family for the individual and society, and the conditions conducive to successful family life.*
5. *Knowledge of how to purchase and use goods and services intelligently, understanding both the value received by the consumer and the economic consequences of their acts.*
6. *Understanding of the methods of science, the influence of science on human life, and the main scientific facts concerning the nature of the world and humanity.*
7. *The development of capacities to appreciate beauty in literature, art, music, and nature.*
8. *The use of leisure time and the budgeting of it wisely, balancing activities that yield satisfaction to the individual with those that are socially useful.*
9. *Respect for other persons, insight into ethical values and principles, and the ability to live and work cooperatively with others.*
10. *Growth of their ability to think rationally, to express their thoughts clearly, and to read and listen with understanding.*[13]

The Central Purpose of American Education.
Feeling the effects of Sputnik, the National Educational Association's Educational Policies Commission addressed the aims of education in 1961. It noted that in the modern world, an expanding role was accorded the rational power of humans. Using these powers, knowledge was increased to solve the riddles of life, space, and time.[14]

Educators were concerned that in a real sense we were losing excellence, especially in mathematics and science. Sputnik had caught us by surprise, and the schools were identified as the cause of our coming up second. America had to meet the demands of the space race and the Cold War. The Educational Policies Commission's 1961 report essentially stressed intellectual excellence and thinking competencies. We needed to challenge our gifted and talented students.

A Nation at Risk. In 1983, the Commission on Excellence in Education was directed to examine the quality of American education and to report its findings. The Commission concluded that our nation was at risk: Our educational system was delivering a mediocre performance and the schools had lost sight of the basic purposes of education. The Commission argued that "learn-

ing is the indispensable investment required for success in the 'information age' we are entering."[15]

The Commission made several recommendations that touched on the directions of education and how to address them. The first recommendation dealt with content. The commission stated:

> *We recommend that State and local high school graduation requirements be strengthened and that, at a minimum, all students seeking a diploma be required to lay the foundations in the Five New Basics by taking the following curriculum during their 4 years of high school: a) 4 years of English; b) 3 years of mathematics; c) 3 years of science; d) 3 years of social studies, and e) one-half year of computer science. For the college-bound, 2 years of foreign language in high school are strongly recommended.*[16]

The Commission focused on the need for higher standards and expectations by urging educators to "adopt more rigorous and measurable standards, and higher expectations, for academic performance and student conduct, and that 4-year colleges and universities raise their requirements for admission . . ."[17] The Commission also made the recommendation that significantly more time be devoted to learning the New Basics. This would require more effective use of the existing school day, a longer school day, and a lengthened school year. Finally, the commission urged that citizens hold educators and elected officials responsible for providing the leadership necessary to achieve these reforms and that citizens provide the fiscal support and stability required to bring about the reforms it proposed.

Challenge for Tomorrow. In looking at the broad sweep of American educational aims, you might ask yourself whether the schools are expected to do more than is feasible. The schools are often seen as ideal agencies to solve the nation's problems, but can they do so? Many people refuse to admit to their own responsibilities in helping children develop their potential and adjust to society.

The importance of various pressure groups also needs to be mentioned. As society changes, and as different groups seek to further their interests and promote their causes, the aims of education must change. Educators are confronted by new, vocal pressure groups—particularly ethnic groups, women's groups, homosexual groups, and the handicapped. These groups all define themselves as a minority entitled to privileges or special treatment not afforded to the majority. These groups have new power! Educators must process the needs and interests of these groups, along with traditional pressure groups such as the National Rifle Association, United Way, labor affiliates, and church groups. In processing the information, educators must maintain professional control, yet address the demands placed on them. The educational aims must be relevant to the times—both the present and future—and furnish direction that is good for society, and not one particular group.

GOALS OF EDUCATION

Goals are statements of purpose with some outcome in mind. Peter Oliva distinguishes between curriculum goals and instructional goals. He defines a curriculum goal as a "*purpose* or *end* stated in general terms without criteria of achievement." In contrast, he identifies an instructional goal as a "*statement of performance* expected of each student in a class, phrased in general terms without criteria of achievement."[18] A sample curriculum goal might be that students demonstrate competence in the application of geographic information. An instructional goal might be that students be familiar with the basic steps of problem solving.

When speaking of goals, we are addressing curriculum goals, or desired outcomes for students as a result of experiencing the curriculum. We are not addressing how teachers would instruct students to achieve these goals, although it is realized that instruction is related to curriculum and that particular methods of instruction are selected mindful of the demands of certain contents and also the demands of students and their abilities and interests.

By analyzing a school's goals, we can determine the scope of its entire educational program. Goals, in contrast to aims, are not open statements. They are specific statements written so that those responsible for program creation can use them as guidelines to achieve particular purposes. Goals are derived from various aims and thus provide teachers and curriculum decision makers with broad statements of what they should accomplish in terms of student learning as a result of a particular subject or educational program.

Levels of Goals

Goals can be written at several levels of generality. At one extreme, they can be written in such broad phrasing that they are similar to aims and reflect a philosophical base. At the other extreme, they can be written rather specifically to indicate a concern about a particular achievement.

The distinction between aims and goals of education is one of generality. Aims deal with the general process of education, such as "building worldmindedness" or "creating technological literacy." No particular program in the school will attain these aims; many aspects of the curriculum quite likely will address them. Aims become goals when they become more specific and refer to a particular school or school system and to a specific subject area of the curriculum. The aim of "building worldmindedness," for example, might become the social studies goal that "students will become aware of the various nations of the world and the roles that they play, in the world community."

Much discussion regards the proper phrasing of educational goals. Some individuals prefer sentences, some phrases, some just a single word. The Association for Supervision and Curriculum Development identified ten major goals for youth that contain several words each: (1) learning self-conceptualization (self-esteem); (2) understanding others; (3) developing basic skills; (4) encouraging interest in and capability for continuing learning; (5) becoming responsible members of society; (6) developing mental and physical health; (7) enhancing creativity; (8) being informed about participating in the economic world of production and consumption; (9) using accumulated knowledge to understand the world; and (10) coping with change.[19] Each of these goals contained several subgoals.

Some educators are more comfortable with goal statements that start with infinitive verbs. These persons would rewrite the preceding list as follows: (1) to develop in students positive self-concepts; (2) to improve students' understanding of others; (3) to develop in students command of basic skills; (4) to stimulate students' interests and capabilities for continual learning, and so forth.

The Phi Delta Kappa honor society has distributed a list of goals; they are:

1. Learn how to be a good citizen.
2. Learn how to respect and get along with people who think, dress, and act differently.
3. Learn about and try to understand the changes that take place in the world.
4. Develop skills in reading, writing, speaking, and listening.
5. Understand and practice democratic ideas and ideals.
6. Learn how to examine and use information.
7. Develop skills to enter a specific field of work.
8. Develop a desire for learning now and in the future.
9. Practice and understand the ideas of health and safety.
10. Appreciate culture and beauty in the world.[20]

In 1990, President Bush and the governors of the United States generated a list of six goals for the nation's schools. During the same year, the National Goals Panel was established to determine just how the nation was progressing toward meeting these goals. The goals identified to lead the schools in the last decade of this century were:

1. *By the year 2000, all children in America will start schools ready to learn.*
2. *By the year 2000, the high school graduation rate will increase to at least 90 percent.*
3. *By the year 2000, American students will leave grades four, eight, and twelve having demonstrated competency in challenging subject matter (English, Mathematics, Science, History, and Geography).*
4. *By the year 2000, U.S. students will be first in the world in science and mathematics achievement.*
5. *By the year 2000, every adult American will be literate and will possess the knowledge and skills necessary to compete in a global economy and exercise the rights and responsibilities of citizenship.*
6. *By the year 2000, every school in America will be free of drugs and violence and will offer a disciplined environment conducive to learning.*[21]

It is both interesting and a bit disconcerting to note that the goals are very similar to those generated by various groups after the Sputnik scare in the late 1950s. The humanities appear not to be adequately addressed. The curriculum suggested by the goals also reveals a rather traditional emphasis. The emphasis tends to be on academics. With the exception of the last goal, there is little mention of the students' social, psychological, or moral development.

Formulating Goals

Goals, like aims, should have a degree of timelessness to them. That is, they should address the particular times in which educators find themselves, but should contain wording also appropriate for future times. While goals address endpoints, they leave a certain degree of freedom in identifying the particulars of the goal. Actually, the particulars are considered in the educational objectives.

The timelessness of the goals is made evident by a recent publication by the Carnegie Council on Adolescent Development. In that document, the council states "Every student should learn to think critically through mastery of an appropriate body of knowledge, lead a healthful life, behave ethically and lawfully, and assume the responsibilities of citizenship in a pluralistic society.[22]

Persons charged with creating curricula certainly do not lack suggestions as to which goals to emphasize. Having so many goal statements actually may make determining goals more problematic. For instance, should we consider equally the goals suggested by the ASCD, Phi Delta Kappa, or the National Goals Panel? Or should the school only attend to those goals primarily within the cognitive realm, leaving goals in the personal realm to other social agencies? Should schools be primarily concerned with the goals of the local community? To what extent should state, regional, and national priorities be incorporated into our goal statements? When do our goal statements need to be modified? Every year?

Every 3 years? How do we educate our teachers so that they can create educational programs that speak to the major goals?

Creating educational goals is really a continuing activity in which educators engage as they consider the philosophies of their schools and work to clarify their educational aims. The needs of society, of students, or of the particular community commonly give rise to initial statements of curriculum goals. When school districts have identified current students' learning and behaviors, they often match those with their views of what an educated person is. When persons analyze their philosophies and the aims of their schools, they come up with general statements of outcomes—results they expect to occur in consequence to educational activity. People then make a final match between students' learning and behavior and the goals they have generated. The goals are sometimes rank-ordered in light of importance or feasibility, or both. Persons involved in goal development—teachers, community members, and even students—are asked to decide if these are the goals they wish to address—if these are the end points toward which the program should strive. If they answer yes, then these goals are accepted by those who are creating and delivering the curriculum. See Curriculum Tips 7-1.

OBJECTIVES OF EDUCATION

Within the context of educational aims and goals, it is necessary to formulate objectives that will indicate in more specific terms the outcomes of the curriculum or project being considered. Throughout much of our history objectives have been stated vaguely; they are often confused with goals and aims. To keep aims, goals, and objectives clearly separated, it is perhaps helpful to remind ourselves that in translating aims into goals and finally into objectives, we proceed from the very general, couched in a long-term framework, to the more specific, couched in a short-term time sequence. The sequence is illustrated as follows:

Philosophy → Aims → Goals → Objectives

For a particular program or project, then, curriculum developers may state a general objective like "improving students' skill in information processing when dealing with science material." Under this rather general objective, which some might call a goal, they must have a series of more specific objectives.

Types of Educational Objectives

When proceeding from the most general statements to the more specific, as illustrated in the sequence above, some curriculum planners denote several levels or types of objectives. These begin with general objectives (which indicate general outcomes relating to specific areas of the curriculum, often courses or subjects and particular grade levels) and go to specific outcomes resulting from classroom instruction.

Hilda Taba asserted that educational objectives can be of two sorts: those that describe school-wide outcomes and those that are more specific and describe behaviors to be attained in a particular unit, a subject course, or a particular grade-level program.[23] Robert Zais classifies the school-wide objectives as curriculum goals and the more specific objectives as curriculum objectives.[24]

George Madaus and James Popham point out that specific objectives are often translated into performance objectives or performance levels; such objectives are usually accompanied by "high-stake" tests, meaning a good deal is riding on the outcomes. Exit tests for high school graduation (whether the student passes or gets a diploma), and tests for college admission (such as the SAT or ACT) are high-stake tests; so are state-wide tests in reading and math, at the lower grades, as well as the National Assessment tests in selected grades and subjects. Not only do these tests drive the curriculum, but also in some states the student performance levels or outcomes pit school districts, or schools within school districts, against each other in terms of competition, reputation, recognition, and even monetary rewards.[25]

Ornstein identifies objectives as to the level for which they are written: (1) program objectives, addressing subjects (science or math) at particular grade levels; (2) course objectives (biology or algebra), relating to particular courses within grade levels; and (3) classroom objectives, which are further divided into unit objectives and lesson plan objectives. The first two types of objectives are usually developed by curriculum specialists working at the state or school district level; however, classroom objectives are designed by teachers in an attempt to achieve program and course objectives.[26]

George Posner and Alan Rudnitsky introduce another term for objectives: intended learning outcomes (ILOs), defining them as statements of precisely what the student is to learn. An ILO is a declaration about the specifics to be learned: facts, concepts, principles, process, techniques, generalizations, etc. Posner and Rudnitsky stress that the words *intended learning outcomes* require our reflection. *Intended* means that the statements are not referring to accidental learning. Learning that is intended is the result of reflecting on information judged to be of worth.

Also, intended means that the educational process is under a type of control for particular purposes. While there may be many unintended learnings, in curriculum planning we are addressing those we *intend* to occur. The term *learning* is also important. As the authors point out, learning implies that the bottom line for planning is student performance. And *outcome* is also a crucial word. Curricular planners are concerned with the results from students interacting and experiencing the curriculum. What has the student achieved from taking a course?[27]

It perhaps rests with the educational professional, and that includes teachers, to decide just what to call objectives. But, whatever they are called, objectives are more specific than goals, and this specificity increases in the progression from general curriculum objectives (subject or grade level), to unit objectives (classroom level), to lesson objectives (also classroom level). Objectives are statements that enable curriculum decision makers—curriculum developers, teachers, and even students and members of the general public—to identify the particular intent of a particular action. Norman Gronlund and Robert Mager state that a meaningful objective is one that communicates effectively to the reader the instructional intent or behavior of the objective as well as specific learning outcomes.[28]

Behavioral Objectives. In our previous discussion, we referred to educational objectives as general or specific statements of expected learner outcomes. Advocates of both types of objectives have, for the past decade or so, debated their value. But the general public and, so it seems, the majority of educators have accepted the view that specific statements are the most effective for educational objectives. Many educators who hold this view believe that objectives that are stated precisely will improve the quality of teaching and learning.

For an objective to be meaningful and therefore useful in guiding educators (whether or not it has been achieved), it should be measurable. To the extent that educators are unable to measure achievement, the meaningfulness of the objective is diminished. Put simply, this means that a behavioral objective is a statement of outcomes in terms of observable behavior expected of students after instruction.

Mager contends that an educational objective must describe (1) the *behavior* of the learner when demonstrating his or her achievement of the objective, (2) the *condition* imposed on the learner when demonstrating mastery of the objective, and (3) the minimum *proficiency* level that will be acceptable.[29] A behavioral objective in science following Mager's counsel might read as follows:

> After studying the unit on energy, the student must complete a 100 item multiple-choice test on the subject. The student must answer correctly 75 items and respond to this exam within a 1-hour period.

An example for mathematics might be as follows:

> Given a worksheet dealing with the process of multiplication, the pupil will be able to multiply sets of three-place numbers at the rate of one problem per minute with 80 percent accuracy.

Most behaviorists are advocates of such objectives. They counsel all who formulate objectives to use verbs in the objectives to signify *observable behaviors,* such as "identify," "describe," "solve," "write," "build," and so on. They urge educators to avoid such verbs as "appreciate," "understand," and "know," because such words are vague and really cannot be easily observed as outcomes of education.

Nonbehavioral Objectives. Perhaps the greatest advantage of behavioral objectives is the clarity of communication they foster. People reading such objectives know precisely what they mean and can determine the extent to which they have been attained. But advocates of nonbehavioral objectives, who are somewhat general in wording, and use such words as "appreciate," "know," and "understand," contend that stating objectives too specifically restricts learning opportunities to those situations that require measurement. Objectives that address higher-order learning (for example, analytic thinking and appreciation of literature) are likely to be eliminated because they frequently do not lend themselves to precise measurement. Many opponents of behavioral objectives reject precise objectives as expressions of behaviorism. They insist that much learning can occur that does not result in overt, measurable pupil behavior. Learning in the affective domain is a more subtle form of learning, and teachers cannot detect the attainment of positive affective states by having pupils take 100-item tests and get 80 responses correct.

Behavioral objectives are also criticized for not taking into account what Michael Polanyi has called *tacit knowing:* having knowledge that we are perhaps unable to verbalize or demonstrate specifically.[30] One example of tacit knowing is being able to recognize a familiar face in a crowd, yet not being able to describe in any detail the person's appearance.

Advocates of nonbehavioral objectives point out that educators must realize that there are many indicators of attainment of an educational outcome. With behavioral objectives, the educational outcome may be considered attained *if, and only if,* such a behavior is demonstrated. Knowledge of subtraction, for example, is attained if and only if a child completes eight out of ten subtraction examples in a 20-minute period. Are we willing to state that 80 percent is the only indicator of achieving this goal? What of the student who gets seven out of ten? Are curriculum designers really willing to enunciate such a narrow interpretation?

Over a decade ago, J. Galen Saylor et al., summarized the objections of many regarding behavioral objectives. They indicated that behavioral objectives only emphasize the teaching of facts (which are easy to measure) at the expense of the more complicated intellectual behaviors (which are difficult to measure). Such objectives place a sameness on the curriculum, assuming all must master identical material and do so almost in identical ways. Precise objectives nurture a rigidity in learning and tend to deny the unique learning outcomes of students, thus resulting in an assemblylike or factorylike educational process. Rigidly following objectives often dehumanizes individuals, overlooks individual outcomes, and stifles creativity and spontaneity. Finally, overemphasis on behavioral objectives negates that learning is much more than the gathering and hoarding of specific facts learned in isolation.[31] While objectives are still being written in behavioral terms and for mastery at the school level, it would appear that the general posture of some educators is opposition to such objectives. Many cognitive and humanist educators would reject the use of behavioral, objectives especially precise ones, as narrow minded, rigid, and silly—even as dysfunctional to the educational process.

Advocates of behavioral objectives advise curriculum makers to create comprehensive lists of behavioral indexes. The behaviors indicated are only to be guides that indicate that a learning outcome has been attained. Other behaviors could also attest that a learner has been successful.

This still is not acceptable to those who completely reject the behaviorist posture. These people still prefer nonbehavioral objectives or objectives that provide direction only on a conceptual basis. The intent of the program is for the student to know something or to appreciate something—not to be able to do twenty pushups or twenty subtraction exercises. As Lorin Anderson asserts, "A well-written instruction objective specifies the desired learning outcome in conceptual terms."[32] It focuses on general learning outcomes, not specific performance.

Those who favor nonbehavioral objectives are still concerned with being precise. All educational objectives should be stated with sufficient precision to make clear what pupils are supposed to learn. The verbs "to know," "comprehend," "be able to," "enjoy," and "encounter" are all clear—they just are not behavioral! Words like "be familiar with" or "become aware of" or "have a feeling for" are vague and are rejected.[33]

Teachers who believe in nonbehavioral objectives sometimes prepare such objectives in broad general terms indicating what students are to do. Some examples follow:

> As a result of this course, the learner will:
>
> Be able to interpret the various map symbols found on the particular types of map projections.
> Understand that a community is a place where people work and play together.
> Understand the functions of nouns and verbs.
> Be able to perform long division of numbers.
> Demonstrate ability to do back flips.
> Enjoy folk music.

Means and Ends.   Much of the argument between behaviorists and nonbehaviorists revolves around the nature of language. Just how precise must the language in educational objectives be? Mauritz Johnson and David Pratt make an interesting and useful distinction between educational intent and the realization of the intent. They note that many educators fall prey to the belief that the objective is in reality the statement that indicates its measure of achievement.[34] They state that an educational objective is really a statement of intent, an expected end product, not an actual product.

Drawing on these arguments, consider the following objective: "The student will write three statements, three questions, three commands, and three exclamations within a 15-minute time period and will have at least ten of the sentences correct as to type and with regard to subjects, predicates, and punctuation."

A person charged with curriculum development should raise the question, "Why do I want the student to do this?" A likely response is that, by engaging in this activity, the student will show a basic understanding of the four types of sentences and punctuation. But does this answer the question? *Why* should a student need to understand these types of sentences? Johnson and Pratt would argue that the real reason is that a student will be able to apply such knowledge of sentence types and write what accurately and effectively expresses his or her feelings or interpretations of a subject. The real objective is not writing three statements, three questions, three commands, and three exclamations; rather, it is writing effectively on subjects of the student's own choosing.

Guidelines for Formulating Educational Objectives

Because objectives indicate end points or expected outcomes or points that lead to other significant outcomes or points in the educational process, careful thought must be given to the creation of educational objectives. Indeed, giving careful thought to objectives increases the probability that a particular program will be judged successful. Educators should consider the following factors when creating objectives.

Matching. Objectives should relate to the goals and the aims from which they are derived. Many curriculum guides include objectives that, although perhaps having merit, are unrelated to the goals. An objective of students' "understanding" certain science contents, for example, is not in alignment with a goal that students be able to utilize particular information-processing approaches to uncover scientific understanding.

Worth. It is often debatable which educational objectives have worth and which do not. Many schools overemphasize detail, especially in the skills subjects such as reading and mathematics. As a result, many objectives are written that have little worth. Even in such subjects as social studies we see evidence of trivial objectives. "The student knows that the Mississippi River empties into the Gulf of Mexico." Does such an objective

have value? Is it essential to know such information? Worth also relates to whether attaining an objective will have value to the student at present and in the future. Indeed, certain subject knowledge needs to be eliminated, modified, or updated because our knowledge base is constantly changing.

Wording. Objectives are only effective if the persons who are to use them as curriculum guides are able to understand from them the same intended outcomes as their writers. Objectives, brief and trimmed of excessive wordiness, are easy to understand and agree on. How appropriately an objective is worded also depends on its level and its scope. Some objectives are written as general subject or grade objectives, some are written as unit objectives, and some, as lesson-plan objectives. Because lesson-plan objectives should be worded to indicate rather specifically the intended outcomes, they may include performance criterion statements. This type of precision is not necessarily needed at the first two levels (subject or grade level and unit plan level).

Appropriateness. Not all objectives need to be attained by all students. Curricularists must ask, What are the needs of the students? What type of learning outcomes do they need to achieve? To determine appropriateness, educators must consider the students who are to receive the instruction and the content within which the curriculum is to be delivered. Some objectives might not be appropriate because they demand of students behavior that they are incapable of performing. Some are not appropriate because they do not cater to the students' interests. Some objectives might be more suitable for students in a particular subject than for students interested in a general program. Some objectives might list outcomes that students have already attained.

Logical Grouping. Objectives should be grouped logically so as to make sense when units of instruction and evaluation are being determined. Frequently, statements of objectives lack organizational coherence. In many cases, objectives that address a general understanding of self, such as understanding the particular effects of lack of exercise on the body, are grouped with objectives that are more specific. Often such general objectives as students' understanding how to process information are listed alongside objectives of students knowing how to write complete sentences. The need is to group objectives according to some common thread or idea, what some observers call a "domain."[35]

Periodic Revision. No objectives should stand for all times; objectives require periodic revision. This is necessary because students change, society changes, the realm of knowledge changes, and instructional strategies change. Educators should occasionally analyze their objectives to determine if they are still of value to the program. At times, the objective may perhaps still be of value in regard to its implied content, but the activities or the behavioral guideline incorporated may no longer be appropriate. See Curriculum Tips 7-2.

In general, an objective is useful if it exists not for its own purpose or end, rather if it exists as a means—as a pathway of educational activity or learning. We can judge whether our objectives are useful if they enable a student to proceed to the next step or to the next part of the unit plan or lesson plan. In this connection, the term *enabling objective* has appeared in the literature in recent years. This concept is worth noting, for most behaviors we wish students to engage in are not done primarily for their own sake. Students do not solve mathematical word problems just for their own sake. They work out these problems because doing so implies that such problems will assist students in the world outside of school.

TAXONOMIC LEVELS

When making curricular decisions, especially when generating objectives, educators ideally consider all domains of learning: The cognitive, the affective, and the psychomotor. Fortunately, several well-known classifications of learning exist for them to use. These classifications have organized various types of learning into taxonomies.

The Cognitive Domain

Of all the classifications of realms of objectives, Benjamin Bloom's *Taxonomy of Educational Objectives: Cognitive Domain* is perhaps the most familiar and certainly has the greatest influence on the formation of objectives.[36] The *Taxonomy* categorizes cognitive learning into six major divisions; each upper division subsumes the previous lower ones: (1) knowledge, (2) comprehension, (3) application, (4) analysis, (5) synthesis, and (6) evaluation.

When forming objectives, effective curriculum makers keep in mind at which cognitive level the objectives are placed. Following is a brief listing, along with illustrative examples, of the types of objectives at each level of the cognitive taxonomy:

1. *Knowledge.* This level includes objectives that are related to knowledge of (1) specifics, such as specific facts and terminology; (2) ways and means of dealing with specifics, such as conventions, trends and sequences, classifications and categories, criteria and methodology; and (3) universals and abstractions, such as principles, generalizations, theories, and structures. Example: The student will name the highest mountain range in Asia.
2. *Comprehension.* This level involves objectives that deal with (1) translation, (2) interpretation, and (3) extrapolation of information. Example: When given various geometric concepts in verbal terms, the student will draw the correct geometric form.
3. *Application.* This level includes objectives that are related to using abstractions in particular situations. Example: The student will be able to predict the effect on a container of exhausting its air contents.
4. *Analysis.* This level includes objectives that relate to the breaking of a whole into parts and distinguishing (1) elements, (2) relationships, and (3) organizational principles. Example: When given a document to read, the student will be able to distinguish facts from opinion.
5. *Synthesis.* This level includes objectives that relate to putting parts together in a new form such as (1) a unique communication, (2) a plan for

CURRICULUM TIPS 7-2   Formulating Objectives

With all the various terms and suggested guidelines for writing objectives, Hilda Taba long ago provided us with some common principles that could and still can guide our creating of objectives. Her guidelines make sense for formulating objectives at both the school level and classroom level.

1. A statement of objectives should describe both the kind of behavior expected and the content or the context to which that behavior applies.
2. Complex objectives need to be stated analytically and specifically enough so that there is no doubt as to the kind of behavior expected or to what the behavior applies.
3. Objectives should be so formulated that there are clear distinctions among the learning experiences required to attain different behaviors.
4. Objectives are developmental, representing roads to travel rather than terminal points.
5. Objectives should be realistic and should include only what can be translated into curriculum and classroom experience.
6. The scope of objectives should be broad enough to encompass all types of outcomes for which the school is responsible.

Source: Hilda Taba, *Curriculum Development* (New York: Harcourt, Brace, 1962), pp. 200–205.

operation, or (3) a set of abstract relations. Example: When confronted with a report on pollution, the student will be able to propose ways of testing various hypotheses.

6. *Evaluation.* This is the highest level in the cognitive taxonomy in terms of complexity. Objectives at this level would address making judgments in terms of (1) internal evidence or logical consistency and (2) external evidence or consistency with facts developed elsewhere. Example: The student will appraise fallacies in an argument.

A key assumption many educators bring to this cognitive taxonomy is that we should proceed from the lower levels to the higher levels. Another is that the higher levels of learning should be stressed. Most of our objectives should be addressing thinking skills rather than the recall of knowledge. However, we sometimes think that we need to spend a great deal of time on knowledge since it has so many categories compared to the other levels in the taxonomy. We believe mistakenly that students first need vast amounts of facts before they can process information and problem solve. If we keep in mind that the upper categories subsume the knowledge category, then we will write objectives that stress the higher mental processes,

realizing that we are not really ignoring the dimension of knowledge.

The Affective Domain

David Krathwohl and others presented to the educational community a taxonomy of objectives, consisting of five major categories, in the affective domain.[37] Following is a brief listing, along with examples, of objectives of the categories of the affective domain:

1. *Receiving.* Objectives at this level refer to the learner's sensitivity to the existence of stimuli. This includes (1) awareness, (2) willingness to receive, and (3) selected attention. Example: From studying various cultures of the Eastern world, the student develops an awareness of aesthetic factors in dress, furnishing, and architecture.

2. *Responding.* Objectives at this level refer to the learner's active attention to stimuli such as (1) acquiescence, (2) willing responses, and (3) feelings of satisfaction. Example: The student displays an interest in the topic of conversation by actively participating in a research project.

3. *Valuing.* Objectives in this level refer to the learner's beliefs and attitudes of worth. They are addressed in the form of (1) acceptance, (2) preference, and (3) commitment. Example: The student will take a viewpoint on advantages or disadvantages of nuclear power.

4. *Organization.* Objectives at this level refer to internalization of values and beliefs involving (1) conceptualization of values and (2) organization of a value system. Example: The student forms judgments about his or her responsibilities for conserving natural resources.

5. *Characterization.* This is the highest level of internalization in the taxonomy. Objectives at this level relate to behavior that reflects (1) a generalized set of values and (2) a characterization or philosophy of life. Example: The student develops a regulation of his or her personal and civic life based on ethical principles.

Although many educators find these categories useful, other educators and many parents view the taxonomy with concern. They feel that the school is responsible for the cognitive dimensions of learning, but has little or no responsibility in the affective or values domains. Arthur Combs has been an effective spokesperson for affective education: "Education must be concerned with the values, beliefs, convictions, and doubts of students. These realities as perceived by an individual are just as important, if not more so, as the so-called . . . facts."[38] Also other educators urge that education should address the social, emotional, and spiritual domains of students.[39]

The Psychomotor Domain

The psychomotor domain has received much less emphasis than either the cognitive or affective domains. Also, fewer persons have worked on delineating it. Anita J. Harrow has, however, developed a psychomotor taxonomy with several categories:[40]

1. *Reflex movements.* Objectives at this level include (1) segmental reflexes (involving one spinal segment) and (2) intersegmental reflexes (involving more than one spinal segment). Example: After engaging in this activity, the student will be able to contract a muscle.

2. *Fundamental movements.* Objectives in this category address behaviors related to (1) walk-ing, (2) running, (3) jumping, (4) pushing, (5) pulling, and (6) manipulating. Example: The student will be able to jump over a 2-foot hurdle.

3. *Perceptual abilities.* Objectives in this division address (1) kinesthetic, (2) visual, (3) auditory, (4) tactile, and (5) coordination abilities. Example: The student will categorize by shape a group of building blocks.

4. *Physical abilities.* Objectives included at this level are related to (1) endurance, (2) strength, (3) flexibility, (4) agility, (5) reaction-response time, and (6) dexterity. Example: The student will do at least five pushups more at the end of the year.

5. *Skilled movements.* Objectives at this level of the domain are concerned with (1) games, (2) sports, (3) dances, and (4) the arts. Example: The student can correctly perform a series of somersaults.

6. *Nondiscursive communication.* Objectives at this final level of the taxonomy relate to expressive movement through (1) posture, (2) gestures, (3) facial expressions, and (4) creative movements. Example: The student will be able to create his or her own movement sequence and perform it to music.

The categories of the three taxonomies are arranged in a hierarchy in which the levels increase in complexity from simple to more advanced. In the cognitive domain, levels 2 through 6 connote various problem-solving skills and abilities. Each level depends on the acquisition of the previous level. For example, for a student to analyze an issue, he or she must be able to apply information, must comprehend information, and must have some level of knowledge. For a student to express a value preference, he or she must be able to respond to situations and must be willing to receive information; that is, he or she must be sensitive to a particular situation. For a child to be skilled at the level of perceptual abilities, he or she must have mastered fundamental movements and reflex movements.

The taxonomies are useful for developing educational objectives and for grouping sets of objectives. One difficulty educators may have is making decisions identifying objectives between adjacent categories. This is particularly true if the objectives are not clearly stated. But, if educators carefully reflect on their objectives, they should find the taxonomies valuable tools for creating objectives. Mindful of these taxonomies, they should be able to move their learners from the lower to the higher levels of learning in each domain. Ideally, effective education calls into play all three major domains of learning. See Table 7-1.

APPROACHES TO EDUCATIONAL OBJECTIVES

Objectives, stated more specifically than goals, are designed to communicate to involved parties—students, teachers, laypersons—the intents of particular actions. However, diverse views exist regarding approaches to curriculum objectives. Some attention was given to defining these approaches in Chapter 1.

Behavioral Approach

In the last two decades, much attention has been given to behavioral objectives. Although such objectives are rather new to educational dialogue, the theoretical basis for them is not; it has been borrowed from behaviorist learning theory (see Chapter 4) in psychology and from the concept of operationalism in science (by which people operationalize or give a tangible or observable condition to a particular learning or disposition of a human being). For example, you may wish to indicate that a person appreciated good art; however, no one has ever seen an "appreciation." What you need to do is to indicate those tangible or observable ways of behaving that comprise "appreciation." Armed with such a tangible definition of appreciate, you have a better indication of what you are looking for or intending with your objectives.

In this connection, B. F. Skinner views the curriculum as being formulated according to behavioristic objectives.[41] To Skinner, the teacher's role is primarily a mechanical one of arranging contingencies of reinforcement, in a sequenced and step-by-step procedure, under which the students are automatically conditioned toward specific terminal ways of behaving. Taking this approach to objectives, we view method as the

scheduling of reinforcement contingencies established by the teacher or the curriculum developer.

The concern for high levels of behavioral specificity has some history in American business and education. It is tied closely to the notion of curriculum as a production system in which the student is a product to be acted on. This view of the curriculum received attention during the early decades of this century, when educators were attempting to relate scientific management to education.[42] This push for precision in planning and then stating what one intended to do or have students do has continued to the present time. It is an approach that pays special attention to curriculum as an end product.

Popham and Baker defined the curriculum as "all planned learning outcomes for which the school is responsible."[43] They viewed curriculum as the ends and instruction as the means. This separating of curriculum and instruction as ends and means continues to affect behavioral objectives. Popham argued, "Measurable instructional objectives are designed to counteract what is to me the most serious deficit in American education today, namely a preoccupation with the process without assessment of consequences." He lists three areas in which "measurable objectives have considerable potential—in curriculum (what goals are selected); in instruction (how to accomplish those goals); and in evaluation (determining whether objectives of the instructional sequence have been realized)."[44]

Gagné et al. made a similar point. They stated that greater precision in the definition of objectives meets two needs: the need for communication of the purposes of instruction and the need for evaluation of instruction.[45] They note that in achieving precision in stating objectives "one is said to be 'defining objectives in terms of human performance [or human behavior].'" When objectives are so stated, an individual is "informed as to what must be observed" in order to determine the achievement of the course's purpose.[46]

A central assumption of this approach to objectives is that one can identify all the essential learnings and behaviors that should result from the curriculum. Teachers who attempt to follow this approach sometimes generate lists of hundreds of objectives. However, the major limita-

TABLE 7-1 Overview of Aims, Goals, and Objectives

EDUCATIONAL STATEMENT	FEATURES	SOURCE	SAMPLES	CURRICULUM IMPLICATIONS
Aims	A general statement that provides direction or intent to educational action.	From national commissions, task forces, and panels.	Cardinal Principles of Secondary Education; The Purpose of Education in American Democracy; A Nation at Risk	Identifies the overall direction of the curriculum.
Goals	Statements of purpose. More specific than aims.	From professional associations, government agencies, state departments of education, and school districts.	ASCD, Measuring and Maintaining the Goals of Education; PDK, Phase III of the Educational Planning Model; National Goals for Education	Identifies specific content areas of the curriculum.
Objectives	Specific statements that indicate either general or specific outcomes. Behavioral objectives indicate the specific behavior the student is to demonstrate to indicate learning. Nonbehavioral objectives use more general words to denote the learning desired, such as to know, to understand.	From school districts, schools, and individual writers.	Taxonomy of Educational Objectives; Posner, Gronlund, Mager	Behavioral objectives tend to make curriculum more sequenced, precise, and compartmentalized. Nonbehavioral objectives allow for a more open ended curriculum and integration of subject matter.

tion of this approach is that we really cannot denote all of the specific competencies and essential behaviors that should result from education. Even if we could, the fact that the teacher is doing it in a major way excludes the student from playing some role in determining the direction of his or her education. The approach is effective in addressing areas of the curriculum that deal with skills and the training of certain performances. But it is deficient in furnishing guidance for showing appreciation and attitudes toward content and values.

Managerial and Systems Approaches

The managerial approach and the systems approach are closely related. Thus they are included here as essentially comprising one approach to the formulation of objectives. These approaches represent a way of thinking that has its roots in the early scientific movement and behavioral approaches to educational decision making. Both school managers and systems personnel rely on organizational theory and are sensitive to the interrelatedness of the units or departments of the organization. According to Roger Kaufman, they rely on problem identification and problem resolution as a means of identifying goals and objectives and implementing and evaluating programs.[47]

Problem identification centers primarily on determining the exact nature of the problem and then considering possible ways to address or solve the problem. Specifying the problem allows us to identify what the objectives should be. For instance, if the problem is poor reading performance, we may reflect on what behaviors need to be addressed for students to read effectively. Whereas problem identification is identifying the particulars of the problem and contemplating and generating possibilities, the second major stage, *problem resolution,* is the actual determining of the objectives to be addressed and selecting the teaching procedures appropriate for these objectives. Problem resolution also refers to the actual carrying out of those strategies selected and engaging in particular actions to evaluate the effectiveness of the strategies employed to teach the objective.

The managerial and systems person has various levels of activities in which to engage: mission analysis, function analysis, and task analysis. The mission analysis is very similar to delineating the aims of education, similar to Charter's discussion in his classic book. Function analysis relates to the general activities, which can be equated to some degree to the activities that Babbitt discussed. Task analysis represents

the end point of what is to be done, what, in our case, the pupil is to do to obtain a particular learning. Gagné is a proponent of such an approach.

Sometimes managerial and systems approaches appear in educational institutions under the guise of management by objectives. Management by objectives (MBO) can be considered as a philosophical approach whereby all school personnel identify their common and uncommon goals as a basis for defining successful criteria for evaluating the degree of goal attainment. Some people call this approach behaviorist. MBO rests on the assumption that school operations can be conducted in a logical and effective pattern. One can identify directions, plot action, implement such action, and evaluate the success of such implementation.[48]

Although MBO is not a complex process, it still includes an acceptance of the managerial and systems posture. When the school functions as a system, it consists of a number of components, each differentiated from the others in terms of particular functions to be performed; all these components contribute in some way to the accomplishment of the organization's purpose. Furthermore, the term *system* implies that the relationships among the various components are characterized by interdependence, regularity, order, and predictability.[49]

Humanistic Approach

All educators realize that they are creating curricula for human beings. However, humanists believe that the function of the curriculum is to provide each learner with intrinsically rewarding experiences that will make for more complete living and more authentic lives. Humanists view the goals of education as personal growth, integrity, and autonomy. Goals and objectives stress the person in contrast to subject matter. Curricula resulting from the formulating of humanistic objectives contain experiences through which individuals can expand their awareness of being human, compassionate, and caring. These human expressions are considered more important than knowing the capital of Nigeria or the chemical formula for carbon monoxide.[50]

Humanists deal with such questions as what is real, what is human, and what is good. In processing such questions, educators can arrange educational objectives and experiences to allow students to attain personal dignity and self-worth. Weinstein and Fantini embrace the notion that education in a free society should have a broad human focus, which is best served by educational objectives resting on a personal and interpersonal base and dealing with students' concerns.[51]

The idea of self-actualization is central to the humanistic approach to education. Carl Rogers, a recognized spokesperson for this approach, indicates that the goals and objectives of such a curriculum should be geared to enabling the individual student to gain an openness to experience, to view living as a process, and to trust his or her own experiencing. The individual is thus able to view himself or herself as becoming a more fully functioning individual.[52]

Abraham Maslow, a major figure in the development of humanistic psychology, viewed self-realization as multidimensional, as relating to life achievement, as continually evolving. Thus the curriculum was constantly changing as well. Every learner is, in part, "his own project" and makes the curriculum fit his own needs.[53] The objectives and goals that humanists favor address openness and tend to be stated in humanistic rather than behavioral or rational terms. The prime criterion is that such objectives must encourage self-actualization; they must relate to peak experiences. For Maslow such experiences are those that give rise to love, hate, anxiety, depression, and joy. Maslow noted that the peak experiences of awe, mystery, and wonder are both the end and the beginning of learning.

Philip Phenix has expanded some of Maslow's thinking. Phenix believes that the curriculum must do more than concentrate on academic knowledge. It must stress transcendence—the limitlessness of experience. Stressing transcendence, the student will experience every event within a context of wider relationships and possibilities. Phenix indicated that certain qualities are associated with transcendence: hope, creativity, awareness, doubt and faith, wonder, awe, and reverence.[54] Focusing on these dimensions permits optimal individual development.

Objectives in the humanistic camp direct the teachers to furnish learners with opportunities to become their own persons, to gain control over their processes of learning, and to realize the complexity of existence. Thus teachers in this camp do not usually write explicit or precise objectives. They allow the objectives, if there are any, to "evolve" from the experiences that students have. If we were looking at a curriculum guide for a humanistic curriculum, for example, we might find such objectives as (1) students will have experiences that will help them become self-directed and involved in the learning process, (2) students will gain in self-confidence, and (3) students will become more considerate of others. Such objectives do not list specific behaviors that the students are to demonstrate, nor do they indicate any criteria of performance. But these so-called "vague" statements are still objectives, for they do present educational outcomes.

Reconceptualism

The concerns and questions asked by advocates of the above approaches to the formation of objectives are not considered by the reconceptualists to be important. Reconceptualists think that curricularists are preoccupied with the practical and technical modes of understanding and action. William Pinar asserts that the key question is not the purposes of the school, but rather why, as an individual, I identify with particular people or certain situations. Why do I read these authors and not others? Why am I fascinated with this play or movie and not others?[55]

In a sense, reconceptualists are like humanists; however, reconceptualists are much more critical of education and view the educational arena from an existential, esthetic, and spiritual framework. For this reason, their objectives are open ended. Reconceptualism is essentially not an approach to objectives, but more of a political and social force offering a critique of current schooling. They urge the reorganization of schools to address the social problems of the times.

Henry Giroux argues that we need to overcome the objectives of schooling as they exist today. For him, the shortcomings of objectives coincide with the shortcomings of schools: narrow focus, standardization of behavior, instruction as one dimensional, oppressive demands, and a technical orientation toward ends. To Giroux, technical processes in curriculum suggest an emphasis on standardization, efficiency, and concrete outcomes, while neglecting questions such as why are we doing what we are doing, why is this knowledge being learned, or why is this type of pedagogical style being used to transmit information in the classroom. Giroux remarks that "While the behaviorists have generally avoided the question of ends [purposes], the humanists have limited questions concerning ends to the immediacy of the classroom setting and have ignored helping students bent on surpassing what is merely given, on breaking through the everyday experiences." [56]

Giroux approaches his critics of education from a neo-Marxist orientation. Thus, he faults curricularists for ignoring those barriers that prevent humans from grasping and discussing the relationship between socially constructed knowledge and how it is employed in the classroom. The ideology behind the knowledge of the curriculum and the manner of instruction is not addressed. Curricularists should develop objectives stressing the importance of critical analysis of subject matter and the politics of knowledge. If this link is established and made known to students, then students will be able to construct connections among themselves and others and the larger social reality. Giroux contends that having such theoretical frameworks allows students to employ them as filters in their viewing of information, in selecting of facts, in considering reality, in formulating problems, and in generating solutions to the problems.

Similarly, David Purpel notes that education should strive in ways that will foster the "cultivation, nourishment, and development of a cultural mythos that builds on a faith in the human capacity to participate in the creation of a world of justice, compassion, caring, love and joy." [57] Reconceptualists and the critical theorists within this camp are concerned with the cultivation and nourishment of those processes requisite for making learning meaningful. They would argue that learning needs to be taken beyond the classroom. Learning is getting students to move beyond the textbook or classroom defined by a particular subject. It is meaningful if it establishes connections between schooling and the

sociopolitical forces th
culture.

Most reconceptualists
specific advice on creating objec
they do seem to have at least acknow
we can take a blended approach to writing
tives, perhaps using behavioral objectives fo
specific parts of a lesson and more global, open-ended objectives for the macro emphasis on the lesson. Still, the major thrust of the reconceptualists has been to critique the field of curriculum and to reinterpret the sociopolitical framework of schooling. See Table 7-2.

CHALLENGES

Educators are challenged by these various approaches to objectives and to the resulting curricula. Although many will not have to decide among these approaches, they will need to know that such approaches to objectives do exist and that each makes various assumptions regarding the schools, education, the curriculum, the students, and the teachers. It is likely that those faced with making decisions about objectives will draw on different aspects of each approach. The idea is to process objectives in light of our assumptions. Those using the behavioral-rational approach will write their curriculum objectives in behavioral terms; those confronted with ensuring that the school program is delivered according to plans, schedules, and programs will draw on the systems-managerial orientation to objectives and their delivery. For certain teaching and learning aspects of the curriculum, some will draw heavily on the humanistic-esthetic approach, and a few may learn to be reconceptualists.

Considering goals and objectives as statements of end points in students' learning raises the issue of how to determine whether the competency implicit or explicit in an objective is stated appropriately. Although behavioral objectives have the virtue of clarity, they usually only indicate the observable levels of learning—some would argue only the trivial or lowest outcomes of the curriculum. [58]

Expanding on the point that objectives tend to trivialize important issues, Joseph Schwab asserted that curriculum developers who overrely

7-2 Overview of Major Approaches to Educational Objectives

PROACH	APPROACH FOCUS	SPOKESPERSONS	CURRICULAR IMPLICATION
Behavioral	Technical-scientific emphasis; concern for specificity. Assumption: we can identify essential learnings.	Bobbitt, Charters, Gagné, Mager, Popham, Tyler	Compartmentalization of curriculum; defined scope and sequence. Convergent emphasis on curricular learnings.
Systems-managerial	Systems theory, organizational theory; interrelatedness of parts of the organization. Objectives are seen as part of the total process of decision making and curriculum implementation. Management by objectives.	Hunkins, Kaufman, Pratt, Saylor	Curriculum viewed as a system of related components.
Humanistic	Focus on the person: personal growth, respect for others, joy of learning.	Eisener, Maslow, Phenix, Purpel, Rogers	Curriculum seen as divergent; opportunities for students to explore to become self-directed.
Reconceptualists	More of a political and social posture with a theoretical critique. Focus on individual's being empowered to be more fully human, socially sensitive, and existential emphasis.	Apple, Giroux, Pinar, Purpel	Curriculum seen as emergent, as concerned with cultivation of those processes that allow for control of one's learning.

on endless strings of objectives tend to separate what should be held together. "They atomize, not only subject matter, but teachers' thoughts about it, the pattern of instruction used to convey it, the organization of textbooks, and the analysis and construction of tests."[59]

Behavioral objectives can easily denote logical and rational thought, but they cannot easily describe creative and intuitive learning or internalized value systems. Behavioral objectives seem to indicate that behavior is unidimensional rather than multidimensional. Advocates assume, for instance, that all students who list the major river systems in the United States have the identical understanding or are exhibiting the same

competency at the same level. The objectives developed seem to be for all students, but for those students who are able to specialize and excel, they would be limiting.

Many curriculum specialists are concerned that behavioral objectives do not seem to focus on higher-order tasks and skills. Other educators, however, are concerned that the focus on precise objectives is likely to cause educators to ignore the unintended consequences, either positive or negative, of the curriculum on the learners.[60]

Curriculum development also deals with the issue of competencies. Educators must question: What competencies? Competencies in what subject areas? An individual's approach to curriculum will influence how he or she processes such questions. The behavioral-rationalists will respond, "Those skills necessary for working in the world." Those involved in managerial and systems approaches might respond, "Those subjects that enable one to obtain a better understanding of the world and its many systems and subsystems." Humanists might respond, "Those competencies that enable individuals to know who they are and that contribute to the development of positive self-concepts." Reconceptualists, on the other hand, might say, "Those competencies needed to engage in self-inquiry and to seek out meaningful relationships in life."

All the approaches to creating objectives have shortcomings. The behavioral approach might be viewed as too structured and trivial. The managerial and systems approaches could be viewed as technocratic and an offshoot of behaviorism. The very strength of the humanistic camp is perhaps also its major weakness; the wording of such objectives is vague and open to interpretation and misinterpretation.

The reconceptualists' approach can also be criticized as not furnishing enough specific guidance about how to form objectives. We might also fault such objectives as being directed more

toward political and social realities than educational concerns.[61]

Both the humanistic-esthetic and the reconceptualist approaches are difficult to assess: When have we attained the end point, the expected outcome? Even though educators can agree that end points are only points that lead eventually to other points in a continuum of existence, they still need some indication that they are at least on the correct track with regard to their purposes. It is not likely that advocates of these approaches will come to any agreement in the near future, because persons in these camps are not just arguing about the wording of objectives, but are debating the basic purpose of education itself, and they are coming up with different answers as a result of their inherent philosophical orientations. See Curriculum Tips 7-3.

CONCLUSION

We have presented in great detail information on aims, goals, and objectives. The chapter began with a discussion of the nature of aims. We presented aims that have been created by various groups and commissions. Aims essentially guide and direct our educational efforts. They are gen-

.d in response to general societal concerns particular times.

Goals are statements that are more specific than aims; they indicate end points or outcomes of education. It was pointed out that often goals are generated by professional associations, but that educators can take more active roles in creating goals. It was also mentioned that creating goals is a continuous activity.

The major portion of the chapter dealt with the objectives of education, giving much attention to both behavioral and nonbehavioral ob-jectives. Discussion centered on the common components of the various types of objectives, which illustrate that objectives differ perhaps more in degree than in kind.

The diversity of levels of objectives was presented in a discussion of the various taxonomies that are available for guiding the creation of objectives. Such taxonomies help educators write objectives. The various philosophical approaches assist as well. We presented these to show the richness of the views that we really need to consider when formulating objectives.

ENDNOTES

1. Decker Walker and Jonas F. Soltis, *Curriculum and Aims* (New York: Teachers College Press, Columbia University, 1986).
2. John Dewey, *John Dewey on Education; Selected Writings,* D. Archambault, ed. (New York: Random House, 1964), p. 74.
3. J. Galen Saylor, William M. Alexander, and Arthur J. Lewis, *Planning Curriculum for Schools,* 4th ed. (New York: Holt, Rinehart and Winston 1981), pp. 144–145.
4. Allan C. Ornstein, "How Do Educators Meet the Needs of Society?" *NASSP Bulletin* (May 1985), pp. 36–47; George J. Posner, *Analyzing the Curriculum* (New York: McGraw-Hill, 1992).
5. Walker and Soltis, *Curriculum and Aims.*
6. Ralph W. Tyler, "Purposes of Our Schools," *NASSP Bulletin* (May 1968), pp. 1–12.
7. Ronald C. Doll, *Curriculum Improvement: Decision Making and Process,* 8th ed. (Boston: Allyn and Bacon, 1992).
8. Herbert Spencer, *Education: Intellectual, Moral and Physical* (New York: Alden, 1885).
9. Commission on the Reorganization of Secondary Education, *Cardinal Principles of Secondary Education,* Bulletin 35 (Washington, D.C.: U.S. Office of Education, 1918), p. 9.
10. Ibid., pp. 11–16.
11. Educational Policies Commission, *The Purpose of Education in American Democracy* (Washington, D.C.: National Educational Association, 1938), p. 89.
12. Ibid.
13. Educational Policies Commission, *Education for All American Youth* (Washington, D. C.: National Educational Association, 1944), pp. 225–226.
14. Educational Policies Commission, *The Central Purpose of American Education* (Washington, D.C.: National Educational Association, 1961), p. 11.
15. Commission on Excellence in Education, *A Nation at Risk* (Washington, D.C.: U.S. Government Printing Office, 1983), p. 1.
16. Ibid., pp. 13–14.
17. Ibid., p. 24.
18. Peter F. Oliva, *Developing the Curriculum,* 3rd ed. (New York: Harper Collins, 1992).
19. ASCD Committee on Research and Theory, *Measuring and Attaining the Goals of Education* (Alexandria, Va.: Association for Supervision and Curriculum Development, 1980).
20. *Phase III of the Educational Planning Model* (Bloomington, Ind.: Phi Delta Kappa Educational Foundation, 1976).
21. *National Goals for Education* (Washington, D.C., U.S. Department of Education, 1990).
22. *Turning Points,* Carnegie Council on Adolescent Development (New York: Carnegie Corp. of New York, 1989), p. 43.
23. Hilda Taba, *Curriculum Development: Theory and Practice* (New York: Harcourt, Brace, 1962).
24. Robert S. Zais, *Curriculum Principles and Foundations* (New York: Crowell, 1976).
25. George F. Madaus, "The Distortion of Teaching and Testing," *Peabody Journal of Education* (Spring 1988), pp. 29–46; W. James Popham, "Can High-Stake Tests Be Developed at the Local Level?" *NASSP Bulletin* (February 1987), pp. 77–84.
26. Allan C. Ornstein, *Strategies for Effective Teaching* (New York: Harper & Row, 1990).
27. George J. Posner and Alan N. Rudnitsky, *Course Design,* 2nd ed. (New York: Longman, 1990).
28. Norman E. Gronlund, *Stating Objectives for Classroom Instruction,* 2nd ed. (New York: Macmillan, 1985); Norman E. Gronlund and Robert L. Linn, *Measurement and Evaluation in Teaching,* 6th ed. (New York: Macmillan, 1990); and Robert F. Mager, *Preparing Instructional Objectives,* 2nd ed. (Belmont, Calif.: Fearon, 1984).

29. Mager, *Preparing Instructional Objectives.*

30. Michael Polanyi, *The Tacit Dimension* (New York: Doubleday, 1966).

31. J. Galen Saylor, William N. Alexander, and Arthur J. Lewis, *Curriculum Planning for Better Teaching and Learning* (New York: Holt, Rinehart and Winston, 1981).

32. Lorin W. Anderson, "Master Learning: One Approach to the Integration of Instruction and Measurement." Paper presented at the annual meeting of the American Educational Research Association, Toronto, March 1978, p. 4. *NASSP Bulletin* (October, 1990), pp. 78–88.

33. David Pratt, *Curriculum: Design and Development* (New York: Harcourt, Brace, Jovanovich, 1980); Richard D. Kimpston, Howard Y. Williams, and William S. Stockton, "Ways of Knowing and the Curriculum," *Educational Forum* (Winter 1992), pp. 153–172; Allan C. Ornstein, "A Look at Teacher Effectiveness Research," *NASSP Bulletin* (October 1990), pp. 78–88.

34. Mauritz Johnson, "Definitions and Models in Curriculum Theory," *Educational Theory* (April 1967), pp. 127–130; Pratt, *Curriculum Design and Development* (New York: Harcourt, Brace, Jovanovich, 1980).

35. Saylor, Alexander, and Lewis, *Curriculum Planning for Better Teaching and Learning.*

36. Benjamin S. Bloom, ed., *Taxonomy of Educational Objectives, Handbook I: Cognitive Domain* (New York: McKay, 1956).

37. David R. Krathwohl, ed., *Taxonomy of Educational Objectives, Handbook II: Affective Domain* (New York: McKay, 1964).

38. Arthur W. Combs, ed., *Perceiving, Behavior, Becoming: A New Focus for Education* (Washington, D.C.: Association for Supervision and Curriculum Development, 1962), p. 200.

39. Henry A. Giroux, ed., *Postmodernism, Feminism, and Cultural Politics* (Albany, N.Y.: State University of New York Press, 1991).

40. Anita J. Harrow, *A Taxonomy of the Psychomotor Domain* (New York: McKay, 1972).

41. B. F. Skinner, *The Technology of Teaching* (New York: Appleton, 1968).

42. Raymond E. Callahan, *Education and the Cult of Efficiency* (Chicago: University of Chicago Press, 1962).

43. W. James Popham and Eva L. Baker, *Systematic Instruction* (Englewood Cliffs, N.J.: Prentice-Hall, 1970), p. 48. Also see Merlin C. Wittrock and Eva L. Baker, *Testing and Cognition* (Boston, Mass.: Allyn and Bacon, 1991).

44. W. James Popham, "Practical Ways of Improving Curriculum via Measurable Objectives," *NASSP Bulletin* (May 1971), p. 48; also see Popham, *Modern Educational Measurement,* 2nd ed. (Boston, Mass.: Allyn and Bacon, 1990).

45. Robert M. Gagné, Leslie J. Briggs, and Walter Wagner, *Principles of Instructional Design,* 3rd ed. (New York: Holt, Rinehart, 1988).

46. Ibid., p. 56.

47. Roger A. Kaufman, *Educational System Planning* (Englewood Cliffs, N.J.: Prentice-Hall, 1972).

48. Robert V. Carlson and Gary Awkerman, *Educational Planning: Concepts, Strategies and Practices* (New York: Longman, 1991); Gerald C. Ubben, *The Principal: Creative Leadership for Effective Schools,* 2nd ed. (Needham Heights, Mass.: Allyn and Bacon, 1992).

49. Max G. Abbott and Terry L. Eidell, "Administration Implementation of Curriculum Performance," *Educational Technology* (May 1970), pp. 62–64. See also Robert G. Owens, *Organizational Behavior in Education,* 2nd ed. (Englewood Cliffs, N.J.: Prentice Hall, 1981).

50. Gerald G. Duffy, "Let's Free Teachers to Be Inspired," *Phi Delta Kappan* (February 1992), pp. 442–447.

51. Gerald Weinstein and Mario D. Fantini, *Toward Humanistic Education: A Curriculum of Affect* (New York: Praeger, 1970).

52. Carl R. Rogers, "Toward Becoming a Fully Functioning Person," in Combs, ed., *Perceiving, Behaving, Becoming,* pp. 21–33.

53. Abraham H. Maslow, "Some Basic Propositions of a Growth and Self-actualization Psychology," in Combs, ed., *Perceiving, Behaving, Becoming,* pp. 34–49.

54. Philip H. Phenix, "Transcendence and the Curriculum," in E. W. Eisner and E. Valance, eds. *Conflicting Conceptions of the Curriculum* (Berkeley, Calif.: McCutchan, 1974), pp. 117–135.

55. William Pinar, "Currere: Toward Reconceptualization," in Pinar, ed., *Curriculum Theorizing: The Reconceptualists* (Berkeley, Calif.: McCutchan, 1975), pp. 396–414.

56. Henry A Giroux, *Teachers as Intellectuals* (Granby, Mass.: Bergin & Garvey, 1988), p. 45.

57. David Purpel, *The Moral and Spiritual Crisis in Education* (New York: Bergin & Garvey, 1989), p. 150.

58. Gail Delicio, "Teaching Alliteration Inductively: Taba's Deductive Thinking Model in Practice." Paper presented at the annual meeting of the American Educational Research Association, San Francisco, April 1986.

59. Joseph Schwab, "The Practical Four: Something for Curriculum Professors to Do," *Curriculum Inquiry* (Fall 1983), pp. 239–266.

60. Bruce W. Tuckman, *Educational Psychology: From Theory to Application* (San Diego: Harcourt Brace Jovanovich, 1992); Wittrock and Baker, *Testing and Cognition.*

61. James T. Sears and J. Dan Marshal, eds., *Teaching and Thinking About Curriculum* (New York: Teachers College Press, Columbia University, 1990).

CHAPTER 8

CURRICULUM DESIGN

Focusing Questions

1. *What are some sources of curriculum design?*
2. *How can curriculum design be defined?*
3. *When contemplating the design of curriculum, what key dimensions need to be considered?*
4. *Which design stresses the unity of knowledge?*
5. *What are the major representative curriculum designs?*
6. *Which curriculum design is the most commonplace in American schools?*
7. *Which design would you consider the most representative in your school?*

The concept of curriculum design brings into focus the way in which curricula are created, especially the actual arrangement of the parts of the curriculum plan. In this chapter the term *curriculum design,* sometimes called *curriculum organization,* refers to the arrangement of the elements of a curriculum into a substantive entity. Which design someone actually selects is influenced by his or her curriculum approach and philosophical orientation.

The parts, sometimes called components or elements, that are arranged in a curriculum design are (1) aims, goals, and objectives; (2) subject matter; (3) learning experiences; and (4) evaluation approaches. The nature of these components and the manner in which they are organized in the curriculum plan comprise what we mean by curriculum design. Although most curriculum plans have within their design these four essential elements, often they are not given equal weight. Frequently, content or subject matter receives the primary emphasis. But, sometimes, schools do create designs that stress primarily objectives and evaluation approaches. Other designs give primary emphasis to learning experiences or activities.

COMPONENTS OF DESIGN

When considering curriculum design, the curriculum decision maker confronts the question: What general structure of the curriculum can I develop so that the parts promote and/or provide insight to the whole?

Thinking about the design, the arrangement of the parts of the curriculum, causes us to reflect on the approaches to curriculum we are contemplating or accepting. Attending to design questions allows us to consider the philosophical and learning theories to determine if we are basing our arrangements of the curriculum components on something that has a rational basis. Posner and Rudnitsky point out that any systematic approach to creating curricula must also be processed within the context of a theoretical framework.[1] The need is to base our design decisions so that they are consonant with our basic beliefs concerning people, what they should learn and how they should learn.

Curriculum design is concerned with the nature and arrangement of four basic curricular parts. These parts are rooted in the classic work of Harry Giles in his report on "The Eight-Year Study." He used the term "components" to show the relationship and included learning experiences under "method and organization."[2] The relationship is shown in Figure 8-1.

The design's four components suggest to the curriculum maker four questions: What is to be done? What subject matter is to be included? What instructional strategies, resources, and activities will be employed? And what methods and instruments will be used to appraise the results of the curriculum? According to Giles, the four components interact with each other; decisions made about one component are dependent on decisions made about the others. While Giles presented the paradigm, it is very similar to a model that Tyler developed several years later. Tyler's model, however, denotes a linear attention to the key elements of the curriculum, while Giles's paradigm shows ongoing interaction among the components.[3]

Curriculum design involves various philosophical or theoretical issues, as well as practical issues. A person's philosophical stance will affect his or her interpretation and selection of objectives, influence the content selected and how it will be organized, affect decisions about how to teach or deliver the curriculum content, and guide judgments about how to evaluate the success of the curriculum developed.

Not all designs need to have the four components noted by Giles. But a curriculum design does need to provide a consistent framework of values and priorities for dealing with the operational decisions necessary for delivering the curriculum.

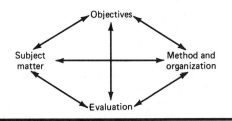

FIGURE 8-1 The Components of Design. From H. Giles, S. P. McCutchen, and A. N. Zechiel, *Exploring the Curriculum* (New York: Harper, 1942), p. 2.

If a curriculum is designed adequately, it defines for the curriculum decision maker the components in the curriculum that are to receive particular attention. Hilda Taba noted that most curriculum designs contain Giles's four components, but that many lack balance, because the elements are poorly defined or are not considered in relation to a theoretical rationale.[4] Indeed, the various types of designs that we discuss in this chapter are really the result of loading on a particular component or element of the curriculum.

In Chapter 6 the distinction between curriculum and instruction was made, pointing out that they coexist in schools. The confusion between curriculum and instruction exists with regard to the design question. There are two levels of confusion. In this chapter on design, we are using the term as a noun; that is, it refers to the "naming" of the arrangement of the curriculum components: objectives, content, experiences, and evaluation means. However, there are some who use design as a verb, that is, to identify a process by which curricula are created or instructional plans are developed. Posner and Rudnitsky in their book on course design are using the term design as synonymous with development.[5]

Also, Ronald Doll points out that there is confusion when people think about curriculum design and instruction. He denotes that curriculum design is the parent of instructional design.[6] That is, curriculum is the total plan that arranges the four components of the curriculum (objectives, content, experiences, and evaluation means). Instructional design refers specifically to one component, the potential experiences for students. Instruction does not address objectives, or content; rather, it "maps" out pedagogically and technologically defensible teaching methods and educational activities that engage students in learning the content of the curriculum. In instructional design, individuals raise questions as to what teaching methods and materials can be employed that will facilitate learning. What resources will be appropriate for the particular lesson indicated in the curriculum plan? How should we arrange our students, and which students should be involved in particular activities?

Ideally, when curriculum workers contemplate a particular curriculum, they should also make instructional design decisions within the context of curriculum.

Sources for Curriculum Design

Those charged with curriculum design must clarify their philosophical and social views of society and the individual learner—or what is commonly called the sources of curriculum. To determine the influences of curriculum design, attention must be given to how such sources will influence education. How the curriculum planner responds to the question of the sources of ideas for education will affect his or her views of curriculum design. For this reason, it is essential for curriculum designers to identify their philosophical and social orientations. If they ignore philosophical and social questions, their curriculum designs will have limited or confused rationales. Taba notes that "much of the distance between theory and practice may be caused by just such lack of rationale."[7]

Ronald Doll describes four sources of ideas that undergird curriculum designs: science, society, eternal verities, and Divine Will.[8] These sources are somewhat similar to those sources of curriculum identified by Dewey and Bode and popularized by Tyler: knowledge, society, and the learner.[9]

Science as a Source.   Curriculum workers who rely on science as a source usually maintain that the scientific method provides meaning for the curriculum design. The design would contain only those elements that can be observed and quantified. In a design based on this stance, problem solving would have a prime position. However, it may be misleading to cite science as a source of ideas for curriculum design; the real emphasis of this design is not just on scientific procedure, but also on procedural knowledge (or knowledge of process). Those designs that stress learning how to learn or "thinking" curricula would emphasize scientific procedures, and the various means by which we process knowledge. But Elliot Eisner has argued that teachers need to understand, besides scientific ways of knowing,

aesthetic modes of knowing, interpersonal modes, practical modes, and even spiritual ideas.[10]

Much of what is stated about thinking processes comes from a knowledge of cognitive psychology. What is advocated in terms of problem-solving procedures is derived from our understanding of science and other organizations of knowledge, such as psychology. Some educators would have these ideas regarding procedural knowledge and thinking strategies stand alone as a prime source of the curriculum. Given the times, when the knowledge realm is exploding so rapidly, the only constant seems to be the procedures by which we process knowledge. A curriculum with this source would teach students a set of rational procedures by which they could process the content of the curriculum. Even thinking strategies, much a part of this design emphasis, would have students learn procedures for processing information.

To be sure, this view of curriculum design coincides with the scientific and rational world of Western culture. But we also live in a pluralistic world with many different cultures. This latter view accepts the universe not as static, but as self-generating, complex, and evolving. It is a universe that *is becoming* rather than just existing for our detached scientific viewing.[11] This new view of the reality goes by many different names, postmodernism, postpositivism, and third-wave thinking, in contrast to the mainstream view, called positivism or modernism that we have been operating under for several centuries. It seems evident that viewing science as a source of ideas for curriculum design needs to be considered with some degree of caution lest we simply think that we are teaching rational processes for dealing with reality.

Society as a Source.   Curriculum designers favoring society as a source for the curriculum believe that school is an agent of society, and thus the school should draw its ideas for the curriculum from the analysis of the social situation. This social foundation has been a most important curriculum foundation. John Dewey certainly realized that educators needed to be in touch with needs of society. It was from a careful study of society that we could determine that which was meaningful and most likely to last. Viewing society as a source would give educators indications of where to modify the curriculum.

While it perhaps has never been easy to get an accurate "reading" of how society is evolving, it is perhaps even more problematic today given an information-based society with large numbers of diverse and well-informed people. The schools must realize that they are not separate from the larger culture and local community in which they are located. Schools are designed to serve the broad social interests of society, as well as the local community. We also know that we cannot ignore in our curriculum design the diversity of our citizens, especially our multiple cultures, ethnic groups, and social classes. The challenge is how to address the unique needs of students and particular demands of diverse social groups and still allow students to gain understanding of the common culture, as well as common, agreed on competencies to engage productively in society. Indeed, the search for a common curriculum presupposes that there is something general and universal for all to know. Those persons arguing for the 3 R's at the elementary school level and basic academic subjects in the secondary schools assume that a common culture exists.

It would seem that if educators are to create curricula with effective designs, they will have to realize the need for collaboration among people and groups. As John Naisbitt has reported, we are at a time of increasing participatory democracy in which the individuals affected by decisions are demanding a role in making those decisions. Perhaps never before in the history of our nation has society as a source influencing curriculum design been more pronounced. It is quite probable that the curricular designs coming from collaborative dialogue will produce some designs currently not even imagined.[12]

Eternal and Divine Sources. Some people consider that designers should simply draw on the past for guidance as to what is appropriate content. These persons believe that the curricular design should be intended to perpetuate society. This traditional view, which reflects a perennialist philosophy, proposes selecting those eternal truths advanced by the great persons of the past. Such designs stress the content element and that certain content (subjects) is more important than other content.

Divine will as an undergirding factor of curriculum design is related to eternal truth and notes that the elements of the curriculum are revealed to humans through the Bible or other religious documents. While this "source" of curriculum design played a significant role in our nation's early colonial schools, for the last century, it really has had little influence in public schools primarily due to the mandated separation of church and state.[13] But, to many private and parochial schools, this source of the curriculum is still valid and a major influence.

An interesting development in recent times is the issue of spirituality and its relationship to knowing. When we hear the word spiritual, we usually think religion. However, while we have believed in separation of church and state, and thus tended to downplay divine sources as influencing curriculum design, we have come to realize the significance of people's values and personal morality. To be sure, one of the criticisms of Western society is its emphasis on science and rationality, its stress on material wealth, at the expense of spiritual and/or moral values.

Dwayne Huebner has argued that talk of the spirit "and spiritual" in education need not refer to a divinity. "The talk is about lived reality, about experience and the possibility of experiencing. . . . The 'spiritual' is of this world, not of another world; of this life, not of another life." For Huebner, to have spirit is to be in touch with the forces or energies of life.[14] Being in touch with spirit allows one to see the essences of reality and to generate new ways of looking at knowledge, new relationships among people, and even new ways of perceiving one's existence. While there will be people who take issue with Huebner, those who design curriculum might need to be a little more cosmopolitan and tolerant in their thinking when contemplating eternal and divine sources as influencing the curriculum.

Knowledge as a Source. As already indicated, some might interpret science as the source of the curriculum design as too limiting because it ignores content from other fields of study. If we consider knowledge itself as one of the prime sources of curriculum, we certainly will not leave out any particular content. Hunkins has gone so far as to suggest that knowledge is perhaps the only source of curriculum, and that society and what we know about learners really serve as filters in the selection of content.[15] Certainly, knowledge cannot be ignored. Herbert Spencer placed knowledge within the framework of curriculum when he asked, "What knowledge is of most worth?" It is the same question that Arno Bellack raised 80 years later when he examined knowledge in relationship to the various disciplines and structure of a curriculum.[16]

Those who place knowledge at the center, or as a key source, realize that it is organized in specialized ways. Disciplined knowledge has a particular structure and a particular method or methods by which its scholars extend its boundaries. Undisciplined knowledge does not have unique content, but has content that is clustered according to the focus of the investigation. Physics has a unique conceptual structure and a unique process. But home economics is undisciplined in that its content is not unique to itself but is drawn from various other disciplines and adapted to a special focus.

The Learner as a Source. Some believe that the curriculum should be derived from what we know about the learner: how he or she learns, forms attitudes, generates interests, and develops values. Progressive curricularists and humanistic educators who favor learner-centered curriculum designs (we discuss both designs later in this chapter) consider the learner as the primary source.

Stressing the learner as the key influencing factor in designing the curriculum causes us to draw heavily on the psychological foundations. Today, much scholarly activity deals with the ways that minds work to create meaning. Much cognitive research has provided curriculum designers with ways to develop educational activities in the curriculum plan to facilitate perceiving, thinking, and learning. The key feature of curricular designs that draw on the learner as source emphasize learning by doing.[17] This, of course, dates back to Dewey who asserted that learning requires students to apply knowledge and solve problems. Just reading about things and

events, without thinking and doing, is incomplete.

There seems to be some overlap between science as a source, where the emphasis is on strategies for processing knowledge, and the learner as source where we draw our design from what we know about how individuals process information in order to learn. Of course, we could argue that all sources of curriculum design do overlap. We do not just draw from one source and consciously exclude the others. In developing a theory of imagination, educators deal with content that can be placed either under science as a source or learner as a source. We might even argue that imagination draws from the eternal truths.[18]

Using the learner as source for curriculum design means that we take those hallmarks of what makes a person a learner and try to emphasize them in the curriculum organization. As we discover more about the complexities of learning and reacting and imagining, we will bring more precision to this design. We are just beginning to recognize that imaginative activity is a factor in thinking and learning—and has been largely ignored in the past. It is perhaps in this realm where much creative thinking regarding curriculum design will occur. See Curriculum Tips 8-1.

Conceptual Framework: Horizontal and Vertical Organization

Curriculum design, the organization of the components or elements of curriculum, exists along two basic organizational dimensions: horizontal and vertical. *Horizontal* organization engages the curriculum worker with the concepts of scope and integration, that is, the side-by-side arrangement of curriculum elements. For instance, arranging content from the separate subjects of history, anthropology, and sociology into a course dealing with contemporary studies involves horizontal organization. Taking content from one subject, such as mathematics, and relating it to content in another, such as science, is another example of horizontal design.

Vertical organization, which centers on the concepts of sequence and continuity, is concerned with the longitudinal placement of curriculum elements. Placing "the family" in first-grade social studies and "the community" in second-grade social studies is an example of vertical organization. Frequently, curricula are organized so that the same topics are introduced and treated in different grades, but at more detailed and difficult levels. This also is vertical organization. For instance, in mathematics the concept of set is introduced in first grade and reintroduced or mentioned at each succeeding year in the elementary curriculum. This corresponds with Bruner's idea of the "spiral curriculum."[19]

Even though design decisions are essential, it appears that curricula in schools are not the result of careful design deliberations. In most school districts, overall curricular designs receive little attention. Curriculum often exists as disjointed clusters of content organized as particular items that frequently duplicate and/or conflict with other items. Robert Zais has noted that many courses in the schools' curricula are really the result of current "educational" fashion and not careful deliberations about design.[20]

DESIGN DIMENSION CONSIDERATIONS

Curriculum design is a statement noting the relationships that exist among the components or elements of a curriculum. Curricularists must, when considering design, view it on several dimensions: scope, integration, sequence, continuity, articulation, and balance.

Scope. When considering the design of a curriculum, educators need to address the breadth and depth of its content, that is, its scope. Tyler, in his classic book, referred to scope as consisting of all the content, topics, learning experiences, and organizing threads comprising the educational plan.[21] By scope we mean all the varieties and types of educational experiences that are to be provided to the students through the school.

Sometimes the scope of the curriculum is represented just simply as a listing of the key topics and activities to be considered.

When teachers and other educators are deciding what content to include in the curriculum and the amount of detail to the content, they are engaged in considering the scope of the curriculum. In many ways, the current knowledge explosion has made dealing with scope almost overwhelming. Many teachers realize that the scope of possible topics and content areas to cover is just too broad. Some teachers respond to the overload of content by ignoring certain content areas or not including new content topics into the curriculum. Others attempt to relate certain topics to each other to create curriculum themes or threads.

Doll suggests that the scope of the curriculum can perhaps be kept at manageable levels by only addressing a limited number of objectives. These objectives would refer to general clusters of content that would be kept from expanding to a number beyond control.[22] The challenge is to achieve consensus with others that the chosen content categories are indeed of greater educational significance than those not selected. The challenge of determining scope goes back to the basic question posed by Herbert Spencer, "What knowledge is of most worth?" It also forces curriculum decision makers to reflect on the curriculum foundations, particularly the philosophical foundation. What is the nature of schooling? What do we mean by an educated person, a literate person? Often, teachers' philosophical views will guide them in responding to these questions.

Peter Oliva notes that, when considering scope, we need to attend to the cognitive, affective, and psychomotor domains of learning. (We might add the moral or spiritual domain.) This further complicates scope, for decisions must be made that determine what will be covered and what will be the detail not only within each domain, but also which domain will receive the most emphasis.[23] Tradition shows that the cognitive domain has received the greatest emphasis, drawing on the realm of knowledge. Frequently, at the secondary level of schooling, we draw upon disciplines of knowledge and their main concepts to determine the scope of the curriculum. However, there has recently been attention to assure that the affective domain, dealing with values and attitudes, and the psychomotor domain, dealing with motor skills and coordination, are addressed. Often, in the past, we have indicated the need to educate the whole child, but our scope charts have frequently indicated otherwise.

Integration.   The major challenge in dealing with scope is integrating the myriad learnings that students are to encounter at a particular grade level of the curriculum. Integration refers to the linking of all types of knowledge and experiences contained within the curriculum plan. It emphasizes horizontal relations among various content topics and themes involving all domains of knowledge recognized.

Integration allows the learners to obtain a unified view of knowledge and an in-depth meaning of the subject matter. In fact, Saylor, Alexander, and Lewis went so far as to say that integration only occurs within the learner. "Although curriculum planners can organize opportunities for learning in such a way as to facilitate integration, it is the learners who integrate what they are learning through various educational experiences."[24] Taba also advanced a similar view, defining curriculum integration as "something that happens in an individual, whether or not the curriculum is organized for that purpose." This conception leads to a concern with the integrative process "in which students organize in a meaningful fashion knowledge and experiences which at first seem unrelated."[25] However, Taba did not just limit integration to that which was happening in the student. She realized that it was also an attempt to interrelate the content components with learning experiences and activities in ways that would facilitate learning.

Over 30 years ago, Taba noted that integration of knowledge was an important issue because of the knowledge explosion, the increasing specialization in society, and expanding technology. If this point was relevant in the 1960s, it is even more relevant in the 1990s when the information age is fully upon us. We might follow Taba's advice that there is a need to develop common knowledge by dealing with ideas that transcend fields of study. We need to move to broader organizations of knowledge. Interestingly enough, there is a major move today for designing curricula into just such global clusters linked together by relational threads. Some schools even call their curricula "integrated curricula," denoting attempts to make common themes the hallmarks of their programs. The integration of curriculum works to interrelate not only the basic ideas within subjects, but to point to the interrelationships with other subjects.

At the elementary school level, whole language learning is an example of an integrated curriculum; reading and writing across content areas is an example at the secondary level. STS, meaning science-technology-society, combines science with social sciences in an attempt to solve practical, everyday problems. The study of science combined with esoteric lab work is deemphasized for an integrated approach that takes the student outside the lab, and away from the textbook, into the local community, where the action is and where solving problems involves integration and application of subject matter.

Sequence. When considering sequence, curricularists are challenged to deal effectively with the curricular elements so that the curriculum fosters cumulative and continuous learning, or what is referred to as the *vertical* relationship among curricular areas. Taba has noted that people dealing with sequence have addressed content but have given little or no attention to the sequences of processes—those skills requisite for dealing with the content. She argued that this failure to pay serious attention to sequence in terms of the cumulative development of intellectual and affective processes has resulted in less-than-optimal curricula, as well as problems articulating among the levels of schooling.[26]

Persons addressing sequence have been aware of the longstanding controversy over whether the sequence of content and experiences should be based on the logic of the subject matter or on the way in which individuals process knowledge. Those arguing for sequence based on psychological principles draw on an understanding of and research on human growth, development, and learning. Piaget's research has provided a framework for sequencing content and experiences (or activities) and relating expectations to what we know about how individuals function at various cognitive levels.[27] Most

school districts, when they formulate curriculum objectives, content, and experiences by grade levels, consider the students' stages of thinking. The curriculum is thus sequenced according to Piaget's theory of cognitive development.

Certainly, in organizing content into a productive sequence, we cannot totally disregard how individuals develop and learn. But neither can we neglect the substantive structure or logic of the content. Nor can we forget that learners have individual and group interests and needs and that these concerns must also be addressed.

Curricularists faced with sequencing content have drawn on some fairly well accepted learning principles. Smith, Stanley, and Shores introduced four such principles: simple to complex learning, prerequisite learning, whole to part learning, and chronological learning.

1. *Simple to complex learning* indicates that content is optimally organized in a sequence going from simple subordinate components or elements to complex components depicting interrelationships among components. It notes that optimal learning results when individuals are presented with easy, often concrete, content and then with more difficult, often abstract, content.
2. *Prerequisite learning* is similar to part to whole learning. It works on the assumption that bits of information or learning must be grasped before other bits of learning can be comprehended.
3. *Whole to part learning* receives support from cognitive psychologists. They urged that the curriculum be arranged so that the content or the experience is presented first in an overview (abstract) fashion to furnish students with a general idea of the information or situation.
4. *Chronological learning* is another organizer for sequencing content. Frequently, history, political science, and world events are organized in this manner. Curricularists refer to this type of organization as "world-related": The content is sequenced as it occurs in the world.[28]

Posner and Strike also furnished the field of curriculum with four other organizers for determining sequence: concept-related, inquiry-related, learning-related, and utilization-related learning.[29] The *concept-related* method draws heavily from the structure of knowledge. It focuses on the interrelationships of concepts rather than on knowledge of the concrete; it overlaps with the ideas of Hilda Taba and today's curriculum theorists such as Alan Bloom and Philip Phenix. The *inquiry-related* sequence is derived from the nature of procedures employed by scholars. The steps they would take in processing a sequence of concepts or principles in their investigations would become the sequence of topics in the curriculum. It coincides with the idea of teaching the syntactical structure of a subject, popularized by Bruner and Schwab. The *learner-related* sequence concerns how individuals learn or should experience content and activities; this is nothing more than old-fashioned progressivism. *Utilization-related* learning draws on how people who use some knowledge or engage in a particular activity in the world actually proceed through it. It closely resembles the "activity analysis" proposed by Bobbitt and Charters many years ago.

Continuity.   Continuity deals with the vertical manipulation or repetition of curriculum components. Tyler indicated that if, for example, reading skills is an important objective, then "it is necessary to see that there is recurring and continuing opportunity for these skills to be practiced and developed. This means that over time the same kinds of skills will be brought into continuing operation."[30]

Continuity accounts for the reappearance in the curriculum of certain major ideas or skills about which educators feel students should have increased depth and breadth of knowledge over the length of the curriculum.

Continuity is most evident in Bruner's notion of the "spiral curriculum." Bruner noted that the curriculum should be organized according to the interrelationships between the structure of the basic ideas of each major discipline. For students to grasp these basic ideas and structures, "they should be developed and redeveloped in a spiral fashion"—in increasing depth and breadth, as the pupils advance through the school program.[31]

The concept of the spiral curriculum relates not only to the vertical integration of knowledge, but also to the horizontal integration, or the adding of breadth. When educators seek to improve the linkages among topics within a given discipline or subject field, they are dealing with the vertical articulation of the curriculum. When they are organizing the curricular elements to stress the interrelationships between and among different elements, disciplines, subject fields, or experiences, they are concerned with the horizontal articulation of the curriculum.

Articulation.   Articulation refers to the interrelatedness of various aspects of the curriculum. The relation can be either vertical or horizontal. Vertical articulation depicts the relationships of certain aspects in the curriculum sequence to lessons, topics, or courses appearing later in the program's sequence. For instance, a teacher might design introductory or ninth-grade algebra so that concepts in the algebra class are related to key concepts in a geometry course. When viewed vertically, we usually are referring to the sequencing of content from one grade level to another. The key reason for addressing vertical articulation is to assure that students receive those learnings that are prerequisite to later learnings in the curriculum. Horizontal articulation refers to the association between or among elements occurring simultaneously. Horizontal articulation takes place, for instance, when curriculum designers attempt to develop interrelationships between eighth-grade social studies and eighth-grade English courses.

When considering articulation horizontally, we are equating it with what some have called correlation. In horizontal articulation, curriculum decision makers are striving to meld those contents in one part of the educational program with those contents that are similar or have a logical or educational link. In those curricula where thinking is being stressed across the curriculum, we are making horizontal linkages dealing with thinking in, say, mathematics with thinking in science. Much of the present-day emphasis on "integrating the curriculum" is really an effort at horizontal articulation.

Articulation is difficult to achieve, and few school districts have developed procedures by which the various interrelationships within and among subjects are clearly defined. One reason for the difficulty is that it is sometimes a difficult task to determine just what these interrelationships are. Curricula arranged by subjects often pay no attention to connections with any other subject matter.

Another reason for the difficulty in attaining articulation is that we are not as far along in cooperative curriculum development as our educational talk might indicate. For example, within school districts, it is sometimes difficult to achieve articulation from one school to another school. Also, we could argue that there is need for articulation among school districts as well as within school districts. This is especially important at a time when the population is mobile. Students new to a school district sometimes experience a repeat of information they had in their former school at a previous grade level. Other times, they experience gaps; that is, they miss a particular concept or topic because it was offered the year prior to their arrival.

It would seem that schools need to develop effective strategies for attaining both vertical and horizontal articulation, especially if we are going to strive to have our students attain continuous progress in experiencing the curriculum. Articulation seems to be particularly difficult in the transitions between elementary and middle schools and middle schools and high schools, and especially among different school districts.

Balance.   When designing a curriculum, educators are also concerned that appropriate weight be given to each aspect of the design so that distortions do not occur. In a balanced curriculum, students have opportunities to master knowledge and to internalize and utilize it in ways that are appropriate for their personal, social, and intellectual goals. To say that the components must be balanced is easier said than done. John Goodlad argues that the curriculum should be balanced in terms of subject matter and the learner. However, he comments, "The prospect of stressing one to the exclusion of the other appears scarcely worthy of consideration. Nonetheless, the interested observer has little difficulty finding school practices emphasizing one component to the impoverishment of the other."[32]

Adding to the complexity of attaining balance in the curriculum is the fact that what might be interpreted as balance today might well be imbalance tomorrow. The times in which schools find themselves are always changing, and what should be emphasized is in a state of flux. Also,

Doll points out that balance is problematic because we are striving to localize and individualize the curriculum in its content and experiences while at the same time addressing a tradition that plans schooling for the masses of students.[33] Thus there is a balancing problem between the needs and interests of the individual students and a common content that all students should know. Do we put emphasis on low achievers, average achievers, or high achievers?

Perhaps the curriculum will never be fully balanced, because schools are slow to adapt to the changing needs of the individual and society and because they are influenced by whim and fads. Educators tend to put too much emphasis on one subject, or a group of subjects, at the expense of others. The criteria for emphasis are often based on pressure and subjectivity, not systematic planning and objectivity. The latest fad often dominates the direction of curriculum design.

It behooves curriculum specialists to maintain a balance in the curriculum despite pressures and fads. Oliva has listed a set of points to consider that can provide guidance in attaining balance in the curriculum:

1. The child-centered and subject-centered curriculum.
2. The needs of the individual and those of society.
3. The needs of common education and specialized education.
4. Breadth and depth of curriculum content.
5. Traditional content and innovative content.
6. The needs of the unique range of pupils regarding their learning styles.
7. Different teaching methods and educational experiences.
8. Work and play.
9. The community and school as educational forces.[34]

Following these suggestions may not make the task of attaining balance easier, but it may increase the probability of attaining it. Keeping the curriculum "in balance" requires continuous fine-tuning of the curriculum as well as balance in one's view of philosophy and psychology of learning so as not to fall prey to a particular drummer or popular tune. See Curriculum Tips 8-2.

REPRESENTATIVE CURRICULUM DESIGNS

Curriculum components can be organized in numerous ways. However, most curriculum designs are modifications and/or integrations of three basic design types: (1) subject-centered designs, (2) learner-centered designs, and (3) problem-centered designs. Each category comprises several examples. Subject-centered designs include subject designs, discipline designs, broad field designs, correlation designs and process designs. Learner-centered designs are those identified as child-centered designs, experience designs, romantic/radical designs, and humanistic designs. Problem-centered designs consider life situations, core designs, and social problem/reconstructionist designs.

Subject-centered Designs

Subject-centered designs are by far the most popular and widely used curriculum designs. This is because knowledge and content are well accepted as integral parts of the curriculum. Schools have a strong history of academic rationalism; furthermore, the materials available for school use also reflect content organization.

The category of subject-centered designs has the most classifications of any of the designs.

This richness may result from our greater understanding of knowledge or from the very strong tradition knowledge or content has in our culture. Concepts central to a culture are more highly elaborated than peripheral ones. In our culture, content is central to schooling; we thus have many concepts to depict our diverse organizations.

Subject Design.   The subject design is both the oldest school design and the best known—to both teachers and laypeople. It is so well known because teachers and laypersons are usually educated and/or trained in schools employing it. It is also popular because it corresponds to textbook treatment and how teachers are trained as subject specialists.[35] This design is based on a belief that what makes humans unique and distinctive is their intellect; the searching for and the attainment of knowledge are the natural fulfillment of that intellect.

An early spokesperson for the subject curriculum was Henry Morrison, who was the state superintendent of public instruction in New Hampshire before he joined the University of Chicago. Morrison argued that the subject matter curriculum contributed most to the literacy of the individual and that literacy skills should be the focus of the elementary curriculum. This orientation to subject matter reflected a mental discipline approach to learning and a perennialist orientation to subject matter. Morrison also felt that such a design could allow a student at the secondary school level to develop interest and competence in one subject area. However, he believed that a variety of courses should be offered to cater to the diverse needs of students.[36]

William Harris, superintendent of the St. Louis schools in the 1870s, also receives credit for fostering this curriculum design. Under Harris's guidance, the St. Louis schools established a subject-oriented curriculum that took firm hold there well into this century. Indeed, some would argue that the subject design is still alive and well. One educator notes that most Americans would recognize this curriculum design, which he classifies as the conservative liberal arts design, as the type they experienced in school.[37] In the mid-1930s, Robert Hutchins indicated what subjects would comprise such a curriculum design: (1) language and its uses (reading, writing, grammar, literature); (2) mathematics; (3) sciences; (4) history; (5) foreign languages.[38]

Today's emphasis on a common core curriculum, exemplified by Boyer, Goodlad, and Sizer (see Chapter 5) and the theme of educational excellence, exemplified by the national task force reports (also Chapter 5) since the mid 1980s reflects a subject orientation.

In the subject matter design, the curriculum is organized according to how essential knowledge has been developed in the various subject areas. With the explosion of knowledge and the resulting specializations in the various fields of knowledge, subject divisions have increased in number and sophistication. For instance, history has been divided into cultural history, economic history, and geographic history. English can be divided into literature, writing, speech, reading, linguistics, and grammar as major subject divisions.

This organization of curricular content also assumes that subjects are best outlined in textbooks. The teacher usually assumes the active role. Lecture, recitation, and large group discussion are major instructional techniques utilized with this design. Usually, discussion proceeds from simple to complex ideas. Logic is emphasized.

Advocates of this design defend the emphasis on verbal activities. They argue that knowledge and ideas are best communicated and stored in verbal form. Many educators today, in fact, agree that learning is primarily a verbal activity. Advocates also note that a prime advantage of the design is that it introduces students to the essential knowledge of society. Also, the design is easy to deliver because complementary textbooks and support materials are commercially available. Tradition, too, is on its side. People are familiar with this format, having gone through schools using it.

Critics, however, say that the design prevents individualization of the program and de-emphasizes the notion of the learner. Other critics contend that stress on subject matter fails to foster social, psychological, and physical development and to some extent fosters a scholarly elite, a ruling class based on knowledge. Another drawback of this design is that learning tends to be compartmentalized and to stress mnemonic skills. A serious problem is that this design stresses content and neglects students' needs, interests, and experiences. Another problem is that, in delivering such a curriculum, the teachers tend to foster in students a passivity for learning.

Dewey was concerned about isolating subject matter from the learner's reality—knowledge divorced from the learner's experiences, essentially second-hand knowledge and other persons' knowledge. Such knowledge tends to be merely verbal, and learning primarily becomes remembering other peoples, ideas.[39] For Dewey, the curriculum did not need to emphasize subject matter or the learner. It should do both. From the analysis of the current scene, it seems that Dewey's and others advice to combine subject matter and pupils' experiences has gone unheeded. For instance, while following much of Tyler's advice on creating curriculum, educators have not reflected on his point that overemphasizing subject matter results in a curriculum that is "too technical and too specialized" for most students. What is needed is a common education that integrates content with the learner's prior experiences; this leads to meaningful, new experiences.[40]

Discipline Design. The discipline design that appeared in the post-World War II era evolved from the separate-subject design. This new design grew rapidly in popularity during the 1950s and reached its zenith during the mid-1960s. Its popularity was tarnished somewhat during the student protests of the 1970s, but it is still present in much curriculum organization in secondary schools and colleges.

Like the separate-subject design, the discipline design's basis is the inherent organization of content. However, whereas the subject design does not make clear the foundational basis upon which it is organized or established, the discipline design's orientation does specify its focus on the academic disciplines.

King and Brownell, proponents of this design, indicate that a discipline is specific knowledge that has the following essential characteristics: a community of persons, an ex-pression of human imagination, a domain, a tradition, a mode of inquiry, a conceptual structure, a specialized language, a heritage of literature, a network of communications, a valuative and affective stance, and an instructive community.[41]

This stress on disciplined knowledge can be likened to a "command" to only teach the disciplines—science, mathematics, English, history, and so on. The assumption used by advocates to support their advice is that the school is a microcosm of the world of intellect and that the disciplines reflect that world.[42] This means that the manner in which the content is to be learned is suggested by the methods scholars employ to study the content of their fields. Students in history would approach the subject matter as would a historian, and students in biology would investigate biological topics following procedures advocated by biologists.

This point is important. Even though proponents of the discipline design view as necessary experiencing the disciplines in the school, they stress understanding the conceptual structures and the processes of the disciplines. This is perhaps the essential difference between the disciplines design and the subject matter design. In the discipline design, students experience the disciplines so that they can comprehend and even conceptualize, whereas in the subject matter design the students are considered to have learned if they just acquire knowledge and information. Sometimes, it is difficult to determine whether in fact a classroom has a subject matter or a discipline design. The key distinguishing characteristic seems to be whether students are involved in actually using some of the methods of the discipline to process information.

In the discipline design, students are encouraged to see the basic logic or structure of each discipline—the key relationships, concepts, and principles—what Joseph Schwab called the "substantive structure" and Phil Phenix called the "realms of meaning."

Considering structure or meaning allows a "deep" understanding of the content and a realization of ways in which such knowledge can be applied to generate additional meaning. This is what Harry Broudy calls "applicative knowledge,"[43] knowledge we can directly use, or apply, such as knowledge of problem-solving procedures.

The student who cultivates fluency with the modes of inquiry really attains mastery of the content area and is able to continue independently his or her learning in the field. The student need not always require the teacher to present information. Ideally, supporters of this design wish students to function as "little" scholars in the respective fields of the school curriculum. When learning mathematics, students would be neophyte mathematicians. When engaged in studying history, the students would employ the methods of historiography.

The emphasis on disciplines and structure eventually leads to Jerome Bruner's classic book, *The Process of Education.* The very title suggests that education, more precisely learning, should emphasize process or procedural knowledge. Bruner states that the "curriculum of a subject should be determined by . . . the underlying principles that give structure to that subject."[44] Organizing the curriculum according to the structure of the discipline will cause relationships to be made clear, indicate how elementary knowledge is related to advanced knowledge, allow individuals to reconstruct meaning within the content area, and furnish the means for advancing through the content area.

A most attractive notion of the disciplines approach expounded by Bruner was that "any subject can be taught in some effectively honest form to any child at any stage of development."[45] Contrary to what many persons had held, Bruner argued that students are able to comprehend the fundamental principles of any subject at almost any age. And children can thus understand the structure and operations of a discipline at any age—such understanding does not need to await adolescence or adulthood.

Bruner has been criticized as having a romantic notion of students as scholars. Developmentalists have disagreed with his thesis that "intellectual activity anywhere is the same," and point out that the processes of the young child, for example, differ in kind and in degree from the thinking processes of adolescents and adults. There are also differences between sexes in the early grades in terms of how children process cognitive information.[46]

Many educators criticized the design for assuming that the students must adapt to the curriculum, rather than that the curriculum must adapt or be modified to meet students' requirements.[47] Additionally, the design was attacked for assuming that all students have a common or at least a similar type of learning style. The design tended to emphasize academically oriented students and to ignore nonacademic students. This later evolved as a major criticism, as educators turned to the needs of the disadvantaged in the 1960s and 1970s and the bilingual and handicapped in the 1980s and 1990s.

Perhaps the greatest shortcoming of the design was that it caused the schools to ignore the vast amount of information that could not be classified as disciplined knowledge. Such knowledge, dealing with esthetics, humanism, personal-social living, and vocational education, is difficult to categorize as a discipline, although Phil Phenix would argue that it can be achieved.[48]

Broad Fields Design.   The broad fields design, another variation of the subject-centered design, appeared as an effort to correct what many educators considered the fragmentation and compartmentalization caused by the subject design. It was an attempt to integrate content that appeared to fit together logically. Thus the separate social sciences of geography, economics, political science, anthropology, sociology, and history were fused into social studies. Linguistics, grammar, literature, composition, and spelling were collapsed into language arts. Biology, chemistry, and physics were integrated into general science.

The idea was both bold and simple. Educators essentially had only to meld two or more related subjects, already well known in the schools, into a single broad or fused field of study. However, it was a change from the traditional subject pattern of the perennialists and essentialists. While the design first appeared shortly after the first decade of this century at the college level, it gained its most popularity at the elementary and secondary levels of schooling. This continues to the present day. Its use today at the college level really is only seen in introductory courses, but it is widespread with the K-12 curriculum.

Harry Broudy et al. offered a unique broad fields design during the Sputnik era. They suggested that the entire curriculum be organized into the following categories: (1) symbolics of information—English, foreign language, and mathematics; (2) basic sciences—general science, biology, physics, and chemistry; (3) developmental studies—evolution of the cosmos, evolution of social institutions, and evolution of human culture; (4) exemplars—modes of esthetic experience that would include art, music, drama, literature; and (5) molar problems that would address typical social problems.[49] This last category would have a yearly variety of courses depending on the social problems of the times.

This broad fields design still receives attention from curriculum specialists. The National Society for the Study of Education recently discussed this design for all students. Its curriculum included mathematics, natural sciences, language and literature, esthetics and fine arts, and social studies.[50]

The broad fields design allows students to discern relationships among the various aspects of the curriculum content, as well as wholeness of meaning. In this connection, one educator has referred to this design as the wave of the future, whereby subject matter "is less compartmentalized and more integrated and holistic. Although traditional subject boundaries will remain, there will be increased cross-subject material." Knowledge will no longer be fragmented or linear, "but multidisciplinary and multidimensional."[51]

Like any design, this one has its problems. One is the issue of breadth versus depth. Having students spend a year studying social studies teaches them a greater and more varied range of social science concepts than they would learn if they just took a year of history. But is their knowledge of the various social sciences superficial? Certainly, a year of history will furnish more historical knowledge than a year of social studies. But then the question arises, at least at the elementary level, is it necessary to have great depth? Is not the purpose of the curriculum to have students understand the entire field of social science knowledge? How this question is answered depends in part on the particular philosophical posture of the school.

Correlation Design. Correlation is a design employed by those who do not wish to go as far as creating a broad fields design, but who realize that there are times when separate subjects require some linkage in order to reduce fragmentation of curricular content. Existing as a midpoint between separate subjects and total integration of content, it attempts to identify ways in which subjects can be related to one another while still maintaining their identity as subjects.

Perhaps the two most frequently correlated subjects are English literature and history at the secondary level and language arts and social studies at the elementary level. While studying a period in history, students in their English class read novels that relate to the same time period. Science and mathematics are also courses frequently correlated. Students in a chemistry course may have a unit in mathematics that deals with the mathematics required, to conduct an experiment. However, the content areas remain distinct, and the teachers of these courses retain their subject matter specialties.

The notion of a correlated design was attractive to many. Alberty and Alberty were famous for their discussion of the correlated curriculum at the secondary level. They presented a variant of this design that employed an "over-arching theme." This version of core retained the basic content of the subjects, but the content was selected and organized with reference to broad themes, problems, or units.[52]

This variation of core required that classes be scheduled in a block of time. So scheduled, teachers of the various content areas to be correlated could work together and have students working on assignments that drew from the correlated content areas. Combining various subjects with other subjects is only limited by our imagination. It is possible to relate literature and art that depicts similar issues in verbal or pictorial form. Science is now being taught through literature. It is conceivable that courses in computer science can be correlated with separate courses in art, music, or economics.

Currently, few teachers are actually using the correlated design, possibly because it requires that they plan their lessons cooperatively. This is somewhat difficult to accomplish because teachers have self-contained classes at the elementary level and often do not have time for such collaboration. At the secondary level, teachers are organized into separate departments that tend to encourage isolation. Teachers must also meet time schedules dictated by specified classes and so may have little time to work with other teachers in team-teaching arrangements. Furthermore, most class schedules do not allow a sufficient block of time for students to meaningfully study correlated subjects. Modular scheduling and flexible scheduling, which would allow for this, really never received wide acceptance.

Process Designs. As indicated when discussing discipline-centered designs, attention is often given to the procedures and processes by which individuals advance knowledge. Thus, students in biology would learn the methods for dealing with biological knowledge; history students would learn the ways of historiography, and students studying anthropology would learn the various ethnographic procedures appropriate for the study of culture and society.

While advocates of the disciplines design urge students to learn process, other educators are suggesting curricular designs that stress the learning of general procedures, general processes not specific to any particular discipline, but applicable to all. The numerous curricula for teaching critical thinking exemplify this procedural design.[53]

Educators have always suggested that students be taught to think in schools. Curricular designs need to address process, or how learners learn, and the application of process to subject matter. Barry Beyer has written extensively on strategies of thinking. His curriculum would be organized around three key thinking strategies: problem solving, decision making, and conceptualizing. Accompanying these thinking strategies are micro-thinking skills such as analysis and synthesis of data necessary for engaging the major thinking strategies.[54]

Marilyn Adams points out that the fundamental assumption motivating all curricula on thinking is that there exists a certain set of skills or processes that are common to thinking in general, regardless of [subject], domain, or purpose. The common goal of the curricula is to teach

those processes and, in that sense, fall under the general rubric of process-oriented curricula.[55] It is this emphasis on processes that is applicable to all fields of knowledge that distinguishes this curriculum design from the disciplines design in which the procedural knowledge is specifically related to the specialized discipline. Thinking critically is not unique to history or physics. Neither is thinking creatively the sole domain of art or literature. Thinking curricula can be organized so that procedural knowledge is integrated throughout the total curriculum. To a large extent, this type of curriculum design coincides with the "critical thinking" section of Chapter 4, highlighted by the works of Matthew Lipman and Robert Sternberg.

Adams played a significant role in the development of a curriculum entitled, "Odyssey: A Curriculum for Thinking."[56] The curriculum was designed by the collaborative effort of Harvard University and the Venezuelan Ministry of Education and was influenced by two basic thinking components: information and interpretion. Thus the curriculum included special types of information and various strategies for interpreting such information or thinking about it. The processes provide the central structure for this curriculum design. Table 8-1 presents the total curriculum. By studying the table, it is evident that the process is not subject or discipline specific. But it is important to note that there is more than procedural knowledge in this curriculum. The units in this thinking series engage students in learning how to process content across subjects. For instance, in learning the content regarding analysis or reasoning, students are acquiring approaches for studying content in any subject. But in reality there is no content-free curriculum; it is the nature of the content that receives a different emphasis. Many of the processes are specific to a subject, or tend to be common in one more than in another, but the examples and exercises tend to be rich in diverse content areas. Instead of recalling knowledge in one subject, students are asked to think, react, and/or explore—to learn processes they can use in many subjects.

Another curriculum exemplifying the process design is the program *Tactics* designed by Robert Marzano and Daisy Arrendondo. Essen-

TABLE 8-1 Odyssey: A Curriculum for Thinking

Theme 1: Foundations of Reasoning
  Unit 1: Observation and classification
  Unit 2: Ordering
  Unit 3: Developing hierarchy
  Unit 4: Employing analogies
  Unit 5: Spatial reasoning and strategies

Theme 2: Understanding Language
  Unit 1: Word relations
  Unit 2: Language, its structure
  Unit 3: Gathering and interpreting information

Theme 3: Verbal Reasoning
  Unit 1: Assertions
  Unit 2: Arguments

Theme 4: Problem Solving
  Unit 1: Linear representations
  Unit 2: Tabular representations
  Unit 3: Simulating representations
  Unit 4: Engaging in trial and error
  Unit 5: Reflecting on implications

Theme 5: Decision Making
  Unit 1: Introduction to decision making
  Unit 2: Gathering and evaluating information
  Unit 3: Analyzing decision contexts

Theme 6: Inventive Thinking
  Unit 1: Design
  Unit 2: Processes as designs

Source: Adapted from Marilyn J. Adams, "Thinking Skills Curricula: Their Promises and Progress," *Educational Psychologists* (Winter 1989), pp. 50–51.

tially a training program for teachers who wish to teach thinking skills in K-12 schools, the curriculum content is comprised of twenty-two skills (tactics), with attention to the various means by which these particular skills can be taught.[57] In elaborating on the means of teaching, the actual procedures of each tactic are presented. As outlined in Table 8-2, several thinking units or topics are presented: concept attainment, concept development, pattern recognition, synthesizing, analogical

reasoning, decision making, solving everyday problems, solving academic problems, etc.

Another example of cognitive processing which is generic involves computer programming. Because there are so many programs available in many subject areas and grade levels, it is not essential to have program knowledge. Nonetheless, according to one educator, computer programming is an active mental endeavor, which fosters critical thinking, rational thinking, and problem-solving skills. Programming may be the only generic subject that succeeds in teaching students about things as a process. Writing and debugging a program force students to think logically and carefully about a subject. In addition, students can learn a repertoire of *templates*, that is, patterns of code using more than a single feature, to perform common tasks and complex mental activities.[58]

Templates can be likened to cognitive schema among teachers—methods for processing information. An analysis of the program can also tell the user about the quality of the thinking that went into the solution. When students master computer programming, it becomes possible for teachers to teach in different ways, and students to think in multiple ways, ways that indirectly foster achievement in traditional subject matter. For these reasons, students should be encouraged to learn how to program.

Seymor Papert argues that the computer is a medium of expression and should be used to build a sense of inquiry to "mess about," to explore, and to improve thinking. He also argues that the main impact of computers on learning is not teaching students practical uses of the computer such as word processing or data filing; the real impact will only come when students are taught how to program.[59] Hence they must process information, think logically, and problem solve.

It is likely that, with the knowledge explosion continuing to explode, as well as the increase in computers and computer programming, curricula with a process design, that is, designs emphasizing procedural knowledge, are going to receive increasing attention. These ways of knowing or processing are essentially "learning

TABLE 8-2 Tactics for Thinking

UNITS	UNITS
1. Attention control	12. Proceduralizing
2. In-depth processing	13. Analogical reasoning
3. Memory	14. Extrapolation
4. Power thinking	15. Determining value of evidence
5. Goal setting	16. Examining value
6. Framing responsibility	17. Decision making
7. Concept attainment	18. Linguistic pattern
8. Concept development	19. Elaboration
9. Pattern recognition	20. Everyday problems
10. Macro-pattern recognition	21. Academic problems
11. Synthesizing	22. Inventing

Source: Adapted from Robert J. Marzano and Daisy E. Arrendondo, *Tactics for Thinking* (Aurora, Colo.: Mid-continent Regional Educational Laboratory, 1986).

how to learn" designs. However, they will not replace the teaching of discipline-specific strategies. Rather, they will probably complement such instruction.

Learner-centered Designs

All curricularists are concerned with creating curricula that are valuable to students. In response to those educational planners who value subject matter, educators early in this century asserted that students are the center or focus of the program. Supporters of this posture, largely progressives, advocated what have come to be called learner-centered designs. These designs are found more frequently at the elementary school level where teachers tend to stress the whole child. At the secondary level, the emphasis is more on subject-centered designs largely because of the influence of textbooks and the colleges and universities at which the discipline is a major organizer for the curriculum.

Child-centered Designs. Advocates of the child-centered or student-centered design believed that if we are to optimize learning then the student must be active in his or her environment. Learning should not be separated from the ongoing lives of students, as is often the case with the subject-centered designs. Indeed, it should be based on students' lives, their needs and interests. Taba noted that the rational for this design was that "people learn only what they experience. Only learning that is related to active purposes and is rooted in experience translates itself into behavior changes."[60]

The shifting of emphasis from the tradition of subject matter to the needs and interests of children was part of Rousseau's educational philosophy demonstrated in his book on the education of Emile first published in 1762. Rousseau believed that children should be taught in context with their natural environment, drawing on their needs and interests in creating an educational program. However, Rousseau did not believe in just letting children run free. They required guidance from the teacher. But the manner in which the teacher stimulated the student's curiosity had to be appropriate for the particular developmental level of the child. In a very real sense, Rousseau was the first to advocate a developmental approach to teaching and learning.

Proponents of this design also drew on the thinking of some other early pedagogical giants. Heinrich Pestalozzi and Friedrich Froebel argued that children would attain self-realization through social participation; they voiced the principle of learning by doing. Their social approach to education furnished a foundation for much of the work of Francis Parker.

The child-centered design, often attributed to John Dewey, was really conceived by Parker, who laid the foundations for this movement. Parker had studied pedagogy in Germany, and he knew well the work of Pestalozzi and Froebel. Like Rousseau, Parker believed that effective education did not require strict discipline. Rather, the approach to instruction should be somewhat free, drawing on the child's innate tendency to become engaged in things that interested him or her. Teachers who involved children in conversations would find that students could effectively participate in their own learning. Parker took his views of teaching into practice in developing school curricula in science and geography. In the teaching of geography, he urged teachers to have children experience the content as would a geographer out in the field, doing observations and recording them in sketch books and later analyzing them. Parker was superintendent of schools in Quincy, Massachusetts, and his approach to curriculum was called the Quincy system.[61]

Dewey deduced similar notions in his early thinking. In 1896, he had a chance to put some of his ideas into action in his laboratory school at the University of Chicago. The curriculum was organized around human impulses: the impulse to socialize, the impulse to construct, the impulse to inquire, to question, to experiment, and the impulse to express or to create artistically.[62]

The emphasis on the child displaced the emphasis on subject matter. In addition, when subject matter was presented, it was no longer separated into narrow divisions, but was integrated around units of experience or social problems. The idea that a solution to a problem required using methods and materials from several subject fields was inherent in the child-centered, experience-centered curriculum. This new emphasis on the learner also led to "life needs," "life-adjustment education," "persistent life situations," "common learnings," and "core"[63] methods for organizing bodies of knowledge and subject matter. Here the idea was to integrate subject matter from various fields as needed for the understanding and solution of social problems, as well as to meet the developmental needs of students.

The child-centered design of curriculum flourished in the 1920s and 1930s, primarily under the work of the progressives such as Ellsworth Collings, who introduced the child-centered curriculum in the public schools of McDonald County, Missouri, and William Kilpatrick who created the "project method" which engaged children in their learning at the Lincoln School in New York City.[64] Although the "Project Method" was written up and discussed extensively in the literature, it only gained limited acceptance.

Currently appearing are learner-centered designs aimed specifically at addressing pressing social problems. One such program, advocated by the National Association of Elementary Principals, is called "Skills for Growing" (for grades K-5); it contains five curriculum units to be incorporated into the regular curriculum: (1) building a school community, (2) growing as a group, (3) respecting you and me, (4) making positive decisions, and (5) choosing to be drug free.[65] Woven into these units are opportunities for students to learn how to get along with their peers and other people, how to communicate effectively, how to make healthy decisions, how to think critically, how to foster attitudes of caring about others and developing a willingness to help others, and how to say no to negative influences.

This particular program is essentially a hybrid curriculum. While it is certainly learner centered, it also emphasizes process, ways of knowing and thinking. It further could be considered a type of problem-centered design, which is discussed later in this chapter. Currently, educators are realizing that often what is required in schools are not pure designer types, but combinations with varied emphases such as this skills program.

Experience-centered Designs. Experience-centered curriculum designs closely resembled the child-centered designs in that they used the concerns of children as the basis for organizing the children's school world. However, they differed from child-centered designs in their view that the interests and needs of children cannot be anticipated and, therefore, a curriculum framework cannot be planned for all children.

This notion—that a curriculum could not be preplanned, that everything had to be done "on the spot" by each teacher reacting to each child—made this design almost impossible to implement. It also put people in a posture of ignoring the vast amount of information they had about children's growth and development—cognitively, affectively, emotionally, and socially.

Those favoring the child-centered or experience-centered curriculum placed heavy emphasis on the learners' interests. Pupils' interests have received much attention throughout this century. However, cautions about relying solely on children's interests have been made frequently. Harold Rugg and Ann Shumaker wrote in 1928, "We do not dare leave longer to chance—to spontaneous, overt symptoms of interest on the part of occasional pupils—the solution of this important and difficult problem of construction of a curriculum for maximum growth."[66]

In the beginning of this century, Dewey noted that the spontaneous power of the child, his demand for self-expression, cannot by any possibility be suppressed. For Dewey, interest was purposeful; it had to be taken into consideration. In *Experience and Education,* he noted that education should commence with the experience learners already possessed upon entering school. Experience was essentially the starting point for all further learning.[67] He further noted that the child exists in a personal world of experiences. His or her interests are those of personal concern, rather than relating to the total body of knowledge with its myriad facts, concepts, generalizations, and theories.

While Dewey believed that experience was a starting point for further learning and that pupils' interests had to be considered, he was never an advocate of making the child's interest actually the curriculum or placing the child in the role of curriculum decision maker. On the child and the curriculum, he noted that "the easy thing is to seize upon something in the nature of the child, or upon something in the developed consciousness of the adult, and insist upon that as the key to the whole problem."[68] If we do this, we get into either/or thinking. We begin to see the situation

as the child versus the subject or the nature of the individual versus the social environment.

Ideally, what Dewey wished educators to do was to analyze the experience of children and to see where in their natural experiences there were already existing ideas regarding organized knowledge of facts and truths. One searched for starting points, for places where the child's natural interests and concerns could be linked with more formalized knowledge. Dewey wanted educators to think of the child's experience as vital and fluid, dynamic as opposed to static. Thus, the curriculum would be ever changing in addressing the needs of students.[69]

Dewey contended that the very subjects studied in the curriculum are themselves the results of experience. They are the formalized learnings that have resulted from children's experiences. The content is not just mere clustering of information; rather, the information is organized systematically as the result of careful reflection.

The current postpositivist view supports this belief that individuals are part of their own experience and knowledge production. Individuals are not isolated from the world. Rather, they are dynamic players influencing their world and in turn being influenced by it. As Dewey indicated, subject matter and an individual's experiences are really parts of one's reality.[70] The child interacts with and modifies knowledge through his or her experiences.

Many current advocates of the learner-centered design have assumed an adversarial position with the subject-centered design. Taking an either-or posture in which we either place content at the center or the child at the center ignores Dewey's admonition.

We need to meld content and experience. Several curricularists have translated the ideas of the experience movement into courses emphasizing touching, feeling, and imagining. Some have emphasized life experiences and career-based activities intended to prepare students for adult responsibility.

Romantic (Radical) Designs.   The view of the child as central has been stressed in more recent times by reformers who advocate radical school modification. Many of these individuals essentially adhere to Rousseau's posture on the value of attending to the nature of individuals and Pestalozzi's thinking that individuals can find their true selves by looking to their own nature. While their thinking has a particular progressive ring, they also are drawing on the views of more recent philosophers: Jurgen Habermans, a German philosopher and Paulo Freire, a Brazilian educator. The radical school reformers are eloquent proponents of learner-centered designs. Some, such as John Holt and Ivan Illich, even go so far as to say that parents should not even send their children to schools since the current practices of schools actually are detrimental to the development of children.[71]

An underlying assumption of the radicals appears to be that the current society is corrupt, repressive, and unable to cure itself. Schools have used their curricula to control and to indoctrinate individuals into a particular cultural view rather than to educate and emancipate them. Paulo Freire, in his book *Pedagogy of the Oppressed,* was influential in shaping the thinking of some present-day radicals. Freire noted that the purpose of education is to enlighten the masses about their present state of being denied their rights, to design situations in which they recognize their state of being and feel dissatisfied with it, and finally to gain those skills and competencies requisite for correcting the identified inequities.[72]

Many radicals draw on critical theory, which has been explained in great detail by Habermans, who emphasizes that emancipation is the goal of education. This emancipation refers to the individuals gaining those awarenesses, competencies, and attitudes to enable us to take control of our lives. No longer are we under the control of others; no longer must we follow social conventions without any thought or reflection. In writing about Habermans and his critical theory of education, Robert Young notes that the theme of emancipation has a rather long history, dating back to Roman times and keenly expressed by many philosophers during the

Age of Enlightenment. Students must accept the responsibility for educating themselves, and they must garner the courage to resist indifference to freedom.[73]

Radical curricularists believe that critical theory "has for its object people as producers of their own historical way of life in its totality."[74] Individuals learn those ways of engaging in a critique of knowledge. Learning is reflective; it is not externally imposed by a person in power. Education leads to freedom and emancipation. In the radical curriculum design, knowledge is not a finished product that sits in a unit plan or course syllabus. Such a document is a curriculum that indoctrinates. Learning is something that results from the interaction between and among people. It comes by challenging content and permitting different views about the content, as well as from critiquing the purposes of the information presented in the curriculum.

Perhaps the biggest difference between mainstream educators and radicals is that the latter view the general society as flawed and that education indoctrinates students to fit into those roles that the controlling groups in society wish youth to enter. According to radicals, the curriculum must be overhauled. But traditional curricularists argue that the content does not indoctrinate. For example, curriculum designs based on disciplines emphasize procedural knowledge: students actively involved with the content, engage in a dialogue with teachers and fellow students, raise questions, and evaluate knowledge. Much of what the traditional curriculum is doing is in agreement with the demands of radicals.

Humanistic Designs.   This design gained prominence in the 1960s and 1970s, partly in response to the excessive emphasis on the disciplines during the 1950s and the early 1960s. It was this perceived imbalance regarding attention to subject matter that caused humanistic education to appear in the 1920s and 1930s as part of progressive philosophy and the whole-child movement in psychology. After World War II, humanistic designs connected to existentialism in educational philosophy.

Much of the underpinning for humanistic designs has been associated with third-force psychology or humanistic psychology. Humanistic psychology developed in the 1950s in opposition to the then dominant psychological school of behaviorism. This new psychological orientation emphasized that human action was much more than a response to a stimulus, that meaning was more important than methods, that the focus of attention should be on the subjective rather than objective nature of human existence, and that there is a relationship between learning and feeling.

It was in this context that the Association for Supervision and Curriculum Development published its 1962 yearbook entitled, *Perceiving, Behaving, Becoming*.[75] It represented a new focus for education, an approach to curricular design and instructional delivery that would allow individuals to become fully functioning persons. Arthur Combs, the chairperson of the yearbook, noted some key questions. "What kind of person would it be who has truly achieved the ultimate in self-realization? How do they come about? What factors went into making this kind of person?" He suggested that the curriculum be designed to stress human potential and to enable the student to be involved in the process of becoming.[76] The emphasis was on empowering individuals—what today is called postpositivistic thinking, whereby a person is involved with his or her reality, participating in it, and is aware of the notion of becoming.

The 1977 yearbook of the Association for Supervision and Curriculum Development, entitled *Feeling, Valuing, and the Art of Growing,* also stressed the affective dimensions of humanistic educational designs. The yearbook made a case for the affective domain, indicating among other things that we need to harness human potential and to allow it to set itself free. It suggested that educators must permit students to feel, value, and grow.[77]

A key influence on this particular curriculum design has been Abraham Maslow and his theoretical concept of self-actualization. His list of characteristics of such a person gave educators indicators that could serve as building blocks for this curriculum. A person who was self-actualized (1) was accepting of self, others, and nature; (2) possessed spontaneity, simplicity, and naturalness; (3) was problem-oriented; (4) possessed openness to different experiences beyond the ordinary; (5) possessed empathy and sympathy toward the less fortunate; (6) had mastered sophisticated levels of interpersonal relations; (7) believed in persons participating in decision making; (8) and possessed a philosophical sense of humor.[78] Maslow emphasized that an individual did not become self-actualized early in life. Rather, a person reaches this state sometime around or after age 40. But, to attain that stage, the individual has to start the process as a student. Some educators miss this point and think that their humanistic designs will have students attain self-actualization as an end product.

Carl Rogers's work has been another major force. He assumes that people can enhance self-directed learning by drawing on their own resources to improve self-understanding, to learn self-concepts and basic attitudes, and to guide their own behavior. The educators' task is to set the educational environment such that these personal resources can be tapped. Such an environment encourages genuineness of behavior, empathy, and respect for self and others.[79]

Individuals given such an environment will naturally develop into what Rogers termed a fully functioning person. Individuals able to take self-initiated actions and responsibility for those actions are capable of intelligent choice and self-direction. Furthermore, having acquired knowledge relevant to the solutions of problems, these persons are critical learners. They also are able to approach problem situations with flexibility and intelligence and to work cooperatively with others. They are internally guided with regard to their socialization process; they do not wait for or work for the approval of others.

Humanistic education in the 1970s absorbed the notion of *confluence*. Essentially, confluence education is a melding of the affective domain (feelings, attitudes, values) with the cognitive domain (intellectual knowledge and problem-solving abilities). This approach adds the affective component to the conventional subject matter curriculum that is already in place.[80] Those who support this design do not favor either content or experience or intellect or feeling; rather, they strive to blend the subjective or intuitive with the objective. They urge that the curriculum be so organized as to provide students with more alternatives from which they can choose what to feel. Students are challenged to take responsibility for and to appreciate their choices and to feel comfortable knowing that they have the power to make choices.

Confluent education stresses participation; it emphasizes power sharing, negotiations, and joint responsibility. It is essentially nonauthoritarian. It also stresses the whole person and the integration of thinking, feeling, and acting. It centers on the relevance of subject matter in light of students' basic needs and lives. Throughout the curriculum, students are confronted with situations that make them realize that the development of self is a legitimate objective of learning.

Humanistic educators realize that the cognitive, affective, and psychomotor domains are interconnected and that the curriculum design should address these dimensions. Some educators in this camp—and in the subject-centered camp—would argue that, in addition to these three domains, the two domains of socialization and spirituality should also be addressed.[81]

Humanistic curriculum designs stress the development of positive self-concept and interpersonal skills. A related design, the transpersonal or transcendence orientation—the consciousness aspect of the humanistic design—takes this orientation a bit further. Here the stress, though still on the individual, encourages intuition and transcendence. Through intuition a person is able to access his or her creative thinking and to generate a holistic perception of reality. An individual's inner and outer worlds tie his or her inner self to the environment. This orientation suggests a curriculum that highly regards the uniqueness of the human personality.

This curriculum is open to human spirituality, which, as used by such curricularists, refers to the links between a person's inner life and the infinite. Transcendence and spirituality are experienced through quality experiences. As Phenix notes, in such a curriculum reality is experienced as a "single interconnected whole, such that a complete description of any entity

would require the comprehension of every other entity."[82]

Transcendent education is lured by the concept of wholeness or comprehensiveness of experience. Certain content needs to be incorporated into the curriculum, but the stress is on giving the students the opportunity to take a journey, to contemplate on that journey, and to relate that journey to others—past, present, and future. It emphasizes the general dispositions of humans for hope, creativity, awareness, doubt and faith, wonder, awe and reverence.[83] See Curriculum Tips 8-3.

Humanistic curriculum designs have many of the same weaknesses as learner-centered designs. They require of the teacher great skill and competence in dealing with individuals. Moreover, available educational materials are often not appropriate.

One serious charge against this design is that humanists focus on their methods and techniques and do not adequately consider them in light of the consequences for learners. Another criticism leveled at the design concerns its apparently inconsistent emphasis on both the human as unique and on activities that all students experience. In contrast, some say that the design places far too much emphasis on the individual and ignores the needs of the overall society. A final criticism is really of third-force psychology itself. Critics charge that it does not integrate what we know about behaviorism and psychiatry or about cognitive developmental theory. Rather, it seems to splinter our knowledge base about human learning and development.

Problem-centered Designs

The third major type of curriculum design, which is problem-centered, focuses on the problems of living—on the perceived realities of institutional and group life—both for the individual and for society in general. Problem-centered curriculum designs are organized to reinforce cultural traditions and also to address those community and societal needs that are currently unmet. They address individuals' problems as well.

Even though these designs place the individual in a social setting, they are unlike learner-centered designs in a major way. Problem-centered

CURRICULUM TIPS 8-3　The Curriculum Matrix

In designing a curriculum, keep in mind the various levels at which we can consider the content component of the curriculum. The following listing of curriculum dimensions should assist in considering content in depth.

1. Consider the intellectual dimension of the content. This is perhaps the most commonly thought dimension of curriculum. The content selected should stimulate the intellectual development of students.
2. Consider the emotional dimension of the content. We know much less about this dimension, but we are obtaining a better understanding of it as the affective domain of knowledge.
3. Consider the social dimension of the content. The content selected should contribute to students' social development. Content stressing human relations contributes to this dimension.
4. Consider the physical dimension of the content. This is commonly referred to as the psychomotor domain of knowledge. Content should be selected not only to develop physical skills, but also to allow students to become conscious of themselves as physical beings.
5. Consider the aesthetic nature of the content. People have an esthetic nature, yet we currently have little knowledge of the place of esthetics in education.
6. Consider the transcendent or spiritual dimension of the content. This dimension is almost totally excluded from our considerations. We tend to confuse this dimension with formalized religions. This dimension of content does not relate specifically to the rational. But we need to have content that causes students to reflect on the nature of their humanness and to strive to transcend their current levels of knowing and action.

Source: Adapted from Arthur W. Foshay, "The Curriculum Matrix: Transcendence and Mathematics," *Curriculum* (Autumn 1990), pp. 36–46.

designs are planned before the arrival of students. However, problem-centered curricularists realize that, because their concern is with genuine life problems, they will sometimes have to adjust or cater to the concerns and situations of learners.

How a curriculum is organized with this design depends in large part on the nature of the problem areas to be studied. The content selected must be relevant to the problem under consideration. For this reason, the content often cuts across subject boundaries. It must also be based, to a major extent, on the needs, concerns, and abilities of the students. This dual emphasis on both content and the development of learners distinguishes problem-centered designs from the other major types of curriculum designs.

Because problem-centered designs draw on social problems and the needs, interests, and abilities of learners, several variations exist. Some focus on persistent life situations, others center on contemporary social problems, others address areas of living, and some are even concerned with the reconstruction of society. What seems to distinguish these various types is the relative degree of emphasis they place on social needs as opposed to individual needs.[84]

Life-situations Design. Interest in this curriculum design emphasizing life functions or life situations can be traced to the nineteenth century and to Herbert Spencer's writings on a curriculum for complete living. His curriculum emphasized activities that (1) sustain life, (2) enhance life, (3) aid in rearing children, (4) maintain the individual's social and political relations, and (5) enhance leisure, tasks, and feelings.[85] This design, which draws its legitimation from society and its social challenges, was part of the recommendation of the Commission on the Reorganization of Secondary Education, sponsored by NEA in 1918. The commission outlined in its report a curriculum that would deal with the life situations of health, command of the fundamentals, worthy home membership, vocation, citizenship, leisure, and ethical character.

Fundamental to the design are three assumptions. The first is that persistent life situations are crucial to a society's successful functioning and that it makes educational sense to organize a curriculum around them. The second assumption is that students will see direct relevance to what they are studying if the content is organized around aspects of community life. Finally, by having students study social or life situations, they will not only study ways to improve society, but will be directly involved in such improvement.[86]

This design was popularized in the 1930s and 1940s, with several states using the design as a framework for creating curriculum guides. For example, the Virginia State Curriculum developed nine areas of life situations for attention in the schools.

1. Protecting life and health
2. Getting a living
3. Making a home
4. Expressing religious impulses
5. Satisfying the desire for beauty
6. Securing education
7. Cooperating in social and civic action
8. Engaging in recreation
9. Improving material conditions[87]

In 1947, this design was the focus of an entire curriculum textbook entitled *Developing a Curriculum for Modern Living*. The book, authored by Florence Stratemeyer, Hamden Forkner, and Margaret McKim, made the case that society could indeed be the basis upon which to develop a curriculum and that education had to function as a positive social force.

Stratemeyer and her coauthors based their argument for a life-situations design on the fact that the industrial age that was at full maturity had altered the traditional pattern of all aspects of life: economic, social, spiritual, even physical as it related to health. The curriculum had to enable students to function effectively in this new world, to process those life situations common in this highly industrialized society that was not only nationwide but worldwide. To address the challenge, she and her colleagues generated an extensive master list of persistent life situations that students would face and

therefore needed to consider in school before entering the world of work and adult responsibilities. The key points of this curriculum are presented in Table 8-3.

Stratemeyer noted that "above everything else a curriculum developed in the manner described . . . depends on an understanding of individual learners. Their purposes must be sensed, their needs determined."[88] However, she pointed out that not all expressed needs and interests will become part of the curriculum. Some needs and interests would already be met adequately by other institutions in society: the family, the church, scouts, and other community organizations. The school would address those needs not met through these organizations.

One of the strengths of the life-situations design is its focus on the problem-solving procedures for learning. Process and content are effectively integrated into the curricular experience. Some critics point out that the students do not learn much subject matter. However, proponents are quick to counter that the design draws heavily from content, and from traditional content at that. What makes the design unique is that the content is organized in ways that allow students to clearly view problem areas.

Another strong feature of this design is that it utilizes the past and current experiences of learners as a means of getting them to analyze the basic areas of living. In this respect, the design is very different from the experience-centered design, which uses the learners' felt needs and interests as the sole basis for content and experience selection. The life-situations design uses students' existing concerns, as well as pressing immediate problems in the larger society, as a starting point.

The design has definite strengths. It presents subject matter in an integrated form by cutting across the separate subjects and centering on related categories of social life. Because it centers on social problems and personal concerns, it encourages students to learn and apply problem-solving procedures. The linking of subject matter to real situations increases the relevance of the curriculum.

But, like the previous designs, life-situation designs have deficiencies and challenges. Per-

TABLE 8-3 A Curriculum for Modern Living

I. Growth in Individual Capacities	II. Growth in Social Participation	III. Growth in Ability to Deal with Environmental Facts and Forces
A. Situations calling for growth in ability to meet health needs	A. Situations calling for growth in ability to act in person-to-person relationships	A. Situations calling for growth in ability to deal with natural phenomena
1. Satisfying physiological needs	1. Establishing effective social relations with others	1. Dealing with physical phenomena
2. Satisfying emotional and social needs	2. Establishing effective working relations with others	2. Dealing with plant, animal, and insect life
3. Avoiding and caring for illness and injury		3. Using physical and chemical forces
B. Situations calling for growth in ability to use intellectual power	B. Situations calling for growth in ability to participate as a responsible group member	B. Situations calling for growth in ability to deal with technological resources
1. Making ideas clear	1. Deciding when to join a group	1. Using technological resources
2. Understanding the ideas of others	2. Participating as a group member	2. Contributing to technological advances
3. Dealing with quantitative relationships	3. Taking leadership responsibilities	
4. Using effective methods of work		
C. Situations calling for growth in the ability to take responsibility for moral choices	C. Situations calling for growth in ability to act in intergroup relations	C. Situations calling for growth in ability to deal with economic, social, and political structures and forces
1. Determining the nature and extent of individual freedom	1. Working with racial and religious groups	1. Earning a living
2. Determining responsibility to self and others	2. Working with socioeconomic groups	2. Securing goods and services
		3. Providing for social welfare
		4. Molding public opinion
D. Situations calling for growth in ability to meet needs for aesthetic expression and appreciation		5. Participating in local and national government
1. Finding sources of aesthetic satisfaction in oneself		
2. Achieving aesthetic satisfaction through the environment		

Source: Adapted from Florence Stratemeyer, Hamden L. Forkner, and Margaret G. McKim, *Developing a Curriculum for Modern Living* (New York: Teachers College Press, Columbia University, 1947).

haps the greatest challenge is to determine what are the scope and sequence of the essential areas of living. Are the major activities of the current time also going to be the essential activities of future times?

Another criticism of this design has been that it does not adequately expose students to their cultural heritage. Moreover, it tends to indoctrinate youth into the existing conditions and thus perpetuates the social status quo. However, if students are educated to be critical of their social situations, then intelligent processing of the social scene is fostered, rather than adherence to the status quo.

There are always some who point out that the life-situations design cannot be mounted by teachers for they lack adequate preparation for it. Others argue that textbooks and other teaching materials inhibit the implementation of this design. Furthermore, many teachers are uncomfortable with it because it departs too much from their training. Finally, this organization departs from the curricular tradition maintained by colleges and universities.

Core Design.   This particular curriculum design, sometimes called "social functions" core, is carefully planned. It centers on general education and is based on problems arising out of common human activities. There are several variations of core designs. Subject matter core designs, for example, would be classified as subject-centered designs. Areas-of-living core designs are rooted in the progressive education tradition. However, making areas of living the core of the curriculum leaves no doubt about the focus of the curriculum.

This type of core is problem centered rather than learner centered. It is carefully planned before the students arrive, but with the notion that adjustment can be made if necessary. This design is usually taught in a block-time format, whereby two or more normal periods for teaching the core component are scheduled together. One teacher assumes responsibility for this block of time and also manages a counseling function. Although content is part of this design, the common needs, problems, and concerns of learners comprise the central focus.

The focus on problems proceeds in different ways in each core class, but certain characteristics for problem solving are recommended by the advocates of core, as illustrated below. These recommendations make sense today, as they did when core was popularized by Faunce and Bossing.

1. The problem is selected by either the teacher or students.
2. A group consensus is made to determine important problems and interest of the class.
3. Problems are selected on the basis of developed criteria for selection.
4. The problem is clearly stated and defined.
5. Areas of study are decided, including dividing the class by individual and group interests.
6. Needed information is listed and discussed.
7. Resources for obtaining information are listed and discussed.
8. Information is obtained and organized.
9. Information is analyzed and interpreted.
10. Tentative conclusions are stated and tested.
11. A report is presented to the class on an individual or group basis.
12. Conclusions are evaluated.
13. New avenues of exploration toward further problem solving are examined.[89]

The advantages of the core design are that it unifies content, presents subject matter relevant to students, and encourages active processing of information. Furthermore, because it presents subject matter in a relevant form, it fosters intrinsic motivation in students. Alberty and Alberty state that this design makes it possible for students to attack directly problems they consider crucial in the contemporary society. It encourages students to view the community as a laboratory for learning.[90] Because the design encourages cooperative learning, its advocates claim it fosters democratic practices in the classroom.

But, the design has weaknesses, too. Perhaps the major one, which may also be its strength, is that it departs too significantly from the traditional curriculum. People attack it as ignoring the fundamentals. It also requires materials that are hard to find. Conventional textbooks, in fact, do not support this core design. Nor is it commonly used because many educators have not accepted the idea that general education is worthwhile. Furthermore, it requires an exceptional teacher, well versed in subject matter, problem-solving skills, and general knowledge.

Social Problems and Reconstructionist Designs. Whereas some educators, such as Stratemeyer, have urged that children's interests should guide the selection of curriculum content and experiences, other educators still feel that the curriculum should address contemporary social problems and even social action projects aimed at reconstructing society. Many such educators consider themselves to be in the social orientation camp, or what some have called social reconstructionism. These individuals, interested in the relation of the curriculum to the social, political, and economic development of society, believe that through the curriculum educators will effect social change and ultimately create a more just society. Interestingly, even though many of the schools' current critics are of this opinion, aspects of reconstructionism actually first appeared in the 1920s and 1930s.

Perhaps this concern for reconstructionism, or social reconstruction, was a response to the Great Depression. To many reconstructionists, the problems lay with the schools, as did the solutions. Some critics during this period classified the reconstructionists as "leftists" or communists who were plotting the overthrow of the government by their urgings for actions in the classroom.

George Counts believed that society had to be totally reorganized to meet the common good. The times demanded a new social order and the schools should play a major role in such a redesign. Counts presented some of his thinking on this issue of new social order in a speech entitled "Dare Progressive Education Be Progressive?"[91] He challenged the Progressive Education Association to broaden its thinking beyond the current social structure. He accused its members of only advocating curricula that would continue the dominance of the middle class and its privileged positions. Counts expanded on his call

for a reconstructed society in his classic book, *Dare the Schools Build a New Social Order.* He argued that if educators would accept the challenge they could involve students in a curriculum for participating in a more just and equitable society.[92]

Harold Rugg also believed that the school should engage children in a critical analysis of society in order to improve it. Rugg's criticisms were directed to those who favored child-centered schools. He stated that their laissez-faire approach to curriculum development only produced chaos, in which subjects were disjointed and unarticulated. "Rarely are they designed in the light of a review of a careful record of the program of earlier years and of the most probably effective year-programs to follow it in the school career of the child."[93] In the 1940s, Rugg observed that the Progressive Education Association still overemphasized the child. All seven purposes of the association referred to the child, and not one took into consideration "man's crucial social conditions and problems."[94]

Theodore Brameld, a spokesperson for the reconstructionists' view well into the 1950s, argued that the reconstructionists were committed to facilitating the emergence of a new culture. The times demanded a new social order; the existing society showed signs of decay: poverty, crime, racial conflict, unemployment, political oppression, and a wasting of the environment.[95] Brameld also believed that the school should help the individual to develop as a social being and as a skilled planner of the social reality. The individual must come to learn that he or she must satisfy his or her personal needs through social consensus. The group would be paramount. The schools not only had this obligation to educate children for the good of society; they also needed to point out the urgency for the change.

The fact that reconstructionists stress the notion of change and the needs to plan for tomorrow brings in mind a series of pressing questions raised by two other reconstructionists, Virgil Clift and Harold Shane, as they explore new directions for American educators and new decisions for curriculum specialists.

1. What policies shall govern our future use of technology?
2. At a global level, what shall be our goals, and how can we reach them?
3. What shall we identify as the "good life"?
4. How shall we deploy our limited resources in meeting the needs of various groups of people?
5. How shall we equalize opportunity, and how shall we reduce the gap between the "haves" and "have-nots"?
6. How can we maximize the value of mass media, especially television?
7. What shall be made of psychological, chemical, and electronic approaches to behavior modification?
8. What steps can we take to ensure the integrity of our political, economic, and military systems?
9. What, if anything, are we willing to relinquish, and in what order?
10. And, what honorable compromises and solutions shall we make as we contemplate the above questions?[96]

These questions deal with social issues that are generic—meaning they were relevant yesterday, they are relevant today, and they will be relevant tomorrow, and they are relevant for most school subjects and grade levels. The way we deal with these issues or problems will make the difference about the society we are and will become.

The social reconstructionist curriculum has the primary purpose of engaging the learner in analyzing the many severe problems confronting humankind. However, the exact content and objectives are to be decided by those who actually create such a curriculum. The curriculum is to engage students in a critical analysis of the local, national, and international community. Also, attention is to be given to the political practices of the business and government groups and their impact on the economic realities of the workforce. Such a curriculum must propose industrial and political changes that will ultimately modify the social fabric of the nation and perhaps the world.

There are still curricularists who believe the society to be unjust, who presume that privilege is not equitably distributed. Few of these current individuals would call themselves reconstructionists, but they do consider that the curriculum and its design should address the key social problems of current society and impart in students a commitment for resolution of these problems. Michael Apple speaks of a curriculum that would address the issues of race, gender, and the poor. He speaks to the issue of the curriculum being designed so that the social inequities of society are not reproduced.[97]

While the reconstructionists and the present-day reconceptualists both believe that the curriculum should provide students with those learnings requisite for adjusting the social, economic, and political realities, there are other curricularists who, while being less politically and philosophically motivated, are still interested in designing curricula that address social problems. Many of the drug- and AIDS-related education programs can be classed in this social problems design. Courses that deal with conservation or various environmental issues can also be categorized as following the social problems design.

CONCLUSION

Curriculum design is more than just making sure that the parts of a curriculum are neatly organized in a document. Design is a complex phenomenon requiring of educators careful attention so that the curriculum conceived will have merit and will succeed in getting students to learn those concepts, attitudes, and skills considered worthwhile and essential.

The issue of design is likely to continue to draw the attention of curriculum specialists and generalists. Designing a curriculum is really dealing with a vision, which most educators have but don't always apply. The concepts related to design help them put flesh on their visions and to increase their probability of becoming reality.

Various design options exist from which curricularists can select—subject centered, learner centered, and problem centered. Each of these, as has been noted in this chapter, has a history and philosophy associated with it. Each has its advocates. Each, when imple-

mented, gives the school a particular character. However, many schools meld these designs, often so much that it is almost impossible to determine just what the curriculum design is. Table 8-4 presents an overview of the major designs.

Advocates of each design face the same design decisions as advocates of all the others.

Regardless of the particular design, educators must be concerned with the scope and sequence of the curriculum elements. They must also pay attention to articulation, continuity, and balance. Overall, their understanding of curriculum design is necessary knowledge for the building of a curriculum, the topic of the next chapter.

ENDNOTES

1. George J. Posner and Alan N. Rudnitsky, *Course Design,* 2nd ed. (New York: Longman, 1990).

2. H. H. Gills, S. P. McCutchen, and A. N. Zechiel, *Exploring the Curriculum* (New York: Harper, 1942), p. 2.

3. Ralph W. Tyler, conversation with one of the authors, April 16, 1986.

4. Hilda Taba, *Curriculum Development: Theory and Practice* (New York: Harcourt, Brace, 1962).

5. Posner and Rudnitsky, *Course Design.*

6. Ronald C. Doll, *Curriculum Improvement: Decision Making and Process,* 8th ed. (Boston: Allyn and Bacon, 1992).

7. Taba, *Curriculum Development: Theory and Practice,* p. 423.

8. Doll, *Curriculum Improvement.*

9. Ralph W. Tyler, *Basic Principles of Curriculum and Instruction* (Chicago: University of Chicago Press, 1949).

10. Elliott W. Eisner, "Aesthetic Modes of Knowing," in E. W. Eisner, ed., *Learning and Teaching the Ways of Knowing,* Eighty-fourth Yearbook of the National Society for the Study of Education, Part II (Chicago: University of Chicago Press, 1985), pp. 23–36.

11. William E. Doll, "Teaching a Post-Modern Curriculum," in J. T. Sears, and J. D. Marshall, eds., *Teaching and Thinking about Curriculum* (New York: Teachers College Press, Columbia University, 1990), pp. 39–47; Henry A. Giroux, ed., *Postmodernism, Feminism, and Cultural Politics* (Albany, N.Y.: State University of New York Press, 1991).

12. John Naisbitt and Patricia Aburdene, *Megatrends 2000* (New York: William Morrow, 1990).

13. Doll, *Curriculum Improvement.*

14. Dwayne E. Huebner, "Spirituality and Knowing," in E. W. Eisner, ed., *Learning and Teaching the Ways of Knowing,* p. 163.

15. Francis P. Hunkins, *Curriculum Development: Program Improvement* (Columbus, Ohio: Merrill, 1980).

16. Arno A. Bellack, "What Knowledge Is of Most Worth?" *High School Journal* (February 1965), pp. 318–332.

17. John D. Bransford and Nancy J. Vye, "A Perspective on Cognitive Research and Its Implications for Instruction," in Lauren B. Resnick and Leopold E. Klopfer, eds., *Toward the Thinking Curriculum: Current Cognitive Research,* 1989 Yearbook (Alexandria, Va: Association for Supervision and Curriculum Development, 1989), pp. 173–205.

18. Mark Johnson, *The Body in the Mind* (Chicago: University of Chicago Press, 1987); James Pusch, "Metaphor and Teaching," *Educational Forum* (Winter 1992), pp. 185–192.

19. Jerome S. Bruner, *The Process of Education* (Cambridge, Mass.: Harvard University Press, 1959).

20. Robert S. Zais, *Curriculum: Principles and Foundations* (New York: Harper & Row, 1976).

21. R. Tyler, *Basic Principles of Curriculum and Instruction.*

22. Doll, *Curriculum Improvement.*

23. Peter F. Oliva, *Developing the Curriculum.* 3rd ed. (New York: Harper Collins, 1992).

24. J. Galen Saylor, William M. Alexander, and Arthur J. Lewis, *Planning for Better Teaching and Learning,* 4th ed. (New York: Holt, Rinehart, 1981), p. 251.

25. Taba, *Curriculum Development: Theory and Practice,* p. 223.

26. Ibid.

27. John Piaget, *The Psychology of Intelligence* (Paterson, N.J.: Littlefield, Adams, 1960).

28. B. Othanel Smith, William O. Stanley, and Harlan J. Shores, *Fundamentals of Curriculum Development,* rev. ed. (New York: Harcourt, Brace, 1957).

29. Gerald J. Posner and Kenneth A. Strike, "A Categorization Scheme for Principles of Sequencing Content," *Review of Educational Research* (Fall 1976), pp. 401–406.

30. Tyler, *Basic Principles of Curriculum and Instruction,* p. 86.

31. Bruner, *The Process of Education,* p. 52.

32. John I. Goodlad, *Planning and Organizing for Teaching* (Washington, D.C.: National Education Association, 1963), p. 29.

TABLE 8-4 Overview of Major Curriculum Designs

DESIGN	CURRICULAR EMPHASIS	UNDERLYING PHILOSOPHY	SOURCE	SPOKESPERSON
SUBJECT CENTERED				
Subject design	Separate subjects	Essentialism, perennialism	Science, knowledge	Harris, Hutchins
Discipline design	Scholarly disciplines (mathematics, biology, psychology, etc.)	Essentialism, perennialism	Knowledge, science	Bruner, Phenix, Schwab, Taba
Broad fields design	Interdisciplinary subjects and scholarly disciplines	Essentialism, progressivism	Knowledge, society	Broudy, Dewey
Correlation design	Separate subjects, disciplines linked while keeping identities of each	Progressivism, essentialism	Knowledge	Alberty and Alberty
Process design	Procedural knowledge of various disciplines; generic ways of information processing, thinking	Progressivism	Psychology, knowledge	Adams, Beyer, Dewey, Papert
LEARNER CENTERED				
Child-centered design	Child's interests and needs	Progressivism	Child	Dewey, Kilpatrick, Parker
Experience-centered design	Experiences and interests of child	Progressivism	Child	Dewey, Rugg and Shumaker
Radical design	Experiences and interests of child	Reconstructionism	Child, society	Freire, Habermans, Holt, Illich
Humanistic design	Experiences, interests, needs of person, and of the group	Reconstructionism, existentialism	Psychology, child, society	Combs, Fantini, Maslow, Rogers
PROCESS CENTERED				
Life-situation design	Life (social) problems	Reconstructionism	Society	Spencer, Stratemeyer, Forkner, and McKim
Core design	Social problems	Progressivism, reconstructionism	Child, society	Alberty and Alberty, Faunce and Bossing
Social problems, reconstructionist design	Focus on society and its problems	Reconstructionism	Society, eternal truths	Apple, Brameld, Counts, Rugg, Shane

33. Doll, *Curriculum Improvement.*

34. Oliva, *Developing the Curriculum,* 3rd ed.

35. Allan C. Ornstein, "Textbook Instruction: Processes and Strategies," *NASSP Bulletin* (December 1989), pp. 105–111.

36. Henry C. Morrison, *The Curriculum of the Common School* (Chicago: University of Chicago Press, 1940).

37. Christopher J. Lucas, *Challenge and Choice in Contemporary Education* (New York: Macmillan, 1976).

38. Robert M. Hutchins, *The Higher Learning in America* (New Haven: Yale University Press, 1936).

39. John Dewey, *Experience and Education* (New York: Macmillan, 1938).

40. Tyler, *Basic Principles of Curriculum and Instruction.*

41. Arthur R. King and John A. Brownell, *The Curriculum and the Disciplines of Knowledge* (New York: Wiley, 1966).

42. Taba, *Curriculum Development: Theory and Practice.*

43. Harry S. Broudy, "Becoming Educated in Contemporary Society," in K. D. Benne and S. Tozer, eds., *Society as Educator in an Age of Transition,* Eighty-sixth Yearbook of the National Society for the Study of Education, Part II (Chicago: University of Chicago Press, 1987), pp. 247–268.

44. Bruner, *The Process of Education,* p. 8.

45. Ibid., p. 33.

46. Patricia Arlin, "Piagetian Tasks as Predictors of Reading and Math Readiness in Grades K–1," *Journal of Educational Psychology* (October 1981), pp. 712–721; Anita M. Meehan, "A Meta-analysis of Sex Differences in Formal Operational Thought," *Child Development* (June 1984), pp. 1110–1124.

47. Elliot W. Eisner, *The Educational Imagination,* 3rd ed. (New York: Macmillan, 1993); Daniel Tanner and Laurel Tanner, *The History of Curriculum* (New York: Macmillan, 1990).

48. Philip Phenix, *Realms of Meaning* (New York: McGraw-Hill, 1964).

49. Harry S. Broudy, B. O. Smith, and Joe R. Burnett, *Democracy and Excellence in American Secondary Education* (Chicago: Rand McNally, 1964).

50. Gary D. Fenstermacher and John I. Goodlad, eds., *Individual Difference and the Common Curriculum,* Eighty-Second Yearbook of the National Society for the Study of Education, Part I (Chicago: University of Chicago Press, 1983); Gary D. Fenstermacher and Jonas F. Soltis, *Approaches to Teaching,* 2nd ed. (New York: Teachers College Press, Columbia University, 1992).

51. Allan C. Ornstein, *Secondary and Middle School Teaching Methods.* (New York: Harper Collins, 1992).

52. Harold B. Alberty and Elsie J. Alberty, *Reorganizing the High School Curriculum,* 3rd ed. (New York: Macmillan, 1962).

53. Allan A. Glatthorn, *Curriculum Leadership* (Glenview, Ill.: Scott, Foresman, 1987); Gene D. Shepherd and William B. Ragan, *Modern Elementary Curriculum,* 7th ed. (San Diego: Harcourt Brace Jovanovich, 1992).

54. Barry K. Beyer, *Practical Strategies for the Teaching of Thinking* (Boston: Allyn and Bacon, 1987); Beyer, *Teaching Thinking Skills* (Boston, Mass.: Allyn and Bacon, 1991).

55. Marilyn J. Adams, "Thinking Skills Curricula: Their Promise and Progress," *Educational Psychologist,* (Winter 1989), pp. 25–77.

56. Ibid.

57. Robert J. Marzano and Daisy E. Arredondo, *Tactics for Thinking* (Aurora, Colo.: Mid-continent Regional Educational Laboratory, 1986).

58. Allan C. Ornstein, "Making Effective Use of Computer Technology," *NASSP Bulletin* (March 1992), pp. 27–33.

59. Seymour Papert, "Computer Criticism vs. Technocentric Thinking," *Educational Researcher* (January-February 1987), pp. 22–30.

60. Taba, *Curriculum Development: Theory and Practice,* p. 401.

61. Francis W. Parker, *Talks on Pedagogics* (New York: E. L. Kellogg, 1894).

62. John Dewey, *The Child and the Curriculum* (Chicago: University of Chicago Press, 1902).

63. Frederick G. Bonser, *Life Needs and Education* (New York: Teachers College Press, Columbia University, 1932); Charles Prosser, *Life Adjustment Education for Every Youth* (Washington, D.C.: U.S. Government Printing Office, 1951); and Florence B. Stratemeyer et al., *Developing a Curriculum for Modern Living* (New York: Teachers College Press, Columbia University, 1947).

64. William H. Kilpatrick, "The Project Method," *Teachers College Record* (September 1918), pp. 319–335; Kilpatrick, *Foundations of Method* (New York: Macmillan, 1925).

65. Quest International, Granville, Ohio.

66. Harold Rugg and Ann Shumaker, *The Child-Centered School* (New York: World Book, 1928), p. 118.

67. John Dewey, *Experience and Education* (New York: Macmillan, 1938).

68. Reginald D. Archambault, ed., *John Dewey on Education.* (Chicago: University of Chicago Press, 1964).

69. Daniel Tanner and Laurel Tanner, *Curriculum Development: Theory into Practice,* 2nd ed. (New York: Macmillan, 1980).

70. Dewey, *The Child and the Curriculum.*

71. John Holt, *How Children Fail* (New York: Pitman, 1964); Ivan Illich, *Deschooling Society* (New York: Harper & Row, 1971).

72. Paulo Freire, *Pedagogy of the Oppressed* (New York: Herder and Herder, 1970); Freire, *The Politics of Education* (South Hadley, Mass.: Bergin and Garvey, 1985).

73. Robert Young, *A Critical Theory of Education* (New York: Teachers College Press, Columbia University, 1990).

74. N. Horkneimer, "On Tradition and Critical Theory," in P. Connerton, ed, *Critical Sociology, Harmondsworth* (New York: Penguin, 1976), p. 244.

75. Arthur W. Combs, ed., *Perceiving, Behaving, Becoming* (Washington, D.C.: Association for Supervision and Curriculum Development, Yearbook, 1962).

76. Arthur W. Combs, "What Can Man Become?" in Combs, ed., *Perceiving, Behaving, Becoming,* pp. 1–8.

77. Louise M. Berman and Jessie A. Roderick, eds., *Feeling, Valuing, and the Art of Growing: Insights into the Affective* (Washington, D.C.: Association for Supervision and Curriculum Development, 1977). Also see Louise M. Berman, et al., *Toward Curriculum for Being* (New York: State University of New York Press, 1992).

78. Abraham H. Maslow, *Toward a Psychology of Being* (New York: D. Van Nostrand, 1962).

79. Carl Rogers, "Toward Becoming a Fully Functioning Person," in Combs, ed., *Perceiving, Behaving, Becoming,* pp. 21–33.

80. Gloria A. Castillo, *Left-Handed Teaching,* 2nd ed. (New York: Holt, Rinehart, 1970); Gerald Weinstein and Mario D. Fantini, *Toward Humanistic Education: A Curriculum of Affect* (New York: Praeger, 1970).

81. Ibid.

82. Philip H. Phenix. "Transcendence and the Curriculum," in Eisner and Vallance, eds., *Conflicting Conceptions of Curriculum,* p. 123.

83. Francis P. Hunkins, "Sailing: Celebrating and Educating Self," *Educational Forum* (Summer 1992), pp. 1–9.

84. Jacqueline C. Mancall, Erica K. Lodish, and Judith Springer, "Searching Across the Curriculum," *Phi Delta Kappan* (March 1992), pp. 526–528.

85. Herbert Spencer, *Education: Intellectual, Moral, and Physical* (New York: Appleton 1860).

86. Saylor et al. *Planning for Better Teaching and Learning.*

87. Taba, *Curriculum Development, Theory and Practice,* p. 398.

88. Florence B. Stratemeyer, Hamden L. Forkner, and Margaret G. McKim, *Developing a Curriculum for Modern Living* (New York: Teachers College Press, Columbia University, 1947), p. 300.

89. Faunce and Bossing, *Developing the Core Curriculum.*

90. Alberty and Alberty, *Reorganizing the High School Curriculum.*

91. George S. Counts, "Dare Progressive Education Be Progressive?" *Progressive Education* (April 1932), p. 259.

92. George S. Counts, *Dare the Schools Build a New Social Order?* (Yonkers, N.Y.: World Book, 1932).

93. Harold Rugg, *Culture and Education in America* (New York: Harcourt, 1931), pp. 302–303.

94. Harold Rugg, *Foundations for American Education* (New York: Harcourt, 1947), p. 745.

95. Theodore Brameld, *Toward a Reconstructed Philosophy of Education* (New York: Holt, Rinehart and Winston, 1956).

96. Virgil A. Clift and Harold G. Shane, "The Future, Social Decisions, and Educational Change in Secondary Schools," in W. Van Til, ed., *Issues in Secondary Education,* Seventy-fifth Yearbook of the National Society for the Study of Education, Part II (Chicago: University of Chicago Press, 1976), pp. 295–315.

97. Michael W. Apple, "Conservative Agendas and Progressive Possibilities: Understanding the Wider Politics of Curriculum and Teaching," *Education and Urban Society* (May 1991), pp. 279–291.

CHAPTER 9

CURRICULUM DEVELOPMENT

Focusing Questions

1. *How would you describe the technical-scientific approach to curriculum development?*
2. *What roles did Bobbitt and Charters play within the field of curriculum development?*
3. *In what ways are the various models of the technical-scientific approach alike?*
4. *Define the nontechnical approach to curriculum development.*
5. *What important stages help define the naturalistic model?*
6. *How does the postpositivist model of curriculum enhance the idea of intuition and/or imagination in education?*
7. *Which components are central to the curriculum development process?*
8. *Who are the key participants in developing a curriculum? Should the roles of students, parents, and community residents be increased?*

Successful education requires careful planning. Educators have come to recognize that without planning, confusion and conflict are likely to characterize curriculum activity. Educators originate curriculum development strategies. They formulate master plans prior to creating or implementing a program for students. How they conceptualize the plan will be influenced by their awareness of and sensitivity to issues—both present and anticipated. Certainly, few people can construct a curriculum without giving some thought to goals; to content; to learning experiences, methods, and materials; and to evaluation.

The need to plan effective curricula is obvious; the difficulty, however, is that there are various ways to define curriculum development. Also, several curriculum designs dictate what factors should receive attention: subject matter, students, or society. Also, it is difficult to be precise or to plan what is not defined with any universality. Not everyone agrees what curriculum is or what is involved in curriculum development. We present here a broad definition to allow

the different views and interpretations to coexist with ours—which posits that curriculum development draws on the principles (usually technical or scientific) and consists of those processes (humanistic and artistic) that allow schools and school people to realize certain educational goals.

Ideally, all those who are to be affected by a curriculum should be involved in the process of development. Although there are numerous models from which to choose, most models can be classified as either technical-scientific or nontechnical-nonscientific. These two general organizers were presented in Chapter 1, which identified specific curriculum approaches. Technical-scientific approaches were (1) behavioral, (2) managerial, (3) systems, and (4) academic. The two nontechnical-nonscientific approaches were (1) humanistic and (2) reconceptualist.

Although these specific approaches are appropriate, in this chapter we refer to the more global categories. As we pointed out in Chapter 1, classifying an approach as nontechnical or nonscientific does not mean presenting it in a negative manner. Rather, it means contrasting the two basic postures. Persons who believe in some subject matter curriculum design usually advocate the technical-scientific approach to curriculum development. Those individuals who favor a learner-centered design frequently advocate the nontechnical-nonscientific approach. Problem-centered designs can fall within either approach.

TECHNICAL-SCIENTIFIC APPROACH

The technical-scientific approach to education and to curriculum is a way of thinking. To those who believe in the approach, it is not a vehicle for dehumanizing education, but rather a way of planning curricula to optimize students' learning and to allow them to increase their output. According to this point of view, curriculum development is a plan or blueprint for structuring the learning environment and coordinating the elements of personnel, materials, and equipment.

A technical-scientific view can enable us to comprehend curriculum from a macro or broad view and to understand it as a complex unity of parts organized to serve a common function—the education of individuals. It also allows us to have a plan in mind.

The technical-scientific approach requires that educators use a rational approach to accomplish their tasks and that they believe that it is possible to outline systematically those procedures that will facilitate the creation of curricula. The various models employ a means-end paradigm that suggests that the more rigorous the means, the more likely the desired ends will be attained. Followers of this approach indicate that such a systematically designed program can be evaluated. However, others question just how precise the evaluation can be.

The various technical-scientific models exhibit what James Macdonald would call a "technological" rationality as opposed to an "aesthetic rationality." Macdonald notes that there is a press for this rationality in the way schools are organized.[1] Persons who have this orientation tend to believe that there is a large body of educational knowledge and that efforts should be made to ensure that students are presented with opportunities to gain such knowledge. Macdonald wrote that those with a technological consciousness

prize optimum growth, maximum efficiency, and effectiveness of the system in delivering education.

History of Technical-Scientific Approach

Students of the history of curriculum development have located the origin and substance of the technical-scientific model in the schools' attempt, at the turn of the century, to adapt the principles of bureaucracy to methods that could be considered scientific. Early educators reasoned that using empirical methods (surveys and analysis of human conduct) would answer the curriculum question: What shall be taught? The push for a science of curriculum making paralleled the rise of science—biology, physics, and chemistry—during the nineteenth and twentieth centuries and also the notion of "machine theory"—time and motion studies—evolving in the world of business and industry. Scientific principles were also being applied to agriculture, manufacturing, and government, as well as to other phases of practical life. In education, especially in curriculum, these models evolved with the work of Bobbitt and Charters.

Bobbitt and Charters. Bobbitt compared creating a curriculum to the task of constructing a railroad. Once the general route is planned, the railroad builder then gets into the particulars of engaging in surveying and eventually laying of track. Developing a curriculum is essentially like planning the route that a person must travel from infancy "to the goals of his growth, his culture, and his special abilities."[2] The educator must, like the railroad engineer, "take a broad overview of the entire field . . . [see] the major factors in perspective and in relation." In doing this, a general plan for the educational program can be formulated. To this general plan could be added specific "surveying actions [for] determining content and experiences necessary for the [learner]."[3]

For Bobbitt the first task of curriculum development was to "discover the activities which ought to make up the lives of students and along with these, the abilities and personal qualities necessary for proper performance."[4] From this activity analysis, educational objectives were derived. Bobbitt was insistent that the analysis address the actual activities of humans being sure to consider the broad range of human experiences. Bobbitt's contemporary, Weret Charters, was also a believer in activity analysis. However, Charters noted that "changes in the curriculum are always preceded by modifications in our conception of the aim of education."[5] The selection of school content and experiences was influenced by our aims, the ideals, we wish to address.

Charters wanted educators to connect aims or ideals with activities that individuals performed. Charters suggested a sequence of steps for curriculum construction that is still rather timely, showing the foundational impact he had on the thinking of his contemporaries and subsequent generations of curriculum decision makers. He noted that curriculum construction had four steps: "(1) selecting objectives, (2) dividing them into ideals and activities, (3) analyzing them to the limits of working units, and (4) collecting methods of achievement."[6]

For Charters, philosophy supplied the ideals that were to serve as objectives and standards. He noted that the curriculum could contain both primary and derived subjects. *Primary subjects* were those found directly within the items of a job analysis, derived from other subjects. Thus educators looking at the task of being a weather reporter would note that the activity required one to fill out various types of reports, indicating that report writing would be included under the subject of English. The job activity of weather reporting, while showing a need for report writing, also required a knowledge of physics and mathematics. Charters defined such information as comprising *derived subjects,* noting that "these are service subjects which are important not because they are directly useful in the performance of activities, but because they are derived from material which has practical service value."[7]

These two men firmly established the scientific movement in curriculum making. They pointed out that curriculum development is a process that will, if followed, result in a meaningful program for pupils. They initiated a concern for the relation of goals, objectives, and activities, pointing out that the selection of goals is a normative process, whereas the selection of objectives and activities is empirical and scientific. They indicated that curricular activity can be planned and systematically studied and evaluated.

Through the efforts of men like Bobbitt and Charters, concern grew for curriculum as a field of study. The field achieved independent status upon the establishment of the Society for Curriculum Study in 1932. In 1938, Teachers College at Columbia University established a department of curriculum and teaching. For the next 20 years, Teachers College dominated the field of curriculum, even surpassing the earlier influence of the University of Chicago.

The Tyler Model: Four Basic Principles. Without doubt, Tyler's is one of the best known, technical-scientific models. In 1949, Tyler published *Basic Principles of Curriculum and Instruction,* in which he outlined a rationale for examining the problems of curriculum and instruction.[8] He mentioned that those involved in curriculum inquiry must try to define the (1) purposes of the school, (2) educational experiences related to the purposes, (3) organization of these experiences, and (4) evaluation of the purposes.

By "purposes," Tyler was referring to objectives. He indicated that curriculum planners should identify these general objectives by gathering data from three sources: the subject matter, the learners, and the society. After identifying numerous general objectives, the curriculum planners were to refine them by filtering them through two screens, the philosophy of the school and the psychology of learning. What resulted from such screening were specific instructional objectives. Note, however, that even though Tyler used the term *instructional objectives* he was not advocating the narrow behavioral objectives that have been advocated in recent years.

Tyler then discussed how to select educational experiences that would allow the attainment of objectives. Learning experiences had to take into account both the previous experience and the perceptions that the learner brings to a situation. Also, the experiences were to be selected in light of what educators know about learning and human development.

Tyler next talked about the organization and sequencing of these experiences. He purported that the ordering of the experiences had to be somewhat systematic so as to produce a maximum cumulative effect. He thought that organizing elements, such as ideas, concepts, values, and skills, should be woven as threads into the curriculum fabric. These key elements could serve as organizers and means and methods of instruction, and they could relate different learning experiences among different subjects. The ideas, concepts, values, and skills could also link content within particular subjects.

Tyler's last principle deals with evaluating the effectiveness of planning and actions. Tyler considered evaluation to be important in curriculum development. He realized that it was necessary if educators were to find out whether the learning experiences actually produced the intended results. Also, it was important to determine whether the program was effective or ineffective. An evaluation should relate to all the objectives.

Although Tyler did not display his model of curriculum development graphically, several other people have. The authors' diagram of this procedure follows in Figure 9-1.

The Taba Model: Grass-roots Rationale. Hilda Taba believed that those who teach curriculum should participate in developing it. She advocated what has been called the grass-roots approach,[9] a model whose steps or stages are similar to Tyler's. Although Tyler did not advocate that his model only be employed by persons in the central office, educators during the early days of curriculum making thought that the central authorities really had the knowledge for creating curricula. This was the top-down or what some have called the administrative or line-staff model. Ideas from curriculum experts were frequently given to teachers to develop, and then administrators supervised the teachers to ensure that the ideas were implemented.

Taba felt that the administrative model was really in the wrong order. The curriculum should be designed by the users of the program. Teachers should begin the process by creating specific teaching-learning units for their students. She advocated that teachers take an inductive approach to curriculum development—starting with specifics and building to a general design—as opposed to the more traditional deductive approach—starting with the general design and working toward the specifics.

Taba noted seven major steps to her grass-roots model in which teachers would have major input:

1. *Diagnosis of needs.* The teacher (curriculum designer) starts the process by identifying the

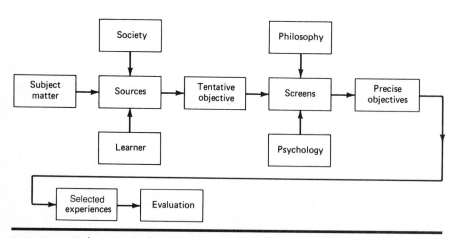

FIGURE 9-1 Tyler's Curriculum Development Model

needs of the students for whom the curriculum is to be planned.

2. *Formulation of objectives.* After the teacher has identified needs that require attention, he or she specifies objectives to be accomplished.

3. *Selection of content.* The objectives selected or created suggest the subject matter or content of the curriculum. Not only should objectives and content match, but also the validity and significance of the content chosen needs to be determined.

4. *Organization of content.* A teacher cannot just select content, but must organize it in some type of sequence, taking into consideration the maturity of the learners, their academic achievement, and their interests.

5. *Selection of learning experiences.* Content must be presented to pupils and pupils must engage the content. At this point, the teacher's instructional methods involve the students with the content.

6. *Organization of learning activities.* Just as content must be sequenced and organized, so must the learning activities. Often the sequence of the learning activities is determined by the content. But the teacher needs to keep in mind the particular students whom he or she will be teaching.

7. *Evaluation and means of evaluation.* The curriculum planner must determine just what objectives have been accomplished. Evaluation procedures need to be considered by the students and teachers.

Taba's model has much merit. Nonetheless, according to some educators, putting such an effort into a grass-roots framework weakens it. Robert Zais maintains that the primary weakness is that it applies the concept of participatory democracy to a highly technical, complex, and specialized process. This does not mean that teachers cannot be involved—indeed, they must if curricula are to be actually used in the classroom. It does mean, however, that a "one person-one vote" rationale will not guarantee effective curricula.[10] Also, the grass-roots design assumes that teachers have the expertise and, perhaps more importantly, the time to engage in such extensive curricular activity. However, we do need to recognize that the grass-roots approach has made it

abundantly clear that a broad base of involvement is essential for curriculum decision making.

Curriculum making requires compromise among administrators from the central office, supervisors from the local school, and teachers, students, and community members. Traditionally, the central office staff is charged with directing those actions that enable the various participators to engage in curriculum development. In a nontraditional approach, members of the community and teaching profession are given primary responsibility for developing the curriculum.

Saylor and Alexander Model: Planning Process. Saylor and Alexander presented a systematic approach to curriculum development.

1. *Goals, objectives, and domains.* Curriculum developers start by specifying the major goals and objectives they wish to address. Objectives are organized within a curriculum domains. There are four major domains that should receive attention: personal development, human relations, continued learning skills, and specialization.

The goals, objectives, and domains selected evolve from careful consideration of the views and demands of the community, the legal requirements of the state, research findings, and the philosophical views of the curriculum specialists.

2. *Curriculum design.* Once this first major step has been accomplished, the curriculum planners next decide on the content, its organization, and appropriate learning opportunities. The manner of delivering these learning opportunities and tying them into the particular domain is also considered. Philosophical views are taken into consideration. Will the curriculum be designed to emphasize the academic disciplines, the learner, or the needs of society?

3. *Curriculum implementation.* When the curriculum design has been decided upon and created, the teachers create instructional plans; that is, they implement the curriculum. Teachers select the methods and materials to use to help the students learn the content.

4. *Curriculum evaluation.* This is the final stage in the model. At this stage, curriculum planners and teachers choose from numerous evaluation techniques those that will furnish an accurate picture of the value and success of the curriculum and its delivery. Evaluation should focus on the curriculum plan, the quality of the instruction, and the learning behaviors of the students. Through such comprehensive evaluation, curriculum developers determine whether to keep the program, modify it, or discard it.[11] The overall process is depicted in Figure 9-2.

It should be noted that once goals have been determined, the faculty commences either to develop a curriculum from the ground up or to begin searching for existing materials or programs that might be adapted for use in the particular school. Rather than creating a master curriculum plan, schools often engage in locating material, usually published, that will address their goals and the problem(s) that has been identified.

The staff may or may not pilot test the materials selected to ascertain their effectiveness in addressing the problem. Once adjustments are made, the program is implemented in the school or district. Afterward, the staff should engage in formative evaluation. Data from such evaluation enable those involved in the curriculum process to monitor the program and to gather information that will be useful in modifying the program. After the program has been in place, the staff might initiate summative evaluation to determine if the program has indeed addressed the perceived problem and whether it should now be institutionalized. If all goes well, the program becomes part of the regular curriculum.[12] See Curriculum Tips 9-1.

Hunkins's Decision-Making Model. Hunkins's model, another technical-scientific example, has seven major stages: curriculum conceptualization

and legitimization; diagnosis; content selection; experience selection; implementation; evaluation; and maintenance.[13] A schema of the model is illustrated in Figure 9-3.

The model represents the essential stages of decision making requisite for developing educational programs. The initial stage, *curriculum conceptualization and legitimization,* makes the model somewhat unique. In this stage, decision makers deal with the conceptualization of the concepts of the curriculum. Just what is the nature of this curriculum that is about to be developed? What are its key components? What are the possible ways in which these components can be designed, or put into a relation with each other? Often, schools begin curriculum development assuming that all parties involved have the same conception of curriculum. Here, the needs of students must be carefully defined, and the curriculum being suggested must be legitimated in light of the needs.

The second stage of the model, *curriculum diagnosis,* involves two major tasks: translating needs into causes and generating goals and objectives from the needs. In some instances, an identified need is caused not by the curriculum void, but by the nonteaching of that curriculum by teachers. Rather than generate a new program, what might be required is an in-service program for teachers to make them committed to and comfortable with the program already in place. When a new curriculum is judged as appropriate for addressing the needs of students, then goals and objectives are generated to serve as guidelines, and sometimes as statements of expected learning outcomes. Such goals and objectives serve as frameworks for determining content, the next stage in the model.

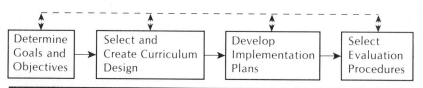

FIGURE 9-2 Saylor and Alexander's View of Curriculum Development.

Source: Adapted from J. Galen and William M. Alexander, *Planning Curriculum for Schools* (New York: Holt, Rinehart, 1974).

CURRICULUM TIPS 9-1   Steps Used in Planning Curricula

There is a commonness to most technical-scientific and top-down approaches to curriculum development. The sameness results from a certain logic implicit in thinking through curriculum planning. Ronald Doll lists a compendium of suggestions for planning programs that reveals this "sameness" in the scientific-technical approach.

1. *Surveying the scene.* It is logical to identify the context within which we are going to create a program. This surveying action is what allows district personnel to ascertain what makes their school system the same as or different from other systems.

2. *Assessing needs.* Needs most often focus on individuals, usually on students and occasionally on teachers. Rarely are the needs of the organization of the school considered in a needs assessment.

3. *Identifying and defining problems.* Once needs are identified, we require some demarcation of the nature of the problem. Not all needs are identified at the outset of the planning process; many emerge as the stages are activated.

4. *Recalling accepted aims and goals.* Needs and problems are shaped in part by the aims and goals of those involved in the planning and those present in the community in which the school is located. From the analysis of aims and goals, curriculum planners are able to generate program objectives or instructional objectives for the curricula.

5. *Marking proposals—and evaluating them.* At this step, we consider essential problems and the means of addressing them. Proposals are considered in light of the general aims and goals previously deemed appropriate for the school.

6. *Preparing designs.* Here, the shaping of the components of design and the selecting of the particular design for the program occur. Instructional materials and methods are reviewed and recommended.

7. *Organizing the work force.* This step seems a bit out of sequence. The school district in its adoption process looks at the work force in their attempt to establish and implement the curriculum.

8. *Supervising the planning process.* For planning to proceed smoothly, the process must not only be administered, but also supervised to determine if all is going as intended. Supervision may be directed by central/district policy, but usually it will be done at the school level by those directly involved in planning and developing the curriculum.

9. *Utilizing the products of planning.* This step is essentially performed by the classroom teacher. The degree of acceptance of the new program/material depends on whether teachers have been involved in the planning process and whether necessary inservice has been provided so that teachers feel comfortable with the new material and/or program.

10. *Applying evaluation means.* This refers to raising questions as to whether the actions of planning and implementation have actually produced some program that effectively addresses the aims, goals, and objectives of the curriculum. The key questions are "Does the program work? To what extent? How can it be improved?"

Source: Adapted from Ronald C. Doll, *Curriculum Improvement: Decision Making and Process,* 8th ed. (Needham Heights, Mass.: Allyn and Bacon, 1992).

Content selection deals with the "what" of the curriculum. Content is the "stuff" of the curriculum. It is the "what" that is to be taught, the "what" that students are to learn. Content is the foundation of the curriculum. Content refers to facts, concepts, principles, theories, and generalizations. Content also refers to cognitive processes that learners employ when think-

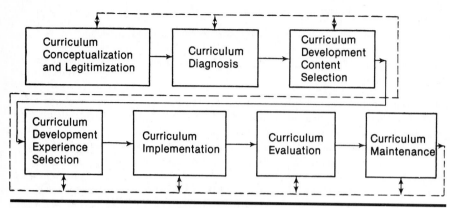

FIGURE 9-3   Curriculum Developmental Model.

Source: Francis P. Hunkins, *Curriculum Development Program Improvement* (Columbus, Ohio: Merrill, 1980), p. 17.

ing about or studying the content. Also, content as process refers to the procedures students learn to use to apply their knowledge and skills and to communicate what they know to others.

The next step in the model is *experience selection.* This stage deals primarily with instruction. The key questions relate to how the content is to be delivered to students or experienced by them. What teaching methods will be employed? What educational activities will be designed to make learning effective and enjoyable? How will the content, the what, of the curriculum be experienced so that the goals and objectives selected for the schools' program are attained? At this stage the teacher decides what instructional materials will be employed: textbooks, software programs, films, reference books, primary materials, maps, pictures, and so on.

After experiences have been selected, organized, and matched with the content of the program, the curriculum is essentially ready for *implementation.* Curriculum implementation has two stages, an initial piloting of the curriculum to work out any minor problems in the program and the final diffusion of the tested program. To assure that the curriculum as designed will be delivered to and experienced by students, a management system needs to be set up by which

the new program is introduced to the staff to develop a commitment to and comfort with the new program.

Once the program is implemented, we then engage in *evaluation.* This stage is usually conducted through the life of the curriculum: to furnish data so that decisions can be made to continue, modify, or discontinue the program. Often, schools only plan a series of student achievement tests to assess the effectiveness of a curriculum. A greater variety of means of gaining information should be considered.

The final stage of this model is *maintenance.* Curriculum maintenance encompasses the methods and means by which an implemented program is managed to assure its continued effective functioning. It deals with issues such as making sure that the new staff is educated into the ongoing system. It makes sure that budgets are sufficient to resupply necessary materials. It means that supervisors are available to assist teachers when a new strategy or content organization is to be tried. It infers communicating with the community, continuing a dialogue, so that parents feel a sense of ownership with the ongoing program. Often, once a curriculum has been implemented, schools forget that there needs to be some management design for continuing the program, for keeping it focused on the goals and objectives of the new program. Curricula not followed by a maintenance plan tend to disappear into the daily routine of the classroom, with teachers sometimes personalizing the programs to the point where they have little resemblance to the original curriculum.

A unique feature of this technical model is the feedback and adjustment loop depicted by the dashed lines. This loop allows decision makers as they proceed through the model to refer back to previous stages and to make necessary modifications.

Other technical-scientific models exist. Even though these model types tend to be used by advocates of subject-centered designs, who are perhaps more in the traditional philosophical and technological camps, the models really can be employed to develop a curriculum for any and all of the curriculum design orientations. Curricularists can be systematic in creating subject-centered, child-centered, or problem-centered curricula.[14] Although good planning cannot guarantee programs of quality, quality programs rarely result from unplanned actions.

NONTECHNICAL-NONSCIENTIFIC APPROACH

The danger in noting that one set of approaches is systematic or rational is the implication that the other camp is nonsystematic or nonrational. Advocates of methods of curriculum development not in the technical-scientific camp, however, are not suggesting disorder. Rather, they are taking issue with some of the key assumptions underlying the technical-scientific approach and questioning some of the consequences that result from utilizing this approach to curriculum development.

The technical-scientific approach to curriculum suggests that the process of curriculum development has a high degree of objectivity, universality, and logic. It works on an assumption that reality can be defined and represented in symbolic form. Knowledge, as it were, can exist as a matter of fact, unaffected by the very process of creating and learning it. It states that the aims of education can be made known, can be stated precisely, and can be addressed in a linear fashion.

In contrast, those in the nontechnical camp stress the subjective, personal, aesthetic, heuristic, and transactional. They stress not the outputs of production but rather the learner, especially through activity-oriented approaches to teaching and learning. Those favoring this approach note that not all ends of education can be known nor, indeed, do they need to be known in all cases. This approach considers that the curriculum evolves rather than being planned precisely.[15]

Thus, in this approach, those persons who are to be most affected by the curriculum are involved in its planning. Individual learners know themselves better than anyone else and therefore are capable of identifying and selecting those learning experiences that will facilitate their cognitive growth and social development. This approach to curriculum development focuses on individuals' self-perceptions and personal preferences, their own assessments of self-needs, and their attempts at self-integration. These are the data points for the curriculum decision-making process.

This differs to some degree from the technical-scientific persons, who rely more heavily on the view of experts and the demands of subject matter and society for determining students' needs. Indeed, some have criticized Taba for being too subject oriented and Tyler for being too accepting of the values of society in determining the direction of the curriculum.[16] The top-down tradition of the technical advocates is challenged by the nontechnical persons. The teacher and the learner have some roles, some autonomy for running the curriculum. Advocates of the nontechnical-nonscientific view stress that curricula deal with humans, both at the teaching and learning levels.

Common among these persons is that the key focus of curriculum activity is not the content, the subject matter per se, but rather the individual. Subject matter tentatively selected in the development process has importance only to the degree that a student can find meaning in it for himself or herself. Subject matter should provide opportunities for a reflection on and the grist for a critique of knowledge, for engaging the student dynamically in the creation of meaning.[17]

Persons with this orientation toward the curriculum and its development view learning as holistic compared to a compendium of discrete parts arranged in some artificial sequence. We cannot really departmentalize learning into precise steps or specific domains such as the cognitive, affective, and psychomotor. Rather than developing curricula prior to students coming to school, teachers actually become co-learners with the students, engaging each other in an educational conversation about topics of mutual interest and concern. Thus, in many of these nontechnical models, the curriculum, rather than being developed, actually evolves from joint teacher-pupil interaction. Part of the students' challenge is to create and interact with that which they will learn. In many ways, those accepting this approach to curriculum development are part of the postmodernist movement that essentially believes that all persons comprise part of the very worlds they attempt to study and create.

Essentially, the technical-scientific view toward curriculum development relies heavily on rationalism (thinking) and empiricism (sensing). The nontechnical-nonscientific orientation relies heavily on intuitionism (feeling) and on what Macdonald has called an "aesthetic rationality" in contrast to a "technological rationality."[18]

Advocates of the nontechnical-nonscientific approach to designing curricula are likely to support child-centered and to a lesser extent problem-centered designs. But as some examples of nontechnical-nonscientific designs will hopefully show, these are still purposeful approaches that can be employed systematically.

Nontechnical-nonscientific approach advocates challenge assumptions about whether all aims and goals of education can be known. They do not accept the position of the logical positivists—that if something exists it can be perceived and measured. This also applies to formulating conclusions about school and society: All of the concerns and subjects nontechnical curricularists examine do not have a means-ends logic as defined by technocratic or behaviorist educators.

Glatthorn: Naturalistic Model. Some models of curriculum development appear to take a middle ground—being systematic in planning, but still recognizing the "messy" involvement of people. One such model is Allan Glatthorn's naturalistic model. He argues that the technological model is limited by its insensitivity to the politics of curriculum making and that curriculum cannot be generated in such a neat, systematic, ends-oriented manner.

Glatthorn's model contains the following eight steps:

1. *Assess the alternatives.* Persons involved in planning should commence the process by systematically examining alternatives to the current curriculum. Those employing the technological approach might also begin at this stage, but such persons seem to advance too hastily to developing the course, not spending time reflecting on and critiquing current practice. While not taking the posture of a critical theorist, he encourages serious reflection on what the school is offering and advocates that people contemplate alternatives.

2. *Stake out the territory.* Here individuals define the course parameters, the learning audience, and learning activities. At the conclusion of this stage, we have in place a tentative course prospectus that addresses for whom the course is designed, whether it will be elective or required, its basic information and knowledge, and how it relates to existing courses in the school.

3. *Develop a constituency.* This step attends to the humanness of curriculum development and to its innately political character. Thus, before proceeding too far along the development process, those charged with program creation should realize their own personal convictions and biases. Likewise, developers should realize that there will be those in the system who oppose the new program because of their personal and professional beliefs. Thus, to advance the course development, participating parties must convince others to join forces. They must communicate with various groups and convince them of the soundness of the program being created.

4. *Build the knowledge base.* Once the curriculum development team has sufficient support among colleagues, it is necessary to create a knowledge base required for program creation. This knowledge base is about content or subject matter, but it also relates to gathering data on the students, on faculty skill and receptivity to the suggested program, community willingness to support the innovation, and what research information might lend credence to the new program.

5. *Block in the unit.* At this step, developers determine the nature and number of the units or parts, attending to the general objectives for the unit as well as how unit topics might be sequenced. Attention is given again to the question of what students are to learn from engaging with these units. In contrast to the technological approach, rather than one particular sequence defined for all students to follow, there are several avenues, all sensitive to students' interests, learning styles, and other differences.

6. *Plan quality learning experiences.* After blocking in the units, developers engage in designing particular sets of learning experiences that will address the general objectives. This stress on learning experiences, rather than on subject matter, distinguishes this approach and qualifies it as nontechnical. We admit the reader may have some difficulty in accepting that this student-centered focus is sufficient to classify this as truly a nontechnical process. But the planning of learning experiences suggests that there is no clear-cut technical delineation of what will transpire in the curriculum unit. The developers are creating possible options that will address numerous curriculum objectives and that will trigger numerous divergent outcomes.

7. *Develop the course examination.* In this naturalistic process, there is more emphasis on divergent means of assessment. Tests (and grades) do not drive the curriculum. Both teacher and student participate in determining the means of documenting whether learning has occurred and the quality of such learning. Student portfolios, biographies, and other alternative forms of assessment are acceptable procedures, as opposed to only standardized forms.

8. *Developing the learning scenarios.* The final step of the process is creating learning scenarios rather than the standard curriculum guide. These scenarios denote a detailed statement of the unit objectives, a suggested number of lessons, and a recommended list of learning experiences, with suggestions as to how to personalize them in the classroom. The scenarios also contain reprints of materials necessary to support the learning experiences.[19]

Weinstein and Fantini Model: A Curriculum of Affect. While Glatthorn's naturalistic model is of recent origin, there have been others before him who have denoted procedures that would place the student centrally in the process deliberations. In the early 1970s, many persons considered that the imbalance placed on the schools by the emphasis on the disciplines could be corrected by redirecting attention to the student.

Gerald Weinstein and Mario Fantini believed that education should have a human focus and objectives should address students' concerns, both personal and interpersonal. To these curriculum thinkers, the curriculum had a humanitarian purpose, serving as a vehicle for developing students' self-concepts and mature images of themselves as members of the human family.[21]

The curriculum model, presented in Figure 9-4, reveals several stages. We might first think it rather technical in layout, but, like Glatthorn's model, it has the basic assumption that the focus of action is on the individual or individuals for whom the curriculum is created. Students' concerns drive the system. "It is the . . . major factor in determining the basic organizing ideas . . . and content areas [stages 4 and 5] of the curriculum." Weinstein and Fantini are quick to point out that their model of curriculum and its development is not a replay of the child-centered approach of the progressive education era. As did Dewey, they define interests as too transitory. As these two curriculum workers argue, student concerns are deeper and more persistent than interests.

The first stage in the model is determining just who are the *learners,* a rather obvious stage if we are to address students' concerns. However obvious it may be, there are times when programs are developed with little or no attention as to just who comprises the audience for the curriculum. At this first stage, curriculum workers denote the demographic and cultural data of the students, also attending to their psychological and developmental levels. However, the characteristics denoted are common to the group, rather than to individual students. The authors carefully point out that they are concerned with the group since most students are taught in groups. This might be modified a bit today, although we would argue that group teaching is still the most common instructional approach.

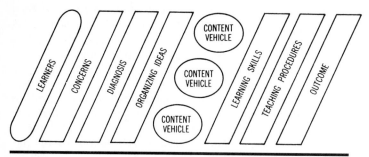

FIGURE 9-4   Model for Developing a Curriculum.
Source: Gerald Weinstein and Marco D. Fantini, *Toward Humanistic Education.* (New York: Praeger, 1970). Reprinted with permission.

The second stage is denoting the particular *concerns* common to the group. The authors identify three major concerns: concerns about self-image, concerns about disconnectedness, and concerns about control over one's life. Certainly, other concerns are possible, and today, students might have somewhat different concerns.

Once concerns are identified, we specify the reasons for the concerns and *diagnose* what can be done to resolve these concerns. This is the third stage. The psycho-sociological factors underlying these concerns must be delimited so that teachers can develop instructional approaches that will actually address the concerns.

In the fourth stage, the decision makers select *organizing ideas:* those ideas, concepts, and generalizations around which particular curriculum content can be generated. Here these authors are very much in line with many mainstream curricularists. But the difference is that the organizing ideas are selected on the basis of learner concerns rather than on the demands of academic subjects. The authors maintain that organizing ideas that cut across numerous disciplines and concerns are more valuable than those that do not.

Fifth, comes the actual selection of *content vehicles;* these vehicles are organized around three personal and social themes. The first is content gained from experiences one has as a growing person. Here content addresses student identity, power, belonging, and connec-tion. The second type of content deals with the affective domain and relates to the learner's feelings and interests. Examples would be feelings and/or interests about friends, sports, and clubs. The third type of content is that which the student has learned from the social context in which he or she lives—his or her "experimental content."

The types of content chosen influence the types of *learning skills* (stage 6) selected as well. What skills will the learner require to deal with the content? The basic skills of reading, writing, and arithmetic can be included as learning how to learn skills. Another set of skills is related to the self: social awareness skills are employed to enable the learner to recognize and describe himself or herself on an individual basis and in relation to others. Here the learner is in touch with himself, peers, and adults; in short, social skills are as important as cognitive skills.

Teaching procedures is the seventh stage. What means can the teacher employ to get students to learn the appropriate contents and skills for power over their own lives? The procedures necessary are those that will address the learning styles of individuals and that will also have the greatest impact on their affective dimensions. The learners, from interacting with teachers and peers, should develop emotionally and strengthen their feelings of self-worth. In this stage, it is important for the teacher to consider the students as individuals—with different learning styles, abilities, and interests—and match procedures with these differences.

The final stage denotes the intended *outcomes* for the curriculum. Here we ask whether the context vehicles have been achieved, and whether the learners' skills and teaching procedures were effective? What can be done to improve the curriculum? While this stress on outcomes may seem to place these thinkers in the technical camp, it is their attention to the human element of education, the social and personal development of the learner, that locates their model in the nontechnical camp.[22]

Postpositivist Models.   Since the time of Isaac Newton, scholars have perceived their world as a finely running mechanical machine. They believed, at least theoretically, that at some level the world is governed by certain fundamental laws. From the study of the world, we could discover order and certainty. Donald Schon argues that this technological rationality, this viewing of the world as a machine that we could study and manipulate objectively as a bystander, means that it is possible to determine with a great deal of certainty exactly what is happening in any given situation. The second assumption indicates that, given the fact of certainty, individuals can understand the phenomena under question on the basis of cause and effect. Third, it is possible to generate the means of obtaining data that will test out the certainty of reality. Finally, the results of such experiments or investigations are amiable to evaluation such that the results can be generalized to other situations.[23]

These assumptions support the technological-scientific approach to curriculum development. However, in the past decade and a half, these assumptions have been challenged by an increasing number of social scientists. Some of these people are called postpositivists in that they are challenging the positivistic thinking that Newton introduced. Others are identified as postmodern thinkers, attributing again to Newton the beginning of modern thought. Regardless of the labels, many persons arguing for a more dynamic curriculum and a more dynamic means of creating it are coming from a multitude of academic positions.

As educators, we need to commence questioning that all meaning is knowable and that all knowledge can be represented by finitary propositions.[24] Curriculum and curriculum making represent an uncertain system and an uncertain set of procedures for dealing with these systems. People such as James Macdonald was fond of arguing about the need for an aesthetic rationality to at least complement our technological rationality.[25] Similarly, Elliott Eisner has suggested that curriculum development is a process of transforming images and aspirations about education into programs. He intentionally uses the terms images and aspirations, believing that the conditions of curriculum development are rarely clear in all dimensions to those who would create educational programs.[26] Eisner does not believe it possible for an educator, or anyone for that matter, to prescribe formulas for another to follow. We cannot delineate content that should be taught to all or suggest prescribed sequences that claim the exact manner in which the content should be taught. However, we can formulate possibilities, realizing that we still will have a high degree of uncertainty, even disorder, as to how these possibilities will occur or what other events they may trigger.

The postmodern view causes curriculum makers to assume an openness to process, an eye for the unexpected, and a willingness to let individuals interact with systems as they evolve. This view allows chaos to occur so that order may result. In the same vein, artistry is considered a special way of knowing or perceiving, of constructing reality. Artistry fills in those spaces left vacant by the application of a technical rationality.[27] Ends are not perceived so much as ends but as beginnings, a view advocated by Dewey, although William Doll points out that postmodernism did not develop until after Dewey's death. Perceiving ends not as ends but as evolving beginnings is essential for examining the relation between being and becoming and between permanance and change.[28]

Traditionalists in the application of the technical approach to curriculum and its development argue for being and permanence. Proponents of the postmodern approach to curriculum believe that the actual planning process assumes its own ethos. Ends are transformed into new beginnings;

people in the process are altered; students, teachers, and even course materials are changed as the dynamics and chaos unfold. The energy driving the actions comes in part from the actions themselves, rather than being applied to the process from outside sources. Curriculum becomes a process of development to be experienced in unique and at first unimagined ways, rather than a static body of knowledge to be presented within a strict time table.

For the postmodernists or postpositivists, curriculum participants are engaged in a critical dialogue with themselves and others in the planning process and interact with an evolving content of the curriculum. The exact nature of the interactions is uncertain. Realizing this uncertainty, planners are open to new ideas, to surprise, to content taking off in new directions in consequence of some unanticipated event. Even when things appear calm, at equilibrium, they will at times behave in disorganized or chaotic ways.[29] Accepting this mode of thought, planners realize that curriculum is not something that is "boxed" or preplanned and given to individuals. Rather, as Young notes, meaning in curriculum results from the interactions of individuals. Meaning does not exist in separate compartments. Meaning results from a person becoming aware of the interconnections between and among the various realms of knowledge, people, and social/political reality.[30]

In short, the curriculum developer or planner looks at the dynamics of the education situation. The individual realizes that the situation at hand is unstable and dynamic. The players in the system, including teachers, students, and parents are not static types. The society in which the school finds itself is evolving. The levels of pedagogic knowledge are changing. This knowledge influences teaching, as well as our understanding about the nature of individuals and their learning, and is in a state of flux. As an overview, we come to realize that many of the systems do not evolve in any set pattern. Also, we realize that, with the diversity of individuals and situations, there is no one set pattern for arranging the content and experiences of the curriculum. Indeed, the plans allow for things to be random, to evolve as the situation develops. However,

once plans are put into place, there is a certain irreversibility. Students will never go back to a prior time of not knowing something once that something has been taught. They will never be younger. But the outcomes to be anticipated are not prescriptive or convergent, are essentially not ends, but new and evolving beginnings, resulting in what we could call "dissipative structures."[31]

Table 9-1 gives an overview of the technical approaches to curriculum development discussed in the previous section. Also included in the table is an overview of the nontechnical approaches discussed in this section.

COMPONENTS TO CONSIDER IN DEVELOPING A CURRICULUM

Curricularists deal with the question, "*What* shall be included for purposes of learning?" After that they deal with *how* to present or arrange the *what* that is selected for learning, so that students can learn or experience it. In other words, first they deal with knowledge and content specifically, and then they deal with teaching and learning experiences. Regardless of their philosophical orientation, they should not ignore these two elements.

Curriculum Content

All curricula have content, regardless of their design or developmental models. How individuals view the content is affected by their view of knowledge and reality—their philosophical postures. Those who believe in the traditional philosophies "discover" knowledge by using their senses. Also, to them knowledge is "objective"; it can be measured and therefore tested.

Those who view the world from a progressive posture "invent" knowledge according to their relationships with others and the environment. The meaning and truth of a child's experience depend on their relationship to the situations in which he or she is acting.

Those who are part of the romantic position view knowledge and likewise content from an existential or phenomenological epistemology. To these individuals, knowledge and reality refer to the immediate inner experience of the self. Knowledge and truth in this view are self-aware-

TABLE 9-1 Overview of Curriculum Development Approaches

APPROACH	MAJOR ASSUMPTIONS	VIEW OF CURRICULUM	MAJOR MODELS
Technical scientific	Major steps can be identified, managed	Knowable components that can be selected and organized	Bobbitt, Charters: Curriculum activities Tyler: Four basic principles
	Curriculum development has high degree of objectivity, logic	A compendium of parts	Taba: Grass-roots rationale
	Curriculum development is rational	A plan for learning opportunities	Saylor, Alexander: Planning process
	Curriculum development involves key decision points	Curriculum is the organization and delivery of contents and experiences	Hunkins: Decision-making model
Nontechnical	Curriculum development is subjective, personal, aesthetic, transactional	Curriculum viewed as quality activities	Glatthorn: Naturalistic model
	Curriculum development relies on intuitive forces	Curriculum viewed as emerging, holistic	Weinstein and Fantini: Curriculum of affect
	Curriculum development is a dynamic process fraught with much uncertainty	Curriculum is an emerging phenomenon with which humans interact; it is a dynamic and uncertain system	Doll, Prigogine, and Schon and Young: Post-positivist models

ness or self-insight. This form of truth is extended beyond the self as a person attempts to understand other human beings.[32]

Individuals within the rather open boundaries of postmodernism view knowledge as dynamic and evolutionary. It is not static, not something that can be observed and manipulated from clinical or detached settings. An individual is part of the very knowledge structure being investigated. We do not observe knowledge, we actually participate in its making. Knowledge is a process that influences the learner and is thereby also influenced by the learner. Knowledge results from a structuring and a reconstructing of perceived and also invented realities. Knowledge is that which results from the environment within which humans find themselves.[33]

Conceptions of Content. Groups charged with curriculum planning have options in content selection that are influenced by their philosophical outlooks. Actually, they have the problem of overchoice. There is too much content to include, and they must somehow make sense of what is available and select that which will enable students to learn the most—whatever curriculum design or developmental model they implement. This task can perhaps be made a bit easier if curricularists think of just how they define curriculum content and what it comprises.

Some educators argue that it is more important to learn process than content. Such a statement dichotomizes content and process, when in reality they should receive equal emphasis in the school's curriculum. Process is a type of specialized content, related to methodology and procedures. Thus, Parker and Rubin indicate that process suggests "random or ordered operations which can be associated with knowledge and with human activities." Varied processes can help create knowledge, as well as "communicate and utilize knowledge."[34]

Emphasis on process does not reduce the value of students' gaining knowledge, but rather affirms that students need to be active in their learning. Furthermore, such underscoring of process indicates that students must progress beyond the simple acquisition of knowledge; they must use the knowledge if they are to gain appreciation and understanding of it.

Content is more than just information to be learned for school purposes. It must be information that relates to learners' concerns and be organized so that the learner finds the information useful and possessing deep meaning. When selecting content the curriculum planner must take into account the potential of the content to address all the cognitive, social, and psychological dimensions of the individual student.

Some curricularists might conclude that content is really another term for knowledge. Content (subject matter) is a compendium of facts, concepts, generalizations, principles, and theories similar to disciplined knowledge. Additionally, school content does incorporate methods of processing information. But, knowledge, whether disciplined, like chemistry, or nondisciplined, like environmental education, is concerned with the advancement of understanding and the exploration of unknown areas. In contrast, content and processes arranged in school subjects do not provide students with opportunities for advancing the realm of knowledge, but rather opportunities for discovering knowledge that is new to them but known by scholars and practitioners outside of the school. School content, then, is distinguished from knowledge by its purpose.

All curriculum content—that is, facts, concepts, generalizations, and so on—should enable students to gain understanding and to apply that understanding to daily living—present and anticipated. Content selected should contribute to the students' knowledge or levels of understanding. Considering content in terms of its meaning as knowledge allows or enables the curriculum planner to be more effective in the content-selection process. Figure 9-5 might make these distinctions clearer.

Organization of Content. The capitalized version of knowledge in the diagram is all information that has been organized by scholars for the advancement of understanding. Such knowledge is organized according to various knowledge theories. Paul Hirst has advanced a "forms of knowledge" theory that organizes knowledge into distinct domains with unique types of concepts in specialized relationships. For instance, he observes that mathematics has unique categorical concepts of number, integer, and matrix. Physics has unique concepts of matter and energy. These concepts are organized into specialized networks whose relationships influence the particular types of meanings that can be derived from them. These specialized organizations of knowledge can be distinguished by the different types of tests, or processes, used by learners in these respective domains as subjects.[35]

How knowledge is organized in "reality" depends on the philosophical views of the scholar. Curriculum planners who favor subject-centered designs would accept most, if not all, of what Hirst discusses. However, those who accept learner-centered curriculum designs might consider that the school curriculum organizes personal knowledge rather than what some would call objective knowledge. Persons like Hirst (and

KNOWLEDGE————————————→ Content ————————————→ Knowledge
(formal organization of   (selected from knowledge   (understanding of school
information)   source for educational   content at levels sufficient
                                                            purposes)   for use)

FIGURE 9-5 World Knowledge to School Knowledge

other subject-centered advocates) in many cases view knowledge as things and relationships that are real and awaiting discovery in the outer world. To the learner-centered design champion, however, knowledge relates to the individual's personal and social world and how he or she defines reality.

Perhaps the best posture for curriculum designers is to recognize the many variations among interpretations of knowledge and its organization. They would be wise to remember what Bruner was quick to point out, that the knowledge they identify and create cannot be conceived of in terms of absolute truth: "Knowledge is a model we construct to give meaning and structure to regularities in experience." The way we organize knowledge is an invention for "referring experiences economical and connected. We invent concepts such as force in physics, . . . motive in psychology, style in literature as a means [for] comprehension."[36]

Faced with organizing content for the curriculum, program planners usually use two organizers: logical and psychological. In following the *logical* organization, they organize content according to certain rules and concepts. In economics, for example, the concepts of supply and demand are major organizers. Without these concepts, the idea of capital and labor or the marketplace cannot be grouped. Arranging economics content in this manner makes sense, but it really does not denote the way an individual might actually learn economics.

To detail this process, curricularists consider a *psychological* organization: How do students learn or process information? Most educators assume that content should be organized by going from the students' immediate environment to a more distant environment. Content, in other words, should be organized so that the concrete is experienced first, then the more abstract. This psychological factor is a key principle of sequencing content.

Criteria for Selecting Content. Regardless of their curriculum design preferences or their philosophical orientations, curriculum planners have to apply criteria in choosing curriculum content. Although the criteria are common to most curricular orientations, educators in the various philosophical camps might place greater emphasis on particular criteria.

Self-Sufficiency. Israel Scheffler argues that the prime guiding principle for content selection is helping the learners to attain maximum self-sufficiency in the most economical manner. He elaborates three types of economy: economy of teaching effort and educational resources, economy of students' efforts, and economy of subject matter's extent of generalizability.[37] This criterion—helping learners to attain maximum self-sufficiency—is also supported by many humanists, radicals, and reconceptualists as a means by which learners can actualize their potential and crystallize their identities.

Significance. Content to be learned is significant only to the degree to which it contributes to the basic ideas, concepts, principles, generalizations, and so on, of the overall aims of the curriculum. Content should also consider the development of particular learning abilities, skills, processes, and attitude formation.

Taba noted that we should not just select content based on the cognitive aspects of learners, but also on their affective dimensions.[38] Even though most curriculum planners note that significance is central, they often disagree as to what is significant. Those who favor subject matter designs think of significance in terms of what knowledge needs to be transmitted to students. Those who favor learner-centered designs think of significance in terms of how it contributes to the meaningful experiences of the pupils. Those who advocate problem-centered designs would consider significance in terms of particular social, political, and economic issues.[39]

Validity. Validity is the authenticity of the content selected. In this time of information explosion, knowledge selected for school content can quickly become obsolete and even incorrect. As new knowledge is discovered, content assumed valid may become misleading or even false. Validity must be verified at the initial selection of curriculum content, but it also needs to be checked at regular intervals through the duration of the curricular program to determine if content originally valid continues to be so.

Validity would seem to be a rather straight-forward criterion. Something is either accurate or inaccurate; something either happened or it did not. Nevertheless, the ideological stance that any individual brings to a situation vastly influences what he or she perceives as valid. This is why some can state that certain information in school content is valid or truthful, while others can consider the same information invalid. Revisionists, radical school critics, reconstructionists, and post-positivists would state that much of the curriculum offered to students is invalid.[40]

Interest.   Another criterion is interest. To those who favor the learner-centered design, this is a key criterion. These persons note that knowledge exists in the learner when it is meaningful to his or her life. When it fails to be meaningful, it dehumanizes education.[41] The interest criterion has been with us since the times of the child-centered school in the 1920s. Advocates of this movement urged that the child should be the source of the curriculum; in other words, the children's interest should determine the curriculum.

Those currently advocating a learner-centered curriculum point out that the content of the curriculum must be selected with students' interests in mind. But the school experience should create and broaden interests as well as address them. A key question is: "Are students' current interests of long-lasting educational value for both the students and society?" Dealing with this question is difficult because it assumes educators possess some degree of perception regarding future society and students' places in that future. The criterion of students' interests should be weighted and adjusted to allow for students' maturity, their prior experiences, the educational and social value of their interests, and the way they are expected to interact within society.

Utility.   Utility concerns the usefulness of the content. Again, how a person defines usefulness is influenced by his or her philosophical view and favored curriculum design. Usefulness to those favoring the subject-centered design is often judged in terms of how the content learned will enable students to use that knowledge in job situations and other adult activities. Usefulness to

those in the learner-centered camp is related to how the content enables the individual to gain an accurate perception of his or her self-identity and to attain meaning in his or her life. Is the content useful for the learner developing his or her human potential? Proponents of the problem-centered mode would think of content as having utility if it has direct application to ongoing life and to social and political issues.

Learnability.   Could anyone select content without considering this obvious criterion? Some critics of the schools say yes. Certain contents are selected that are out of the range of experiences of particular students and are thus difficult, if not impossible, to learn. Furthermore, selected contents are sometimes arranged and presented in ways that make their learning difficult for some students. Critics often say that content selected reflects a middle-class bias and that it is organized to favor those who have convergent (and right-answer) learning styles. The learnability criterion relates to the optimal placement and appropriate organization and sequencing of content. Furthermore, it addresses the issue of appropriateness for the intended student audience.

Feasibility.   Feasibility, the last criterion, forces curriculum planners to consider content in light of the time allowed, the resources available, the expertise of current staff, the nature of the political climate, the existing legislation, and the amount of public monies available. Although educators may think that they have an entire world of content from which to choose, they do have limitations on their actions. Even the number of days in the school calendar, for example, limits what can be taught. So do the size of the classroom and the personnel of the school. Content selection has to be considered within the context of the existing reality, which usually boils down to economics and politics.

In this connection, David Pratt analyzes economic and political feasibility in terms of "constraints." The curriculum, he argues, is "largely governed by [such] constraints, [and] unfeasibility is commonly due to the magnitude of the constraints." It may be necessary to "ask whether any of the constraints can be changed."[42] Here we allude to economic compromises, shifting funds, altering public opinion, compromising or negotiating with pressure groups, and/or becoming involved in school-community politics.

Curriculum Experiences

Curriculum content is the "meat" of the curriculum plan, but we can consider the experiences planned for the students as the "heart." Experiences are the key factors that shape the learners' orientations to the content and, ultimately, their understanding of it. Taba noted that "perhaps the first important consideration in achieving a wider range of objectives is the fact that the learning experiences, and not the content as such, are the means for achieving all objectives besides those of knowledge and understanding."[43]

Curriculum experience involves the instructional component of the curriculum. Instruction refers primarily to the human interaction between teacher and student in ways that are designed to achieve the goals of the school. It is specialized behavior planned in light of particular objectives. It consists of teaching methods and activities that take place in the classroom for the purpose of attaining the schools' goals. There are a multitude of both teaching methods and educational activities. Examples of teaching methods are inquiry strategies, lecture, discussion, and demonstration. Examples of educational activities are viewing films, conducting experiments, viewing videos, interacting with computer programs, taking field trips, and listening to speakers. Both are integral parts of the curriculum and must be carefully considered in light of the content selected.

At a theoretical level, instruction includes all the actions of teachers necessary to influence the students' behavior and, ultimately, their learning. The particular actions of a teacher may vary according to the teaching method and/or educational activities, but they all have the purpose of influencing students' behavior and learning.

Experiences Versus Activities. When discussing curriculum, we do not make a fine distinction between teaching methods and educational activities. Rather, we group all the actions of both teachers and students under the title learning experiences. But this was not always the case. At the turn of this century, the terms *learning activities* and *learning experiences* were absent in the educational literature. We read instead about *recitations, exercises,* and *projects.* But with the evolution of the field of psychology, and also the work of progressivism led by Kilpatrick and Ellsworth Collings (a doctoral student of Kilpatrick's), the activities of the learners received more attention in the educational equation."[44]

Educators began to realize that the term *learning activities* did not describe adequately the dynamics of the teaching-learning situation. Many children could be engaged in the same learning activities, but the experiences each pupil derived might be quite different. By 1935, the term *learning activities* was being replaced with the term *learning experiences.* Most writers of curriculum today talk of learning experiences, especially since Tyler used the term in his classic text, *Basic Principles of Curriculum and Instruction.*

Wholeness and Continuity. Students' curriculum experiences should be such that they see life's wholeness and continuity in activity. Students should see that every concrete entity is experienced within a context of wider relationships and possibilities. Conscious life is always open to a never-ending web of entailments and unfoldings. No content of experience is just what it appears to be here and now without any further prospects or associations.[45]

Means and Ends. Persons who favor learner-centered designs and problem-centered designs tend to view learning experiences as means— as valuable in themselves. Means-oriented curricularists seem to be looking at effects that are more personal and individual and that perhaps address human needs. They are looking at the effects of the experiences to determine whether or not students gain a sense of personal fulfillment and power over their own lives and a commitment to responsible action.

But many in the curriculum field, though they do not necessarily ignore completely the process aspect of the educational experience, place major emphasis on the ends of education. These individuals favor subject-centered curriculum designs. Curriculum development activities and implementation strategies are performed with the intention of achieving the aims and goals of the school. Instruction is the means for attaining the content that has been selected and the overall goals of the program. Ends-oriented curricularists view learning opportunities not as valuable in themselves but as instrumental in attaining specified consequences. These persons are product-oriented. They look at the outcomes resulting from the interface of students, teachers, and the curriculum. They are interested in results, not just inherent attributes of experiences. See Curriculum Tips 9-2.

Criteria for Selecting Experiences. Some criteria are useful for considering potential content and experiences. Validity, especially congruence of objectives and goals, is an appropriate example. Other criteria are expressed by the question: "Will the experience do what we wish it to do in light of the overall aims and goals of the program and specific objectives of the curriculum?" Following are specific extensions of this question. Are the experiences

1. Valid in light of the ways in which knowledge and skills will be applied in out-of-school situations?
2. Feasible in terms of time, staff expertise, facilities available within and outside of the school, community expectations?
3. Optimal in terms of students' learning the content?
4. Capable of allowing students to develop their thinking skills and rational powers?
5. Capable of stimulating in students greater understanding of their own existence as individuals and as members of groups?
6. Capable of fostering in students an openness to new experiences and a tolerance for diversity?
7. Such that they will facilitate learning and motivate students to continue learning?
8. Capable of allowing students to address their needs?
9. Such that students can broaden their interests?
10. Such that they will foster the total development of students in cognitive, affective, psychomotor, social, and spiritual domains?[46]

Relationship of Content and Experiences. No curriculum, regardless of its design, can ignore content and experiences. Although subject-centered designs stress content, they also consider its delivery. Learner-centered designs focus on the students and their experiences, but they, too, consider the experiences in relation to what is learned.

What educators need to remember is that, in reality, content and experiences do not exist apart. If students are reading a book, they are combining both an experience and content. Content and learning experiences always comprise curriculum unity. Students cannot just engage in learning or in studying without experiencing some activity and some content. Likewise, teachers cannot deal with content without being engaged in some experience or some activity.

Curriculum planners sometimes separate content from experience. However, they realize that in the actual delivery of educational programs both elements coexist. Taba noted, "One can speak of effective learning only if both content and process are fruitful and significant."[47]

Educational Environments

As we cannot separate content from experiences in the actual delivery of a curriculum, neither can we divorce the experiencing of content from the space within which experience occurs. Until recently, educators have not given much attention to the environment of the school other than to make sure that the children had adequate light, places to sit, desks upon which to write, and places to hang their clothes. As John Holt pointed out, "We would have to worry a lot less in our schools about 'motivating' children, about finding ways to make good things happen, if we would just provide more spaces in which good things *could* happen." Space, Holt noted, creates activity; it allows students "to generate places and moods."[48]

Educational space is crucial to meaningful educational experiences. Children who experience a creative environment are much more likely to be stimulated, to realize their potential, and to be excited about learning. The environments educators design should facilitate students' attending to the experiences and content that they have selected and organized. The environments should stimulate purposeful student activity. They should allow for a depth and range of content and experiences that facilitate learning.[49]

Persons who favor subject-centered designs might give only scant consideration to the educational environment. They might feel that it matters little where learning is to occur. But even these persons would have to admit that if, for example, a teacher were presenting science information the laboratory environment would, at times, be more appropriate than the lecture hall. Persons who favor learner-centered designs, on the other hand, might be more inclined to take seriously the planning of meaningful environments. Space is needed to allow individuals to grow; they are part of the quality of experience for students. Ideally, persons creating programs, regardless of their design preference, will take into consideration the nature of the space in which the curriculum is to be realized by both teachers and students. See Curriculum Tips 9-3.

Criteria for Environment. Educational environments should address social needs, security needs, and belongingness needs, as well as the

development of inner awareness, appreciation, and empathy for others. In addition, they should enable students to master intended learnings. The environments should stimulate purposeful student activity, and they should allow for a depth and range of activities that facilitate learning.

Brian Castaldi has suggested that, when contemplating and designing educational environments, planners keep in mind four criteria: adequacy, suitability, efficiency, and economy.[50] _Adequacy_ refers to the space planned: Is it of sufficient size to accommodate the students for whom the space is intended? Adequacy also refers to environmental controls: Is the light sufficient so that students can read with ease? Are the visual displays big enough so that students can see them? Are the materials serviceable for the learning styles of the students? Are the acoustics appropriate so that students can hear?

When dealing with the criterion of adequacy, we also consider the relationships between the various spaces within a school. How do spaces designed for individual investigation relate to spaces planned for storage and retrieval of educational materials? How do spaces created for small-group investigation relate to spaces designed for small-group viewing of educational

**CURRICULUM TIPS 9-3   Dealing with the Physical and
                        Health Factors of the Environment**

Until recently curriculum leaders did not give much attention to the curriculum environment. One way of viewing this environment is to look at the physical and health factors that impact on student learning. The factors considered below represent a "nuts and bolts" view, typical of a supervisor or practitioner who deals in the real world of classrooms and schools as opposed to the theoretical world.

1. **Arrangements.** Identify the activities that will take place and the best way to combine or arrange the physical layout or setting. Different configurations must be evaluated on the basis of how they will accommodate lectures, demonstrations, experiments, etc. Other factors include storage space, electrical/telephone outlets, teacher work space, student learning space (open/closed) and grouping patterns (whole group, small group, and independent learning) or spaces.
2. **Floors, Ceilings, Windows.** There is a need to consider carpeting vs. tile in terms of cost, durability, and esthetics. Electro-static charges are important, too, in terms of human sensitivity and technical equipment (especially computers). Ceiling materials and window treatments affect acoustics and lighting.
3. **Temperature.** The research data suggest that students learn best when the temperature is 70 to 74 degrees Fahrenheit, since they are seated and somewhat inactive in most classroom situations. They also learn best when the relative humidity is between 40 to 60 percent.
4. **Electrical.** Electrical wires should run parallel to the walls, and when they run across floors they should be taped down to prevent accidents. Equipment and adapter plugs should be stored when not in use, and in no one's way when in use. There should be more than one circuit in a classroom to guard against possible line failure, and surge suppressors need to be installed in schools/classrooms that cannot risk data loss in the event of a power surge.
5. **Lighting.** In most cases windows are suitable for providing adequate light, coupled with the standard fluorescent lighting to save money. In small learning areas, recessed lighting is more effective than fluorescent light.
6. **Acoustics.** Room noise can be a problem, especially when students are active or involved in an open classroom setting and are permitted to talk or engage in multiple activities at the same time. Neutralizing noise with appropriate floor, ceiling, and window treatments are basic considerations; some schools are experimenting with soft background music, and in other schools special window panes have been installed to reduce outside noise.
7. **Security.** Physical security is a consideration in entryways, hallways, and schoolyards, especially in terms of unwarranted intruders. It is also a factor when storing office and instructional equipment, as well as with student lockers and teacher closets. Schools are increasingly installing special locks and bolts, steel plates with locking cables, electronic trackers, closed circuit television, and alarm systems connected to police departments.
8. **Dust.** Elimination of dust has always been a concern. When remodeling or designing a new school, all chalkboards should be replaced with dry marker boards. Special consideration should also be given to paper and disk storage.
9. **Safety.** To protect students (or teachers) from injury and school and liability, the smart administrator learns to identify and eliminate as many hazards as possible. Science labs, gyms, cafeterias, and schoolyards are major places where accidents take place, but also injuries do occur in classrooms, hallways, and auditoriums.

Source: Allan C. Ornstein, "Components of Curriculum Development," *Illinois School Research and Development* (Spring 1990), pp. 208–209.

media? Will students be able to move around the room without disrupting other students?

Closely related to adequacy is *suitability*. Is the shape of the environment suitable for the type of activity planned? If some information is going to be demonstrated, is the environment such that all students can see with ease? If students are to engage in discovery, does the environment help or hinder such activity?

Ensuring *efficiency* involves attending to those characteristics of educational space that are likely to improve its instructional effectiveness or operational characteristics: Does the environment allow the educational activity to be carried out with a minimum of effort? Will the environment facilitate the greatest amount of learning with the least amount of effort by students and teachers? If students are to listen to audio tapes at their desks, can they be placed where they will not be disturbed by unnecessary noise or by students engaged in other activities?

The final criterion, *economy*, relates to actual savings, in terms of capital outlay, that can be achieved by the initial architectural design or by a modification of an existing environment for a particular aspect of the curriculum. Economy deals with the cost of teaching some part of the curriculum in the environment provided. It also relates to economy of students' and teachers' efforts. Time is a resource, and curricula are designed to make maximum use of time to achieve basic program goals and objectives. Sometimes, for example, students spend a major part of their day just waiting for the teacher to get to them. Sometimes, teachers spend too much time going from one part of the school to another to engage in a different school activity. It could be that planners can design educational environments so that students and teachers are very near to the appropriate spaces for their different activities.

PARTICIPANTS IN DEVELOPING THE CURRICULUM

Developing or designing a curriculum involves a large number of persons, both school based and community based. It also involves different levels of planning: the classroom level, the school level, the national level, and even the international level. Sometimes the designers work in

harmony, and sometimes they are at odds with each other. In fact, concern among people or groups for certain types of curricula makes curriculum development largely a political activity in which there is competition for authority and control, for scarce resources, and for primacy of certain values.

Political Arena Participants

Most educators work to have their particular views or purposes of education become dominant. The politics of education is concerned with who benefits and how those benefits are determined. Curriculum is concerned with providing programs for learners. Curriculum participants, both educators and noneducators have to determine what types of curricula will benefit what students, how to select those curricula, who will receive the benefits of particular curricula, and how to deliver those benefits.[51]

School Arena Participants

Macdonald advocated that all parties affected by the curriculum should be involved in deciding its nature and purpose. He presented a model that showed several groups, all directing their thinking, feelings, and knowledge to curriculum activity. The model, shown in Figure 9-6, depicts the major players in continuous interactions.

Teachers.   The teacher occupies a central position in curriculum decision making. The teacher decides what aspects of the curriculum, newly developed or ongoing, to implement or stress in a particular class. The teacher also determines whether to spend time, and how much of it, on developing basic skills or critical thinking skills. Observers point out that when teachers shut the classroom door they determine the details of the curriculum regardless of the curriculum plans of others. Teachers are clearly the most powerful implementers regarding curriculum.[52]

In addition to being curriculum participants at the classroom level, teachers are also involved with curriculum committees. Some of these committees are organized by grade level, for example, a fifth-grade curriculum committee; others are organized by subject area. Some might be

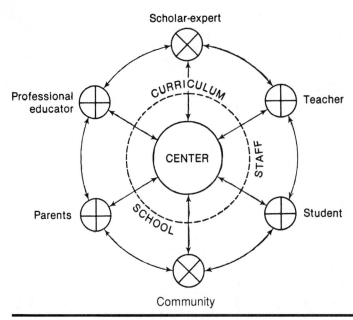

FIGURE 9-6 Continuous Interaction Model for Curriculum Activity.
Source: Adapted from James B. Macdonald, "Responsible Curriculum Development," in E. W. Eisner, ed., *Confronting Curriculum Reform* (Boston: Little, Brown,
1971), p. 71.

organized according to the type of student under
consideration; for example, a committee for the
gifted or a committee for the learning disabled.
The committee format is the standard way of
involving teachers in curriculum activity outside
the classroom level.[53]

Actually teachers should be involved with
every phase of curriculum development. Although not all teachers wish to be involved in
all stages of curriculum development, all teachers, by the nature of their role, are involved in
the implementation of the curriculum: Teaching is implementing the curriculum. Teachers
need to be part of the total curriculum-development activity, from the formation of aims and
goals to the evaluation and maintenance of the
curriculum.[54]

Teachers should by their very roles be practicing intellectuals. Indeed, Henry Giroux argues
that the teacher should be viewed as an intellectual engaged in some form of thinking. Teachers
should be viewed not as "performers professionally equipped to realize effectively any goals

set for them. Rather [teachers] should be
viewed as [professionals] with a special dedication to the values of the intellect and the
enhancement of the critical powers of the
young."[55] Schon advances that teachers should
be reflective practitioners engaged in actions
resulting from careful considerations of the
nature of the task.[56] Going one step further,
teachers need to work in school-university
and school-community partnerships to improve curriculum and teaching, to build the
knowledge base in curriculum and teaching,
and to professionalize teaching and the teachers'
role in curriculum development.

Students. If we accept that all who are affected by the curriculum need to be involved in
its planning, we cannot ignore the students.
Students seldom have formal influence on what
they will learn or even on the manner of their
experiencing the content. This is, however,
changing in some schools. Students, especially
at the secondary level, are sometimes involved

in curriculum committees. Many schools are also involving secondary students in conducting surveys and needs assessments. As Ronald Doll notes, students are the "consumers" of education and they deserve to supply input to educators regarding curricular matters.[57]

Educators are ill advised to ignore what learners think and feel. Also, we would advance that, if we are attempting to empower teachers in the curriculum process, we also need to empower students to assume some control, to a degree appropriate for their ages, over their learning. If the curriculum is to truly evolve from the conversations of involved parties, we cannot keep students out of the conversation in which we plan what they are to learn.

Principals. Principals long have been considered to be the curriculum leaders in the school setting. However, this still may be more the ideal than absolute fact, since many principals are still go-betweens from the central office to parents and the school staff. Currently, it appears that the roles of principals, along with the roles of teachers, regarding curriculum activity are changing. Part of this is due to the effort to restructure the schools. As Mary Raywid notes, those who consider themselves restructuralists have proposed two broad strategies for attaining their goals regarding changes in authority and governance. The first is to return authority for decision making to the school site and to democratize the process of decision making. The other is to extend to teachers the right to choose or develop the program for which they are responsible.[58]

There seems to be growing support for school-site management. John Goodlad in his major study of schools recommended that the school be recognized as the primary unit of education. If the school site is to be the "place of action" with regard to curriculum decision making, then the principal must be a visionary leader possessing a clear view of the mission of the school and a strong belief in his or her professional values.[59] The principal must be able to communicate the sense of mission to teachers and others affected by the curriculum and to engage teachers and others in the actual refinement of the mission of the school. Principals must exert care to be the curriculum and instructional leader in the school and not just the person in charge of the managerial functions of the school.

Principals realize, especially those involved in school-site management schemes, that effective functioning and managing change results, when those at the school recognize themselves as a community with shared values and ideology. Ideally, principals acknowledge that with school site-based management there will be many committees, and these committees will involve community members and even students in decision making. While such committees are a part of "restructured" schools, there is still some debate as to whether community members will have advisory roles or decision-making authority and set policy for the school. In either case, it is the principal's responsibility to guarantee that the actions of the players in the school, in the curriculum arena, are not counterproductive.

In large schools, we envision the principal as a facilitator of curriculum: furnishing time for curricular activities, arranging for in-service training, sitting on curriculum advisory committees as a resource agent, and refining the mission of the school. In small schools, we would expect principals to serve more actively as curriculum initiators, developers, and implementers. Regardless of the specific roles that principals will play, the shift to site-based management can make the principal a much more powerful figure, since he or she is now the visible person to both teachers and community members; or the principal can share responsibilities in curriculum planning with other participants. See Curriculum Tips 9-4.

Curriculum Specialists. Curriculum specialists play a major role in curriculum development and implementation activities. They are known by many titles: chairpersons, supervisors, coordinators, or directors. An individual's title usually gives some idea of his or her responsibilities. Persons called curriculum coordinators or directors are usually educators who are known as curriculum generalists.[60] They have a broad knowledge of the nature of curriculum and are experts in creating and implementing curricula. They usually do not have a content major. Other generalists in a school district are known as directors of elementary or secondary education.

CURRICULUM TIPS 9-4   Sharing Curriculum Leadership

The NEA has introduced a new five-year, school-based improvement program to explore ways of overcoming the isolation of the traditional roles of teachers and administrators. Nine stages toward shared leadership are listed; they suggest how staff members are better able to share ideas, solve problems together, and contribute to curriculum planning and practice.

1. *Testing.* Teachers and administrators determine their willingness and desire to change. Each staff member can decide whether or not to participate.
2. *Exhilaration.* The teachers are elated to learn they will be treated as professional and given new authority and resources to improve curriculum and instruction.
3. *Commitment.* The staff commit their energies to solving curriculum/instructional problems they have identified; they modify the school structure to support this work. New leaders emerge.
4. *Dispiritedness.* The staff discover no one from outside the school is going to provide solutions. Some staff members drop out of the program; others confront the reality that they are on their own.
5. *Regeneration.* No more than 50 percent of the staff remain active participants, but they begin again—reassessing what needs to be done and talking at length about commitment, mission statements, and empowerment.
6. *Seeking small successes.* The staff focuses on smaller and simpler ideas; they become realistic as to what they can accomplish. Small successes are used as springboards to more comprehensive projects.
7. *Using research.* Staff members begin to rely increasingly on relevant research and practical information from many sources. They no longer write off all research as a bunch of theory; they see the need to bring in consultants from nearby regional laboratories, universities, and professional associations.
8. *Experimentation.* Together teachers and administrators select and introduce new ideas and pilot test and assess their outcomes. If successful, they move to the adoption stage at the school level.
9. *Comprehensiveness.* The staff moves from fragmented curriculum/instructional efforts to comprehensive reform. The staff's readiness for this stage is signaled by nonparticipants being won over, increased communication among teachers, and greater interest by school supervisors and administrators to support the activities of teachers.

Source: Adapted from Robert M. McClure, "The Evolution of Shared Leadership," *Educational Leadership* (November 1988), pp. 60–62.

Usually, these persons have expertise in administration as well as curriculum, but their focus is either elementary or secondary.

Persons with specific content specialties are often titled as supervisors, chairs, or heads of a particular subject area, for example, supervisor (chair, head) of science. These persons have some background in curriculum, but they have a content major and are often more concerned with supervising instruction.[61]

Curriculum specialists are responsible for ensuring that programs are conceptualized, designed, and implemented. This requires a high level of understanding of curriculum and skill in managing people. Curriculum specialists need knowledge of curriculum design and development, in translating curriculum theory into practice, and in supervising and evaluating instruction. Unruh and Unruh have noted that curriculum specialists must be sensitive, patient, and skilled in human relations. Additionally, they need competence in decision making and leadership. The authors identified ten tasks of the curriculum specialist: (1) defining goals and objectives; (2) developing needs and problems; (3) creating conceptual models of curriculum development; (4) developing plans, strategies, and procedures that encourage people to work together; (5) fostering interrelationships and comprehensiveness in curriculum development; (6) involving people in curriculum development; (7) communicating within and outside of the schools; (8) increasing professionalism regarding curriculum; (9) planning implementation; and (10) evaluating the curriculum.[62]

Assistant (Associate) Superintendent. In many school districts, the person with the primary responsibility for curriculum activity is the assistant or associate superintendent. This person, a line administrator, reports directly to the superintendent, who is in the forefront. In large school districts curriculum directors or coordinators report to the assistant or associate superintendent. Ideally, this assistant or associate superintendent (1) chairs or serves as advisor to the general curriculum advisory committee; (2) is responsible for informing the superintendent of the major trends occurring in the field of curriculum and how these trends are being translated in the school system; (3) works with elementary and secondary directors or coordinators regarding curricular activity; (4) is in charge of the budget for curricular activity; (5) provides input in the statement of philosophy, aims, and goals; (6) guides evaluation relevant to aims and goals; and (7) manages long-term and short-term activities designed to strengthen programs.[63] This educator also helps formulate policies concerning curriculum innovation.

Superintendent. The chief administrator of the school system is the superintendent, who is charged with keeping the system running. The superintendent responds to matters before the school board, initiates curriculum activity, starts programs for the in-service training of teachers, informs all district personnel of changes occurring in other schools, and processes demands coming from outside the system for change or maintenance of educational offerings.

Good superintendents also inspire change and enable curricula to be responsive to changing demands. They are directly responsible to the

school board for the total educational action in the district. They must establish the means for curricular action, interpret all aspects of the school's program to the board, and set up communication networks to inform the public of and involve the public in the curriculum process.

Boards of Education. Boards of education are the legal agents for the schools. Comprised of laypersons usually elected as representatives of the general public, these boards are spokespersons for the community who are responsible for the overall management of the schools. They are also responsible for being informed about the realm of curriculum and for relating the existing curriculum to the goals of the school system. School boards, in fact, have the final say about whether a new program is funded or implemented districtwide. They enact district policies that facilitate the development and implementation of new curricula. They vote the funds that enable curricula to go from an idea to reality.

School boards, along with the central administrative staffs, seem to be losing some control in running school districts. In some cases, control has been taken away by the actions of state legislatures defining just what basic education is. In other cases, special-interest groups have gone to court to alter board policies if such policies are found unacceptable. In some communities, board members have been recalled by angry community members. In many school districts the school board, rather than being the leader in determining curriculum and policy, plays a secondary role. Federal, state, and local professionals carry the charge for creating new curricula.

Lay Citizens. Few people would contest that the schools belong to the public. But, although laypeople have been assuming increasing roles in curriculum activity, the role of the lay community in curriculum matters is still minimal. Most of the public, though perhaps concerned in general terms with the schools, are really not interested in becoming actively engaged in curriculum development. Most possess little knowledge about course content, course designs, or models of curriculum development. In general, parent involvement in school affairs drops off considerably as students grow older and enter middle level and high school; also, the secondary schools often neglect the importance of parental involvement in their student's education, much less school affairs.[64]

Research indicates that citizen participation in curriculum policy making tends to be superficial and reactive. Citizens sometimes participate, however, when goals are being determined and often when the changes have been completed. This may be because considering and implementing new programs involves needs analysis, and so receives media coverage. Most authorities maintain that the community should be involved in curriculum activity. However, there is still some discussion as to the extent and manner of its participation. Ideally, citizens should be involved in real problems and should be members of formal committees or groups established by the school district. They can, for example, be members of school-sponsored committees. Parents and citizens should play greater roles in curriculum matters if site-based management becomes fully implemented.

Participants outside the School District

Many participants outside the school district affect the nature and scope of the curriculum and influence who will plan the curriculum. These participants exist at various levels.

The Federal Government. For much of this century, the federal government was content to allow the states and the local districts to deal with curricular matters. But beginning in the 1960s the federal government became a powerful force in determining the kinds of educational materials and their uses in the schools. This corresponded with the post-Sputnik era, followed by the War on Poverty. Federal dollars established and maintained regional laboratories and centers, first for science and math and then later for disadvantaged and minority groups.

Today, controversy exists over the role and extent of involvement by the federal government in curriculum matters. It has been suggested, for example, that the federal government might well assume five specific roles. The federal government:

1. Could identify critical educational issues, many of which are related to curriculum, such as the demand for back to the basics or a common curriculum for all students.
2. Could synthesize the vast amount of knowledge regarding education, specifically curriculum.
3. Could promote research regarding curriculum materials.
4. Could support the application and dissemination of knowledge about curriculum.
5. Could encourage the preparation of persons interested in the field of education, including curriculum.[65]

Currently, the federal government, despite fostering the creation of national goals for education, appears to be withdrawing from playing a major role in education, leaving the key responsibilities with the states.

State Agencies. States have increased their role in educational policymaking. Much of this growth has been at the expense of the local school district. In many states, the state board of education has made formal recommendations and issued guidelines as to what the curriculum should contain and how it should be organized. The growing involvement of the states is based in part on the position that the management of education is truly a state function, a posture that is augmented by the decrease in federal funds.[66]

States affect the curriculum in many ways. State legislatures frequently publish guidelines on what shall be taught. They also mandate such courses as driver education and drug education to deal with perceived social problems. Pressure groups operating on a state basis frequently push their interests upon the curriculum. Often these associations or groups lobby in the legislatures to treat particular content and/or address certain students. With the publication of the numerous reports on the reform of education, state agencies throughout the nation have initiated minimum competency testing and gate-keep tests aimed at upgrading academic content and standards.

State boards of education seem to be taking a more active role in determining competencies and certification requirements of teachers, supervisors, and administrators. In some states, a special certificate, with specific curriculum courses is needed to become a supervisor or administrator. State legislators are taking a more active role in financing education, and thus indirectly affect new programs and funding of old programs. Then there are the state governors who have assumed the recent role of educational innovators—in context with the national reform movement in education.

Regional Organizations.   States often participate voluntarily in curriculum matters. Two regional organizations have become formalized to ensure such participation: regional educational laboratories and research and development (R and D) centers. Regional educational laboratories influence school curricula by providing guidance in the production of materials and by furnishing consultants who serve on planning teams. R and D centers investigate specific curricular problems, among other problems, whose results can be of value to curriculum planners. R and D centers also aid curriculum specialists by documenting the effectiveness of particular programs or approaches.

Another type of regional organization is the intermediate school district. The term "intermediate district," "educational service district," or "educational service agency" refers to an office or agency in a middle position between the state department of education and local school districts. About 40 states have some form of intermediate school district. The average intermediate district comprises twenty to thirty school districts in about fifty square miles.[67]

In recent years, intermediate districts have provided school districts with resource personnel in such general areas of education as curriculum, instruction, and evaluation; in specialized areas, such as education of the handicapped, gifted and talented, and bilingual students; and in more specific areas, such as prekindergarten education, vocational education, data processing, and computer education.

Other Participants

1. *Educational publishers.* In large part, publishers have given the country an unofficial national curriculum. In most schools, the textbooks used frequently determine the curriculum. The power of the textbook is particularly evident when we realize that nearly 75 percent of the students' total classroom time is spent engaged with instructional materials. An even greater percentage of time, 90 percent, is spent with instructional materials when students are doing homework. What students "know" usually reflects their textbooks' content.[68]

2. *Testing organizations.* Along with educational publishers, testing organizations, such as the Educational Testing Service or Psychological Corporation, have also contributed to the making of a "national" curriculum. By standardizing the content tested, these organizations have affected what content the curriculum will cover and how much emphasis will be given to particular topics.

3. *Professional organizations.* Organizations such as the Association for Supervision and Curriculum Development, the National Council of Teachers of English, the National Council for the Social Studies, and the American Educational Research Association have indirectly influenced the curriculum. Their members bring messages and goals set forth at state and national conferences back home to be tried out in the local schools. Increasingly, such professional organizations are formalizing networks of schools (and school districts) to communicate curricular concerns and to mount studies whose published reports set guidelines and standards for the creation of curricula.

Other Groups.   Many other people and groups outside of the schools also influence the curriculum one way or another. Colleges and universities directly and indirectly influence curriculum development. Many educational consultants to the schools come from the colleges. Business and private industry are building closer connections to schools by providing special personnel, donating equipment and materials, and funding programs of special interest. Groups who define themselves as minorities, entitled to special treatment in content areas and special programs, often organize to affect the curriculum. Sometimes, individual educators and lay critics assume the role of educational reformers, and they attempt, mostly through their writings, to give direction to curriculum development. Various foundations have also influenced curriculum formation, largely by supplying funds. The Ford, Rockefeller, Carnegie, and Kettering foundations have made the most active efforts to modify the curriculum through pilot and experimental programs.

CONCLUSION

Curriculum planners really have an over-choice of curriculum development models from which to choose. Which models they select are influenced by their philosophical orientations and approaches to curriculum. Several subject-centered models emphasize a technical-scientific approach to curriculum development, the major approach to curriculum creation today.

Likewise, several models of a nontechnical-nonscientific approach to curriculum exist; these consider curriculum from a more "evolutionary"

viewpoint. Educators who accept learner-centered designs tend to favor these models.

Diversity of approach characterizes curriculum creation; however, certain curriculum elements are universal and require attention from all curricularists. Content, experiences, and environments, for instance, are constants regardless of design or development, that is, whether a particular curriculum is being systematically planned or evolving naturalistically. A curriculum without content is no curriculum. A curriculum without experiences cannot be delivered or encountered by students. And a curriculum without a planned environment cannot be implemented by teachers.

The various models available and the numerous elements of curriculum present challenges to a vast array of participants, who exist at many levels—from the local to the national. People will no doubt continue to argue about who should have the major part in curriculum decision making.

ENDNOTES

1. James B. Macdonald, "The Quality of Everyday Life in School," in J. B. Macdonald and E. Zaret, eds., *Schools in Search of Meaning* (Washington, D.C.: Association for Supervision and Curriculum Development, 1975), pp. 76–94.
2. Franklin Bobbitt, *How to Make a Curriculum* (Boston: Houghton Mifflin, 1924), p. 2.
3. Ibid., p.9.
4. Franklin Bobbitt, *The Supervision of City Schools: Some General Principles of Management Applied to the Problems of City School Systems,* Twelfth Yearbook of the National Society for the Study of Education, Part I (Bloomington, Ill.: 1913), p. 11.
5. W. W. Charters, *Curriculum Construction* (New York: Macmillan, 1923), p. 5.
6. Ibid., p. 101.
7. Ibid., p. 105.
8. Ralph Tyler, *Basic Principles of Curriculum and Instruction* (Chicago: University of Chicago Press, 1949).
9. Hilda Taba, *Curriculum Development: Theory and Practice* (New York: Harcourt Brace, 1962).
10. Robert S. Zais, *Curriculum: Principles and Foundations* (New York: Harper and Row, 1976); Posner, *Analyzing the Curriculum.*

11. J. Galen Saylor and William M. Alexander, *Planning Curriculum for Schools* (New York: Holt, Rinehart and Winston, 1974). See also J. Galen Saylor, William M. Alexander, and Arthur J. Lewis, *Curriculum Planning for Better Teaching and Learning,* 4th ed. (New York: Holt, Rinehart and Winston, 1981).
12. Ibid.
13. Francis P. Hunkins, *Curriculum Development: Program Improvement* (Columbus, Ohio: Merrill, 1980); Hunkins, "A Systematic Model for Curriculum Development," *NASSP Bulletin* (May 1985), pp. 23–27.
14. Rhonda M. Wilkerson, "Integrated Teaching and Learning: A Developmental Perspective," *Kappa Delta Pi Record* (Spring 1992), pp. 93–96.
15. Catherine Cornbleth, *Curriculum in Context* (New York: Falmer Press, 1990); George O. Posner, *Analyzing the Curriculum* (New York: McGraw-Hill, 1992).
16. Herbert M. Kliebard, "The Tyler Rationale," in J. R. Gress and D. E. Purpel, eds., *Curriculum: An Introduction to the Field* (Berkeley, Calif.: McCutchan, 1978), pp. 256–267.
17. M. Frances Klein, "Approaches to Curriculum Theory and Practice," in J. T. Sears and J. D. Marshall, eds., *Teaching and Thinking about the Curriculum* (New York: Teachers College Press, Columbia Uni-

versity, 1990), pp. 3–14; Robert Young, *A Critical Theory of Education* (New York: Teachers College Press, Columbia University Press, 1990).

18. James B. Macdonald, "Curriculum Theory," in W. Pinar, ed., *Curriculum Theorizing: The Reconceptualists* (Berkeley, Calif.: McCutchan, 1975), pp. 5–13; Macdonald, "Theory, Practice and the Hermeneutic Circle," in W. Pinar, ed., *Contemporary Curriculum Discourses* (Scottsdale, Ariz.: Gorsuch, Scarisbrick, 1988), pp. 101–113.

19. Allan A. Glatthorn, *Curriculum Leadership* (Glenview, Ill.: Scott, Foresman, 1987).

20. Gerald Weinstein and Mario D. Fantini, *Toward Humanistic Education: A Curriculum of Affect* (New York: Praeger, 1970).

21. Ibid., p. 109.

22. Ibid.

23. Donald A Schon, *Educating the Reflective Practitioner* (San Francisco: Jossey-Bass, 1990).

24. Mark Johnson, *The Body in the Mind* (Chicago: University of Chicago Press, 1984).

25. J. Macdonald, "The Quality of Everyday Life in School."

26. Elliott W. Eisner, *The Educational Imagination,* 3rd ed. (New York: Macmillan, 1993).

27. Mark Johnson, *The Body in the Mind* (Chicago: University of Chicago Press, 1984); Schon, *Educating the Reflective Practitioner.*

28. William E. Doll, "Teaching a Post-Modern Curriculum," in James T. Sears and J. Dan Marshall, eds., *Teaching and Thinking about Curriculum* (New York: Teachers College Press, Columbia University, 1990), pp. 39–47.

29. Ibid.

30. Young, *A Critical Theory of Education.*

31. Ilya Prigogine and Isabelle Stengers, *Order Out of Chaos* (New York: Bantam Books, 1984).

32. Richard D. Kimpston, Howard Y. Williams, and William S. Stockton, "Ways of Knowing and the Curriculum," *Educational Forum* (Winter 1992), pp. 153–172.

33. Young, *A Critical Theory of Education.*

34. J. C. Parker and Louis J. Rubin, *Process as Content: Curriculum Design and the Application of Knowledge* (Chicago: Rand McNally, 1966), p. 2.

35. Paul Hirst, *Knowledge and the Curriculum* (Boston: Routledge & Kegan Paul, 1974).

36. Jerome S. Bruner, *On Knowing: Essays for the Left Hand* (Cambridge, Mass.: Harvard University Press, 1963), p. 120.

37. Israel Scheffler, "Justifying Curriculum Divisions," in J. Martin, ed., *Readings in the Philosophy of Education: A Study of Curriculum* (Boston: Allyn and Bacon, 1970), pp. 27–31.

38. Taba, *Curriculum Development: Theory and Practice.*

39. Asa G. Hilliard, "Why We Must Pluralize the Curriculum," *Educational Leadership* (December-January 1992), pp. 12–15; John O'Neil, "Preparing for the Changing Workplace," *Educational Leadership* (March 1992), pp. 6–9.

40. Henry A. Giroux, *Postmodernism, Feminism and Cultural Politics* (Albany, N.Y.: State University of New York Press, 1991).

41. James A. Beane, *Affect in the Curriculum* (New York: Teachers College Press, Columbia University, 1990).

42. David Pratt, *Curriculum: Design and Development* (New York: Macmillan, 1980), p. 116.

43. Taba, *Curriculum Development: Theory and Practice,* p. 278.

44. Allan C. Ornstein, "Curriculum Contrasts: A Historical View," *Phi Delta Kappan* (February 1982), pp. 404–408; Ornstein, "Components of Curriculum Development," *Illinois School Research and Development* (Spring 1990), pp. 204–212.

45. Maxine Greene, *The Dialectic of Freedom* (Teachers College Press, Columbia University, 1988); Philip H. Phenix, "Transcendence and the Curriculum," in E. W. Eisner and E. Vallance, eds., *Conflicting Conceptions of Curriculum* (Berkeley, Calif.: McCutchan, 1974), pp. 117–135.

46. Doll, *Curriculum Improvement: Decision Making and Process;* Ornstein, "Components of Curriculum Development," p. 206.

47. Taba, *Curriculum Development: Theory and Practice,* p. 290.

48. John Holt, "Children Are Sensitive to Space," in T. G. David and B. D. Wright, eds., *Learning Environments* (Chicago: University of Chicago Press, 1975), p. 83.

49. Francis P. Hunkins and Patricia A. Hammill, "Quality Curriculum: Determining the Urban Vision," *Education and Urban Society* (May 1991), pp. 292–301.

50. Brian Castaldi, *Educational Facilities: Planning, Modernization, and Management,* 3rd ed. (Boston: Allyn and Bacon, 1987).

51. Ann Lieberman, *Rethinking School Improvement: Research, Craft, and Concept* (New York: Teachers College Press, Columbia University, 1986).

52. M. Frances Klein, "A Conceptual Framework for Curriculum Decision Making," in M. Frances Klein, ed., *The Politics of Curriculum Decision Making* (Albany, N.Y.: State University of New York Press, 1991), pp. 24–41.

53. Richard D. Kimpston and Douglas H. Anderson, "The Locus of Curriculum Decision Making and Teachers' Perceptions of Their Own Attitudes and Be-

haviors toward Curriculum Planning," *Journal of Curriculum and Supervision* (Winter 1986), pp. 100–110.

54. Anne Reynolds, "What Is Competent Beginning Teaching? A Review of the Literature," *Review of Educational Research* (Spring 1992), pp. 1–35.

55. Henry A. Giroux, *Teachers as Intellectuals* (Granby, Mass.: Bergin & Garvey, 1988), p. 125.

56. Schon, *Educating the Reflective Practitioner.*

57. Doll, *Curriculum Improvement, Decision Making and Process.*

58. Mary Anne Raywid, "Rethinking School Governance," in R. F. Elmore, *Restructuring Schools: The Next Generation of Educational Reform* (San Francisco: Jossey-Bass, 1990), pp. 152–206.

59. John Goodlad, *A Place Called School* (New York: McGraw-Hill, 1984).

60. James A. Beane, Conrad E. Toepfer, and Samuel J. Alessi, *Curriculum Planning and Development* (Boston: Allyn and Bacon, 1986).

61. Carl D. Glickman, ed., *Supervision in Transition* (Alexandria, Va.: Association for Supervision and Curriculum Development, 1992).

62. Glenys G. Unruh and Adolph Unruh, *Responsive Curriculum Development,* 2nd ed. (Berkeley, Calif: McCutchan, 1984).

63. Roald F. Campbell et al., *The Organization and Control of American Schools,* 6th ed. (Columbus, Ohio: Merrill, 1990); Thomas J. Sergiovanni et al., *Educational Governance and Administration,* 3rd ed. (Needham Heights, Mass.: Allyn and Bacon, 1992).

64. Joyce L. Epstein, "Parent Reactions to Teacher Practices of Parent Involvement," *Elementary School Journal* (January 1986), pp. 277–294; Bob Stouffer, "We Can Increase Parent Involvement in Secondary Schools," *NASSP Bulletin* (April 1992), pp. 5–8.

65. Keith Goldhammer, "The Proper Federal Role in Education Today," *Educational Leadership* (February 1989), pp. 350–353.

66. Michael Fullan, *The New Meaning of Educational Change,* 2nd ed. (New York: Teachers College Press, Columbia University, 1991).

67. Allan C. Ornstein and Daniel L. Levine, *Foundations of Education,* 5th ed. (Boston: Houghton Mifflin, 1993).

68. David L. Elliott and Arthur Woodward, eds. *Textbooks and Schooling in the United States.* Eighty-ninth Yearbook of the National Society for the Study of Education, Part I (Chicago: The University of Chicago Press, 1990).

CHAPTER 10

CURRICULUM IMPLEMENTATION

Focusing Questions

1. *Why is implementation considered a restructuring activity?*
2. *How does planning relate to implementation?*
3. *What role does communication play in the implementation activity?*
4. *To what extent does the nature of change coincide with curriculum implementation?*
5. *Why do people tend to resist change?*
6. *How can we improve people's receptivity to change?*
7. *What factors influence the implementation process?*
8. *What roles can people assume in the educational change process?*

It makes little difference how appropriate or valued a school curriculum is if it does not get "delivered" to students. A curriculum, however well designed, must be implemented throughout a school district if it is to make any impact. Much that is planned and developed often does not get implemented. Many new programs do nothing more than gather dust on shelves. They get blunted at classroom doors.[1]

Part of the problem is that implementing a curriculum often has not been considered a crucial stage. Even today, with much discussion about change and the restructuring of the schools, attention is more often directed to organizational and management problems than to curriculum change. Few efforts to actually restructure the curriculum seem to be evident. Also, many charged with curriculum activity have neither had a good macro view of the process nor realized that innovations need to be monitored. Implementation should not be viewed as a clear-cut yes or no—to use or not use a new program. The process is developmental and occurs at different levels. Successful implementation of a curriculum, regardless of its design, rests on delineating at the outset of the development process the stages necessary for implementation.

The present authors view implementation as a separate component in the curriculum action cycle. It is the logical step once a program has been developed and piloted. It involves extensive actions by many parties, not just, for example, an offer to staff one workshop. Note, however, that implementation also involves attempts to change individuals' knowledge, actions, and attitudes. It also suggests that implementation is an interaction process between those who have created the program and those who are to deliver it.

THE NATURE OF IMPLEMENTATION

Leslie Bishop stated that implementation requires restructuring and replacement. It requires adjusting personal habits, ways of behaving, program emphases, learning spaces, and existing curricula and schedules. It means getting educators to shift from the current program to the new program, a modification that can be met with great resistance. The ease with which a curriculum leader can trigger such behavior changes in staff depends in part on the quality of the initial planning and the precision with which the steps of curriculum development have been carried out up to this point.[2]

Although experienced leaders of curriculum activities have realized that implementation is an essential aspect of curriculum development, only in the last 10 or 15 years has implementation become a major educational concern. Such interest has evolved partly because even though millions of dollars have been spent developing curriculum projects, especially for reading and math, many of these projects have not succeeded.

When evaluating implementation, we need to consider the various assumptions educators bring to the process. Many assume that implementation is simply another step in the curriculum planning process and that they can expect to proceed from the planning and design stages to the actual implementation stage with relative ease. After reviewing several innovative projects, Fullan and Pomfret presented some sobering comments:

> Effective implementation of . . . innovations requires time, personal interaction and contacts, in-service training, and other forms of people-based support. Research has shown time and again that there is no substitute for the primacy of personal contact among implementers, and between implementers and planners/consultants, if the difficult process of unlearning old roles and learning new ones is to occur.[3]

For implementation of a program or process to occur, changes must be made in the behaviors of all affected parties. Teachers must be clear about the purpose, the nature, and the benefits of the innovation.

A high degree of district-wide and school-wide implementation involves educating individuals about the worth of a new program or program component, such as a new content area or a new set of materials. Implementation also attempts to influence behavioral change in a direction or directions deemed necessary. It occurs in stages; it takes time to win people over to an innovation.

To win people over, we need to assure them that there is recognition or reward in making the effort to change, to implement the new curriculum. Indeed, what is rewarding gets done. Some have claimed that we really do not pay teachers enough to be innovators, to implement truly novel curricula. However, Kouzes and Posner note that educational leaders of curriculum need to be concerned if staff have to justify their involvement in a new program solely on economic bases.[4]

Involvement in curriculum change and implementation solely for financial reasons only contributes minimum effort to the venture. To be institutionalized, an innovation must elicit internal motivation. Too much reliance on external incentives actually constrains people. Individuals contribute their best talents when they accept the new program, when they derive a good feeling from being involved, and when they view their contributions as adding to the quality of students' education. People perform well when challenged, when the involvement is exciting, when the change process seems worthwhile.

Relationship of Implementation to Planning

Successful implementation of curricula results from careful planning. Planning processes address needs and resources requisite for carrying out intended actions. It involves establishing and determining how to administer policy that will govern the planned actions. Planning takes place prior to program creation and/or delivery. Edgar Morphet et al. have indicated that, if the processes of planning and implementation are to be effective and meaningful, the relationship between the two must be carefully considered. Effective planning must relate to a desired and identifiable change that is to be implemented.[5] Essentially, the planner, whether a politician, a businessperson, or an educator, is the agent of change. He or she must be concerned with instituting change in an orderly fashion.

Matthew Miles and Karen Louis note that for planning to occur there must be vision building. In their research, they found that those schools successful in implementing change and improving their programs had staff who passionately held similar images of what the school should become. Teachers were committed to the new program and had developed enthusiasm about the innovation. Implementing the new program afforded an opportunity to make vision reality, to give vision form.[6] Ideally, from the outset of curriculum development curriculum leaders have furnished those involved with occasions for such an attitude.

Only recently has vision become part of the management lexicon. Previously, managers discussed purpose, but not vision. Today, vision is receiving attention, as opposed to purpose, for vision suggests images and pictures. It suggests a dynamic future.[7] Curriculum implementation is not just for the immediate. It is created to generate future results and future dynamics. People get excited about a new program not so much for the particulars of what is there, but for the potential.

Implementation requires planning, and planning focuses on three factors: people, programs, and processes. Although these three factors are inseparable, some individuals consider that dealing primarily with only one factor will facilitate implementation. Some persons feel, for example, that to facilitate implementation of a major change educators must deal primarily with people. If the people change, so does the program and/or process. Others consider that the primary focus should be the program. People will adapt if they are furnished with different ways to meet the objectives of the schools' programs.[8] Still others think that attention should center on the organizational processes within which the people work. If departments are reorganized, if spaces are remodeled, then people will adjust in the directions necessary for successful implementation.

A leader may wish to stress one factor more than another, but no skillful leader will ignore any one factor altogether. Many school districts have failed to implement their programs because they ignored the people factor and spent time and money modifying only the program or process. One reason why many curriculum projects fail is that the curriculum innovators, especially from universities, center most of their energies on changing the program but pay scant attention to the needs of teachers, and minimal attention to the organization of their own schools.[9] The reason why they focus on programs is that is how to obtain funds or money for research.

Incrementalism

People want to change; yet they are also afraid of change, especially if it comes quickly or if they feel they have little control or influence over it. People become accustomed to the status quo and prefer to make modifications in new behavior in small and gradual steps. Most people, when they talk about change, and say they welcome it, often would prefer that other people within the organization change.

The world of the teacher does not allow for much receptivity to change. Both Fullan and Goodlad have described the teacher's daily routine as presenting little opportunity for interaction with colleagues. This isolation results partly from the school's organization into self-contained classrooms and partly from the teaching schedules.[10] Seymour Sarason has also commented on the isolation of teachers in the school organization and on how that isolation negatively impacts change. He contends that the reality of the school has made teachers feel that, professionally, they are on their own. It is their responsibility, and theirs alone, to solve their problems.[11] This posture causes teachers to view change introduced into the program as an individual activity. Viewing their struggles as solitary, teachers often develop a psychological loneliness that results in hostility to administrators and outside change agents who seem insensitive to the teachers' plight. Dan Lortie has noted that, in fact, many factors affect the teachers' receptivity to change:

> *Teachers have a built-in resistance to change because they believe that their work environment has never permitted them to show what they can really do. Many proposals for change strike them as frivolous and wasteful—not addressing the real issues which deal with student disruptions or discipline, student reading problems, administrative support, etc.*[12]

In an investigation of maturation during adulthood, one investigator noted that several principles can guide changing adults' behaviors. These principles include fostering multiple perspectives, allowing time for integration of ideas, and creating a supportive environment in which learning becomes more autonomous.[13] Drawing on these principles, the curriculum implementor facilitates the active involvement of teachers to allow for experiential learning, fosters the creation of an environment that encourages openness and trust, and gives feedback so that participants realize that their contributions are appreciated and their talents considered worthwhile.

Teachers need time to "try" the new program to be implemented. They need time to reflect on new goals and objectives, to consider new contents and learning experiences, and to try out new tasks.

Teachers also need time to reflect on the new program in relation to the mission of the school. For any new program to be successfully implemented, it must be perceived as central to the mission of the school. This congruence is especially important in turbulent times: "The more . . . change . . . is related or linked to [the] central . . . mission the more likely its survival in the face of shifting, but less central priorities."[14]

Implementation, therefore, does not occur all at once with all teachers. Ideally, an implementation process allows sufficient time for certain groups of teachers to try out the new curriculum in pieces. Loucks and Lieberman have found that teachers go through levels of use with a new curriculum. First, they orient themselves to the materials and engage in actions that will prepare them to deliver the curriculum. Their beginning use of the new curriculum is mechanical. They follow the guide with little deviation. Planning is largely day by day. Their delivery of the curriculum becomes rather routine, and they take little initiative to make any changes in the curriculum. As they become more comfortable with the curriculum, they may begin to modify it, either to adjust it to their own educational philosophies or to better meet students' needs.[15]

Communication

It is almost an axiom that whenever a new program is being designed, communication channels must be kept open so that the new program comes not as a surprise. Frequent discussion about a new program among teachers, principals, and curriculum workers is a key to successful implementation.[16]

But communication is a complex phenomenon. It has been defined as the transmission of facts, ideas, values, feelings, and attitudes from one individual or group to another. Put simply, communication deals with message processing

between the sender and the receiver of a message. The receiver can either accept or reject the message. Communication is not a one-way street; however, the process can be reversed to make a two-way channel.

Knowing that communication deals with message sending and receiving is not sufficient to ensure that communication will be effective or that messages sent will be accurate or of high quality. To assure that the communication network is comprehensive and the message sending avenues are in place, the curriculum specialist must understand both the formal and informal channels of communication within the school or school system. Formal channels of communication follow the established arrangement of the levels of organization. Communication can flow throughout these levels of organization both vertically (upward or downward) or laterally (horizontally) among peers.

If message sending, however, is from superior to subordinate, then the message sender needs to realize that the recipients of the message are more likely to attend to the message content. Messages coming from the opposite direction may not be attended, especially if the administration is run by a top-down model. Teachers must feel that the person in the "front office" understands the curriculum and will provide necessary support staff and released time to perform what is expected of them. Teachers need to grasp that what is being proposed not only affects them as individuals but also the entire school program.

Maintaining open communication channels upward is important, too, for teachers possess the hands-on experiences with curriculum. If a program needs to be modified, teachers are the first to know and perhaps even have the ways of addressing the perceived difficulty. Also, teachers will be much more willing to be involved in curriculum implementation if they realize that they truly have a communication route to their principal or curriculum director. See Curriculum Tips 10-1.

Lateral communication is perhaps the wave of the future. Horizontal networking among peers is being encouraged in many school restructuring efforts. Communication flows more easily among persons who consider themselves equals and equally involved in some change or curriculum implementation. There is much attention to teamwork within organizations. Also, many curricular activities involving combining of subject areas or integrating of major segments of the curriculum presuppose effective lateral communication.

While formal lines for lateral communication may exist in schools, much lateral message sending and receiving occurs informally. Ideally, effective curriculum leaders encourage the emergence of numerous channels of information communication. Informal communication networks result primarily from teachers' actions.

Networks get people together to share similar interests and concerns. By computer, people communicate with others who are not in their schools. Such networking should be encouraged by those engaged in any aspect of curriculum implementation, for it allows opportunities for gaining numerous perspectives on educational programs and the means of delivering such programs.

Whether the communication challenge is formal or informal, upward or downward or lateral, messages are relayed both orally and in written form. Information about new programs can be communicated by means of letters, memos, articles, books, bulletins, research reports, and speeches. The vehicles we use to communicate are only limited by our imaginations. With fax machines and electronic mail, messages can be delivered with a minimum of transit time. Interactive video allows meetings without individuals taking time to travel to meeting places.

There are still times when we wish face-to-face communication. Such communication is superior to other means of communication, for it allows the receiver of the message to raise questions and to furnish immediate feedback. Also, persons engaged in personal interaction can gain information from nonverbal aspects of the communication situation. Much can be learned from the tone of voice, the body language, and the facial expressions of the parties involved. The fact that people are brought together to discuss a new program gives testimony that the new program has significance. It also sends the message that feedback and input by faculty are crucial to the success of the new program and that people as individuals and professionals are valued.

Support

Curriculum designers need to provide the necessary support for their recommended programs or program modifications to facilitate their rapid implementation. They have to do this so as to build self-confidence among those affected. Educators often require in-service training or staff development time to feel comfortable with new programs. Research efforts have catalogued the characteristics of effective professional in-service programs. Such programs must be designed so that they can be integrated into and supported by the organizations within which they are designed to function. In-service programs that work have resulted from collaborative efforts and have addressed the needs of those who are to be affected by the new curricula.[17] Effective in-service training has the necessary flexibility to respond to the changing needs of the staff. Not all details of in-service training can be planned prior to implementation; nor can all problems and concerns be anticipated.

Because in-service programs must reach their intended audiences, they should be accessibly scheduled for curriculum implementors. Open discussions on the new programs should be scheduled throughout the implementation process. Such discussions allow implementors to voice their objections or concerns and consequently reduce opposition. Effective in-service programs must also evaluate whether they are achieving their objectives and whether they are in harmony with the underlying philosophy and approach of the district.[18]

Without adequate financial support, efforts to get a program going district-wide will fail. When federal monies were flowing, many school districts were quite innovative, but they failed to add funding for their innovations into their regular school budgets. When the federal monies ran out, which were essentially meant to be start-up monies, the districts discontinued their new programs, citing lack of necessary funds. If school districts, today, create new programs using federal or state grant money, called "soft money," they need to devise ways to support these programs once implemented with "hard money"— money that is part of the regularly allocated school budget.

Money is required for materials and equipment to institutionalize a new program. Money is also necessary to provide often-overlooked human support for the implementation effort. At the local level, five steps are involved in budgeting for new programs: preparation, submission, adoption, execution, and evaluation. The third step, adoption, involves the school board whereby it appropriates specific amounts for specific categories. The other four steps involve the superintendent at the district level and principal (or chair) at the school level.[19]

A trusting relationship must exist among all parties in the school, especially between the administration and the teachers. The principal is a key guarantor of successful innovation and implementation. Disagreement does exist, however, on how principals should furnish human support. Still, those considered to be successful principals are knowledgeable of and committed to the curriculum; they also view their role as providing encouragement for it, on one end of the continuum, and to serving as the curriculum leader, on the other end of the continuum.[20]

Implementation is a collaborative and emotional effort. Peer support is vital if implementation is to be successful. Dan Lortie points out that teachers spend the majority of their working time in individual classrooms with their students, therefore, they have minimal communication with their peers. By and large, they are left on their own with little input or assistance from colleagues or supervisors unless a crisis develops.[21] Opportunities for teachers to work together, share ideas, jointly solve problems, and cooperatively create materials greatly enhance the probability of successful curriculum implementation.

IMPLEMENTATION AS A CHANGE PROCESS

The purpose of curriculum development, regardless of level, is to make a difference—to enable students to attain the school's, the society's, and, perhaps most importantly, their own aims and goals. Implementation, an essential part of curriculum development, brings into reality anticipated changes. Simply put, curriculum activity is change activity.

But what happens when change occurs? What is the source of change? Can people predict the consequences of change? Can educators control those changes that directly affect them? Indeed, people can exert some control over the process of change, but to do so requires that they understand change. Understanding the concept of change and the various types of change allows individuals to determine sources of change. It also helps them realize that, even though they cannot really predict the consequences of change, they can make "best-guess" forecasts about its results.

Change can occur in several ways. The two most obvious differences are slow change (as when minor adjustments are made in the course schedule, when some books are added to the library, or when the unit or lesson plan is updated by the teacher) and rapid change (say as the result of new knowledge or social trends impacting on schools, such as computers being introduced into classrooms).

According to the research, for curriculum change to be successfully implemented, either slowly or rapidly, five guidelines should be followed to help avoid mistakes of the past.

1. *Innovations designed to improve student achievement must be technically sound.* This means that changes should reflect research about what works and what does not work, as opposed to whatever designs for improvement happen to be popular today or tomorrow.

2. *Successful innovation requires change in the structure of a traditional school.* By structural change, we mean major modification of the way students and teachers are assigned to classes and interact with each other.

3. *Innovation must be manageable and feasible for the average teacher.* We cannot innovate ideas concerning critical thinking or problem solving when students cannot read or write basic English or refuse to behave in class.

4. *Implementation of successful change efforts must be organic rather than bureaucratic.* Strict compliance, monitoring procedures, and rules are not conducive for change; this bureaucratic approach needs to be replaced by an organic or adaptive approach that permits some deviation from the original plan and recognizes grass-roots problems and conditions of the school.

5. *Avoid the "do something, do anything" syndrome.* The need is for a definite curriculum plan, to focus one's efforts, time, and money on content and activities that are sound and rational, not a scam or simplistic idea.[22]

The data indicate that the guidelines "are systematically interrelated, and that with the possible exception of the guideline regarding structural change, they apply equally well to all levels of education." Curricularists will benefit by "considering their applicability in the particular context of their own schools and school districts."[23]

A Theory of Change

Change results from new knowledge; however, the presence of new knowledge is not sufficient for change. People must recognize a need for change. And they are more likely to recognize that need if they understand change and how it works. Lovell and Wiles present a theory of change that incorporates five processes: (1) leadership, (2) communication, (3) release of human potential, (4) problem solving, and (5) evaluation. These processes can lead to system (school) tension and conflict or cooperation and cohesion. Every system has this choice, and the choice depends on the participants involved in the change.[24]

Adding further complexity is the fact that the system's process for change, according to these two system experts, is affected by external forces. Feedback from the external environment, for instance, furnishes new information, new expectations, and rewards or problems for system members. Such data inputs from external factors can cause tension within the system and generate a state of disequilibration among members within the system. This condition then sets in motion an attempt by the system to achieve a new state of equilibration.

Hence, change is achieved through the continuous process of disequilibration and reequilibration through problem-solving activities. Curriculum leaders, in short, must react to external factors, as well as internal factors, through the five change processes. Each one of these processes—leadership, communication, release of human potential, etc., will determine whether change is constructive or unproductive.

In contrast to Lovell and Wiles's theory, Kurt Lewin, considered to be the father of change theory, advanced a much simpler idea. His theoretical model appears in Figure 10-1.

Lewin considered that all persons find themselves in environments comprised of competing forces: driving forces and restraining forces. When these two groups of forces were equal, a balance or equilibrium existed enabling a steady state or status quo. This status quo is true regardless of whether we are discussing the actions of people or groups or the functioning of organizations. However, at times the driving forces begin to overpower the restraining forces, initiating change action. As long as these driving forces are the more powerful, the change activity will continue. When the restraining forces regain momentum, change will slow down. Once reestablished, restraining forces serve to inhibit change.[25]

Lewin conceptualized the change process as consisting of three stages. The first stage changes the current situation in which we find ourselves, an unfreezing, if you will, from a point A. This unfreezing actually means a decrease in the restraining forces in order to stimulate the driving forces. Lewin believed that to stimulate change, it was better to reduce the power of the restraining forces than to increase the driving forces. Such action allowed driving forces to act more naturally within the situation.

The second stage is getting the individual group or organization to move from the unfrozen point A to point B; the destination or goal point. Here the person or group or system engages in the actions necessary for attaining the change now desired. Upon successfully attaining point B, a refreezing occurs, the third stage of change. The process appears diagrammatically as follows:

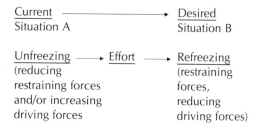

Lewin was instrumental in the development of laboratory training, also known as sensitivity training, T-groups, and encounter groups. The

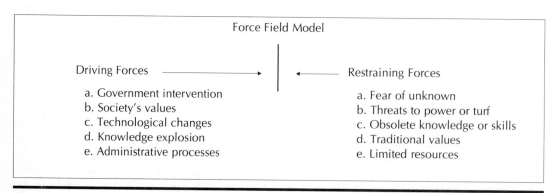

FIGURE 10-1 Force field model

National Training Laboratories (NTL) refined these programs in the 1950s and 1960s—and they emerged as widely used strategies to stimulate change in organizations. Training sessions are carried out in small groups of 10 to 15 members. The main idea of these sessions is to get participants to better understand themselves and each other, and to become more aware of group processes, to facilitate constructive change.[26] By analyzing one's own behavior, and the behavior of others, communication, interpersonal relations, and subordinate–superior relations tend to improve within an organization; the atmosphere is thus conducive for constructive change.

Large business and government organizations have adopted this strategy for change, much more so than schools. Nonetheless, today, curriculum leaders, supervisors, and adminstrators can enroll in these training sessions at the university level, often in departments of Educational Administration and/or Educational Leadership which stress organizational theory and organizational change.

Change Typologies

Persons with curriculum responsibilities, specifically those of implementation, need to understand the nature of change. With understanding, the change process can challenge and excite those who must be involved. Those who do not comprehend the complexities of change are likely to initiate actions that will result in discord within the school organization, either at the school level or district level or both.

Warren Bennis has identified several types of change:

1. *Planned change* is change in which those involved have equal power and function in a prescribed fashion. People identify and follow precise procedures for dealing with the activity at hand. Planned change is the ideal.

2. *Coercion* is characterized by one group determining the goals and intentionally excluding others from participating. The group in control has the major power and maintains the unequal power balance.

3. *Interaction change* is characterized by mutual goal setting and a fairly equal power distribution among groups. But those involved often lack a deliberateness of effort; they are uncertain how to follow through with the plans of development and implementation. Few procedures are carefully developed.[27]

The opposite of planned change is *natural* or *random change*. This type of change occurs with no apparent thought and no goal setting on the part of the participants. Often natural change is what occurs in schools. Curricula are adjusted or modified and implemented not as a result of careful analysis, but as a response to unanticipated events. For example, demands by legislatures or pressure groups that certain programs be implemented are inconsistent and based on whim or rhetoric.

Robert Chin has discussed three types of change strategies that can be considered as change typologies as well:

1. *Empirical-rational* strategies stress the importance of knowing the need for change and having the competence to implement it. Often schools lack this approach to change because they neither know they need a change nor have the skill to implement it.

2. *Normative-reeducative* strategies are based on the rationality and intelligence of humans. Humans will change if they are approached rationally and made to see that they need to modify their values, attitudes, understandings, and skills.

3. *Power strategies* require that individuals comply with the wishes of those who are in positions superior to theirs. Although outright strategies of coercion are rarely used in schools, it is not uncommon for those in power to "coerce" people into compliance by offering material and symbolic rewards in exchange for accepting new programs.[28]

We can also consider change according to its complexity. John McNeil has investigated the change process by using complexity as the organizer:

1. *Substitution.* This depicts alteration in which one element may be substituted for another. A teacher can, for example, substitute one textbook for another. By far, this is the easiest and most common type of change.

2. *Alteration.* This type of change exists when someone introduces into existing materials and programs new content, items, materials, or procedures that appear to be only minor and thus are likely to be adopted readily.

3. *Perturbations.* These changes could at first disrupt a program, but can then be adjusted purposefully by the curriculum leader to the ongoing program within a short time span. An example of a perturbation is the principal's adjusting class schedules, which would affect the time allowed for teaching a particular subject.

4. *Restructuring.* These changes lead to modification of the system itself, that is, of the school or school district. New concepts of teaching roles, such as differentiated staffing or team teaching, would be a restructuring type of change.

5. *Value-orientation changes.* These are shifts in the participants' fundamental philosophies or curriculum orientations. Major power brokers of the school or participants in the curriculum must accept and strive for this level of change for it to occur. However if teachers do not adjust their value domains, any changes enacted are most likely going to be short-lived.[29]

Although change that occurs in the schools cannot be fit into precise categories, curricularists need to realize that types do exist and that planned change is the ideal. But change is not synonymous with improvement. Education is a normative activity. A person's advocating and then managing change means, in effect, making a statement about what he or she thinks is valuable. This is why people can use the same change procedures and generate different curricula. They have different values and different perceptions of what education should be.

Resistance to Change

A curriculum leader who accepts that people are the key to successful curriculum activity and implementation is cognizant of the barriers that people place between themselves and change efforts. Perhaps the biggest barrier is inertia—among the staff, the administration, or the community. Many people think it is just easier to keep things as they are. If we think of ourselves as systems,

we realize that we like to maintain steady states. We have traditions to which we adhere and institutions that we cherish, and we do not wish to change them. Many people are happy with the current school setup as a bureaucracy.

Wanting to keep things as they are is often mixed with believing that things do not need to be changed or that the change being suggested is unwise and will thus be unproductive in meeting the objectives of the school. Educators themselves argue this point. Some say that the schools are fine and just need to be modified. Whereas others posit that the schools are not responsive to the times and require major modification. The status quo tends to be maintained if those suggesting change have not presented precise goals of the new program being suggested; that is, they have not planned adequately what the new program will look like or indicated ways in which the new program will be superior to the existing one.[30]

Often, teachers have not been able or willing to keep up with scholarly developments. They have not stayed abreast of the knowledge explosion, which would allow them to feel committed to curriculum change and the implementation of new programs. Teachers frequently view change as just signaling more work—something else to add on to an already overloaded schedule for which little or no time is allotted. Usually, no extra money or reward is earmarked for the extra work either. Many educators, in fact, are overwhelmed by changes proposed and their implications. Often they view new curricular programs as requiring them to learn new teaching skills, develop new competencies in curriculum development, or acquire new skills in interpersonal relations.

Another reason curriculum leaders have difficulty getting teachers to accept innovation is, according to Edgar Friendenberg, that people who go into teaching tend to be conformist in nature, not innovative. These people have succeeded in the school system as it has existed. They have learned to play it safe and to keep a low profile in a bureaucratic system run by administrators who do not like to create "waves."[31] They have found success and fulfillment as students and now as teachers in this system, and for this reason many see no reason to change it. To many beginning teachers, the bureaucracy in place is a welcome and familiar support system, and they are often slow to change it.

Can educators cope with the demands for more change or for assuming new roles? Uncertainty fosters insecurity. Often educators who feel comfortable with the present are reluctant to change for a future they cannot comprehend or see clearly. People often prefer to stay with certain known deficiencies than venture forth to uncertain futures, even if the changes most likely would be improvements. Bringing new students or parents or content into the curriculum realm or organizing the program in new ways makes many teachers uneasy.

Another factor that causes people to resist change is the rapidity of change. Many people feel that if something is implemented this year, it will most likely be abandoned when another innovation appears and will thus make all their efforts useless. There have, in fact, been enough "bandwagons" in education to make educators "innovation shy."

Sometimes people resist innovation and its implementation because they lack knowledge. They either do not know about the innovation at all or they have little information about it. Curriculum leaders must furnish all affected parties—teachers, pupils, parents, community members—with information about the nature of the program and its rationale. Ideally, all affected parties should be informed either directly or indirectly by school representatives of the reasons for the new program.

People often resist change, too, if no financial or time support are given the effort. A project for which no monies are budgeted is rarely destined to be implemented. Often, school districts budget monies for materials but fail to allocate funds for the creation of the curriculum plan, its delivery within the classroom, or necessary in-service training.[32] Finally, we raise the question whether a person who earns $25,000 to $40,000 is supposed to be a change agent. Teachers are not paid enough to innovate; that is not the role of a teacher—rather of a leader. Teachers are required to help implement change, but the school leader (principal) or school district leader (superintendent) should be the one to initiate change and provide the ingredients and processes for constructive change. On the other hand, teachers are virtually an untapped source of energy and insight, capable of profoundly changing the schools if they act as a group and direct their energies to local and state policy matters.

Thomas Harvey, writing on the nature of change, provides an analysis of the obstacles to getting people involved in change—and why they resist it.

1. *Lack of ownership.* Individuals will not accept change if they consider it alien or coming from outside their organization; interestingly, much of the current demand for reform and restructuring in the schools is coming from external sources, from national commissions or state legislatures.

2. *Lack of benefits.* If teachers are unconvinced that a new program will make things better for students (in terms of learning) or themselves (say, greater recognition, respect, or reward), they are likely to resist the suggested change.

3. *Increased burdens.* Often change just means more work, increased burdens; today, teachers are frustrated, even hostile, toward outside groups prescribing what needs to be done and lacking sensitivity to the issue of adding work to the teachers' already heavy schedule.

4. *Lack of administrative support.* People will not embrace change unless those officially responsible, often legally responsible, for the program have shown or guaranteed their support for the change.

5. *Loneliness.* Few people desire to innovate alone. Colleagual action is necessary for successful implementation of new programs.

6. *Insecurity.* People resist that which appears to threaten their security. The instinct to survive is strong and few will venture into programs with obvious threat.

7. *Norm incongruence.* The roles and assumptions of new programs must be congruent with the norms and expectations held by personnel in the system. Sometimes new programs represent philosophical orientations to education that are at odds with the staff's.

8. *Boredom.* No one accepts a new program believing that he or she is not going to enjoy the experience. Successful innovations are presented as alluring, enticing, and thought provoking.

9. *Chaos.* If a change is perceived as lessening control or of generating chaos, it is likely to be opposed. We desire changes that make things more manageable, allow for greater control, and enable us to function more effectively.

10. *Differential knowledge.* If we perceive those persons advocating change to have considerably more information than we, we may well consider those persons as having excessive power.

11. *Sudden wholesale change.* People tend to resist major changes, especially about-faces requiring a complete redirection.

12. *Unique points of resistance.* Sometimes, it is the unknown or the unexpected that surfaces and retards change. Not everything can be planned in advance; people or events (i.e., a death of a friend) outside the organizaiton can dampen our innovative spirit.[33]

Considering the points raised in the above list may make it seem that curriculum specialists face insurmountable problems. But such need not be the case. Being mindful of these points and sensitive to the needs of persons involved in the change will greatly enhance the smoothness with which change can be introduced and curriculum can be implemented. Also, we should realize that resistance to change does have the benefit of requiring change agents to think carefully about the innovations and to consider the human dynamics involved in implementing programs. Having to fight for change protects the organization from becoming a proponent of random change and educational fads.

Improving Receptivity to Change

Curriculum activity involves people thinking and acting. Leaders of curriculum development, and especially implementation, realize that the human equation is of paramount importance and that, therefore, they must understand how people react to change. Often, people say they are willing to change, but act as though they are unwilling to adjust. A successful change agent knows how people react to change and how to encourage them to be receptive to change.

Curriculum implementation requires face-to-face interaction—person-to-person contact. Those persons charged with implementation must understand the interpersonal dimension of leadership. Curriculum implementation is also a group process involving individuals working together. Not only does the group enable certain actions to occur, it also serves to change its individual members.

Of course, if a group is to change individuals, it must be attractive to its members. The ideas and values the group expresses must be acceptable to them. This is why curriculum leaders need to make sure that the members of the group are clear about the platform upon which they are to build the curriculum. This is why members must understand the rationale for the various curriculum designs and the consequences of accepting a particular design. As groups talk about the need to change and the strategies for implementation, they create a pressure for change within the educational system.[34] Creating a well-formed group with a clear sense of mission and confidence that it can bring about change is one way to make individuals receptive to the notion of change.

Curriculum leaders can also increase educators' willingness to change by "linking" the needs and expectations of the individuals with those of the organization. Each person has certain needs and expectations that he or she expects to fulfill within the school organization. Rarely, however, are institutional expectations absolutely compatible with individual needs. Getzels and Guba have created a model (Figure 10-2) that depicts the major relationships between the individual's personality and needs and the institution's role expectations.

Every individual who comes into a system plays a multitude of roles; each professional brings to his or her role his or her personality as well. Each person has certain needs he or she expects to fulfill within the system—in this discussion, the school—or the school district. Rarely is there absolute congruence between institutional roles and expectations and individual personality and needs. Misalignment can cause conflict. Curriculum leaders need to recognize that they cannot always avoid this conflict; they must manage it. The way they manage it is reflected in the social behavior of the individual.

Following the guidelines outlined next can help individuals increase their receptivity to curriculum innovations:

FIGURE 10-2 The Dimensions of Social Behavior.

Source: From Jacob W. Getzels and Egon G. Guba, "Social Behavior and the Administrative Process," *School Review* (December 1957), p. 429.

1. *Curriculum activity must be cooperative.* If a program is to be implemented and institutionalized, it should be perceived by all parties as their program. This sense of ownership is achieved by involving people directly and indirectly with the major aspects of curriculum development and implementation. When people participate in planning and implementing a program, they gain understanding of it and commitment to its goals and underlying philosophical basis.

2. *Some people like to change; some people do not like to change.* Resistance to any new idea is often natural. Curriculum leaders should anticipate it, and should prepare procedures for dealing with it. They must also identify well in advance of the action questions that will arise about the innovation being implemented: How will people feel about the change? What worries will people have? What are some likely points of conflict? What can be done to lessen the anxiety levels of individuals who will be affected by the change?

3. *Innovations are subject to change.* Nothing should be viewed as permanent. A new curriculum is presented as a response to a particular time and context. As time passes and contexts change, other modifications, sometimes even new programs, will be required. Change is a constant, and people need to realize that all programs will be constantly reviewed to determine if they should be continued.

4. *Proper timing is a key to increasing people's receptivity to an innovation.* If the school community is demanding that a new program be created to respond to a perceived need, then a new program addressing that need is likely to meet with success and acceptance. However, if people are satisfied with the current program, and there is little demand for change from either the staff or community, then a major curriculum change

should not be attempted. Also, if staff have just completed a major revision or created a major program, it is most likely not a good idea to involve the same people in another major curriculum development effort.[35] See Curriculum Tips 10-2.

CURRICULUM IMPLEMENTATION MODELS

We live in a time of overchoice not only of products, but also of orientations to action, as well as of models for guiding our actions. Considering the total process of curriculum activity can help educators select a particular approach to implementation. Their views are often influenced by their overall curriculum approaches and philosophical preferences.

Ben Harris has pointed out that strategies for improving educational offerings are not easy to identify. But scholars and practitioners continue to dialogue about the need for effective means of improving the curriculum and its delivery. Harris observes that from the present dialogue we can ferret out common suggestions for possible strategies of change: (1) clarifying lines of authority; (2) involving affected parties in goal setting, staff selection, and evaluation; (3) specifying roles and responsibilities of teachers; (4) training personnel in change strategies and conflict-resolution techniques; and (5) furnishing impacted parties with necessary support.[36]

Implementing change in any organization, and schools are no exception, requires a multitask approach. Those involved in implementing new programs should be encouraged by the fact that much of the work of the last two decades has furnished tactics on how to effect change in schools. Change agents can employ several strategy types to solve a variety of specific problems and to enhance change. We examine a number of change models next.

Overcoming Resistance to Change Model

The overcoming resistance to change (ORC) model rests on the assumption, according to Neal Gross, that the success or failure of planned organizational change efforts is basically a function of the ability of leaders to overcome staff resistance to change that is present just prior to, or at the time of, the introduction of the innovation.[37]

To implement a new program, that is, to introduce change, we must gain advocates for the new program. Glatthorn talks of developing a constituency for the planned curriculum change. To get a program implemented, we need persons willing to engage in something new, to push boundaries, to explore new territories. And these advocates must be able to attract colleagues.[38] To establish a community of supporters for a new program, we must address their fears, misgivings, misapprehensions, and other factors that could inhibit the acceptance of change. We must convince all that their values, assumptions, beliefs, indeed visions, are included in the new program proposed.

One strategy to overcome resistance to change is power equalization between management and organizational members—school administrators and teachers in this case. The leaders of an innovation accept that subordinates will initially be negatively predisposed toward the innovation and will hence resist it. This resistance can be avoided if staff members are involved in the deliberations that initially create the program and in the deliberations to develop it. Curriculum leaders, mindful of this fact, share their power with subordinates by allowing them to participate in decisions about program change. When leaders adopt this strategy, staff members tend to view the innovation as self-imposed and thus express ownership of it and commitment to it. Power equalization has thus become a key concept in several theories of organizational change. It has been constructed as an initial subgoal, a necessary predecessor to creative change.

Curriculum leaders using the ORC model realize that they must identify and deal with the concerns of the staff. In their research on the implementation of innovations in schools and colleges, Hall and Loucks have noted that concerns can be grouped into four broad developmental stages:

Stage 1: Unrelated concerns. At this level teachers do not perceive a relationship between themselves and the suggested change. For example, if a new science program is being created in a school, a teacher at this stage would be aware of the efforts, but would not consider that he or she would be affected by or concerned with the effort. The teacher would not resist the change, because he or she really does not perceive the change as affecting his or her own personal or professional domain.

Stage 2: Personal concerns. At this stage, the individual reacts to the innovation in relation to his or her personal situation. He or she is concerned with how the new program compares to the ongoing program—specifically, to what he or she is doing. In the science example, the teacher would perceive that he would have to be involved with the new program. The teacher would face the question of how well he could teach the innovation.

Stage 3: Task-related concerns. Concerns at this level relate to the actual use of the innovation in the classroom. Continuing the science example, the teacher would now be concerned with how to actually implement the new program. How much time will be required for teaching this new program? Will adequate materials be provided? What are the best strategies for teaching the new program?

Stage 4: Impact-related concerns. When reacting at this stage, a teacher is more concerned with how the innovation will affect others—the total organization. The teacher is interested in how the new program might influence students, colleagues, and the community. The teacher might want to determine the program's impact, too, on what he or she is teaching. Will the new science program, for example, enable students to live in the future world?[39]

When working with the ORC model, educators must deal directly with the concerns at stages 2, 3, and 4. If they ignore them, then people will either not accept the innovation or will deal with it in ways that are not intended in the program's conception. Such concerns can be addressed by curriculum leaders' keeping all staff informed of the innovation and by their involving those persons who will be directly affected in the early decisions regarding the innovation. Often, faculty can be called together to share concerns and to map strategies for dealing with those concerns. Sometimes information can be gathered from questionnaires that allow for open-ended questions. When concerns are shared, often persons with some insecurity regarding the program find that they really have nothing about which to worry. This does not mean that they do not have to make changes. Perhaps teachers will find that they do have to change their strategies and that they do have to teach different content. By sharing concerns, they may realize, however, that they are capable of making any changes necessary in order to deliver the new program in its intended fashion.

Organizational Development Model

Schmuck and Miles hold the positions that many approaches to educational improvement do not succeed because the leaders assume that adoption is a rational process. Taking such a view forces leaders to overrely on the technical aspects of innovation and diffusion. They assume that systematic properties of local school districts are constants. They do not perceive that the organizations need self-renewal or that various parts of the districts experience change as a result of interaction with the environment. Schmuck and Miles suggest organizational development (OD) as a better approach.[40] Organizational development has come to mean a rather specific approach for bringing about change and improvement in an organization. It is a long-range effort to improve an organization's problem-solving and renewal processes, particularly through collaborative diagnosis and management. The emphasis is on team work and organizational culture.

French and Bell depict seven characteristics that separate organizational development from more traditional ways of intervening in organizations.

1. Emphasis on the work team for addressing issues.
2. Emphasis on group and intergroup processes.
3. Use of action research.
4. Emphasis on collaboration within the organization as the dominant culture.
5. Realization that the culture must be perceived as part of the total system.
6. Realization that those in charge of the organization serve as consultants–facilitators.
7. Appreciation of the ongoing dynamics of the organization within a continually changing environment.[41]

Organizational development views the process of curriculum implementation as an ongoing interactive process. The task of implementation is never finished for there are always new ideas to bring to the new program, new materials and methods that we might wish to try out. Each year we have new students experiencing the new program; thus there is a need to implement and try out on a manageable scale new content and new instruction strategies. Organizational development works to orchestrate the various events of "teaching the new program" so that the actions of all persons involved are coherent and share a common purpose.[42]

Applying the organizational development model continually engages those concerned with

the new program in working to improve it and the conditions under which it is delivered. organizational development represents planned change, as opposed to random change. However, the change is not change for the sake of change. It is change as a result of careful deliberation and the consideration of alternatives. It is planned change that seeks to have people confront their own values, their perceptions of what is valued in the organization, and how the new program fits into the organization.

Organizational Parts, Units, and Loops

The system of relations that forms the whole makes or defines an organization. If no system of relations draws the parts into a whole, then there is no organization, just free-floating parts. These parts, in our case people, work in such ways that their areas of responsibility overlap others within the organization. An interplay or overlap exists among these groups. According to Rensis Likert, persons in these overlapping work groups serve as "linking pins." The notion of linking pins coincides with the idea of team work and organizational development. The interplay of the dynamics of these work teams, as conveyed by the "linking pin" incumbents, has a powerful effect on the attitudes and behavior of people in both groups.[43]

This means that the manner in which those in the higher teams work with those in the lower teams will rub off on the lower teams. If persons responsible for a major portion of an innovation treat their team players with respect, support, and trust, it is likely that those team players when interacting with others throughout the organization will also exhibit a similar style. This central assumption applies to all people whether placed on standing or ad hoc committees. The entire culture is affected.

Educators are coming to realize that the school is actually an organization of loosely coupled units—departments, classrooms, and persons. Also, these parts have rather flexible relationships. Although a central administration is defined, most schools have little centralized control, especially over what occurs in the classroom. For this reason it is difficult for curricular change to be implemented as an edict from the central office.

Viewing implementation from an organizational stance, educators realize that organizations can create conditions that significantly influence how individuals will perceive the innovation and the ways in which they will be involved in implementing it. Chris Argyris addresses this point in a discussion of the concept of organizational learning. He notes that learning occurs when an organization achieves what it intended—a match between what it planned for action and the actual outcome of the implemented plans. He asserts that organizations can address learning, or what we can call effective action, by either a single- or double-loop approach.[44]

As depicted in Figure 10-3, single-loop learning takes place when an organization detects an error and corrects it without questioning or altering the underlying values of the system. It just asks whether it achieved its objectives in light of the problem defined. Single-loop learning is routine and repetitive. Argyris gives the example of a thermostat for a single-loop learner. The thermostat is programmed to detect states of "too cold" or "too hot" and to correct the situation by activating the furnace. If the thermostat were to ask itself *why* it was too cold or too hot, then it would be a double-loop learner. Double-loop learning is more advanced and complex than single-loop. It involves reasoning processes among people affected by the change.

For the most part, students in school organizations learn by a single-loop approach. Generally, teachers note that students are deficient in

certain skills, and they set out to correct the deficiencies through a program of change. They do not always ask *why* the students are deficient. Sometimes teachers are not successful in meeting certain objectives, but they still may not ask themselves if the objectives are indeed appropriate in light of the current times.

Planned change within the organization, the school in our situation, should attempt to be perceived as "win-win" or match not "win-lose" or mismatch. In implementing change there will be the potential for conflict between people and groups, even departments. While conflict will occur, it must be managed so that people realize that everyone can win. The new program being implemented in the school presents an opportunity for all involved parties to gain: students, teachers, chairs, and principals. However, successful implementation requires energy, time, and patience. Implementation to be successful must be perceived as an effort requiring a long-range time frame and major involvement and cooperation among people and departments. See Curriculum Tips 10-3.

Educational Change Model

While there are numerous models of implementation at our disposal, our effectiveness in employing them depends in part on how well we grasp the entire concept of implementation. Michael Fullan has discussed key factors that affect implementation, a list that curriculum workers would do well to keep in mind.[45] Table 10-1 lists these factors.

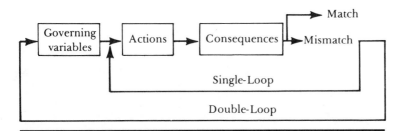

FIGURE 10-3 Single- and Double-Loop Learning.

Source: Chris Argyris, "How Learning and Reasoning Processes Affect Organizational Change," in P. S. Goodman, ed., *Change in Organizations* (San Francisco: Jossey-Bass, 1982), p. 50.

CURRICULUM TIPS 10-3 Unconventional Wisdom for Promoting Change

The human equation is an important consideration for curriculum implementation. Agents of change and leaders of change must understand people and how they react to change. Here are some unconventional ideas to consider.

1. *Progress from certainty to ambiguity.* Rather than making sure that everything is in place before you begin implementation, realize that some unexpected things will happen.
2. *Allow for some chaos in your order.* In your implementation journey, allow time for serendipity, surprise, and a little chaos. In dealing with "planned chaos," we may stimulate creative modifications in our implementation order and bring into existence relationships that we never imagined possible.
3. *Look beyond the person to the behavior.* We will get people to try out new ideas if, instead of personalizing disagreement, we address the behavior or issue. Rather than state that a person is acting unprofessionally or resisting a change, indicate that the person has raised issues of concern that need to be addressed.
4. *Realize that people do not resist change, but victims do.* People do not want to be shaped up or made victims in the change process. Getting people to be partners in innovation can reduce this feeling of being victimized.
5. *Use your fallibility to build your credibility.* The effective manager of change realizes that he or she is human and therefore fallible. Those who come across as all knowing can bring smiles to wiser players who know otherwise. Worse yet, others may become angry at the omniscient person. People who admit their mistakes and even indicate that future mistakes will be made in the implementation process are likely to be accepted as strong leaders of innovation.
6. *Be sensitive.* People who realize their own fallibility are more likely to be sensitive to others. They operate with people in open, honest interaction, with a true sense of who they are. They have recognized their personal space and the personal boundaries of others.
7. *Upgrade permanent to temporary.* Any new program is only designed for a particular time period, a particular audience. Times and audiences will change, and even the best of programs will have to be modified, perhaps discarded.
8. *Have humor.* Remember that most plans carried out are not so crucial that a missed date or a few snags will cause lives to be lost. Yes, education is serious, but we can deal with ourselves and others with some degree of humor. People who can see humor in missed cues, who realize the need to laugh at themselves, are likely to be much more willing to be involved in implementation on a continuing basis.

Source: Adapted from Thomas L. Quick, *Unconventional Wisdom* (San Francisco: Jossey-Bass, 1989).

Persons who wish to implement the new curriculum *need* to understand the characteristics of the change being considered. Often people will resist the innovation because the need for the change is not made known or, if made known, not accepted by those persons to be affected by the change. Needs are influenced by the values we hold. When people view change to coincide with their values, they are more willing to accept the innovation being suggested.

What the program will do and what it will involve are two questions that persons raise regarding innovations. People want to know the purpose for the innovation and how it is going to be conducted. *Clarity* about goals and means is always an issue in any change activity.[46] If we are going to persuade others that the suggested innovation is worthwhile, then we must be clear at the outset as to what the goals are and specify the manner in which people will be involved. Often

TABLE 10-1 Factors Affecting Implementation

A. Characteristics of the change
   1. Need and relevance of the change
   2. Clarity
   3. Complexity
   4. Quality and practicality of program
B. Characteristics at the school district level
    5. History of innovative attempts
    6. Adoption process
    7. Central administrative support and involvement
    8. Staff development (in-service and participation)
    9. Time-line and information systems
   10. Board and community characteristics
C. Characteristics at the school level
   11. Principal characteristics and leadership
   12. Teacher characteristics and relations
   13. Student characteristics and needs
D. Characteristics external to the local system
   14. Role of government agencies
   15. External funds

Source: Adapted from Michael Fullan, *The New Meaning of Educational Change,* 2nd ed. (New York: Teachers College Press, Columbia University, 1991).

people are not clear as to why a particular innovation is actually different from what they are doing.

    Complexity refers to the difficulty, which is relative to many factors. For staff experienced in curriculum development, extensive change can be rather easy. For inexperienced staff, the same change can be quite challenging. In most organizaitons, the idea is to remember the KISS theory: keep it short and simple. However, simple changes may be less satisfying, simple changes often do not make much difference. We need to recognize our innovation for what it is and have a realistic perception of its difficulty level.

    To accept an innovation people need to perceive its *quality,* worth, and practicality. While we would hope that any curriculum innovation would have evident quality, developers often miss the mark when it comes to practicality. The ideas are sound, but teachers just do not have the time to carry out the suggestions. Sometimes curricula are hapazardly implemented that could be practically implemented if those in charge had made sure that the necessary materials were available for teachers. Often teachers in new programs soon realize that technical or support staff are unavailable to answer questions.

    Curriculum implementation is "putting the show on the road." We all want a "hit play." Recognizing the characteristics of change will not guarantee a hit, but it can make one more likely. We need to keep in mind the community in which the play will be performed, the characteristics of the school district and school, as well as the key players in tables 10-1 and 10-2.

CHANGE AGENT ROLES

Any attempt at change requires change agents. Change agents may be students, teachers, administrators, consultants, state employees, university professors, parents, lay citizens, and political officials interested in education. Often such people can play different roles at different times in the change process, depending on their skills. Other persons are formally educated to assume particular roles as consultants, researchers, or systems

TABLE 10-2 Overview of Curriculum Implementation Models

MODEL	AUTHOR-ORIGINATOR	ASSUMPTIONS	KEY PLAYERS	RELATIONSHIP TO CHANGE TYPOLOGY
Overcoming resistance to change (ORC)	Neal Gross	Resistance to change is natural Need to overcome resistance at outset of innovation activities Must address concerns of staff	Administrators, directors, teachers, supervisors	Power strategy Empirical strategy Planned change
Organizational development	Richard Schmuck and Matthew Miles	Top-down approach (vertical organization) Stress on organizational culture Implementation an ongoing interactive process	Administrators, directors, supervisors	Empirical, rational Planned change
Organizational parts, units, and loops	Rensis Likert Chris Argyris	Parts, units, and departments of the organization compromise the whole Linkages between people and groups Implementations consist of corrective actions	Administrators, directors, teachers, supervisors	Normative, rational Planned change
Educational change model	Michael Fullan	Successful change involves need, clarity, some complexity, and quality of programs	Administrators, teachers, students, school board, community and government members	Centralized policies External/internal factors

experts. Often the job a person holds allows him or her to gain the expertise necessary to play that role in the change process.

Someone has to initiate the change process—or at least elicit a reaction to a demand. Almost anyone in the educational community can be an initiator. As we move up the administrative hierarchy, there is a greater chance for an individual, because of his or her role, to serve as an initiator.

Sometimes school districts pay one or more people to be internal initiators or change agents. These persons are charged with scanning the current scene to detect problems, demands, or deficiencies that require attention. These persons may get others to consider change by writing papers, forming ad hoc committees to analyze particular issues, submitting proposals, or simply sending memos to staff expressing concern for some action.

In some cases, an initiator stays with the change effort during its entirety. This frequently happens when the initiator is an internal member of the organization. Other times, the initiator is a catalyst and is not actively involved in any of the stages of curriculum change. The most successful change projects usually have an initiation phase with some person (or group) who is the initiator.

Students   Rarely do educators think of students as agents of change. We are just beginning to realize that students, even in the elementary grades, can contribute to meaningful educational change. How much we involve them will not only depend on their maturity, but also on the complexity and scope of change we are considering. Just as teachers must accept a new program for it to be successful, so students must also be willing to participate in the program. If students see little relevance in the curricular activities planned, they are not going to be motivated to participate—or learn. Ideally, we want students to react with heightened interest, with enthusiasm.

While we have been discussing empowering students to be more in command of their own learning, we have perhaps been a bit slow in furnishing them with opportunities for gaining the competencies requisite for assuming a more active role in determining the nature of their school experiences. There is still limited research to guide us on how to involve students. We have little information that tells us how students react to innovation.

Involving students in the change effort is not suggesting that teachers and students working on change should take time off from the curriculum of the school. The act of being engaged in considering the "what" of their education and "how" they will experience it can be very much a part of the students' actual curriculum.

Teachers as Initiators   We are now in a period of reform where we are involving teachers in the change process. Until recently, we tended to only give lip service to the active participation of teachers. Of course, teachers even when not formally involved in implementation are involved. They cannot be excluded because much of curriculum implementation is introduced in the classroom. But now we are involving them in the entire process of curriculum change.

For Henry Giroux, teachers are integral to the thinking that drives program creation and implementation. Teachers are reflective. They are aware of the assumptions behind the process, and they are involved in making the process of curriculum development and implementation even more effective. Many educators realize that, of all the people within the educational organization, teachers often are the most knowledgeable about the practice of teaching; teachers often represent the best clinical expertise available.[47] Of course, not all teachers are going to become actively involved in reform or change. But they can be involved in modifying and fine-tuning the work of their colleagues and outside professionals who have participated in curriculum development.

The key to getting teachers committed to an innovation is involvement. Good curriculum development is a cooperative venture. However, involvement means more than having teachers on the curriculum development advisory committee. For implementation to occur, many teachers will need to experience skill-training workshops. As Fullan and Joyce mention, they also will require numerous opportunities for one-to-one and group encounters where ideas can be exchanged and assistance given. "Talking up" an innovation is a way to make teachers eager to become involved in it. Being an advocate for an innovation is a new role for many teachers.[48] As teachers become involved, they realize the professional rewards of being players in the implementation process. There is a general satisfaction in generating ideas and assisting peers in mastering new competencies. And, teachers are realizing that being involved in change is not something that occurs in cycles. While there are periods of major revision or implementation of new programs, change is an ongoing process in innovative schools.

Supervisors   The processes of curriculum development and implementation must be supervised. Someone must monitor what is occurring and determine whether these actions are appropriate. Frequently, the word *supervision* is associated with instruction. Certainly, instructional supervision is important, especially at the level of implementation, but, in fact, the entire process of curriculum development needs to be supervised. Moreover, during the implementation phase, not only the manner of teaching but also the content that is actually being addressed need to be supervised as well.

The supervisor provides direction and guidance and makes sure teachers have the skills to carry out the change. Those charged with supervising curriculum development and implementation are responsible for overseeing or directing the work of others. This requires making certain decisions, engaging in particular actions, and interacting with others involved in the change effort.[49]

Effective supervisors realize that they must alter their tactics depending on the situation and the participants. Supervisors can place much responsibility in the hands of seasoned and experienced, teachers. However, they might have to provide beginning teachers with much more structure. They might need to schedule more supervisor–teacher conferences and more in-service training for such staff members to deliver the new curriculum.

Ronald Doll points out that supervisors have three major tasks: (1) assisting the total faculty in determining the purposes of education and monitoring the actions of professionals to see that these purposes are adhered to in the delivery of the program; (2) furnishing democratic instructional leadership; and (3) keeping channels of communications within the school organization and between the school and the community open.[50]

Supervisors can carry out their responsibilities in numerous ways. A few popular ways are classroom observation, demonstration teaching, supervisor–teacher conferences, staff development meetings, and grant funding.

If supervisors are effective, it is likely that the teachers within the system will feel committed to and comfortable with the new program being implemented. Teachers will be satisfied and thus the organization will run smoothly.

Principals as Initiators   Principals play a major role in program improvement. They can determine organizational climate and they support those persons involved in change. If a principal creates an atmosphere in which good working relationships exist among teachers, and teachers are willing to take the risks necessary to create and deliver new programs, then it is more likely that program changes will be implemented.

While we have known that the principal is central to the success of having innovative programs delivered in schools, it is recently that we have asked principals to assume the role of curriculum leader as well as instructional leader. In their review of hundreds of innovative projects, Berman and McLaughlin point out the role of the principal:

> *The importance of the principal to both short- and long-run outcomes of innovative projects can hardly be overstated. When teachers thought that principals disliked a project, we rarely found favorable project outcomes. Some projects with neutral or indifferent principals scored well, particularly in the percentage of goals achieved; but these projects typically . . . had highly effective project directors who compensated for the lukewarm principals. Projects having the active support of the principal were the most likely to fare well.[51]*

In their survey of secondary-school principals, Barney Berlin et al. determined the top ten curriculum functions that principals contend they do as curriculum leaders. In rank order, they were: (1) develops an orientation program for new teachers, (2) develops a clear set of goals and objectives, (3) involves individual departments in curriculum development, (4) encourages communication among schools within the district, (5) handles controversial issues involving curriculum, (6) spends time visiting the teachers in the classroom, (7) plans staff development programs, (8) rewards curriculum innovation, (9) encourages use of library and media services by the teachers, and (10) modifies school environment to improve instruction.[52] To be sure, there are few who would contest that the principal is indeed a principal player in implementation. This person is critical to the success of the change effort.

Curriculum Directors   The director of curriculum concentrates on the overall process of curriculum development, including implementation and evaluation. Large school districts have full-time centralized directors who oversee curriculum activities. Some directors oversee the entire K-12 program, whereas in other school districts there is a separate director of elementary education and a separate director of secondary education. In small school districts, the superintendent or associate (assistant) superintendent assumes responsibility over curriculum matters.

In schools where there has been successful change, the curriculum director assists teachers and principals in furnishing pedagogic and curricular knowledge. Teachers within the system expect these people to keep abreast of the latest research and theorizing about any particular innovation and to communicate these results to the school staff. Directors of curriculum can assist teachers, supervisors, and principals in the implementation process by inspiring and providing necessary support for the staff. For example, Edward Pajak points out that curriculum directors provide assistance to school people by (1) clarifying the districts goals and values, (2) conducting curriculum surveys, (3) communicating district policies and guidelines, (4) working cooperatively with local business groups to obtain funds, (5) coordinating federal/state programs, (6) organizing curriculum/instructional school teachers or committees, (7) coordinating staff development activities, and (8) assisting supervi-

sors in the supervision of instruction.[53] Directors also serve as resource agents, information agents, and consultants for selected programs and schools. They serve as a "linking pin" between the central office and school site, between the superintendent's office and school principal (as supervisor). Directors should inspire change and implementaiton through personal conferences, participation in committees, and staff development activities. See Curriculum Tips 10-4.

Curriculum Consultants   There are times when a school district will wish to bring in an external facilitator or coordinator. Often, in small school districts, there are no internal experts to consult regarding change or innovation. However, large school districts may also find that an outside facilitator is required. School districts do not usually employ curriculum consultants over extended periods of time. Rather, schools bring in consultants to do one- and two-day workshops. However, such workshops are not really effective—in curriculum development and implementation for such activities require a much longer time frame. Consultants are also used to analyze and/or assess programs, as well as to assist in grant funding. Most of these consultants are based at colleges and universities and have a specific skill that many small school districts lack in terms of central personnel who can do this particular job.

Joseph Murphy discovered from his research that when consultants were good, they were very good, and when they were bad, they were an obstacle. Good external consultants assisted by furnishing practical advice to teachers on how to utilize the materials. Often these persons conducted workshops to allow teachers to try out the innovation during the implementation stage. These consultants did not solve the teachers problems; rather, they worked with teachers so that they could solve their own problems. Bad or ineffective consultants often furnished information that was far too abstract to be useful.[54]

Most consultants will not work with a school district throughout the entire curriculum development and implementation process; there is just not enough time. This problem can be addressed in part by having consultants establish peer support systems, peer coaching, and networks for working with internal facilitators and suggesting information that teachers can use to gain comfort and expertise with the innovation.

Parents and Community Members We have known for some time, say since the 1960s when community control became a controversial issue in the big cities, that parents and community members want participatory influence in school matters and can be change agents. Certainly, school boards have always had a legal responsibility for approving and overseeing change efforts. But now we are witnessing the creation of temporary ad hoc committees comprised of community members and parents to assist in furnishing input into curriculum development and change efforts. After all, the schools belong to the community; they are not the possession of educators. Indeed, some critics argue that education is too important to be left just to the educators. Bringing in parents and members from the community should enable the change process to incorporate the diverse views of the community.

Just as we have not asked our students in past times what they thought about an innovation, so have we neglected to tap parents and other community members for their perceptions of new programs being considered for implementation. This is changing. More and more schools are involving parents in the stages of curriculum development from the formulation of goals to evaluation. This is all for the good, especially if we wish to promote participatory democracy, but many parents are unsophisticated and still others lack time or interest. In short, they are unable to provide us with much assistance in educational reform. But we have to start somewhere. We have to realize that we have a cadre of potential consultants who can furnish guidance in curriculum implementation, perhaps even contributing to the entire process of curriculum development.

CONCLUSION

Those who understand that implementation is much more than handing out new materials or courses of study realize that, if a new curriculum is to be successfully implemented, then those involved need to be able to visualize the purposes of the program, the roles people will play within the system, and the types of individuals who are to result from the interaction with the new curriculum. Such persons also realize that even though planning is central to the change and implementation process, the process cannot be rigidly planned. Human beings require plans that are flexible; we must be able to adapt the plans to unintended consequences of implementation efforts. Because change is a process—not an event that happens at a point in time—we are never really finished with the implementation task. Successful implementation of a program or procedure requires perpetual fine tuning.

Persons who have worked on creating a new curriculum or a new course are anxious to have it implemented and accepted with enthusiasm by all involved in the school or school district. However, new curricula often fail to become established in the schools because the importance and complexity of the implementation stage were not understood.

We have presented this chapter in hopes of making the case that curriculum implementation is crucial. We have shown that curricularists can bring various perspectives to implementation and that they can employ numerous strategies.

We have presented implementation as a change process. We have pointed out the complexity of change and that planned change is essential if innovation is to occur systematically in the school. Those in charge of change strategies must understand the relationship of change to planning and the interaction of individuals, groups, and systems.

ENDNOTES

1. John I. Goodlad and Frances Klein, *Behind the Classroom Door* (Worthington, Ohio: Charles A. Jones, 1970); Thomas S. Popkewitz, *A Political Sociology of Educational Reform* (New York: Teachers College Press, Columbia University, 1991).

2. Leslie J. Bishop, *Staff Development and Instructional Improvement: Plans and Procedures* (Boston: Allyn and Bacon, 1976).

3. Michael Fullan and Alan Pomfret, "Research on Curriculum and Instruction Implementation," *Review of Educational Research* (Winter 1977), pp. 391–392.

4. James M. Kouzes and Barry Z. Posner, *The Leadership Challenge* (San Francisco: Jossey-Bass, 1990).

5. Edgar L. Morphet, Roe L. Johns, and Theodore L. Reller, *Educational Organization and Administration* (Englewood Cliffs, N.J.: Prentice-Hall, 1982).

6. Matthew B. Miles and Karen Seashore Louis, "Mustering the Will and Skill for Change," in *Educational Leadership* (May 1990), pp. 57–61.

7. Kouzes and Posner, *The Leadership Challenge.*

8. Ronald C. Doll, *Curriculum Improvement: Decision Making and Process,* 8th ed. (Boston: Allyn and Bacon, 1992).

9. Michael Fullan, *The New Meaning of Educational Change* (New York: Teachers College Press, Columbia University, 1991).

10. Fullan, *The Meaning of Educational Change*; John I. Goodlad, *The Dynamics of Educational Change* (New York: McGraw-Hill, 1975).

11. Seymour B. Sarason, *The Culture of the School and the Problem of Change,* 2nd ed. (Boston: Allyn and Bacon, 1981); Sarason, *Human Services and Resource Networks* (San Francisco: Jossey-Bass, 1988).

12. Dan C. Lortie, *Schoolteacher: A Sociological Study* (Chicago: University of Chicago Press, 1975), p. 235.

13. David Heath, *Maturity and Competence: A Transcultural View* (New York: Gardner, 1977).

14. Thomas R. Harvey, *Checklist for Change* (Boston: Allyn and Bacon, 1990), p. 112.

15. Susan Loucks and Ann Lieberman, "Curriculum Implementation," in F. W. English, ed., *Fundamental Curriculum Decisions* (Alexandria, Va.: Association for Supervision and Curriculum Development, 1983), pp. 126–141.

16. David P. Crandall et al., *People, Policy and Practices: Examining the Chain of School Improvement* (Andover, Mass.: The Network, 1982).

17. Ann Lieberman and Lynne Miller, *Teachers—Their World and Their Work* (New York: Teachers College Press, Columbia University, 1991); Milbrey W. McLaughlin, Joan E. Talbert, and Nina Bascia, eds., *The Contexts of Teaching in Secondary Schools*

(New York: Teachers College Press, Columbia University, 1990).

18. Bruce Joyce and Beverly Showers, *Student Achievement Through Staff Development* (New York: Longman, 1988).

19. Harry J. Hartley, "Budgeting," in R. A. Gorton, ed., *Encyclopedia of School Administration and Supervision* (New York: Oryx Press, 1988), pp. 40–41.

20. Laurence Iannaconne and Richard Jamogochian, "High Performing Curriculum and Instructional Leadership in a Climate of Excellence," *NASSP Bulletin* (May 1985), pp. 28–35; Allan C. Ornstein, "Curriculum, Instruction, and Supervision: Their Relationship and the Role of the Principal," *NASSP Bulletin* (April 1986), pp. 74–81.

21. Lortie, *Schoolteacher.*

22. Daniel U. Levine, Rayna F. Levine, and Allan C. Ornstein, "Guidelines for Change and Innovation in the Secondary School Curriculum," *NASSP Bulletin* (May 1985), pp. 9–14.

23. Ibid, p. 14.

24. John T. Lovell and Kimball Wiles, *Supervision for Better Schools,* 5th ed. (Englewood Cliffs, NJ.: Prentice Hall, 1983).

25. Kurt Lewin, *Field Theory in Social Sciences* (New York: Harper & Row, 1951).

26. Chris Argyris, *Reasoning, Learning, and Action* (San Francisco: Jossey-Bass, 1982).

27. Warren Bennis, *Changing Organizations* (New York: McGraw-Hill, 1966); Bennis, *On Becoming a Leader* (Reading, Mass.: Addison Wesley, 1989).

28. Robert Chin, "Basic Strategies and Procedures for Effecting Change," in E. L. Morphet and C. O. Ryan, eds., *Planning and Effecting Needed Changes in Education* (Denver: Designing Education for the Future, 1967), pp. 39–57.

29. John D. McNeil, *Curriculum, A Comprehensive Introduction,* 4th ed. (Glenview, Ill.: Scott, Foresman, 1990).

30. Roald F. Cambell et al., *The Organization and Control of American Schools,* 6th ed. (Columbus, Ohio: Merrill, 1990); John P. Miller and Wayne Seller, *Curriculum: Perspectives and Practice* (New York: Longman, 1985).

31. Edgar Z. Friendenberg, *Coming of Age in America* (New York: Random House, 1965).

32. Seymour B. Sarason, *The Predictable Failure of Educational Reform* (San Francisco, Jossey-Bass, 1990).

33. Harvey, *Checklist for Change.*

34. Dorwin Cartwright, "Achieving Change in People," in W. Bennis, K. Benne, and R. Chin, eds., *The Planning of Change* (New York: Holt, Rinehart, 1976), pp. 36–67.

35. William W. Savage, *Interpersonal and Group Relations in Educational Administration* (Glenview, Ill.: Scott, Foresman, 1968).

36. Ben M. Harris, *Supervisory Behavior in Education,* 3rd ed. (Englewood Cliffs, NJ.: Prentice Hall, 1985); Harris, *Inservice Education for Staff Development* (Needham Heights, Mass.: Allyn and Bacon, 1989).

37. Neal Gross, "Basic Issues in the Management of Educational Change Efforts," in R. E. Herriott and N. Gross, eds., *The Dynamics of Planned Educational Change* (Berkeley, Calif.: McCutchan, 1979), pp. 20–46.

38. Allan A. Glatthorn, *Curriculum Leadership* (Glenview, Ill.: Scott, Foresman, 1987).

39. Gene E. Hall and Susan Loucks, "Teacher Concerns as a Basis for Facilitating and Personalizing Staff Development," *Teachers College Record* (September 1978), pp. 36–53; Hall and Loucks, "The Concept of Innovation Configurations: An Approach to Addressing Program Adaptation." Paper presented at the annual meeting of the American Educational Research Association, Los Angeles, April 1981.

40. Richard S. Schmuck and Matthew Miles, eds., *Organizational Development in Schools* (Palo Alto, Calif.: National Press Books, 1971); Schmuck et al., *The Second Handbook of Organizational Development in Schools* (Palo Alto, Calif.: Mayfield, 1977).

41. Wendell L. French and Cecil H. Bell, *Organization Development,* 4th ed. (Englewood Cliffs, N.J.: Prentice Hall, 1990).

42. Ibid.

43. Rensis Likert, *New Patterns of Management* (New York: McGraw-Hill, 1961), p. 113; Rensis Likert and Jane G. Likert, *New Ways of Managing Conflict* (New York: McGraw-Hill, 1976).

44. Chris Argyris, *Personality and Organization* (New York: Harper & Row, 1957); Argyris, *Increasing Leadership Effectiveness* (New York: Wiley, 1976).

45. Fullan, *The New Meaning of Educational Change.*

46. French and Bell, *Organizational Development.*

47. Henry A. Giroux, *Teachers as Intellectuals* (Granby, Mass.: Bergin & Garvey, 1988).

48. Fullan, *The New Meaning of Educational Change;* Bruce Joyce, ed., *Changing School Culture Through Staff Development* (Alexandria, Va.: Association for Supervision and Curriculum Development, 1990).

49. Carl Glickman, *Supervision and Instruction,* 2nd ed. (Boston, Mass.: Allyn and Bacon, 1990); Peter F. Oliva, *Supervision for Today's Schools,* 3rd ed. (New York: Longman, 1989).

50. Doll, *Curriculum Improvement: Decision Making and Process.*

51. Paul Berman and Milbrey W. McLaughlin, *Fed-*

eral Programs Supporting Educational Change: Implementing and Sustaining Innovations (Santa Monica, Calif.: Rand Corporation, 1980), p. 95.

52. Barney M. Berlin, Jack A. Kavanugh, and Kathleen Jensen, "The Principal as Curriculum Leader: Expectations vs. Performance," *NASSP Bulletin* (September 1988), 43–49.

53. Edward Pajak, "A View from the Central Office," in C. Glickman, ed., *Supervision in Transition* (Alexandria, Va.: Association for Supervision and Curriculum Development, 1992), pp. 126–140.

54. Joseph Murphy, *Restructuring Schools* (New York: Teachers College Press, Columbia University, 1991).

CHAPTER 11

CURRICULUM EVALUATION

Focusing Questions

1. *How can we define evaluation?*
2. *What important questions should be considered for evaluation?*
3. *How does measurement compare with evaluation?*
4. *Explain the differences between formative and summative evaluation.*
5. *Identify some of the evaluation models that follow each of the two major approaches.*
6. *How do positivists view evaluation?*
7. *How do naturalists view evaluation?*
8. *What are the major issues of evaluation?*
9. *What roles can educators play in evaluation?*

Few educators would dispute the importance of curriculum evaluation. Even if they did, many persons in the general public would counter that evaluation is indeed crucial to the health of education and its programs. In the last 40 or so years, there has been much curriculum activity at a national, state, and local level. Along with these curriculum activities has come a demand that the results of such actions be identified and communicated. Funding agencies and consumers want evidence as to the effectiveness of programs. They wish to assess the content, materials, and teaching methods used. They also want to know the cost of new programs and whether they are effective. They also desire evaluation of what is occurring at every level within the school system: at the classroom level, the school level, and the district level. The general public wishes to know the quality of education at the local, state, and national levels—even how we compare with the rest of the world.

Part of this demand is connected with a new realization of the importance of education and making the schools accountable. To meet this continuing demand for accountability requires that educators conceive and carry out an effective evaluation and reporting process. It requires educators to possess an in-depth understanding of the nature and purpose of evaluation.

THE NATURE AND PURPOSE OF EVALUATION

Although a simple definition of the concept of evaluation can be misleading, it can nonetheless serve to clarify the term for our discussion. Evaluation is a process or cluster of processes that people perform in order to gather data that will enable them to decide whether to accept, change, or eliminate something—the curriculum in general or an educational textbook in particular. In evaluation people are concerned with determining the relative values of whatever they are judging. They are obtaining information that they can use to make statements of worth regarding the focus of the evaluation. They are interested in conducting evaluation to determine whether the expected or the planned for has occurred or is occurring in relation to the intended. Applied to curriculum, evaluation focuses on discovering whether the curriculum as designed, developed, and implemented is producing or can produce the desired results. Evaluation serves to identify the strengths and weaknesses of the curriculum before implementation and the effectiveness of its delivery after implementation.

The purpose of gathering such data about strengths and weaknesses is to allow curricularists to either revise, compare, maintain, or discontinue their actions and programs. Evaluation enables them to make decisions, to draw conclusions, and to furnish data that will support their decisions regarding curriculum matters. Not all evaluation efforts are aimed at securing data and making judgments regarding students' success in a program. Often, evaluation efforts center on determining how to modify the staff's in-service education. Sometimes evaluation is directed toward making judgments on just how educators can communicate with and educate the community.

Evaluation Questions

Harriet Talmage has pointed out that a good part of educators' disillusionment with evaluation results because they misunderstand what it can and cannot do for them. We have perhaps been asking unrealistic or inappropriate questions of evaluation. Talmage discussed five types of value questions pertinent to evaluating curricula. An individual's approach to evaluation depends on which question or set of questions he or she poses.[1]

The Question of Intrinsic Value. This question addresses the goodness and the appropriateness of the curriculum. It deals with the curriculum as it is planned and also with the finished curriculum as it is delivered. Essentially, if a school were dealing with a new language arts curriculum, it would ask whether the curriculum incorporates the best thinking to date on what is known about the content of language arts, the arrangement of that content, and the presentation of that content. Would specialists in linguistics, composition, grammar, and communication give the curriculum planned "high marks"?

But raising such questions is not a simple matter of getting experts to analyze the curriculum document. People bring to this question of intrinsic value their philosophical and psycholog-

ical views. They perceive the curriculum in light of the purpose of education they see as paramount (Should we stress critical thinking, citizenship, or preparation for employment?) and what learning theory they prefer. (Behaviorists, cognitivists, and humanists have different views about content and methods for presenting it.)

The question of intrinsic value is difficult to process precisely, partly because there are subject areas in the school whose underlying principles are not carefully formulated. In science, there are underlying scientific principles about which most scientists and science educators agree. In contrast, bilingual educators would most likely express more diverse opinions about the underlying principles of their area of study.

The Question of Instrumental Value. This question posits, "What is the curriculum good for, and who is its intended audience?" Educators deal with the first part of this query by attempting to link up the curriculum planned with the goals and objectives stated for the program. Essentially, they judge whether what is planned in the program is going to address the goals and objectives stated. They can make this evaluation judgment by looking at the finished document; they also raise this question once the curriculum has been delivered.

The question of instrumental value also addresses whether what is planned in the curriculum will be attained, or to what extent, and by which students. In addition, this question concerns whether the philosophical or psychological orientation of the curriculum will be maintained, given the suggested contents, materials, activities, and methods. If a curriculum developer is a humanist, he or she might ask if the specifics planned for the curriculum are going to be instrumental in fostering in students a humanistic orientation toward themselves and others. A behaviorist, on the other hand, might ask if the encounters planned in the program are such that students will attain the specific behavior at the intended level of competence.

The audience to be evaluated must be identified at the outset. The second part of the instrumental value question addresses this audience factor. Not all curricula planned may be of value to all students. Evaluation efforts should identify the types of students who are likely to benefit the most from the curriculum being planned.

The Question of Comparative Value. This question is often asked by those faced with possible new programs. Is the new program better than the one it is supposed to replace? Usually, new programs are created because people feel that the existing program is inadequate. Often, when dealing with the question, people get caught up in making comparisons between different programs with different goals. Is a program that stresses skill training better than a program that stresses contemporary issues of the world? Certainly, the two are different. Whether one is better than the other relates to the values people hold as educators. But, still, if the program being suggested for implementation is of the same type as the existing program, the question of comparative value should be considered.

Educators need to consider this question, in fact, more than just in terms of student achievement. They need to compare the two programs' ease of delivery, cost, demand on resources, role in the existing school organization, and responsiveness to expectations of the community.

The Question of Idealization Value. When dealing with evaluation, educators are not just concerned with determining whether what was planned actually happened. They are interested in engaging in actions that will furnish data that can help them decide how to make the program the best possible. They are concerned with taking their information on how the program is working and asking themselves if there are alternative ways to make the program even better—to heighten students' achievement or to involve students more fully in their own learning. This question requires continued action throughout the delivery of the new program. Educators must constantly ask themselves how they might fine-tune the program's content, materials, methods, and so on, so that students can derive optimal benefits from experiencing it.

The Question of Decision Value. If the previous four evaluation questions are addressed, the decisions made should be quality decisions. The evaluator and the curriculum decision maker should now have evidence documented in such a manner that they can decide whether to retain, modify, or discard the new program. Decisions have consequences, however. The question of decision value keeps the curriculum evaluator cognizant that the value of the decision or decisions made needs to be assessed as the curriculum is delivered in the school classrooms.

Definitions of Evaluation

The questions presented in the previous section suggest that evaluation is a process or group of processes by which evaluators gather data in order to make decisions. Like most concepts in education, there is no consensus as to the meaning of evaluation. Worthen and Sanders define evaluation as "the formal determination of the quality, effectiveness, or value of a program, product, project, process, objective, or curriculum." Evaluation includes inquiry and judgment methods: (1) "determining standards for judging quality and deciding whether those standards should be relative or absolute; (2) collecting relevant information; and (3) applying the standards to determine quality."[2]

Bruce Tuckman has defined evaluation as "the means of determining whether the program is meeting its goals: that is, whether . . . a given set of instructional inputs match the intended or prescribed outcomes."[3]

Ronald Doll defines evaluation as "a broad and continuous effort to inquire into the effects of utilizing content and process to meet clearly defined goals."[4] Somewhat similarly, Daniel Stufflebeam has defined evaluation as "the process of delineating, obtaining, and providing useful information for judging decision alternatives."[5]

What is the difference between research and evaluation? Stake and Denny point out that the difference deals with generalizability and application. "Almost always the steps taken by the researcher to attain generalizability tend to make his inquiries artificial or irrelevant in the eyes of the practitioner. The evaluator sacrifices the opportunity to manipulate and control but gains relevance to the immediate situation."[6]

Essentially, the researcher is interested in advancing knowledge. The evaluator wishes primarily to gather information so as to make a judgment as to the worth of the phenomenon being evaluated. Even this needs to be qualified, since many educators are engaged in action research in which the variables in a new program are manipulated so as to improve the program in question, rather than to produce some generalizable results.

Further enriching our discussion of just what is evaluation is the view of evaluation as critical inquiry. In some ways, this is related to evaluation as disciplined inquiry, that is, studying phenomena so as to make informed judgments. However, evaluation as critical theory emphasizes that most models of evaluation advanced in this century and their approaches to utilization have seemed to neglect the very concept central to the word evaluation, *value*. Many models discussed in this chapter share a common feature; they appear to be value free, that is, objective. What some evaluators want to do is to determine if the values implicit or explicitly stated in the program are in fact attained. Does the program have worth or meaning? Is the program or curriculum valuable in the sense that its goals are attained? There is no attempt to judge the worth of the goals themselves or the social purposes to which the goals are employed in schools or society.

Kenneth Sirotnik and Jeannie Oakes expand on this concept of evaluation as critical inquiry. They argue that we should inquire into the assumptions undergirding the values we hold, the positions we advocate, the actions we undertake.[7] Many current evaluation models appear to fail to make explicit what the "good" is in evaluation activities. Most evaluators maintain that, while the presence and importance of values cannot be ignored, they can only be considered within a particular context. We judge whether the program attained its values and if those in charge of a curriculum have made their values explicit. Then what we evaluate is whether these goals have been attained. Thus, the evaluator approaches the task as a value neutral person. However, it can be argued that inquiry is not value free and evaluation cannot be value free.

Measurement versus Evaluation

Sometimes educators confuse measurement with evaluation. Other times they use the terms interchangeably to denote a general process of appraisal. Fred Kerlinger defines measurement as the assignment of numerals to objects or events according to rules. He points out that a numeral is a symbol of the form 1, 2, 3, ... It has no quantitative meaning unless someone chooses to give it such.[8] People use symbols to label objects, such as boxes of strawberries or learning packets. It is important to remember that they must also assign value and meaning to numerals. For example, an evaluation of 70 percent means nothing unless someone has stated that 70 percent means "passing" or "successful performance."

Measurement is really nothing more than the description of a situation or a behavior using numerical terms in order to avoid the value connotations that people can easily associate with words. A gym teacher can thus measure the number of times a student does pushups, a reading teacher can record the number of pages per hour a person reads, or a classroom teacher can indicate the score a child gets on a language skills test.

Measurement enables educators to record students' degrees of achieving particular competencies. Nonetheless, educators must do something with the data gathered; they must decide whether doing so many pushups is good, whether reading so many pages per hour indicates reading ability, whether a certain test score denotes success or failure. They must evaluate the data and make value judgments. Such judgments will be influenced by their understanding of the purposes of the program in particular and of education in general.

APPROACHES TO EVALUATION

Evaluation is a methodological activity that really is not content specific. The same procedures can be used to evaluate the effectiveness of any curriculum. Essentially, evaluation consists of gathering and combining data in relation to a weighted set of goals or scales so as to allow people to make judgments about worth. In determining the value of a curriculum plan, educators must eventually ask whether the results they expect to obtain are worth what the cost of delivering them is likely to be.[9]

How people specifically go about processing data is influenced by their philosophical and psychological postures. If they are behaviorists or if they believe in approaching evaluation from a prescriptive or sequenced orientation, they are likely to want to spell out specific entities of curriculum and instruction. They will want to have clearly stated objectives so that they can enact procedures that will furnish them with precise indicators of whether they—or, more precisely, their students—have achieved the intended outcomes of the program. If they are humanists, they are likely to be more interested in determining whether the situations planned have enabled students to improve their self-concepts. They may not pay as much attention to the students' specific achievements demonstrated by particular objective tests.

Whether educators are looking at achievement or self-concept, they will realize that an evaluation will still involve a managerial aspect as well as a decision-making dimension. They have to plan how they will obtain the data necessary for making judgments; how they will communicate to students and to others the effectiveness of the curriculum; how they will manage themselves and their evaluation actions as well as the actions of others who might be involved; and how they will determine the criteria they will employ to judge some aspect of the program.

In general, evaluation focuses on and results in decisions in one of three areas: (1) decisions about course improvement; (2) decisions about individuals, teachers, and students; and (3) decisions about administrative regulation—actually judging how good the school system is and how good individual staff members are.[10]

Scientific and Humanistic Approaches to Evaluation

Lee Cronbach had identified the scientific and humanistic approaches to evaluation as opposite extremes on an evaluation continuum. Advocates of the scientistic end favor clinical or objective

experiments; advocates of humanistic approaches consider experiments misinformative. Cronbach presented the *scientific* person as a believer in the true experiment:

> *A true experiment . . . concentrates on outcome or impact and embodies three procedures: (1) Two or more conditions are in place, at least one of them being the consequence of deliberative intervention. (2) Persons or institutions are assigned to conditions in a way that creates equivalent groups. (3) All participants are assessed on the same outcome measures.*[11]

Persons in this camp tend to concentrate their efforts on the learners. Data, frequently in the form of test scores, are employed to compare students' achievement in different situations. Information collected is quantitative, so it can be analyzed statistically. The decisions about the program or programs are made on the basis of the comparative information gained through the evaluation effort.

Cronbach described the *humanistic* ideal as very different from the scientistic ideals approach:

> *Writers at the humanistic extreme find experiments unacceptable. For them, naturalistic case studies are the panacea. A humanist would study a program already in place, not one imposed by the evaluator. If persons are assigned to a treatment, that is because the policy under study calls for assignment; assignments are not made for the sake of research. The program is to be seen through the eyes of its developers and clients. Naturalistic investigators would ask different questions of different programs. Benefits are to be described, not reduced to a quality. Observations are to be opportunistic and responsive to the local scene, not prestructured.*[12]

Those who approach evaluation from a humanistic or naturalistic posture analyze data collected in a way that differs significantly from that found in a scientistic evaluation. The data gathered in a naturalistic investigation are more qualitative than quantitative in nature. The evaluator relies more on impressions of what was observed. He or she engages in what are called "thick" descriptions of actual incidents that were observed during the evaluation effort. Data gained from interviews and discussions with participants are included in the evaluation. Patterns observed from the many observations form much of the data for analysis.

Today, the issue of approach to evaluation is not as clear cut. As Ernest House asserts, evaluation has moved from monolithic to pluralistic conceptions, to multiple methods, multiple criteria perspectives, and multiple audiences. Evaluators, who once for the most part viewed the methods of evaluation as primarily quantitative, are now coming to realize that qualitative methods are indeed appropriate means of processing data. Rather than viewing these two basic approaches as in conflict with each other, evaluators increasingly advocate mixed data collection methods.[13] A plurality of approaches seems to be the advice of the day. While we can argue that evaluators are still attempting to determine which programs work effectively, evaluators realize that they need more than just test scores to make that judgment.

But some persons still consider quantitative and qualitative methods as essentially different ways of viewing the world. These people possess different senses of reality. Those firmly in the *quantitative* camp seem positivistic in their orientation to the world. Those favoring the *qualitative* approaches are perhaps post positivistic. According to House, most evaluators would not place themselves in either camp, but rather would attest to the fact that the qualitative and quantitative methods are complementary.[14] However, we maintain that most evaluators would still consider themselves as favoring one approach more than the other. While they might settle on an approach somewhere between the two extremes, if given the charge to make a forced choice to identify themselves, they will favor one over the other.

There are several other ways to identify the approaches to evaluation other than the scientific (quantitative) and humanistic (qualitative). Evaluation can be classified as either utilitarian or intuitionist. The *utilitarian* is closely linked to the scientific, while the *intuitionist* is tied to the humanistic approach. The utilitarian evolution operates under the premise that the greatest good is that which will benefit the greatest number of individuals.[15] This approach to evaluation looks at large groups such as an entire school or school district. Attention is on total group performances.

Programs will be judged effective by considering how they affect the larger school student population. Those programs that allow the greatest number of students to attain the objectives will be judged of worth and appropriate to continue.

At the other end of the continuum is the intuitionist evaluation. Evaluators taking this approach are interested in gathering data to make judgments on the impact of the program on each individual. These approaches mirror those advocated by supporters of humanistic, qualitative evaluation. Persons taking this approach are interested in how individual students and subgroups of individuals are doing. Since attention is on individuals or small groups of individuals, there can be no one criterion of good. Rather, numerous criteria are employed to make judgments as to the worth of programs. Each person is the best judge of the quality of the program, not some outside or defective evaluator. All those affected by the program can make judgments about the program; their opinion is considered more important than a clinical analysis of the program.[16]

Intrinsic and Pay-off Evaluation

In addition to looking at evaluation from quantitative-qualitative or utilitarian-intuitionist continuum, we also can look at evaluation as either intrinsic or pay-off.

Evaluators can study the curriculum plan separately or they can study the effects of the curriculum after it is delivered to the students. Michael Scriven calls the first type *intrinsic evaluation*. The criteria for evaluation are not usually operationally formulated; evaluators are merely trying to answer the question: How good is the curriculum?[17] The criteria employed in such evaluation refer directly to the curriculum itself.

To evaluate curricula intrinsically, evaluators study the particular content included, the way in which the content is sequenced, the accuracy of the content, the types of experiences suggested for dealing with the content, and the types of materials to be employed. They might assume that if a curriculum plan has accurate content and a firm basis for its particular organization, it will be effective in stimulating particular student learning.

Although it may seem obvious that evaluators need to engage in intrinsic evaluation—that is, they must determine if the curriculum has value—some persons do neglect it. Rather than asking the prior question, "How good is the curriculum?" they ask, "How well does the course or curriculum achieve its goals?" Unless educators have some judgment about the worth of the goals and objectives and the attendant content, they cannot be sure that attaining the goals through a particular course or curriculum is a good thing.

Once the basic worth of a curriculum has been evaluated, its effects when delivered must be examined. Scriven calls this *pay-off evaluation.* Often the outcomes are operationally defined. Evaluators can consider the effects not only on the students, but also on teachers, parents, and perhaps administrators. This approach to evaluation may involve making judgments regarding the differences between pre- and post-tests and between experimental group tests and control group tests on one or more criterial parameters. Pay-off evaluation draws the most attention from educators. Its defenders assert that it is really the only one that counts, because it supplies information that allows them to determine the effects of the curriculum or course on learners.

Advocates argue that with their present state of knowledge, evaluators can only do "arm-chair" intrinsic evaluation. They cannot unequivocally defend the worth of some content or experience, but they can document whether in fact learners have attained a stated objective. Supporters of the intrinsic approach would counter that the important values do not really show up in the outcomes noted in a curriculum—outcomes to which pay-off people limit themselves. This is partly due, intrinsic people argue, to the deficiencies of present test instruments and scoring procedures. Also, the results reported in pay-off evaluation studies are usually short-term results of a curriculum. Little attention is given to the long-term outcomes of a particular program. If educators wish to have an idea of the relevance and perhaps elegance of a curriculum, they will best look at the materials directly, not at students' test scores.

Formative and Summative Evaluation

Another way to view evaluation is to distinguish between formative and summative evaluation. *Formative evaluation* encompasses those activities undertaken to improve an existing program. Evidence is sought so that decisions can be made about how to revise a program while it is being developed. That is, data are collected during the developmental phase of the program in order to modify the program before it is fully implemented in the school or district. During the developmental and early piloting stages of a curriculum, the evaluation effort provides frequent, detailed, and specific information to guide the developers. Formative evaluation takes place at a number of specified points during the curriculum development process. It provides the opportunity for the evaluator(s) to modify, reject, or accept the program as it is evolving. It provides a second chance, or third chance, to make some changes.

How educators conduct formative evaluation varies widely. If they are evaluating only one unit plan, their manner of evaluation may be very informal, perhaps only involving those persons teaching the unit. However, if they are engaged in creating a new program for the entire school district, then the procedure of formative evaluation may be more formal and systematic.

Because curriculum development takes place over time, formative evaluation is especially well suited for guiding the creation and fine tuning of a curriculum. According to Gronlund and Linn, it allows the teacher and others involved in the evaluation not only to determine what intended effects are occurring, but also to record and examine the presence of unintended effects. It uses the process of feedback and adjustments and thus keeps the curriculum development process "open."[18]

Summative evaluation aims at getting the total picture of the quality of the produced curriculum. It is usually undertaken after the project has been completely developed and after it has been implemented school wide or district wide. It focuses on the effectiveness of the total course or total curriculum. Summative evaluation's major purpose is to enable the involved parties to draw conclusions about how well the curriculum or particular curriculum unit has worked. The name *summative* has been applied not because of any particular method employed, but rather because this type of evaluation obtains evidence about the "summed" effects of various components or units in a particular curriculum.[19]

In contrast to formative evaluation, which often uses informal methods and frequently focuses on processes, summative evaluation is likely to use more formal means of gathering data for analysis. Tests for measuring attainment of objectives will be more carefully designed. Surveys given to assess teachers' reactions to the new curriculum will be formally prepared. Tests for students will be designed for use at the end of the course or at the end of the school year.

SCIENTIFIC- POSITIVISTIC EVALUATION MODELS

Formal evaluation has a very long history. The ancient Chinese were giving civil service examinations to candidates as early as 2000 B.C. Early Greek teachers employed verbally mediated evaluation in their teaching. The first large-scale formal evaluation was reported in the United States in Joseph Rice's 1897 to 1898 comparative study of spelling performance of over 30,000 students in an urban school system. Also, Robert Thorndike's contributions to the issue of evaluation in the early 1900s cannot be ignored. Thorndike was instrumental in getting educators to measure human change.[20] Finally, the "Eight-Year Study," from 1933 to 1941, was a turning factor in educational evaluation.[21] In our view, it represented the beginnings of the modern era of program evaluation. The evaluation plan was organized in seven sequential steps: Focusing on the goals and objectives of the program, classifying objectives, defining objectives in behavioral terms, finding situations in which achievements can be shown, developing or selecting measurement techniques, collecting student performance data, and comparing data against objectives.

Metfessel-Michael Evaluation Model

In the late 1960s, Metfessel and Michael presented the academic community with a variation of the model set forth in the Eight-Year Study. Their model presents eight major steps in the evaluation process. Evaluators should:

1. Involve both directly and indirectly members comprising the total educational community— teachers, professional organization members, students, lay citizens.
2. Develop a cohesive paradigm of broad goals and specific objectives and arrange them in hierarchical order from general to specific outcomes.
3. Translate the specific objectives produced in step 2 into a form that will be communicable and applicable to the conduct of the curriculum program.
4. Create the instrumentation necessary to furnish criterion measures from which individuals can draw inferences regarding the program's effectiveness in light of the objectives stated.
5. Conduct periodic observations throughout the implementation and maintenance of the program using tests, cases, and other appropriate instruments.
6. Analyze the data gathered.
7. Interpret the data in terms of particular judgmental standards and values that reflect the philosophical orientation of the curriculum. The conclusions derived will enable those involved in the evaluation to judge the direction of learners' growth, their progress in specific areas of education, and the overall effectiveness of the total program and its impact on all affected parties.
8. On the basis of information gathered, generate recommendations that will furnish a basis for further implementing the program or for modifying the elements of the curriculum, broad goals and specific objectives, specific content, experiences, and materials. At the conclusion of this step, the process is ready to be repeated.[22]

Arranged as a system of activities, the paradigm looks like Figure 11-1.

Provus's Discrepancy Evaluation Model

The model developed by Malcolm Provus combines evaluation with systems-management theory and consists of four components and five stages of evaluation. The four components are as follows: (1) determining program *standards,*

FIGURE 11-1 The Metfessel-Michael Model.

(2) determining program *performance,* (3) *comparing* performance with standards, and (4) determining whether a *discrepancy* exists between performance and standards.[23] This is shown in Figure 11-2. Discrepancy information is reported to decision makers, who in turn must make a decision (or act) at each stage. The choice of decisions is: To go to the next stage, recycle to a previous stage, start the program over, modify performance or standards, or terminate the program. It is the job of the evaluator to report to the decision maker and to identify problems and suggest what corrective actions are possible. When discrepancies exist, the decision maker is the key person in making decisions.

There are five stages in the Provus model, and they are described in Table 11-1. In all five stages, program performance is compared to program standards—criteria that have already been established.

1. *Design.* This involves a comparison of the program's design with a prescribed standard or criteria. The program is examined to determine if it is internally sound (adequacy of space, personnel, resources, materials, and so on) and externally sound (comparisons with similar programs that seem to work). The initial problems of the program are identified. Any discrepancy that exists between the program design and design standard is reported to the decision maker, who must decide whether the program should be rejected, modified, or accepted.

2. *Installation.* The actual operation of the program is compared with the installation standard

or fidelity criteria. The characteristics of the program are evaluated, including facilities, media, methods, student abilities and staff qualifications. Discrepancies between program installation and installation criteria are noted and reported to the decision maker for appropriate action.

3. *Processes.* Specific program processes are evaluated, including student and staff activities, functions, and communications. If the processes are inadequate, they should be reported to the decision maker who should make the appropriate adjustments.

4. *Products.* The effect of the whole program is evaluated in terms of the original goals. The products to be assessed can be in terms of student and staff products, as well as products related to the school and community. The information gained will assist decision makers about whether the program is worthwhile and should be continued as is, modified, or terminated.

5. *Cost.* The program products should be compared to products of similar programs; also, it should be evaluated in terms of cost-benefits. The methods of cost-benefit are not clearly explained. However, we must always ask whether the results are worth the cost—not only in terms of money but also morale and time taken away from other tasks. This answer has economic, social, and political implications.

Provus claimed that his evaluation plan could be used to make evaluations of ongoing programs, in any stage, from the planning stage to the implementation stage. It could be used at

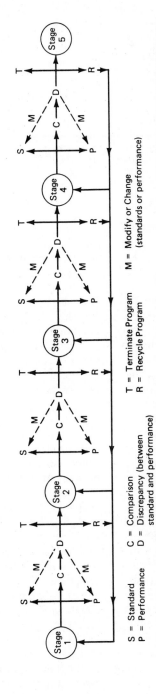

FIGURE 11-2 Components of Provus's Discrepancy Evaluation Model

Source: Malcolm Provus, "The Discrepancy Evaluation Model," in P. Taylor and D. M. Cowley, eds., *Readings in Curriculum Evaluation* (Dubuque, Ia.: Brown, 1972), p. 118; Provus, "Evaluation of Ongoing Programs in the Public School System," in R. W. Tyler, ed., *Educational Evaluation: New Roles, New Means.* Sixty-Eighth Yearbook of the National Society for the Study of Education, Part II (Chicago: University of Chicago Press, 1969), pp. 252–253.

TABLE 11-1   Stages of Provus's Discrepancy Evaluation Model

STAGES	PERFORMANCE	STANDARD
1	Design	Design Criteria
2	Installation	Installation fidelity
3	Processes	Process adjustment
4	Products	Product assessment
5	Cost	Comparisons and cost-benefit

Source: From Malcolm Provus, "The Discrepancy Evaluation Model," p. 118; Provus, "Toward a State System of Evaluation," *Journal of Research and Development in Education* (September 1971), p. 93.

the school level, school district level, and regional or state level.

Stake's Congruence-Contingency Model

In his discussion of evaluation, Robert Stake distinguishes between formal and informal evaluation procedures. While recognizing that educational evaluation continues to depend on casual observation, implicit goals, intuitive norms, and subjective judgment, he notes that educators should strive to establish more formal evaluation procedures. Formal procedures are objective rather than subjective and aim at furnishing data so that descriptions can be made and judgments rendered regarding the program being evaluated.[24]

Stake indicates that evaluation specialists seem to be, and rightly so, increasing their emphasis on providing full objective descriptions and on collecting and reporting hard data. Stake asks that evaluators collect and process more extensive types of data and that they consider the dynamics among the people involved in the curriculum process. Not only should evaluators assess the roles various people play, but they should be sure to allow those people more extensive participation in judging programs. Stake further maintains that those involved in curriculum evaluation must make judgments in addition to reporting data; they should even take positions on the worth of the program being evaluated. Many evaluation specialists note that they are willing to

let the local community make judgments about worth. Stake accepts that making judgments is difficult, but points out it is part of the professional role of the evaluator.

Stake maintains that data can be organized into three bodies of information: antecedents, transactions, and outcomes. An *antecedent* is any condition that exists prior to teaching and learning that may influence outcomes. Antecedents are such things as the status or characteristics of the students prior to their lessons: their aptitudes, previous achievement scores, psychological profile scores, grades, discipline, and attendance. Antecedents also include teacher characteristics such as years of experience, type of education, and teacher behavior ratings. Antecedents are "entry behaviors," sometimes described as "inputs" by other evaluators.

Stake notes that *transactions* occur between and among students and teachers, among students and students, and among students and resource people. Transactions are interactions the students have with certain curriculum materials and classroom environments dealing with time allocation, space arrangements, and communication flow. Transactions comprise what is commonly called the "process" of teaching and instruction.

In our approach to evaluation, we have been concerned with *outcomes,* also called "products," of programs—particularly achievement, sometimes attitudes and motor skills. Evaluators also need to attend to such outcomes as the impact of a new program on teachers' perceptions of their competence. They need to evaluate the influence of a program's outcomes on the actions of administrators. They also need to consider outcomes that are not directly evident at the conclusion of a program. And they should attend to long-range effects, too. Stake contends that outcomes are the consequences of education—immediate and long-range, cognitive and affective, personal and community wide.[25]

Stake's model for planning an evaluation study provides an organizational framework that points out data to be considered and contrasts what is planned and what has occurred. This model arranges the three types of data into a matrix. Figure 11-3 shows the matrix. The model shows the antecedents, transactions, and outcomes—the elements of evaluation—both intended and observed.

The challenge to the evaluator is to identify contingencies, and later congruencies, among these antecedents, transactions and outcomes. *Contingencies* are the relationships among the variables in the three categories: antecedents, transactions, and outcomes. Ideally, it should be demonstrated that the outcomes are a result of antecedents and transactions. If it can be shown that transactions are related to prior antecedents, then the transactions are logically contingent on the antecedents. Similarly, the outcomes should be logically contingent from the transactions. In short, one category is expected to lead to observable and/or measurable variables in another category.

The model shows that the evaluator is also concerned with *congruence* between the intended and the observed outcomes. In dealing with congruency, he or she strives to match what is intended and what is observed. Did what was intended actually happen? To be completely congruent, all the intended antecedents, transactions, and outcomes would have to occur.

Stufflebeam's Context, Input, Process, Product Model

Perhaps the most important contribution to a decision-management-oriented approach to educational evaluation has been that presented by Daniel Stufflebeam. His approach to evaluation is recognized as the CIPP (context, input, process, product) model.[26] This comprehensive model considers evaluation to be a continuing process.

Information is provided to management for the purpose of decision making. It is a three-step process: *delineating* the information necessary for collection, *obtaining* the information, and

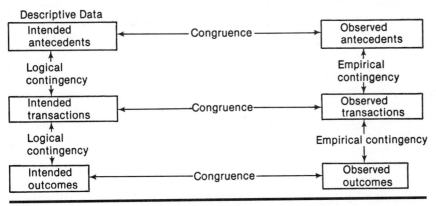

FIGURE 11-3 Congruence-Contingency Model.

Source: from Robert E. Stake, "Language, Rationality, and Assessment," in W. H. Beatty, ed., *Improving Educational Assessment and an Inventory of Measures of Affective Behavior* (Washington, D.C.: Association for Supervision and Curriculum Development, 1969), p. 20. Used with permission.

providing the information to interested parties. Any evaluation study must include these three steps. Corresponding to these decision types are four types of evaluation: (1) context, (2) input, (3) process, and (4) product.

Context Evaluation. Context evaluation involves studying the environment of the program. Its purpose is to define the relevant environment, portray the desired and actual conditions pertaining to that environment, focus on unmet needs and missed opportunities, and diagnose the reason for unmet needs. Context evaluation is really a "situation analysis,"—a reading of the reality in which individuals find themselves and an assessment of that reality in light of what they want to do. This diagnosis stage of evaluation is not a one-time activity. It continues to furnish baseline information regarding the operations and accomplishments of the total system. See Curriculum Tips 11-1.

Input Evaluation. The second stage of the model, input evaluation, is designed to provide information and determine how to utilize resources to meet program goals.

Input evaluators assess the school's capabilities to carry out the task of evaluation; they consider the strategies suggested for achieving program goals, and they identify the means by which a selected strategy will be implemented. At this stage, we might consider alternative designs in terms of how they will contribute to the attainment of objectives in terms of resources, time, and budget. Here we are focusing on what is feasible or practiced.

Input evaluates specific aspects of the curriculum plan or specific components of the curriculum plan. It deals with the following questions: Are the objectives stated appropriately? Are the objectives congruent with the goals of the school? Is the content congruent with the goals and objectives of the program? Are the instructional strategies appropriate? Do other strategies exist that can also help meet the objectives? What is the basis for believing that using these contents and these instructional strategies will enable educators to successfully attain their objectives?

Process Evaluation. This stage addresses curriculum implementation decisions that control and manage the program. It is used to determine the congruency between the planned and actual activities. It includes three strategies. "The first is to detect or predict defects in the procedural design or its implementation stage, the second is to provide information for decisions, and the third is to maintain a record of procedures as they occur."[27]

In dealing with program defects, or the first strategy, it is important for educators to identify and monitor continually the potential sources of the project's failure. They must pay attention to the logistics of the entire operation, and they must maintain communication channels among all affected parties. The second strategy involves decisions to be made by project managers during the implementation of a project. For example, some decisions may require that certain in-service activities be planned and carried out before the program's actual implementation. The third strategy addresses the main feature of the project design, for example, the particular content selected, new instructional strategies, or innovative student–teacher planning sessions.

Process evaluation, which includes the three strategies, occurs during the implementation stage of curriculum development. It is a piloting process conducted to "debug" the program before district-wide implementation. From such evaluation, project decision makers obtain information they need to anticipate and overcome procedural difficulties and to make preprogrammed decisions.

Product Evaluation. Product evaluators gather data to determine whether the final curriculum product now in use is accomplishing what they had hoped. To what extent are the objectives created being attained? Product evaluation provides evaluators with information that will enable them to decide whether to continue, terminate, or modify the new curriculum. It allows them to link actions at this stage of the model to other stages of the total change process. For example, a product evaluation might furnish data that shows that the science curriculum planned for talented science students has successfully allowed students to attain the program objectives. The program is now ready to be implemented in other schools in the system.

Judicial Approach to Evaluation

Many educators still believe that the evaluator should judge in an impartial and nonvalue-laden manner. However, even within the scientific camp, individuals are coming to realize that evaluations are made by humans and humans have values. A rather new model being used in making evaluations sets up an encounter, rather than precisely spelling out steps to take. This model is the judicial model or what some call the adversary evaluation approach.[28]

This procedure encompasses numerous evaluation activities in which time is scheduled for opposing points of view to be heard. One evaluator or team member serves as the program's advocate, presenting the positive view of the program. Another evaluator or team member plays an adversarial role, stressing problems in the program. The encounter is very much like a court trial. People to be affected by the new program have their day in court. By allowing individuals to present both sides or opposing views of the new program, a more accurate view of the new program is attained.

The program stands or falls on the weight of the evidence furnished.

In addition to following judicial court proceedings, this adversary approach to evaluation can also be used in congressional hearings, community town meetings, and formal debates. With the current emphasis on participant involvement in the evaluation process, this adversary approach may well serve to not only judge the value and effectiveness of a program, but give both the community within the school and outside the school a broad view of the program and also the underlying rationale. Not only are people apprised of the evaluation data, but the entire process can be considered educational for all parties.

The judicial evaluation method is often used for the passage of legislation, such as with the Civil Rights Act, Education for All Handicapped Children Act, and in educational finance laws such as Proposition 13 or more recently in finance cases involving the states of Kentucky, New Jersey, and Texas. People get the opportunity to express their sentiment and participate in educational policy. With the growing concern among educators, policy makers, and the public about education, we can expect this model (or its derivatives) to be increasingly used in the future. See Curriculum Tips 11-2.

Humanistic and Naturalistic Evaluation Models

The previous models draw heavily on the quantitative and technical posture of evaluation. However, some evaluation theorists take issue with these scientific approaches to evaluation. They feel that evaluators have become much too concerned with observing or measuring specific behavioral objectives and generating elaborate evaluative schemes to measure program success.[29] In many ways, these critics reflect the growing awareness that educators have become obsessed with a positivistic paradigm, a mechanistic view of the world that consists of competencies, checklists, and tiny behaviors that can be assessed.

A new approach to evaluation has taken form, a thinking that places the evaluator in the center of things. Evaluators not only visit sites, but they are often personally involved in arguing their values and cases with colleagues. Evaluators are not separated from the system, looking on as disinterested parties; rather, they are viewed as integral parts of the very process they are evaluating. These persons believe in more humanistic or naturalistic methods of inquiry.

Numerous approaches to evaluation can be included under humanistic methods. However, all share the view that there are many realities and that the evaluator is influenced by his or her own values. In essence, these evaluators realize, accept, and even appreciate the "messiness" of the arena within which evaluation efforts are undertaken. Those urging use of humanistic or naturalistic procedures argue for a more holistic engagement that presents us with much more detail. With these methods, we get portraits of the situations we are evaluating. Evaluation reports are less lists of numbers than they are written descriptions of what was found or what occurred. The approach focuses more on human interactions than on outcomes and more on the quality than on the quantity of classroom or school life.

Scientific approaches may have revealed data that depicted what people did, but naturalistic approaches, while interested in that, are also concerned about delving into the *why* behind the *what* of performance. The stress is on interpretative understanding rather than on objective explanation.[30]

Where scientific evaluators might just ask what did students learn, humanistic or naturalistic evaluators might query the actual value of the knowledge that is known or presented in the curriculum. They observe the curriculum through political and social lenses. The pictures we get of programs are not only about content but also about the social significance of the content. We begin to judge the moral overtones of what we are doing with our programs, of what we are trying to accomplish. Such evaluation efforts are a far cry from the traditional position that inquiry is value free.

Eisner's Connoisseurship Evaluation Model

The previous models draw heavily on the quantitative, technical posture of evaluation. Elliot Eisner has recommended a process, called educational criticism and connoisseurship, that will supposedly produce more than hard data and outcomes. It will furnish a rich or qualitative description of educational life as a consequence of new programs.[31] Eisner notes that, to employ the procedure of educational criticism, evaluators should ask such questions as "What has occurred during the school year at a particular school as a result of the new program? What were the key events? How did such events arise? How did students and teachers participate in these events? What were the reactions of the participants to these events? How might the events have been made even more effective? Just what do the students learn from experiencing the new program?[32] These questions focus on process, on school life, and on school quality. They differ in kind from questions raised in the quantitative camp.

Eisner's case for educational criticism and connoisseurship draws heavily from the arts. If an individual is to be an illuminating critic of painting, opera, theater, film, or even wine, he or she must first be a connoisseur—that is, he or she must possess knowledge about and experience with the type of phenomenon he or she is to criticize. A good critic has an awareness and appreciation of the subtle qualities of the situation; he or she can detect and write about the nuances of the situation in ways that help others to become more aware of the phenomenon under consideration.

Eisner points out that educational connoisseurship is "the art of appreciating the educationally significant."[33] But such appreciation is made public through criticism—the description, interpretation, and assessment of the situation. In discussing his approach to evaluation, Eisner relies on personal observations, expert opinion, and group corroboration instead of scientific validity.

Eisner would have the evaluators engaged in such qualitative activities as being participant classroom observers and asking many questions about the quality of the school and the curriculum. An evaluator following Eisner's model would also engage in a detailed analysis of pupils' work. He or she would use films, videotapes, photographs, and audio tapes of both teachers and students in action; the person would also note what is done, what is said, and, perhaps more importantly, what is not done and not said. The evaluator would strive to describe the *tone* of the curriculum in action.

Additionally, an evaluator with this orientation might well employ evaluation by using portfolio analysis. Portfolios are collections of the students' works that exhibit their progress and achievement in one or more areas. The collection must include student participation in selecting contents and the criteria for judging merit.[34] Portfolios allow people to supply what they think is important for others to judge in order to make an evaluation as to the nature and degree of learning. They allow an educator to picture students in a broader context, in effect to get a more complete view about which to reflect and evaluate.

Eisner makes the point that evaluation should allow for some form of communication to some public—parent, school board, local or state agency—about what has been and is occurring in the school. The evaluator presents or describes the educational scene. To some extent, such evaluation takes on a subjective and esthetic approach; for this reason, it is considered controversial by those who believe in objective and scientific documentation. Finally, the connoisseurship model has many characteristics of what is sometimes called responsive evaluation.

Stake's Responsive Evaluation Model

Responsive evaluation is a term popularized by Robert Stake and is more concerned with evaluating curriculum or program activities and processes than intents or outcomes; it relies more on informal and natural communication than formal and standard communication.[35] Like with the Eisner evaluation model, the responsive approach is more concerned with the portrayal of the program than standardized data, test scores, and goals—what some people might label as methodological or objective data. Responsive evaluation requires planning and development, but it relies less on formal statements and research-oriented information than do technical-scientific models of evaluation. Using the responsive approach, the evaluator tells the story of the program, presents its features, describes the clients and personnel, identifies major issues and problems, and reports the accomplishments. The evaluator assumes the posture of a critic reviewing a play or a painter depicting a landscape scene.

To conduct responsive evaluation. Stake maintains that the evaluator develop a plan that deals with the scope and activities of the program. He or she must arrange for people to make observations, prepare narratives and portrayals, and provide product displays. Because all of us have particular biases, the various audiences of the report must be identified; their feelings and expressions of what is worthwhile and important should be considered. The data reported must be analyzed in terms of the audience's biases, and they (as well as personnel of the program) must have a chance to react to the findings. To perform this task, the evaluator will probe and ask questions. Various participants and audiences may become defensive and seek to avoid or confront the evaluator. However, important questions about quality must be examined and processed.

Stake outlines the steps of responsive evaluation as applied to evaluating a curriculum. (Nine steps are listed; number four is the authors' based on interpretation of the entire model.)

1. Negotiate a framework for evaluation with the sponsors.
2. Elicit topics, issues, and/or questions of concern from the sponsors.
3. Formulate questions for guiding the evaluation.
4. Identify the scope and activities of the curriculum; identify the needs of clients and personnel.
5. Observe, interview, prepare logs and case studies, and so on.
6. Pare down the information; identify the major issues or questions.
7. Present initial findings in a tentative report.
8. Analyze reactions and investigate predominant concerns more fully.
9. Look for conflicting evidence that would invalidate findings, as well as collaborative evidence that would support findings.
10. Report the results.[36]

Many of these steps are related to goal-free evaluation, which is concerned with the biases of evaluation. In goal-free evaluation, the evaluator is expected to be objective, not influenced by the goals or objectives of the program or the values of the program developer or sponsors.

Illuminative Evaluation Model

Another naturalistic approach to evaluation is illuminative evaluation, sometimes called explication. It strives to furnish a complete picture of the educational program. Originally, developed by Parlett and Hamilton, this procedure illuminates problems and significant features of an educational program. The method allows the evaluator to discern the total program and to gather data about the particular workings of the program. There are three steps to the model: observation, further inquiry, and explanation.[37]

1. *Observation.* The first stage involves a general look at the program to orient oneself to the program and to describe the context within which the curriculum is being delivered. Attention is given to all factors that might influence the program. Thus, data can be gathered on the arrangement of school subjects, the types of teaching and learning styles evident, the materials being used, and even the types of evaluation methods employed by the teacher.

2. *Further inquiry.* Here the evaluator brings a focus to the evaluation, separating the significant from the trivial. During this second stage, the evaluator strives to get the individuals affected by the program to gain an understanding of it, not just to know if the program works, but also why it works. Further inquiry or progressive focusing emerges out of continually examining the program in action. This means that the evaluator spends extended time in the field. He or she also gathers data by examining school documents and portfolios of the students' work and from interviews and questionnaires with staff and parents.

3. *Explanation.* The evaluator using this model is not attempting to pass judgment on the program, but rather to furnish data on what is happening with the program and why. The evaluator's explanations are presented to those affected by the program. Upon receiving such information, these people can then engage in decision making.

The illuminative model assumes an artistic perspective, insisting that education is a complex and dynamic set of interactions. These interactions are to be observed and evaluated holistically and subjectively because they cannot be broken down into artifical ways or discrete categories for objective measurement. The scientific evaluation method asserts that to understand something, we need to break it down into manageable parts and evaluate these parts; this is the only way of establishing a base for understanding and for making generalizations. All this is admirable and rooted in the Tyler and Taba models of evaluation. Illumination deals with the unintended categories and parts; it deals with the subtle aspects of the environment, the items that are often missed or discarded by the strict behaviorist or so-called objective observer.

Illuminative evaluators try to avoid taking sides, that is, which perspective is correct. They wish to accept the validity of both scientific and humanistic approaches to evaluation; they contend there are weaknesses and strengths in both approaches.[38] Hence, other humanistic/naturalistic models become acceptable to the field.

Portraiture Model

While not strictly an evaluation model, portraiture can be used much like illuminative evaluation or Eisner's connoisseur model. Sara Lawrence Lightfoot developed this method, drawing from the field of anthropology.[39] In conducting a portraiture, an evaluator would go into a school, the field, and observe what was occurring regarding the curriculum. This individual would observe teachers and students in classrooms and look at school documents and students' work. He or she would conduct interviews and employ questionnaires. From these sources the evaluator would create a thin description. This description is basically a narrative in which what is actually occurring is recorded. If teachers teach a particular topic in the curriculum, or if teachers and students behave in particular ways, it is jotted down in the evaluator's journal.

Once the evaluator has completed a thin description, he or she then creates a "thick" description, which is an attempt to interpret what is recorded in the thin description. In creating this report, the evaluator engages in a process similar to that of explanation in illuminative evaluation. This thick description or portrait is then presented to the school or to those in charge of evaluating the curriculum.

A portrait is a compressed ethnography in which the evaluator attempts to capture the spirit of the school program, to not only tell what was done, but to offer some thought on the reasons behind actions. The portrait writer draws on his or her creative or aesthetic abilities in addition to his or her scientific abilities. There are usually five elements to a thick description: (1) description of the setting and activities, (2) recording and commentory about people in the systems, (3) inclusion of dialogue, (4) interpretation of the situation, and (5) impressionistic records.

When writing a portrait, the evaluator allows his or her feelings to enter into the document. However, the portrait should be such that those who receive it will recognize it as referring to them and their program. Ideally, the portrait is outlined in a manner that allows the emergence of themes or patterns to occur.

Well-done portraits capture the insider's views of what is central to the conduct of the curriculum. Table 11-2 contrasts the scientific and humanistic approaches and Table 11-3 presents an overview of all the evaluation models.

PRACTICES AND ISSUES OF EVALUATION

The previous models involve a variety of practices. Although there is some disagreement about the precise steps that evaluation would take, some notion of how to proceed through the evaluation process is useful. Presented next are phases of evaluation that educators can follow. These steps draw heavily from the technical-scientific approach to curriculum. But, even a humanistic approach to evaluation would have to focus on the curricular phenomena being evaluated. Evaluators would also need some means, whether objective or subjective, of collecting the information.

Phases of Evaluation

As just mentioned, to carry out an evaluation, an evaluator must have a plan of action. Much has been written on what steps are necessary to accomplish this. The following steps seem to be common to most evaluators' discussions:

1. *Focusing on the curricular phenomena to be evaluated.* In this step, evaluators determine just what they are going to evaluate and also what design they will use. They determine the focus of the evaluation: Will it be the total school system or a particular school? Will it be one particular subject area or grade level within that school? In this connection, evaluators spell out the objectives of their evaluation activity and identify the constraints and policies under which the evaluation will be conducted.

2. *Collecting the information.* In this step, evaluators identify the sources of information essential for consideration and also the means they can use to collect that information. They also map out stages for collecting the information in terms of their time schedule.

3. *Organizing the information.* Here evaluators organize the information so that it becomes interpretable and usable to the final intended audience. They note means of coding, organizing, storing, and retrieving the information.

4. *Analyzing the information.* At this stage, evaluators select and employ appropriate analysis techniques. The specific techniques they choose depend on the focus of the evaluation.

5. *Reporting the information.* Here evaluators decide the nature of the reporting, keeping in

TABLE 11-2   Contrasting Scientific-Positivist and Humanistic-Naturalist Approaches

AXIOMS	SCIENTIFIC-POSITIVIST PARADIGM	HUMANISTIC-NATURALIST PARADIGM
Nature of reality	Reality is single, tangible, and fragmentable	Realities are multiple, constructed, and holistic
Relationship of knower to the known	Knower and known are independent, a dualism	Knower and known are interactive, inseparable
Possibility of generalization	Time and context-free generalizations are possible	Time and context-bound working hypotheses are possible
Possibility of causal linkages	There are real causes, temporally precedent to or simultaneous with their effects	All entities are in a state of mutual simultaneous shaping, so it is impossible to distinguish cause from effect
Role of values	Inquiry is value free	Inquiry is value bound

Source: Yvonna S. Lincoln and Egon Guba, *Naturalistic Inquiry* (Beverly Hills, Calif.: Sage, 1985), p. 37. Used with permission.

TABLE 11-3 Overview of Evaluation Models

MODEL	AUTHOR	APPROACH	VIEW OF REALITY	POSSIBILITY OF GENERALIZATION	ROLE OF VALUES
Metfessel-Michael model	Metfessel and Michael	Scientific	Reality is tangible, single	Yes	Value free
Provus discrepancy model	Provus	Scientific	Reality is tangible, single	Yes	Value free
Congruence-contingency model	Stake	Scientific	Reality is tangible, single	Yes	Value free
Context, input process, product model	Stufflebeam	Scientific	Reality is tangible, single	Yes	Value free
Judicial model	Wolf, Worthen and Sanders	Scientific	Reality is tangible, single	Yes	Value free
Connoisseurship model	Eisner	Humanistic	Realities are multiple, holistic	No	Value bound
Responsive-evaluation model	Stake	Humanistic	Realities are multiple, holistic	No	Value bound
Illuminative model	Parlett and Hamilton	Humanistic	Realities are multiple, holistic	No	Value bound
Portraiture model	Lightfoot	Humanistic	Realities are multiple, holistic	No	Value bound

mind the audience for the report. They might engage in an informal reporting, such as giving opinions and making judgments based on general perceptions. They might, however, decide that their evaluation should more rigorously collect, treat, and report the data. The final report would have detailed statistical data.

6. *Recycling the information.* The need for current information involves continuous reevaluation and reassessment—a continuous attempt to improve the curriculum. Even if the curriculum appears to be viable, continuous feedback, modifications, and adjustments are necessary

because forces affecting the schools are always changing.

In relaying information to the intended audience, the evaluators need to do more than just report—that is, tell the results. They should also relay their interpretations of the data, drawing from the analysis stage, and make recommendations for action. They need to help determine how the information and the results will be used. They need to make judgments. If they have been working for those responsible for the overall curriculum, then they may just submit their recommendations to the curriculum decision makers to do with as they wish. Sometimes, evaluators are also charged with ensuring that their recommendations are carried out. This is especially true when the evaluators are working directly for the central school office. In such instances, evaluators may indicate means by which their recommendations can be accomplished.

Of course, some person or persons must be in charge of these phases of evaluation. Schedules and budgets have to be determined. Ideally, the management aspects of evaluation should be carefully planned at the outset of the evaluation effort, whereby various stages of evaluation are outlined with timetables, divisions of labor (people assigned to tasks), and cost allocations per task and then totaled.

The Nature and Form of Objectives

A common focus of evaluation has been to determine the extent to which objectives have been achieved. In this context, evaluators must first make clear what they mean by objectives. Perhaps during the last 15 years, one issue in curriculum which has received much attention has been the value of and the appropriate form for objectives. Part of the reason for such continued interest in objectives is philosophical. Behaviorists believe that an objective must specify the exact behavior that the learner will display as a consequence of experiencing the curriculum. At the other extreme are individuals who state that the curriculum must have a humanistic bent and, therefore, that objectives must evolve from the experiences of individuals. Each student has the responsibility of forming his or her own objectives.

Although a particular behavior can specify that an objective has been attained, the behavior can denote covert as well as overt action. Some curriculum specialists have noted that an objective really should show the educational intent rather than indicate realization of the intent.[40] These educators maintain that, when creating objectives, evaluators should also consider why they want students to perform these actions. Having a student run a mile in eight minutes indicates a behavior (run), a situation (a mile), and even the

criterion of performance (eight minutes). But the objective does not indicate *why* they would want a person to run a mile in the first place, much less in eight minutes.

Part of the problem of determining just what objectives are or should be and how to write them is that groups do not always consider sufficiently the many purposes of objectives. Objectives also can be listed at several levels. Curriculum objectives, for example, can be written to communicate general direction for the entire curriculum or for only the grade or subject level. Also they can be more specific—designed to guide the selection of particular contents and instructional experiences at a unit or lesson-plan level.

It is likely that discussion will continue to center on objectives. But few persons would accept that objectives should not be used at all. Most consider them to be valuable guides for curriculum planners and evaluators. How specific someone is in forming objectives is affected by his or her curriculum orientations and philosophical views. Objectives, however formed, give evaluators a view of just where they think they are going, which will help them realize when they have "arrived."

Measurement of Student Exit Requirements

Evaluators need to measure how students are performing at the conclusion of the program. But some evaluators distinguish between evaluating the *program* and evaluating the *students*. Program evaluation centers on instructional outcomes in the program and determines whether these outcomes are the result of groups of students' experiencing the program. The thrust of such evaluation is on the program. It assesses the worth of the program and holds those who deliver it accountable.

Student evaluation, in contrast, involves gathering data about students' performances to decide whether they are qualified for course completion or, for that matter, for graduation. The burden of responsibility shifts to the individual student. If evaluators take this stand, they really have no reason to modify the program or to hold teachers accountable. The student failed, not the program. Who an evaluator holds accountable, of course, can generate a good deal of conflict; it often reflects the individual's philosophical and political views of schools and society.

In this connection, there is a dramatic growth of "high-stake" testing of students: Test results are used to make important decisions about students, schools, and/or the curricula. About 40 states have mandated minimum competency testing programs for students.[41] In some cases, student promotion or diplomas are at stake; in other cases, the reputation of teachers or schools are at stake; and in still other cases, school monies are allocated as cash awards.

Intended Outcomes versus Goal-free Evaluation

Mauritz Johnson, who states that curriculum is a series of intended learning outcomes, argues that evaluators should indicate at the outset just what they want their program to accomplish in order to determine how to evaluate it.[42] Tyler has also, on occasion, told educators that they must define the objectives of a program and to indicate the situations in which students would be given the opportunity to accomplish the objectives. Most evaluators favor using objectives for this purpose.

This seems logical, especially if evaluation is considered purposeful behavior—actions meant to determine the worth of the curriculum or whether the curriculum allowed students to attain the objectives stated. But for many years Scriven has been advocating a goal-free approach to evaluation.[43] Scriven argues that sometimes people wish to engage in evaluation just to examine the effects of an educational innovation and to judge the quality of the effects produced. He calls such evaluation goal-free evaluation; its purpose is to determine the actual effects of the program by recording and interpreting what occurred during and as a result of the program.

Taking this approach, an evaluator does not confine his or her energies to the stated objectives of the new program, but instead gathers data to assess and evaluate the outcomes, whatever they may be. The educator employs a wide variety of measures to do this. He or she uses both quantitative and qualitative measures to get a picture of the program in action and also a reading of what has happened to students from having experienced the program.

If educators employ goal-free evaluation measures, they may get a more accurate picture of both the intended and the unexpected results of how the curriculum functions. The trouble is, many educators are not goal free; they are compelled by strong views about schools and society and have already made up their minds about the worth of certain programs and curriculum before the outcomes are known.

Norm-referenced and Criterion-referenced Measurement

Two basic approaches to testing dominate curriculum evaluation. Norm-referenced measurement is the most common. In this approach, the student's performance on a particular test is compared with the performance of other students who also took the same test. The students as a group establish a norm. Student norms can be grouped by age of grade level, ethnicity, sex, geographical location, or any other easy to categorize factor.

Standardized achievement tests, probably the most well known norm-referenced tests, identify persons of varying ability. They have, however, questionable value for measuring the quality of a curriculum or the instruction. Such tests do not relate specifically to the goals and content of a particular curriculum. These tests are designed to measure what a student knows in a particular subject (say reading or math) in relation to other students at a given time. However, they do not measure effectively what has been taught.[44] Despite their limitations, standardized tests are often administered to determine the success of the curriculum and for evaluating the effectiveness of teaching.

The alternative to the norm-referenced test is the criterion-referenced test. These tests are designed to report how a student performs or demonstrates a skill or task or understands a concept with respect to some fixed criterion. Such tests indicate a learner's performance that can be stated as some specific educational objective, such as the ability to identify longitude and latitude lines on a map or the ability to multiply two-digit numbers.[45] With these tests, students either attain mastery or nonmastery of each objective to which a test item refers. While the test produces a total score, it is the score on each item or related items that is of interest to the evaluator.

Criterion-referenced tests indicate what the students can and cannot do with regard to specific content, skills, and attitudes. In effect, they indicate changes in learning over time, compared to normative tests, which compare students and measure learning at a specific time. The student has either learned or not learned to do something, understands or does not understand something, or shows progress in understanding something as a result of experiencing the curriculum.

Criterion-referenced tests focus on the specific tasks and competencies that have been stressed in a particular curriculum. Because these tests are curriculum specific, they have special value to those who wish to evaluate a new curriculum in their school district. Evaluators can use such tests to gather data that will enable educators to determine what has been taught and the overall effectiveness of the curriculum.

Criterion-referenced tests can also reveal whether a student has mastered particular material. Thus, these tests can be used for student evaluation as well as program evaluation.[46] Educators can use the results of such tests to determine what specific remedies are necessary for particular students. Test results can be employed to indicate that students are ready to proceed to other stages in the curriculum.

Even though the criterion-referenced test enables educators to correct some of the shortcomings of the norm-referenced test, it does have some problems or disadvantages of which educators should be aware. One is that it addresses specific objectives. A great number of such tests, up to ten or fifteen, are thus necessary to get a thorough picture of the curriculum. Second, it is not easy to determine the standards for acceptable performance that criterion test items are supposed to measure. Just what is the cutoff score for mastery of an objective? However, educators usually get around this difficulty by setting the passing score arbitrarily; for instance, they may require the student to get three out of four correct. But, is three out of four really mastery?

Perhaps the most serious criticism of criterion-referenced tests is that most lack reliability

information; in fact, most of these tests are constructed without any attention to reliability. Whereas norm-referenced tests usually have strong content validity (the items measure what they are intended to measure), criterion-referenced tests have curricular validity (the items usually coincide with the objectives of the curriculum).[47] Table 11-4 presents a comparison of these two types of tests.

Human Issues of Evaluation

Many good evaluation reports, valid in all technical details, have failed because of interpersonal insensitivity, ethnic or racial considerations, or political naivete.[48] Educators increasingly realize that evaluation is not just a technical exercise set apart from people. Evaluation reports are presented to and received by important stakeholders. The manner of the presentation determines in part if the evaluation results will be buried or misused, or misinterpreted, or just ignored. Human, ethical, and political factors comprise many aspects of curriculum evaluation.

Ernest House has indicated that the social conflict of the last two decades has placed the problems of values into prominence. If the evaluation process encapsulates the values, then where do the values come from and fit in an evaluation effort? Whose values are most worthwhile? In large part, programs have been evaluated in terms of goals and objectives, and whether they have been attained. However, increasingly we are being forced to ask if the goals and the objectives are of value. Just whose values are they? From where do the criteria of merit come?[49]

Different groups, jockeying for power and to have their views represented, point to the increasing politicalization of curriculum evaluation. Over the years, evaluation has come to be seen as part of the political process. Often schools release tests results not to improve programs but to impress various power groups within the community or to demonstrate to legislators that an educational program is effective. Sometimes, test results are broadcast to convince various minority groups that their children are experiencing equity within the school system.

TABLE 11-4 Comparison of Norm-Referenced Tests (NRT) and Criterion-Referenced Tests (CRT)

CHARACTERISTIC	NRT	CRT
1. Comparisons Made	Score to group average	Score to minimum standard
2. Purpose	Survey or achievement test	Mastery or performance test
3. Validity	Content, criterion or construct	Content <u>and</u> curricular
4. Degree of Validity	Dependent on instruction	Usually high
5. Reliability	Usually high	Usually unknown
6. Importance of Reliability to Test Model	Important	Unimportant
7. Traits Measured	Exist in varying degrees	Present or not present
8. Usability		
Diagnoses	Low general ability	Specific problems
Estimation of Performance	Broad area	Specific area
Basis for Decision Making	How much was learned	What has been learned
9. Item Difficulty	Medium	Easy items
10. Administration	Standardized	Variable
11. Size of Group Tested	Large	Small
12. Content Covered	Broad	Narrow
13. Skills Tested	Integrated	Isolated
14. Control of Content	Publisher	Instructor or School
15. Limitations	Inability of school personnel to interpret tests on local level	Difficulty of constructing quality tests
16. Versatility	Extensive	Limited
17. Comparison of Results Between Schools	Readily available	Not yet developed
18. Distribution of Scores	Normal (one)	Rectangular (two)
19. Range of Scores	High	Low
20. Repetition of Test if Test Is Failed	No, one test	Until mastery occurs
21. Basis for Content	Expert Opinion	Local Curriculum
22. Quality of Items	High	Varies, depending on ability of test constructor
23. Pilot Testing	Yes	No
24. Basis of Item Quality	High Discrimination	Content of items
25. Student Preparation	Studying for test does not help much	Studying for test should help
26. Teaching to Test	Difficult to do and unethical	Encouraged
27. Standards	Averages	Performance levels
28. Scores	Ranking, standard score, or number correct	Pass or fail
29. Type of Measure	Relative	Absolute
30. Purpose	Ranking students	Improving instruction
31. Revision of Test	Not possible	Often necessary
32. Student Information about Test Content	Little available	Known in advance
33. Motivation of Students	Avoidance of failure	Likelihood of success
34. Competition	Student to student	Student to criterion
35. Domain of Instruction	Cognitive	Cognitive or psychomotor

Source: Allan C. Ornstein and David A. Gilman, "The Striking Contrasts Between Norm-Referenced and Criterion-Referenced Tests," *Contemporary Education* (Summer 1991), p. 293.

Considering multiple interests and how they should be woven into the evaluation process places us within the realm of social justice. One educator states that the evaluation community to some degree is reluctant to confront issues of social justice in the educational system. Part of this reluctance stems from a misunderstanding of what the evaluation process should accomplish and the reluctance to consider the politics of education.[50] Evaluators are hesitant to engage in conducting evaluation or in reporting results in ways that will alienate the numerous audiences. Evaluators often realize that reporting on certain data will only add fuel to discontented groups. Additionally, these specialists sometimes fear being perceived as non-objective arbitrators, mean spirited, or anti-minority, anti-female, or anti-handicapped. When scholars or evaluators are attacked by the political left, the issue is rarely whether these educators have a case but how the attack can be explained as manifestations of Reganism, racism, technocraticism, capitalism, or just simple ideology of white or heterosexual males. Indeed, the political realities of the arena within the academic world and in which evaluation occurs weaken the overall process of scientific procedures and frank discussion.

This objective stance, as noted previously in this book, is increasingly being challenged. This view rests on the desire to discredit tenets of scientistic/technocratic processes, logical positivism and empiricism. Some critics have actually argued that scientific ideas of causation and methodology are actually incompatible with the values and ethics of a democratic society.[51] We would argue that the traditional scientific procedures are not about to be discarded as useless or antidemocratic. However, evaluation is a human activity, and we do need to deal with "messy" topics such as ethical and political issues when evaluating our programs.

Influence of Testing

While discussion focuses on using a variety of means for gathering data to make judgments about the success of curricula, the test still exerts enormous force on the curriculum and those charged with delivering it. George Madaus notes that proponents of testing actually think that mea-surement-driven instruction is beneficial. Tests can determine what is taught, how it is taught, and even what is learned and the manner of such learning. Madaus indicates that measurement-driven instruction leads to cramming, narrows the curriculum, centers attention on those skills most easily measured by our current tests, dampens creativity among teachers and students, and essentially takes from teachers the opportunity to make professional judgments.[52]

Madaus offers seven principles that indicate the influence of tests.

Principle 1. The power of tests and examinations to affect teachers, institutions, curriculum, or instruction is a perceptual phenomenon. If individuals perceive the test as important, it will influence their actions, whether the test is important or not.

Principle 2. The more any quantitative social indicator is used for social decision making, the more likely it will distort and negatively impact the social processes it is intended to monitor.

Principle 3. If important decisions are presumed to be related to test results, then teachers will teach to the test. The practices of schools publishing test results to compare students and schools often makes the stakes so high for educators that they forego a well-founded educational experience for students in lieu of having their students do well on the test.

Principle 4. In every setting where a high-stake test operates, tradition of past exams develops, which eventually de facto defines the curriculum.

Principle 5. Teachers pay particular attention to the form of the questions on a high-stakes test (for example, short answer, multiple choice, essay) and adjust their instruction accordingly. In other words, the name of the "educational game" is pass the test, not become educated.

Principle 6. When test results are the sole or even partial arbiter of future educational or life choices, society tends to treat test results as a major goal of schooling rather than as a useful but fallible indicator of achievement.

Principle 7. A high-stakes test transfers control over the curriculum to the agency which sets or controls the exam.

These principles are applicable whether we are discussing externally or internally created tests. While the test is an important means of gathering data, it is only one means. We are realizing that we need expanded means of gathering evaluative data. Rather than being driven by tests, and more tests, we need various methods of testing and grading teachers. We need portraits of classrooms and schools offering different curricula. We need to disregard the belief that only a score on a test will indicate the quality of curriculum or instruction or accurately reflect the grade a student deserves.

Tests actually do more than drive the curriculum. The amount of test-tampering and cheating on standardized tests by teachers and administrators has grown dramatically. Depending on which recent survey you read. The percentage of reported incidents by respondents run from 10 to 40 percent.[53] Why this rise of test cheating among educators? Standardized tests are being used for determining teacher and school awards, high-paying administrative contracts, even a school district's or community's reputation, as well as for awarding U.S. Department of Education effective school awards and state bonus awards. And, by 1992, new state accountability measures in 14 states included potential teacher and/or administrative loss of jobs and takeovers by state officials; these decisions were tied to achievement scores, in this case low scores.[54]

The outcome is that parents are denied true pictures of their children's performance and taxpayers are being misled about the performance of the schools they fund. And just at the point when schools are being asked to teach critical thinking and problem-solving skills, today's standardized skill tests are driving down the level of instruction to rudimentary skills and low-level knowledge on what teachers think (and sometimes know) the test will cover. See Curriculum Tips 11-3.

ROLES PLAYED IN EVALUATION

Over two decades ago, Hilda Taba maintained that evaluation is a cooperative activity. This cooperation is as necessary to the process of evaluation as it is to the various activities of the total curriculum.[55] It is necessary in forming the overall evaluation plan, in selecting the instruments and evaluation model to be applied, and in carrying out all stages of evaluation.

In a school-wide evaluation effort, teachers, administrators, evaluators, and even students and parents need to cooperate to determine what is necessary to make judgments regarding the curriculum. They need to coordinate the gathering and formating of data. Evaluation decisions are not made by one teacher or one administrator in isolation, and they are not made about only one aspect of the curriculum. Usually, such decisions relate to the entire curriculum and all the people responsible for delivering it.

Taba indicated that perhaps the best reason for cooperative evaluation of the curriculum is that such a collective effort allows all involved to get a total curriculum picture. For example, teachers can work together to provide evidence of the effects of the curriculum on various types of students. If they work alone, teachers only realize how the program worked with their own students. If they collaborate, they can ascertain the program's effectiveness with all types of students.

Students

Mention has been made in several places in this book that students should be active learners. This being the case, students also should assume some responsibility for evaluating not only their own learning, but also for assessing the curriculum. Students can work with teachers in classrooms and curriculum committees in deciding the worth and effectiveness of various curriculum components. Of course, their involvement will be geared to their maturity and age levels. Students should play increasing roles in determine what procedures of evaluation will be applied to judge how much learning is occurring. Educators are now giving students responsibilities for creating portfolios containing their own work and their comments on how well they liked and how much they learned from particular curriculum units.[56]

And students are not just being asked to evaluate their own work. They are getting opportunities to work cooperatively to assess the quality of their peer's learning. In other schools, they participate in evaluating teachers—and these evaluations are sometimes considered for merit and tenure. It is likely that students will play increasing roles in evaluation to personalize their own learning and to work as a partner in the curriculum process.

Teachers

Teachers are perhaps the most obvious professionals who should assume evaluation roles. In some cases, they have worked alone in evaluating the curriculum, and in other cases, they have been shut off from the evaluation process. Indeed, teachers should be involved in cooperative curriculum work, and they should have partial responsibility for program evaluation. Today teachers realize that they can play several roles in evaluation.

Evaluators

Cooperation among all parties engaged in curriculum development and delivery is necessary. Even though various people can play particular roles in an overall evaluation, it is wise to have one person in charge. This person, the evaluator, should work with the central school office, which administers the curriculum.

The evaluator can be a member of the school system. There are several advantages to this. The person knows the system and its goals. It is usually less expensive to conduct an evaluation if the evaluator is already on the school payroll. Because the person is an insider, the results of his or her evaluation may be accepted more easily. However, there are also disadvantages to having an insider as the key evaluator. An insider may not be willing to issue an evaluation report that is critical of the system. He or she may also have too many other responsibilities to be able to undertake a major evaluation effort. Furthermore, his or her expertise might not be considered to be at the same level as that of an outside expert.

The evaluator is one of the agents of the evaluation team and is usually an observer. He or she designs the means of gathering data so that knowledge can be supplied to decision makers. Note that the evaluator does not supply the values with which the data gathered will be used; rather he or she helps the decision maker to clarify his or her values so that they can be addressed.[57]

In theory, the evaluator serves as the eyes and the ears of the decision maker. In this role, he or she furnishes data gathered from observations about how the curriculum is functioning in the school. It is up to the curriculum coordinators, curriculum advisory committees, and the administrators to take the data gathered, to judge their value, and to then act on them. The evaluator is essentially a support person to the curriculum-development and implementation efforts.[58]

As we employ more humanistic or naturalistic approaches to evaluation, teachers will play an involved, ongoing role in curriculum evaluation. They may well create journals or stories that record the successes and failures of various curricula being attempted. They may generate portraits of their class to compare how students have responded to the curriculum over time. Teachers may even evaluate their own and their students feelings regarding a program in action. Eventually, teachers will become key players in an expanded conception of the evaluation process. They will likely determine the nature of their involvement in evaluation. The time is past when teachers only passed out tests or answered questionnaires designed by evaluators.

Consultants

It is sometimes wise for a school district to hire an outside consultant to conceptualize the evaluation approach and to coordinate the evaluation effort. Often small schools do not have any staff persons trained especially for evaluation. When they require such activity, a common procedure is for them to bring in an outside person. In fact, some educators argue that the evaluator of a new program should always be an outsider.[59] Such a person, having no "professional turf" to guard,

can be much more objective and truthful in reporting findings.

The resources of the school district, the extent of the evaluation effort, and the level of the staff's expertise should guide educators deciding whether to bring in an outside consultant for evaluation. An outside consultant should have expertise, but he or she may be viewed as an intruder from outside the system or as a representative of the central office, which would impede the evaluation process. The person in charge of the curriculum-development effort must take these factors into consideration.

Parents and Community Members

Unquestionably, education involves politics. Those affected by education should be involved in some aspects of decision making about education, including curriculum matters. Parents, and even community members without children, should be involved curriculum evaluation efforts. The particulars in such involvement can be worked out with school officials. The point is that parents should not just be readers of evaluation reports or receivers of test results. Parents and community members should be contributing participants of curriculum teams engaged in all aspects of curriculum—and that includes evaluation.[60]

CONCLUSION

The nature and purpose of evaluation are associated with making decisions about curriculum matters. A number of questions dealing with the value of evaluation were examined, along with several definitions. Most scientific definitions involve inputs and outputs, or determining goals and then assessing results. Humanistic definitions deal with the values we hold and our biases within the evaluation process. We made the case that evaluation is an essential aspect of curriculum development; it requires expertise and resources, just as the other major stages in curriculum development.

Evaluation is a complex stage. This was keenly illustrated by the evaluation models that were examined. These evaluation models were divided into scientific and humanistic ap-

proaches. The field of curriculum evaluation is not without argument. To illuminate some of the dynamics of the field, we discussed methodological issues relating to evaluation. These ranged *from selecting and forming objectives to choosing the types of tests to employ when gathering data. The chapter closed by pointing out various roles that people can play in the evaluation effort.*

ENDNOTES

1. Harriet Talmage, "Evaluating the Curriculum: What, Why and How," *National Association for Secondary School Principals* (May 1985), pp. 1–8.
2. Blaine R. Worthen and James R. Sanders, *Educational Evaluation: Alternative Approaches and Practical Guidelines,* 2nd ed. (New York: Longman, 1987). pp. 22–23.
3. Bruce W. Tuckman, *Evaluating Instructional Programs* 2nd ed. (Boston: Allyn and Bacon, 1985), p. 1.
4. Ronald C. Doll, *Curriculum Improvement, Decision Making and Process,* 8th ed. (Boston: Allyn and Bacon, 1992). p. 237.
5. Daniel L. Stufflebeam, *Educational Evaluation and Decision Making* (Itasca, Ill.: Peacock, 1971), p. 25.
6. R. E. Stake and T. Denny, "Needed Concepts and Techniques for Utilizing More Fully the Potential of Evaluation," in R. W. Tyler, ed., *Educational Evaluation: New Roles, New Means.* The Sixty-Eighth Yearbook of the National Society for the Study of Education, Part II, (Chicago: University of Chicago Press, 1969). pp. 370–390.
7. Kenneth A. Sirotnik and Jeannie Oakes, "Evaluation as Critical Inquiry: School Improvement as a Case in Point," in K. A. Sirotnik, ed., *Evaluation and Social Justice: Issues in Public Education* (San Francisco: Jossey-Bass, 1990), pp. 37–60.
8. Fred N. Kerlinger, *Behavioral Research: A Conceptual Approach* (New York: Holt, Rinehart and Winston, 1979).
9. Michael Scriven, "The Methodology of Evaluation," in J. R. Gress and D. E. Purpel, eds., 2nd ed. *Curriculum: An Introduction to the Field* (Berkeley, Calif.: McCutchan, 1988), pp. 340–412; Blaine R. Worthen and Vicki Spandel, "Putting the Standardized Test Debate in Perspective," *Educational Leadership* (February 1991), pp. 65–69.
10. Lee J. Cronbach, "Course Improvement through Evaluation," *Teachers College Record* (May 1963), pp. 672–683.
11. Lee J. Cronbach, *Designing Evaluations of Educational and Social Programs* (San Francisco: Jossey-Bass, 1982), p. 24.
12. Ibid., p. 25.
13. Ernest R. House, "Trends in Evaluation," *Educational Researcher* (April 1990), pp. 24–28.
14. Ibid.

15. Ernest R. House, "Assumptions Underlying Evaluation Models," in G. F. Madaus, ed., *Evaluation Models: Viewpoints on Educational and Human Services* (Hingham, Mass.: Kluwer Publishers, 1983), pp. 45–64; Worthen and Sanders, *Educational Evaluation: Alternative Approaches and Practical Guidelines.*
16. I. E. Seidman, *Interviewing as Qualitative Research* (New York: Teachers College Press, Columbia University, 1991); Worthen and Sanders, *Educational Evaluation: Alternative Approaches and Practical Guidelines.*
17. Scriven, "The Methodology of Evaluation."
18. Norman E. Gronlund and Robert L. Linn, *Measurement and Evaluation in Teaching,* 6th ed. (New York: Macmillan, 1990).
19. Robert M. Gagné, Leslie J. Briggs, and Walter W. Wager, *Principles of Instructional Design,* 3rd ed. (New York: Holt, Rinehart and Winston, 1988).
20. Robert L. Thorndike, *Applied Psychometrics* (Boston: Houghton Mifflin, 1982).
21. H. H. Giles, S. P. McCutchen, and A. N. Zechiel, *Exploring the Curriculum* (New York: Harper & Row, 1942); R. E. Smith and Ralph W. Tyler, *Appraising and Recording Student Progress* (New York: Harper & Row, 1942).
22. Newton S. Metfessel and William B. Michael, "A Paradigm Involving Multiple Criterion Measures for the Evaluation of the Effectiveness of School Programs," *Educational and Psychological Measurement* (Winter 1967), pp. 931–943.
23. Malcolm Provus, *Discrepancy Evaluation for Educational Program Improvement and Assessment* (Berkeley, Calif.: McCutchan, 1971).
24. Robert E. Stake, "The Countenance of Educational Evaluation," *Teachers College Record* (April 1967), pp. 523–540.
25. Ibid.
26. Daniel Stufflebeam, *Educational Evaluation and Decision Making* (Itasca, Ill.: Prosuch, 1971).
27. Ibid, p. 229.
28. Robert L. Wolf, "The Use of Judicial Evaluation Methods in the Formulation of Educational Policy," in G. F. Madaus, ed., *Evaluation Models,* pp. 189–204; Worthen and Sanders, *Educational Evaluation: Alternative Approaches and Practical Guidelines.*
29. Sigrun Gudmundsdottir, "Story-maker, Storyteller: Narrative Structures in Curriculum," *Journal of Curriculum Studies* (May–June 1991), pp. 207–218;

Gene I. Maeroff, "Assessing Alternative Assessment," *Phi Delta Kappan* (December 1991), pp. 272–281.

30. Sirotnik and Oakes, "Evaluation as Critical Inquiry: School Improvement as a Case in Point."

31. Elliot W. Eisner, *Educational Imagination: On the Design and Evaluation of School Programs,* 3rd ed. (New York: Macmillan, 1993).

32. Elliot W. Eisner, "What Really Counts in Schools," *Educational Leadership* (February 1991), pp. 10–17.

33. Eisner, *Educational Imagination: On the Design and Evaluation of School Programs,* p. 226.

34. Linda Darling-Hammond, "Instructional Policy into Practice," *Educational Evaluation and Policy Analysis* (Fall 1991), pp. 233–242; F. Leon Paulson, Pearly R. Paulson, and Carol A. Meyer, "What Makes a Portfolio a Portfolio?" *Educational Leadership* (February 1991), pp. 60–64.

35. Robert E. Stake, *Evaluating the Arts in Education* (Columbus, Ohio: Merrill, 1975).

36. Robert E. Stake, *Program Evaluation: Particularly Responsive Evaluation* (Kalamazoo, Mich.: Evaluation Center of Western Michigan University, 1975); Robert E. Stake and James A. Pearsol, "Evaluating Responsively," in R.S. Brandt, ed., *Applied Strategies for Curriculum Evaluation* (Alexandria, Va.: Association for Supervision and Curriculum Development, 1981), pp. 14–28.

37. M. Parlett and D. Hamilton, "Evaluation as Illumination: A New Approach to the Study of Innovative Programs," in G. V. Glass, ed., *Evaluation Studies Review Annual,* (Beverly Hills, Calif.: Sage, 1976).

38. Kent L. Koppelman, "The Explication Model: An Anthropological Approach to Program Evaluation," in G. F. Madaus, ed., *Evaluation Models,* pp. 349–356.

39. Sara Lawrence Lightfoot, *The Good High School.* (New York: Basic Books, Inc. 1983).

40. David Pratt, *Curriculum: Design and Development* (New York: Harcourt, Brace, 1980); Robert Young, *A Critical Theory of Education* (New York: Teachers College Press, Columbia University, 1990).

41. Ronald A. Berk, "Setting Passing Scores on Competency Tests," *NASSP Bulletin* (February 1987), pp. 69–76; Allan C. Ornstein, "National Reform and Instructional Accountability," *High School Journal* (October–November 1990), pp. 51–56.

42. Mauritz Johnson, "Definitions and Models in Curriculum Theory," *Educational Theory* (April 1967), pp. 127–139.

43. Scriven, "The Methodology of Evaluation."

44. Dale Findley and Robert Estabrook, "Teacher Evaluation: Curriculum and Instructional Considerations" *Comtemporary Education* (Summer 1991), pp. 294–298; B. Worthen and V. Spandel, "Putting the Standardized Test Debate in Perspective."

45. W. James Popham, *Modern Educational Measurement,* 2nd ed. (Englewood Cliffs, N.J.: Prentice Hall, 1990).

46. Norman E. Gronlund, *Stating Objectives for Classroom Instruction,* 2nd ed. (New York: Macmillan, 1978); Gronlund, *How to Construct Achievement Tests,* 4th ed. (Englewood Cliffs, N.J.: Prentice Hall, 1988).

47. Allan C. Ornstein, "Comparing and Constructing Norm-Referenced and Criterion-Referenced Tests," *NASSP Bulletin* (in press 1993); Allan C. Ornstein and David A. Gilman, "The Striking Contrasts Between Norm-Referenced and Criterion Referenced Tests," *Contemporary Education* (Summer 1991), pp. 287–293.

48. Worthen and Sanders, *Educational Evaluation: Alternative Approaches and Practical Guidelines.*

49. Ernest R. House, "Trends in Evaluation," p. 281.

50. David P. Ericson, "Social Justice, Evaluation and the Educational System," in K. A. Sirotnik, ed., *Evaluation and Social Justice: Issues in Public Education,* pp. 5–22.

51. House, "Trends in Evaluation"; Yvonna S. Lincoln and Egon G. Guba, *Naturalistic Inquiry* (Beverly Hills, Calif.: Sage, 1985).

52. George F. Madaus, "The Influence of Testing on the Curriculum," in L. N. Tanner, ed., *Critical Issues in Curriculum,* Eighty-seventh Yearbook of the National Society for the Study of Education, Part I (Chicago: University of Chicago Press, 1988), pp. 83–121.

53. Thomas Toch and Betsy Wagner, "Schools for Scandal," *U.S. News and World Report,* April 27, 1992, pp. 66–72.

54. Allan C. Ornstein and Daniel U. Levine, Foundations of Education, 5th ed. (Boston: Houghton Mifflin, 1993).

55. Hilda Taba, *Curriculum Development: Theory and Practice* (New York: Harcourt, Brace, 1962).

56. Paulson, Paulson and Meyer, " What Makes a Portfolio a Portfolio?"

57. Stufflebeam, *Educational Evaluation and Decision Making.*

58. Rebecca K. Hawthorne, *Curriculum in the Making* (New York: Teachers College Press, Columbia University, 1992); Peter F. Oliva, *Developing the Curriculum,* 3rd ed. (New York: Harper Collins, 1992).

59. James A. Beame, Conrad E. Toepfer, and Samuel J. Alessi, *Curriculum Planning and Development* (Boston: Allyn and Bacon, 1986); Ernest House, *Evaluating with Validity* (Beverly Hills, Calif.: Sage, 1980).

60. Warren Chapman, "The Illinois Experience: State Grants to Improve Schools, Through Parent Involvement," *Phi Delta Kappan* (January 1991), pp. 355–358.

CHAPTER 12

CURRICULUM ISSUES AND TRENDS

Focusing Questions

1. *Should the federal government become more involved in setting national goals, academic subject matter, and/or standards of achievement? Why? Why not?*
2. *How can school people deal with censorship issues? How does one determine an appropriate school curriculum?*
3. *What are the characteristics of a good textbook?*
4. *Why are textbooks often criticized?*
5. *How can the curriculum be made more relevant to the needs and interests of students?*
6. *What are the major detractors from academic time? How can academic time be improved in the classroom?*
7. *What are the major issues involving compensatory education? How has compensatory education influenced curriculum development?*
8. *What is multicultural education? What are its major benefits and dangers?*

Various trends and events that have affected curriculum in recent years are likely to continue in the near future. Many issues related to these trends confront the schools and, in turn, curriculum workers. As society changes and new forces and factors influence our lives, we are required to appraise the realities of the times and modify the curriculum, and on a regular basis. We live in a setting of change, and as curriculum workers we must be sensitive to changing issues and trends.

In this chapter we examine seven broad curriculum issues and trends: (1) national curriculum, (2) censored curriculum, (3) textbook curriculum, (4) academic time, (5) irrelevant curriculum, (6) compensatory education, and (7) multicultural education.

NATIONAL CURRICULUM

Starting in the 1980s under President Reagan and continued by President Bush, a new federalism evolved that called for a dramatic shift in federal policy and programs. Driven by a belief that the federal government was too meddlesome and involved in too many activities and regulations, the last two presidents (Reagan and Bush) reduced federal funds (vis-à-vis inflation), activities, and regulations in education as well as other social sectors of the economy.[1] In addition, monetary and program responsibilities have been shifted to state and local agencies. Federal rules and regulations governing education were revoked or more loosely enforced.

The new federalism, according to two educators, can be viewed in terms of three policy moves by the executive branch of government: (1) deregulation, the reduction of federal bureaucratic rules and regulations; (2) consolidation, the reduction of government proliferation of agencies and programs; and (3) cutbacks, the move to reduce social and educational spending.[2] Similarly, the new federalism has been analyzed in terms of five policy shifts, or the "five D's" in education: (1) diminution, reduction of federal expenditures in education; (2) deregulation, revocation of federal enforcement of rules and regulations; (3) decentralization, the belief that the ills of education are related to federal intrusion into what should be a state or local responsibility; (4) disestablishment, limiting the powers of the Department of Education and other federal agencies; and (5) deemphasis, the sum of the preceding aspects or the narrowing of the focus and scope of the federal role in education.[3]

At the same time that the new federalism has been shaping education, another conservative trend at the federal level has been growing in momentum, called the national standards movement, a deepening concern for declining student scores on national and international achievement tests and the declining quality of the teaching work force as evidenced by a large percentage of entry teachers having difficulty passing basic skills tests.[4] There is also concern for insufficient investment in human capital and the nation's economic decline and lack of international competitiveness.

A new consensus is developing, one that promotes national needs and goals as more important than local or pluralistic needs and goals, supports more rigorous teacher training and national testing and professional standards for teachers, and seeks a common core of subjects, content, and values in the Adler-Bloom-Hirsch mode as well as to upgrade the curriculum and drive it with achievement tests for students.

Similarly, a growing number of educators and policy makers maintain student achievement will not increase unless national goals, standards, and tests are introduced, whereby progress is monitored and teachers and schools are held accountable.[5] While a national consensus for high standards and planned curricula is evolving, and the U.S. Department of Education is promoting this reform, the control, special programs, and policies that produce the outcomes should come from the states. Nonetheless, the politics of Bennett, Finn, and Ravitch, all federal education policy makers, point to a national strategy for curricular change supported with money, technical assistance, and federal–state networks. It is a strategy quite different from the traditional one that saw reform tied to increased federal spending for target students (such as the poor, minority, and handicapped) and in terms of special programs and personnel (such as compensatory edu-

cation, bilingual education, and handicapped education).

The national curriculum seems driven by an essentialist philosophy, as opposed to the progressive and reconstructionist philosophy that drove the old idea of federal reform; it promotes the recent idea of a core curriculum, that is, a common curriculum that every student should be required to take, as opposed to the idea of a relevant and a student-centered curriculum; it puts emphasis on national assessment testing, framing high-stake tests (there are real consequences riding on the tests results), imposing and meeting standards for students and teachers, putting more emphasis on outputs (what criteria or outcomes students must meet) and not inputs (spending money), and comparing these outputs with other industrialized nations.

The competency movement in education, whereby the states are imposing "gatekeeping" tests for promotion, "exit" tests for high school graduation, and "certifying" tests for beginning teachers, is a spin-off of the national movement to establish standards and a common curriculum. By 1989, some twenty-five states had implemented competency tests for high school graduation and thirty-seven states had implemented it for certifying beginning teachers.[6]

Within the context of nationalization of standards, some critics are asking, why raise standards that students cannot meet to begin with? Why talk about a nationalized set of goals or curriculum when the focus has always been on local control of the schools and when there is little agreement on goals, standards, or requirements among the fifty states and 85,000 public schools? Why talk about a national commitment to education reform when the federal government is reducing education spending in real dollars?

On the other side of the coin is the fact that most industrialized nations already have a ministry of education in place at the federal or national level, supplemented by regional, state, or provincial agencies in education. The federal ministry creates a policy climate capable of fostering an integrated and organizationally coherent response to national problems and/or trends and makes it easier to restructure schools (a new trend shaping American schools) in a focused manner by making marginal changes (such as adding new programs) or reshuffling organizational responsibilities.[7]

Similarly, most ministries of education (since they represent the federal government) work hand in hand with business and education groups. The result is that the roles and responsibilities of institutions connected with education are clarified and compliance regulations exist that force students and teachers to meet minimum standards or competency levels; in addition, an explicit curriculum exists with intended learning outcomes, and national employment needs are fine-tuned in conjunction with vocational and academic programs (including college admissions).

There is no free market college system in many European or Latin American countries, as in the United States; rather, the government controls the number of college seats or students permitted to study for a future occupation. The result is minimal supply-demand correction trends or job dislocations (for example, there are few Ph.D.s driving taxi cabs or waiting on tables). Poor advice from school authorities, which sometimes leads to dead-end programs and unemployed youth in this country, rarely exists in other industrialized countries; elsewhere, the ministry allocates and coordinates the college openings and academic programs; it helps track students by placing them into one of several programs that prepare the young for economically productive and socially responsible positions. An important component of German, Korean, and Japanese success in the world economy is that the ministries of these countries direct and invest in their youth.

Clarifying the Federal Role in Education

The federal government's role in education is compelling, because how we educate our children and youth will determine the kind of nation we become. The issue is not whether we do or don't reduce the federal role or nationalize standards in education, but rather to clarify and determine how the federal government can and should use its resources and dollars to effectively promote schools and society. Federal leadership should support and work with state and local education agencies not for the purpose of promoting the needs of one group versus another group, but for the priorities of all of us, as a people or nation.

According to the National School Boards Association (NSBA), the future federal role in education should be ninefold: (1) define and clarify federal responsibility to education, (2) increase our competitive edge through education, (3) advance equal educational opportunity, (4) promote effective use of technology, (5) strengthen the quality of teaching, (6) serve special need students, such as the economically deprived, minorities, bilingual, and handicapped, (7) improve and fund rural schools, (8) continue to support urban schools, and (9) increase the federal interest in education.[8]

All these recommendations suggest increased federal presence and funding of education. Without a strong federal commitment, school effort will be sporadic and inconsistent, relying mainly on local and state wealth. The NSBA agenda suggests that we are at a critical period in our history, where policies and actions in education by the federal government can enhance or hinder our future. The priorities suggest that federal leadership can work hand in hand with local school districts and that the focus should be on enhancing academic achievement for all students and ensuring that students with special needs have equal opportunity to succeed. In no way should the priorities suggest that schools be nationalized or the federal government establish national standards of educational performance or a core curriculum; this is certainly not the goal of the NSBA, which represents some 97,000 local school board members in some 15,000 school districts; it prefers a local school focus for reform, and values local education efforts.

Actually, the federal role in education should be based on helping local schools and school districts build consensus and confidence in educating their clients. Many educational problems are national, state, and local. The problem is national because it occurs in many parts of the country and because world or national events help construct it. It is a state problem because states have legal responsibility for schools, and governors and state legislators are playing a much greater role in school reform. It is also local in the sense that the composition and needs of the student population differ from place to place, and local efforts and resources are needed to resolve the problem. If state and local efforts and resources are not available, then the services or personnel will not always be provided. See Curriculum Tips 12-1.

There seems to be agreement that a new federal strategy is needed—one that stimulates local school planning and reform and supplements local efforts and resources. Beyond that point there tends to be controversy as to whether the federal government should become involved in national minimum standards, national goals, national testing, or a national core curriculum. The concern over national activities regarding student achievement and subject matter is somewhat reminiscent of the post-Sputnik era, some 35 years ago, when the perceived threat was from the USSR. Today the threat is more economic than military and has changed to those who are outproducing us. Indeed, our future jobs and standard of living will depend partially on the academic and work goals and standards that we establish, to the extent we track our progress, create conditions most likely to increase our output and produce quality, and support first-rate teachers and schools.

CENSORED CURRICULUM

A certain amount of curriculum censorship has always existed, not as a matter of policy or law, but rather as a customary practice. During the eighteenth and nineteenth centuries, content in curriculum was restricted to traditional American values that centered around the family, church, work, and nation. Textbooks portrayed, according to authorities, the Puritan morality, work ethic, individualism, achievement, American patriotism, and the melting pot theme.[9]

As late as the mid twentieth century, history, civics, and English literature textbooks barely included, or even excluded, such topics as poor people, immigrants, minorities, women, and organized labor. Many even ignored our Democratic presidents. In a strict sense, the curriculum was not censored. Rather, it only included information educators considered appropriate. Readers or textbooks presented an idealistic American society with traditional, patriotic, and majority core values. Information considered too sensitive or too controversial was simply excluded. This policy elicited no fanfare or controversy, only occasional criticism. The problem was, however, that some of the content in the textbooks was racist and sexist, at least by today's standards. It mirrored what some call the "established curriculum," the interests of dominant groups.

Today, publishers exercise self-censorship to appease dissenting factions and to avoid alienating pressure groups. As Elliott Eisner says, textbook editors "take no risks" and design textbooks the same way. Textbooks "alienate no one. They are usually models of the dull, the routine, and the intellectually feckless." In general, textbooks shape the curriculum and are stabilizing factors that serve "to resist change."[10] The need for publishers, and now textbook authors, is to be "politically correct," to reflect the cultures of all students. But some are willing to succumb to popular rhetoric, to the extent of showing contempt to the dominant culture and for nearly everything that is European or white. Some of the more ardent critics disparage the "common culture," as if it was a vehicle for sexism, racism, and oppression. Sadly, in some schools the goal of the curriculum is to find new textbooks and teachers who will urge separate identities and separate cultures.[11]

As a matter of practical concern, textbook editors must have a keen sense of the educational marketplace and they must be highly cognizant of a variety of pressure groups. Like other businesspeople, publishers attend to what their customers want, and they are sensitive to the wishes of textbook selection committees. Current data show that all the major textbook companies conform to the preferences of the larger educational markets—the most populous states, such as California, Illinois, New York (which together accounted for more than 23 percent of the total national expenditure on curriculum materials in one recent year—or to the major adoption states—California, Texas, and Florida.[12] These few states greatly influence the books available for study in other states; most other school systems have little choice but to go along with the dictates, specifications, and price maintenance of a handful of school systems in a few states.

**CURRICULUM TIPS 12-1   Clarifying the Federal
                              Role in Education**

The federal role in education is important and needs to be clarified. The following tips outline a set of federal priorities.

1. Establish a national task force for continually reviewing and modifying the aims of education and targeting the funding of education programs.
2. Coordinate efforts with the Department of Education and Department of Labor to upgrade human capital and to ensure adult workers have minimal literacy skills.
3. Create a federal-higher education-corporate task force to assess future personnel needs, high school-college-university programs, and admission standards.
4. Develop a coordinated public-private program in education technology, with assistance for computers and computer software, video instruction, robotic education, and satellite-based education.
5. Expand funding in math, science, foreign languages (especially Mandarin), and computer literacy.
6. Establish incentive programs to attract math, science, and foreign language teachers.
7. Increase research and development in education in order to establish a knowledge base for teacher education programs, as well as for teaching and learning.
8. Expand international education and global awareness and support exchange programs for students and teachers.
9. Increase funding for talented and gifted students including enrichment programs in math, science, and computer education at the elementary school level and academic honor programs at the secondary school level.
10. Increase funding for at-risk, bilingual, handicapped, and immigrant children and youth.
11. Coordinate a public-private funding program to expand educational programs in urban and rural schools.
12. Increase assistance for vocational education, farm-related, and marine-life programs that consider our future needs.
13. Provide funding for comprehensive homework and latchkey programs, which utilize preschool and after school hours.
14. Establish environmental, fuel conserving, and hazardous waste educational programs for all students.
15. Increase funding in drug, AIDS, homeless, and nutrition education.
16. Develop an intergovernmental policy that incorporates state and local agencies such as libraries, parks, and museums with schools as the center of community education.
17. Underwrite a system of education that makes use of and incorporates our aging populace with the education of our youth.
18. Require the states to require the schools to establish education programs that consider the following:
    a. Local resources (money and personnel, community people and business people) that can be reasonably provided
    b. Projected needs (short and long term)
    c. Educational goals (short term and long term)
    d. Programs for attaining the goals
    e. Specific activities to achieve the goals
    f. Methods of implementation and follow-through
    g. Necessary staff and training procedures
    h. Evaluation procedures to assess the programs

Source: Allan C. Ornstein, "The Federal Government and Education in a New Era," *High School Journal* (in press 1993).

Recent Censorship

As the 1980s unfolded, covert censorship changed to overt censorship, and criticism began to mount. Widely publicized textbook battles and school library book battles fanned censorship flames in many parts of the country. Depending on the incident, the focus of controversy focused on one of six major issues: (1) the sanctity of the family, (2) criticism of the free enterprise system, (3) anti-Americanism or disrespect toward traditional American values, (4) obscene language, (5) racial bias or criticism, and (6) creationism versus evolution. By 1990, 244 censorship incidents were reported in 39 states, up 75 percent from the previous 3 years and 150 percent over 7 years.[13]

The ban on books, which has spread to school libraries, curriculum councils, and classrooms across the country, has involved all types of school districts: suburban and city, rich and poor, predominantly minority and predominantly white, and so on. Various community groups, parent groups, and taxpayer groups involved with censorship concerns have exhibited different "zones of tolerance," ranging from heated school-community conflicts and serious watchdog committees to mild newspaper editorials and questions at PTA meetings.

Today, almost any book that contains strong political or economic messages, obscenity, sex, nudity, profanity, slang or questionable English, or ethnic or racially sensitive material or that is considered by a pressure group as antifamily, antireligious, or anti-American is subject to possible censorship. The list of books for potential censorship has included *Madame Bovary, Grapes of Wrath, Mary Poppins,* and *Catcher in the Rye* and even such classics as Shakespeare's *Hamlet* and Mark Twain's *Huckleberry Finn.* Even harmless nursery rhymes, such as "Mother Goose," "Muffin Man," and "Humpty Dumpty," are on the hit list in some states and banned from the primary grades because of so-called subliminal messages about sexism, drugs, or religion.

Caught in the middle of book-censoring controversies are publishers of school texts and materials, who are forced to compromise; boards of education, both state and local, who are pressed by special-interest groups to censor books; and librarians, teachers, and school administrators, who are afraid to stir citizen wrath. On one side are some parents and other community members, who contend that certain passages or pictures in textbooks or library books are warping traditional American or community values that should be inculcated in students; on the other side are advocates of intellectual freedom and most education associations, who say that schools and libraries should be forums for ideas that students can question and examine.

In general, the current community-school conflict over censorship has several causes. One is the schools' unwillingness to recognize the role of the community in selecting books. A second is the schools' inability to define or clarify the community's role in the selection process. A third cause is that certain community groups may be overzealous in pushing their ideas on other parents and public institutions.

One way to deal with this confrontation is to recognize the citizens' reasons for concern and their right to express views about the merit and appropriateness of the school curriculum and materials. Such concerns should be communicated to school authorities and responded to promptly and professionally. Censorship battles will continue, but appropriate selection policies with well-defined procedures worked out in advance by school and community representatives should alleviate some of the fury that has erupted in the past over curriculum materials and textbooks.

Censorship as a Condition

Censorship will always be with us in terms of what content is included and excluded, in terms of the pictures and diagrams we encourage or discourage. (Some publishers count the pictures of Democrat versus Republican presidents, while others count the number of white versus minority pictures or boys versus girls.) We must continually guard against censorship, "at least be alert to it," according to Anne Meek, "because it is always hanging around" under the guise of one slogan or another,"[14] and if we may add one ism or another. Even so-called "traditional" professional associations have impact and seek changes in what students learn. By advocating reform and embracing new ideas, the associations indirectly censor, or at least modify, subject boundaries. For example, the major subject areas, such as English, social studies, math, science, and foreign language, all have their professional associations that make basic recommendations for certain changes in content and influence the funding of programs. Perhaps the most influential group of professional associations today are the National Geographic Society, National Endowment for the Humanities, National Council of Teachers of Mathematics, and National Science Foundation. They all have substantial influence on the curriculum, and each of these groups has produced recent reports recommending a change in goals and related content in their respective subject areas.

In this connection, Michael Apple reinterprets Herbert Spencer's fundamental question about schooling, "What knowledge is of most worth?" to "Whose knowledge is of most worth?" This is simply not a theoretical question, but a practical and strikingly clear one that "calls for censorship and controversies over the values that our schools teach" or don't teach.[15] Apple asserts that the context of curriculum has become "a political football in school districts throughout the country" and is increasingly subject to legislative mandates and state reform measures.

Although Apple may be termed a "liberal" critic or "reconceptionist," he argues that conservative groups have gained the advantage and momentum in the reform movement in education, as characterized by tax credits for private schools, higher academic standards, mandated teacher and student competency tests, and the increased concern by parents and school officials for patriotism, discipline, moral character, free enterprise, and other content and values that suggest a western tradition. He concludes that curriculum scholars are considered irrelevant in the great debate involving reform or change in subject boundaries.

In this connection, Eisner maintains that most curriculum specialists have had little influence over the content of curriculum. They seem more concerned to express philosophical concerns that reflect a neo-Marxist or highly liberal view; they have lambasted the schools and have little to say about what is right or how to make schools better.[16] The result is that the educational establishment, the local, state, and national associations, school administrators and school board members, have been reluctant to consult with or take seriously curriculum scholars. These professors are left on the sidelines to debate irrelevant and esoteric topics in the professional literature and at professional meetings. Who listens to them? Until better messengers are found, that is, scholars who are practical and sensitive to the concerns of school people, the message by curriculum scholars will rarely be heard or taken seriously.

TEXTBOOK CURRICULUM

Textbooks, tests, and college admission standards drive and stabilize the curriculum. What is emphasized by texts, tests, and colleges becomes the formal or explicit curriculum. From a theoretical stance, teachers are in a position to influence the curriculum, but they have little authority to recommend changes, little time to plan the curriculum, and even less time to interact with their colleagues about curriculum concerns. Principals are in a better position to make curriculum changes at the school level, and some make an honest attempt, but most principals have time constraints and managerial concerns that supersede curriculum responsibilities. According to research surveys, principals may see themselves as "curriculum" or "instructional" leaders or wish they had more time for such items, but they are more burdened by everyday administrative and supervisory matters.[17]

Of all three factors, it is the textbook that has had the longest and most obvious influence on the curriculum, to the extent of standardizing teaching and instructional practices. Traditionally, the textbook has been the most frequently used instructional material at all grade levels beyond the primary grades, and in some cases it is the only one used by the teacher. In terms of purchasing, it receives the highest priority, with the recent exception of costly hardware such as computers and copying machines. Textbooks can have a strong influence or even dominate the nature and sequence of a course and thus profoundly affect the learning experiences of students.

Reliance on the textbook (as well as its companion, the workbook) is consistent with the stress on written words as the main medium of education, as well as the way many teachers themselves were educated. Dependence on the textbook is also linked to the time when a majority of teachers were poorly prepared in subject matter or teaching out of license and read the text one day in advance of the students. Many of today's teachers, while better educated than their predecessors, sometimes lack the time or training to prepare new materials; thus, they continue to rely on the textbook and workbook.

Advantages and Disadvantages

In many classes the textbook becomes the only point of view in the course. In effect, the course is based on the theories and biases of the author of the text. Even though the author may try to maintain objectivity, what is selected, what is omitted, and how the discussion is slanted reflect the author's views.

To have wide application and to increase potential sales, textbooks tend to be general, non-controversial, and bland. They are usually written for a national audience, so they do not consider local issues or community problems. Because they are geared for the greatest number of average students, they may not meet the needs and interests of any particular group of students. Moreover, issues, topics, and data that might upset potential audiences or interest groups are omitted.[18]

Textbooks summarize large quantities of data and in so doing may become general and superficial and may discourage conceptual thinking, critical analysis, and evaluation. With the exception of those on mathematics, most textbooks quickly become outdated because of the rapid change of events; but, because they are costly, they are often used long after they should be replaced. Even worse, many textbooks are suffused with factual errors. One recent study, for example, discovered 231 errors in 10 widely used history textbooks, published by the major publishing companies. Among the gaffes: One book maintained "Truman settled the War in Korea by dropping 'the bomb,'" although atomic or nuclear bombs were not used in Korea and Eisenhower was president when the Armistice was signed. Another book asserts that "American troops encountered powerful resistance" during the Bay of Pigs invasion; however, Cuban expatriates were the attacking force. One book claims "53,000 Americans were killed during the Great War"; but the official dead count was 126,000.[19]

Considering these criticisms, you might ask why teachers, when they have access to other instructional materials, rely so heavily on textbooks. The answer is, of course, they do have many advantages. A textbook (1) provides an outline that the teacher can use in planning courses, units, and lessons, (2) summarizes a great deal of pertinent information, (3) enables the students to take home in convenient form most of the material they need to learn for the course, (4) provides a common resource for all students to follow, (5) provides the teacher with ideas regarding the organization of information and activities, (6) includes pictures, graphs, maps, and other illustrative material, which facilitate understanding, (7) includes other teaching aids, such as summaries and review questions, and (8) relieves the teacher of preparing material for the course, thus allowing more time to prepare the lesson.[20]

Unless a curriculum committee or teachers can develop materials that are substantially better than a text in meeting evaluative criteria, there is little reason for them to spend much time, effort, and money on "homemade" materials that are sometimes put together for the sake of throwing away the textbook. Given the facts that textbooks take several years to write and revise and that publishers often spend considerable effort developing and refining them through market analysis, subject and methods consultants, writing staffs, and copy editors, it makes little sense to condemn them as a whole as being ineffective or harmful to the educational process.

Good textbooks have many desirable characteristics. They are usually well organized, coherent, unified, relatively up to date, accurate, and relatively unbiased. They have been scrutinized by scholars, educators, and minority groups. Their reading level and knowledge base match the developmental level of their intended audience. They are accompanied by teacher's manuals, test items, study guides, and activity guides. The textbook is an acceptable tool for instruction as long as it is selected with care and is kept in proper perspective so that it is not viewed as the only source of knowledge, and it does not turn into the curriculum.

Readability

Concern about student reading problems has prompted educators to identify textbooks and other reading materials that are suitable for specific student populations, especially below-average readers. Reading formulas, first devised in the 1920s to estimate the reading difficulty of a text, have increased and are widely used by authors, publishers, teachers, reading consultants, and textbook adoption committees.

Some reading formulas count the number of syllables or the number of letters in a word, some count the number of words not on a specific word list, others measure sentence length, and still others remove words in a passage and test whether students can fill in the exact word that was removed. Some formulas use graphs, regression statistics, and percentiles and range scores to calculate reading difficulty, and computer programs are now available for doing the counting and calculation chores involved in reading level determinations.

The best-known reading formula was developed by Edward Fry. An estimate of the approximate grade level of the reading material is obtained by plotting on a graph the average number of sentences and the average number of syllables in three 100-word passages taken at random.[21]

The Raygor Reading Estimate, developed by Alton Raygor, is a graph procedure, too, but is easier to use than the Fry method. Raygor's procedure is based on counting the number of words of six or more letters, instead of syllables, It has been validated with the Fry formula and is of equal accuracy.[22] There are many other reading formulas and methods for determining the reading level of instructional materials and textbooks.

Critics of the various reading formulas say that (1) they fail to consider students' prior knowledge, experience, and interests, all of which influence reading comprehension; (2) they assume that words with fewer syllables and shorter, simpler sentences are easier to comprehend than words with more syllables and longer

sentences with subordinate clauses, which is not always true; (3) publishers have reacted to these formulas by adjusting sentence and word length to give the appearance of certain levels of readability without necessarily providing them; and (4) strict adherence to formulas robs prose of the connective words, vocabulary, and sentence structure that make it interesting and comprehensible and contribute to a style that makes the text worth reading.[23] In short, rigid following of reading formulas often results in a boring and bland text.

Whatever their faults, reading formulas do help teachers to assess reading difficulty and to select printed material that is appropriate to the students' abilities. Since most teachers work with groups of students in which there is a range of abilities, it is advisable that the difficulty of the material not be more than 1 year below or above the average reading grade level of the group. If there is more than a 2-year spread in reading ability in a group, the teacher should use more than one set of instructional materials.

Comprehension and Cognition

Some educators now urge that comprehendability, not readability, is the major quality to consider when adopting a text. Teachers and textbook committees are identifying various textbook aids, such as structural overviews, introductory objectives, summaries, and review exercises, as devices that contribute to comprehendability. One reading expert lists more than forty reader aids that might be considered in selecting a text.[24] This applies not only to reading books, but also to all texts. Table 12-1 lists four levels of cognition and corresponding reading activities and reader aids or what the author calls pedagogical aids. Whereas the cognitive processes, operations, activities, and outcomes appear to be hierarchal, in theory only, the pedagogical (textbook) aids are not hierarchical. These aids commonly appear in textbooks, and when used as a tool by the learner, they can promote meaningful learning.

Without good textbook aids, it is assumed that poor readers will learn little and capable readers will develop *default* strategies, that is, partially ineffective strategies for processing text information. A default strategy is likely to in-

TABLE 12-1 Levels of Cognition and Reading, with Implications for Using Textbook Aids

COGNITIVE PROCESSES	COGNITIVE OPERATIONS	READER ACTIVITIES	OUTCOMES	TEXTBOOK AIDS
Identifying	Focusing on selective information Sequencing selective information	Copying Underlining Simple note-taking or discussion	Retention of target information	Overviews Instructional objectives Prequestions Key words or terms Margin notes Summaries Review Exercises
Conceptualizing	Classifying main ideas of text Comparing main ideas of text	Logical or structured note-taking or discussion Distinguishing relevant information Relating points to each other	Retention of key concepts of text Internal connections (relations among ideas of text)	Headings Margin notes Point-counterpoint discussions Summaries Postquestions Problems Review exercises
Integrating	Analyzing main ideas of text Modifying ideas of text into variations or new ideas Deducing main ideas of text Expanding main ideas of text	Elaborate note-taking or discussion Making generalizations Hierarchical ordering of items Making inferences from text information	Understanding implications of text (explicit and implicit) External connections (relations between ideas of text and ideas outside of text)	Headings Graphs, tables Models, paradigms Postquestions Case studies Problems Activities (or things to do)
Transferring	Applying main ideas of text to problems Evaluating text information Verifying text information Going beyond text information Predicting from text information	Elaborate note-taking or discussion Evaluating, problem solving, and inferring based on text information Using text information to create new information	Establishing dimensions of a problem Understanding causal relations in text information Assessing the degree of universality of text information for predicting	Graphs, tables Models, paradigms Simulations Case studies Problems Activities (or things to do)

Source: Allan C. Ornstein, "Textbook Instruction: Processes and Strategies," *NASSP Bulletin* (December 1989), p. 109.

volve focusing on topic sentences or unusual and/or isolated information instead of on concepts or major ideas.[25] A default strategy also leads to students copying and memorizing long lists of information rather than organizing, inferring, or transferring text ideas (see Table 12-1, columns 1, 2).

Critics have found that textbooks in nearly every subject and grade level cover too many topics, the writing is superficial, choppy, and lacking in depth and breadth (the phenomenon is called "mentioning"), and content wanders between the important and the trivial.[26] They fail to capture the imagination and interest of the students or to make students think and spurn current knowledge about cognitive information and linguistic processing. The so-called best textbooks are often designed to entertain and to be decorative, but they provide only tidbits of information, lack adequate integration of subject matter, and do not stretch the student's mind. They are unintentionally geared to oversimplify and to limit thinking.

Textbook adoption committees have contributed to the problem with their demands for topic coverage and easy to read prose. Special-interest groups, with their passions and legal challenges, have added to the problem, causing publishers to become politically sensitive to the content at the expense of linguistic and cognitive processes. Teachers have done their part, too, since most teachers emphasize answers to be found, not problems to be solved or thinking processes to be used. See Curriculum Tips 12-2. In this connection, it would benefit students if teachers would take time out to help students to organize ideas, in terms of reading, writing, and notetaking, along the organizational structure of textbooks.[27] Teaching students how their textbooks organize content would increase reading comprehension, report and essay writing, and note taking in studying for tests. Students need to learn to read and write in sequential and descriptive ways similar to the ways their books are organized.

Neville Bennett and his colleagues analyzed 417 language and math tasks assigned in texts by teachers and found that 60 percent were practice tasks or content already known to the students. New tasks accounted for 25 percent, and tasks requiring students to discover, invent, or develop

a new concept or problem made up 7 percent of the tasks.[28] In another study, approximately 84 percent of the teachers relied on *textually explicit* instruction, a method of using printed material in which a correct answer can be obtained by selecting verbatim information from the textbook or workbook. Rarely do teachers employ *textually implicit* instruction, in which a correct answer requires students to make an inference from the textual information supplied. Even more rarely do they use *scripturally implicit* instruction, in which a correct answer requires students to go beyond the information given and call on prior knowledge and reasoning skills.[29]

Most teachers are right-answer oriented in their teaching and testing. Hence, they are unwilling or unable to change from textbooks that are characterized by low-level cognitive demands and are divorced from how students think or reason. One might expect at least science teachers to exhibit textually implicit or scripturally implicit instruction, since they deal with scientific problems and laboratory experiments, yet the above conclusions were based on observations of seventh-grade science classes.

Teachers of mathematics, especially at the upper elementary and junior high school grades, are not much different. Some data strongly suggest that many of these "teachers don't know mathematics. They assign the basic problems but skip word problems because word problems are harder to teach."[30] Students may learn to deal with simple right-answer problems (Which number is closest to 27: 20, 31, 22, 25?), but they rarely learn how to think. (A better question would be, Suppose you have seven coins and have at least one quarter, dime, nickel, and penny. What is the least amount of money you could have?) Kids who cannot handle this "penny-ante" problem are in trouble, but then some teachers have trouble handling it—and that is trouble for the nation.

IRRELEVANT CURRICULUM

Almost everyone likes to criticize the schools. And such critics often claim that the curriculum is irrelevant in some way or another. When people say that the curriculum is irrelevant, they often mean either that it does not meet the needs

**CURRICULUM TIPS 12-2   Appraising the Worth
of a Textbook**

Here are some questions to keep in mind in assessing the worth of a textbook for teachers and curriculum committees.

Content

1. Does the text coincide with the content and objectives of the course?
2. Is it up to date and accurate?
3. Is it comprehensive?
4. Is it adaptable to the students' needs, interests, and abilities?
5. Does it adequately and properly portray minorities and women?
6. Does it foster methodological approaches consistent with procedures used by the teacher and school?
7. Does it reinforce the type of learning (such as critical thinking and problem solving) sought by the teacher and school?
8. Does it provide the student with a sense of accomplishment because it can be mastered and is still challenging?

Mechanics

1. Is the size appropriate?
2. Is the binding adequate?
3. Is the paper of adequate quality?
4. Are the objectives, headings, and summaries clear?
5. Are the contents and index well organized?
6. Is there a sufficient number of pictures, charts, maps, and so on, appropriate for the students' level?
7. Does it come with instructional manuals and study guides?
8. Is it durable enough to last several years?
9. Is it reasonably priced relative to its quality? To its competitors?

Overall Appraisal

1. What are the outstanding features of the text?
2. What are the shortcomings of the text?
3. Do the outstanding features strongly override the shortcomings?

Source: Allan C. Ornstein, "Textbook Instruction: Processes and Strategies," *NASSP Bulletin* (December 1989), p. 110.

of the social situation or the students and so the subject matter needs to be modified. Such a broad view permits educators to consider the irrelevant curriculum in several ways: (1) The curriculum is *fixed* or not relevant to society, which suggests that the sweep of change in society is more rapid than that in curriculum; (2) the curriculum is *antiseptic,* which connotes that the materials or textbooks are divorced from the students' sense of reality; (3) the curriculum is *trivial,* which implies that its facts and figures are remote, meaningless, and/or nonessential to students; and (4) there is *hidden* curriculum that has little to do with the formal or established curriculum.

The Fixed Curriculum

This interpretation suggests that a relationship exists between changes in society and changes in the curriculum. It is rooted in Dewey's interpretation of the *curriculum as experience,* which links curriculum to the importance of perpetuating, transferring, and reconstructing society. "The scheme of a curriculum must take into account . . . the intention of improving the life we live in common so that the future shall be better than the past,"[31] asserted Dewey. This idea suggests that the cumulative knowledge and total culture of society must be reflected in the curriculum, what such reconstructionists as B. Othanel Smith and his colleagues called *curriculum as race experience*. They wrote: "The curriculum is always [or should be], in every society, a reflection of what the people think, believe, and do . . . [A] universal relationship [exists] between the curriculum and the culture of a society."[32]

The idea that the curriculum had become static or fixed was proclaimed by another early reconstructionist as well. In 1939, Harold Benjamin described a society whose curriculum was based on perennial beliefs, dating back to the Paleolithic era. The wise men of society argued that "the essence of true education is timeless . . . something that endures through changing conditions like a solid rock standing squarely and firmly in the middle of a raging torrent."[33] Benjamin's message was simple: Eventually the curriculum became outdated.

Today's explosion of knowledge and the swiftness of change underscore the need for curricula to be relevant. Some educators have contended that a curriculum can become obsolete every few years. This claim is based on the facts that knowledge increases exponentially and that the rate of obsolescence of scientific knowledge equals that of an automobile.[34] This premise is somewhat questionable, however, because it assumes that the explosion of knowledge can go on indefinitely, and it does not consider that trends change or that the rate of change varies over time. Moreover, it considers our resources to be limited.

The effects of the knowledge explosion on curriculum are tempered by the fact that new knowledge is assimilated as existing knowledge is revised and modified to accommodate it. In the same vein, new subject matter is systematically incorporated into existing subject matter, and new teaching and learning methods are fused with existing methods to produce new instructional approaches. These curriculum and instructional processes are continuous and to some extent reflect new knowledge in the social sciences. In assessing the onrush of new knowledge, Orlosky and Smith contend that as "knowledge continually expands so does the curriculum. Old areas grow and new ones emerge. . . . These developments give rise to new perspectives, new goals,"[35] and, if we may add, new content. Indeed, if schools are to maintain their health and vitality, the curriculum cannot remain fixed in a world of change.

The Antiseptic Curriculum

An antiseptic curriculum is safe and sterile; it does not deal with student or societal reality. The stories, characters, and illustrations in reading material tend to be one-dimensional or monolithic, not multicultural (in terms of ethnicity, religion, sex, and class).

The term antiseptic curriculum was first used to describe basic readers in the 1960s when they were considered to be irrelevant to the social realities and culture of disadvantaged (minority and low-income) groups. These readers portrayed an almost exclusively white and middle-class world, and they treated the few minorities they did include as exotic or different, not part of the American landscape. The Indians, for example, were called "Big Horn" or "Shining Star," and peddlers or organ grinders wore red scarves, not ties, and ragged clothes, not suits. Their appearances or names were typically Italian, Greek, or Polish. When "Dick and Jane" or "Johnnie" visited their grandmothers in the South, or in the country, either no mention was made of blacks or one black boy might be inserted in the background. Yellow or dark people were depicted in the illustrations for the stories about China, India, and Africa, but they were always different in appearance and custom. Women were usually portrayed as mothers, nurses, or teachers, and religion was rarely mentioned except, perhaps, in relation to church attendance on Sunday mornings. In short, these readers were presented with a monocultural view of our society. Put in different words, in 1960, approximately 6.5 million nonwhite children were learning to read books that either scarcely mentioned them or omitted them entirely.

According to Fantini and Weinstein, life was depicted in these books in terms of "happy, neat, wealthy, white people whose intact and loving families live only in clean, grassy suburbs. . . . Ethnic groups comprising so much of our population are often omitted," or else they are included under "units as 'Children From Other

Lands.' "[36] Fantini and Weinstein concluded that these books had no relationship to the culture or reality of the disadvantaged child.

Otto Klienberg was more outspoken in his review of the most popular readers of the period. Americans, when illustrated, were almost exclusively white and blonde, were relatively comfortable financially (but not wealthy); were nicely dressed; lived in clean, pleasant homes with nice furniture; and provided their children with toys, bicycles, and spending money.[37] Every family had a father and mother at home and usually a grandmother or grandfather to visit. The parents always had time to take their sons to ballgames or their daughters shopping or to take both children on train rides to visit relatives, on car rides to learn about farmers, or to the seashore on family vacations. In summary, life in America was portrayed through a white, middle-class lens; life was comfortable, frustrations were rare, and people were invariably generous, kind, honest, and hardworking. Other kinds of people did live in the world, and some of them may have had problems, but they lived far away and had no place in the American scene. For Klienberg, the basic readers displayed both "ethnocentrism" and "socioeconomic-centrism."[38] Critics argued that the great distance between the schools' curricula and reality for minority and poor children contributed to their academic failure.

Most of these abuses were corrected by the late 1960s to the extent that Harry Passow could summarize the instructional materials as being (1) multiracial, multiethnic, and multisocial class; (2) urban-oriented rather than suburban or rural; (3) historically and culturally accurate regarding the contributions of various minority groups; (4) nationally and internationally pluralistic; and (5) positive in the treatment of emerging and third-world nations.[39]

Today, readers, workbooks, and textbooks unquestionably exclude racial, ethnic, religious, and sexual stereotyping. Obscenity, violence, and sexual topics are still generally avoided, as are such unpleasant issues as disease and death. Story characters and pictures tend to be well represented by major racial and ethnic groups, including the handicapped and elderly. Girls now rarely play with dolls, and women are depicted as airplane pilots, police officers, construction workers, lawyers, and doctors. Blacks, Hispanics, and other traditional minorities have professional and managerial jobs. Minorities are not basketball players or musicians, unless surrounded by a host of whites, and boys rarely play baseball, and least not without girls.

One might even argue that the "correction" factor has gone too far to the other side of the continuum: The curriculum has become Afrocentric, multiculturalist, and gender pure at the expense of reducing or purging white, male political leaders and authors as well as traditional Western thought from the curriculum. In some schools, Christopher Columbus is now an evil white colonialist, Johnnie Tremain and his band of radicals are sexists and therefore irrelevant, and Washington and Jefferson are little more than slave masters whose historical contributions are cast aside into second place. History and English books and courses must be revised, with the intent of pruning away Plato, Erasmus, and Shakespeare so that minority and female contributors, what is "politically correct," can receive equal attention.

In our desire that all people and groups gain recognition and be shown as contributors to American history and culture, certain basic information and ideas are now deemed irrelevant. The mood is to increase the African-American, Hispanic, Asian-American, and female perspective and to reduce the Eurocentric and male representation. Frederick Douglass is more important and gets more coverage than Henry Clay, as does Cesar Chavez over Samuel Gompers. Elizabeth Cady Stanton and Betsy Ross are "in" and Sam Adams and Tom Paine are "out."

Finding good literature or good texts that meet all these requirements (and many more) is difficult. To accommodate some of the new criteria, many classic works of literature have been eliminated from the curriculum, and many bland texts and instructional materials have been included. The idea is to please all and offend none and thus many textbooks and related materials have no clear point of view.[40] Although many new books portray the majority and minority populace more accurately, however, they remain sterile and safe; they tacitly perpetuate the antiseptic curriculum. This, in turn, can lead to student boredom. Considering that readers, workbooks, and/or textbooks have become the basis for curriculum and classroom instruction and that they represent 70 to 95 percent of the total curriculum program (depending on the subject), this is a serious problem indeed.[41]

The Trivial Curriculum

A trivial curriculum is one that emphasizes rote learning and irrelevant facts and figures that teachers must insist that students learn. Teachers may ask students, for example, to memorize a good deal of nonessential and meaningless information, such as the names of all the American presidents in order, the capital of each state, the products of Brazil, the lines to the "Highwayman" or the "Rhyme of the Ancient Mariner," or the coefficient of an angle. This type of teaching and learning is almost useless, and it occurs at the expense of important academic time that could be utilized more efficiently by introducing significant content.

Most students have had facts and figures drummed into them repeatedly during their school careers, perhaps even in college. Most of them cannot remember what they memorized for their last exams, much less what they memorized a year or more ago. More than 75 percent of various kinds of facts learned in a subject is forgotten over a twelve-month period of time.[42] For a single lecture, as contrasted with a whole course, retention over one hour is also unimpressive—as low as 60 percent.[43] Obviously, the drop-off or loss of retention differs for students with varying ability. Bright students retain more than slow students, and college students do better than elementary school students. For content, what is perceived by the learner as trivial material—useless, arbitrary or disconnected—the ability to recall data declines very rapidly, often within minutes.

Both Ausubel and Wittrock make a critical distinction between rote and meaningful learning. They argue that, to the extent that instruction concerns simple rote learning and meaningless data, the curriculum is essentially irrelevant to the learner and little is learned.[44] In contrast to memorizing a host of facts or words (for a short period of time), meaningful learning takes place if the curriculum relates to what the learner already knows, deems personally useful, and considers relevant to his or her personal experience.

If trivial facts and figures have little value or relevance to adults, how can we expect them to have meaning for children? Information, including the names of the American presidents, state capitals, coffee beans, sonnets, and quadratic equations, can have meaning to students *if* it can be related to existing ideas in the students' cognitive and affective backgrounds or *if* it can be subsumed within existing mental and personal structures. If data are learned only as random facts or only because of the dictates of the formal curriculum, students' memory-storing processes will be limited and what they remember will be remote and arbitrary.

E. D. Hirsch's list of "essential 5000 names, phrases, dates, and concepts," what he feels every literate American needs to know, might be considered important ideas and information to be mastered, the kind of stuff that "trains the mind."[45] For critics, however, the list is considered silly, a compilation of fragmented data, and we should not expect students to remember an extensive curriculum as a mere catalogue of information.

Using satire, Harmin and Simon illustrate how teaching facts can dominate the entire curriculum and how educators' misplaced ingenuity can stifle real learning. Their scenario takes place during "the year the schools began teaching the telephone directory" to the seventh grade.[46] Each seventh grade teacher, working in conjunction with his or her immediate supervisor, was responsible for developing appropriate methods to make this memorization task easier. The students began from A to Z: " 'What is Gregory Arnold's phone number?' asked the teacher. 'Who lives at 174 N. Maple?' "[47] (Everyone knew because it was the principal's address.) The task continued, with frequent quizzes, a midterm through M, and a final exam at Z: "Oh the cram sessions which were organized by eager mothers, the withheld allowances which were used as bludgeons, the diligent studying which went on! Never before did so many telephone numbers, addresses, and names get committed to so many memories."[48]

Students who did not learn the phone book were labeled as slow learners and were placed in remedial classes the following term. In general, the telephone directory curriculum was deemed a success and was admired by the entire community. It was even extended down to the sixth and fifth grades the following year. To integrate subject matter, sixth graders were required to memorize the Paris, France, telephone directory as well. To make learning more relevant, fifth graders were also assigned the local community directory. New seventh graders were assigned the "exciting" task of learning the state capitol directory.

Although Harmin and Simon's criticism is directed at reforming the curriculum, their wit has implications for the way teachers still require students to commit to memory much trivial information. The real issue is how educators can help students move from memorizing random facts to developing useful concepts and problem-solving skills. Learning useless or arbitrary facts in isolation, a process that characterizes a good deal of classroom activity, is not conducive to real learning, that is, to concept thinking or problem solving. At best a trivial curriculum can encourage students with good memories to retrieve information in order to please the teacher or pass an examination. But computers can now do a better job of retrieving information than students. Learners must instead be taught to think and solve problems.

The Hidden Curriculum

Every school has a planned or formal curriculum, that is, a stated and structured set of objectives, with related content and learning experiences and expected outcomes. There are intended, explicit, and operational plans, usually organized around subjects and grades, whereby the roles of the curriculum leader and teacher are well defined. But there is also an unplanned and informal curriculum, or what we call the hidden curriculum. Some observers also use the term "unofficial," "masked," or "covert" curriculum to refer to the hidden curriculum.[49] There are behaviors and attitudes conveyed in classrooms and schools that often go unnoticed and unmentioned because they were never explicitly stated as expected. Most educators prefer to deal with only the planned curriculum; however those who are aware of the attitudes and feelings of students are well aware of the influence of the hidden curriculum.

The hidden curriculum is best illustrated in the sexual roles and ethnic strategies that are conveyed in textbooks and sometimes in the student-student and student-teacher interactions. Although most teachers would be offended and reject the idea that they admonish girls to act "ladylike" or boys to "act like a man" or that their instructional materials sometimes emphasize an ethnocentric (Afrocentric, Hispanic, or Western) view of the world, hidden biases do emerge in classrooms and schools. To be sure, pictures in textbooks convey all types of messages, as do such innocent classroom activities as the Pledge of Allegiance (patriotism), independent assignments (individualism), and obeying rules (conformity).

Another aspect of the hidden curriculum is the social messages, the roles and norms of classrooms. For example, who is nominated as class representative, which students sit next to each other or play with each other on the playground and who is left out or standing alone. What happens when Sally is in front of the class and doesn't know the answer, how the teacher greets particular students, or who the teacher calls on to answer easy (or difficult) questions all convey messages about self-esteem and self-worth of students.

Things always happen in classrooms and schools, and they are not always planned or expected; they can be happy and healthy experiences or frightening and humiliating. According to Philip Jackson, school "is a place [where students] sit, listen, wait, raise their hands," converse, work together, and "stand in line."[50] Many of these experiences are routine and go unnoticed. But these interactions convey messages and affect how students are socialized in classrooms and schools, and eventually affect academic achievement.

The teacher's role is to recognize the hidden aspects of the curriculum, especially potential dysfunctional or negative learning experiences, and wherever possible to control and improve the situation. "To the alert teacher," according to one curriculum specialist, "there is no such thing as the hidden curriculum."[51] The competent educator removes the hidden practices and harmful consequences of the curriculum. He or she is supposed to orchestrate and direct the implicit or unstated behaviors and attitudes of the curriculum in subtle and unofficial ways. The trouble, however, is that most curriculum leaders and teachers, when asked to define what happens in classrooms, tend to be vague and unsure. They lack a technical or scientific vocabulary, unlike other professionals, to describe the social interaction processes in classrooms. They often simplify the complexity of the classroom into three or four underlying events or global terms such as motivation, questioning, homework, or review.

Indeed, much of our professional behavior is based on intuitive hunches and impulses, since events in classrooms and schools occur at a very rapid rate. Content and learning experiences and corresponding curriculum sequences and consequences cannot be easily predicted or planned. There is a great deal of spontaneity in classrooms, and this is how it should be unless we wish stillness and conformity to dictate pedagogy. The interplay among students and teachers is crucial and cannot always be carefully controlled or planned in advance.[52] To some extent, the implementation of curriculum, which encompasses the act of teaching, must be considered in part intuitive and interactive, not prescriptive or predictable. Likewise, there will always be a hidden curriculum—unplanned, unofficial, and unintended. But we need to be sensitive about it, reflect on it and explore our hidden feelings and attitudes—the social and educational messages our instructional materials and we as teachers convey in classrooms when we implement the curriculum.

ACADEMIC TIME

In Chapter 5, the classic question, "What is the most worthwhile content?" was asked and discussed. Now we discuss its supplementary question: "How much time do we devote to specific content?" Determining the content and the time we spend on instruction to teach the content are key considerations in developing curriculum. Together they determine "opportunity to learn." If students have not been taught some content or have had little time for learning or practicing the specific knowledge, skill, or task, they simply

cannot do well on tests relevant to the topic or on future learning that involves previous mastery of the work, when the content should have been covered. We now look at some aspects of academic time.

Mandated Time

Mandated time in the nation's schools averages about 178 days per year and about 5 hours and 8 minutes per day. The longer school term and days of Japan (220 days and more than 6 hours per day), Korea and western European nations (200 to 230 days) lead some educators to conclude that one reason for poor performance of U.S. students is the shorter time in school. But research indicates that increasing time in school by itself, without changing other aspects of instruction, does not result in increased achievement.[53] Nonetheless, common sense suggests that, if instructional quality is kept constant, then extra instructional quantity should have positive effects. Students who have more time to study specific knowledge, skills, and tasks should learn more than students who have less time. Increasing school time in U.S. public schools about 40 minutes per day would add 119 hours in one school year, about 290 school days over 12 years, and 1.6 extra years of schooling.[54] This is an important point that has future consequences in terms of U.S. human capital, productivity and, in turn, our standard of living for all age groups.

Allocated Time

Allocated time is the portion of the school day (or school year) the school assigns to academic and nonacademic instruction. About 60 to 80 percent of the school day is allocated to academic content.[55] Secondary schools are subject oriented and allocate more time to academic content than do elementary schools. The younger students have need for more time for socialization and personal growth.

More than half of the states make recommendations, and some have requirements for allocating time in curriculum content by subjects at the elementary grade levels. School districts can and usually do modify the recommendations or requirements upward, especially in math and English (perhaps because of the recent publicity given to the results of statewide programs to test performance in math and reading). Modifications of allocated time at the school level also reflect the philosophy of the local community, district superintendent, and school principal; for example, a "progressive" educator might allocate more time for socialization than an "essentialist," who might put more emphasis on the three R's and subtract time from a sports or music/art program.

Although state policies vary, as illustrated in Table 12-2, English (language arts) receives the most allocated time in the early grades, after which the time decreases. Math receives the second most attention and remains relatively constant throughout the grades. Note, however, that the *difference* in recommendations among the states for allocated time in English is 102 minutes per day in the third grade and 75 minutes in the sixth grade. In math the *difference* is as much as 45 minutes. The time allocated to science and social studies increases from the early grades to grade 8, when it is equal to the time for other subjects (except in Illinois). If standardized testing in grades 3 to 6 included science and social studies, then there would most likely be more

allocated time for them in those grades. The states that do not establish time allocations (such as California, Florida, and New York) focus on instructional objectives and test performance in subject areas, especially at the middle school and high school levels.

At the secondary level, allocated time is better defined and is influenced by the nature of the students' program (academic, technical, or vocational). In response to national demands for upgrading academic requirements and increasing academic productivity, the curriculum has undergone modification (in the 1980s and 1990s) with more emphasis on such core subjects as English, social studies, math, and science, and academic course requirements for graduation were also increased.

Table 12-3 shows that there has been a marked increase in required course work for public high school graduation in all major academic subjects, especially in math and science, between 1981 and 1988. Graduation requirements in English and social studies for public schools are now only slightly below the recommendations of the National Commission on Excellence in Education; they are still substantially below the rec-

TABLE 12-2 Allocated Time (by minutes) by Subject and Grade Level

SUBJECT	GRADE	ILLINOIS (minimum recommendations)	MICHIGAN (minimum recommendations)	TEXAS (minimum requirements)
Math	3	50	15	60
	6	49	15	60
	8	47	15	45
Science	3	26	9	20
	6	39	9	45
	8	44	15	45
English (language arts)	3	142	40	120
	6	107	32	90
	8	87	15	45
Social studies	3	45	4	20
	6	42	9	45
	8	44	15	45

Source: Based on telephone conversations with curriculum specialists from the respective state departments of education, January 27, 1989, and September 17, 1990.

TABLE 12-3 Average Years of Course Work Required for Public High School Graduation

	SUBJECT AREA				
SCHOOL YEAR	MATHEMATICS	SCIENCE	ENGLISH	FOREIGN LANGUAGES	SOCIAL STUDIES
1981–1982	1.6	1.5	3.6	a	2.6
1984–1985	1.9	1.8	3.8	0.1	2.8
1987–1988[b]	2.3	2.0	3.9	0.2	2.9
Recommendations of National Commission on Excellence in Education[c]	3.0	3.0	4.0	2.0[d]	3.0

Source: The Condition of Education 1987 (Washington, D.C.: U.S. Government Printing Office, 1987), Table 1.37B, p. 84.

[a] Less than 0.05 year.

[b] Expectations as of fall 1985 about requirements for seniors graduating in 1988.

[c] Another half year of coursework was recommended in computer science. Almost no school districts had requirements in this area in 1981–82. That situation changed by 1984–85, when the average for all school districts was 0.1 year of coursework required for graduation in computer science; the expected average for 1987–88 was 0.2 year.

[d] The Commission's recommendations about foreign languages applied only to the college-bound, not to all students. The figures for actual requirements represent requirements for all graduates.

ommended level in math, science, and, especially, foreign languages.

Academic Instructional Time

This refers to the actual amount of time the teacher spends in the various curriculum areas and is sometimes referred to as academic learning time or content covered. This time rarely exceeds the school's allocated time, and, when it does, it connotes that the teacher is spending more time on a particular subject or aspect of a subject than is expected by the school district or curriculum guidelines.

Goodlad and Klein observe that teachers devote most academic learning time to reading activities at all elementary grade levels (except kindergarten). This includes related activities in phonics instruction, listening to stories, and discussion of library books and elements of language. In terms of time allocation, this curriculum area is followed by "independent activities," such as filling in workbooks, looking up words in the dictionary, writing in journals, spelling words, and attending to class projects (almost all of which deal with language skills and have a reading component). Mathematics was the third most popular activity.[56]

Recently, Ornstein analyzed the academic coverage devoted to teaching third grade and sixth grade language arts. In general, the ranges for each content area are wide, although they seem wider at the sixth grade than for the third grade. For example, one third grade teacher devotes 140 minutes per year to spelling, while another devotes 852 minutes. One teacher spends 206 minutes on vocabulary, whereas another spends 1,615 minutes.

In the sixth grade, one teacher devotes 124 minutes each year to creative writing, while another spends 967 minutes. One teacher spends 261 minutes on grammar and another

1,486 minutes. One spends 71 minutes on spelling, another spends 216 minutes. We can make a safe bet about which students will perform better as a whole in certain content-related tests. See Table 12-4. A question arises: Why is it that one teacher spends seven or eight times more academic time in such content areas as library skills, creative writing, grammar, or vocabulary than another teacher in the same school district?

Even in junior high and senior high schools, where departmentalization forces common time allocations for each subject, teachers must still decide how much actual time to spend on lesson units or topics. How much time should be spent on subjects such as library skills or creative writing that achievement tests don't usually evaluate?

Two cautionary observations should be noted. First, we should not necessarily conclude that "more is always better." Instructional quality is crucial, and we must remember that a diminishing point is reached where "more" of the same thing becomes boring. On the other hand, teachers must allocate sufficient and sometimes extra time so that their students can learn the required subject matter.

Second, teachers vary in the way they efficiently use time—or avoid wasting time. According to research data, no more than 50 to 60 percent of an elementary school day and 30 to 45 percent of a high school day is devoted to academic instruction. The rest of the time is spent on nonacademic subjects, recess, lunch, and/or study time, transitions between classes, announcements, and clerical procedures and maintenance tasks. The biggest time waster, especially at the secondary level, is considered to be the changing and beginning of classes; an estimated 75 hours or 15 days in the school year is lost each year.[57]

Also, there is a problem of absenteeism, and in many inner-city schools the absenteeism among students is high. When a student is absent or late, it does not matter how much time the teacher devotes to instruction. A student who is not present receives no instruction.

To increase academic learning time, teachers should have a system of rules and procedures that facilitates noninstructional tasks and reduces disruptions and disciplinary problems. Similarly, schools need to implement policies that decrease absenteeism and lateness. See Curriculum Tips 12-3.

TABLE 12-4 Allocated Time in Language Arts in Grades 3 and 6

LANGUAGE ARTS	Grade 3 MINUTES PER YEAR	Grade 6 MINUTES PER YEAR
Library skills	96–248	63–886
Spelling	140–852	71–216
Creative writing	92–649	124–967
Grammar	43–298	261–1,486
Reading		
Vocabulary	206–1,615	112–991
Comprehension	391–992	444–1,841

Source: Allan C. Ornstein, *Institutionalized Learning in America* (New Brunswick N.J.: Transaction, 1990), Table 6.4, p. 74.

Note: Based on self-reports from nine third grade teachers in three schools and seven sixth grade teachers in two schools in Illinois suburbs.

CURRICULUM TIPS 12-3 Increasing Academic Time

Too much instructional time is wasted in today's classrooms. Two educators contend that as much as 50 to 60 days or nearly one-third of the school year may be wasted, but could be regained by improving or changing some procedures. Here are some major time wasters to resolve.

1. *Working on homework during the school day.* It is not uncommon to find teachers allocating 20 to 30 minutes in class for students to work on homework assignments. This is equivalent to about 10 school days if only one teacher per day is guilty of this practice. *Action to be taken:* Time used for homework in class should be converted to instructional time. Teachers should still explain the homework assignment and review common problems, but not permit work on homework in class.

2. *Excessive viewing of films.* Two many teachers use too many films, especially on Fridays. Viewing films for one hour per week uses up 36 hours or 7 days. *Action to be taken:* The use of instructional tools should be justified in terms of student results. A cumulative record of film time used by teachers should perhaps be kept.

3. *Changing and beginning classes.* In most middle and senior high schools, students move from room to room. It is not unusual for teachers to use 5 to 10 minutes per class to take attendance and make announcements. If only 5 minutes were used, 75 hours or 15 days would be saved. *Action to be taken:* Teachers need to devise systems, such as assigned seats, printed lists, or diagrams, to show quickly who is absent from class.

4. *Teacher absences.* Learning suffers when teachers are absent (the average teacher is absent three to five times a year), since most substitute teachers are unable to reach desired academic objectives. *Action to be taken:* Excellent substitute teachers need to be identified by the school principal. Also, the regular teacher needs to make available the lesson plan for the day, along with related materials, when he or she expects to be absent.

5. *Registration and testing.* About 3 days a year are lost on registration and another 3 on schoolwide testing. In both cases, students are often free for portions of the day. *Action to be taken:* Registration should be scheduled prior to the school year. Schoolwide testing and standardized testing should be incorporated into the regular class time, not treated as a separate testing day.

6. *Extracurricular activities.* Although it is impossible to state the exact number of days lost by students who are dismissed early for athletic events, school tournaments, community and state activities, music and dance workshops, band, and other activities, a good estimate is 5 to 10 days. *Action to be taken:* Students must be encouraged to make up their academic work. Special events should be scheduled on activity days, not regular academic days, or during after-school hours (in the afternoon, evenings, or on weekends), not during class time.

Source: Adapted from Robert Lowe and Robert Gervais, "Increasing Instructional Time in Today's Classroom," *NASSP Bulletin* (February 1988), pp. 19–22.

Academic Engaged Time

Academic engaged time is the time a student spends attending to academic tasks or content. For some educators, it also means that students must perform the tasks or be engaged in the content with a high success rate (80 percent or more).[58] Although actual classroom instructional time is a more important variable than engaged time in the sense that it shows a higher correlation with improved performance, there are more data on engaged time because it is easier to measure. Moreover, different teachers use different materials and methods to cover the same content, and they focus on different aspects of content. Since researchers have not developed a method for coding content in such situations, they often turn to academic engaged time as a proxy for instructional time or content covered.[59]

Barak Rosenshine's review of instruction in reading and mathematics in 50 classrooms, grades 2 and 5, shows the importance of how time is spent in the classroom. About 58 percent of the school day is allocated to academic activities, about 23 percent to nonacademic activities (music, art, physical education), and about 19 percent to noninstructional activities (transitions between activities and class business). On the average, students are engaged about 73 percent of the time allocated to academic activities in reading and math. Students in the lower grades (grade 2) spent 1 hour and 30 minutes on these two activities daily, and older students (grade 5) spent 30 minutes longer on an average.

During time allocated for academics, students are not engaged about 16 minutes an hour, during which they are passing out and collecting papers, waiting for help, or completely off task. Overall, students spend about two-thirds of the allocated time in seatwork (or self-paced activities), mainly practice and drill, and about one-third engaged with an adult. Student engagement is higher in teacher-directed settings (about 84 percent) than in other seatwork settings (about 70 percent).[60] Thus, if a teacher divides a class into three groups and engages one group at a time while the other two groups work alone, student academic engaged time substantially falls off. Many educators object to emphasis on teacher-directed activities and would prefer more independent activities for students—just what seems to create academic waste of time.

In a study of 19 social studies classes and 20 mathematics classes in Chicago and its surrounding suburban school districts, Susan Stodolsky found in social studies a much greater amount of time spent on group work (11 percent), student reports (7 percent), and audiovisual materials (7 percent) than in mathematics (0.01, 0, 0, respectively). Although students in both subjects spent a goodly amount of time on uniform seatwork (22 percent versus 30 percent in math) and recitation (31 percent versus 29 percent in math), they spent no time on individualized seatwork in social studies, but 11 percent in math classes.[61]

In general, the source for new knowledge and learning how to learn in math was the teachers. These teachers were expected to present new materials and explain how to do problems. In contrast, social studies students were expected to learn on their own by reading the text and other materials. They were supposed to develop research skills by gathering and using information from many sources, whereas math students were expected to first learn the fundamentals and then become problem solvers.

In the final analysis, both the quantity and quality of academic engaged time (as well as actual instructional time) are considered to be important in improving the outcomes of student learning, although quantity is easier to agree on and measure. Students of teachers who provide more academic engaged time (as well as actual instructional time) learn more than students of teachers who provide relatively less time. In a review of more than 20 different studies, the correlations between student achievement in reading and mathematics and learning time was between 0.40 and 0.60.[62] In a review of 22 studies, Herb Walberg concluded that *corrective feedback,* a component or aspect of academic time, had one of the most powerful effects (.45) on achievement. When necessary, effective teachers provide additional time for practice.[63]

Since academic time, both instructional and engaged, seems to be a scarcer commodity than most of us probably realized, what we might focus on in the future is how curriculum workers and teachers can better utilize their time when they are allocating instruction time and how students can better utilize their time when on task (academic engaged time).

COMPENSATORY CURRICULUM

A massive movement into compensatory education, begun in the 1960s and 1970s, was designed to overcome the educational (and to some extent social and psychological) deficiencies or disadvantages of lower-class and minority children. The movement was widespread and intense; it took on more than just bandwagon status. Nonetheless, surprisingly little mention is made of this trend in other curriculum texts.

The various programs and projects can be categorized by *target population* (kindergarten through college, student or teacher), *treatment* (remedial, enrichment, and therapeutic), *service* (curricula, instructional, counseling, school wide, and community), *setting* (urban and rural), and *policy* (local, regional, state, and national). Most compensatory programs were experimental or additive and were not designed for fundamental or system-wide reform. They operated from the theoretical premises that cognitive, social, and psychological development are mainly the consequence of environmental influences, and that improving the environment of the child can reverse whatever learning deficits exist. Beginning with the Johnson administration, special personnel and services were usually funded by the federal government, under Title I of the Elementary and Secondary Education Act (ESEA). Chapter I was introduced (to replace Title I) by the Reagan administration and continued by the Bush presidency.

The 1990s: New Concerns for "At-Risk" Students

Although the term "disadvantaged" has been replaced by "at-risk" and "special needs" students, concern for these children and youth has increased as the proportion of these students grows every year and is probably one major reason for our declining student achievement. This at-risk population tends to encompass the following major groups: poverty children (21 percent of student enrollments K–12); minority students (some 30 percent), especially immigrant children who speak a language other than English (15 percent); and handicapped students (12 percent).[64] Somewhat unnoticed is another group of at-risk students; hungry and/or malnourished, some 5.5 million under the age of twelve (and not necessarily all from poor home environments) and another 6 million considered borderline hungry.[65]

Although most at-risk students are poor (some 13.5 million as of 1990), estimates are that approximately 60 to 65 percent of our students, increasingly from the middle class, are latchkey children or potentially at risk, that is, without adult supervision after school.[66] In addition, a category of the "new needy" has emerged, including some 250,000 to 500,000 homeless children, 250,000 to 300,000 crack-exposed babies born each year, and some 500,000 to 600,000 migrant children.[67]

Also, an increasing number of children are being raised in foster care centers, juvenile detention centers, and mental health facilities (in total predicted to reach 850,000 to one million by 1995);[68] the critical needs of these children go ignored to the extent that many are abused and the schools really have minimal programs to assist them. Although there is significant overlap between the old needy groups (poor, minority, non-English speaking, and handicapped) and the new needy groups, the full depth of our educational problems are just beginning to surface as we identify new at-risk groups.

In addition, some educators are expanding the notion of at-risk to include students who fall into one or more of these categories: (1) prematurely born, (2) abused or neglected, (3) substance addicted, (4) pregnant, (5) gang or cult members, (6) school-dropout parents, (7) teenage parents, (8) single-family parent, (9) AIDS children or parent, (10) divorced parents, (11) drug or alcohol-dependent parents, and (12) incarcerated parents.[69] Add these twelve groups to the traditional poor (minority, immigrant or bilingual, and handicapped categories) as well as the latchkey and new needy, and more than 90 percent of the U.S. student enrollments may be at risk and can use some extra assistance in school.

Where is all this help or money going to come from? Given our shrinking tax base and that the elderly poor, a powerful political force, are vying for the same human-service dollars, the future is not promising for young Americans—who lack the vote.

One way to put all these trends in perspective is as follows: the U.S. student population K–12 is expected to grow in this decade, from 46 million to 50 million by 2001.[70] But teaching in that year, and beyond, will be more difficult than today, especially in our big cities where the underclass (poor, minority, handicapped, and others) is growing rapidly. In more dramatic terms, our human capital is at stake; an increasing number of educationally disabled students are in part creating long-term American decline. All our new slogans and fuzzy buzzwords—"higher national standards," "restructuring schools," and "reforming education"—may be doomed before they get off the ground as a growing flood of at-risk children each year enter our classrooms, basically unprepared for school and later unprepared to enter our skilled workforce and information age.

Problems and Prospects

Much of the efforts during the early period of compensatory education has been raising the cognitive levels of disadvantaged students. Basically, four failure trends emerged:

1. In many of the best-known and heavily funded programs, such as Headstart and Follow-Through, no significant differences showed in learning between the target children and matched controlled groups.

2. In the early stages of compensatory funding, input increments had a discernible effect, but they gradually diminished until input was wasted because there was virtually no increase in output. The conclusion was that the programs had reached a "flat area"—less output in relation to input, or even worse, no return.

3. Longitudinal studies of several programs also revealed a "fade out" process; that is, the early gains made by these youngsters (if any) eventually leveled off and, after a few years of schooling, were equivalent to gains made by those without such funding.

4. Many so-called "successes" were generally based not on hard data, but on impressions and testimonies (in many cases suspect). When evaluated on the basis of measurable data, most of these programs proved to be ineffective. For example, of the more than 1200 projects evaluated in the 1970s and originally judged to be successful, only ten were found to be effective on the basis of statistical reanalysis.[71]

The same problems were exhibited in the 1980s, when several well-publicized and so-called outstanding early-childhood programs were analyzed and proved to have limited cognitive outcomes despite early claims of success. Some programs tended to be subject to fade-out within a few years; others had no data available with which to verify successes or to conduct critical reviews in scientific journals. What educators experienced in the early stages of compensatory programs was reality. Intervention efforts of a few hours a day in one or two school years could not compensate for several years of impoverishment, despite the claims of many environmentalists and behaviorists.[72]

In general, compensatory education has been criticized for (1) its hasty planning and piecemeal approach; (2) its mismanagement and misappropriation of funds; (3) its dependence on unethical grantspeople who justify their conduct on the basis that "everyone does it"; (4) the large consultant fees charged for unaccomplished or shoddy work; (5) its use of inadequately trained personnel at the state and local levels; (6) the high salaries it pays people at the administrative levels; (7) its disregard for and lack of teacher participation; (8) its vague objectives; (9) its poor evaluation procedures; and (10) the increased quantity of services it substitutes for change in the quality or content of the program.[73]

In addition, opponents have criticized the attitude of educators that the money was there for them to give away even if they expected no real benefits. Lawmakers who allocate funds for compensatory programs have become increasingly concerned about putting money into areas in which little worth has been empirically shown.

Advocates of compensatory spending claim that most of these problems can be remedied over time and that the real problem is the concern that disadvantaged children will not succeed. Americans are obligated to find solutions that will reach these children and provide them with the necessary equality of opportunities. Moreover, advocates contend that, in most instances, (1) money was made available in such haste that the quality of planning and development was limited; (2) many programs have been operative for too brief a period to be effectively evaluated; (3) many programs were funded at insufficient levels; and (4) some student successes have been reported in the affective domain.[74]

Effective Teachers and Schools

The kind of research that holds out the most promise today for giving direction to compensatory education is not research on the educational disadvantaged, at risk, or compensatory programs, but research on effective teachers and effective schools. In this sense, the emphasis now is on an integrative and school-wide approach, as opposed to a piecemeal or experimental approach based on one or two compensatory programs. For example, in a review of two decades of research on low-income students, Levine and Ornstein list six characteristics of effective teaching and instruction.

1. *Classroom management.* Effective teachers make sure that students know what to expect; they hold students accountable, provide smooth transitions between activities, and do not respond emotionally to discipline problems.

2. *Direct instruction/explicit teaching.* The terms are sometimes used interchangeably to connote a systematic and structured method of teaching; instruction is teacher directed, material is presented in small steps and systematic feedback and corrections are provided by the teacher.

3. *Time on task.* Effective teachers make use of classroom time and bring about high levels of students' time on task. Students are actively engaged in relevant activities and are not doing busy work.

4. *Questioning.* Effective teachers stimulate engagement in learning by asking appropriate questions. They mix or alternate the difficulty of questions and provide sufficient "wait time" (as long as 3 seconds) for students to respond.

5. *Explicit comprehension instruction.* Such instruction emphasizes review and preview, feedback and correctives, monitoring of student comprehension, and step-by-step guidance to facilitate students' thinking. Students learn to monitor and assess their own learning process (called *metacognition*) and *learn how to learn strategies.*

6. *Cognitive instruction.* Emphasis is on extensive reading and writing across the curriculum, critical thinking programs, cooperative learning techniques, and other approaches that de-emphasize mechanical and rote learning. Direct and mastery approaches are used, but without passive learning and only low-level skills.[75]

In general, what seems to work, to a large extent, is teaching and instructional programs that provide teachers and students with assistance and support. Instruction is prescriptive and diagnostic; emphasis is on basic skill acquisition, monitoring of student progress, providing prompt feedback to students, and mastery learning op-portunities. Also, students are actively involved in learning and engage in more than just low-level learning.

Also, programs that exhibit the most promise tend to be well organized and targeted toward preschool and primary grade children. This approach corresponds with environmental research data that indicate that intervention is most critical in the early stages of human development, because the most rapid period of cognitive development is in the initial years of growth (50 percent by age 4, according to Bloom).[76] The need for school nutrition programs, extended day and preschool programs, and parenting education is also crucial if we are to meet the challenges of disadvantaged and/or at-risk students.

At the elementary and secondary level, the more effective school literature holds the most promise for meeting the needs of our target population. By identifying effective schools in terms of student achievement (most of the studies have been conducted in low-income and inner-city schools), we are really talking about strategies for educating disadvantaged student populations. In this connection, the research has identified fourteen characteristics of effective schools:

1. A *safe and orderly environment* that is not oppressive and is conducive to teaching and learning.

2. A *clear school mission* through which the staff shares a commitment to instructional goals, priorities, assessment procedures, and accountability.

3. *Instructional leadership* by a principal who understands and applies the characteristics of instructional effectiveness.

4. A climate of *high expectations* in which the staff demonstrates that all students can attain mastery of basic skills.

5. *School pride and spirit* are systematically emphasized.

6. Frequent *monitoring of student progress,* using the results to improve individual performance and to improve the instructional program.

7. *Homework* is assigned and promptly checked by teachers; students are held accountable for homework, but teachers explain and review homework before teaching new content.

8. Positive *home-school relations* in which parents support the school's basic mission and play an important part in helping to achieve it.

9. Substantial *staff development* time is provided for participating faculties, preferably during the regular teacher work day.

10. *Remedial and tutorial programs* are established in all major subject areas, from the primary grade level through high school; these programs should supplement the regular school day for 1 or 2 hours per day and on Saturdays.

11. *Work-study programs* based on learning opportunities in the community are made available to a growing number of students after the ninth grade.

12. Effective schools' programs seek out and *consider* using materials, methods, and approaches that have been successful in *schools and programs elsewhere.*

13. Effective schools' programs are *data driven:* that is, appropriate information is collected and utilized to guide participants and make decisions to carry out plans for improvement.

14. The success of effective schools' programs depends on a *judicious mix of autonomy and teamwork* among school faculties and leadership from the school principal and central office.[77]

With the exception of items 10 and 11, the above approach costs very little and depends more on school climate, administrative leadership, teacher attitudes, and student/parental motivation and commitment. Money is not the key, nor is the approach piecemeal, as with the old compensatory movement. The focus is on a macro level, understanding and implementing the big picture, not a specific program, overhauling the roles, values, and beliefs of *all* those concerned with the teaching and learning process.

Probably the most important factor is the need for teachers to change their expectations for students in compensatory, remedial, and/or basic skills programs. At-risk students must learn to link their successes and failures to their own efforts. And parents must learn that they have responsibilities in providing support structures and a home environment that is conducive to proper socialization, personal growth, and learning. A joint accountability plan that includes teachers,

students, and parents is what is needed if education is to succeed.

MULTICULTURAL EDUCATION

America is a pluralistic society, a nation with many different ethnic groups and cultures. For most of our history, we have perceived of our country as a *melting pot* whose different peoples have joined to form a "new" race. We expected the schools to contribute to this melting pot process by socializing and acculturating immigrant children to the American ways and by instructing them in English. Today the melting pot concept is in disfavor, because it is perceived as stripping different ethnic groups of their cultures and identities. In contrast, *cultural pluralism* calls for understanding and appreciating differences among people, so that ethnic groups can maintain their customs, folk mores, and languages and still work together with other groups. Ideally, cultural pluralism promotes a sense of wholeness within society, based on the strengths of each of its parts or groups, and maintains that ethnic group interests can coincide with the interests of the nation.

Although this country continues to attract hundreds of thousands of immigrants from around the world each year, Hispanics represent the fastest growing ethnic population in the country. In 1980, 15 million was the legal Hispanic population. Based on current immigration and fertility trends, shown in Table 12-5, the Hispanic population should reach 30 million in the year 2000 (10.8 percent of the total population) and 47 million in 2020 (14.7 percent), surpassing the U.S. black population (14 percent) as the largest minority group. On the heels of the Hispanic population is the Asian group, the next fastest growing minority group. It is expected to total 12 million in 2000 (4.3 percent) and 20 million in 2020 (6.4 percent), compared to 4 million (2 percent) in 1980. The composition of the United States is undergoing considerable ethnic change, due largely to immigration trends, and the federal government is responding in the schools by requiring that the states and local education agencies meet the needs of these children.

Multicultural education values and believes in the ideal concept of cultural pluralism; it seeks the cultural enrichment of all children and youth

TABLE 12-5 Total U.S. and Minority Population, Based on Current Immigration Rates and Fertility, 1980–2020 (in millions)

	1980		2000		2020	
	NUMBER	PERCENT	NUMBER	PERCENT	NUMBER	PERCENT
White (non-Hispanic)	181.0	79.9	200.3	71.7	205.6	64.9
Black	26.5	11.7	36.4	13.0	44.4	14.0
Hispanic	14.6	6.5	30.3	10.8	46.6	14.7
Asian	4.4	2.0	12.1	4.3	20.3	6.3
Total	226.5	100.0	279.1	100.0	316.9	100.0

Source: Allan C. Ornstein, "Urban Demographics for the 1980s: Educational Implications," *Education and Urban Society* (August 1984), Table 2, p. 486. Also see Allan C. Ornstein, "Enrollment Trends in Big-city Schools," *Peabody Journal of Education* (Summer 1989), Table 1, p. 65.

through the curriculum, and at all levels of education, kindergarten to grade 12. In particular, national professional associations, state and local education agencies, colleges and universities, and curriculum developers have introduced various guidelines for promoting constructive multicultural education. In general, they have emphasized curriculum materials and instructional techniques. They have specifically proposed (1) introducing materials that are multiracial, multiethnic, and nonsexist; (2) teaching values that promote cultural diversity and individuality; (3) incorporating various cultural and ethnic activities in the classroom and school-community program; (4) encouraging multilingualism and multiple dialects; and (5) emphasizing multicultural teacher education programs.[78]

Multicultural Instruction. Educators are also trying to identify effective instructional approaches for teaching students of various racial and ethnic backgrounds. Some of the more important approaches have been concerned with student learning, or what is called a "biocognitive" approach to student learning. For example, Ramirez and Castañeda concluded that Hispanic students tend to be more "field sensitive" than nonminority children.[79] Field sensitive children are described as being more influenced by personal relationships and by praise or disapproval from authority figures, including teachers, than are "field independent" students, who are more abstract thinkers. A field sensitive curriculum is "humanized through use of narration, humor, drama and fantasy and should be "structured in such a way that children work cooperatively with peers or with a teacher in a variety of activities."[80]

Another effort to identify instructional approaches suited to students' ethnic backgrounds has been provided by researchers who have worked with native Americans.[81] These researchers conclude that schooling for native American children would be most successful if the curriculum took better account of their "primary learning" patterns (learning outside the school) and organized instruction in a manner more compatible with these patterns. These researchers contend that primary learning tends to take place in personal communication with emotionally important individuals and in tutorial (face-to-face) situations in which learning is adaptive (linked to the concerns and needs of the community). Primary learning also includes verbal instruction, exploratory play, and concrete (as opposed to abstract) learning. It involves monitoring the activities of elders who are particularly important to the children, say, uncles or aunts.

Some caution is necessary. The value of field-oriented and primary learning approaches is not well documented. What appears to be as or more important, according to some observers, are the basic, old approaches—friendliness, understanding, democratic teacher behaviors, positive teacher expectations, English proficiency, and parental support for the students.[82]

Bilingual Education. Bilingual education, which provides instruction for non-English speaking students in their native languages, has been an expanding activity in public schools in the United States since the late 1960s. Although the federal and state governments fund bilingual projects for more than sixty groups speaking various Asian, Indo-European, and Native American languages, the large majority (70 percent) of children in these projects are Hispanics.

Bilingual education has been expanding for various reasons: (1) partly because of the United States Supreme Court decision in the *Lau* case, which requires that school districts initiate some type of bilingual program if they enroll more than twenty students of a given language group at a particular grade level; (2) partly because of the subsequent pressure of the federal Office of Civil Rights (OCR), which insists that educational opportunities be provided for limited-English speaking (LES) and non-English speaking (NES) students; and (3) partly because of the continuous federal funding of bilingual programs, even today, even though other categorical programs are being merged within block grants.

Bilingualism is intertwined with such sensitive issues as our attitudes toward immigrants, that is, our accepting or rejecting those legal and illegal immigrants who work for less money and thus replace American-born citizens on the job and our deciding who can enter the United States: who is a political refugee, economic refugee, and/or undocumented worker.

Controversies over bilingual education have become somewhat embittered emotionally as federal and state guidelines have led to the establishment of various programs. Those who would "immerse" children in an English-language environment argue with those who believe initial instruction will be more effective in the native language; and both of these groups argue with those who wish that a mixture of both English and the native language be taught in school. Ethnic and community leaders have engaged in bitter struggles over the establishment of bilingual programs in the public schools.

Educators and laypeople concerned with NES (no English speaking) and LES (limited English speaking) students also argue whether emphasis should be placed on teaching in the native language over a long period (maintenance) or proceeding to teach in English as soon as possible (transitional). On the one side are those who favor maintenance because they think it will help build or maintain a constructive sense of identity among ethnic or racial minorities.[83] On the other side are those who believe that cultural-maintenance programs are harmful because they separate groups from one another or discourage students from mastering English well enough to function successfully in the larger society.[84] The latter or transitional approach is reflected in current federal guidelines.

Adherents and opponents of bilingual education also differ on the related issues of whether bilingual programs sometimes or frequently are designed to provide teaching jobs for native language speakers and whether individuals who fill these jobs are competent in English. Observers who favor bilingual/bicultural maintenance tend to believe that the schools need many adults who can teach LES or NES students in their own languages; many observers who favor transitional programs feel that relatively few staff are required for a legitimate program.

Another major controversy involving bilingual education concerns whether this approach is effective in improving the performance of low-achieving students. Most scholars who have examined the research agree that bilingual education has effected little, if any, improvement in the performance of participating students.[85] In fact, critics argue that multicultural and bilingual education is spearheaded not by current immigrants, but rather by black and (to a lesser extent) Hispanic educational leaders in big-city schools and universities to mask the academic failure of such students. Combined with the weak preparation of teachers in history and geography and the responsiveness of textbook publishers to organized pressure, most educators are trapped into going along with an Afrocentric and Hispaniccentric curriculum, or risk being labeled as mean-spirited or worse.[86]

Other scholars partially disagree; they argue that well-implemented programs can result in significant individual and group self-esteem, achievement gains and enriched cultural experiences.[87] In general, however, educators agree that much more than bilingual/bicultural education is needed to improve the performance of economically disadvantaged LES and NES students.[88]

On the whole, bilingual education is too frail a device in and of itself to significantly change the learning experiences of the minority-native tongue. Many other factors not related to language explain why such children achieve poorly. Removing only the language problem does not usually change the situation, regardless of the approach. There are many factors related to academic achievement, self-esteem, and economic outcomes. Putting too much emphasis on one approach usually results in an "ism" and can lead to errors, distortions, and overzealousness. The best approach is to maintain a balance, enlist support, and recognize diversity. Yes, there is a black perspective, Hispanic perspective, Asian-American perspective—and also an Armenian perspective, Croatian perspective, and Iraqi perspective, and so on. The need is to recognize these perspectives, especially when teaching students of these ethnic roots. But there is no need to rewrite history or our language and culture.

CONCLUSION

This chapter has been concerned with contemporary philosophical, social, and political issues in curriculum. Indeed, the search to improve school curricula is a continuing process that reflects the current issues and trends affecting schools and society. The curriculum trends noted in this chapter are controversial. Surely, debate over them will continue in the near future.

There are no simple solutions to these debates and issues. The idea is not to be swept away by a particular point of view or pressure group. Curriculum workers need to maintain a balance with subjects, programs, and projects, noting that at a given time specific subjects and programs are more fashionable than others. But the pendulum does swing, and on a continuous basis. In a democracy, corrective factors and countergroups surface, and today's bandwagon often becomes tomorrow's quaint and forgotten concerns.

Given the fact that we are a nation of immigrants—from all parts of the world—curriculum change should proceed on the basis that all cultures and all groups have strengths and that there is worth and there is something to be learned from the whole human population. A wealth of multicultural and multiethnic data exists and should be included in the school curriculum without having to distort history or invent myths. But a politically correct curriculum is unnecessary, even dangerous; hopefully, sufficient academic freedom and integrity exist among educators to neutralize coerced conformity and liberation rhetoric.

ENDNOTES

1. Norman Amaker, "Reagan Record on Civil Rights," *Urban Institute Policy and Research Report* (Fall 1988), pp. 15–16; Thomas R. McDaniel, "Demilitarizing Public Education: School Reform in the Era of George Bush," *Phi Delta Kappan* (September 1989), pp. 15–18.
2. Paul T. Hill, "The Federal Role in Education: A Strategy for the 1990s," *Phi Delta Kappan* (January 1990), pp. 398–402; Allan C. Ornstein, "The Federal Government and Education in a New Era," *High School Journal* (in press 1993).

3. David L. Clark and Mary A. Amiot, "The Reagan Administration and Federal Education Policy," *Phi Delta Kappan* (December 1981), pp. 258–262; Larry Cuban, "Four Stories about National Goals for American Education," *Phi Delta Kappan* (December 1990), pp. 265–271.
4. John O'Neil, "Drive for National Standards Picking up Steam," *Educational Leadership* (February 1991), pp. 4–8; Richard J. Stiggens, "Assessment Literacy," *Phi Delta Kappan* (March 1991), pp. 534–539.

5. Diane Ravitch, "A Message from Assistant Secretary Diane Ravitch," *OERI Bulletin* (Winter 1991–92), p. 2; Theodore R. Sizer, "No Pain, No Gain," *Educational Leadership* (May 1991), pp. 32–34.

6. Allan C. Ornstein, "National Reform and Instructional Accountability," *High School Journal* (October–November 1990), pp. 51–56.

7. Dale Mann, "Conditional School Deregulation," *Executive Educator* (January 1990), pp. 26, 28; Thomas Timar, "The Politics of School Restructuring," *Education Digest* (May 1990), pp. 7–10.

8. *A National Imperative: Educating for the 21st Century* (Arlington, Va.: National School Board Association, 1989).

9. Charles P. McFadden, "Author–Publisher–Educator Relationships and Curriculum Reform," *Journal of Curriculum Studies* (January–February 1992), pp. 27–42; Sandra Stotsky, "Whose Literature? America!" *Educational Leadership* (December–January 1992), pp. 53–56.

10. Elliott W. Eisner, "Who Decides What Schools Teach?" *Phi Delta Kappan* (March 1990), p. 523.

11. Diane Ravitch, "A Culture in Common," *Educational Leadership* (December–January 1982), pp. 8–11, 75; Sandra Stotsky, "Cultural Politics," *American School Board Journal* (October 1991), pp. 26–29.

12. *Fifty-state Survey of Textbook Adoption Procedures and Policies* (Washington, D.C.: Education Commission of the States, 1984); Ray Gerke, "American Textbooks: Perspectives on Public Controversies and Censorship," *High School Journal* (October–November 1983), pp. 59–64.

13. *Attack on the Freedom to Learn, 1989–90* (Washington, D.C.: People for the American Way, 1990).

14. Telephone conversation with Anne Meek, managing editor of *Educational Leadership,* September 4, 1990.

15. Michael Apple, "Is There a Curriculum Voice to Reclaim?" *Phi Delta Kappan* (March 1990), pp. 526–530

16. Eisner, "Who Decides What Schools Will Teach?"

17. Carrol A. Bartell, "Outstanding Secondary Principals Reflect on Instructional Leadership," *High School Journal* (December–January 1990), pp. 129–132; Barney M. Berlin, Jack Kavanagh, and Kathleen Jensen, "The Principal as Curriculum Leader—Expectations vs. Performance," *NASSP Bulletin* (September 1988), pp. 43–49.

18. Allan C. Ornstein, "Textbook Instruction: Processes and Strategies," *NASSP Bulletin* (December 1989), pp. 105–111.

19. Gary Putka, "Readers of Latest U.S. History Textbooks Discover a Storehouse of Misinformation," *Wall Street Journal,* February 12, 1992, pp. B 1–2.

20. Ornstein, "Textbook Instruction."

21. Edward Fry, "Fry's Readability Graph: Clarification, Validity, and Extensions to Level," *Journal of Reading* (December 1977), pp. 242–252.

22. Alton L. Raygor and George B. Schick, *Reading at Efficient Rates,* 2nd ed. (New York: McGraw-Hill, 1980).

23. Margret T. Bernstein, "The Academy's Contribution to the Impoverishment of America's Textbooks," *Phi Delta Kappan* (November 1988), pp. 193–198; Marily J. Chambliss and Robert C. Calfee, "Designing Science Textbooks to Enhance Student Understanding," *Educational Psychologist* (Summer 1989), pp. 307–322; Karen A. Shriver, "The Impact of Reader's Self-evaluations in Comprehending Poorly Written Instructional Text," paper presented at the annual meeting of the American Educational Research Association, Chicago, April 1991.

24. Robert A. Pavlik, "Tips on Texts," *Phi Delta Kappan* (September 1985), p. 86.

25. Richard E. Mayer, "Aids to Text Comprehension," *Educational Psychologist* (Winter 1984), pp. 30–42.

26. Margret T. Bernstein, "The New Politics of Textbook Adoption," *Education Digest* (December 1985), pp. 12–15; Marcy L. Stein, "Helpfulness of Context Plus Number of Exposures," paper presented at the annual meeting of the American Educational Research Association, New Orleans, April 1988.

27. Hines Cronin, et al., "Combining Writing with Text Organization and Content Instruction." *NASSP Bulletin* (March 1992), pp. 34–45.

28. Neville Bennett et al., *The Quality of Pupil Learning Experiences* (Hillsdale, N.J.: Erlbaum, 1984).

29. John R. Mergendoller et al., "Task Demands and Accountability in Middle-grade Science Classes," *Elementary School Journal* (January 1988), pp. 251–265.

30. Ezra Bowen, "Flunking Grade in Math," *Educational Psychologist* (Spring 1988), pp. 181–202.

31. John Dewey, *Democracy and Education* (New York: Macmillan, 1916), p. 125.

32. B. Othanel Smith, William O. Stanley, and J. Harlan Shores, *Fundamentals of Curriculum Development,* rev. ed. (New York: Harcourt, Brace, 1957), pp. 4–5.

33. Harold Benjamin, *The Saber-tooth Curriculum* (New York: McGraw-Hill, 1939), pp. 43–44.

34. Bentley Glass, *The Timely and the Timeless* (New York: Basic Books, 1979); Joseph J. Schwab, "The Concept of the Structure of a Discipline," *Educational Record* (July 1962), pp. 197–205.

35. Donald E. Orlosky and B. Othanel Smith, *Curriculum Development: Issues and Insights* (Chicago: Rand McNally, 1980), p. 192.

36. Mario D. Fantini and Gerald D. Weinstein, *The Disadvantaged: Challenge to Education* (New York: Harper & Row, 1968), p. 133.

37. Otto Klienberg, "Life Is Fun in a Smiling, Fair-skinned World," *Saturday Review* (February 16, 1963), pp. 75–77, 87.

38. Ibid.

39. A. Harry Passow, "Urban Education for the 1970s," in A. H. Passow, ed. *Urban Education in the 1970s* (New York: Teachers College Press, Columbia University, 1971), pp. 1–45; Passow, "Urban Education for the 1980s: Trends and Issues," *Phi Delta Kappan* (April 1982), pp. 519–522.

40. Dennis Doyle, "The Unsacred Texts," *American Education* (Summer 1984), pp. 3–13; Connie Muther, "What Every Textbook Evaluator Should Know," *Educational Leadership* (April 1985), pp. 4–8; and Allan C. Ornstein, "Textbook Instruction."

41. Dolores Durkin, *Is There a Match between What Elementary Teachers Do and What Basal Readers Manuals Recommend?* (Champaign, Ill.: Center for the Study of Reading, University of Illinois, 1983); Patrick Shannon, "The Use of Commercial Reading Materials in American Elementary Schools," *Reading Research Quarterly* (Fall 1983), pp. 68–85.

42. J. P. Guilford, *General Psychology,* 2nd ed. (Princeton, N.J.: Van Nostrand, 1952); Ralph Tyler, *Constructing Achievement Tests* (Columbus, Ohio: Ohio State University, 1934).

43. Francis P. Hunkins, *Teaching Thinking through Effective Questioning* (Boston: Christopher-Gordon, 1989); John McLeish, *The Lecture Method* (Cambridge, Eng.: Cambridge Institute of Education, 1968).

44. David P. Ausubel, *Educational Psychology: A Cognitive View* (New York: Holt, Rinehart and Winston 1968); Merlin C. Wittrock and Eva L. Baker, *Testing and Cognition* (Boston, Mass.: Allyn and Bacon, 1991).

45. E. D. Hirsch, *Cultural Literacy: What Every American Needs to Know,* rev. ed. (Boston: Houghton Mifflin, 1987).

46. Merrill Harmin and Sidney B. Simon, "The Year the Schools Began Teaching the Telephone Directory," *Harvard Educational Review* (Summer 1965), pp. 326–331.

47. Ibid., p. 327.

48. Ibid., p. 328.

49. Barry Kampol and Eva Weisz, "The Effective Principal and Curriculum: A Focus on Leadership," *NASSP Bulletin* (April 1990), pp. 15–18.

50. Philip W. Jackson, *Life in Classrooms,* 2nd ed. (New York: Teachers College Press, Columbia University, 1990), p. 4.

51. Elizabeth A. Poliner, *Modern Curriculum Design* (Lexington, Mass.: Ginn, 1983), p. 53.

52. Margaret C. Needels and N. L. Gage, "Essence and Accident in Process-Product Research on Teaching," in H. C. Waxman and H. J. Walberg, eds., *Effective Teaching: Current Research* (Berkeley: McCutchan, 1991), pp. 3–32; Allan C. Ornstein, "A Look at Teacher Effectiveness Research," *NASSP Bulletin* (October 1990), pp. 78–88.

53. Gene V. Glass, "What Works: Politics and Research," *Educational Researcher* (April 1987), pp. 5–11; Nancy Karweit, "Should We Lengthen the School Term?" *Educational Researcher* (June 1985), pp. 9–15.

54. Allan C. Ornstein, "Academic Time Considerations for Curriculum Leaders," *NASSP Bulletin* (September 1989), pp. 103–110.

55. Nancy Karweit, "Time on Task: The Second Time Around," *NASSP Bulletin* (February 1988), pp. 31–39.

56. John I. Goodlad and Francis Klein, *Behind the Classroom Door* (Worthington, Ohio: Jones Publishers, 1970). Also see John I. Goodlad, *A Place Called School* (New York: McGraw-Hill, 1984).

57. Walter Doyle, "Academic Work," *Review of Educational Research* (Summer 1983), pp. 159–199; Allan C. Ornstein, "Emphasis on Student Outcomes," *NASSP Bulletin* (January 1987), pp. 88–95; and Ornstein, "Academic Time Consideration for Curriculum Leaders."

58. James H. Block, Helen E. Efthim, and Robert B. Burns, *Building Effective Mastery Learning Schools* (New York: Longman, 1989); Benjamin S. Bloom, *Human Characteristics and School Learning* (New York: McGraw-Hill, 1976).

59. Allan C. Ornstein, *Institutionalized Learning in America* (New Brunswick, N.J.: Transaction, 1990); Barak Rosenshine, "Content, Time, and Direct Instruction," in P. L. Peterson and H. J. Walberg, eds., *Research on Teaching: Concepts, Findings and Implications* (Berkeley, Calif.: McCutchan, 1979), pp. 28–56.

60. Barak Rosenshine, "How Time Is Spent in Elementary Classrooms," in C. Denham and A. Lieberman, eds., *Time to Learn* (Washington, D.C.: National Institute of Education, 1980), pp. 107–126.

61. Susan Stodolsky, *The Subject Matters* (Chicago: University of Chicago Press, 1988).

62. Bloom, *Human Characteristic and School Learning.*

63. Herbert J. Walberg, "Productive Teaching and Instruction," in H. C. Waxman and H. J. Walberg, eds., *Effective Teaching: Current Research* (Berkeley, Calif.: McCutchan, 1991), pp. 33–62.

64. *A National Imperative: Educating for the 21st Century* (Arlington, Va.: National School Boards Association, 1989); "Children of Poverty," *Phi Delta Kappan* (June 1990), pp. K1–K12.

65. Ellen Flax, "One in Eight Children in Households With Insufficient Food, Study Finds," *Education Week,* April 3, 1991, p. 13.

66. Lynette Long and Thomas J. Long, "Latchkey Adolescents: How Administrators Can Respond to their Needs," *NASSP Bulletin* (February 1989), pp. 102–108.

67. Martha R. Burt, "Roots and Remedies of Homelessness," *Urban Institute Policy and Research Report* (Summer 1991), pp. 1–5; *The Effects of Migrant Children* (Washington, D.C.: U.S. Office of Education, 1989); Marilee C. Rist, "The Shadow Children," *American School Board Journal* (January 1989), pp. 19–24.

68. Deborah L. Cohen, "Foster-care Reforms Ignore Problems Children Face in School," *Education Week,* June 5, 1991, pp. 1, 15; "The New Needy," *Education Digest* (February 1990), pp. 70–71.

69. Allan C. Ornstein, "Enrollment Trends in Big-city Schools," *Peabody Journal of Education* (Summer, 1989), pp. 64–71; David C. Smith and Edward E. Greene, "Preparing Tomorrow's Principals Today," *Principal* (September 1990), pp. 20–24.

70. *Projections of Education Statistics to 2001* (Washington, D.C.: U.S. Government Printing Office, 1990), Table 1, p. 4.

71. Richard L. Fairley, "Accountability's New Test," *American Education* (June 1972), pp. 33–35; Daniel Moynihan, *Coping On the Practice of Government* (New York: Random House, 1975). Also see Mary J. LeTendre, "Improving Chapter I Programs: We Can Do Better," *Phi Delta Kappan* (April 1991), pp. 576–581.

72. Arthur R. Jensen, "Compensatory Education and the Theory of Intelligence," *Phi Delta Kappan* (April 1985), pp. 554–558; A. Harry Passow, "Urban Schools a Second or Third Time Around," *Education and Urban Society* (May 1991), pp. 243–255.

73. Allan C. Ornstein and Daniel U. Levine, "Compensatory Education: Can It Be Successful?" *NASSP Bulletin* (May 1981), pp. 1–15.

74. Consortium for Longitudinal Studies, *As the Twig Is Bent* (Hillsdale, N.J.: Erlbaum, 1983); Jacqueline J. Irvine, *Black Students and School Failure* (Westport, Conn.: Praeger, 1991); and Nancey A. Madden et al., "Success for All," *Phi Delta Kappan* (April 1991), pp. 593–599.

75. Daniel U. Levine and Allan C. Ornstein, "Research on Classroom and School Effectiveness and Its Implications for Improving Big City Schools," *Urban Review* (July 1989), pp. 81–95; Allan C. Ornstein and Daniel U. Levine, "Urban School Effectiveness and Improvement," *Illinois School Research and Development* (Spring 1991), pp. 111–117.

76. Benjamin S. Bloom, *Stability and Change in Human Characteristics* (New York: Wiley, 1964).

77. Lorin W. Anderson and Leonard O. Pellicer, "Synthesis of Research on Compensatory and Remedial Education," *Educational Leadership* (September 1990), pp. 10–16; Allan C. Ornstein and Daniel U. Levine, "School Effectiveness and Reform: Guidelines for Action," *Clearing House* (November–December 1990), pp. 115–118; and Kenneth A. Sirotnik, "Improving Urban Schools in the Age of 'Reconstructing,'" *Education and Urban Society* (May 1991), pp. 256–269.

78. *Relating Knowledge to Teacher Education* (Washington, D.C.: American Association of Colleges for Teacher Education, 1989); *Toward High and Rigorous Standards for the Teaching Profession,* 2nd ed. (Washington, D.C.; National Board for Professional Teaching Standards, 1990).

79. Manuel Ramirez and Carlos Castañeda, *Cultural Democracy: Biocognitive Development and Education* (New York: Academic Press, 1974).

80. Ibid., p. 142.

81. Paul E. Greenbaum, "Nonverbal Differences in Communication Style between American Indian and Anglo Elementary Classrooms," *American Educational Research Journal* (Spring 1985), pp. 101–116. Lindra Grant, "Regenerating and Refocusing Research on Minorities and Education," *Elementary School Journal* (May 1988), pp. 441–448.

82. James A. Banks, *Multiethnic Education: Theory and Practice,* 4th ed. (Boston, Mass.: Allyn and Bacon, 1992); Pamela L. Tiedt and Iris M. Tiedt, *Multicultural Teaching,* 3rd ed. (Boston: Allyn and Bacon, 1990).

83. Jose A. Cardeñas, "The Role of Native Language Instruction in Bilingual Education," *Phi Delta Kappan* (January 1986), pp. 359–363; Henry A. Giroux and Paulo Freire, eds., *Culture and Power in the Classroom: A Critical Foundation for Bicultural Education* (Westport, Conn.: Praeger, 1991).

84. Noel Epstein, *Language, Ethnicity, and the Schools: Policy Alternatives for Bilingual-Bicultural Education* (Washington, D.C.: George Washington University Press, 1977); Joshua A. Fishman, *Language and Ethnicity in Minority Sociolinguistic Perspective* (Bristol, Pa.: Taylor & Francis, 1989).

85. Keith Baller, "The Effectiveness of Bilingual Education." Paper presented at the annual meeting of the American Educational Research Association, New Orleans, April 1988; Epstein, *Language, Ethnicity, and the Schools;* and Martin Ridge, *The New Bilingualism: An American Dilemma* (New Brunswick, N.J.: Transaction, 1990).

86. Nathan Glazer, "In Defense of Multiculturalism," *New Republic,* September 2, 1991, pp. 18–22.

87. Joseph E. Barry, "Politics, Bilingual Education and the Curriculum," *Educational Leadership* (May 1983), pp. 56–60; Asa G. Hillard, "Why We Must Pluralize the Curriculum," *Educational Leadership* (December–January 1992), pp. 12–15; and Ann C. Willig, "Examining Bilingual Education Research," *Review of Educational Research* (Fall 1987), pp. 363–376.

88. Josha A. Fishman, *Reversing Language Shift* (Bristol, Pa.: Taylor & Francis, 1991); Christine H. Russell, "The Research on Bilingual Education," *Equality and Choice* (Winter 1990), pp. 29–36.

CHAPTER 13

FUTURE DIRECTIONS FOR CURRICULUM

Focusing Questions

1. *What is futurism?*
2. *How has the information age affected curricularists' thinking about education?*
3. *Identify some future trends that can affect the curriculum.*
4. *What procedures can educators employ in planning for the future?*
5. *Which constants in education are likely to continue in the future?*
6. *What new curricular areas are likely to evolve in the future?*

This century has been characterized by a high rate of diverse and extensive changes affecting many aspects of our world. This rapidity and extensiveness of change have given to this century a high degree of uncertainty. In dealing with the various changes, many curricularists have come to realize that the relationship between school and society reflects a mutual give and take. During this century, society has been forcefully dynamic. It continues to exhibit this energy. Change is always present. It is a dangerous practice for educators to base education, specifically, the curriculum, on any static portrait of society. Indeed, curricularists in tune with current times realize that it is even more important today than yesterday that individuals be educated not for the present, but for a better future.

The ultimate purpose of education is to present programs and thus opportunities for students to gain the knowledge, skills, beliefs, and values that will enable them to create productive lives for themselves and others. The central question curriculum planners ask is: "What kind of educational program will achieve this central goal?" How they respond to this central question rests on their understanding of current and, more importantly, future times. They need to consider what one futurist has called a fan of alternative futures; they need to identify which of the potential futures could at any time emerge into reality given

the probabilities of the different possibilities under existing trends and cycles.[1] They must not just ask what are the *likely* futures, but what are the *desirable* futures. Educators should ask: "When, where, by whom, how intensely, under what conditions, and with what consequences are different futures desired?" To deal with these questions, educators need to analyze innovations and educational trends in terms of their overriding frameworks and their histories.

Curricular activities, by their very nature, should be future-oriented. All education, to be relevant, should consider some image of the future. What educators think appropriate for the future will be influenced by their visions of the future. If their visions or images are inaccurate, then the education they design will miss its mark.

In general, they can deduce their images of the future from their knowledge of the past and their reading of the present. The accuracy of our views will affect what we project for the future. Alvin Toffler notes that people cannot totally view their images of the future as predictive in the sense that what they see is what they will get. He points out that the possible future is not singular, but plural. It is not the result of one event or one decision, but the results of choices that people make from a myriad of options. Also, their future or futures may result from factors that they cannot control or about which they have little choice.[2] Their choices for dealing with and identifying possible and desirable futures are still limited by the tools they currently have. Even so, they do have available some methods that will allow them to discern which lines of development are more likely than others.

FUTURE AND FUTURISM

The industrial age is ending; it is being replaced with the information age. John Naisbitt asserted that current society is caught between two eras: the age in which industry was the leader and an age built on information. He argues that the second wave, that of industrial might, is being swept aside by the third wave, which is the age of the information industry. He suggests that we really are in the early stages of the information age.[3] Perhaps the key question for educators, especially curricularists, is: "Are the schools in the same time period?"

In this connection, Phillip Schlechty asserts that much of the driving force behind recent and current school reform is the realization that schools must shift focus so that students can compete in an emerging information-based world community. He argues that schools must contemplate and actualize redesigned curricula and school organizations to prepare students for life in the twenty-first century.[4] A challenge for curricularists is to ask themselves what needs to be addressed in designing curricula for students who will spend most of their lives in the next century, in the information age.

In the information age, people are engaged in "knowledge work," the employment of ideas and symbols to produce meaning and some purposeful results. Knowledge work is mental work as compared to physical work, which was paramount in the industrial work age. In reading this book, in contemplating the questions and issues raised by this and previous chapters, you are engaged in knowledge work. Schlechty notes that "in an information-based society, knowledge is the primary mode of work, since information provides the primary means by which work is accomplished.[5]

Today, more individuals are involved in knowledge work than in physical work. The shift occurred in the mid 1950s when, for the first time

in American history, white-color workers in technical, managerial, and clerical positions outnumbered blue-color workers. At this juncture, we experienced for the first time more people working with information than producing material goods.

The rate at which the information, or postindustrial age, has appeared has clouded their images of the future. They have to generate new paradigms to organize their social and work worlds. This makes many people unclear about the roles they are to play. Indeed, many are finding that their secure jobs are being phased out and that they have to almost "start again."

Not only are people being informed that they must start again, they are being advised to be prepared to actually "keep starting again." There is no end in sight for change. Indeed, Thomas Quick has urged us to change the permanent to the temporary.[6] Those in education currently embracing notions on the restructuring of schools and the curriculum need to keep this caveat in mind; our organizations must be considered temporary in order to be responsive to a rapidly changing future, a future that is actually being managed for change and modification.

In discussing this temporary mode of thinking, Warren Bennis refers to adaptive organizations creating temporary systems to confront emerging problems quickly and effectively. In responsive organizations, there will be "task forces composed of groups of relative strangers with diverse professional backgrounds and skills organized around problems to be solved. The groups will be arranged on an organic rather than mechanical model, meaning that they will evolve in response to a problem rather than to represent, programmed expectations. . . . Organizational charts will consist of project groups rather than stratified functional groups."[7] The future requires that those designing curricula function similarly: groups of curricularists evolving in response to educational demands emanating from myriad sources.

Keeping our organizations temporary and our roles fluid points to the rapidity with which things are changing. The European shift from an agricultural to an industrial society took several centuries; the same shift evolved over a century in the United States. However, the shift from an industrial to an information society has occurred in only two or three decades! The times have not allowed us either the opportunities to reflect on the nature of the change or "breathing room" in which to react. And to heighten our discomfort, the rate of change currently is increasing.

Megatrends: Beyond 2000

The ten megatrends that Naisbitt reported are well established and yet continuing to evolve. We are ever deeper into an *informational society* (megatrend 1). We are embraced by a *high tech/high touch world* (megatrend 2). We are in a *world economy,* in which changes in any part of the world almost immediately affect us (megatrend 3). We are becoming more comfortable in engaging in *strategic planning,* in going from *short term to long term* (megatrend 4). The school restructuring move is only part of the shift from *centralization to decentralization* (megatrend 5). The press for independent learners, to empower teachers and parents in the educational game, represents a move from *institutional help to self-help* (megatrend 6), a move to *participatory democracy* (megatrend 7) within our schools. Restructuring also is part of the move to *networking,* rather than the hierarchical arrangements of yesterday (*megatrend 8*). And we are beginning to plan options and programs that will emerge in our schools, reflecting the move from *either/or thinking to that of multiple options (megatrend 9).* Megatrend 10 refers to demographic shifts from north to south.[8]

In *Megatrends 2000,* Naisbitt identified additional trends that will also affect education and its offerings. The booming *global economy,* trends 1 and 2 in Naisbitt's list, certainly will mean that our students will have to possess an increasing global education expertise. Ideally, the *renaissance in the arts* will affect the curriculum, forcing educators to realize that we must educate the whole person, all those dimensions that address human spirit. New *lifestyles and cultural nationalism* should make students come to realize what it means to participate as a world citizen. The *expanding role of women* will further influence college environments and the job sector. The *age of biology,* will affect what educators know about individuals, biological dis-coveries may allow us all to participate in our evolution, or at least extend our life span. For this reason, life-long education and two or three different employment careers should become more common in the future.[9]

Perhaps the key trend for educators to consider is that the individual changes him or herself first before attempting to change society. We are now recognizing ourselves as futurists. Our challenge as curriculum planners is to create programs that enable students to adapt to the future, to participate in its planning, to maximize themselves for the benefit of all. See Curriculum Tips 13-1.

Dealing with the Future

Although educators may not have perfected the tools for dealing with all aspects of the future, they do have the means for viewing and creating futures. These tools partly comprise the field of *futuristics,* sometimes called *futurism* or *future studies.* Whatever it is called, it embraces both the science of forecasting and the art of imagining.[10] This discipline views both technological and social events not as separate and independent occurrences, but as twin components linked in a system or process. Reality and the events comprising it are holistic. Events affect other events, which in turn affect still other events. Knowing the strength and direction of an interaction allows people to "preview" what are the likely consequences of such interactions—to "visualize" the future.

Futurism is a systematic attempt to meld creative forecasting, planning, and action. Those engaged in this new field, and curriculum leaders should be among them, are studying and developing alternative futures and generating supporting scenarios elaborating specific areas of society including its institutions. From the tentative futures, these professionals draw significant variables likely to influence events or behavior and then deduce the kinds of educational programs that have a high probability of meeting the projected conditions. Using the tools of educational futurism, educators can proact rather than react.

The majority of futures techniques are really types of forecasting. Note that *predictions* are statements about occurrences that are to happen in a specific future. *Forecasts* tell us not what will happen, but rather what can happen if certain conditions or certain events occur or continue. The accuracy and inclusiveness of forecasts depend on the data fed into the deliberations, the decision systems employed, and the diversity of the techniques utilized.

One researcher has provided a useful overview of the major approaches to future planning. These approaches involve either exploratory forecasting or normative forecasting.[11] *Exploratory forecasting* means processing data to discover possible capabilities, changes, opportunities, and problems that may or are likely to appear in the future, assuming the continuance of certain events. Attention is given to identifying likely futures. Often such forecasting expands various trends that have been identified. *Normative forecasting* deals with attending to various goals or norms to be actualized in the future. Here forecasters are "inventing" the future of their choice. They actually set the norms for the future and then indicate what needs to be accomplished to attain such norms or goals.

Following is a listing of some major approaches to forecasting:

Simulation Forecasting. This technique generates the future by activating models of known physical, social, and environmental laws and determines how they will most likely impact the future. The models, designed and used to predict future probabilities, denote sets of variables or entities and their interactions.[12] They allow forecasters to discover what can be or should be controlled, what can be or needs to be designed, and ultimately what needs to be forecasted.

For example, educators might create a model of the future school system denoting the key variables and then, using various mathematical formulas, design a computer program that will enable them to project results or alternative actions and thus make particular choices. Using this technique, educators might be able, for example, to accurately picture what might happen if all the students in a school experienced a particular curriculum. By obtaining a readout of possible consequences, educators can decide whether to enact their current plans.

Trend Forecasting.   To use this procedure, an educator plots mathematically the path of discovered events and extends them into the future. Such forecasting assumes that the rate of change noted in the past and present will continue uninterrupted into the future. For example, educators may be interested in the amount of new knowledge that is being discovered in a subject or discipline. The number of discoveries can be either plotted on a graph or compared against specific points in time, such as decades, years, or months, and arranged in increasing order. Arranging the information in this manner, educators can see if the variable, for example, the number of discoveries in biology, is increasing or decreasing with time. A straight line may be fitted to the points and then extended beyond the most recent point. If the line denotes an increase, then educators can forecast that they will likely need to expand coverage in the biology curriculum.

Intuitive Forecasting.   This procedure is something everyone can do. It relates to the images or feelings people have about the future. These perceptions of what is to come influence their decisions and actions, such that many of their views become reality. For example, someone may feel that in the future there will be a greater need for more science and mathematics courses in light of the increasing technological nature of our society. In other words, their intuition about the increasing technology becomes essentially a tool for their forecasting what will be a useful educational future.

Delphi Forecasting.   Along with brainstorming, Delphi forecasting is perhaps the most well known futures procedure. It is a process of extracting "expert" opinions about the future and then furnishing the "experts" with the preliminary results. This process is repeated several times until the "experts" achieve consensus of opinion regarding the future. According to one observer, "Delphi . . . operates on the principle that several heads are better than one in making subjective conjectures about the future, and that experts . . . will make conjectures based on rational judgment and shared information rather than merely guessing, and will separate hope from likelihood in the process."[13]

Educators might use a Delphi technique to obtain a "reading" of what they believe the future will demand of the curriculum with regard to specific content to be covered. Each educator might be given a questionnaire that asks him or her to note ten major content areas that will be needed for future education. An analysis of the results of the first questionnaire is used to develop a second questionnaire. This second questionnaire is sent to the same group of educators with the results of the first questionnaire to indicate those areas considered essential for inclusion in the curriculum. Educators are asked to respond to this second questionnaire after considering the responses of the "experts" to the first questionnaire. They are also asked to indicate why they revised their responses if they did so.

A third questionnaire is then created to summarize the previous responses and the reasons individuals changed those responses. As before, the educators are asked to consider the questionnaire items, to revise their responses if they think it necessary, and to explain their actions. Ideally, by this third round, educators have a fairly good consensus of how they and their colleagues "read" the future.

Scenario Forecasting.   This procedure is also quite well known to the public. It involves creating a scenario, which is basically a well-thought-out story or description about how a possible future state of affairs might occur. The story must draw on current happenings and likely trends. Often it notes how people can go from the present reality to some possible future period.[14] Scenario writing puts into prose form innovative, imaginative, and plausible futures for people to contemplate.

There is really no one method for creating a scenario, but there are certain approaches to scenario forecasting. Usually, the general process requires those involved to begin with a checklist of the aspects of society that deserve attention. The scope of the checklist depends on the writer's definition of the system that is to be the focus of the scenario. If, for example, a teacher is going to write a scenario about the schools of the future, the list will be much more detailed than if he or she is writing a scenario about only one subject area in the curriculum.

The writer would then propose specific questions on the checklist items. For curriculum, they might include: What new contents might be produced? How will the new contents be organized? What old contents are likely to remain? How will these old contents be organized? What are some likely new teaching methods? How will computers interface with students? What new staff members will be needed? How will change agents, researchers, and instructional designers be used in formulating curriculum? The writer reviews the answers to these questions for accuracy and arranges them in chronological order or in a time period. This arrangement of the responses to the questions really forms the basis for the scenario. In essence, the scenario writer has created an outline for his or her "story."

Force Analysis Forecasting.   To use this procedure, educators note and analyze forces (sets of events, pressures, problems, and/or social events) and their probable impact on future events or areas. For example, people start out by selecting a topic, say, an area of the curriculum. Next, they define a force as a set of events, pressures, or technologies, whose impact on the curriculum will impel those who design the curriculum to make modifications in it. Next, they ask persons knowledgeable about the curriculum to scan the present and immediately past environment for forces, as they have defined them. Recent discoveries in knowledge might be listed as one force, and the public's increasing demands that certain contents be covered might be another. National needs might also be noted, as could the changing nature of students.

Once these forces have been selected, each is described. After descriptions have been written, the forecasting team draws upon data gathered and the inferential summaries made to describe the nature of each force and the impact it has previously had on, in this case, the curriculum. Last, the forecasting team uses the data gathered to forecast the nature of each force and how it will affect the curriculum in the time frame indicated.[15]

Although the preceding discussion has listed six types of forecasting (see Table 13-1), it is not all-inclusive. Nonetheless, it does indicate that educators have options. Rarely would they employ just one technique; rather, they would usually combine various types of forecasts to obtain a useful reading of a possible future.

But forecasting the future is still challenging, because the future is the consequence of the dynamics between events current and events yet to happen. The future, in a real sense, is always evolving. For this reason, a curriculum that is to be responsive to the times must also be evolving. See Curriculum Tips 13-2.

FUTURE DIRECTIONS

We in this century have seen unprecedented change in every aspect of life. More change has occurred in this century, in fact, than has occurred in all the previous centuries of human existence. Harold Shane notes the rapidity of change. From a historical point of view, it seems reasonable to conclude that for the first time in human history, we have been propelled from yesterday into tomorrow with no familiar "today" during which we can become acclimated to change.[16]

Toffler states "at the rate at which knowledge is growing, by the time the child born today graduates from college the amount of knowledge in the world will be four times as great. By the time that same child is fifty years old, it will be 32 times as great and 97 percent of everything known in the world will have been learned since the time he was born."[17] Toffler's projection, however, assumes a linear extrapolation of current events. It does not consider changes in either rate or direction (see Chapter 5), nor does it consider unseen variables or events, what some people call system breaks. Still, it is safe to accept that the knowledge explosion, though it may not be as dramatic as Toffler indicates, will still be formidable.

Daniel Bell has noted that the world is becoming increasingly empirical, worldly, secular, humanistic, pragmatic, utilitarian, contractual, epicurean, and hedonistic. Bourgeois, bureaucratic, and meritocratic elites also seem to be forming. More and more decisions are being made by fewer and so-called highly qualified individuals. Scientific and technological knowl-

TABLE 13-1 Overview of Futures Techniques

TECHNIQUE	FORECAST TYPE	POSSIBLE USES	POSSIBLE BENEFITS
Simulation	Exploratory, normative	To play out consequences of employing various curriculum designs.	Permits educators more control over programs; introduces more creativity in school programs
Trend forecasting	Exploratory	To plot the path of events into the future	Gives curricularists insights into future demands and needs for planning curriculum
Intuitive forecasting	Exploratory, normative	To get a feel for what the future may hold for education	Provides educators a sense of readiness to deal with new events, demands
Delphi procedure	Exploratory, normative	To obtain conjectures regarding future needs in education, or to outline preferred future events	Allows educators to survey views of knowledgeable persons regarding future developments affecting education
Scenario writing	Exploratory, normative	To outline a future story of how curriculum will or should look	Gives educators a usable written document on possible future times for which the curriculum is designed
Force analysis	Exploratory	To plot those events that will affect each other and the school	Allows curricularists to design programs that will influence future events in society

edge is accumulating that leaves many areas of decision-making beyond the scope and participation of many people.[18]

Michael McDaniel has listed seven factors that have contributed to the rapidity and nature of change. They basically deal with social and cultural trends and the way society is undergoing change:

1. *Demographic change:* sex and age patterns death rates, lifespans, family size, balance of youth versus old, and so on.

2. *Technological innovation:* adaptive changes in existing machines and productivity.

3. *Social innovation:* new arrangements, systems, or styles in educational, political, economic, military, and other dimensions.

4. *Cultural-value shifts:* changes in cultural axioms or values and ideas.

5. *Ecological shifts:* changes in the natural ecology, catastrophic events, pollution of rivers.

6. *Information-idea shifts:* scope, quality, and manipulability of knowledge; new conceptions of how things work.

CURRICULUM TIPS 13-2   Curriculum Forecasting

Forecasting identifies and describes possible future developments or events pertinent to a particular topic. It also makes estimates about the probabilities that these developments or events will occur. Curriculum planners who proact engage in some forecasting activities. The following points should assist:

1. Identify the particular topic or event about which the forecast is to be made. Be sure that those involved actually are knowledgeable about the topic.
2. Be sure that the necessary data about the topic have been gathered in order to have a good reading of current and past situations.
3. Identify the continuities that exist in the topic considered. (Continuities refer to any observed relations among specific aspects of a topic or between topics.)
4. Identify or estimate discontinuities likely to affect the topic considered. (Discontinuities refer to any significant change in relations among identified aspects of a topic or between topics.) Determining discontinuities is a bit more challenging than identifying continuities, for discontinuities tend to be sudden and unanticipated.
5. Have the group estimate the timing of the event. When and under what circumstances might what is forecast occur? The rate of past and current change in the topic can be used to estimate the scheduling. Are the change rates likely to remain constant? How much confidence can we place in these change rates?
6. Determine the manageability of the topic in question. How well will people at some future time be able to regulate the various aspects of the topic?

Note: Some ideas for these tips came from David Miller and Ronald Hunt, *Survey of Future Studies,* Final Report, U.S. Department of Health, Education and Welfare, 1972.

---

7. *Cultural diffusion:* transfer of ideas, values, or techniques from one culture to another through war, invasion, advertising, and increased travel.[19]

Certainty Versus Uncertainty

While rapid change in all aspects of life has been and continues to be a hallmark of this century, this does not mean that individuals have accepted change with ease and grace. Indeed, much has been and still is traumatic. We realize that the times are uncertain. We increasingly grasp the difficulty of generating projections that are both accurate and on target. While appreciating that making accurate projections is increasingly problematic, we also understand that the costs of failure to make such readings, to generate such forecasts, is indeed high. If we as educators misread the future, we may create curricula that do not address students' needs. We may even educate students in ways that may add to social problems, for example, by preparing students for obsolete jobs and thus unemployment.

One thing is certain: "Knowledge is

power." Those individuals who develop new thoughtways to create understanding will indeed have meaningful roles in the future. The uncertainty as to how to create in our students new thoughts should not make us withdraw from the challenge. Rather, we should grasp that uncertainty will compel us to think of options and alternatives; uncertainty will challenge our creativity. Decisions made under uncertainty are different from those generated under certain conditions. When a situation is certain, we have only to decide to achieve whatever it is that we want to maximize and then focus our resources and schedule time to do it.[20] At other times, it is good procedure to leave options open and to denote contingency plans. Being unsure about what the future may demand, we should arrange for possible options; that is, we should suggest several avenues or programs that can be delivered in a multitude of ways. In this way, we anticipate future problems and ways to deal with them before they actually materialize.

In accepting uncertainty as a constant, we approach the concept of time, both present and future, in a somewhat different mind frame. Time is emergent; time is uncertain as to rate and duration. Huebner has spoken of time in this manner:

> Time is not a dimension in which we live—a series of "nows" some past and some in the future. Man does not have so many "nows" allotted. He does not simply await a future and look back upon a past. The very motion of time arises out of man's existence, which is an emergent. The future is man facing himself in anticipation of his own potentiality for being . . . human life is never fixed but is always emergent . . .[21]

In many instances, the futures perceived are nothing like the past. Answers currently considered correct will be frequently wrong in future times. Students who consider education as more than the gathering of answers will find themselves challenged by time. The explosion of knowledge has indeed furnished new information that has questioned the validity—even the occurrence—of previously held conclusions. A constant challenge for us all will be to abandon existing answers and perceptions. Distancing ourselves from current answers and indeed from the means of processing information is a crucial first step in dealing with unanticipated futures. From chaos theory, we realize that ways of processing information will often emerge from the very situations that demand our attention. The successful student of the future may be that person who can change his or her mind and identify those situations that require such change.

Human life as emergent makes individuals major players in their own lives. Empowering people means that we educators have a responsibility to assure that individuals, our students, gain those competencies to act so that they indeed can take control of their lives. If this is to be the age of the empowered individual, then schools must furnish opportunities so that students can be fully unique and in control of themselves and their destinies.

The times demand that individuals function autonomously. Technology is putting individuals in control of information. Students in our schools will not only be asked to receive information from teachers, but also to search out information of their own choosing and, perhaps even more importantly, to create information from their investigations. This stress on the individual does not mean that people will be duped into believing that they are indeed alone in the world and that they can function in isolation from their societies. Quite the opposite. Naisbitt states that the triumph of the individual does not mean that "the individual is condemned to face the world alone. Stripped down to the individual, one can build community, the free association of individuals. In community there is no place to hide either. Everyone knows who is contributing and who is not. Individuals seek community."[22]

Focusing on the individual, educators realize that the school curricula needs to be adjusted and created so that students do develop as individuals, as enlightened persons. Educators are now thinking of modifying the schools to fit the students rather than demanding that the students change to fit the schools. Increasingly, curricularists are creating specialized environments to meet individuals' needs, and they are contemplating requisite support services. We have new curricular designs to integrate content in more meaningful ways. In addressing the empowered individual, educators are creating varied program options and alternatives and multiple career programs. Furthermore, educators are recognizing and addressing the different forms of intelligence that individuals possess—not just in the cognitive domain—but also musical, artistic, spatial, kinesthetic, and interpersonal.

FUTURE INTELLIGENCE

Toffler believes that the intelligent environment that is so dramatically altering our info-sphere may indeed transform our minds. It may even alter the chemistry of our brains.[23] While that may be a bit extreme, students having access to various types of computers may actually think about problems, synthesize information, and generate options for actions in ways far different from current students. Students may indeed have different language forms and employ different types of symbols as yet unimagined. Certainly, our verbal skills will be affected by the available means of sending skills via technological links and electronic impulses.

In his more recent book, *Power Shift,* Toffler discusses extra-intelligence. Our technological equipment can now create "added value" to our messages. Currently, businesses employ electronic networks to gather and even analyze data patterns. Toffler notes that companies are growing very dependent on their networks for billing, ordering, tracking data, and trading. Design information is exchanged, schedules are communicated, and even production is controlled from distant places.[24]

This networking is occurring within the general community and the schools. Currently, students can get their own electronic mail, E mail. In some schools, students can actually call in to see how their teacher "liked" their papers, which were also sent to the teacher electronically. Students can access entire textbooks, even encylopedias, on compact disks through satellite linkages. Students are now able to access the views of other students in the world regarding any conceivable school topic.

At one time these electronic networks only relayed information. Now, as Toffler reports, we are seeing the rapid development of the self-aware network. These networks have "intelligence" built into them. They are like the double-loop systems that Argyris talked about in management systems. (See Chapter 9.) These networks now monitor the messages; they can even decide which routing of the message will be the most efficient. As Toffler notes, it is "as though a once-dead organism . . . [can] suddenly . . . [check] its own blood pressure, pulse, and breathing rate."[25] Such self-aware networks are crisscrossing the world in increasing density. Millions of computers are tied into them. Individuals taking notes with lap-top computers and fax machines are now able to tie into these networks and then communicate around the world in a matter of seconds. The current networks are what Toffler calls "second stage." Researchers are working on third-stage networks. The results will most likely give even more intelligence to our info-sphere. One thing is certain, however, the future is uncertain; it is this uncertainty that challenges our intelligence.

For schools, such networks used by students will certainly influence the manner in which students learn, process information, and experience school. Learning styles should be influenced as networks interact with the student using them, as networks carry on conversations and act as critics of the information being sent. Such networks will have students of the future thinking more multidimensionally and creatively—utilizing visual, computer, and communication tools to enhance the way they process and utilize information. Many students in the future will think and process information in ways that may challenge and even differ from their teachers, who might still rely on traditional thinking patterns. It is very possible that future students will think more future oriented than their teachers; youth should be able to adapt to the world of optical fibers, lasers, and electronics much easier than the older generation.

Some Constants

So much instability overwhelms some people. However, we can take some comfort in the realization that the four commonplaces of the curriculum depicted by Schwab will remain: students, teachers, content, and context. The basic organizers for our thinking most likely will remain. Schools, despite the increasing demand for choice, will not disappear. School will continue to be considered the most efficient means of bringing students into contact with their culture, with themselves, and with others. Certainly, schools will have curricula. We may not recognize the content, but we will have content, and we will plan experiences for students.[26]

Schools are, however, likely to play a less important role, or at least a shared role, in learning. More learning will occur as a result of students' interacting with the mass media, especially television and tapes. But, the mass media will not be a few media sources presenting a rather common "picture." Rather the media is likely to be what Toffler calls demassified.[27] The media industry will create both written and visual materials for specialized markets. Already in the United States, mass magazines are no longer a powerful influence in national life. Such magazines as *Life* and *The Saturday Evening Post* have even been phased out as an explosion of minimagazines address particular audiences. The media also cover an expanded range of topics: addressing young children, teenagers, middle-aged persons, and senior citizens. These trends are likely to continue.

The same trends characterize television and radio. No longer are there just three major channels; there are potentially hundreds. No longer does just one radio station play rock music; numerous stations specialize in all rock of all styles, from soft to hard—and now heavy metal.

FUTURE CURRICULA

While this section addresses some possibilities regarding school curriculum content and also ways of organizing such content, it does not spell the demise of the traditional subject-centered design. Indeed, because it is the most pervasive design not only in the United States, but also in the rest of the world, it is unlikely to disappear in the future. Subject-centered designs regard intellect as central to humanness, even though they have partly resulted from historical accident, institutional inertia, and social demand.

At the elementary school level, the subject-centered design comprises such subjects as language arts, social studies, mathematics, science, and the arts. At the secondary level, the traditional academic subjects are English, mathematics, science, history, geography, and foreign language. These subjects, many would agree, will be part of the educational future of schools. Miller and Seller have noted that those who accept this as the most likely future, indeed the preferred future, believe that schools of tomorrow will be much like schools of today. Schools and their curricula will be organized to essentially transmit the general society.[28] This is not to say that schools will not be responsive to the times and evolving futures. Rather, those individuals who believe schools are primarily created for transmitting the culture will exert their energies to maintain and continue a relatively traditional curriculum.

New Curricular Designs

While traditional designs have served us fairly well in the past, we realize that the future demands of schools different curricular designs and novel curriculum content. Education is more than mere accumulation of facts and mastery of skills. As Schlechty states: "In this age, . . . it is not more facts that people need. Citizens need ideas, concepts, and refined sensibilities to make sense out of the facts that bombard them daily and overwhelm their instincts as well as their understanding."[29]

Much current talk on integration of the curriculum, even within the standard content areas, reflects a beginning realization that individuals need ideas, concepts, and refined sensibilities for making meaning of their world. We are at a threshold in our curricular thinking. We are realizing that our programs must be designed so that students not only transmit that which is good in society and world culture, but also can transform themselves and their cultures. Many of us are commencing to grasp that being alive is not only *being,* but *becoming.*[30]

Those suggesting new designs for curriculum appear to be accepting this notion of humans as becoming, rather than just humans as being. This is a major conceptual shift, a moving away from viewing the world as a giant mechanical clock with knowable or potentially knowable causes generating anticipated effects.[31] It is a departure from viewing the world, and the school for that matter, with a feeling of certainty and control.

This major shift in thinking is seeping into educational discourse, into new curriculum designs. Many of these new designs draw on the dynamics of reality and humans in action. These designs draw on existentialist, moral, and spiritual ideas, what some call "Third Force" psychology. Abraham Maslow, a pioneer in humanistic psychology, considered this type of psychology to be a transitional preparation for a higher Forth Force or transpersonal psychology. Transpersonal psychology focuses on the cosmos, rather than on human needs and interests, and on intuition and transcendence.[32] Through intuition, an individual thinks creatively and views the world holistically.

Some curricularists are suggesting that education and its curricula address the moral and even spiritual ideas of students. Although most educators find little problem with the moral dimensions of teaching and learning, they do with the spiritual dimension. We are not advocating the teaching of religion but trying to show via experiences within schools that human nature is more than intellect. We learn by our relationships with our world, with all peoples. Students also are learning that they need to go beyond their narrow self-centered views; they need to transcend themselves—at least to see themselves as part of a community (local, state, national, international) of people. What we do can affect others and often does, and what others do can affect our lives.

Arthur Foshay addresses the transcendent issue within the curriculum. He maintains that the transcendence is the most ignored of all universal dimensions of human experience. Perhaps schools ignore it because educators think that the transcendent, also called the spiritual, suggests religion. Indeed, we are sensitive about maintaining the separation of church and state.[33] However, students are more than mere rational beings who can only grasp cognitive ideas. Both educators and students need to realize that reflecting on the purpose of being is essential in this highly complex world.

David Purpel speaks of the moral and spiritual crisis in education. He discusses liberation theology. While such theology is not taught directly in the schools, many are attending to the issue of poverty and oppression, which reflects this orientation. Bringing into the curriculum attention to compassion and justice for the less fortunate of the world is also part of the concern for the transcendent.[34]

While some might counsel resisting any semblance of incorporating the transcendent in the curriculum or drawing ideas from theology, most of us would accept the broad educational goals central to this orientation. Purpel presents these goals as an educational credo, as basic values and assumptions about education that are "nonnegotiable."

1. *The examination and contemplation of the awe, wonder, and mystery of the universe.*
2. *The cultivation and nourishment of the processes of meaning making.*
3. *The cultivation and nourishment of the concept of the oneness of nature and humanity.*
4. *The cultivation, nourishment, and development of a cultural mythos that builds on a faith in the human capacity to participate in the creation of a world of justice, compassion, caring, love, and joy.*
5. *The cultivation, nourishment, and development of ideals of community, compassion, and interdependence within the traditions of democratic principles.*
6. *The cultivation, nourishment, and development of attitudes of outrage and responsibility in the face of injustice and oppression.*[35]

These new designs of the curriculum, essentially humanistic, are currently more talk than reality. They emphasize putting the student more in control of his or her learning. In these designs the teacher acts as facilitator and catalyst rather than as transmitter of knowledge. These designs orient the curriculum to prizing the primacy of personal meaning; they include higher-level psychological and philosophical experiences.

The real challenge confronting educators is selecting the specific content for such new designs and determining the particulars of how to arrange and organize the content. Perhaps this is why many of these new designs are not present in the school. Designs that stress humanistic and transpersonal orientations are really addressing the inner realms of individuals. In a way, the content of the curriculum is created by the individual, emerging from significant encounters. Educators might be able to list significant encounters, but often the significance of an encounter is determined by the student rather than by the teacher.

New Curriculum Areas

The curriculum in the future will no doubt contain some entirely new areas of information. Currently, for example, we have the beginnings of several new content areas.

Informatics. Informatics deals with computers and their use. It has been described as a science for dealing with information. The computer, a central aspect of this new discipline, will afford students access to vast amounts of currently unattainable information. Students will be able, for example, to process documents written in other languages, because the computers will translate them. Computers will also enable students to network with other students in other schools, even in other countries. Joint investigations by students in different states or countries can become commonplace.[36]

As students think of ways to program their computers, they will begin to conceptualize different ways of organizing information. "Presenting" the computer to students will really give them power and control over the curriculum. If they control the machine, they can control the information; if they control the information, they may in effect gain increased influence in the classroom. This shift in classroom power from teacher to student could be a real system break in how school is "played": Learning could come to dominate teaching.[37]

The computer is much more than a tool. Indeed, it can be a "partner" the students can use not only for "joint" inquiry but even for suggesting and creating new curricular areas into which they can delve. The computer has the potential of personalizing the curriculum of the future.

Not all learning with the computer will occur in schools. Much of it will occur in the home or perhaps in public learning centers. Computerized call-up systems and intercontinental networks, as well as closed circuit and cable telecourses, should be commonplace by 2000, and video and/or auditory discs and tapes should replace many textbooks and written materials. Students may even have available a dial-access facility that permits access, via laser or a telephone, to a central learning center equipped with high-speed computers that can communicate with computers in any home or learning center anywhere in the world.[38]

The Future as Curriculum Content. It would seem unusual if future curricula did not include courses on the future itself. Such courses already exist in a few secondary schools. Some objectives of future studies courses are to give students a more sophisticated approach to thinking about the future and to help students learn forecasting techniques. Such courses will most likely increase in number; they may also extend into elementary schools.

Draper Kauffman has presented six areas of competence that could comprise a possible future-oriented curriculum: (1) having access to information; (2) thinking clearly; (3) communicating effectively; (4) understanding humanity's

environment; (5) understanding the individual and society; and (6) enhancing personal competence.[39]

As part of the future studies curriculum, students should learn about planning procedures, the nature of decision making, various types of heuristics for dealing with information, and procedures for handling stress caused by the rapidity of change. They should learn not only how to think critically about the future, but also perhaps how to distinguish between logic and nonlogic.

New Areas of Content. Whereas some courses on the future are predictable, other courses on the future are not so predictable. Nevertheless, we venture some predictions. Many courses may reflect hybrid fields of study—courses in biostatistics and molecular biology, for example.

Courses in dieting and exercise should increase as we become more health conscious. Research linking good nutrition and exercise for children with positive social behavior and academic achievement should encourage the schools to incorporate increased nutrition and exercise into the curriculum—and possibly lead to the elimination of junk food (especially excessive sugar and fats) from school vending machines and lunch counters.[40]

Some new courses may deal with the changing nature of society. Courses in aging, for instance, may become commonplace because students will be faced with an increasingly large "maturing" populace. Eventually the curriculum should treat many of the problems of aging as a form of discrimination, as another "ism." This emphasis should parallel changes in the curriculum concerning racism, "ethnicism," and sexism.[41] Special courses may offer students the opportunity to study about lifelong education and the ways in which it can be accessed.

As society continues to become culturally and ethnically pluralistic, more courses will deal with cultural diversity, international, and global education. Courses in valuing will appear so that students can gain insight into the attitudes, feelings, and emotions of themselves and others.[42]

Not all new courses will be related to emerging fields in the public sector. Some new courses may deal with the brain and ways of thinking. Secondary schools may assign textbooks on courses entitled "Your Brain," "Metacognition," "Left-Brain/Right-Brain Thinking," and "Trans-ductive Thinking." Specific courses in self-man-agement of one's intellect, emotions, and stress are probable as well. Courses on inner awareness, T-groups, and encounter groups may reappear. See Curriculum Tips 13-3.

CURRICULUM CONSIDERATIONS AND CHOICE

Much current discussion of new content areas does not actually suggest particular courses for students. Rather, general areas of content or program focus are proposed. This globalness of proposals allows each of us concerned with cur-riculum to reflect on ways to make the curricu-lum unique to particular students, yet beneficial to the general society. Schools are knowledge-work organizations. It is the purpose of future schools to invent knowledge work for students to nurture those competencies and attitudes requi-site for living in an information age.[43]

Schlechty states that in the school as a knowledge-work organization, the curriculum is perceived in a fundamentally different manner. No longer is it something to be passed on to students. Neither is it perceived as a mechanical assembly line on which students travel while things are done to them. In the knowledge-work school the curriculum becomes a body of mate-rial to be worked on by students, processed by students, and molded and formed by students. In effect, the curriculum becomes the raw material for the knowledge-work process.[44]

The designs for curriculum as the raw ma-terial for the students' knowledge-work pro-cess are as diverse as our imaginations and are primarily influenced by our educational and world philosophies and the resultant visions we hold for the school. As mentioned earlier, there are many educators, indeed some argue that these persons make up the vast majority of edu-cators, who think that the knowledge-related curriculum of the future will be essentially the one we currently have. Ornstein presents a very traditional view of the curriculum of the future as comprising five basic subject areas: mathe-matics, science, social studies, English, and modern language.[45] These subject areas would be presented so that students not only learned the central concepts but also how to use such knowl-edge, how to combine the basic knowledge with problem-solving strategies and learning how-to-learn strategies.

This curriculum basically brings to the future a belief that the current curriculum is soundly organized. The prime shift for the future school curriculum is seen in its delivery or in the ways in which students experience it. The ways of dealing with the content of the curriculum com-prise the new basics of the information age. Peo-ple of the future must be capable of manipulating images and sounds in addition to the printed word. Students will need new forms of abstrac-tion that will go far beyond simple book knowl-edge as we know it today. It is highly likely that this traditional design of the curriculum will re-main prominent as we go into the next century.

An Extreme Future Curriculum Design

While most schools will bring into the next cen-tury curricular organizations more like those of today than of some far-off future, some current curricularists suggest curricula that do push at the boundaries of possibility. The following cur-riculum represents a radical shift in what are con-sidered appropriate raw materials with which students can interact. The curriculum centers on areas of emphasis rather than specific course con-tent.[46]

Empowerment and transformation. In this cur-riculum component, students come to understand the power of knowledge; they are engaged in actions that unblock their minds. Students center on the relationships of various types of knowl-edge and how people interact with that knowl-edge and also with other people. Students come to realize that they are both producers and con-sumers of knowledge. It is their task to take knowledge and to make it their own, to personal-ize it.

Intellectual processes and forms. The central thrust of this curriculum organizer is to furnish students with opportunities to study the structures of the well-accepted disciplines and the new emerging disciplines. In their study, students will

CURRICULUM TIPS 13-3   **Guidelines for Curriculum Reform**

Since the times are dynamic, we need to realize that the curriculum is never completed; it is ongoing. We never arrive at the perfect curriculum for the times. History is added to each day. Science makes new discoveries. The following guidelines can help us meet the ongoing challenge of curriculum for evolving futures.

1. Consider curriculum improvement as a continuous process.
2. View broadly what your school can contribute to your students and the general society.
3. Realize that there are numerous resources that can assist you in improving your curriculum.
4. Understand that attempts at change require time and will usually occur in small increments.
5. Realize that we must maximize the continued growth and professionalization of teachers and staff.
6. Be vigilant in monitoring your vision for your school regarding its curriculum and its practices.
7. Adopt a spirit of inquiry in your school; become students of education as well as deliverers of curriculum.
8. Realize that there will be a continued need to involve others from outside the school in curriculum activities.

Source: Adapted from Frances M. Klein, *Curriculum Reform in the Elementary School* (New York: Teachers College Press, Columbia University, 1989).

begin to grasp the ways in which knowledge is created, the ways in which meaning is developed, and the means by which people generate conclusions. They will study the nature of language, the essential character of modes of inquiry, and the different forms of evidence.[47]

Social Skills. Kenneth Benne states that rather than presenting a notion "of the self as passive, reactive, in continual need of motivation and socialization from outside itself—a self divided, with its intellect segregated from its feelings and emotions—and from the interpersonal community that sustains it in being," we in education need to "apply a conception . . . of self as inherently active and creative, a self proactive, going out to select, to choose, to shape through its actions its environment toward a habitat more supportive of human living."[48]

In this rather radical curriculum, students learn requisite skills for functioning in an increasingly dynamic community. Students learn skills of doing, rather than skills of learning about. Students learn to develop commitment to act, to utilize their skills within the community arena.[49]

Historical sense. Dwayne Huebner notes that human life is anticipatory, never fixed, but always emergent.[50] In this suggested curriculum, content and experiences are arranged so that students come to truly understand the relationship of past, present, and future. Students come to realize that events in time, at least human events, are or can be under our control. We have created our histories and our views of past events. We are currently managers of our present time, and we have the power to manage our futures.

Critical awareness and competence. Few would argue against students today being active thinkers. This segment of the curriculum relates to developing in students both a disposition to question and process information and the competence to actually do so. In the present and future world, students must possess critical awareness and know how to process their questions in order to deeply comprehend their world.[51] Critically aware students realize their potential to create their own knowledge; they grasp the richness and diversity of the world, and they accept their responsibility for being active in contemplating the world and their places within it. Critical consciousness makes individuals aware of their presence in the world in an existential sense.[52]

Imagination and visioning. Imagination and creativity are central to meaning making. Indeed to develop meaning requires imagining, visioning, and dreaming. Such creative processes partly define our humanness. In this curriculum, time is given to individuals to imagine schemata and their metaphorical and qualitative projections of life. Students learn to think creatively.[53]

These content areas are not to be presented separately. Rather, they serve as markers of encounters designed to integrate all these contents into events in which students can participate and from which they can generate meaning.

A More Traditional Curriculum Model

We need not change the curriculum as dramatically as suggested in the previous model in order to attain a curriculum responsive to a dynamic future. We can have a curriculum divided into three rather familiar categories: academic curriculum, creative curriculum, and socialization curriculum.[54]

The academic curriculum would embrace the traditional school subjects such as language arts, social studies, mathematics, biology, and chemistry. The courses could stand alone or could be integrated. The courses could also be presented as a required core or offered as options for student selection. But the academic curriculum would not be delivered in a traditional way. Students would have opportunities to work both alone and collaboratively.

The creative curriculum, scheduled alongside the academic curriculum, would contain contents from the arts and also from areas not traditionally included in the curriculum: courses such as cooking, dance, and graphic design. Here the emphasis would be on students satisfying their creative urges, perfecting their aesthetic ways of knowing.

The socialization curriculum would furnish students with opportunities to learn about problem solving, health maintenance, interpersonal communications, and purpose in life.[55] Students would develop their social intelligence and their social competence. Social intelligence is knowing oneself and knowing other people. Social competence is the ability to act on one's knowledge so that a desire to interact among self and others is achieved.[56] In a world that is becoming globalized, both social intelligence and social competence are essential.

THE CHALLENGE OF DEALING WITH THE FUTURE

To create the extreme curriculum design would indeed be a challenge. It would call for bold reconceptualization of the curriculum and the manner in which students experience it. The extreme design is no superficial rearrangement. Yet, it is really not advocating departing from those things that all educators consider essential for a fully functioning individual—to be in control of oneself, to have command of intellectual processes, to have a sense of one's history, to be socially literate, to possess essential knowledge, to be a critical thinker, and to be imaginative and creative.

Even the more traditional model comprised of the academic, the creative, and the social divisions would require some modification of our thinking. But the design demands less stretch of vision. For this reason, future curriculum might be more like this design than the more extreme one. It already is in place.

Although most traditional designs maintain the basic curriculum organizations of the current time, they can be taught in ways that get students active in their learning and committed to participating in their local, state, and national societies. No design can remain totally static.

These designs are not presented with any particular one being advocated. Rather, they are offered as grist for our thinking. We mentioned at the beginning of this chapter that all education springs from some image or vision of the future. It is important to remember that dealing with visions is not a casual activity; it requires careful planning, intense reflection, and deliberate action. We educators must assume the posture of futurists to deal with anticipated visions, even to create and manage those visions, those future directions of schools and their curricula. Being futurists will allow us to design curricula that are responsive to students' needs not only in the practical sense of application to job situations but also in the totally humanistic sense of allowing them to understand, manage, and appreciate their realities.

Toffler pointed out several years ago that no educational institution can address the challenges placed on it until all its members, including students, subject their views of the future and related challenges to critical analysis. Toffler cautioned "to design educational systems for tomorrow . . . we need not images of a future frozen in amber, as it were, but something far more complicated: sets of images of successive and alternative futures, each one tentative and different from the next."[57]

Our challenge as curriculum designers and developers is to create programs so that all students will function optimally in a just future society. The task is difficult and complex and perhaps at times unmanageable. But those with curriculum responsibilities should realize that they must rise to the challenge. Society depends upon it.

CONCLUSION

In this chapter, we have attempted to define what futurism is and to relate it to the field of curriculum. Futurism was presented as a systematic attempt to meld creative forecasting, planning, and action. In using futurism, educators can proact rather than react to events. Certainly, educators have past habits to break, because it has been their posture to react to events affecting the schools and their programs. Often educators are unaware of how to influence the future, how to modify public or client demands to more manageable dimensions, or how to be more in tune with accepted purposes of education.

We live between eras, and we have uncertainty in our lives. Nonetheless, we need to approach this uncertainty as a plus rather than a minus. Uncertainty forces people to engage in decision making that is liquid, flexible, and adaptable. This should encourage the creation of more diverse curricular offerings.

In this chapter, we discussed various directions of the 1990s and beyond that appear likely for our schools and society. We discussed procedures that we can muster that will enable us not only to react to directions but also to play a role in their creation. We presented various forecasting procedures for consideration. We presented, too, a general overview of some of the developments within the curriculum field. We mentioned what might be expected in new curricular areas and we outlined possibile future curricula.

The challenge for curricularists is to generate images of the future and then to fit schools and their programs into those images so that the curriculum that is actualized serves the needs and desires of all those within the school and society. To attain this is no small task. The health and vitality of society depend to a significant degree on how well curricularists meet this challenge.

ENDNOTES

1. Wendell Bell, "Social Science: The Future as a Missing Variable," in A. Toffler, ed., *Learning for Tomorrow: The Role of the Future in Education* (New York: Vintage Books, 1974), pp. 75–102.
2. Alvin Toffler, "The Psychology of the Future," in Toffler, ed., *Learning for Tomorrow,* pp. 3–18.
3. John Naisbitt, *Megatrends* (New York: Warner Books, 1982), John Naisbitt and Patricia Aburdene, *Megatrends 2000* (New York: William Morrow, 1990).
4. Phillip C. Schlechty, *Schools for the 21st. Century* (San Francisco: Jossey-Bass, 1990).
5. Ibid., p. 35.
6. Thomas Quick, *Unconventional Wisdom* (San Francisco: Jossey-Bass, 1989).

7. Warren Bennis and Paul Slater, *The Temporary Society* (New York: Harper & Row, 1968); W. Bennis, *Why Leaders Can't Lead* (San Francisco: Jossey-Bass, 1989), p. 155.
8. Naisbitt, *Megatrends.*
9. Naisbitt and Aburdene, *Megatrends 2000.*
10. Harold L. Strudler, "Educational Futurism: Perspective or Discipline?" in Toffler, ed., *Learning for Tomorrow,* pp. 173–180.
11. Earl C. Joseph, "An Introduction to Studying the Future," in S. P. Henley and J. R. Yates, eds., *Futurism in Education* (Berkeley: McCutchan, 1974), pp. 1–26.
12. Roy Amara, *Some Methods of Future Research* (Menlo Park, Calif.: Institute for the Future, 1975);

Elizabeth Vallance, "Ways of Knowing and Curricular Conceptions," in E. Eisner, ed., *Learning and Teaching the Ways of Knowing,* Eighty-fourth Yearbook of the National Society for the Study of Education, Part II (Chicago: University of Chicago Press, 1985), pp. 199–217.

13. John W. Sutherland, "Architecturing the Future: A Delphi-based Paradigm for Normative System Building," in H. Linstone and M. Turoff, eds., *The Delphi Method* (Reading, Mass.: Addison-Wesley, 1975), p. 467.

14. Robert V. Carlson and Gary A. W. Kerman, *Educational Planning: Concepts, Strategies and Practices* (New York: Longman, 1991); Department of Defense, *Military Standard: Human Engineering Design Criteria for Military Systems* (Washington, D.C.: U.S. Government Printing Office, 1988).

15. Joseph, "An Introduction to Studying the Future."

16. Harold G. Shane, "Future-Planning as a Means of Shaping Educational Change," in R. M. McClure, ed., *The Curriculum: Retrospect and Prospect,* Seventieth Yearbook of the National Society for the Study of Education, Part I (Chicago: University of Chicago Press, 1971); Shane, "Improving Education in the Twenty-first Century," *Educational Horizons* (Fall 1990), pp. 10–15.

17. Toffler, *Future Shock,* pp. 157–158.

18. Daniel Bell, "The Year 2000—The Trajectory of an Idea," *Daedalus* (Summer 1967), pp. 642–644.

19. Michael A. McDaniel, "Tomorrow's Curriculum Today," in Toffler, ed., *Learning for Tomorrow,* pp. 103–131.

20. Kenneth E. Boulding, "Predictive Reliability and the Future: The Need for Uncertainty," in Lewis Rubin, ed., *The Future of Education: Perspectives on Tomorrow's Schooling* (Boston: Allyn and Bacon, 1975), pp. 57–82.

21. Dwayne Huebner, "Curriculum as Concern for Man's Temporality," in W. Pinar, ed., *Curriculum Theorizing, The Reconceptualists* (Berkeley, Calif.: McCutchan, 1975). p. 362.

22. Naisbitt and Aburdene, *Megatrends 2000,* p. 300.

23. Alvin Toffler, *The Third Wave* (New York: Bantam Books, 1980), p. 168.

24. Alvin Toffler, *Power Shift* (New York: Bantam Books, 1990).

25. Ibid., p. 114.

26. Don Glines and Kathleen Long, "Transitioning Toward Educational Futures," *Phi Delta Kappan* (March 1992), pp. 557–560.

27. Alvin Toffler, *Previews and Premises* (Boston: Sound End Press, 1983).

28. John P. Miller and Wayne Seller, *Curriculum: Perspectives and Practice* (New York: Longman, 1985).

29. Schlechty, *Schools for the 21st Century,* p. 32.

30. Ilya Prigogine and Isabell Stengers, *Order Out of Chaos* (New York: Bantam Books, 1984).

31. Toffler, *Power Shift.*

32. Jerry L. Patterson, Steward C. Purkey, and Jackson V. Parker, *Productive School Systems for a Nonrational World* (Alexandria, Va.: Association for Supervision and Curriculum Development, 1986); Donald Vandenberg, *Education as a Human Right: A Theory of Curriculum and Pedagogy* (New York: Teachers College Press, Columbia University, 1990).

33. Arthur Foshay, untitled paper presented at Professors of Curriculum Meeting, Chicago, 1988.

34. David Purpel, *The Moral and Spiritual Crisis in Education* (New York: Bergin & Garvey, 1989).

35. Ibid., pp. 113–118.

36. Harlan Cleveland, "Educating Citizens and Leaders for an Information-Based Society," *Educational Leadership* (March 1986), pp. 62–63; M. Francis Klein, "Beyond the Measured Curriculum," *Theory into Practice* (Winter 1986), pp. 1–17.

37. Daniel Barron and Timothy J. Bergen, "Information Power," *Phi Delta Kappan* (March 1992); Cleveland, "Educating Citizens and Leaders for an Information-Based Society."

38. Paul E. Merril et al., *Computers in Education,* 2nd ed. (Boston: Allyn and Bacon, 1992); Decker F. Walker, "Computers and the Curriculum," in J. A. Culbertson and L. L. Cunningham, eds., *Microcomputers and Education.* Eighty-fifth Yearbook of the National Society for the Study of Education, Part I (Chicago: University of Chicago Press, 1986), pp. 22–39.

39. Draper Kauffman, *Teaching the Future* (Palm Springs, Calif.: ETC Publications, 1976).

40. Judith Herr and Winifred Morse, "Food for Thought: Nutrition Education for Young Children," *Young Children* (November 1982), pp. 3–11: Allan C. Ornstein, "Controversy and Trends in Curriculum for the 1980s," *Contemporary Education* (Summer 1985), pp. 242–251.

41. Allan C. Ornstein, "Emerging Curriculum Trends: An Agenda for the Future," *NASSP Bulletin* (February 1989), pp. 37–48.

42. James A. Banks, "Multicultural Education: For Freedom's Sake," *Educational Leadership* (December-January 1992), pp. 32–36; Martha Ozturk, "Education for Cross-Cultural Communication," *Educational Leadership* (December–January 1992), pp. 79–81.

43. Schlechty, *Schools for the 21st Century.*

44. Ibid., p. 42.

45. Allan C. Ornstein, "Problem Solving: What Is It? How Can We Teach It?" *NASSP Bulletin* (November 1989), pp. 113–121.

46. Purpel, *The Moral and Spiritual Crisis in Education.*

47. Ibid.

48. Kenneth D, Benne, *The Task of Post-Contemporary Education* (New York: Teachers College Press, Columbia University, 1990), p. 170.

49. Purpel, *The Moral and Spiritual Crisis in Education.*

50. Huebner, "Curriculum as a Concern for Man's Temporality."

51. Vandenberg, *Education as a Human Right: A Theory of Curriculum and Pedagogy.*

52. Maxine Green, *The Dialectic of Freedom* (New York: Teachers College Press, Columbia University, 1988).

53. Purpel, *The Moral and Spiritual Crisis in Education.*

54. Timothy D. Evans, Raymond J. Corsini, and George M. Gazda, "Individual Education and the 4Rs," *Educational Leadership* (September 1990), pp. 52–55.

55. Ibid.

56. Ellen Berscheid, "Interpersonal Modes of Knowing," in Elliot Eisner, ed., *Learning and Teaching the Ways of Knowing,* Part II. Eighty-fourth Yearbook of the National Society for the Study of Education, 1985), pp. 60–76.

57. Alvin Toffler, "The Psychology of the Future," in Toffler, ed., *Learning for Tomorrow,* p. 5.

NAME INDEX

SUBJECT INDEX